कल्पागमसंग्रहाख्या वाधूलश्रौतसूत्रव्याख्या

Prakashika Series
No. 14

General Editor
DIPTI S. TRIPATHI

आचार्य-आर्यदासप्रणीता

कल्पागमसंग्रहाख्या

वाधूलश्रौतसूत्रव्याख्या

खण्ड 1

सम्पादक

व्रजबिहारी चौबे

इत्याख्येन विदुषा सम्पादितम्
विशदभूमिकया विविधाभिरनुक्रमणीभिश्च समलङ्कृतं
पाठविमर्शादिभिर्युतं समालोचनात्मकं संस्करणकम्

राष्ट्रीय पाण्डुलिपि मिशन
नई दिल्ली
तथा
देव पब्लिशर्स एण्ड डिस्ट्रीब्यूटर्स

प्रकाशक :

राष्ट्रीय पाण्डुलिपि मिशन

11, मानसिंह रोड,

नई दिल्ली-110 001

दूरभाष: 2338 3894; फैक्स: 2307 3387

E-mail: directornamami@nic.in

Website: www.namami.nic.in

सह-प्रकाशक :

देव पब्लिशर्स एण्ड डिस्ट्रीब्यूटर्स

द्वितीय तल, प्रकाशदीप बिल्डिंग,

22, दिल्ली मैडिकल एसोसिएशन रोड

नई दिल्ली-110002

दूरभाष: 43572647

e-mail: devbooks@hotmail.com

website: www.devbooks.co.in

ISBN 978-93-80829-02-9 (Series)

ISBN 978-93-80829-22-7 (Vol. XIV)

प्रथम संस्करण: 2013

मूल्य : ₹ 650.00 (दोनों खण्ड)

Ācārya Āryadāsapraṇītā

KALPĀGAMASAṂGRAHĀKHYĀ

Vādhūlaśrautasūtra Vyākhyā

Part I

Critically edited with Introduction
and
Various Indices
by

Braj Bihari Chaubey

National Mission for Manuscripts

Dev Publishers & Distributors

Published by:
National Mission for Manuscripts
11 Man Singh Road
New Delhi 110 001
Phone: 91 11 2307 3387
E-mail: directornamami@nic.in
Website: www.namami.nic.in

and Co-published by:
Dev Publishers & Distributors
2nd Floor, Prakash Deep,
22, Delhi Medical Association Road,
Darya Ganj,
New Delhi-110002
Phone : 011-43572647
e-mail: devbooks@hotmail.com
website: www.devbooks.co.in

ISBN 978-93-80829-02-9 (Series)
ISBN 978-93-80829-22-7 (Vol. XIV)
First published 2013

विषयानुक्रमणिका

खण्ड 1

खण्ड 2

आमुख

वैदिक साहित्य के अन्तर्गत संहिता, ब्राह्मण, आरण्यक और उपनिषद् की गणना होती है। संहिताओं में ऋग्वेद, सामवेद, यजुर्वेद, अथर्ववेद हैं जिसमें से प्रत्येक की अनेक शाखाएँ स्वीकृत और प्रचलित थीं। पतंजलि के अनुसार यजुर्वेद की 101 शाखाएँ थीं (एकशतमध्वर्युशाखा, महाभाष्य)। इसके अतिरिक्त प्रत्येक संहिता के ब्राह्मण, आरण्यक और उपनिषद् अलग-अलग हैं। वेदों के अध्ययन के लिए विभिन्न प्रकार के अंगभूत शास्त्रों का भी विकास हुआ, जिन्हें वेदों का षडंग कहा गया। शिक्षा, व्याकरण, निरुक्त और छन्द वेदों की भाषा से सम्बद्ध हैं। शिक्षा में उच्चारण की प्रक्रिया, व्याकरण में शब्दों की व्युत्पत्ति एवं सिद्धि, वाक्यों में स्वरों का विधान आदि, निरुक्त में शब्दों का निर्वचन तथा छन्द में मन्त्रों के छन्द-प्रकार का विश्लेषण एवं प्रस्तुतिकरण हुआ है।

यज्ञ-प्रक्रिया के विकास के साथ ही उनको नियमबद्ध करने की आवश्यकता का अनुभव हुआ। अन्य दो वेदांग कल्प तथा ज्योतिष वैदिक यज्ञ प्रक्रिया से जुड़े हुए हैं। कल्प साहित्य यज्ञों के प्रायोगिक स्वरूप के नियमों का उपस्थापन करता है। कल्पसूत्र के तीन खण्ड हैं जिन्हें क्रमशः श्रौतसूत्र, गृह्यसूत्र एवं शुल्वसूत्र कहा जाता है। श्रौतसूत्र और शुल्वसूत्र का सम्बन्ध विशिष्ट यज्ञों से है जिनका विधान राजा अथवा बहुत धनी लोग ही कर सकते हैं। गृह्यसूत्र अपने नाम के ही अनुसार गृहस्थों के लिए आजीवन किये जाने वाले अनुष्ठानों का विधान करता है। अतः गृह्यसूत्रों का सम्बन्ध व्यक्ति के सामाजिक जीवन से जुड़ा होता है। वैदिक संस्कृति के विस्तार के साथ यज्ञ की विधियों में भी परिवर्तन स्वाभाविक था। इसमें कहीं तो प्राचीन विधियों का परित्याग किया गया और कहीं कतिपय नवीन विधियों को स्वीकार किया गया। इन परिवर्तनों को जब आचार्यों ने नियमबद्ध कर दिया तो कल्पसूत्रों की रचना हुई। जैसा कि इस साहित्य की प्रवृत्ति से समझा जा सकता है, कल्पसूत्र वैदिक शाखाओं को सुव्यवस्थित करने का भी आधार थे। सूत्रों की व्याख्या, वृत्तियों एवं कारिकाओं के रूप में, उपलब्ध होती है।

कृष्णयजुर्वेद की चार मुख्य शाखाएँ हैं। जिन्हें काठक, कपिष्ठल, तैत्तिरीय और वाधूल के नाम से जाना जाता है। इनमें से तैत्तिरीय सर्वाधिक प्रसिद्ध शाखा है। वैदिक साहित्य के लिखित रूप में प्रकाशन की प्रक्रिया शुरू होने के बाद इस शाखा के अनेक ग्रन्थ प्रकाश में आये, किन्तु अन्य तीन शाखाओं का प्रचार कम होने से तत्सम्बन्धी ग्रन्थों का प्रकाशन भी सीमित रहा। प्रो. कैलान्ड ने सर्वप्रथम वाधूलश्रौतसूत्र एवं वाधूलान्वाख्यान का कुछ अंश प्रकाशित किया। प्रो. विट्ज़ल और प्रो. यासुके भी वाधूलश्रौतसूत्र, वाधूलान्वाख्यान एवं वाधलगृह्यसूत्र को प्रकाश में लाने में सक्रियता से संलग्न हैं। भारतवर्ष में प्रो. ब्रज बिहारी चौबे ने वाधूलशाखा को पुनरुज्जीवित करने में महत्वपूर्ण योगदान किया है। इन्होंने सर्वप्रथम 1993 में वाधूलश्रौतसूत्र का प्रकाशन किया तदनन्तर वाधूल शाखा के निम्नलिखित ग्रन्थ भी क्रमशः प्रकाशित किये:

1. वाधूलस्मृति, हिन्दी अनुवाद सहित (सन् 2000)
2. वाधूलान्वाख्यान (2001)
3. वाधूलयज्ञप्रायश्चित (2001)
4. नारायण मिश्र कृत वाधूलगृह्यागमवृत्तिरहस्य (2006)
5. शिवश्रोण कृत वाधूलश्रौतप्रयोगक्लृप्ति (2011)
6. वाधूलगृह्यसूत्र वृत्तिसहित (2012)

सन् 2012 में राष्ट्रीय पाण्डुलिपि मिशन ने प्रो. चौबे द्वारा सम्पादित वृत्ति सहित वाधूलगृह्यसूत्र का प्रकाशन किया। तदनन्तर विभिन्न पाण्डुलिपियों के आधार पर वाधूलश्रौतसूत्र की व्याख्या का सम्पादन वाधूलशाखा को प्रकाश में लाने की दिशा में महत्वपूर्ण प्रयास है। प्रौ. चौबे ने शास्त्र एवं सम्पादन दोनों में ही अपने लम्बे अनुभव के आधार पर इस व्याख्या का सम्पादन किया है। उन्होंने विवेचकता का परिचय देते हुए वाधूलश्रौतसूत्र में दो प्रपाठकों में वर्णित अग्निष्टोम यज्ञ का, व्याख्या में, एक ही प्रपाठक में सम्पादन किया है। ऐसा करना उन्होंने व्याख्याकार के मन्तव्य का अनुसरण करने की दिशा में आवश्यक एवं उपयोगी माना है। कुछ इस प्रकार के परिवर्तन अन्य सन्दर्भों में भी किये गये हैं। अनेकत्र जहाँ मूल सूत्र उपलब्ध नहीं होते वहाँ व्याख्या के आधार पर उनकी सत्ता भी प्रमाणित होती है। अथातो बृहस्पतिसवः, अथातो ओदनसवः, अथातो मृत्युसवः आदि जैसे प्रयोगों की व्याख्या के आधार पर सूत्र ग्रन्थ में उनकी सत्ता का अनुमान, इस बात का प्रमाण है कि वाधूलशाखा के सम्पूर्ण स्वरूप को निर्दुष्ट रूप से जानने में अभी और शोध की आवश्यकता है।

आर्यदास की व्याख्या श्रौत प्रक्रियाओं को हमारे समक्ष प्रकाशित करने में सहायक सिद्ध होगी।

कल्पागमसंग्रह को विद्वानों के समक्ष उपस्थापित करते हुए मुझे सन्तोष एवं हर्ष का अनुभव हो रहा है। प्रो. चौबे के अथक प्रयासों से यह लुप्तप्राय शाखा पुनः विद्वानों के लिए अध्ययन का विषय बन रही है, इसके लिए प्रो. चौबे का साधुवाद। देव पब्लिशर्स एण्ड डिस्ट्रीब्यूटर्स के सर्वेसर्वा श्री पंकज जैन सुरुचिपूर्ण एवं समय सीमा में प्रकाशन करने में समर्थ एवं सन्नद्ध हैं। शास्त्र के प्रति उनके इस भाव के लिए मिशन उनका धन्यवाद करता है। इन ग्रन्थों के प्रकाशन से शोधकर्ताओं को वाधूलशाखा के विषय में जानने में सुविधा होगी, ऐसा विश्वास है।

दीप्ति त्रिपाठी

नयी दिल्ली — निदेशक

23 जून 2013

Preface

My critical edition of *Vādhūlaśrautasūtra* which was published for the first time in 1993 was mainly based on Manuscript deposited at Government Oriental Manuscript Library, Madras under the title '*Vādhālakalpa-Vyākhyā*' No. R 4375. From the nomenclature of the MS one could easily understand that it would be a commentary on *Vādhūla-Śrautsūtra.* But contrary to this, it was a copy of original *sūtra*-text of *VādhŚS.* This mis-nomenclature of the text was because of the fact that the first 28 pages of MS belonged to *Gṛhyasūtra*, and from page 29 onward that to the original *Śrautsūtra*-text. Again from p.545, line 6 onword there was a text of *Vādhūla Anvākhyāna* (incomplete) upto the end of p.488.

In 1995, when I went to Madras to attend a three-day National Seminar on 'Palmleaf and other Manuscripts in Indian Languages', organised by the Institute of Asian Studies, Madras, I got an opportunity to visit the Government Oriental Manucript Library there. I was astonished to see a MS No. 923 on the front page and R 2978 on p.399, which was different in nature from MS No. R 4375. It was actualy a commentary on *VādhŚS.* I requested the authorities to kindly give zerox copy of the said MS. Very kindly they accepted my request and promised to send the said MS in a few days. They very kindly supplied the zerox copy of the said MS very soon.

Immediately after receiving the MS, I started preparing my base copy of the text. During the course of copying the MS, I found a large number of displacements of folios and inclusion of two other texts, *viz, Prayogakḷpti* or *Prayogakalpnā* of Śivaśroṇa and *Vādhūlagṛhyasūtravṛtti.* First, I decided to separate the two small texts, *viz Vādhūla Prayogakḷipti* of Śivaśroṇa and the *Vādhūla Gṛhyasūtra with Vṛtti,* both belonging to the *Vādhūla*-tradition. The critical editions of both the texts with detailed introductions, now have already been published from the National Mission for Manuscripts, Delhi under Kṛtibodha Series (No. 2) in 2010, and the *Vādhūla Gṛhyasūtra* with *Vṛtti* under Prakashika series (No. 5) in 2012. Now after publication of *VādhūlaPrayogakḷipti* and *VadhGSV* of the composite MS, only the commentary-part of *VādhŚS* had remained to be critically edited and published.

Since my critical edition of the *VādhŚS* had already been published, I first tried to arrange the text of commentary following the *Prapāṭhaka, Anuvāka* and *Paṭala* orders of that text. Even after separating the two said texts, I was confronted with the problem of displacements of folios even within the *Prapāṭhakas, Anuvākas,* and *Paṭalas*. A large portion of the text dealing with *Agnihotra* had entered in *Rājasūya Prapāṭhaka*. Similarly a large portion of text dealing with *Ekāhas* XI. 10-15 had entered in *Vādhūlagṛhya-sūtravṛtti*. Due to these displacements, the order of the *Anuvāka*-numbers were not given at proper places.

Besides such displacements of folios, there were a large number of lacunae on almost all folios and lines of the text. Struggling with these problems, I started confining and separating the length of the text of commentary sūtrawise. But where there were displacements of folios, there it became almost impossible to trace where the text of commentary of the concerned *sūtra* was.

While arranging the *sūtra*wise-texts of commentary, I found that the length of commentary on some *sūtras* was very big, while that of others was very small, and some of the *sūtras* have been left uncommented upon. At some places many *sūtras* had been commented together in brief and sometimes confined to a single word of the *sūtra.* Where the text of commentary was long or very short, I have given the number of that *sūtra.* But where the text deals with more *sūtras* together, I have given the number of all those *sūtras* together at the end. Where the *sūtras* have not been commented upon their numbers have been left.

In my previous edition of the *VādhŚS* I had given the *Sūtra*-text of *Agniṣṭoma* under two *Prapāṭhakas* (VI and VII), comprising of eight and seven *Anuvākas* respectively. But here, on the basis of commentary, which gives 15 *Anuvākas* together in continuation, I have given here entire text together under one *Prapāṭhaka,* (VI), as a result of which the serial numbers of the following *Prapāṭhakas* have been changed lessening one upto the *Aśvamedha.*

Again after *Aśvamedha*, the serial numbers of the following *Prapāṭhakas* have been changed because of the existence of texts of commentary on *Dvādaśāha, Aupānuvākya, Ahīna* and *Ekāhas.* In none of the MSS of the *VādhŚS* available so far, the *sūtra*-texts dealing with *Dvādaśāha, Aupānuvākya, Ahīna* and *Ekāhas* are found. But on the basis of the existence of commentary-text on them, we will have to accept that once the *VādhŚS* must have had the original *Sutra*-texts of which the commentary is available.

My conjecture about the existence of *Sūtra*-texts on these rituals is supported by the *Vyākhyā* by giving introductory first *sūtras* of each of the *Ekāhas* by mentioning their title as under—

अथातो बृहस्पतिसवः- १४.१.१
अथात ओदनसवः- १४.२.१
अथातो मृत्युसवः- १४.३.१
अथातः सद्यस्क्रीः- १४.४.१
अथातः पञ्चशारदीयो वत्सरः- १४.५.१
अथातोऽपचरणीयानि- १४.६.१
अथातो व्रात्यस्तोमाः- १४.७.१
अथात ऋषभसवः- १४.११.१
अथातो वाजपेयम्- १४.१३.१
अथातो वाङ्नामक्रतुः- १४.१४.३ *etc.*

To show the very existence of the texts on these rituals, I have given the first *sūtras* of each *Paṭala* in bold letter in the commentary on the *Ekāhas*.

Again after *Ekāhas*, the original number of *Prapāṭhakas* dealing with *Aptoryāma, Pravargya, Yājamānāgniṣṭomika-Prāyaścitta* and *Yājñapariśeṣa* have been accordingly changed. But it is to be pointed out that the texts of commentary on these *Prapāṭhakas* are not found in the present MSS of the *Kalpāgamasaṇgraha*. We can only surmise that once the commentary on these texts must have existed, but not discovered so far.

In my previous edition of *VādhŚS* there were a large number of texts which were given in the MSS of *sūtra*-text in abridged form. These abridged texts were of two-types one belonging to *mantra*-text and the other to a large extent of *ritual*-texts. So far the abridged texts, belonging to *mantra*-text are concerned, the *Sūtrakāra* gives the opening few words of the mantras followed by injuction of the ritual concerned to be performed and again the remaining text of mantra in abridged form. For example—

'अयं ते योनिर्ऋत्वियः' इत्यरण्योरग्निं समारोहयते। '०यतो जातो=अरोहाथा नो वर्धया रयिम्' (*VādhŚS* 1.1.3.1)

'इडा स्त मधुकृतः' इति ता एव। '०स्योना=श्रयन्ताम्' इति। (*VādhŚS*

1.2.4.7) *etc.*

In the second type of *abridged* texts, sometimes a group of *sūtras* and sometimes the entire *Paṭala* was given in *abridged* form, *e.g.*

यावदेत=प्रत्यागृणाति, (*VādhŚS* 6.12.3.25-34; cf 6.12.2.47-56)

'आयुष्मन्तं त्वाऽग्ने आयुष्मान् समिन्धे' इति गार्हपत्यः समिन्धे। ०आयुषे त्वा=स कामः पद्यते। (*VādhŚS* 1.5.3.3-17; cf 1.3.3.4-17)

'ज्योतिष्मन्तं त्वाऽग्ने ज्योतिष्मान् समिन्धे।' मनसे त्वा सुवर्गाय=सः हैवास्मै स कामः पद्यते य एतेनोपतिष्ठते। (*VādhŚS* 1.6.3.1-17; cf 1.3.3.2-17)

In the first type of *abridged* texts there was no difficulty to understand the length of the *sūtra*-text, but in the second type of *abridged* texts, where a number of *sūtras* have been given in abridged form, it was very difficult to understand the rituals for their performances. Moreover, some of the texts were indicated in the *Vyākhyā* mentioning the text already explained before where the *sūtras* were given in full. In such cases, where the large number of *sūtras* were given in *abridged* form, I gave the full text of all *sūtras* with their continuing *sūtra*-numbers under bracket and showed them with star-mark (*) in the *sūtra*-text under bracket.

In my previous edition of *VādhŚS* I had wrongly given the *sūtra* द्वादशहाय दीक्षिष्यमाण समवस्यन्ति and अप्तोर्यामेण यक्ष्यमाणः भवति as forming first two *sūtras* under अप्तोर्याम. Now I have placed the four *Prapāṭhakas viz Dvādaśāha, Aupānuvākya, Ahīna* and *Ekāhas* between *Aśvamedha* and *Aptoryāma,* which are justified by the presence of the texts of commentary on the above *Prapāṭhakas.* Now the serial numbers of these *Prapāṭhakas* have been accordingly changed as 15th, 16th and 17th *Prapāṭhakas* on which commentaary is not available.

Again after याजमानाग्निष्टोमिकप्रायश्चित्तम्, there was a *Prapāṭhaka* under title 'अथ परिशेषः'. Under this *Pariśeṣa* there were two types of texts one belonging to *Gṛhya*-rites and other to the *Śrauta*-rituals. Since this text mainly belongs to the *Śrauta*-rituals, I have taken only those *Pariśeṣas* which were related to the *Śrauta*-rituals. Thus, among them I have given only— उपव्याहरणम्, स्वस्तिवचनम्, पाप्मनो विनिधयः, *etc.* up to the end. Their parallel texts are also found in *Baudhāyana Śrautasūtra* with many differences. No text of commentary is available to us on these *Pariśeṣa-sūtras.*

Now I am happy to say that my journey of preparing critical editions of the texts of *Vādhūla*-tradition, which I had strated in 1972 with the *VādhūlaŚrautsūtra,* which appeared in 1993 followed by *VādhūlaSmṛti* (2000), *Vādhūla-Anvākhyāna* (2001), *Vādhūla-Yajña-prāyaścitta* (2001), *Vādhūla-Gṛhyāgamavṛttirahasya* of Nārāyaṇa Miśra (2006), *Vādhūla Śrauta-Prayogakḷpti* of Śivaśroṇa (2010) and *Vādhūla-Gṛhyasūtra* with *Vṛtti* (2012), has come to successful completion with the publication of *Kalpāgamasaṅgraha* of Āryadāsa, a commentary on *Vādhūla-Śrautsūtra* at present. No more material in manuscript-form belonging to *Vādhūla*-tradition is available to me. Now, I am happy to present this critical edition of the *Kalpāgamasaṅgraha-Vyākhyā* of Āryadāsa for the first time in the hands of scholars, which I had started long ago.

Now I take this opportunity to express my deep sense of gratitude to the Instititutions, scholars and well-wishers, who helped me in any way in preparing and bringing out the critical edition of the present text *Kalpāgamasaṅgraha* of Āryadāsa, a very important text containing a store of knowledge regarding the *Śrauta*-rituals, coming through generation to generation in *Vādhūla*-tradition, and preserved in its time with many differences.

First of all I am thankful to the authorities of (i) Government Oriental Manuscript Library, Madras, (ii) Adyar Library and Research Centre, Madras and (iii) Oriental Research and Manuscript Library, University of Keral, specially to Dr. Vishalakasi, the then Director of the Institute, for providing me photo copies of the MSS.

I am very thankful Prof. Yasuke Ikari whose work I have utilized in revising the original *sūtra*-text of *Agnyādheya.*

I am heartily grateful to the Honorable members of the Advirsory committee and Prof. Dipti Tripathi Director, National Mission for Manuscripts (NMM), Delhi, Dr. Sanghamitra Basu, Co-ordinator, publications (NMM), Delhi for accepting this important text and taking keen interest for its publication under *Prakāśikā Series.*

I am also thankful to Dr. N.D. Sharma, HOD, IGNCA, Dr. T.N. Dharmadhikari, Dr. Vijay Shankar Shukla, Dr. Hridaya Ranjan Sharma, Shri Radheshyam Shastri, Dr. Ghanashyam Uniyal for providing their valuable suggestions in selection of correct readings in the case of textual variants.

At the end I would like to place on record my appreciation of the work done by Smt. Sandhya Chaubey, Dr. Aruna Shukla, Shri Krishna Kumar Chaubey, Smt. Rashmi Chaubey who assisted me in preparing various Indices of the text, proof-reading, transcription and colation work, and to Shri Yogesh Chaubey for composing and type-setting of the text. I always wish them all succes in their life.

B.B. Chaubey

Makara Sankranti, VS 2069 (13th Jan., 2013)

Professor Emeritus, Panjab University,
Director, Sangyan Vedic Studies & Research Centre, Hoshiarpur
Former Director, VVBIS & IS (P.U.), Hoshiarpur

संक्षेपाः

आश्वश्रौ.	- आश्वलायनश्रौतसूत्रम्	पु.	- पुटे
तैब्रा.	- तैत्तिरीयब्राह्मणम्	बौधाश्रौ.	- बौधायनश्रौतसूत्रम्
तैसं.	- तैत्तिरीय-संहिता	मनु.	- मनुस्मृति
निघ.	- निघण्टु	माशब्रा.	- माध्यन्दिनीयशतपथब्राह्मण
निरु.	- निरुक्त	वाधूअन्वा.	- वाधूल-अन्वाख्यानम्
पं.	- पंक्तौ	वाधूश्रौ.	- वाधूलश्रौतसूत्रम्
पा.	- पाणिनि	वा.प्रा.	- वाजसनेयि प्रातिशाख्य

Abbreviations

abri	- Abridged	Nir	- *Nirūkta*
ĀpŚS	- *Āpastamba Śrautasūtra*	Om	- Omitted
ĀśvaŚS	- *Āśvalāyana Śrautasūtra*	p.	- Page
Bṛhdd	- *Bṛhaddevatā*	ŚānkhŚS	- *Śāṅkhāyana Śrautasūtra*
cf	- Compare	ŚatBr	- *Śatapatha Brāhmaṇa*
Comm.	- Commentary	TaitBr	- *Taittirīya Brāhmaṇa*
e.g	- For example	VādhAnvā	- *Vādhūla Anvākhyānam*
i.e	- That is	VādhGS	- *Vādhūlagṛhyasūtra*
etc	- Etcetera	VādhGSV	- *Vādhūlagṛhyasūtra Vṛtti*
fn.	- Foot note	VādhŚS	- *Vādhūla Śrautasūtra*
Intro.	- Introduction	Vyā	- Vyākhyā
KātyŚS	- *Kātyāyana Śrautasūtra*		
MS	- Manuscript		
MSS	- Manuscripts		

Key to Transliteration

VOWELS

अ a	आ ā	इ i	ई ī	उ u	ऊ ū
(but)	(palm)	(it)	(beet)	(put)	(pool)
ऋ ṛ	ए e	ऐ ai	ओ o	औ au	
(rhythm)	(play)	(air)	(toe)	(loud)	

CONSONANTS

Guttural	क ka	ख* kha	ग ga	घ gha	ङ ṅa
	(skate)	(blockhead)	(gate)	(ghost)	(sing)
Palatal	च ca	छ cha	ज ja	झ jha	ञ ña
	(chunk)	(catchhim)	(john)	(hedgehog)	(bunch)
Cerebral	ट ṭa	ठ* ṭha	ड/ड़ ḍa	ढ*/ढ़ ḍha	ण* ṇa
	(start)	(anthill)	(dart)	(godhead)	(under)
Dental	त ta	थ tha	द da	ध dha	न na
	(path)	(thunder)	(that)	(breathe)	(numb)
Labial	प pa	फ* pha	ब ba	भ bha	म ma
	(spin)	(philosophy)	(bin)	(abhor)	(much)
Semi-vowels	य ya	र ra	ल la	व va	
	(young)	(drama)	(luck)	(vile)	
Sibilants	श śa	ष ṣa	स sa	ह ha	
	(shove)	(bushel)	(so)	(hum)	
Others	क्ष kṣa	त्र tra	ज्ञ jña	ळ* l	ॠ* ṝ
	(*kṣātriya*)	(*triśūla*)	(*jñānī*)	(play)	

अं *(—) ṁ* or *ṃ amusūra* (nasalisation of preceding vowel) like *saṁskṛti/or soṃskṛti*

अः *visarga* = *ḥ* (aspiration of preceding vowel like (*prātaḥ*)

ऽ *Avagraha* consonant #' consonant (like-*imé vasthitā*)

Anusvāra at the end of a line is presented by m (म्) and not *ṁ*

*No exact English equivalents for these letters.

Introduction

1. Critical Apparatus used for the present edition—

The following MSS have been used for the critical edition of the *Kalpāgamasaṅgraha* of Āryadāsa, a commentary on the *VādhŚS*—

M¹— A MS deposited in the Government Oriental Manuscript Library, Madras under No. R 4375, Devanagari script, written on both sides.

At the top of the first page the MS gives the heading :

श्रीः अथ वाधूलगृह्यकल्पव्याख्या

The word गृह्य of this title has been corrected as श्रौत with question mark (not by the scribe but probably by the user). Upto page 8 each page bears the folio heading वाधूलगृह्यकल्पव्याख्या Rest of the pages bear no folio-headings.

The *Śrautsūtra*-portion begins with—

अथ ग्रन्थपातः ...

प्रार्थनामुपक्रमे यन्नत्वा कृतकृत्यास्स्युस्तं नमामि गजाननम्। अग्नीनानाधास्यमानः संभारन्सभरते, *etc.*

and ends with —

इमा द्वादश शतं गावोस्याग्निष्टोमस्य दक्षिणास्तासान्तव भाग ब्रह्मन् प्रतिगृह्णीष्व त्वत्पुरुषैस्सह इमा = होतः प्रति = स्सह इमाः = मध्वर्यो प्रति = मुद्गातरग्रे गृह्णीष्व सदस्य प्रतिगृह्णीष्व इति। (p.454, line 3)

On p.120, at the foot of the page it is written: K.A. कृष्णशास्त्रिणा सह परिशोधि and signature is put after that. On the left foot-corner the date 22/10/4 (4.10.22) is given. Again on p. 216 at left foot-corner the date is given as 17.11.22 on p. 392 at the left foot corner the date is given as 1.9.23 with signature in right foot-corner. On last page two dates have been given 2.11.23 in the right foot-corner and 10.11.23 in the left foot-corner. These dates have been given by the checkers who compared this transcript with original one. From these dates it is obvious that this transcript was prepared and checked in instalments. The original one from which it was prepared seems to have been frequently broken. The broken texts have been shown by dots.

M— A MS deposited in the Government Oriental Manuscript Library, Madras under No. R 2978, given at the top of page 399, but on the first page No. is given as 923. It starts with—

श्री:

अथ वाधूलकल्पव्याख्या

...प्रमाणं वेद: सचपुरुषार्थाञ्चोदयति.

and ends with—

इतिवाधूलकल्पसूत्रव्याख्या समाप्ता

समाप्तश्चायं ग्रन्थ: ।

This manuscript has been copied from a MS in possesson of Nedumpilli Mana and compared with that of Kaḍaṅgaśeri Mana by K.C. Venkatasvami Mana Sastry as indicated in colophon—

"Transcribed from Nedumpilli Mana compared with that of Kaḍaṅgaśeri Mana by K.C. Venkatasubrahmanya Sastry Mana".

Actually this MS is a composite MS having three texts in it—

1. *Vādhūlakalpasūtravākhyā* p.1-377
2. *Vādhūla Śrauta Prayoga Klṛpti* of Śivaśoṇa p.377, line 4 - p.498, line 12
3. *Vādhūlagṛhyasūtra* with *Vṛtti* p.498, line 13- p.552 up to last.

It may be pointed out that the original MSS from which this MS was first transcribed into Devanāgarī script and compared with were in Malayālam script.

Ad— A composite MS copied in three volumes comprising of three texts—

1. *Vādhūlakalpavākhyā* of Āryādasa (p.1-772),
2. *Vādhūla Prayoga Klṛpti* of Śivaśona (p.772-974) and
3. *Vādhūlagṛhyasūtravṛtti* (p.982-1071), deposited in the Adyar Manuscript Library, Madras, under No. TR 636.1, 63371

MS begins with—

श्री गणपतये नम:

वाधूल कल्प सूत्र व्याख्या

...प्रमाणं वेद:. स च पुरुषार्थान् चोदयति.

and ends with

इति कल्पसूत्रव्याख्या

समाप्ता

समाप्तश्चायं ग्रन्थ:

मद्रपुरस्थराजकीयपुस्तकशालायां मूलमातृकाया: विलिखितं पुस्तकं नारायणशर्मा 18/11/23

From the last colophon it is obvious that thia MS was copied from the Devanāgarī MS No. R-2978, deposited in the Government Oriental Manuscript Library, Madras. It is just a copy of that MS without making any emmendation in it.

T— A MS deposited in the Oriental Research and Manuscript Library, University of Keral, Trivendrum, under No. 1147. Actually it is not a copy of M or Ad, or any of the orignal Malayalam MSS which were preserved in two families Nedumpilli Mana and Kaḍaṅgaśeri Mana. As a matter of fact it was an effort, made by the Paṇḍits of the Oriental Research Institute, to prepare an edition of the comm. of Āryadāsa on *VādhŚS.* It was deposited in the form of MS along with other MSS under No. 1147.

The MS begins with—

॥ श्री ॥

महागणपतये नम:

श्रीवाधूलमहर्षिप्रणीतं

कल्पसूत्रम्

आर्यदासकृतकल्पागमसंग्राहाख्यव्याख्योपेतम्

अग्निष्टोमप्रकरणम् (wrongly for अग्न्याधेयप्रकरणम्)

अग्नीनाधास्यमान: संभारान् संभरते ॥ १ ॥

... प्रमाणं वेद: । स च पुरुषार्थान् चोदयति.

पञ्चदश:

समाप्त एकाहाख्य: काण्ड: p.656

2.a Nature of the MSS M and Ad—

The present edition of the *Kalpāgamasaṅgraha* of Āryādas is based on the above mentioned 3 MSS- M, Ad and T. It is natural, as well as, expected that the MSS of a particular text must follow the order of the original text. But this does not happen always. The original MS written by the author must have been in a proper order. But in course of time, due to bad condition of the MS, breakage in order of the folios takes place and this goes on in subsequent copies of that MS, resulting into displacement of folios. As a result of this, a number of displacements take place in the subsequent copies of the MSS. Thus a big or small text dealing with one ritual mixes with the text dealing with another ritual. Sometimes a portion of the text dealing with the same ritual is displaced and copied down in subsequent copies of the MSS. Such displacements badly affect the proper order of the rituals creating great problem for the editor to edit the text properly. At the time of comparing or checking of the MSS by an expert of the subject, such displacements come to his notice and he gives his remarks about this displacement in marginalia notes. When I started editing this text I found many such displacements in both M and Ad, which I would like to point out here-

1. A text, begining with कर्तव्य° (M p.13, line 5, Ad p.32, line 3) up to °तस्याहिता (M p.14, line 16, Ad p.35, line 13) between मातारिश्वा श्वसितीति and मातरिश्वाऽन्तरिक्षे, has been wrongly given in both M and Ad. But T gives this text at its proper place (See fn. 2 on p.13; fn. 1 on p.16).
2. After the text °तस्याहिता in both M and Ad, the text has been disturbed by the displacement of the folio (M p.14, line 15, Ad p.35, line 13) after °तस्याहिता, the concerned text begins in M on p.16, line 16 and Ad p.40, line 7. (See fn. 2 on p.18).
3. Due to displacement of folios in the original Malayalam MS, a large portion of the text dealing with *Agnihotra* beginning with 'ज्वलितान् तथा' (M p.288, line 7; Ad p.605, line 9) and ending with पर्वणि (M p.293, line 7; Ad p.615, line 11) has wrongly been copied under *Rājasūya*

Prapāṭhaka. It has rightly been noticed by the scribe in marginalia note in both the MSS : अत्र ग्रन्थपात: अध्यायद्वयस्याभावश्च (M p.288; Ad p.605, line 11). T rightly gives this text at its proper place under *Agnihotra* (vide fn. * p. 31). Thereafter the remaining text of *Agnihotra* begins with ...गमनम्। अन्यत्र *etc* (M p.21, line 1; Ad p.49, line 7); also see fn. * on p.444.

4. A large portion of text after यथाग्न्येयादीनां beginning with 'ऊर्जे त्वेति' (M p.26, line 11; Ad p.67, line 5) and ending with उत्तरत्र आहवनीय (M p.30, line 1; Ad p.67, line 5) dealing with *Darśapūrṇamāsa*, has wrongly come under *Agnyupasthāna*. This displacement has been noticed by the scribe within the text पाठोऽनुमेय: । ऊर्जे त्वेति (M p.26, line 11; Ad p.67, line 7). T gives the entire text in a proper order (vide fn. 6 on p.45; fn. under * on p.45).

5. Both M and Ad show the sign of *abridged* text as: =, *eg.*

   ऋतुपात्रे लभते = ब्राह्मणं (M p.207)

   आग्रयणे = श्यामाकांश्च (M p.83)

   whereas T shows such *abridged* text by the sign (+), *eg.*

2.b Nature of T—

As I have already mentioned above, T is not a manuscript in the sense that it has been copied from the original Malayalam MS, but an effort was made by the Paṇḍits of Oriental Research and Manuscript Library, University of Kerala, to edit the text on the basis of Kerala MSS, available to them. Here I would like to point out the nature of this edited MS as under—

1. In form of this MS it was the first effort to prepare a critical edition of the *Kalpāgamasaṅgraha* of Āryadās by the Paṇḍits of the Oriental Institute.
2. A large number of textual displacements which have occured in original Malayalam MSS have been arranged in proper order of the text dealing with the ritual concerned.
3. Different readings have been recorded, some readings with question mark have been suggested under footnote on the back of the previous page. Sometimes different

readings from two Malayalam MSS *viz.* क, ख have been given below on the same page. Where the reading is doubtful it gives under bracket with questionmark (?), I have shown it by T[1].

4. At one place T shows the liberty of an editor to change the prose-text making it a verse. M Ad give a text—
शीक्षा व्याकरणं निरुक्तं छन्दोविचितिर्ज्योतिषामयनं कल्प इति M Ad p.1
T gives this text in a verse-form as under—
शिक्षाव्याकरणं छन्दो निरुक्तं छन्दोविचिति ज्यौतिषं तथा।
[कल्पश्चेति षडङ्गानि वेदस्याहुर्मनीषिणः] T p.1

5. T has tried to supply the text where it was broken in both M and Ad *e.g.*
इतिकरणस्याप्रकारवाचित्वाद्वानस्पत्य...ज्ञायुधाना॰ (M p.4, line 10-12)
T gives the text filling the gaps caused by broken text (T p.7). Such texts given in T helped me to construct the broken texts at several places.

6. I have also noticed at certain places that the text given in M is correct in comparison to T and also sometimes vice-versa. I have mentioned it in the footnotes of the concerned texts.

7. The pagination number has been very much disturbed in T. It appears that after preparing the text as per order given in MSS from which it was prepared, but after going through the text it was found that the topic dealt with therein was not in proper order, so those pages were shifted at another places affecting the original order of pagination, so new pagination numbers were given in those pages.

8. Sometimes T wrongly takes the text of MS as additional and gives the same under fn. see *Vyākhyā* on 3.1.125, fn. 11 *etc.* T wrongly gives the text beginning with दर्शनात् and ending with करोति in fn. not under the body of the comm., whereas both M and Ad give it as a part of comm. See fn. under *-*, the comm. on 2.2.2.30-36 (p.67).

9. Sometimes T suplies the texts (T p.447, line 3-9; p.450, line 6-9) which have been ommited in both A and Ad (vide fn. 8-8 on p. 365).

3. Order and division of the *Vyākhyā*-text as found in the MSS—

1. MSS are not unanimous about the title of the

Prapāṭhakas. Both M and Ad do not mention the title of the first *Prapāṭhaka* in the beginning. At the end also 'इति षष्ठोऽध्याय प्रथमः प्रपाठकः' is given without mentioning the main topic of the *Prapāṭhak*a (M p.30, line11; Ad p.68, line 4). On the other hand T gives wrong nomenclature of the topic of the first *Prapāṭhaka* as 'अग्निष्टोमप्रकरणम्' in the beginning of the first *Prapāṭhaka*.

2. Both M and Ad do not give the title as well as the serial number of the second *Prapāṭhaka* (M p.30; Ad p.68). Ad only gives the benedictory word 'श्रीः'. T gives the title of the *Prapāṭhaka* as 'दर्शपूर्णमासः', without mentioning the serial number of the *Prapāṭhaka* (T p.56). Both M and Ad show the end of *Prapāṭhaka* as : इति तृतीयः समाप्तश्च. Here one may be misguided to take it as the closing number of the *Prapāṭhakas*. Actually, 'इति तृतीयः' refers to the end of the third *Anuvāka,* not to the end of *Prapāṭhaka*. However, the second *Prapāṭhaka,* too, ends here, though not mentioned in any of the MSS. T also shows the end with- 'इति तृतीयः प्रपाठः समाप्तश्च।' (T p.117).

   Here it should have been : 'इति तृतीयोऽध्यायः। प्रपाठकश्च समाप्तः।'

3. Both M, Ad neither give the serial number of the *Prapāṭhaka* nor the title of the *Prapāṭhaka* (M p.69). Ad starts with श्रीः। अथ प्रथमः (Ad p.153). It refers to the *Anuvāka* number अथ प्रथमः, not the number of the *Prapāṭhaka*. However, T gives the title of the *Prapāṭhaka* ॥ याजमानम् ॥ (p.120) and at the end refers to the end : तृतीयः प्रपाठकः (p. 149).

4. M Ad and T without giving the nomenclature of the *Prapāṭhaka* give the serial number अथ चतुर्थः as they generally do for indicating *Anuvāka* (M p.91; T p.149). Ad, however uses the benedictory word श्रीः before अथ चतुर्थः (Ad p.202).

   M mentions the close of the fourth *Prapāṭhaka* as : चतुर्थप्रपाठकः without using इति before समाप्तः or after it (p.116). Ad wrongly shows the end of the fourth *Prapāṭhaka* twice इति चतुर्थः प्रपाठकः समाप्तः (Ad p.263) and इति चतुर्थः

प्रपाठकः समाप्तः (Ad p.265). This first इति चतुर्थः प्रपाठकः समाप्तः was a mistake for इति चतुर्थः which was used for चतुर्थ अनुवाक. T refers to the end of *Prapāṭhaka* as चतुर्थः प्रपाठकः neither using the word इति in the beginning nor समाप्तः at the end (T p.194).

5. M, Ad, T without mentioning the *Prapāṭhaka* number as : पञ्चमः प्रपाठकः give the nomenclature of the topic : अथ पशुबन्धः (M p.116, Ad p.265, T p.194).

   Ad wrongly gives इति प्रथमः प्रपाठकः समाप्तः (Ad p.287) instead of इति प्रथमः (अनुवाकः) under *Paśubandha*.

   M does not mention the end of the *Prapāṭhaka*, only gives इति तृतीयः (for *Anuvāka*).

   Ad and T, however, mention the end of the third *Anuvāka* as well as the end of the fifth *Prapāṭhaka* : इति तृतीयः; पञ्चमः प्रपाठकः समाप्तः. Here it may be pointed out that both Ad and T make mention of the end of the *Haviryajajña* which comprises of *Agnyādheya, Agnihotra, Darśapūrṇamāseṣṭi, Cāturmāsyeṣṭi* and *Paśubandha,* which have been dealt here in first five *Prapāṭhakas* : 'आहविर्यज्ञः समाप्तः०' (Ad p.314, T p.228).

6. In M there is no mention of the end of the fifth *Prapāṭhaka*. However, Ad and T make mention of closing of the fifth *Prapāṭhaka* : पञ्चमः प्रपाठकः समाप्तः (Ad p.314, T p.228). But inspite of mentioning the end of the fifth *Prapāṭhaka* they do not mention the serial number of the following *Prapāṭhaka* as : षष्ठः प्रपाठकः, but following M they wrongly mention अथ चतुर्थः. None of the MSS gives the title of the *Prapāṭhaka* as : अथ अग्निष्टोमः or अथ षष्ठः प्रपाठकः.

7. The entire text of seventh *Anuvāka* (comprising of four *Paṭalas*) of the sixth *Prapāṭhaka,* is given in two sentenses : 'इषे त्वे'त्ययमपि व्याख्यातः। कृत्स्नाम्नानप्रयोजनं तत्रैव व्याख्यातम् (See comm. on *VādhŚS* 5.2.1.1-33 under *Paśubandha*) (M p.179, Ad p. 391).

8. Due to displacement of folios T gives a big text (T p.276, line 6- p.279, line 7) dealing with दर्शपूर्णमास under

Agniṣṭoma. Remaining text after p.279, line 7 belong to *Agniṣṭoma*.

9. All MSS mention the end of *Prapāṭhaka* after इति अष्टमः अष्टमोनुवाकः समाप्तः प्रपाठकः (M p.182, Ad p.396, T p.292). But actually the *Prapāṭhaka* dealing with *Agniṣṭoma* does not end here. The continuety of the text of the 8th *Anuvāka* is also evident from the repetition of last *sūtra* पञ्चदश नक्षत्राणि at the beginning of next *Anuvāka*. The *Anuvāka*-numbers of this *Prapāṭhaka* continue upto the 15th *Anuvāka*. In the original *VādhŚS* MS M No. R 4375, after the end of the 8th *Anuvāka* a text is given : इति प्रथमः प्रश्नः (p.194). This indicates the end of half of the *Prapāṭhaka*, not the end of the *Prapāṭhaka*. This is also supported by the fact that after this *Anuvāka*, the serial numbers of the *Anuvākas* continue, till the 15th *Anuvāka*, where this *Agniṣṭoma-Prapāṭhaka* ends. All the MSS show here the end of the *Prapāṭhaka*.

   This is also evident from the colophon, given at the end of *Prapāṭhaka*, as under :

   इति पञ्चदशः (अनुवाकः)

   समाप्तः प्रपाठकः।

   अग्निष्टोमाख्यं काण्डमार्यदासस्य कृतौ कल्पागमसंग्रहे समाप्तम्

   हरनमश्शिवाय गुरवे शरणम्। रामचन्द्राभयं देहि मे कमलालयालयाय ते नमः (M p.226, Ad p.486)

   अग्निष्टोमाख्यं काण्डम् आर्यदासस्य कृतौ कल्पागमसङ्ग्रहे समाप्तम्॥ (T p.369)

   Here it may be pointed out that all MSS call it अग्निष्टोमाख्यं काण्डम्. Here it is also to be pointed out that both M and Ad unanimously mention समाप्तः प्रपाठकः after इति पञ्चदशः. But T wrongly gives सप्तमः प्रपाठकः (T p.369).

   Here on the authority of both M and Ad we may take सप्तमः प्रपाठकः as given in T as a corrupt reading for समाप्तः प्रपाठकः.

10. None of the MSS gives the serial number of the *Prapāṭhaka* which deals with *Agnikalpa*. It begins with अथाग्निकल्पे प्रथमोऽध्यायः प्रारभ्यते (M p.226, Ad p.487, T p.370). It may be pointed out that here 'अध्यायः' is the subsitute for अनुवाकः.

M Ad T, unlike preceding *Prapāṭhakas,* mention the title of the topic also at the close of the first *Anuvāka*—

इति अग्निकल्पे प्रथमः (M p.232, Ad p.499, T p.379) and also at the end of 15th *Anuvāka*—

इत्यग्निकल्पे पञ्चदशोऽध्यायः (M p.274, Ad p.518, T p.436).

11. It may be pointed out that all MSS mention at the beginning as well as at the end of the 6th and 7th *Prapāṭhakas* as *Kāṇḍa*, not as *Prapāṭhaka*—

 समाप्तं चाग्निकाण्डम् (M p.274, Ad p.518, T p.436).

 What is difference between *Prapāṭhaka* and *Kāṇḍa* ? Both 6th and 7th *Prapāṭhakas* have equal number of 15 *Anuvākas* in each. It appears that in these two *Prapāṭhakas*, some rituals comming under *Iṣṭi* have also been prescribed to be performed. *Kāṇḍa* refers to a bigger division than the *Prapāṭhaka*. Both *Agniṣṭoma* and *Agnikalpa* comprise of 15 *Anuvākas* or *Aadhyāyas* each. A *Kāṇḍa* may consist of many *Prapāṭhakas* as we find in the case of *Taitt.S* and *Taitt.Br.*

12. M, Ad, T after *Agnikalpa* deal with *Vājapeya*, without mentioning the *Prapāṭhaka* number (M p.274, Ad p.679, T p.246). M and Ad mention the topic अथ वाजपेयः and then starts the text. But T without mentioning the topic, directly starts the text—

 अथ वाजपेयेन यक्ष्यमाणः° (T p. 446).

 None of the MSS mentions the serial number of the *Prapāṭhaka* at the end. They only mention the name of the ritual—

 वाजपेयः समाप्तः (T वाजपेयं समाप्तम्।) (M p.283, Ad p.576, T p.461).

13. All MSS without mentioning the *Prapāṭhaka*- number begin with : 'अनन्तरं राजसूयो वक्ष्यते' (M p.283, line 15). Actually, the text given in M is the beginning of the commentary, not the title of the text. Ad rightly gives the title : ॥ श्रीः ॥ अथ राजसूयः ॥ (Ad p.596, line 8-9). T does not give the title (T p.461). At the end of the text of *Rājasūya* इति राजसूयः समाप्तः is given, but the number of *Prapāṭhaka* is not given (M p.297, Ad p.624, T p.484).

14. M T begin with the title of the ritual : अथाश्वमेधः प्रारभ्यते (M

p.297, T p.484) without mentioning the number of the *Prapāṭhaka*. Actually this line is not the title of the text, but a part of the commentary. Only Ad gives the title श्री: 'अथ अश्वमेध:' and 'अथ अश्वमेध: प्रारभ्यते' as a part of the text of comm. At the end all the MSS clearly mention समाप्तश्चाश्वमेधाख्य: प्रपाठक: (M p.313, Ad p.664, T p.530).

15 M Ad deal with *Dvādaśāha* without mentioning the number of the *Prapāṭhaka* : अथ द्वादशाह: (M p.313, Ad p.655). T, too, does not mention the title of the *Prapāṭhaka*. It directly commences with the text : 'द्वादशाहाय दीक्षिष्यमाण: समवस्यन्ति' (T p.530). The end of the *Dvādaśāha* has been shown as : इति द्वादशाहे चतुर्थोऽध्याय: समाप्त: (M p.325, Ad p.679). T however, on the authority of Kaḍaṅṅśśeri MS, does not accept the use of the word 'समाप्त:'. It merely gives : 'द्वादशाहे चतुर्थ:'. In fn. it mentions : चतुर्थोऽध्याय: समाप्त: इति ग्रन्थसमाप्तिर्दृश्यते। कडङ्डश्शेरिपुस्तकरीत्या तु ग्रन्थसमाप्तिर्न दृश्यते (T fn. 4, p.553 (543)). On the authority of T can we think of existence of some more *Anuvākas* under *Dvādaśāha* ? But no marginalia note is given in M, which was compared with Kaḍaṅgaśeri MS by K.C. Venkatasvamin.

16. After द्वादशाह, all M, Ad, T deal with *Aupānuvākya* in four *Anuvākas* without mentioning the *Prapāṭhaka* number : अथ औपानुवाक्य: (M p.326, Ad p.679, T p.553 (543)). It ends with four *Anuvākas*: 'इतिसमाप्तमौपानुवाक्यञ्चतुर्थ:' (M p.344, Ad p.716, T p.577 (587)).

17. After *Aupānuvākya* all MSS deal with *Ahīnas* in ten *Anuvākas* without mentioning the number of the *Prapāṭhaka* : अथ अहीनाख्य: प्रारभ्यते (M p.344, T p.577 (587)). It may be pointed out that the text अथ अहीनाख्य: प्रारभ्यते, as given in both M and T, is the part of the beginning of the commentary, not the title of the *Prapāṭhaka*. Ad, however, gives the title श्री: । अथ अहीनाख्य: (Ad p.716). But mention of *Prapāṭhaka* is found in none. However, at the end of *Ahīna* all MSS unanimously mention the end of the *Prapāṭhaka* :

इति, समाप्तश्चाहीनाख्य: प्रपाठक: (M p.357, Ad p.738, T p.606 (596)).

18. None of the MSS gives the title or serial number of the

Prapāṭhaka as : अथ एकाहाः. All give the title 'अथ बृहस्पतिसवः' (M p.356, Ad p.738, T p.606 (596)), which is one of the *Ekāhas*. M Ad give अथातो बृहस्पतिसवाः as the main title of the *Prapāṭhaka*, but T under body of the text, not as a title.

It is important to point out that a large part of remaining text of *Ekāha* beginning with सहोवाचेत्यादि (M p.377, line 3 to p.541, line 11; Ad p.1040, line 6 to p.1053, line 8) and ending with इति समाप्तः एकाहाख्यः काण्डः, has been misplaced in both M and Ad, under *Vādhūlagṛhyasūtra* (see fn. 14 on p.510). This large displaced text has been given at its proper place in T under *Ekāhas* (T p.632(642), line12-p.646, line 6).

19 In the *sūtra*-text there were certain places where some long texts were given in *abridged* forms. For example, a long text 5.2.2.2-31 was given as ब्रह्मा=अवेक्षन्ते in *Agniṣṭoma*. Āryādasa has explained the text in *Paśubandha*. Since that text was given in *abridged* form in *Agniṣṭoma* 6.7.2.2-31, Āryādas has mentioned that 'इषे त्वे'त्ययमपि व्याख्यातः। कृत्स्नाम्नानप्रयोजनमपि तत्रैव व्याख्यातम् (6.7.1.1-33). The entire text of three *Paṭalas* of *Paśubandh* has been given in *abridged* form (See 6. 7.1.1-4).

20. T wrongly gives the text दर्शनात् = करोति in fn. not in the body of the text. M Ad rightly give the text under the body of the text as the part of commentary on *sūtra* 2.2.2.30-36 (See fn. *-* on p.73).

21. T wrongly takes the text between 'अर्थवादोऽपि = कल्पित०' as additional and gives it in fn. : (०दोऽपि 'नास्तीत्ययं छन्दोब्राह्मणमेतन्मन्त्रलिङ्ग' इति मध्ये वर्तते). Actually, this text is a part of commentary on *sūtra* 3.1.1.25 (See fn. 1-1 on p.97).

22. T also takes the text 'देवत्वस्य दैव्यं नामैतदुपस्थानम्। अथातो' 'दैव्यं नामैतदुपस्थानम् अथा' इति मध्येऽस्ति'. Actually it is the text of commentary on *sūtra* 3.1.2.26-27 (p.97).

23. T takes the text 'अन्यत्राम्नातानामन्यत्र कतिपयान्येव दृश्यन्ते। अथ परिसंख्यानमिति' as given in both M Ad, as additional and gives the same in fn. as 'किं प्रमाणम्। अन्यत्राम्नातानामन्यत्र कतिपयान्येव दृश्यन्ते। अथ परिसंख्या' इति मध्ये वर्तते। (See fn. 13-13

on p.110).

24. The text beginning with 'श्रुतिवाक्ये तु' (comm. on 4.2.1.23) and ending with 'जातीयानि कर्त...' (comm. on 4.2.1.28) is missing in both M and Ad. However, this missing text has been given in T from p.162, line 17 to p.164, line 12. T notices this ommision in the fn. 5 as : 162 पु 17 पं श्रुतिवाक्ये + 164 पु. 12 पं जातीयानि कर्त० इति पर्यन्तं नास्ति. But the text at the end is repeated. As a matter of fact, the text at the end is missing upto (तुल्यजाती)यानि not कर्तव्यानि, as given in T.

4. Displacement and intermingling of texts in the MSS—

1. Due to displacement of folios in both M and Ad the text beginning with सादयित्वा (M p.26, line 11, Ad p.60, line 7) and ending with निदधाति (M p.30, line 1, Ad p.67, line 5) dealing with *Darśapūrṇmāsa* has wrongly come under *Agnyādhāna*. This text has been shifted at its proper place. Also see fn. 6, p.45, T rightly gives this text at its proper place.
2. T wrongly gives a long text beginning with 'ने प्रागग्रमपद्रहव्यन्तरा' (p.276, line 6) and ending with 'अतएव' (p.279, line 7) belonging to *Darśapūrṇamāseṣṭi* under *Agniṣṭoma* between ब्राह्मण and आम्नातमपि. I have put this text at its proper place under *Darśapūrṇamāsa* (comm. on 2.1.1.31- 2.1.2.2).
3. Due to displacement of folios all MSS wrongly give the text beginning with अध्वर्युवुपह्वयस्व (M p.208, line 7; Ad p.450, line 4; T p.332, line 9) and ending with मन्यामहे (M p.209, line 11; Ad p.452, line 11; T p.334, line 8) along with commentary on 6.9.1.16.
4. Due to displacement of folios in the original MS the text of commentary on 6.9.2.28 beginning with 'धाना: करम्भ: विसृजति' (M p.185, line 4; Ad p.402, line 9; T p.296, line 19) and ending with विसृजति (M p.188 line 2; Ad p.406, line 8; T p.299, line 19) has been wrongly given between निर्वाप and प्रस्थितकर्मैतत् (6.9.1.17- 6.9.2.1) See fn. 17 (p.266). Actually this text is commentary on 6.11.1.28. (See fn. 7 on p.286).

5. M Ad T, due to displacement of folio, wrongly give the text 'वसुमद्गणस्य = भक्षयन्तीति' (comm. on 6.1.4.18) after the commentary of *sūtra* 6.11.4.19 (M p.207, line 7-9; Ad p.447, line 12- p.448, line 12). See fn. 2-2 on p.293; fn. 8 on p.294.

6. Due to displacement of folios the text beginning with अध्वर्युवुपह्वयस्व in the MSS (M p.208, line 7; Ad p.450, line 4; T p.332, line 9) and ending with मन्यामहे (M p.209, line 11; Ad p.452, line 11; T p.334, line 8) has been wrongly given at another place. Also See fn. 11 (p.300). This text has been placed at its proper place as the text of commentary on *sūtra* 6.12.2.39-69 (p.300-302).

7. Due to displacement of folios M Ad T wrongly give the text beginning with 'धानाः करम्भः पयस्या' (M p.185, line 4; Ad p.402, line 9; T p.296, line 19) and ending with च प्रस्तरे विसृजति (M p.187 line 2; Ad p.406, line 8; T p.299, line 19) after the commentary on 6.9.1.17. Actually, this text is commentary on 6.11.1.28 (p.286-87). (See fn. 7 on p.286).

8. T takes the text between संख्या and प्रतिभागेन देया as extra : संख्या इत्यनन्तरं 'सम्बन्धा दक्षिणा सप्तदशेभ्य ऋत्विग्भ्यस्समप्रविभागेन देया' इत्यधिकं मध्येऽस्ति तदनु एवं सप्तदश इत्यादि (T fn.1, p.444, line 2). Actually the text after भवति beginning with 'स्वरथं च' upto विदांकुर्वन्तु, has wrongly been copied in MSS between भवति (M p.279, line 4; Ad p.588, line 2; T p.444, line 3) and विष्णुक्रमा (M p.279, line 8; Ad p.588, line 8; T p.444, line 11). Actually, this text is commentary on the *sūtras* 8.3.1.2-3. (See fn. *-* on p.427).

9. Due to displacement of folios the text after रथानां विशेषा (M p.280, line 19; Ad p.593, line 11) upto कोऽत्र प्रतिकारः (M p.283, line 8) is wrongly given in M on p.282, line 5- p.283, line 8; Ad p.593, line 11- p.596, line1. The text being commentary on *sūtra* 8.2.3.3 has been placed at its proper place. (cf fn. *-* on p.427; fn. 1-1 on p.525).

T under fn. 11(p.446) notices this displacement and justifies its placing at its proper place as under :

'अयं पाठः कडङ्डश्शेरिग्रामस्थ पुस्तकानुसारी वर्तते। उपरि विद्यमान तृतीयाध्यायान्तग्रन्थोऽपि तदनुसार्येव यथावस्थित एव च वर्तते। परन्तु अत्र

दृश्यमानलिखितपुस्तके तु इत्थं वर्तते। 446 पुटे 20 पंक्तौ विशेषा इत्यनन्तरं 448 पु. 19 पंक्तौ एभिर्मन्त्रैः इत्यारभ्य द्वितीयाध्यायः समापितः। तदनु तृतीयेऽध्याये 450 पु. 17 पं. राजक्रयानन्तरं इत्यत्र राजक्रया इत्यनन्तरं अनन्तरमित्यतः पूर्वं मध्ये 446 पु. 20 पं. अन्ते ऽनन्तानावगतेः। इत्याद्यारभ्य 448 पु. 19 पं- एभिर्मन्त्रैः इत्येतावत्पर्यन्तो ग्रन्थः लिखितः। पूर्वमुत्तरं चान्यत् समानम्।'

This displacement has also been noticed in the marginalia note on p.280 in M by K.C. Venkatasubrahmaṇya Sastry stating: 'विशेषेति पदमारभ्य 282 भागे 6 पंक्तौ 'आजिसृद्भ्य' इति पदं गृहीत्वा 283 भागे 19 पंक्तौ 'कोऽत्र प्रतीकारः' इत्यन्तं पठित्वा 280 भागे 14 पंक्तौ मन्त्रैरवरोहतीति यथाक्रमपाठेन इयमेव रीतिः समीचाना इति मे मतिः' : (See fn. 2 on p.428).

10. The text after रथानां विशेषा (M p.280, line 19, Ad p.593, line 11) up to कोऽत्र प्रतिकारः which was wrongly given in M on p.282, line 5 - p.283, line 8, Ad p.593, line 11 - p.596, line 1, is commentary on *sūtra* 8.2.3.5-40. (See fn. 2 on p.428).

11. Due to displacement of folios a long text beginning with ज्वलितान् तथासति धार्यपक्षे (M p.288, line 7, Ad p.605, line 9) and ending with पयसा वा स्वयं पर्वणि (M p.293, line 7, Ad p.615, line 11) dealing with *Agnihotra* has wrongly come under *Rājasūya*. This text has been shifted to its proper place under *Agnihotra* (See fn. * on p.31). M p.288 in marginalia note refers to अत्र ग्रन्थपातः अध्यायद्वयाभावश्च.

12. A large portion of the text of commentary between कर्मणा and दक्षिणेनाग्निष्ठं (M p.303, line 6, Ad p.636, line 2) is missing in both M and Ad. T clearly mentions : कर्मणा इत्यनन्तरं 502 पु. 8 पं स्वधितिभिः. ये' इत्येतावत्पर्यन्तो ग्रन्थः नास्ति लुप्त इव भाति (T p.494, fn. 6). However, T supplies the text on the basis of the Kaḍaṅgaśeri MS which was in possession of the Paṇḍits working for preparation of an edition of the text. In absence of the other MSS the textual variations have not been recorded. The omitted text of M, Ad is given here on the basis of T (See pp 419-435) : commentary on *sūtras* 10.3.2.6- X.6.1.1 (pp.478-496).

13. Both M Ad wrongly give the text beginning with 'याभिः

सह' and ending with 'अत्याका तत्रस्था' (M p.304, line 18-19, Ad p.639, line 5-7) at the end of 6th *Anuvāka*. This text is also given in both M and Ad in the opening lines of the next 7th *Anuvāka*. As the proper place of the text is in the beginning of the 7th *Anuvāka*, the extra text given at the end of the 6th *Anuvāka* has been removed.

14. A text beginning with यमाना (M p.306, line 4, Ad p.641, line 11) and ending with अभिमेथिकानाम् covering the commentary on *sūtra* 10.7.1.29-30 is missing in both M and Ad. This text has been supplied by T from Kaḍaṅgaśeri MS (See fn. *-* on p.503).

15. A text beginning with अहीनपक्षा° and ending with याजयन्तीति has been supplied by T, which informs the omission of the text in M under fn. 2: अहीन + याजयन्तीति नास्ति (T p.533).

5. Intermingling of Different types of texts in the MSS—

1. Due to displacement and enter-mingling, some texts of different titles have entered in the commentary. After 'स होवाच' the text of *Vādhūla- Prayogaklṛpti* has come in both M (p.377, line 3- 498, line 10) and Ad (p.772, line 8) and runs up to M (p.498 line 10) and Ad (p.979, line 1). About the remaining text of the commentary, T informs that : "स होवाच... इत्येतावत्पर्यन्तमेव कल्पसूत्रव्याख्यायामुपलभ्यते। अनन्तरं 377 पु. 3 पं. to 398 पु. 10 पं. प्रयोगकल्पनाख्यो ग्रन्थः लिखितः। 502 पु. पं. 1 'अथ ऋतुसंवेशनं इत्यारम्भ। 552 पु. 15 पं. ततः को नामासीत्याचार्यः ततोऽसौ नामास्मि' इत्येतदन्तं वाधूलपूर्वापरप्रयोगव्याख्या लिखिता। मध्ये 498 पु. 10 पं. आरभ्य 502 पुट, पर्यन्तं तत्र विद्यमानो ग्रन्थः कुत्रान्तर्भूत इति न ज्ञायते॥

'वोचेत्यादि स बृहस्पतिर्भवद्वर्तमान' इत्यारभ्य (M p. 533, line 14) एकाहाख्याकाण्ड खण्ड समाप्तिपर्यन्तं अत्र विद्यमानो ग्रन्थः तत्र पूर्वापरप्रयोगव्याख्यायां मध्ये 532 पुटादारभ्य दशभिः पुटैः लिखितः" (See fn. 6, on p.570).

Actually, due to displacement of the folios in original MS, the remaining text of *Ekāha* has entered in the text dealing with *Vādhūlagṛhyasūtravṛtti* at p.533 line 14 to p.541, line 10 in M and p.1040, line 6 to p.1053, line 8 in Ad. Now that text has been shifted at its proper place in the present edition.

6. Texts quoted in *Vyākhyā*—

अछिद्रकल्प (*Acchidrakalpa*)—

1. **अच्छिद्रकल्पे** 'परिस्तरणानन्तरकालं निष्ठितं वेदमभिमन्त्रयंते' इत्याह। निष्ठितग्रहणं पर्वद्वयकालवेदापेक्षमिति मन्यामहे। (*Vyā.* 2.1.2.2)
2. अथवाऽ**च्छिद्रकल्पे** कालमात्रे यथा स्यादिति। (*Vyā.* 2.1.3.1)
3. स एव गुणाधिकोऽ**छिद्रकल्पे** विहितः। (*Vyā.* 2.2.1.1)
4. **अच्छिद्रकल्पे**ऽध्वर्योर्भक्षाभावो दृश्यते। तत्प्रश्नोऽस्ति 'अध्वर्यो प्राशीदग्नीदि'त्यादीति। (*Vyā.* 2.3.2.19-20)
5. अयञ्च कालः पत्न्या योक्त्रविस्त्रंसनस्य। तथा **अछिद्रकल्पे** विधानात्। (*Vyā.* 2.3.3.101)
6. **अच्छिद्रिको**पादानेऽनाज्ञाताहुत्यनन्तरं हूयते अत्याक्रम्य। (*Vyā.* 4.1.3.50)

अनुकल्प (*Anukalpa*)— In favour of such options in applications of mantras or injunctions in the text, Āryadāsa uses the term *Anukalpa.* He defines *Anukalpa* as under—

1. **अनुकल्प**मिति च श्रुत्यन्तरे विहितं वदति न स्वमनीषिकया कल्पितम्। श्रुत्यन्तरे विहितानामाचार्येणाम्नातानां सर्वत्र प्रकृतावेव वैकल्पिकत्वमुक्तम्। तदेतेषामपि यथाकामं प्रयोगः। अनुब्राह्मणस्य प्रयोगः। (*Vyā.* 3.3.2.4-5)

अनुपद (*Anupada*)— The *GobhilaGṛhyakarmaprakāśikā* mentions *Anupada*[1] as one of the ten *sūtra*-texts belonging to the *Kauthuma Śākhā* of the *Sāmveda.* Dr. K.N. Bhatnagar in his Introdution to the *Nidānsūtra* of Patañjali has referred to a MS of *Kalpasūtra* of Maśakācārya (No. 297 Chamber 100) in the Berlin Library. In the colophon of the said MS following verses are given—

लाट्यायन **अनुपदं** निदानं कल्पमेव च।

उपग्रन्थाश्चक्षुद्राश्च तण्डालक्षणमेव च॥

---

1. कल्पसूत्रं तथा क्षुद्रं लाट्यायनकमेव च।
उपग्रन्थः पञ्चविधो निदानं ताण्ड्यजक्षणम्॥
अनुपस्थादनुस्त्रोत्रं कल्पानुपदमेव च।
एतद् दशविधं सूत्रं सामगेषु च विश्रुतम्॥ (7-8)

सूत्रं पञ्चविधेयं च कल्पा**नुपद**मेव च।

अनुस्तोत्रं च विज्ञेय दशसूत्रप्रकीर्तितम् ॥

But no text of *Anupadasūtra* is available to us.

Anupada, a very unique text, dealing with *Śrauta*-rituals, unknown so for, has been mentioned and quotations therefrom have been given frequently in the *Vyākhyā* as under—

1. सर्वकर्मापवर्गे यज्ञायुधानां वृक्षनियमप्रमाणाकृतिविशेषा **अनुपदाद**गमयितव्याः। विध्यवशेषा हि तत्राभिधीयन्ते। (*Vyā.* 1.1.1.5)
2. अतो**ऽनुपद** उक्ताः शेषाः। (*Vyā.* 1.1.1.5)
3. **अनुपदे** पुरस्तात् प्रत्यङ्ङध्वर्युरुपविशति। (*Vyā.* 1.1.2.10)
4. सर्वकर्मकर्तृकरणेऽग्न्यगारसंमार्जनोपलेपनसंमार्जनपात्रप्रक्षालनादि स्मृतिशास्त्राद-**नुपदाद**ाचाराच्चागमयितव्यम्। (*Vyā.* 1.5.1.2)
5. अत्र केचिदाहुः- **अनुपद**वचनाभिप्रायम् एतदिति। (*Vyā.* 1.5.2.24)
6. तथा चोक्तम**नुपदेन** 'प्रातर्ब्रह्मवर्मणोपतिष्ठते'। (*Vyā.* 1.5.4.20)
7. महापितृयज्ञादौ पितृदानस्य याजमानत्वदर्शनाद**नुपदे** च सर्वपितृयज्ञस्य याजमानत्वम्। (*Vyā.* 2.1.2.42)
8. अत्र पुरोडाशसंस्थानविशेषोत्तुंगमित्याद्य**नुपदे** द्रष्टव्यम्। (*Vyā.* 2.2.1.47)
9. आश्रावणादीनां प्लुतं लक्षणशास्त्राद**नुपदा**द्वा ग्राह्यम्। (*Vyā.* 2.3.1.19)
10. पुरोडाशमुखत्वानुजिघृक्षयाऽपि वा नवानामेवाग्नेयं निर्वपेदित्य**नुपदम्**। (*Vyā.* 3.4.1.1)
11. तस्याहवनीयप्रणीतादीनाम**नुपद**समत्ववचनाद् 'दक्षिणमाहवनीयं ब्रह्मायतनम् उत्तरवेद्यै दक्षिणेनाग्निमि'ति विकृतिषु दर्शनाच्च। (*Vyā.* 3.5.1.5)
12. दृष्टार्थत्वाय उपांशुजपं जपित्वोच्चैः प्रसूयोपांशु कर्म निर्दिशेदिति **अनुपदम्**। (*Vyā.* 3.5.1.8)
13. अन्यत्र ग्रहेभ्यः प्राजापत्यं वायव्यं सावित्रं सारस्वतं द्यावापृथिव्यं वैश्वकर्मणमादित्यं सौर्यमिति विध्यवशेषेष्वन्यत्रापि वाचःस्थानान्य**नुपदाद**ागमयितव्यानि। (*Vyā.* 4.1.1.18-30)
14. पञ्चवृत्त्वम**नुपद** आम्नातम्। (*Vyā.* 4.1.2.12)

15. क्षुद्रहोतर्निनुवर्तयेद् द्वौ द्वौ प्रतिदिशमित्य**नुपदम्**। (*Vyā.* 4.1.4.28)
16. **अनुपद** उक्तम्— यावन्तो गृह्या अविच्छिन्नपिण्डास्तेषां प्रतिपूरुषं करम्भपात्राणि कुर्याद्। (*Vyā.* 4.2.1.40)
17. तथाऽ**नुपदे**- 'अध्वर्योरेव गार्हपत्यान्वाहार्यपचनसंयुक्तानि' इति। (*Vyā.* 4.2.3.67-68)
18. 'अनीकवतेऽग्निहोत्रं सवनकालात्प्रतिकर्षेदि'त्य**नुपदम्**। (*Vyā.* 4.3.1.1)
19. 'प्राची योयोपनान्तं वेदिं कृत्वाऽन्वाहार्यपचनादग्निं प्रहृत्य मध्यतो वेद्यै सादयित्वोपसमाधायान्वादध्यात्। तस्मिन्नाहवनीयधर्माः प्रवर्तेरन्' इत्य**नुपदम्**। (*Vyā.* 4.4.1.3)
20. तथा चा**नुपदे** नर्त्विङ्नामधेयान्यभिपद्येत, न यजमानस्य। (*Vyā.* 4.4.1.3)
21. **अनुपद**यज्ञपार्श्वयोः पितृयज्ञे व्रताभाव उक्तो यदि तदिष्यते। (*Vyā.* 4.4.1.29)
22. तथा चा**नुपदे** 'अत्रेडापशुं समञ्ज्यात्'। (*Vyā.* 5.2.1.23)
23. मदन्तीभ्यः स्रुवेणादायानयन्ति। 'प्रोक्षणीशेषेण संयुयादित्येके' इत्य**नुपदम्**। (*Vyā.* 5.3.1.3)
24. 'त्र्यङ्गाणि प्रत्यनक्ती'त्य**नुपदम्**। (*Vyā.* 5.3.1.57)
25. 'हृदयशूलान्ते पत्नीं विसर्जयती'त्य**नुपदम्**। (*Vyā.* 5.3.2.68)
26. **अनुपदो**क्ताश्च पञ्च किणादयः। (*Vyā.* 6.1.1.2)
27. अर्हणमप्य**नुपद** एवाम्नातम्। (*Vyā.* 6.1.1.2)
28. सोमाहरणम**नुपद** उक्तम्। (*Vyā.* 6.1.1.4)
29. अशनविशेषोऽप्य**नुपद** उक्तः—अथाशनमकोशीधान्याशनम्। दध्यश्नीयान्मध्वश्नीया—दुदुम्बरशलून्यश्नीयाद् वत्सान्वा, शालुकान्वा प्ररोहान् वाऽश्नीयात्। (*Vyā.* 6.1.1.7)
30. 'अनुपृष्ठ्यां व्युदजती'त्य**नुपदम्**। (*Vyā.* 6.1.1.10)
31. तथा चा**नुपद** उक्तम्—'ब्राह्मणस्यैव सनिवननमि'ति। (*Vyā.* 6.1.4.7)
32. राजक्रयणेष्वनुद्दिष्टेष्वित्यपरम् इत्य**नुपदम्**। (*Vyā.* 6.2.3.22)
33. 'परिपालनीयमजां वास इति सोमविक्रयिणेऽपाकरोती'तित्य**नुपदम्**। (*Vyā.* 6.3.1.43)
34. एवम**नुपद** आम्नातम्। (*Vyā.* 6.3.3.11)

35. 'दक्षिणोत्तरिणा प्रातःप्रचरणे सव्योत्तरिणा सायंप्रचरणे' इत्य**नुपदम्**। (*Vyā.* 6.3.4.23)

36. 'समग्राङ्गुलिस्रुवमादायास्यन्निवोपसदं जुहुयादि'त्य**नुपदम्**। (*Vyā.* 6.4.1.62-64)

37. 'उपांशुसप्तमा ग्रावाण' इत्य**नुपदे** वचनम्। (*Vyā.* 6.6.1.9)

38. तथा**नुपद** उक्तम्—'मृतसंस्कृतबौधानि तोदमन्योऽन्यं बोधयन्ती'ति। (*Vyā.* 6.9.1.3)

39. **आनुप**दिकोऽपि पुरोडाशशेषभक्षकालोऽनुगृहीतो भवति। (*Vyā.* 6.9.1.16)

40. 'त्रयोऽभिषुणुयुश्चत्वारोऽभिषुणुयुरि'ति उदितम**नुपदे**। (*Vyā.* 6.10.1.3)

41. 'अरिक्त ऋतुपात्रे कृत्वे'त्य**नुपदम्**। (*Vyā.* 6.10.4.1)

42. प्रशास्तरिति मैत्रावरुणं, ब्रह्मन्निति ब्राह्मणाच्छंसिनमिति सौशारदेऽ**नुपद** आम्नातम्। (*Vyā.* 6.11.4.19)

43. 'विश्वकर्मसम्पातेन वैश्वकर्मणानि जुहुयाद्' अन्यत्र 'तं 'विश्वकर्मन् प्रमुञ्चा स्वस्तये' इत्यस्मादि'त्य**नुपदम्**। (*Vyā.* 6.12.2.32)

44. **अनुपद** उक्तं—'वसतीवरीभ्यो निग्राभ्यां कृत्वा सह पेषणांशून्प्रातःसवनवदभिषुत्याधवनीय आशिरि संभृत्य संस्रवयेदि'ति। (*Vyā.* 6.13.1.2)

45. 'नाशिरः कुप्रावृत' इत्य**नुपदम्**। (*Vyā.* 6.14.2.5)

46. तथा ह्य**नुपदं**—'शिक्यं द्वादशोद्यामम्' इति। (*Vyā.* 7.4.1.2)

47. वैणवीभिर्नियम्यन्ते इति ता ऊरीकृत्य सर्वाचार्येऽभिहितं, शर्करा इत्य**नुपदे**। (*Vyā.* 7.7.5.6-10)

अनुपदकार (*Anupadakāra*)— Here I would like to point out that some MSS of *Anupada-sūtra* belonging to *Sāmaveda* are said to have been deposited in the following MSS-collections—

1. Royal Asiatic Society, Calcutta.
2. National Museum, Calcutta.
3. Government Sanskrit College, Calcutta.
4. Sampurnananda Sanskrit University, Varanasi.
5. Rajasthan Oriental Research Institute, Jodhpur.

Dr. Bhaskara Bhattacharya, Associate Professor, School of Vedic Studies, Rabindra Bharati University, Kolkata. on basis of these MSS is working no preparing a critical edition of the text. As per his information the text is divided into ten *Adhyayas,* and in none of the MSS the name of its author is given. But that text is different from this *Anupada,* because that belongs to *Sāmaveda*. But who is the author of this text is not known. Āryadāsa in his *Vyākhyā* very frequently refers to the author by the title *Anupadakāra,* not by any proper name, and gives quotations from *Anupada* as under—

1. **अनुपदकार**स्य 'भृगूणामङ्गिरसामादित्यानामृभूणामि'त्येवमादिषु 'त्वा देवानाम्' इत्यनुषङ्गः। (*Vyā.* 1.1.3.21-26)
2. **अनुपदकार** आह—'यद्युद्गाता न स्यात् तर्हि यजमानः स्वयमेवोत्थायाभिहिंकृत्य योनिभिरुपतिष्ठेते'ति। (*Vyā.* 1.1.4.4)
3. **अनुपदकार** आह– संयुक्ततन्त्राणां बर्हिराहरेत्। (*Vyā.* 1.3.4.28)
4. **अनुपदकार**स्तत्रोपवसिथकायाः नित्यत्वमाह। (*Vyā.* 1.4.4.27)
5. 'एतावन्मात्रे' इति सामान्येनोक्तम**नुपदकारो** विशिनष्टि। (*Vyā.* 1.5.2.11-12)
6. **अनुपदकार** आह— शाखापवित्रस्यौषधानां त्रिवृतं पृथ्वीं रज्जुं वाऽपाकृत्य ग्रन्थ्यासंज्यात्। (*Vyā.* 2.1.2.2)
7. तथाऽ**नुपदकार** आह। (*Vyā.* 2.1.3.1)
8. तस्याग्नीषोमीयादिधर्ममध्ये विधानं स्थानसंबन्धमात्रमिति दक्षिणस्य पुरोडाशस्य ज्यायस्त्वम् प्रयोजनापेक्षयाऽ**नुपदकारो** वदति। (*Vyā.* 2.1.4.13-14)
9. तथा चा**नुपदकारः** 'षट्कपालसप्तकपालेष्विति परिचिन्मन्त्रमूहेदि'त्याह। (*Vyā.* 2.2.1.13)
10. तथा चा**नुपदकार** आह—'दिवे त्वे'त्यग्राणि, 'अन्तरिक्षाय त्वा' इति मध्यानि 'पृथिव्यै त्वेति मूलानि' समस्तैरित्यपरमि'ति। (*Vyā.* 2.2.4.34)
11. **अनुपदकारे**णाम्नातम्—'दक्षिणं पक्षं प्राञ्चं स्तृणुयात्, प्रत्यञ्चं मध्यमं, प्राञ्चमुत्तमम्। (*Vyā.* 2.2.4.44)
12. 'ब्राह्मणांस्तर्पयत वा' इति प्रैषं चा**नुपदकार** आमनति। (*Vyā.* 3.3.3.22)
13. अत्रा**नुपदकार** आह— अन्यदेवत्ये सान्नाय्य ऊहोपाकरणान्तं च न प्रश्नवाग्विसर्गमन्त्रेषु तथा वोपवेषयोः सदेनवकालावधो (?) न इतीह। (*Vyā.* 4.1.1.48-49)

14. **अनुपदकार**स्तु सन्नतां दक्षिणामाह। (*Vyā.* 4.2.1.23)

15. तथा चा**नुपदकार** आह—'अध्वर्योरेव प्रतिवचनाश्रावणसंवादसंप्रैषा यौगपद्य एव तूष्णीं कर्म प्रतिप्रस्थातु'रिति। (*Vyā.* 4.2.1.28)

16. तुल्यबलत्वं मन्यमानेना**नुपदकारे**णोक्तम्–'इष्टिनाऽऽदित्यमाकाङ्क्षेत्साकं वा रश्मिभिः प्रचरेदि'ति। (*Vyā.* 4.3.1.1)

17. तथा चा**नुपदकारो** विशिनष्टि–'अग्रेणान्वाहार्यपचनं यजमानमात्री वेदिर्भवति। (*Vyā.* 4.4.1.1-2)

18. तथा चा**नुपदकार** आह—'पितृयज्ञे यावच्छ्रुतधर्माः प्रवर्तेरंस्तथैक आहुर्धर्मवदेव देवप्रवादेषु देवान् पितॄंनि'ति कुर्युरन्यत्र संस्कारेभ्यः इति। (*Vyā.* 4.4.1.3)

19. **अनुपदकार**स्तु—'अवभृथपितृयज्ञयोर्न समानयनमि'त्याह। (*Vyā.* 4.4.1.9-10)

20. **अनुपदकार** आह—'देवप्रवादेषु देवान् पितॄंनिति कुर्युरन्यत्र सांस्कारिकेभ्यः' इति। (*Vyā.* 4.4.2.18-76)

21. **अनुपदकार**श्चाह—'तमनीजानं षण्मासः संवत्सरो वा नाभ्यतीयात्, यद्यतीयान्मांसं नाश्नीयाद्। अथ कालातिनये अग्नये पथिकृते पुरोडाशमष्टाकपालं निर्वपेत्। वैश्वानरं द्वादशकपालम्, अग्नये व्रतपतये पुरोडाशमष्टाकपालं निर्वपेत्। सर्वेषां दर्शपूर्णमासप्रकृतीनां कालातिनय एतामेव निर्वपेत्। अथ सोमस्य कालातिनय एतां च सवनीयेष्टिञ्च निर्वपेत्। आग्नेयमष्टकपालमैन्द्रमेकादशकपालं वैश्वदेवं द्वादशकपालमि'ति। (*Vyā.* 5.1.1.1)

22. तथा चा**नुपदकार** 'इष्टिं विधाय धार्यत आहवनीय' इत्याह। (*Vyā.* 5.1.1.28)

23. **अनुपदकार** उत्तरवेदिं प्रकृत्याह—'अत्र परिमाणमन्त्रानेके प्रयुञ्जते' इति। (*Vyā.* 5.1.1.36)

24. 'त्रिराग्नीध्रश्चात्वालाद्धरेदुत्तरनाभ्यर्थमि'त्य**नुपदकार** आह। (*Vyā.* 5.1.1.43)

25. **अनुपदकार**स्तु दशपशोः प्रतिषेधति। (*Vyā.* 5.1.2.21)

26. तथाऽस्मिन्नेव पशावविशेषेणा**नुपदकारे**णाम्नातम् 'उद्यत इध्मे शालामुखीये स्रुवाहुतिं जुहुयात्— 'यत्ते पावक चकृमा कच्चनागः पूर्वो यः सन्नपरो भवासि। घृतेन त्वं तनुवो वर्धयस्व मा मा हिंसीरधिगतं पुरस्तात् स्वाहे'ति। (*Vyā.* 5.1.2.21)

27. पशुः परिहरणीय इति प्रकृतत्वात् प्राप्ते पशोः शृङ्गमिति परिहरणस्य

विशेषम**नुपदकार** आह—'उदीचः प्राणानुत्सृजती'ति। (*Vyā.* 5.2.1.13)

28. **अनुपदकार** आह—'पञ्चतयमिह पर्यग्निकुर्यात् पशुं यूपमाहवनीयं शामित्रदेशं स्रुचश्च। चात्वाले पशुपचनीं निधाय तां पचनीम् पशुमेवेत्येक' इति। (*Vyā.* 5.2.2.17-18)

29. **अनुपदकार** आह—'पृषदाज्यं गृहीत्वा तूष्णीमन्यस्मिन् पात्रे तयैवावृता पृषदाज्यं गृह्णीयात् ततो वनस्पतिं यजेद् हृदयं चाभिघारयेदित्येक' इति। (*Vyā.* 5.3.1.32-33)

30. तथा चा**नुपदकार** आह—'वसन्ते वसन्ते ज्योतिष्टोमेन यजेते'ति विज्ञायते। (*Vyā.* 6.1.1.2)

31. तथा चा**नुपदकार** आह—'रथन्तरसामैव प्रथमाहारश्चतुष्टोमोऽग्निष्टोम' इति। (*Vyā.* 6.1.1.2)

32. **अनुपदकारो**ऽपि 'यथाऽन्वाख्यानमृत्विजां वरणमि'त्याह। (*Vyā.* 6.1.1.2; cf *Vādh.Anv.* 4.3.1.4)

33. **अनुपदकार**श्चान्वाधानस्य धारणार्थत्वे देवतापरिग्रहणवर्जस्यावृत्तिं ब्रुवन् अभ्याधानस्यावृत्तिं न्याय्यां मन्यते। (*Vyā.* 6.1.1.14)

34. **अनुपदकार** आह—'क्रय उत्कर्षेत् प्रातर्व्रतमपराह्णे तानूनप्त्रेण प्रयच्छन्नोत्कर्षेदि'ति। (*Vyā.* 6.1.4.4-6)

35. **अनुपदकार**श्च गृहमेधीयवद्वेदिसंयुक्तानीत्याह। (*Vyā.* 6.3.4.30)

36. **अनुपदकार**स्तु माहावेदिकस्य तूष्णीकत्वं तृणकलाप्या धर्मवत्वं चामनति। (*Vyā.* 6.4.3.3-33)

37. ऊर्ध्वपात्राणामनाम्नातवृक्षविशेषाणामौदुम्बरताम**नुपदकार** आह। (*Vyā.* 6.6.1.9)

38. महापरिधीनां प्रमाणम**नुपदकार** आह—'एकादशपदो मध्यमो द्वादशपदो दक्षिणो दशपद उत्तरः' इति। (*Vyā.* 6.8.3.26)

39. **अनुपदकारे**ण 'अपूर्वेषु यावत् श्रुतधर्मा प्रवर्तेरन्' इत्युक्त्वा 'यथा घर्मो दधिघर्म' इत्युदाहृतम्। (*Vyā.* 6.8.3.30)

40. **अनुपदकार**स्तु हविषां निर्वापं विदधाति 'इन्द्राय हरिवते चतुरो मुष्टीन्, इन्द्राय पूषण्वते चतुरः, इन्द्राय सरस्वतीवते भारतीवते चतुरः, इन्द्राय चतुरः प्रदाने सर्व ऐन्द्राः' इति। (*Vyā.* 6.9.1.17)

41. 'अध्वर्युर्ब्रह्मयजमानौ' इत्य**नुपदकार** आह। (*Vyā.* 6.10.1.3)

42. पयः सक्तूनां हिरण्यशल्केन समुच्चयम**नुपदकार** इच्छति। (*Vyā.* 6.10.2.1-2)

43. **अनुपदकारेण** च परिभाषितम् 'प्रत्यगाशिषो मन्त्राः कर्मकरणाः सह जप्या याजमान इतर' इति। (*Vyā.* 6.10.4.1)

44. 'ललाटमुन्मृज इत्यपरमि'**त्यनुपदकारस्य** वचः। (*Vyā.* 6.10.4.1)

45. प्रति निग्राह्याणां मार्जनश्रयणे इच्छत्य**नुपदकारः**। (*Vyā.* 6.11.1.26)

46. **अनुपदकारः** 'संयावा परिवापः' इत्याह। संयाव' इति वक्तुं शक्यते। (*Vyā.* 6.11.1.28)

47. **अनुपदकार**स्तु 'सोमपूर्वो यजमानस्य भक्षः पुरोडाशपूर्व इतरेषाम्'। (*Vyā.* 6.11.4.5)

48. 'स चेत्पशुपुरोडाशं कुर्यात् पुरस्तात् पशुपुरोडाशेभ्यः प्रचरेत् समानस्विष्टकृदिडामि'**त्यनुपदकार**स्य वचः। (*Vyā.* 6.12.1.51)

49. चन्द्रं हिरण्यम्। तस्य परिमाणं शतमानम**नुपदकार** आह। (*Vyā.* 6.12.2.14)

50. तथा चा**नुपदकारे**णाभिहितं—'द्वादश द्वादश मध्यतकारिभ्यः, षट् षडर्धिभ्यश्चतस्र-श्चतस्रस्तृतीयिभ्यस्तिस्रस्तिस्रः पादिभ्यः, एवं शतविभागः। एवं शेषं विभजेदि'ति। (*Vyā.* 6.12.2.27)

51. **अनुपदकारो**ऽत्र सख्यविसर्जनमामनति 'अत्र सख्यानि विसृजेयुर्— 'उभा कवी युवाना सत्यादा धर्मस्पती। सत्यस्य ब्रह्मणस्पते वि सख्यानि सृजामहे' इत्यहर्गणेषूत्तमेऽहनि सख्यानि विसृजेयुरि'ति। (*Vyā.* 6.15.1.39)

52. **अनुपदकार** आह—'परिशाययेत् स्थालीः सोमलिप्तास्ताभिरनूबन्ध्यस्य पशुपरोडाशमनु देविकाहवींषि निर्वपेत् व्युदितम्। देवीनां ताश्चेन्निर्वपेत् तासामपि स्थालीर्लिम्प्यात् सोमेने'ति। (*Vyā.* 6.15.3.103)

53. जातेऽग्नौ क्रमुकस्य फलमित्य**नुपदकार**स्य वचः। (*Vyā.* 7.4.1.19)

54. 'प्रत्यगाशिषो मन्त्राः कर्मकरणाः सहजप्या' इति चा**नुपदकार**स्य वचनमेवमुपपद्यतेतराम्। (*Vyā.* 7.15.1.60-61)

अन्वाख्यान (*Anvākhyāna*)— Āryadāsa in his *Vyākhyā* quotes a large number of passages from a text *Anvākhyāna* which for a long time remained unknown to the Vedic scholars till Prof. Caland pointed for the first time the existence of this text on the basis of references found in the *Kalpāgamasaṅgraha* of Āryadāsa. Since the text of *Vyākhyā* was not edited at that time, it was not possible for him to give all such quotations from the *Vyākhyā*. Now the complete text of *Anvākhyāna*[1] has been edited and published for the first time by the present editor. All references have been given from that edition. I would like to give here those references as under—

1. 'मनसा संकल्पयत्यग्नीनाधास्ये = स वाचा व्याहरत्याधास्ये' इत्य**न्वाख्याने** (*Vādh.Anvā.* 1.6.1) दर्शनात्, तयोश्च प्रथमं कर्तव्यत्वात्। (*Vyā.* 1.1.1.6)

2. अग्नौ सावित्रकाणां कल्प आदिग्रहणेन लक्षितानाम**न्वाख्याने** 'सुवर्ग्याय शक्त्या इन्द्रं दानाय हूमहे' (*Vādh.Anvā.* 5.3.3) इति साधिकदर्शनादित्येवमादि। (*Vyā.* 1.1.1.6)

3. **अन्वाख्याने**क्तं च—'तां पुरा दीप्तोरिति परीप्सोर्' इत्यादि (*Vādh.Anvā.* 2.8.1)। (*Vyā.* 1.5.2.11)

4. उभयोरपि पक्षयोर्हुत्वोपसादयन्ति 'अग्नये गृहपतये स्वाहा' (*Vādh.Anvā.* 2.4.1) इत्य**न्वाख्याना**म्नातेन विकल्पते। (*Vyā.* 1.5.2.13-14)

5. अथापि दीक्षणीया**न्वाख्यान** इदमुक्तम्। उदवसानीयासमाप्ते सोमे कथं पुनः प्रकृतस्याष्टाकपालस्येह प्रवेशः। प्रकृतमष्टाकपालं स्तुत्वोत्तरस्मिन्ननुवाक्येऽष्टाकपालस्य दीक्षाप्रयोजनसाधकत्वं दर्शयित्वा पुनर्दीक्षणीयमेकादशकपालानि स्तौति। (*Vyā.* 2.1.4.2)

   This discussion has reference to *Vādh.Anvā.* 4.6.2-4; 4.7.7. It is pertinent to note that here the treatment of *Aṣṭākapālpuroḍāśa* has been justified under *Dīkṣaṇīyān-vākhyāna*.

6. अतः प्रकृतस्यैवाष्टाकपालस्या**न्वाख्यान**मिदम्। (*Vyā.* 2.1.4.2; cf *Vādh.Anvā.* 4.6.2-4.7)

7. अतः व्रीहियवयोरन्यतरस्य पुरोडाशीयत्वमाग्नेया**न्वाख्यान**त्व-मग्नीषोमीयादीनामपि प्रदर्शनमध्यवदानीयस्तुतौ च। (*Vyā.* 2.1.4.2)

8. ना**न्वाख्याने** ब्राह्मणमस्ति। विधायकं वाक्यं नास्तीत्यर्थः। ब्राह्मणेन विहितं हि कल्पकारैरन्वाख्यायते। (*Vyā.* 3.1.1.24)

   Here Āryadāsa makes a clear difference between *Brāhmaṇa* and *Anvākhyāna. Brāhmaṇa* gives injunction

---

1. *Vādhūla Anvākhyānam*, edited by Prof. B.B. Chaubey, and published from Kātyāyana Vaidik Sāhitya Prakashan, Hoshiarpur, 2001.

for a ritual, but *Anvākhyāna* gives various interpretations based on *Adhidaiva* and *Adhyātma*, in *Ākhyāna*-style to justify the Brāhmaṇic injuntions as prevalent in *Vādhūla*-tradition.

9. सदसो दक्षिणार्ध उद्गातुर्दक्षिणत उदङ्मुख उपविशति। 'तस्मादुद्गातारमभ्यावृत्यास्ते यथा स्वं धिष्णियमि'त्य**न्वाख्याने** उक्तत्वात्। (*Vyā.* 3.6.2.12; cf *Vādh.Anvā.* 4.40.4)

10. उद्यत्यादित्ये निर्वपति। द्रव्यदेवतासंबन्धविधिवाक्ये श्रूयमाणो गुणो भवत्यत एष कालो यागस्य। ननूक्तं कल्पवाक्यं न विधायकम्, ब्राह्मणवाक्येन विहितस्या**न्वाख्यान**मिति। (*Vyā.* 4.3.1.1)

11. 'य: पालाशं पशुबन्धयूपं कुरुत' इत्यादिनाऽ**न्वाख्याने** पलाशस्य नियमितत्वात् पालाश एव भवति। (*Vyā.* 5.1.1.6; cf *Vādh.Anvā.* 3.1.3)

12. हविर्यज्ञविधे व्रतमुपयन्ति न सवविधे। **अन्वाख्यानो**क्तव्रतादीनां सप्तानामभाव: सवविध:। (*Vyā.* 5.1.2.21; cf *Vādh.Anvā.* 3.7.1-2)

13. अनुपदकारोऽपि 'यथाऽ**न्वाख्यान**मृत्विजां वरणमि'त्याह। (*Vyā.* 6.1.1.2)

14. नन्व**न्वाख्याने** आप्तैकोन्नतादिनामर्थं ब्रुवताऽऽचार्येणर्त्विग्विशेषा अभिप्रेता:। (*Vyā.* 6.1.1.3)

This has reference to *VādhAnvā* 4.76.2-6 where the qualities of the *Ṛtiviks* have been prescribed. It may be pointed out that Āryadāsa has clearly mentioned this fact also that the *Anvākhyāna* is the work of Ācārya Vādhūla. Since Āryadāsa was a follower of *Vādhūla Śākhā*, he accepts the views of Ācārya as authentic in the matter of ritualistic controversies.

15. अन्तर्वेदि कृष्णाजिने इत्याद्य**न्वाख्याने** 'तस्या उ हैके योगं विदुर्मनोयुगस्युत प्रजाते०' (*Vādh.Anvā.* 4.19.8) इत्यादिना मन्त्रेणासंजनार्थं कृष्णाजिनमास्तृणाति। स्तीर्णं वा यजमानोऽनुमन्त्रयते'। (*Vyā.* 6.1.2.27)

16. दीक्षितचरणा**न्वाख्याने** न दीक्षितचरणे नासौत्याह्न: प्रवर्तेतेत्यभिप्राय:। (*Vyā.* 6.1.4.54-56)

This has reference to *Dīkṣitacaraṇāvkhāna* (*Vādh.Anvā.* 4.11.1-7).

17. आचार्येणाप्य**न्वाख्याने** 'तदाहुर्यद्देवस्य त्वे'त्युपक्रम्य 'स यदेतस्मिंश्चरौ=देवता: प्राश्नन्ती'ति (*Vādh.Anvā.* 4.27.1) ब्रुवता आचार्येणाभिप्रेत इव लक्ष्यते। (*Vyā.* 6.2.2.5)

18. **अन्वाख्याने** 'ब्रह्म च गाथां च पुरस्तात् सोमस्य क्रयादभिव्याहरेदि'ति (*Vādh.Anvā.* 4.29.16) विहितयोर्ब्रह्मगाथयोः। (*Vyā.* 6.3.1.1)

19. एकं तृणमुष्टिमसिदादानादिभिः संस्कारैः संस्कृत्यापवृत्तात्तेनातिथ्यप्रस्तरेण सह सन्नह्य उपसदर्थं निदधातीत्यर्थः। कथमेवं गम्यते। 'तस्माद्यदेवातिथ्यं बर्हि= भवति इति दृश्यतेऽ**न्वाख्याने**। (*Vyā.* 6.3.4.30)

This text refers to *Vādh.Anvā.* 4.33.3. Here Āryadāsa has given the text in abri. form. The full text as given in *Vādh.Anvā.* is as under—

'तस्माद् यदेवातिथ्यं बर्हि(र्भवति तत्र स्तीर्णमेव तदुपसदां बर्हि-) र्भवती'ति। (*Vādh.Anvā.* 4.33.3)

20. अन्यस्मिन्नपि पक्षे प्राशित्रमवदायैतद् 'द्वावाघारौ द्वावाज्यभागावि'त्य**न्वाख्याने** (*Vādh.Anvā.* 4.43.3) दर्शनाद्धविर्यज्ञविधत्वम्। (*Vyā.* 6.6.2.40)

21. 'अथ यद्धिरण्यशल्का भवन्ति' (*Vādh.Anvā.* 4.86.23) तदग्निना शुचिना एवं नु ह सोमः शृतो भवति, इत्य**न्वाख्यान** उक्तम्। (*Vyā.* 6.9.4.9)

22. 'मध्येऽग्नेरन्नाहुती=अन्तेषु सोमाहुतीरि'त्य**न्वाख्याने** वचनं द्रष्टव्यम्। (*Vyā.* 6.9.4.37)

This has reference to *Vādhu.Anvā.* 4.57.3, where the full text is given

'मध्येऽग्नेरन्नाहुती(राज्याहुतीः पुरोडाशाहुतीः पश्वाहुतीश्च जुहुयाद्) अन्तेषु सोमाहुतीरि'त्य**न्वाख्याने** (*Vādh.Anvā.* 4.57.3) वचनं द्रष्टव्यम्।

23. 'तस्मात् तृतीयसवन ऋजीषमभिषुण्वन्ती'ति (*Vādh.Anvā.* 4.30.3) ब्राह्मणेऽ**न्वाख्याने** च। (*Vyā.* 6.9.4.38)

24. **अन्वाख्याने** 'अन्तःस्तोत्रेषु पुरोडाशाः श्रप्यन्त' (*Vādh.Anvā.* 4.78.3) इति ब्रुवत आचार्यस्यायमेवाभिप्राय। (*Vyā.* 6.12.2.68-69)

Here *Brāhmaṅa* refers to *Brāhmaṇa* portion of *TS* 6.1.6.9-4

25. 'तस्मात् तृतीयसवन ऋजीषम् अभिषुण्वन्ती'ति ब्राह्मणेऽ**न्वाख्याने** (*Vādh.Anvā.* 4.30.3) च वचनाद् उपांशु हुत्वोपांशुपात्रेंऽशुमवाप्य तं तृतीयसवने विसृज्याभिषुणुयादि'ति विहितस्यानारभ्याधीतस्य प्रकृत्यर्थत्वाच्च उभयोः सवनयोर्गृहीतरसे सोमकिट्टे प्रातःसवने निहितमंशुमुपास्या-धवनीयादपनीता अपो निःषिच्याभिषुत्याभिषुत्याशिरि संभरेत्। (*Vyā.* 6.13.1.2)

26. तथा च 'तस्मान्नु हैतद्वाचि हूयते यत्समिष्टयजुः' 'जूरसि धृता मनसा' (*Vādh.Anvā.* 4.27.9) इत्य**न्वाख्यान** उक्तम्। (*Vyā.* 6.15.3.78-80)

27. तदुक्तम**न्वाख्याने**—'तस्मान्नु हैनमुखयैव पूर्वया प्रतिपद्येरन्' (*Vādh.Anvā.* 5.7.6) इति। (*Vyā.* 7.1.1.1)

28. घर्मेष्टकादीनि लोकबाधीनि द्रव्याण्यवटेषूपदध्यात्। **अन्वाख्याने** (cf. *Vādh.Anvā.* 5.17.3) बहुवचननिर्देशात्। (*Vyā.* 7.5.4.3)

29. **अन्वाख्याने** त्वसपत्नानधिकृत्योच्यते—'चतस्रश्चतस्रश्च बृहत्यः संपद्यन्ते, त्रयोविंशतिश्चाक्षराणी'ति (*Vādh.Anvā.* ?)। (*Vyā.* 7.6.4.20-21)

30. यत्र यत्तद् **अन्वाख्याने** 'सप्त च शतानि विंशतिश्चेष्टका' (*Vādh.Anvā.* 5.34.1) इति 'सहस्रं च द्वे शते' इति। (*Vyā.* 7.7.5.6-10)

31. अन्य आहुर्यदेतद**न्वाख्याने** विहितम् 'अथ यद्यष्टापदी स्यात्' (*Vādh.Anvā.* 3.4.7) इति तस्यास्य च समुच्चयो मा भूदिति। (*Vyā.* 12.2.3)

32. यदीदम**न्वाख्याने** 'तन्नु हैतद् एके स्कन्नेऽग्निहोत्रे बिभ्यति (नो ह वै तदेवंविदाद्रियेतापि ह प्रायश्चित्तं कर्तुं)नाद्रियेत' (*Vādh.Anvā.* 2.1.6) इति वचनम्। (*Vyā.* 12.4.1)

Besides these direct references to the text *Anvākhyāna*, Āryadāsa quotes several passages from *Anvākhyāna* without mentioning the text as under—

1. 'जनको ह वैदेहः सोमेन यक्ष्यमाणः' इत्याद्यारभ्य दृष्टत्वादग्न्याधेयविषये चादर्शनाच्च। (*Vyā.* 1.1.1.6)

   This text has reference to *Vādh.Anvā.* 2.1.12-13

2. 'अमृताहुतिर्ह वा एषा हूयते=हु' ता भवती'तीयमृताहुतिममृतायां जुहोमी'त्यस्य मन्त्रावयवस्यार्थमभिप्रेत्याचार्येणोक्तमिति मन्यामहे। यद्यपि प्रायश्चित्ते दृष्टोऽयं मन्त्रस्तथापीतः प्राप्तस्यानुवादः। (*Vyā.* 1.5.1.2)

   Here Āryadāsa has quoted the text in *abridged* form. For the full text see *Vādh.Anvā.* 1.11.5

3. ततो दक्षिणत उपसृजतीत्यादिना विधानेन दोग्धि। पूर्वौ दुह्यादपरौ पूर्वौ दुह्यादिति। तथा 'तस्मान्नु ह सर्वेषामेव स्तनानामग्निहोत्रं दुह्यादि'ति पाक्षिकं वचनं न स्यात्। (*Vyā.* 1.5.1.7; for the full text see *Vādh.Anvā.* 2.2.1)

4. गार्हपत्यं प्रतीक्ष्य इत्यत्र गार्हपत्यशब्देन गार्हपत्याहुतिरभिप्रेता। तथा चोक्तम्—'स यस्यैषा हू=येत' इत्यादि। (*Vyā.* 1.5.2.13-16)

Here Āryadāsa has quoted the text in *abridged* form. The full text is given in *Vādh.Anvā.* as under—

'स यस्यैषा हू(येत स एव प्रत्यवक्षेताथ यस्यैषा न हू)येत स न प्रत्यवेक्षेत'। (*Vādh.Anvā.* 2.4.1)

5. आरुणिपक्षोऽत्राचार्येणाम्नातम्। कौषीतक्यादीनां तु श्रोत्रियाणां समिध्येव द्वयोराहुत्योर्होमकल्पविहितस्यास्य प्रशंसार्थमाह—'उभौ हि स लोकाववेदिमञ्चामुञ्च' इति। (*Vyā.* 1.5.2.13-16)

This has reference to *Vādh.Anvā.* 2.11.1-5

6. 'अग्निरमुष्मिँल्लोक आसी'दित्यस्मिन्ननुवाके 'तेऽग्निं पशुभूतमग्नये मेधायालभन्ते'त्यारभ्य 'तस्मात् सीरलाङ्गलेन कृष्ट्वाऽनुसीतं वपन्ति; तौ प्राजायेतामि'त्येवमन्तेन ग्रन्थेनार्थवादरूपेण व्रीहियवौ विहितौ। (*Vyā.* 2.1.4.2)

This has reference to *Vādh.Anvā.* 4.4.1-13

7. 'का देवता भवतीति आहुर् यक्ष्य'= इति 'व्याहृत्य' इति ब्रुवन्नियमेन संकल्प्योपव्याहरणयोः कर्तव्यतां दर्शयति। (*Vyā.* 6.1.1.2)

Here Ārydāsa has quoted the text in *abridged* form. The full text is given in the *Vādh.Anvā.* as under—

का देवता भवतीत्याहुर्यक्ष्य (इति संकल्प्य। मन एव, मनो वै प्रजापतिः, प्रजापतेर्व्याप्तिमनुव्याप्नोति प्रजापतेः सायुज्यं सलोकतां जयति॥ १ ॥ का देवता भवतीत्याहुर्यक्ष्य) इति व्याहृत्य। (*Vādh.Anvā.* 4.1.1-2)

8. तत उत्तरकालं 'ब्राह्मणो ह वाव देवयजनं तमृत्विजं वृण्वीते'त्यैतैश्चतुर्भिर्गुणैरुपेतानृत्विजः परिगृह्णीयादित्याह। अनूचानो विद्वान्। बन्धुमान् प्रशस्तबान्धवः, अभिजात इत्यर्थः। चरणवान् प्रशस्तचरणः, विहितस्य कर्ता प्रतिषिद्धानां वर्जयितेत्यर्थः। संशितव्रतः यमवान् यमाः। सर्वेषु तितिक्षावैराग्यादयः, अन्तःकरणशुद्ध इत्यर्थः। प्रतिषिद्धाश्च शङ्कूलाङ्गुष्ठकुनखादयो वर्जनीयाः। (*Vyā.* 6.1.1.2)

This text of *Vyākhyā* has reference to *Vādh.Anvā.* 4.3.1-4. Here Āryadāsa is not only quoting *Vādh.Anvā.*-text without naming it, but also explains the four words *viz Anūcāna, Bandhumān, Caraṇavān* and *Saṁśitavrata,* denoting qualities of a *Ṛtvik*, which *Vādh.Anvā.* prescribes.

9. अथ श्रद्धां निवेदयते। 'अस्ति मे देवयजनं पृथिव्यै मे सुस्थलमिच्छे'ति ब्राह्मणम्। ब्रूयादित्येकवचनेन चोदितत्वादध्वर्युरेव निवेदयते। (*Vyā.* 6.1.1.2)

This has reference to *Vādh.Anvā.* 4.77.5-6

10. पुरस्तादवनतं देवयजनस्य रूपमित्येतत्सामान्यं पुरोहविरादीनां प्रतिष्ठितवर्जानां सर्वेषामन्वेति। प्रतिष्ठितं तु सर्वतः सममेव भवति। (*Vyā.* 6.1.1.2; cf *Vādh.Anvā.* 4.77.6)

11. 'पुरोहविषि देवयजने याजयेदि'त्यारभ्य पुरुषार्थानि देवयजनान्यनुक्रान्तानि। तेषां मध्ये यदभिप्रेतं तस्मिन्नित्यर्थः। कतमत्पुनः क्रत्वर्थं गृह्यते। प्राथम्यात् तत्फलस्य सर्वैः प्रार्थयितव्यत्वाच्च पुरोहविषमिच्छन्ति। (*Vyā.* 6.1.1.3)

This has reference to *Vādh.Anvā.* 4.76.1-8, where various types of *Devayajana* have been discussed.

12. अथ 'यजमानो राजानं देवयजनं याचती'ति नैदेशिकेन विधिना। तत्र च पक्षद्वयम्। 'राजन् देवयजनं मे देहि' इत्युक्तो राजाऽऽदित्यमुपतिष्ठते 'नमस्त आदित्य' इत्यादिना ददातीत्यन्यः संशिष्टो ब्रूयात्। (*Vyā.* 6.1.1.7)

'ये ह पूर्वजनाः आसु' इति ब्रह्म= 'या स्त्रीणां प्रथमा वर्या' इति गाथा। (*Vyā.* 6.3.1.1-2)

Āryadāsa shows a difference between a *Brahma* and *gāthā*—

This has reference to *Vādh.Anvā* (4.29.13-14) where the entire text is given.

From these above quotations and references from *Anvākhyāna* and *Anupada* in the *Vyākhya,* I have arrived at the conclusion that these two, texts belong to *Vādhūla*-tradition. Among these two again *Anvākhyāna* is definitely the work of Ācārya Vādhūla. About the authorship of the *Anupada-sūtra* I can only say that this must be a work of some other Ācārya who was the follower of *Vādhūla*-tradition. Nowhere the name of the author is mentioned. He is always mentioned by the term *Anupadakāra,* the author of the *Anupada*-sūtra, as we have seen above. This text was very important in dealing with sacrificial rituals, *etc.* Āryadāsa himself says—

सर्वकर्मापवर्गे यज्ञायुधानां वृक्षनियमप्रमाणाकृतिविशेषा अनुपदादागमयितव्याः। (*Vyā.* 1.1.1.5)

औपानुवाक्य *(Aupānuvākya)*— Āryadāsa refers to the existence of an *Aupānuvākyakāṇḍa* in *Vādhūla*-tradition. Since the *Vyākhyā* of Āryādasa was not edited before, it was regarded that this text constituted only the part of *Taittirīya-Saṁhitā*, under fifth *Khāṇḍa*, *Prapāṭhkā* 6-7. *BaudhŚS* (XIV. 1-30) deals with *Aupānuvākya* under thirty *Khāṇḍas*. In none of the MSS of the *VādhūŚS* available so far, the original *sūtra*-text is found. However, in all MSS of the *Kalpāgamsaṇgraha*, the text of commentary is given. On the basis of the authority of Āryadāsa, we are sure that the original *sūtra*-text must have existed. The difference between the two traditions, *Vādhūla* and *Taittirīya* has been noticed by Āryadāsa at places. We find following references to *Aupānuvākya* in *Vyākhyā*—

1. तत्रायमाचार्य एतच्छाखाधीता अवश्यं विकल्पन्त इति मन्यमानोऽन्यशाखागतानामनति। तद् द्वयोर्वैकल्पिकत्वं भवति। तथा च क्वचित् क्वचिद् दृश्यते। अग्निष्टोमे ग्रहावकाशानाम्नाय पुनर**ौपानुवाक्ये** ग्रहावकाशैश्चरन्ननुवर्तयति। (*Vyā.* 1.1.1.6)

2. एते होमा **औपानुवाक्यै**र्विकल्पन्ते। (*Vyā.* 1.3.4.28)

3. आत्मसमारोपणे **औपानुवाक्या**म्नातेष्वेव द्रव्येषु प्रत्यवरोपणम्। (*Vyā.* 1.6.4.14-16)

4. इह सर्वमनुवाकं मनसा ध्यात्वा पुनर**ौपानुवाक्ये**न विधानेन यथाविभागं यजमानं वाचयति। अथवा तत्र वाचनं विहितम्, इह तेनैव विभागेन मानसत्वम्। मानसवाचनयोर्विकल्पः। (*Vyā.* 3.6.2.3-4)

5. दीक्षितवादम**ौपानुवाक्ये** व्याख्यातम् 'सत्ये भूय इव यतेते'त्यादि। (*Vyā.* 6.1.3.20)

6. **औपानुवाक्यै**र्वक्ष्यमाणैः। हविर्यज्ञविधे पशावत्राध्वर्यू व्रतमुपेतः। (*Vyā.* 6.9.2.14)

   Here it is pertinent to note that the word 'औपानुवाक्य' occurs in the *sūtra*-text too 'औपानुवाक्यैरभिमृशति' (*VādhŚS.* 6.9.2.14)

7. 'उपांशुं हुत्वोपांशुपा=भिषुणुयादि'ति **औपानुवाक्ये** विधानमस्ति। (*Vyā.* 6.9.4.38)

   Here one may notice that since the text is given here is in

abridged form, it must have been in full in the original text of the *Aupānuvākya*.

8. **औपानुवाक्ये** 'ग्रहावकाशैश्चरन्ननुवर्तयती'ति बहुवचनेनैवोपक्रम्य 'त्रिर्देवेभ्यो वपथ' इत्याद्युक्त्वा 'परिभूरग्निं=रायस्पोषस्य ददितारमस्ये'त्यन्तं गृहीत्वा 'तस्य मे रास्व' इति समानमित्याह। (*Vyā.* 6.10.4.2-13)

   Here also, the text is given in *abridged* form.

9. 'ध्रुवं ध्रुवेण हविषा तेऽव सोमं नयामस्यसावि'त्यौ**पानुवाक्ये** विधिरनेन विकल्पते। (*Vyā.* 6.14.2.24)

10. का पुनरुदवसानीया। ब्राह्मणे **औपानुवाक्ये** विहिता। 'आग्नेयं पञ्चकपालमुदवसानीयं निर्वपेदि'ति विधाय पञ्चकपालमपोद्याष्टाकपालः कार्य इति विहिता। (*Vyā.* 6.15.4.1-6)

11. ऋजुहोत्राः संमादयन्तीति **औपानुवाक्यो**क्तस्य पक्षस्यात्र नियमः। (*Vyā.* 10.8.1.14)

12. **औपानुवाक्यं** व्याख्यास्यामः। **औपानुवाक्यं** नाम काण्डम्। तस्मिन् यद्यदाम्नातं तदौपानुवाक्यमित्युच्यते। तानीह कर्माणि कस्येतिकर्तव्यतां प्रतिपद्यन्ते। (*Vyā.* 12.1.1)

13. अयमाचार्यो गवामयनं संवत्सरसत्राणां प्रकृतिभूतं विधाय सर्वाः प्रकृतयोऽनुक्रान्ता इति कृत्वा तदनन्तरमौ**पानुवाक्यं** विदधदनारभ्याधीतानां प्रकृत्यर्थतां बोधयति। (*Vyā.* 12.1.1)

14. तस्य यदन्यत्र क्लृप्तं व्याख्यानं तदौ**पानुवाक्य**स्यावयवभूतम्। (*Vyā.* 12.1.1)

15. न हि पाठक्रमेणानुष्ठानक्रम **औपानुवाक्या**नाम्। (*Vyā.* 12.1.1)

   These above references and existence of commentary on *Aupānuvākya*, clearly establish the fact that orignal *Aupānuvākya*-text of Vādhūlas must have existed.

कल्प *(Kalpa)— Kalpa* is one of the six *Vedaṅgas*, comprising of four sub--branches *viz Śrauta, Gṛhya, Śulba* and *Dharamasūtra* as we understand. But mostly it has been used for *Śrauta*-text in *Vyākhyā*.

1. तद्यथा—शीक्षा व्याकरणं निरुक्तं छन्दोविचितिर्ज्योतिषामयनं **कल्प** इति। (*Vyā.* 1.1.1.1)

2. **कल्पा**ख्येन चाङ्गेन यज्ञस्य क्लृप्तिरभिधीयते। (*Vyā.* 1.1.1.1)

3. सा च क्लृप्तिः **कल्प**सूत्राण्यन्तरेण न सिध्यति। (*Vyā.* 1.1.1.1)

4. **कल्प**स्त्वेकां शाखामारभ्याविरुद्धां वा मिथः काश्चिदारभ्य प्रवर्तते। (*Vyā.* 1.1.1.1)

5. अथायमपि वाधूलेना**चार्येण** रचितः **कल्पः**। (*Vyā.* 1.1.1.1)

6. इमामेव शाखामारभ्यायं **कल्पो** रचित **आचार्येण**। (*Vyā.* 1.1.1.6)

7. तथा 'धूरसी'ति मन्त्रो हि शकटाभिधायी तथाऽग्निष्ठस्य वाऽनस इति। **कल्पे**ऽपि शकटस्य विद्यमानत्वे लिङ्गम्। (*Vyā.* 2.1.4.34)

8. आद्ये **कल्पवाक्य**स्योत्तरयोः श्रुतिवाक्येनाविगीतिः। (*Vyā.* 2.3.1.4)

9. क्रमं पाठात्प्राप्तमपोह्य पौरोडाशिके अवान्तरावकाशादनन्तरं **कल्प** आम्नातमेतं क्रमं स्तौति। (*Vyā.* 3.2.2.27-29)

10. एतत् ज्ञापयति ब्राह्मणेन **कल्पे**न वाऽविनियुक्तानामपि मन्त्राणां लिङ्गेन विनियोगः कर्तव्य इति। (*Vyā.* 3.5.1.1)

11. ननूक्तं **कल्प**वाक्यं न विधायकम्, ब्राह्मणवाक्येन विहितस्यान्वाख्यानमिति। (*Vyā.* 4.3.1.1)

12. **कल्पे** च 'गार्हपत्ये गृहमेधीयं चरुं श्रपयती'ति गार्हपत्यश्रवणात्। लोकाग्नावपि श्रपणमाशंकमानेनैव हि गार्हपत्यग्रहणं कृतम्। सिद्धं हि गार्हपत्ये हविषां श्रपणम्। (*Vyā.* 4.3.1.31)

13. अधिश्रयणमप्युत्तरतो निर्वापपक्ष एवेत्युच्यते। पक्षाश्रितत्वमेषां ब्राह्मणे **कल्पे** वा नोपलभ्यते। (*Vyā.* 4.4.1.3)

14. **कल्पे** तु 'दीक्षास्वग्निहोत्रकाले व्रतयितव्यमि'ति वक्ष्यते। इह प्रातर्व्रतं विधाय तदुत्तरकालं वागुपाकरणदर्शनाद् विकृतौ च 'आगते व्रतं प्रदाय वाचमुपाकरोती'ति दर्शनात्। (*Vyā.* 6.1.4.4-6)

15. पराडतिक्रम्य होमदर्शनाद् गुणत्वात् **कल्पे** चाज्यग्रहणकाल एव ग्रहणदर्शनात् स्रुगादापनदर्शनाच्च। (*Vyā.* 6.4.1.35-36)

16. **कल्पे** तावत् क्वचित्सवनीयस्य पशुपुरोडाशो दृश्यते, न च प्रतिषेधः। (*Vyā.* 6.11.1.1)

17. अथवा ब्राह्मणे **कल्पे** च पठितानां पाठानामानर्थक्यं मा भूदिति बह्वृच्यविहितेन विकल्पते। याजुर्वेदिकस्यापि प्रकृतौ विकृतिषु च विशेषाभावो वा। (*Vyā.* 6.12.2.50-56)

18. **कल्पे** च कृष्णाजिनस्यार्धमिति सामञ्जस्येन भवति। (*Vyā.* 7.1.3.14-15)
19. 'आज्येन संयौतीत्याज्यसंयुतमि'ति च ब्राह्मणे **कल्पे** च दर्शनात्। (*Vyā.* 7.4.1.19)
20. निनयनं मुख्यकल्पः, भक्षणमनु**कल्पः** । (*Vyā.* 8.2.3.13-14)
21. **कल्पे** वैश्वदेवी। उदवसानातिप्रणयनयोर्विकल्पः प्राकृत एवानूद्यते। (*Vyā.* 10.1.2.4)
22. **कल्पे** बहुवचननिर्देशात् सर्वे तूष्णीं प्रोक्षेयुः। (*Vyā.* 10.2.1.33)

कल्पकार *(Kalpakāra)* and **सूत्रकार** *(Sūtrakāra)*—Āryadāsa has mentioned the authors of the ritual-texts by the common titles *Kalpakāra* and *Sūtrakāra* in both singular and plural. Where he uses these titles in singular he means *Vādhūla,* the author of the *Vādhūlasūtra* and where that in plural he means others as we may see in the following references—

(a) **कल्पकार** *(Kalpakāra)*—

1. वाक्यैरभिहितानामर्थानां सन्निवेशविशेषमात्रमेव **कल्पसूत्रकारैः** क्रियते। (*Vyā.* 1.1.1.1)
2. **आचार्येणा**श्रितायाः शाखाया दुर्ज्ञातत्वात्कल्पपदानि मुख्यवृत्त्या व्याख्येयानि। **कल्पकारप्रामाण्या**च्छ्रुतिवचनं कल्पनीयम्। (*Vyā.* 7.1.1.35-36)
3. 'विंशत्याश्च रथाक्षाणामेकविंशत्या अश्वपदानामष्टाङ्गुलस्य च चतुर्विंशं भागमाददीत। स प्रक्रमः स्यात्। तेन वेदिं मिमीत' इति कथयता **कल्पकारेणा**श्वमेधप्रकरण एव रथाक्षान्तरालवचनं द्रष्टव्यमित्यवगन्तव्यम्। (*Vyā.* 7.4.4.15)
4. यागसाधनत्वाय गमनमन्त्रश्च 'द्वे स्रुती' इति प्रत्याम्नायः, यावदुक्तं वा **कल्पकारा**भिप्रायात्। (*Vyā.* 9.4.4.29-31)

(b) **सूत्रकार** *(Sūtrakāra)*—

1. आज्ये दर्भाग्रयोः प्रत्यानयनं **सूत्रकार** आमनति। (*Vyā.* 1.5.1.12)
2. पञ्चावत्तीनामेव **सूत्रकार** आमनति। (*Vyā.* 1.5.2.5)
3. उलूखलभेदे तन्त्रत्वे तु हविष्कृदध्रिगु पुरोनुवाक्यामन्त्रो तस्यावृत्तिर्भिन्नकालेष्विति **सूत्रकार**परिभाषा। (*Vyā.* 2.1.5.19)
4. यथा **सूत्रकारेणा**म्नातं– 'स्फ्यमाज्यस्थालीमुदकमण्डलुमाग्नीध्र' इति। (*Vyā.* 2.3.3.33)

5. पूर्वोक्त**सूत्रकार**वचनादर्शनादिह चाप्रतिषेधात् कामसंयोगेन वैकल्पिकी राका। तथा कर्मसंयोगेनाम्नायते। (*Vyā.* 2.3.3.44-47)

6. तथा च **सूत्रकारेण**ाम्नातम् 'होतृप्रवरे चाध्वर्युप्रवरे च जपती'ति। (*Vyā.* 3.2.3.21-24)

7. तथा हि **सूत्रकार** आमनति–'षडवत्तं पञ्चावत्तिनां, पञ्चावत्तं च चतुरवत्तिनां द्विः प्रथमस्यावद्येत् पञ्चावत्तिन' इति। (*Vyā.* 4.4.2.8-14)

8. तथा च **सूत्रकारः**—'पृथिवी देवपितृयजनी'त्यादीन्युदाहृत्य पुनराह—'अविकारो वा परवाक्यश्रवणादि'ति। (*Vyā.* 4.4.2.18-76)

9. हविष्कृदध्रिगुपुरोनुवाक्यामनोतरस्यावृत्तिर्भिन्नकालेष्विति **सूत्रकारवचनम्**। (*Vyā.* 6.11.1.28)

10. तदाहुः—'यदृचा होता करोती'त्यादिषु महर्त्विग्भिस्तुल्यवत् प्रसंख्यानात्संदीक्षणेत्येताननु सदस्यमित्युक्त्वा यथैव महर्त्विजामानुपूर्व्यमिति वचनाद्विद्यमानेऽपि सदस्ये प्रधानदक्षिणां नासौ लभत इति **सूत्रकारस्य** मतम्। (*Vyā.* 6.12.2.27)

11. तथा च **सूत्रकार** आह—'अग्निष्टोम उत्तरवेदिरुत्तरेषु क्रतुष्वग्निरि'ति। (*Vyā.* 7.1.1.1)

12. **सूत्रकार**मतानुसारेण समुदायुत्य मिश्रयित्वा यथालक्षणं सम्यगभिधाय निदध्यात्। (*Vyā.* 9.4.1.21)

13. यथा **सूत्रकारैः** उपयामेषु सुरास्थालीषु सक्तुलोमैः सक्तुभिर्लोमैश्च यथाक्रमं द्वन्द्वशोऽनुक्रान्तैः तथानुक्रमणस्यार्थवत्त्वाय। (*Vyā.* 9.4.3.17-25)

14. ऐदंयुगीनास्तु **सूत्रकारैः** कल्पितं प्रयोगं स्वल्पेनैव कालेन सुन्वाना इत्येवं कुर्वन्तीति। (*Vyā.* 11.4.1)

15. **सूत्रकार** आह—'यदनाहुतिमात्रा विप्रुडेव से'ति। आहुतिमात्रं च स्रुवपरिमाणं भवितुमर्हति तत्र पुनरुन्नयनं पुनर्होमश्च नेष्यते। (*Vyā.* 12.4.1)

कौषीतकिब्राह्मण (*Kauṣītaki Brāhmaṇa*)—

1 केचित् **कौषीतकादी**नामेव समुच्चयमिच्छन्ति, **ब्राह्मण**ग्रहणात्। (*Vyā.* 1.6.5.4-5)

गणब्राह्मण (*GaṇaBrāhmaṇa*)— An unknown text referred to only once in the *Vyākhyā*—

1. **गणब्राह्मणे** चर्चामष्टौ कृत्वा संस्तुतिरेवमृक्संबन्धादुपपद्यतेतराम्। (*Vyā.* 7.1.1.36)

गणितशास्त्र *(Gaṇitaśāstra)*—

1. तत्रार्धशब्दो यदि समप्रविभागे स्याच्छ्लोकार्थो न गच्छति। असमप्रविभागवाचित्वेऽप्य-गणितज्ञैः विभागप्रकारो ज्ञातुं न शक्यते। अतो **गणितशास्त्रा**देवंविधेषु प्रकार आगमयितव्यः। **गणितशास्त्र**मूरीकृत्य उपाध्यायेन कारिका कृता—

   'यैर्भागाः समतां यान्ति तैः समस्तैर्भजेद् दिशि।

   तत्र लब्धेन ते व्यस्ता विज्ञेया गुणितांशकाः॥' इति। (*Vyā.* 6.12.2.27)

छन्दोगसूत्र *(Chandogasūtra)*— A rare *sūtra*-text related to *Sāma-chanting*

1. आम्नानमुद्गात्रर्थमिति चेत् **छन्दोगे**ऽप्याम्नातस्येहाम्नानमनर्थकं स्यात्। (*Vyā.* 6.5.2.22)
2. **छन्दोग**बह्वृचविषयाः आध्वर्यवा अपि सूत्रान्तरेषु मार्गणीयाः। (*Vyā.* 9.5.1.13-14)
3. तेषां **च्छन्दोग**प्रत्ययो विभागं छन्दोमविधः स्वयमेव विशिनष्टि। (*Vyā.* 13.2.4)
4. तथा च **छन्दोगसूत्रं**— विनशने दीक्षते' इति। (*Vyā.* 13.5.1)

छन्दोब्राह्मण *(ChandoBrāhmaṇa)*—

1. न नृम्णेये बलाधानेऽर्थवादोऽपि नास्तीत्ययं **छन्दोब्राह्मण**भेवैतन्मन्त्रलिङ्गादेव कल्पितम् इत्यर्थः। (*Vyā.* 3.1.1.25)

छन्दोम *(Chandoma)*— A rare *sūtra*-text related to *Sāmaveda.*

1. भूयस्त्वाद्वाच्यस्यार्थस्य **छन्दोम**ग्रहणस्यापि छन्दोमत्वाय दशमग्रहणं दशरात्रस्यैव विकृतौ प्रवृत्तिं ज्ञापयितुं हविष्मतीरित्यस्य प्रत्याम्नायः। (*Vyā.* 11.3.1)
2. तेषां च्छन्दोगप्रत्ययो विभागं **छन्दोम**विधः स्वयमेव विशिनष्टि। (*Vyā.* 13.2.4)
3. सप्तमस्योक्थ्यस्य **छन्दोम**पवमाने चतुर्विंशच्चतुश्चत्वारिंशच्चाष्टा-चत्वारिंशच्छन्दोमाः पवमानबह्वीभिः सस्तोमः पृष्ठ्यः षडह इत्यादि। (*Vyā.* 13.6.1)

छन्दोविचिति *(Chandoviciti)*— Among the six *Vedāṅgas* known as *Kalpa Chandoviciti* generally known as *Chandas*, has been mentioned and sometimes quoted by Āryadāsa in his *Vyākhyā* as under—

1. वेदशब्दश्च मन्त्रब्राह्मणयोः प्रसिद्धः। तस्याङ्गानि षट्। तद्यथा—शीक्षा व्याकरणं निरुक्तं **छन्दोविचिति**ज्योतिषामयनं कल्प इति। (*Vyā.* 1.1.1.1)
2. 'गायत्र्या तेजस्कामस्य परिदध्या'दित्यादिषु छन्दसां मन्त्राणां विनियोगः श्रूयते। स च विनियोगः **छन्दोविचिति**मन्तरेण ज्ञातुं न शक्यते, इति **छन्दोविचिते**रङ्गभावः। (*Vyā.* 1.1.1.1)

   Here I would like to point out that this *Chandoviciti* is not a separate text, but a part of *Nidānasūtra*[1] which comprises of ten *Prapāṭhakas,* the former comprising of *Khaṇḍas* 1-7 of the first *Prapāṭhaka*. The author of the entire text is *Patañjali.* Āryadāsa seems to have taken this nomenclure from that text. अथातश्छन्दसां विचयं व्याख्यास्यामः। (*Nidānasūtra* 1.1.1).

छान्दोग्ये *(Chāndogya)*—

1. एतत्सत्रेष्वेव दक्षिणानां नयनमित्युभयसामा हि भवतीति। प्रसिद्धवद्धेतुत्वेनोपदेशः **छान्दोग्ये** प्रसिद्धमवेक्ष्य अत्रोभयसामत्वं, न निमित्तानि स्युः। (*Vyā.* 11.2.1)
2. रथन्तरवैराजयोरन्यतरत्पुरस्तादुपरिष्टाच्च गीयते। अन्यन्मध्ये भवति। तथोत्तरेष्वपि। गर्भवासमिति **छान्दोग्ये** व्यवहारः। (*Vyā.* 14.5.4)
3. अन्ये वर्णयन्तियानि **छान्दोग्ये** दक्षिणात्वेन प्राकृतावाम्नातानि दशद्रव्याणि गौश्चाश्वश्चाश्वतरश्चेति तेषामन्यतरस्य दक्षिणात्वेन दृश्यमानस्य वाऽनेकगुणविधानप्राप्तौ आद्येन च वारितस्येह ग्रहणं गुणविधानार्थम्।

ज्योतिषामयनम् *(Jyotiṣāmayanam)*— Here one may take notice of the fact that Āryadāsa has used the term *Jyotiṣāmayanam* denoting the movement of all luminaries in the sky, affecting

---

1. The complete text of *Nidānasūtra* of Patañjali has been critically edited by Dr. K.N. Bhatnagar, and published for the first time by Meharchand Lachhmandas, Delhi, 1971.
   Now a seprate text of *Chandoviciti* of Patañjali with *TattvaSubodhīnī-Vṛtti* of Śri Tātaprasāda and *Chandoviciti Vṛtti* of Śri Pedda Śastri, critically edited by Prof. B.R. Sharma, has been published from Rashtriya Sanskrit Vidyāpeetha, Tirupati, 2000.

the functioning of the world related to time and space. All sacrifiecs dealt with in the *Brāhmaṇas* and *Kalpasūtras* follow the rules of *Ayanas* (*uttarayaṇa* and *dakṣiṇāyana*), *Ṛtus* (seasons), *Māsa* (month), *Tithi* (days), *etc.* The performance of sacrifical rituals are very much related to the movements of the sun, moon, stars and planets. They could not be performed without the appropriate knowlege of the hevenly luminares.

1. तद्यथा—शीक्षा व्याकरणं निरुक्तं छन्दोविचिति**र्ज्योतिषामयनं** कल्प इति। (*Vyā.* 1.1.1.1)
2. 'कृत्तिकास्वग्निमादधीत', 'अमावास्यायाममावास्यया यजेत' इत्यादिषु कालज्ञानं **ज्योतिषामयनेन** क्रियते। अतस्तस्याप्यङ्गभावः। (*Vyā.* 1.1.1.1)
3. **ज्योतिषामयना**न्तानामङ्गानां वेदभेदेन शाखाभेदेन च भेदो नास्ति। (*Vyā.* 1.1.1.1)

तैत्तिरीय *(Taittirīya)*— Differences of the *Taittirīya-Śākhā* from *Vādhūla-Śākhā* as noticed by Āryadāsa—

1. ननु तैत्तिरीयश्रुत्याऽयं कल्पो न घटते। कस्माद् ? 'देवो वः सविता प्रेरयतु' इत्यादीनां मन्त्राणाम् एकदेशविकृतानां दर्शनात्। 'असिदमादत्ते' इत्येवमादीनामेतद् ब्राह्मणविहितेभ्योऽन्येषां द्रव्याणां दर्शनात्। अग्नौ सावित्रकाणां कल्प आदिग्रहणेन लक्षितानामन्वाख्याने 'सुवर्गेयाय शक्त्या इन्द्रं दानाय हूमहे' (वाधू.अन्वा. ५.३.३) इति साधिकदर्शनादित्येवमादि। अतः स्थालीपुलाकन्या-येनान्येषामप्येतच्छ्रुत्युक्तमनेन कल्पेनासंबद्धम्। उच्यते। इमामेव शाखामारभ्यायं कल्पो रचित आचार्येण। कुतः ? संप्रदायमार्गे अविच्छिन्नपारंपर्यस्य द्रढिम्नो नोपपद्यते च शाखा विनष्टा तत्क्लृप्त्यर्थं कल्पो न विनष्ट इति। उपनयनात्प्रभृति हि गुरवः शाखां पूर्वमध्यापयन्ति, पश्चात् कल्पम्।

   नन्वेतच्छाखाश्रयणे दोषा उक्ताः। उच्यते। बह्वीरपि शाखा आरभ्य कल्पसूत्राणि प्रथयन्ति, इति पूर्वमुक्तम्। तत्रायमाचार्य एतच्छाखाधीता अवश्यं विकल्पन्त इति मन्यमानोऽन्यशाखागतानामनति। तद् द्वयोर्वैकल्पिकत्वं भवति। तथा च क्वचित् क्वचिद् दृश्यते। अग्निष्टोमे ग्रहावकाशानाम्नाय पुनरौपानुवाक्ये ग्रहावकाशैश्चरन्ननुवर्तयति। 'त्रिर्देवेभ्योऽववथा' इत्यन्यशाखागतं मन्त्रमाम्नाय 'परिभूरग्निम्' इत्यादि मन्त्रस्यान्तं गृहीत्वा 'तस्य मे रास्वे'ति समानम् इत्यग्निष्टोमोक्तमनुजानाति। तथा 'अग्निना देवेन' इत्यादीनां चतुर्थशाखान्तरपठितं समस्तं पठित्वा 'इन्द्रेण सयुजो वयम्'

इत्यवसानादित्येतच्छाखाधीतमनुज्ञाय 'अपि वा तेजस्वी' इत्यन्यशाखागतं वैकल्पिकं पठति। उदाहरणमात्रं प्रदर्शितम्। अन्यान्यप्येतच्छाखाश्रयणे बहूनि लिङ्गानि सन्ति। अतो ब्राह्मणे मन्त्रे वा यद् दृष्टमिहानुक्तमपि परिग्राह्यम्। अतो मन्त्रैः संभरणं कर्तव्यम्। इहानाम्नानं किमर्थमिति चेदविकल्पार्थम्। तथा च वाजसनेयिनः समामनन्ति 'न संभारान् संभरेद्' इति। तच्च संभाराभावो न भवतीति इतिकर्तव्यतया संभरणस्य प्रतिषेधार्थः (*Vyā.* 1.1.1.6)

2. मीमांसा विकल्पना। काञ्चिच्छाखामपेक्ष्याद्य विकल्पना। **तैत्तिरीय**मपेक्ष्येतरा। अथवाऽद्यापि **तैत्तिरीय**कापेक्षैव। (*Vyā.* 7.3.3.56-59)

3. **तैत्तिरीय**के ब्राह्मणे पदैर्मानमाम्नातम्, शुल्बे च किष्कुभिः, कल्पे प्रक्रमैः। (*Vyā.* 7.4.4.15)

4. अस्ति च **तैत्तिरीयक**प्रवचने पक्षद्वयं 'पञ्चचितयो भवन्ति षट्चितयो भवन्ती'ति। (*Vyā.* 7.7.5.6-10)

5. यद्यप्यविशेषेण **तैत्तिरीय**के प्रवचने 'ऋतुस्थाँ यज्ञाज्ञियेन पुच्छ'मित्युक्तम्, तथापि शाखान्तरविशेषवचनं दृष्टमित्यवगन्तव्यम्।(*Vyā.* 7.13.3.14-15)

6. **तैत्तिरीय**के तावत् प्रवचनेऽञ्जलेः करणत्वं समाम्नातम्। इह स्रुवधारणेऽञ्जलिः करणभूतः, न साक्षाद्धोमं प्रति। अतः शाखान्तरस्थोऽयं विधिः 'अञ्जलिना जुहोतीत्यनेन विकल्पत' इति द्रष्टव्यम्। (*Vyā.* 7.14.4.17)

7. **तैत्तिरीय**के समस्तेन हस्तग्रहणम्। शाखान्तरस्थोऽयं विभागविधिर्द्रष्टव्यः। तयोर्विरोधे विकल्पः। (*Vyā.* 7.15.1.54)

8. 'तस्यै गृहे जुहुयादि'ति **तैत्तिरीय**के वचनमनेन विकल्पते।(*Vyā.* 9.2.4.8)

9. प्रातःप्रचरणे आग्नेयोऽष्टाकपाल इत्यादि यत्तत् **तैत्तिरीय**कस्थेन कल्पेन विकल्पते। न ह्युभयोरैकरूप्यम्। तत्र ये सौम्यत्वाष्ट्रवैष्णवाः उपसत्कालम् इहाग्नेयसौम्यवैष्णवाः। कालभेदश्चाधर्मका इवाग्नेयाय आचार्याभिप्रायाद् भजनाभजनीया इत्यादीनि।(*Vyā.* 9.3.2.14)

10. अविशेषात्सर्वाभिः तिसृभिरेव वा 'तिसृभिरुपतिष्ठन्त' इति **तैत्तिरीय**प्रवचने विशेषितत्वात्। (*Vyā.* 9.4.4.32)

11. एवं **तैत्तिरीय**के विशेषात् तद्वच्च मुसलं सैन्ध्रकम्।(*Vyā.* 10.1.1.41)

12. उन्मोऽभिवदनसामान्यं **तैत्तिरीय**के दृष्टस्याहुतिचतुष्टयस्यानिराकरणाय। (*Vyā.* 10.5.2.16)

13. **तैत्तिरीय**केऽन्नशेषस्यानुपसंहृतस्यान्नशेषस्याप्यवघ्रापणेऽस्य मन्त्रस्य विनियोगः। (*Vyā.* 10.6.1.21)

द्वैध *(Dvaidha)*— A text comprising of four *Praśnas* (XX-XXIII), dealing with differences and similarities of views of Baudhayana and Śalīke every where, and sometimes other Ācāryas like Āñgigavi, Ātreya, Ādya, Ārtabhāgiputra, Aupamanyava, Aupamanyavīputra, Kātya, Kātyāyana, Kauṇapatantri, Gautama, Dīrghavātsya, Mangala, Maitreya, Maudgalya, Dakṣiṇākāra, Rathītara and Rathantar. It does not seem to be a work of Bodhāyana, but, perhaps composed by some pupil of Bodhāyana or pupil's pupil.[1] Ācāryas in the matter of ritualistc performances given in *BaudhŚS,* is traditionally known as *Dvaidha-sūtra*. Āryadāsa quotes this text in his *Vyākhyā* as under—

1. 'यत् त्रेधाग्निराधीयते' इत्याहवनीयाधानगुणवाक्यमध्ये श्रवणादनयोरपि ततो विहरणमिति। तथा च **द्वैधे** 'आहवनीयादेवैनौ विहरेदिति शालीकिरि'ति। (*Vyā.* 1.2.1.1)
2. यस्मिन्पर्वसन्धिः तस्मिन्नहन्युपवसथ उत्तरेद्युर्यागः। तथा चोक्तं **द्वैधे**— 'यत्रैतदुपवसतोऽस्तमित आदित्ये पुरस्ताच्चन्द्रमा लोहितीभवन्निवोदियात्, तमुपवसथं जानीया'दिति। (*Vyā.* 2.1.1.1)
3. तथा च **द्वैधे** शालीकिपक्षः 'प्रातःसवन एव सर्वेभ्य सवनेभ्यः सवनीयान् निर्वपेदि'ति। (*Vyā.* 6.9.1.17)
4. तथा चोक्तं **द्वैधे**—'एतानि च नित्यानि च दद्यादि'ति बोधायनः।'एतान्येवेति शालीकिरिति। (*Vyā.* 14.9.3)

निरुक्त *(Nirukta)*— One of the six *Vedaṅgas*, dealing with the principles and methods of etymological interpretation of the Vedic mantras. Since this text is not related to the rituals it has been quoted by Āryadāsa only once. Āryadāsa specifically pointed out that its knowledge is essential for the ritualists also, because without knowing the meaning of the mantras they cannot apply them properly in the rituals.

1. तद्यथा—शीक्षा व्याकरणं **निरुक्तं** छन्दोविचितिर्ज्योतिषामयनं कल्प इति। (*Vyā.* 1.1.1.1)

---

1. Kashikar C.G., 'Survey of Śrauta and other Sūtras', p.44-45.

1. **निरुक्त**मपि मन्त्रार्थप्रत्यायनादिना। अर्थाभिधानसंयोगाद्धि मन्त्रेषु शेषभावः। (*Vyā.* 1.1.1.1)

नैदान *(Naidāna)*— One of the schools of Vedic ritualistic interpretations, mentioned by Āryadāsa. Yāska, too, has referred to the views of *Naidānas* twice in his Nirukta (6.9; 7.12). But no name of any Ācārya is given by him. *Bṛhaddevatā* of Śaunaka refers to a *Naidāngrantha* of the *Chandogas.* The *Nidānasūtra* of Patañjali which we have seen in connection with *Chandoviciti* which constitutes the first seven *Khaṇḍas* of the first *Prapāṭhka* of *Nidānasūtra,* is not intended by Yāska as Patañjali is posterior to Yāska. But the *Nidānasūtra* of Patañjali belonged to *Sāmaveda.* Pt. Satyarvata Sāmaśramī had prepared a text of *Nidānasūtra* which was published from Calcutta. The author of the text is not mentioned in his edition. On the title page of the text it bears simply 'ऋषिप्रोक्तमिदम्'. It was earlier published for the first time in 1896 in *Uṣā* Patrikā, but later on in form of a book by Satyavrata Sāmaśramī. Caland for the first time mentioned the name of its author Patañjali. Dr. Kailash Nath Bhatnagar for the first time prepared a critical edition of the complete *Nidānasūta*[1] comprising of ten *Prapāṭhakas* and assigned its authorship to Patañjali, as Dr. Caland held. In the time of Yāska there was a seprate school of Vedic interpretation known as नैदान *(Naidāna).* In his Nirkuta he has twice mentioned it as:

1. स्याल आसन्नः सं योगेनेति नैदानाः। (*Nir.* 6.9)
2. साम सम्मितमृचाऽस्यतेर्वा, ऋचा समं मेन इति नैदानाः। (*Nir.* 7.12)

These references to *Naidāna* in plural indicate the existence of many *Nidānasūtras* in the time of Yāska. Bṛhaddevata too refers to a *Nidānasūtra* of Bhāllavins-

एष एव परामृष्टो भालविब्राह्मणे द्वृचः।

निदानसंज्ञके ग्रन्थे छन्दोगानामिति श्रुतिः॥ (*Bṛhdd.* 5.23)

Āryadāsa in his *Vyākhyā* seems to have referred to only the school of *Naidānas*, not any particular text under this title.

1. Vide supra fn. 1 Intro. p.37.

1. अतिरात्रस्य प्रथमाहारत्वं **नैदानै**रपि वैस्पष्ट्येन नाभिहितम्। तस्मादग्निष्टोम एव प्रथमाहारे प्रतिषेधः। (*Vyā.* 6.4.1.2)

यज्ञपार्श्व *(Yajñapārśva)*— We find references to an important text *Yajñapārśva* of Vādhūlas in *Vyākhyā*—

1. यथा **यज्ञपार्श्व** उक्तम्—'श्वः परिग्रहणं लुम्पेदन्यश्चेति वा वदेदि'ति। (*Vyā.* 4.1.1.18-30)

2. **यज्ञपार्श्वे** न वक्तव्यो 'यजे'ति। एष द्वारप्रभृतिषु त्रिषु साधारणेन सिद्धो हि, यद्युच्येताधिको भवेत्। (*Vyā.* 4.1.2.39)

3. तथा **यज्ञपार्श्वे**—

'दार्शिकी दक्षिणा वेदिः पाशुकी चोत्तरोच्यते।

आयामतः समे च स्तां वेदी बाहू इति श्रुतेः ॥' इति

सा यदि सन्नता स्याच्छ्रोण्योरंसयोरिति प्रथमात्रादसम्भेदः। (*Vyā.* 4.2.1.23)

4. अग्निप्रणयनीयाग्निमन्थनीयसामिधेनीनामनूहत्वं **यज्ञपार्श्वे**षूक्तम्–

'सामिधेन्यस्त्वनूह्याः स्युर्नर्चमूहेदिति श्रुतेः।

अग्नेः प्रणयनीयाश्च मन्थनीयास्तथैव च ॥' इति। (*Vyā.* 4.2.1.30)

5. उभयार्थं यवान् पृथङ् निधत्तः। व्रीहियवयोः प्रकृतितः प्राप्तेस्तुल्यत्वादिह विशेष-वचनभावात्प्रयोगसौकर्यार्थं यवमयानि सर्वाणि हवींषि स्युः। उक्तं च **यज्ञपार्श्वे**—

'करंभपात्राणि तु मेषमेष्यौ धानाश्च मन्थश्च यवैः क्रियन्ते।

यावानि सर्वाणि हवींषि वा स्युर्यानि प्रघासे पितृयज्ञ एव'॥ इति। (*Vyā.* 4.2.1.37)

6. निर्मथितं विभज्य प्रहृत्याभिजुहुतः। उक्तं तु **यज्ञपार्श्वे**—

'निर्मन्थञ्चातिमुक्त्याश्च संभाराः पृषदाज्यकम्।

वाजिनञ्चोभयत्र स्युराचार्यास्तूत्तरे विदुः ॥

केचिन्निर्मथितस्याग्नेः विभज्य चरन्ति च'॥ इति। (*Vyā.* 4.2.2.9)

7. तथैव द्वेधा **यज्ञपार्श्वे** च। अतो विकल्पः। (*Vyā.* 4.3.1.1)

8. अनुपद**यज्ञपार्श्व**योः पितृयज्ञे व्रताभाव उक्तो यदि तदिष्यते। (*Vyā.* 4.4.1.29)

Here I would like to point out that two texts of *Yajñapārśva* have been edited one by Dr. C.G. Kashikar[1] and the other by Dr. Nabanarayan Bandopadhyay[2]. Dr. Bandopadhyay has published a *Laghu Yajñapārśva* along with *Mahad Yajñapārśva*. But in none of these printed texts the above quoted verses from *Yajñapārśva* are found. On the basis of the absence of these verses in the published *Yajñapārśva*-texts, we may say that there was a separate text of *Yajñapārśva*, belonging to the *Vādhūla*-tradition. The mention of both *Anupada* and *Yajñapārśva* together justifies my conjecture.

रहस्य *(Rahasya)*— A text of *Vādhūlagṛhyāgamavṛttirahasya*[3], belonging to the *Vādhūla*-tradition, of Nārāyaṇa Miśra has been published. But this *Rahasya* is different from that text, because it seems to be related to *Kalpa.* Āryādasa has referred to a text *Rahasya* in *Vyākhyā* twice. This text is also found referred to in *Nidānsūtra*[4] of Patañjali many times as under—

1. अथापि **रहस्य**ब्राह्मणे दर्शयति- याथाकामीति याथाकामानमिति। (*Nidānsūtra* p.28, line 5)
2. यद्वेतद्र**हस्य**ब्राह्मणे दर्शयतीति सर्वाभिप्राय एतदुपपद्यते। (*Nidānsūtra* p.28, line 13)
3. एवं च **रहस्य**ब्राह्मणे दर्शयति- अप्यनेन षोडशिसंस्थेन यजेतेति। (*Nidānsūtra* p.39, line 2)
4. एवं च **रहस्य**ब्राह्मणे दर्शयति। (*Nidānsūtra* p.77, line 23)
5. अपि चैवं **रहस्य**ब्राह्मणे दर्शयति ज्योतिष्प्रायणा ज्योतिरुदयतः। (*Nidānsūtra* p.81, line 17-18)
6. तथापि **रहस्य**परिपठितेषु वैकल्पिकेषु रात्रिं च कृत्वा अहस्त्वकृत्वेति च

---

1. 'यज्ञपार्श्वम् परिशिष्टम्' शुक्लयजुर्वेदानुसारि कात्यायनीयम् ed. by Dr. C.G. Kashikar, published from Bhandarkar Oriental Research Institute, Pune, 1980.
2. '*Laghu-Yajñapārśva Pariśiṣṭa*' and '*Mahad-Yajñapārśva Pariśiṣṭa*', edited by Nabanaryana Bandopadhyay, School of Vedic Studies, Rabindra Bharati University, Kolkata, 2006.
3. *Vādhūlagṛhyāgamavṛttisrahasya* of Nārāyaṇa Miśra, edited by Prof. B.B. Chaubey, published from National Manuscripts Mission (NMM), New Delhi, and D.K. Printworld (P) LTD, New Delhi, under Kṛtibodh Series No. 1.
4. *Nidānasūtra* of Patañjali, edited by Dr. K.N. Bhatnagar, and published for the first time by Meharchand Lachhmandas, Delhi, 1971.

कालद्वयेऽप्यनपायस्तस्यां विधीयते। (*Vyā.* 1.5.4.20)

7. अवदानानां बदरीपलाशमात्रत्वं **रहस्ये**षु दृश्यते 'बदरीपलाशमात्रेणावदानेने'ति। (*Vyā.* 2.3.1.44)

लक्षणशास्त्र *(Lakṣaṇaśāstra)*—

1. आश्रावणादीनां प्लुतं **लक्षणशास्त्रा**दनुपदाद्वा ग्राह्यम्। (*Vyā.* 2.3.1.19)

वाजसनेयिन *(Vājasaneyin)*—

1. तथा च **वाजसनेयिनः** समामनन्ति 'न संभारान् संभरेत्' इति। तच्च संभाराभावो न भवतीति इतिकर्तव्यतया संभरणस्य प्रतिषेधार्थः। (*Vyā.* 1.1.1.6)

विधिशेष *(Vidhiśesa),* **विध्यवशेष** (*Vidhyavaśeṣa)*— Āryadāsa refers to the existence of a text *Vidhyavaśeṣa.* This text is also found mentioned in 11th section of the first *Prapāṭhka* of the *Nidānasūtra* under the title विधिशेष *(Vidhiśesa).* This section is devoted to *Vidhiśesa,* that is the ways to be observed in the performance of rites *i.e.* what kinds of wood and the bark of wood would do and how *Kuśa* is to be used. It further deals with the variety of cloths to be wrapped round the *audumbari* pillar and the way how the *udgātā* priest should sit while performing a rite. I think the *Vidhyavaśeṣa* which Āryadāsa has mentioned in his *Vyākhyā* must be separate type of text which might have discussed some more new rituals which might have remained unnoticed, or might have come into ritualistic practices later on. This title indicates the existence of such types of texts containing rituals, which had remained undealt in the main body of the texts of the concerned *Śākhā.* Āryadāsa frequently referes such types of texts both in singular and plural, as we may see in the following references as under—

1. **विध्यवशेषा** हि तत्राभिधीयन्ते। कस्य पुनस्ते विध्यवशेषाः ? चतुर्णां वाधूलानामिति। के ते चत्वारो वाधूलाः ? कौण्डिन्याग्निवेश्यगालवशाङ्खानां कल्पाः। (*Vyā.* 1.1.1.5)

2. शाखान्तरे तादृशस्य सादयित्वा संभृतेष्वपि तन्न विरुध्यते। इतरेतरयुक्तान्येव भवन्ति। तेषां वृक्षनियमः परिमाणञ्च **विध्यवशेषे**षु संख्याविकल्पनमुक्तम्। तत्रैव वक्ष्यामः। (*Vyā.* 2.1.1.7)

   Here the prhrase 'तत्रैव वक्ष्यामः' indicates the authorship of one of the *Vidhyavaśeṣa* texts to Āryadāsa himself.

3. 'उर्वन्तरिक्षमन्विहि' इत्यन्तरा वेदिं चोत्करं च वेद्युत्करावन्तरेण ऋत्विग्यजमानानां पत्न्याश्च यज्ञपात्राणां मेधादीनां चायमेव पन्था: । तत् क्वचित् क्वचित् प्रदर्शयति। 'विसंस्थिते संस्थिते च संचर' इति **विध्यवशेषे**षु च तथैवाम्नातम्। (*Vyā.* 2.1.1.16)

4. **विध्यवशेषे**षु सप्तबर्हिर्जातयस्तुल्यविकल्पा इवाम्नायन्ते कुशाश्च दर्भाश्च क्षीरदर्भाश्च मुञ्जाश्चाश्ववालाश्चैक्षवाश्चेति। (*Vyā.* 2.1.1.17)

5. परिमाणानि च ब्राह्मणे सामान्यशब्देन 'इयन्तम्' इत्युक्तानि **विध्यवशेषे** विशेषितानि 'स्रुग्दण्डमात्रः स्रुवदण्डमात्र ऊर्वस्थिमात्र' इति। अपरिमित इत्युक्तपरिमाणविकल्पः। (*Vyā.* 2.1.1.19-20)

6. तेषां वृक्षनियमः परिमाणं च **विध्यवशेषेषु** संख्याविकल्पनमुक्तम्। तत्रैव वक्ष्यामः। (*Vyā.* 2.1.1.34)

7. शाखया चोदितस्य शाखापवित्रेणापाकरणस्यायुक्तत्वादुद्गृह्य तयैव शाखयापाकृत्य तत्रैव पुनरुपगूहन्ति केचित्। तदानीमेवान्यां शाखामाहृत्य दर्भैर्वा प्रातर्दोहाय वत्सानपाकृत्य प्रातर्दोहाय संविशेदिति **विध्यवशेषः**। (*Vyā.* 2.1.3.30-31)

8. 'स्फ्येन पुरोडाशीयान् सादये'दिति **विध्यवशेषे**षूक्तम्। (*Vyā.* 2.1.4.1)

9. प्राशिते प्राशिते सर्वेषां मार्जनं 'सन्ततमा ब्रह्मण' इत्यस्य शेषो **विध्यवशेषो**ऽथापः संप्रयच्छेयुरग्नीदध्वर्यवेऽध्वर्युर्होत्रे होता यजमानाय सन्ततमाब्रह्मण इति। (*Vyā.* 2.3.2.23-29)

10. वेदमाञ्जसं **विध्यवशेषे**षु पथ्यन्तरमुक्तम्। (*Vyā.* 3.5.1.4)

11. अन्यत्र ग्रहेभ्यः प्राजापत्यं वायव्यं सावित्रं सारस्वतं द्यावापृथिव्यं वैश्वकर्मणमादित्यं सौर्यमिति **विध्यवशेषे**षु। (*Vyā.* 4.1.1.18-30)

12. हविषां तन्त्राणां चोच्चैरुपांशुता **विध्यवशेषा**दागमयितव्येति। (*Vyā.* 4.1.3.29)

13. अथ समस्ते यथादेशं निवर्तनमन्ते वपनमिति **विध्यवशेषः**। (*Vyā.* 4.1.4.30)

14. तथाहि **विध्यवशेषे**षु 'आप्लुतछागमकुण्यङ्गमि'त्याद्युक्तम्। (*Vyā.* 5.1.1.1)

15. रशनादीनां दर्भाणां मुञ्जानां वेत्यादयो विशेषा **विध्यवशेषे**षु द्रष्टव्याः। (*Vyā.* 5.1.1.1)

16. प्रक्रम उत्तरार्धाद् 'वेद्यैव वा चात्वालस्योत्करस्येति प्रक्रमान्तरमि'ति **विध्यवशेषे**षूक्तम्। (*Vyā.* 5.1.1.34)

17. 'एषा तेऽश्रिः स्पष्टाऽस्त्वि'ति। एषा त्वया श्रीरपि स्मृता भवतु। किं प्रयोजनम्। अस्य विशेषो **विध्यवशेषे**ष्वाम्नातो विज्ञायते। (*Vyā.* 5.2.2.14)

18. 'सा त्रिवली पञ्चवली सप्तवली वे'ति **विध्यवशेषः**। (*Vyā.* 6.1.1.2)

19. तयोरितिकर्तव्यता **विध्यवशेषेभ्य** आगमयितव्या। (*Vyā.* 6.1.1.2)

20. तस्या आयामव्यासरूपाणि **विध्यवशेषे**षूक्तानि—'द्वाद्वशप्रक्रमायामा प्राची शाला स्यात्। षड् व्यासकालातिस्थूणाराजां पुरस्तादुन्नते'ति। (*Vyā.* 6.1.1.3)

21. 'अकृत्स्नासूत्पन्नानि समापयेदि'ति **विध्यवशेषः**। (*Vyā.* 6.1.1.14)

22. राजासन्द्या विशेषो **विध्यवशेषेषु**। (*Vyā.* 6.2.1.2)

23. 'समपिधाय द्वारं प्रायणीयमासादयेदि'ति **विध्यवशेषः**। (*Vyā.* 6.2.3.2)

24. **विध्यवशेषेषु** 'प्राङ्छन्दोमेभ्यो ब्रह्म च गाथां चाभिव्याहरेदि'त्युक्तम्। (*Vyā.* 6.3.1.1-2)

25. एकयैकयोत्सर्गमित्यस्य **विध्यवशेषे**ष्वनेकधा व्याख्यानं कृतम्। (*Vyā.* 6.3.1.6-8)

26. 'योगे विमोके च दक्षिणपूर्व' इति **विध्यवशेषः**। (*Vyā.* 6.3.2.29)

27. 'उदपात्रनिनयनमर्घ्यप्रदानप्रदर्शनमि'ति **विध्यवशेषः**। (*Vyā.* 6.3.3.11)

28. 'प्रातर्दोहं दोहयित्वा तस्योपधाय कपालानि प्रातर्दोहं दोहयेदि'ति **विध्यवशेषः**। (*Vyā.* 6.9.1.17)

29. तथा च **विध्यवशेषेषु** 'अत्रोत्तरयोः सवनयोः व्यावर्तनान्ताः पिण्डकृताः परिशयीरञ्छृताः प्रागुद्वासनादित्येके' इति। (*Vyā.* 6.9.1.17)

30. **विध्यवशेषेषु** 'यथालिप्तं दशापवित्रेण परिमृज्य नैदेशिकान्मृजनान् कुर्यादि'ति तेषां मार्जनान्तरत्वमभ्यधायि। (*Vyā.* 6.9.4.32)

31. तथा स यद् ग्रहान् ग्रहीष्यन् 'भूरि'त्याह। तत्रापि 'सुव'रित्यसीदत्सु होम' इति **विध्यवशेषः**। (*Vyā.* 6.9.4.36)

32. गृहीते च 'पात्राणां तासु परिप्लावनमि'ति **विध्यवशेषो**क्तं ग्रहीतव्यम्। (*Vyā.* 6.10.1.60)

33. 'पुरोरुचः पुरस्तात् 'भूरि'त्याह, ग्रहणमन्त्रान्ते 'भुव' इति, सादनमन्त्रान्ते 'सुवरि'ति **विध्यवशेषः**। (*Vyā.* 6.10.2.31)

34. 'सर्वे विप्रुषां होमं जुह्वती'ति **विध्यवशेषः**। (*Vyā.* 6.10.3.10)

35. 'अधिषवणचर्मणि सर्वेषु समन्वारब्धेषु ऋत्विक्षु विमोचनीयाञ् जुहोती'ति **विध्यवशेषः**। (*Vyā.* 6.15.1.51)

36. **विध्यवशेषे**षु पुनराहवनीयेऽवभृथयजूंषि जुहुयात्। (*Vyā.* 6.15.2.2-3)

37. 'अनूबन्ध्यस्य वपान्ते दक्षिणे वेद्यन्ते परिश्रिते यजमानः केशश्मश्रूणि वापयेदि'ति **विध्यवशेषः**। (*Vyā.* 6.15.3.102)

शतपथ *(Śatapatha)*—

1. श्रुतपथे विज्ञानार्थत्वादिति केचित्। तथा च **शतपथे**। (*Vyā.* 1.5.1.10)

शिक्षा *(Śikṣā)*—

1. तद्यथा—**शीक्षा** व्याकरणं निरुक्तं छन्दोविचितिर्ज्योतिषामयनं कल्प इति। (*Vyā.* 1.1.1.1)

शुल्ब *(Śulba)*— Āryadāsa refers to the existence of a *Śulba* and *Śulbakārikā*-text of Vādhūla as under—

1. तथा हि **शुल्ब** उक्तम् —'वाधूलकाः सवाधूलाश्चत्वारो विहिताः क्रमादि'ति। (*Vyā.* 1.1.1.5)

2. ऊर्ध्वाग्रं **शुल्बा**ग्रं प्रत्यञ्चमायम्य विस्त्रस्य बर्हिरित्यादि। (*Vyā.* 2.2.4.37)

3. ब्राह्मणकल्प**शुल्बो**क्तानां पदप्रक्रमकिष्कूनामन्यतमेन वेदिर्मातव्या। तेषां परिमाणानि **शुल्बे** द्रष्टव्यानि। (*Vyā.* 6.4.2.4-29)

4. **शुल्बि**ण्याख्या शरावप्रोतकूर्च इति केचित्। अन्ये शूर्प इति। अपरे रज्जुसन्निवेशविशेष इति। (*Vyā.* 6.4.2.78)

   It may be pointed out the word शुल्बिणी does not occur in any of the *Śrautasūtras* or *Śulbasūtras* except the *VādhŚS* 6.4.2.78

5. धिष्णियानां विष्कम्भान्तरालानां प्रमाणं **शुल्बे** द्रष्टव्यम्। अन्युप्तधिष्णियानप्यत्रैव केचिदनुदिशन्ति। (*Vyā.* 6.5.4.21)

6. उखामृच्छेशेण कासांचिदिष्टकादीनां कर्तव्यत्वात्। त**च्छुल्बे** द्रष्टव्यम्। (*Vyā.* 7.1.1.26-27)

7. **शुल्बकारेण** व्यायाममात्रे चयनविधानात् देवरथचक्रप्रमाणमित्याचार्येणाभि-प्रेतमिति केषांचिद्दर्शनम्, तत्प्रमाणं तज्ज्ञेभ्य आगमयितव्यम्। **शुल्बोक्तं** तेन विकल्पत इति। (*Vyā.* 7.4.4.15)

8. तैत्तिरीयके ब्राह्मणे पदैर्मानमाम्नातम्, **शुल्बे** च किष्कुभिः, कल्पे प्रक्रमैः। (*Vyā.* 7.4.4.15)

9. त्रिस्तावाश्वमेधे **शुल्ब**कारेणाभिप्रेता। (*Vyā.* 7.4.4.15)

10. **शुल्बो**क्तेन विधानेन पुरुषमात्रेण वेणुना स्पन्द्यया वा मित्वा धर्ममात्रं वेणुना कुर्यात्। (*Vyā.* 7.4.4.16)

11. **शुल्बो**पधानवशात् सूत्रमाक्षिप्योपधानं प्रतिपद्यते। उपधाय वा सर्वं **शुल्ब**वशान्मन्त्रैरनुपूर्वमभिमृशेत्। (*Vyā.* 7.5.1.19)

12. **शुल्बे** च द्वयोः पक्षयोरिष्टका सहस्त्रोपधानप्रकारः परिकल्पितः। (*Vyā.* 7.7.5.6-10)

13. उक्तं च **शुल्ब**कारेण—'घृताच्छिन्नाद् उपदध्यात्। घृतेष्टका' इति श्रुतिः। (*Vyā.* 7.11.3.29)

14. व्यक्तञ्च **शुल्ब**कारेणाभिसंख्याहारि 'अन्यासां चोत्तमयोरि'ति। (*Vyā.* 7.11.3.103-104)

15. नक्षत्रेष्टकास्तावन्न चतुर्विधा वेणुपर्णवदिति **शुल्बे** विहिताः। (*Vyā.* 7.12.1.4)

16. द्विस्तावां वेदिं मिमीते **शुल्बो**क्तेन विधानेन। (*Vyā.* 10.4.1.22)

सदस्यकल्प (*Sadasyakalpa*)— This text is still unknown.

1. **सदस्यकल्पे**—'उत्तरा देवता उपतिष्ठन्त' इति दर्शनाच्चैवमुपपद्यते सुतराम्। एतावदध्वर्योर्यजमानस्य ब्रह्मसदस्ययोश्च समानम्। (*Vyā.* 6.11.1.14)

सरस्वती (*Sarasvasti*)— This text is still unknown.

1. स्तम्बयजुषोर्हरणे प्रतिप्रस्थातोत्तरां वेदिमग्रेण। **सरस्वत्या** चोक्तम्—

   'अग्रेणैवोत्तरामग्निं प्रतिप्रस्थातृसञ्चरः।

   अपरेणापि वा वेदिं हविषां चापि सञ्चरः॥' इति। (*Vyā.* 4.2.1.25)

2. स एवोपभृति स्रुवायां हवींषि गच्छति 'अभिघारणे तदि'ति ब्रुवत्याः **सरस्वत्या** न बर्हिरर्थमेव समानयनमित्यभिप्रायः। (*Vyā.* 4.4.1.9)

सर्वाचार्यक (*Sarvācāryaka*)— This text is still unknown.

1. **सर्वाचार्यके**ऽप्युक्तम्—

   'बाहोस्तु भागा यदि द्वादश स्युः कर्णं दशत्रीन्विदुः पञ्चकोट्याः।

   प्राग्वंशमाने भवेत् सापि वेद्याः वेद्यास्तु भागांस्त्रिकिष्कून्वदन्ति'॥ इति। (*Vyā.* 6.1.1.3)

2. वैणवीभिर्नियम्यन्ते इति ता ऊरीकृताः। **सर्वाचार्ये**ऽभिहितं। (*Vyā.* 7.7.5.6-10)

सामवेद *(Sāmaveda)*—

1. 'अभि त्वा शूर नोनुमः' इति रथन्तरेणोपतिष्ठते। रथन्तरेणेति सामनामग्रहणाद् ब्राह्मणे च गानविधानात् **सामवेदे** च विधानात् साम्नोपस्थानम्। ऋग्द्वयस्य साम्नि नित्यत्वादृगनुक्रमणस्यानर्थक्यप्रसङ्गादृचा साम्ना वेति विकल्पः प्रतिषिद्धः। नह्येतेषां सामानि गायेत्। तदभावेऽपि योनिभिरुपतिष्ठेत। नैतदेवम्। सामश्रवणसामर्थ्याद्धि उद्गाता कल्प्यते। सः कथं तदभावे गृह्येत। दक्षिणादानादिषु न क्वचिच्छ्रूयते। कस्तर्ह्यर्थः। अनुपदकार आह—'यद्युद्गाता न स्यात् तर्हि यजमानः स्वयमेवोत्थायाभिहिंकृत्य योनिभिरुपतिष्ठेते'ति। (*Vyā.* 1.1.4.4)

सौशारद *(Sauśārada)*— This text is still unknown.

1. तथा च **सौशारद** उक्तम्— 'अग्नीषोमीयविकारेष्वविशेषं कुर्यात्, न चास्मिन्नर्थात् कुर्वीते'ति। (*Vyā.* 5.1.2.21)

2. समाख्याभक्षे सर्वे होतारं, होताऽध्वर्युं, होत्रका होतारमध्वर्युं च। कथमनुज्ञापनम् ऋत्विङ्नामधेयेन संबुद्ध्यन्ते नासावुपह्वयस्वेति। प्रशास्तरिति मैत्रावरुणं, ब्रह्मन्निति ब्राह्मणाच्छंसिनमिति **सौशारदे**ऽनुपद आम्नातम्। (*Vyā.* 6.11.4.19)

   It is to be pointed out that here both *Anupada* and *Sauśārada* have been mentioned together. From this we may conjecture that like *Anupada Sauśārada*, too, might have belonged to the *Vādhūla*-tradition.

स्मृति *(Smṛti)*— Here, I would like to point out that in the above *Vyākhyā*-texts Āryadāsa has used the word *Smṛtiśāstra* four times in singular and once in plural in which he quotes Manu in support of speaking lie to save life of a person of any of the four *Varṇas.* But in remaining cases he referes to *Yajñopavita* and *Ācamana-Vidhis,* which, in my opinion, have been dealt with in *Vādhūla-Smṛti*[1] verses 21-30 in my critical edition of *Vādhūla-Smṛti* which was based on a MS in Grantha script, deposited at the Government Oriental Manuscripts Library,

---

1. *Vādhūla-Smṛti*, critically edited with Hindi translation by Prof. B.B. Chaubey, published from Katyayan Vaidika Sahitya Prakashan, Hoshiarpur, 2000.

Madras, under No R.2180. In my opinion Āryadāsa must have seen *Vādhūla-Smṛti.*

1. स यज्ञोपवीतं कृत्वाऽप आचम्य **स्मृति**शास्त्रस्य शेषत्वाद्यज्ञोपवीताचमनयोर्नित्यत्वाद् यज्ञकर्मसु, इह विधानस्यानर्थक्यं स्मृतिशास्त्रप्राप्तस्य प्रदर्शनार्थं भवति। एवं तर्हि अभावे यज्ञोपवीतिना चान्तेन प्रक्रान्तत्वादनुवाक एवेह वचनम्। अथवा नित्यादाचमनादन्यदाचमनं स्मृतावेव विहितमस्ति। (*Vyā.* 1.6.1.7)
2. **स्मृति**शास्त्रस्य शेषत्वमुक्तम्। (*Vyā.* 2.1.3.2)
3. अथापि च यत्र **स्मृति**शास्त्रेष्वनृतमनुक्तं तत्तत्परिग्रहार्थम्—
   'शूद्रविट्क्षत्रविप्राणां यत्रोक्तेऽर्थे भवेद्वधः।
   तत्र वक्तव्यमनृतं तद्धि सत्याद्विशिष्यते॥' (मनु. ८.१०४) इति मनुनाऽभिहितम्। (*Vyā.* 12.1.1)

7. Differences of *Vādhūla*-tradition from other *Śākhās* as noticed by Āryadāsa.

(a) **अस्मत्पक्षे, अस्माभिः, अस्मदीयाः**— In the matter of ritualistic controversies among the different Ācāryas, Āryadāsa gives stress on his own *Śākhā* by using the terms अस्मत्पक्षे, अस्माभिः, अस्मदीयाः *et c.* as we may see in the following references in the *Vyākhyā*—

1. मध्यमं पक्षमाश्रित्या**स्माभिः** प्रयोगे उक्ताः, यद्यत्र क्रियते। (*Vyā.* 1.1.1.6)
2. **अस्म**च्छ्रुत्यपेक्षमाचार्येणाम्नातमिति किमत्रायुक्तम्। **अस्माकं** तु सर्वास्वर्धर्चेन सन्दधातीत्येव। (*Vyā.* 2.3.1.4)
3. प्राशित्रस्य चाग्रेण परिहरणं यच्चाचार्येणोक्तं ब्राह्मणे वा विद्यते तद**स्माकं** प्रमाणम्। (*Vyā.* 2.3.2.22)
4. येषामुत्तरपदार्था यजमानकर्तृकास्तेषां निधाय स्थालीमिति निहितायां स्थाल्यामिति व्याख्येयम्। आध्वर्यवत्वे नास्ति वक्तव्यम्। किन्त्वाशीराशासनेऽध्वर्युर्यजमानस्य तत्पुत्राणां च नामानि गृह्णाति। नैतदेवम्। आत्मनोऽग्रे नाम गह्णातीत्युक्तम्। यद्येवमभिप्रेष्येद् यजमानस्येत्येवावक्ष्यत्। उच्यते। एवं कर्तव्यमिति **अस्माभि**र्न शक्यते वक्तुम्। एवमुक्ते कोऽर्थ इति विचारणीयम्। (*Vyā.* 2.3.3.102-104)
5. निरुप्यमाणाभिमन्त्रणादिषु वचनेषु वाच्यमानो ब्रवीतीति। तत्र इहाभिमन्त्रयत इति। **अस्मत्पक्षे** वाच्यमानानामभिमन्त्रयत इति नास्ति विरोधः। एवमन्येष्वपि

तत्रतत्र द्रष्टव्यम्। (*Vyā.* 3.3.1.1)

6. उभयविरहितेऽन्यस्मिन् प्रकरणे वेदवति वाचने....विनियोक्तुम**स्माकं** नास्ति शक्तिः। (*Vyā.* 3.3.2.3)

(b) **आचार्य** *(Ācārya)*— Through out the commentary Āryadāsa always uses the honourable word *Ācārya* in singular for Vādhūla, not as the promulgater but reviver of this *Śākhā*. He has raised a question on behalf of the complainent *Pūrvapakṣin,* that this *Kalpasūtra* is not the work of Vādhūla, as he has mentioned many options regarding the performance of the rituals. Had this text solely belonged to Vādhūla, he would not have prescribed the options in the matter of their performance. Here Āryadāsa has also pointed out that upto his time the *Vādhūla Śākhā* has become almost extinet and it had also become very difficult to understand and interprete the *Kalpasūtra* of that *Śākhā.* However he tried his best and gave his suggation to interpret the text —

1. अथायमपि **वाधूलेनाचार्येण** रचितः कल्पः। तस्य सुखज्ञानार्थमस्माभिर्निगदसिद्धवर्जमस्मद् बुद्ध्यागमानुरूपं व्याख्यायते। (*Vyā.* 1.1.1.1)

2. कस्य पुनस्ते विध्यवशेषाः ? चतुर्णां **वाधूला**नामिति। के ते चत्वारो **वाधूलाः** ? कौण्डिन्याग्निवेश्यगालवशाङ्खानां कल्पाः। तथा हि शुल्ब उक्तम् — '**वाधूलकाः** स**वाधूला**श्चत्वारो विहिताः क्रमादि'ति। (*Vyā.* 1.1.1.5)

3. इमामेव शाखामारभ्यायं कल्पो रचित **आचार्येण**। कुतः ? संप्रदायमार्गे अविच्छिन्नपारंपर्यस्य द्रढिम्नो नोपपद्यते च शाखा विनष्टा तत्क्लृप्त्यर्थं कल्पो न विनष्ट इति। उपनयनात्प्रभृति हि गुरवः शाखां पूर्वमध्यापयन्ति, पश्चात् कल्पम्। (*Vyā.* 1.1.1.6)

4. नन्वेतच्छाखाश्रयणे दोषा उक्ताः। उच्यते। बह्वीरपि शाखा आरभ्य कल्पसूत्राणि प्रथयन्ति, इति पूर्वमुक्तम्। तत्रायमा**चार्य** एतच्छाखाधीता अवश्यं विकल्पन्त इति मन्यमानोऽन्यशाखागतानामनति। तद् द्वयोर्वैकल्पिकत्वं भवति। तथा च क्वचित् क्वचिद् दृश्यते। अग्निष्टोमे ग्रहावकाशानाम्नाय पुनरौपानुवाक्ये ग्रहावकाशैश्चरन्ननुवर्तयति। 'त्रिर्देवेभ्योऽववथा' इत्यन्यशाखागतं मन्त्रमाम्नाय 'परिभूरग्निम्' इत्यादि मन्त्रस्यान्तं गृहीत्वा 'तस्य मे रास्वे'ति समानम् इत्यग्निष्टोमोक्तमनुजानाति। तथा 'अग्निना देवेन' इत्यादीनां

चतुर्थशाखान्तरपठितं समस्तं पठित्वा 'इन्द्रेण सयुजो वयम्' इत्यवसानादित्येतच्छाखाधीतमनुज्ञाय 'अपि वा तेजस्वी' इत्यन्यशाखागतं वैकल्पिकं पठति। उदाहरणमात्रं प्रदर्शितम्। अन्यान्यप्येतच्छाखाश्रयणे बहूनि लिङ्गानि सन्ति। अतो ब्राह्मणे मन्त्रे वा यद् दृष्टमिहानुक्तमपि परिग्राह्यम्। (*Vyā.* 1.1.1.6)

5. अथवा इहा**चार्येणा**विनियुक्तानां यथालिङ्गं विनियोगः कर्तव्यः। (*Vyā.* 1.1.2.9)

6. अयमप्या**चार्यो** यत्रेच्छति तत्र 'तमेत एव चत्वारो महर्त्विजः प्राश्नन्ति' इति वदति। (*Vyā.* 1.1.2.10)

7. 'सूर्यमग्निमादधे' इति समापयति यजुः। किमर्थमिदमुच्यते, लिङ्गविरोध इवात्र दृश्यते। मातरि श्वसितीति मातरिश्वा। अन्तरिक्षे गच्छतीत्यर्थः। तथा चोक्तं— 'माताऽन्तरिक्षं, निमीयन्तेऽस्मिन् भूतानि' इति। 'सूर्य आदित्यः। स च दिवि गच्छति' इति। तस्माद् विरोधः। मातेति द्यौरप्यभिधातुं शक्यते, 'निमीयन्तेऽस्मिन् नक्षत्राणी'ति। अतो न विरुध्यत इत्या**चार्या**भिप्रायः। एतत् ज्ञापयति लिङ्गाविरोधेन विनियोगः कर्तव्य' इति। (*Vyā.* 1.1.5.10)

8. अयमप्या**चार्यः** चातुर्मास्यपशुसोमेष्वप्येमवेवोपदिशति। (*Vyā.* 1.3.4.4)

9. 'अमावास्यायामग्नय आधीयन्त' इत्युपक्रम्य विधानात्। तेषामुपक्रान्ते पौर्णमास्यास्तन्त्रे क्रियमाणाऽन्वारंभणीया सद्यस्काला क्रियेत। **आचार्य**प्रवृत्त्या ज्ञायते तन्त्रप्रसंगाभावौ न स्त इति। (*Vyā.* 1.3.4.28)

10. अमृताहुतिर्ह वा एषा हूयते=हु' ता भवती 'तीयमृताहुतिमममृतायां जुहोमी 'त्यस्य मन्त्रावयवस्यार्थमभिप्रेत्या**चार्येणो**क्तमिति मन्यामहे। (*Vyā.* 1.5.1.2)

This has reference to *Vādh.Anvā.* (1.11.5), where complete text is given as:

'अमृताहुतिर्ह वा एषा हूयते (यदग्निरुद्ध्रियते; यावत्कृत्वो हैष एवंविदा उद्ध्रियते सत्यो हास्यामृताहुतयो) हुता भवन्त्यमृतस्यैषाधारा प्रवृज्यते।'

11. 'वैकङ्कतं स्रुक्स्रुवं निष्टप्ये'त्या**चार्येण** प्रतिपत्तौ नासिकयोः स्रुचाविति। (*Vyā.* 1.5.1.2)

12. वाचंयमोऽग्रेणाहवनीयं परीत्य परिस्तीर्णमग्निं परिषिञ्चति 'ऋतं त्वा' इत्यादि। परिषेकाभावोऽपीष्यते **आचार्येण**। (*Vyā.* 1.5.1.8)

13. 'संहितासि विश्वरूपी 'रिति पुंल्लिङ्गत्वं दृष्ट्वा पुंवत्सत्वं विहितमा**चार्येण**।

उपलक्षणत्वाद् वत्सशब्दस्य पुंल्लिङ्गत्वाद्वा। स्त्रीवत्सत्वेऽपि न दोष इति स्त्रीवत्सैवापीत्याह। (*Vyā.* 1.6.1.19)

14. एतत्प्राक्संस्थं परिधिवचनं चेह न विरुध्यते। त्रयः पक्षाः। प्रथमो द्वितीयो वा **आचार्येण**ष्यते। (*Vyā.* 1.6.2.10-17)

15. **आचार्य**स्तु प्रायेणानुदितहोममेवोपदिशन् क्वचिदुदितहोमं स्पृशति। तदभिप्रायेणा–संसृष्टहोममेवामनतीति मन्यामहे। उदितहोमानुदितहोमावादि–विकल्पावेवेष्यते। (*Vyā.* 1.5.2.11)

16. अयमप्या**चार्यः** 'आपूर्णां पौर्णमासीमुपवसेत्, यदा न पुरस्तान्न पश्चाच्चन्द्रमसं पश्येदथामावास्यामुपवसे'दिति वक्ष्यति। (*Vyā.* 2.1.1.1)

17. पश्चात्तदस्य देवतापरिग्रहार्थमा**चार्यो** व्यक्तीकरोति। (*Vyā.* 2.1.1.4)

18. क्रत्वर्थाभावे च पुरुषार्थस्य ग्रहणं न्याय्यं दर्शयति च **आचार्यः**। (*Vyā.* 2.1.2.2)

19. अयमा**चार्यः** शाखान्तरस्थमपि विधानं केनचित्प्रकारेण सूचयति। अतो नास्ति दोषो वचनस्य विद्यमानत्वात्। (*Vyā.* 2.1.2.14)

20. 'एतद्वः पितामहाः प्रपितामहाः' इति हैव जीवत्पिता दद्यात्। 'एतद्वः' इत्यादिर्मन्त्रः आद्यपदद्वयमनुषज्य द्वौ मन्त्रौ कृत्वा द्वौ पिण्डौ जीवत्पिता ददाति। देवताद्वित्वाच्छन्द वा द्वित्वम्। नन्वनुषङ्गस्य वाक्यसामर्थ्यत्वादेक–वाक्यगतस्योक्तानुषङ्गो न युक्तः। सत्यम्। **आचार्येण** क्वचित् क्वचित् प्रदर्श्यते। (*Vyā.* 2.1.2.21)

21. **आचार्येणो**क्तं पटलावसानम्। (*Vyā.* 2.1.2.42)

22. अतोऽन्तरा गार्हपत्यं चाहवनीयं च सादनमिष्यत इवा**चार्येण** स्फ्यादीनि वर्जयित्वा। (*Vyā.* 2.1.4.1)

23. तथा 'धूरसी'ति मन्त्रो हि शकटाभिधायी तथाग्निष्ठस्य वाऽनस इति। कल्पेऽपि शकटस्य विद्यमानत्वे लिङ्गम्। तदभावेऽप्या**चार्येण** 'धू'र्मन्त्रस्य विहितत्वात् निवृत्तिः। (*Vyā.* 2.1.4.34)

24. इह पुरोडाशं चाधिश्रयत्याज्यं चेति द्वन्द्वसंपादने दर्शनाद्विहितमा**चार्येण**। (*Vyā.* 2.2.1.51)

25. इह विप्रतिषेधादा**चार्येणा**ग्नीच्चोदितो न वचनाद्यश्चार्थादर्थो न तच्चोदकः प्रापयतीति न्यायविदां दर्शनम्। (*Vyā.* 2.2.3.5-25)

26. एव शब्द उक्तस्यैवार्थस्य संवृत्यर्थ **आचार्येण** प्रयुज्यते प्रायेण। (*Vyā.* 2.3.1.2)

27. अस्मच्छ्रुत्यपेक्षमा**चार्येणा**म्नातमिति किमत्रायुक्तम्। अस्माकं तु सर्वास्वर्धर्चेन सन्दधातीत्येव। (*Vyā.* 2.3.1.4)

28. व्यवायपरिहरणपक्षे गार्हपत्यसमीपादागतानां हविरादीनां द्रव्याणां परिहरणं कर्तव्यम्। तच्च दृश्यते—'पूर्वेण ब्रह्माणं च यजमानं चातिहृत्यान्तर्वेद्यासादयती'त्या**चार्यस्याय**मभिप्राय इव लक्ष्यते। (*Vyā.* 2.3.2.22)

29. 'अमर्त्यस्ये'ति क्रमाद्धोतृप्रवरे प्राप्ते **आचार्येणा**ध्वर्युप्रवरे विनियुक्तः। (*Vyā.* 3.2.3.21-24)

30. तत ऊर्ध्वं काममिन्द्रं वा महेन्द्रं वा यजेत। गतश्रियां नित्यं महेन्द्रः। एवमभिप्रेत्या**चार्येण** महेन्द्रयाजीत्यभ्यधायि। (*Vyā.* 3.2.3.36-37)

31. अस्मिन् कल्पे शाखान्तरविहिता एव मन्त्रा **आचार्येण** विनियुज्यन्ते। ते विज्ञातुं न शक्यन्ते इमे याजमाना आम्नाता, इमे आध्वर्यवा इति। **आचार्य** एव प्रमाणमित्यध्यवसाय कर्तव्यः। (*Vyā.* 3.3.1.1)

32. अनुकल्पमिति च श्रुत्यन्तरे विहितं वदति न स्वमनीषिकया कल्पितम्। श्रुत्यन्तरे विहितानामा**चार्येणा**म्नातानां सर्वत्र प्रकृतावेव वैकल्पिकत्वमुक्तम्। (*Vyā.* 3.3.2.4-5)

33. क्व पुनराग्नेयस्यात्रोत्पत्तिः। **आचार्येण** विहितत्वाच्च श्रुत्यन्तरे विद्यत इत्यवगन्तव्यम्। (*Vyā.* 3.4.1.1)

34. 'भूपते भुवनपते' इत्यनेन मन्त्रेण लिङ्गात् ब्रह्मणो वरणं प्राप्तमविधायैवानुवदत्या**चार्यः**। एतत् ज्ञापयति ब्राह्मणेन कल्पेन वा अविनियुक्तानामपि मन्त्राणां लिङ्गेन विनियोगः कर्तव्य इति। (*Vyā.* 3.5.1.1)

35. तथाऽयमप्या**चार्यः** 'इन्द्रवन्तः स्तुतेति निराह' इति पठति। (*Vyā.* 3.5.1.8)

36. तथा चाश्वलायनेन ब्रह्मत्व उक्तम् 'बहिर्वेदि यां दिशं व्रजेयुः सैव तत्रः प्राची'ति (*ĀśvaŚS.* 1.12.4)। अथवा प्राङ्मुखैरेवावभृथो गन्तव्य इत्या**चार्या**भिप्रायः। (*Vyā.* 3.6.2.19)

Here the difference between *Vādhūla* and *Āśvalayana-Śākhā* has been noticed.

37. 'ता वसन्ता प्रसुवो भवन्ति' इत्युक्त्वा 'फल्गुनी पूर्णमासे वै वैश्वदेवमि'ति

विदधत **आचार्यस्या**यमभिप्रायः शिशिरादेव कक्षं दर्भस्तम्बं दहति। (*Vyā.* 4.1.1.1)

38. अस्या**चार्यस्या**भिप्रायः सर्वत्र वैश्वानरचोदनायां तावत एव देवतात्वमिति। (*Vyā.* 4.1.1.18-30)

39. तदुक्तम्—'पयो वा कालसामान्यादि'ति। **आचार्येण** तूभयोर्दोहयोर्मन्त्रवत्वमाम्नातम्। तद् वाचनिकन्यायाद्धि वचनं बलीयः। (*Vyā.* 4.1.1.52)

40. 'दर्शपूर्णमासावालभमान' इत्यादिभिर्वाक्यैस्तस्य तस्य कर्मण आरम्भात् प्राग्विहितानां होतर्णिां कालान्तराणि वदत्ययमा**चार्यः**। (*Vyā.* 4.1.2.1)

41. तथा यदेवाध्वर्युः करो=ब्राह्मणमिति ब्रुवत **आचार्यस्या**भिप्रायः। (*Vyā.* 4.2.1.28)

42. अतो देवतासंबन्धं यथासम्भवं यथासंख्येनानुवर्त्य मारुती मेषी वारुणो मेष इति देवतासंबन्धं कृत्वा सधर्मकत्वं कल्पयन्ति। अयं पक्ष **आचार्यस्या**नभिप्रेतइव लक्ष्यते। (*Vyā.* 4.2.1.37)

43. तत्र प्रतिकर्षं ब्रुवत **आचार्यस्या**पि प्रतिकर्ष एवाभिप्रेतः स्यात्। (*Vyā.* 4.3.1.1)

44. 'अवन्त्वस्मानिमां वयं सुसंदृशं त्वा वयमि'ति दर्शनाद् वयमित्यादीनां निवृत्तिर्नेष्यत **आचार्येण**। (*Vyā.* 4.4.1.3)

45. 'पञ्चकृत्वोऽवद्यति' 'सन्ततमवद्यती'त्यनयोरर्थ **आचार्येण** कल्पितः। (*Vyā.* 4.4.2.8-14)

46. तथाऽयमप्या**चार्यः** 'ब्राह्मणमु वै भवति नासोमयाजी =ततो दीक्षितमेवोपपरेयादि'ति प्रतिषेधोऽनर्थकः स्यात्। (*Vyā.* 5.1.1.1-2)

47. **आचार्य**प्रभृतिभिरप्युभयत्र धर्माणां कृत्स्नाम्नानमन्योऽन्याविकारत्वं ज्ञापयति। (*Vyā.* 5.1.2.21)

48. अतः पात्रान्तरेऽवदानमा**चार्येणा**नभिप्रेतमिति। यद्यप्या**चार्यस्यै**वमेवाभिप्राय इति ज्ञातुं शक्यते, तथापीडार्थान्यवदानान्यनुपस्तीर्य पृथक् कृत्वाऽभिघार्येडां प्रयच्छेत्। (*Vyā.* 5.3.1.23-24)

49. **आचार्यो**ऽपि 'पञ्चदशनक्षत्राणि रात्रिं नयन्ति' (वाधूश्रौ. ६.९.१.१) इति ब्रुवन्नेतद्वचनं परिगृह्णाति। (*Vyā.* 6.1.1.2)

50. नन्वन्वाख्याने आप्तैकोन्नतादिनामर्थं ब्रुवताऽऽ**चार्येण**र्त्विग्विशेषा अभिप्रेताः। (*Vyā.* 6.1.1.3)

51. एवं ब्रुवताऽऽ**चार्येण** गम्यमाना अप्यर्था न परित्यक्ता इति ज्ञायते।

अतस्तेषामन्यतमे देवयजने प्रागतवंशा शाला मिता भवति।(*Vyā.* 6.1.1.3)

52. चरुनिष्कासं निधाय तस्योपर्युदयनीयं कर्तव्यमा**चार्य**प्रामाण्यादेवंविधं वचनमस्तीति गम्यते। (*Vyā.* 6.2.2.3)

53. **आचार्येणा**प्यन्वाख्याने 'तदाहुर्यद्देवस्य त्वे'त्युपक्रम्य 'स यदेतस्मिंश्चरौ=देवताः प्राश्नन्ती'ति (*Vādh.Anvā.* 4.27.1) ब्रुवता **आचार्येणा**भिप्रेत इव लक्ष्यते। (*Vyā.* 6.2.2.5)

54. 'रोहिते चर्मन् राजा विचितो भवती'ति पूर्वानुवाकं समाप्य तथैवास्यारम्भः किमर्थः। **आचार्यशीलम्**, क्वचिदेवं करोति। अन्योऽप्यर्थो वक्तुं शक्यते। राजा अविचितो भवतीति। पूर्वान्त्ये राजा विचितो भवतीति। कुत एतद्विचित्यः। 'सोमा न विचित्या' इत्यारभ्य 'यदीतरं=णमर्पयती'ति वैकल्पिकमभिप्रेत्याचार्येणैवमभ्यधायीति। (*Vyā.* 6.3.1.1-2)

55. तन्त्रे तन्त्रे च वेद उपादीयते परित्यज्यते च। **आचार्या**भिप्रायेणाग्नीषोमीये बर्हिषोऽन्यत्वाद्वेदोऽप्यन्य एव। (*Vyā.* 6.4.1.2)

56. 'प्रस्तरे जुहूमि'ति ब्रुवताऽऽ**चार्येण** प्रकृतौ पात्रद्रव्यसंस्कारः सादनमिति मत्वैवमभ्यधायीति यथाप्रकृत्येव सादनम्। (*Vyā.* 6.4.1.8-9)

57. न दिग्ग्रहणस्यैषा रात्रिः कालः। कुतः। पूर्वमेव गृहीता दिगित्या**चार्य**प्रवृत्त्या ज्ञायते। (*Vyā.* 6.4.2.3)

58. दोहतादिति पयस्यया तुल्यवद्विधानादयमा**चार्या**भिप्रायः। अन्यैर्धर्मवद्भिर्यागैरतुल्यत्वं च दृश्यते। (*Vyā.* 6.8.3.30)

59. उपांश्वन्तर्यामयोः शेषस्यैकदेशमाग्रयणस्थाल्यामवनीय शिष्टं सदो गत्वा भक्षयित्वाऽऽगत्य पात्रे सादयति। **आचार्यस्य** नायमभिप्रायः। (*Vyā.* 6.9.4.38)

60. मनसा ग्रहा गृह्यन्त आऽऽग्रयणादिति। 'वाग्वा' इत्यादि। 'ते देवा वाच्यपक्रान्तायां तूष्णीं ग्रहानगृह्णीते'ति। तूष्णींशब्देन मन्त्राभावे मन्त्राम्नानानर्थकत्वं स्यात्। तस्मात् तूष्णीमिति मानसत्वं विधीयते इति कृत्वा मनसेत्या**चार्येणा**भ्यधायि। तूष्णीमित्युपांशुत्वं विधीयत इति केचिन्मन्यन्ते। (*Vyā.* 6.10.1.75)

61. तत्र पात्नीवंते गृहीते चतुर्थं विहरणं व्याघारणं चाम्नातमा**चार्येण**। सैवात्रापीतिकर्तव्यता। अन्ये द्रोणकलशात् परिप्लुना पात्रेणादायाग्नीध्रीयमार्जालीयेषु स्वे स्वे क्रमे स्वेन स्वेन मन्त्रेण व्याघारयन्ति। (*Vyā.* 6.10.3.26)

62. साद्यस्क्रियायामपि कर्मप्रश्लेषं ब्रुवताऽग्नीषोमीयानूबन्ध्ययोः पुरोडाशावनुक्रान्तौ, न सवनीयस्य। तस्मादविद्यमानत्वमिव दृश्यते। तत्र वचनमा**चार्येण** दृष्टं, न्यायो वा इत्यवगन्तव्यम्। (*Vyā.* 6.11.1.1)

63. धर्मेषु दीर्घसत्रिणामाग्रयणभक्तिं ब्रुवताऽऽ**चार्येण** 'यवाग्रयणभक्तौ सत्रे यवानां परिवापेणैवोपाप्नुयात्। अनुपदकारः 'संयावा परिवापः' इत्याह। (*Vyā.* 6.11.1.28)

64. **आचार्येणै**तदनभिहितमिति चेदनभिहितमपि प्रकृतं प्राप्तिमदप्रतिषिद्धं कर्तव्यमेव। (*Vyā.* 6.11.4.5)

65. अन्वाख्याने 'अन्तःस्तोत्रेषु पुरोडाशाः श्रप्यन्त' (*Vādh.Anvā.* 4.78.3) इति ब्रुवत **आचार्यस्याय**मेवाभिप्राय इति मन्यामहे। (*Vyā.* 6.12.2.68-69)

66. 'यद्वा मे अपरागतमि'ति लिङ्गात् नैमित्तिकत्वनिवृत्यर्थं मन्यमानेनैवा**चार्येणा**विशेषेण विहितम्। (*Vyā.* 6.14.1.57)

67. उदग्रे देवयजनान्मथित्वा स्वरूपहृतं वा विहृत्योदवसानीययेष्ट्या यजेत। कुत एतत्। अनूबन्ध्यस्य सन्तीति मन्यमानेना**चार्येण** चोक्तम्। (*Vyā.* 6.15.4.1-6)

68. अग्निष्टोम इत्यादि ब्रुवत **आचार्यस्य** नायमभिप्रायः। किं तर्हि ? प्रकृत्यर्थ एवेति। (*Vyā.* 7.1.1.1)

69. पुरुषः संशिष्टो वैश्यः शूद्रो वा तिष्ठति। अविशेषाभिधानाद् यः कश्चित् त्रैवर्णिक इत्या**चार्या**भिप्रायः। (*Vyā.* 7.1.1.30)

70. तथा स्वयंचितिजपश्चानुवित्तिहोमादावनुक्तोऽप्याज्यसंस्कारस्रुक्स्रुव-संमार्गश्चैतेषां सादनं चानुक्तमपि आचारप्राप्तत्वाद्दर्विहोमवत् क्रियेत। एवं प्रदर्शयति **चाचार्यो** बहुकृत्वः। (*Vyā.* 7.1.1.32)

71. अस्याश्चर्चस्तन्त्रसमाम्नाताया विनियोगान्तराभावादेव तामृचं तस्यैव यजुषः पाठक्रमेणावस्थितस्यान्तत्वेन संकल्प्य तया होतव्यमित्येवमभ्यधाय्या**चार्येण**। गणब्राह्मणे चर्चामष्टौ कृत्वा संस्तुतिरेवमृक्संबन्धादुपपद्यतेतराम्। 'एतद्यजुरन्तं करोती'त्यत्राप्येतन्मन्त्रवाक्यं यजुषोऽन्तत्वेनापादयेदिति शक्यते व्याख्यातुम्। अस्मिन् पक्षे न किञ्चित्कल्पाक्षरं लक्षणया वृत्तम्। यद्यपि तावद् ब्राह्मणार्थो न घटते, तथापि त्वा**चार्येणा**श्रिताया: शाखाया दुर्ज्ञातत्वात्कल्पपदानि मुख्यवृत्त्या व्याख्येयानि। कल्पकारप्रामाण्याच्छ्रुतिवचनं कल्पनीयम्। चतुर्थं दर्शनं 'ऋचा स्तोमं समर्धये'त्येतद्यजुरन्त्यं कृत्वा जुहोतीति। अस्मिंश्च पक्षे नास्ति कल्पपदानां लक्षणावृत्तिः, न च पाठक्रमबाधः। किन्तु ऋचि

यजुःशब्दोऽप्रसिद्धः कल्पितः स्यात्। तत्र यद् युक्तं तत्प्राज्ञैः प्रतिपत्तव्यम् । (*Vyā.* 7.1.1.35-36)

72. वैश्वानरस्य नित्यत्वमविशेषाभिधानादा**चार्येणा**भिप्रेतमिति केचित्। (*Vyā.* 7.4.1.2)

73. यज्ञतनूर्मन्त्राश्चतुस्त्रिंशदित्या**चार्या**भिप्रायः। उपधाने तावदन्त्याभ्यासेनेष्ट-कोपधेयेत्युक्तम्। वाचने तु पुनश्चतुस्त्रिंशत् पृथगेव विनिविष्टाः। (*Vyā.* 7.4.1.5)

74. शुल्बकारेण व्यायाममात्रे चयनविधानात् देवरथचक्रप्रमाण-मित्या**चार्येणा**भिप्रेतमिति केषांचिद्दर्शनम्, तत्प्रमाणं तज्ज्ञेभ्य आगमयितव्यम्। (*Vyā.* 7.4.4.15)

75.. 'महावेदिं मित्वे'त्यविशेषाभिधानाद् यावत्यनग्निके वेदिस्तावत्येव साग्निकेऽपीत्या**चार्यो**ऽभिप्रैति स्म। (*Vyā.* 7.4.4.15)

76. अथ च 'द्विस्तावां वेदिं मिमीत' इति ब्रुवत **आचार्यस्या**भिप्रायः। (*Vyā.* 7.4.4.15)

77. गणंगणं वोपधाय मन्त्रैरभिमृश्य गणान्तरोपधानमारभेत। एवमिव ह्या**चार्य**भिप्रायः। (*Vyā.* 7.5.1.19)

78. न प्रतिसीतं च प्रयत्नभेदोऽस्तीति प्रतिसीतं त्वभ्यावृत्तिरिति। तत्रैवमेवेति ब्रुवत **आचार्यस्या**भिप्रायो नियोगतः प्रयत्नान्तरे कर्मभेदस्तन्त्रो मन्त्रेऽभ्यावृतिर्न्याय्येति। (*Vyā.* 7.5.3.11-15)

79. इदमेव च पञ्चचितीकसद्भावे लिङ्गम्, 'एकचितीकं चिन्वीते'त्यस्मिंश्चानुवाके सर्वेऽग्नयः पञ्चचितीकाश्रयाः। अत **आचार्येणा**पि पञ्चचितीकत्वं षट्चितीकत्वं च विकल्पेनेष्यत इत्यवगन्तव्यम्। (*Vyā.* 7.7.5.6-10)

80. 'याः पुरेध्मस्य प्रहरणादग्नावाहुतयो हूयन्ते प्रजापतावु हैव ता हूयन्त' इति चैतस्मिन् पक्षे युज्यते। अयमेवा**चार्या**भिप्रायः। (*Vyā.* 7.7.5.12)

81. अनुपरिक्रम्यानुपरिक्रम्य हि होमे क्रियमाणे 'या अग्नेः पर्यन्ता इष्टकास्ताः सर्वाः प्रसक्ता' इति विशेषवचनमर्थवत्। असत्यप्या**चार्या**भिप्राये विरोधाभावे च प्रत्यक्षश्रुत्युदितो विशेष उपसंहार्य एव। (*Vyā.* 7.13.2.16)

82. 'तमुत्करे न्यस्येदि'ति दीर्घस्य वंशस्य ब्राह्मणम्। नान्यस्यासञ्चर इति विध्यन्तरमा**चार्येणा**भिप्रेतम्। (*Vyā.* 7.13.3.11)

83. उदित आदित्ये प्रवर्ग्योपसत्प्रचरणमा**चार्येणा**भिधीयते स्म। (*Vyā.* 7.14.1.4)

84. द्वादशे द्वादशेऽनवानमिति शाखान्तरविहितस्यार्थवादमभिधातुमिति ज्ञापयत्या**चार्यः**। (*Vyā.* 7.14.3.43)

85. आग्नीध्रीयेऽष्टानामिष्टकानामुपधानस्या**चार्येणा**म्नातत्वादाग्नीध्रीयेऽश्मनिधानं धिष्णियादन्यत्रेत्यवगन्तव्यम्। (*Vyā.* 7.15.1.6)

86. उष्णीषविशेषणं दर्भमयमिति। 'पुनात्येवैनमि'ति पुंल्लिङ्गदर्शनादिति केचित्। पत्न्याः परिधानं दर्भमयम्। तथा हि सूत्रान्तरे दृष्टमित्यपरे। प्रायेणा**चार्यस्या**भिप्रायश्चैष एव। यस्यां शाखायां पुंल्लिङ्गनिर्देशस्तच्छाखान्तरापेक्षोऽयं पक्षो द्रष्टव्यः। (*Vyā.* 8.2.1.3-4)

87. राजसूयेनेति हि नियमो राजशब्दः समधिगतः। राजयज्ञेषु बौधायनादिभिरा**चार्यैः** परिगण्यते। अनेन चा**चार्येण** 'राजा राजसूयेन यक्ष्यमाणः कामयत' इत्यन्यार्थे वाक्येऽनूद्यते। (*Vyā.* 9.1.1.1)

88. सेनानीर्यः सेनां नयति त्रैवर्णिक **आचार्या**भिप्रायत्वात्। क्षत्रियश्च सामर्थ्यात्। (*Vyā.* 9.1.3.32)

89. तत्र ये सौम्यत्वाष्ट्रवैष्णवाः उपसत्कालम् इहाग्नेयसौम्यवैष्णवाः। कालभेदश्चाधर्मका इवाग्नेयाय **आचार्या**भिप्रायाद् भजनाभजनीया इत्यादीनि। (*Vyā.* 9.3.2.3-14)

90. अग्नीषोमीयविकारोऽक्षरसाम्यात्। ऐन्द्राग्नविकारो वा कपालसामान्यात्। सुरौदनेन धर्मकेण भवितव्यम्, पशुपुरोडाशयागत्वे ग्रहयागस्याधर्मक इत्या**चार्याभि**प्रायः। (*Vyā.* 9.4.1.16)

91. रथवाहनं हैवैवातियुजामिति वैकल्पिकं वचनमुभयत्र, तथा दृष्टमा**चार्येणे**त्यवगन्तव्यम्। (*Vyā.* 9.4.4.44)

92. यस्त्वेवमशक्यो निश्चितः प्रतिदानमेवाभ्युपायो वशीकरणे साम्नः कृतपूर्वत्वान्न भेदनदण्डयोश्च तं प्रत्यसाधनत्वादित्या**चार्या**भिप्रायः। (*Vyā.* 10.1.1.18)

93. ततः शतकृत्वो निगदतीत्युक्त्वा 'ताः सहस्रमि'ति ब्रुवन्नभिप्रैति स्म **आचार्यः**। (*Vyā.* 10.2.2.32-36)

94. तस्यैवमेव धृतीः पत्सु जुहोतीत्या**चार्येण** विशेषितत्वादौखीयकत्वाच्च। (*Vyā.* 10.2.2.49-51)

95. 'कस्त्वा युनक्ति स त्वा युनक्तु' इत्येको मन्त्रः साकाङ्क्षत्वाद्, विभागे संख्या नैवमुपपद्यते। **आचार्यस्या**भिप्रायोऽयमेव। 'अमुष्मै कामाय' इत्यत्राभीप्सितः। (*Vyā.* 10.4.3.22)

96. एतयोर्बर्हिषोरित्यश्वतूपरगोमृगाणां प्राजापत्यत्वमा**चार्य**प्रवृत्त्या ज्ञायते। (*Vyā.* 10.5.3.33-40)

97. 'शमिताराविं'त्यादि ब्रुवत **आचार्यस्या**भिप्रायः। (*Vyā.* 10.7.4.20)

98. एवम् अरण्येऽनुवाक्यग्राह्यशब्दस्य च लौकिकत्वादकर्मनामत्वमिति पुनरा**चार्येणा**त्रापि कालनिर्देशः कृतः। (*Vyā.* 10.8.3.24)

99. अपि च सान्तपनीये विवर्तनमभिधाय गृहमेधीये संवर्तनमभिहितवान् **आचार्यः**। (*Vyā.* 11.2.2)

100. परे तूष्णीमुभयं कृत्वा मन्त्रं जपेयुः। **आचार्य**शीलातिक्रमप्रशंसा चेत्यन्ये। न ह्येत**दाचार्य**शीलं यदुत पूर्वं पदार्थमुद्दिश्य पश्चान्मन्त्रकथनम्। (*Vyā.* 11.2.3)

101. दशममहरथातिरात्र इत्यभिधाय पुनरनुवाकान्तरे दशमस्य क्लृप्तिः क्रियते स्म **आचार्येण**। (*Vyā.* 11.3.1)

102. छन्दोलक्षणमनुद्धरण अभिचिक्रीरथा अभ्यास **आचार्य** एवं ह्यस्य शब्दस्यार्थं विवृणोति स्म। (*Vyā.* 11.3.2)

103. अयमा**चार्यो** गवामयनं संवत्सरसत्राणां प्रकृतिभूतं विधाय सर्वाः प्रकृतयोऽनुक्रान्ता इति कृत्वा तदनन्तरमौपानुवाक्यं विदधदनारभ्याधीतानां प्रकृत्यर्थतां बोधयति। (*Vyā.* 12.1.1)

Here Āryadāsa explicitly mentions the existence of *Gavāmayana* before *Aupānuvākya* in the *VādhūlaŚS*. But neither the *Sūtra*-text nor the commentary on *Gavāmayana* is available in the present text.

104. त्रीणि वाव सवनानीत्यन्यत्रानवानं व्याख्यातमा**चार्येण**। ब्राह्मणत एव सिद्धत्वादत्र वक्तव्यं नास्तीत्यभिप्रेत्य न व्याचष्टे। (*Vyā.* 12.1.3)

105. 'उदयवसानीयाः क्वचित् क्वचिदिष्ट्योदवस्येदि'ति पृथगुदवस्यन्ति। पृथगुदवसानीयाभिरिष्टिभिरित्यनूद्यते। न क्वचित् तस्याः क्लृप्तिर्व्याख्याता। तस्याः क्लृप्तिरनुज्ञाताऽऽ**चार्येणे**ति न ज्ञायते। (*Vyā.* 12.3.6)

106. केचिदाहुः पञ्चकपालमपोद्याष्टाकपालोऽस्या ब्राह्मणे विहितः। पौनराधेयिक्यां पञ्चकपाल एव विहितः। तस्या **आचार्येणा**ष्टाकपाल आम्नातः। उभयोस्तुल्यतां मन्यमानो व्याख्यातेति कृत्वा सेति पौनराधेयमिवेति इमां व्यवहरन्ति। नैतया पुनराधेयानिष्ट्वाऽग्निहोत्रं जुहुयादिति। (*Vyā.* 12.3.6)

107. आग्नेयविकारेष्वाग्नेयवदग्नीषोमादिविकारेषु च तद्वदित्यभिषेके विशेषमात्रमे-वा**चार्येणा**भिधित्सितम्। (*Vyā.* 14.1.2)

108. सप्ताहे पुरस्तादिति ब्रुवन्नाग्रयणहविषामनन्तर्भावमिच्छत्या**चार्यः**। कथमाग्रयणह-विर्भ्योऽर्वाचीनाः षडिष्टयोऽन्वहं सारस्वतयोरारम्भणीयायाश्च समानेऽहनि प्रवृत्तिरिति मन्यमानेनैवमभ्यधायि। (*Vyā.* 14.1.3)

109. 'प्रणीता हि प्रायणीयस्ये'त्यादि ब्रुवत आचार्यस्याभिप्रायः। (*Vyā.* 14.4.1)

आचार्याः *(Ācāryas)*— Āryadāsa in his *Vyākhyā* has used the word *Acarya* in plural also, but in these cases he means other *Ācāryas*, not Vādhūlas as we may see in following references—

1. केचिदा**चार्याः** प्रतिपदं संस्कारान् वर्णयन्ति। (*Vyā.* 1.1.1.1)
2. आग्नेयादिसमुदायो यत्र गच्छति कुण्डपेयादिषु प्रवर्तत इत्या**चार्याणा**मुपदेश इत्याग्नेयादिसमुदायमध्ये पठितः। (*Vyā.* 2.1.2.42)
3. उभयथाप्या**चार्या** व्याचक्षते। (*Vyā.* 3.3.2.24)
4. अत्र विप्रतिपत्तिरा**चार्याणाम्**। (*Vyā.* 5.1.2.21)
5. त्रसरेणुलिक्षायूकायवाङ्गुलानां पूर्वस्योत्तरमुत्तरमष्टगुणम् इत्या**चार्या** ब्रुवते। (*Vyā.* 6.4.2.4-29)
6. राजसूयेनेति हि नियमो राजशब्दः समधिगतः। राजयज्ञेषु बोधायनादिभिरा**चार्यैः** परिगण्यते। (*Vyā.* 9.1.1.1)
7. इध्माबर्हिः प्रोक्षतीत्येवमादिप्राकृतपदार्थानुक्रमणं प्रायशः प्रतिपत्तिलाघवाया**चार्यैः** क्रियते, न चात्र ग्रन्थगौरवमवगतपूर्वत्वात्। यत्रानवगतं तत्रापि प्रतिपत्तिगौरवाद् ग्रन्थस्य गरिमा न्याय्य इत्यभिप्रेत्योच्यते कल्पकारैः। (*Vyā.* 9.4.3.1-3)

उपाध्याय *(Upādhyāya)*— Besides quoting the views of others by the name of Ācāryas, Āryadāsa once quotes a *Kārikā* from his own teacher's work respectfully calling him *Upādhyāya*—

गणितशास्त्रमूरीकृत्य **उपाध्यायेन** कारिका कृता—

1. 'यैर्भागाः समतां यान्ति तैः समस्तैर्भजेद् दिशि।

   तत्र लब्धेन ते व्यस्ता विज्ञेया गुणितांशकाः ॥' इति। (*Vyā.* 6.12.2.27)

ब्राह्मण *(Brāhmaṇa)*— Āryadāsa very frequently refers to the *Brāhmaṇa*-texts in general, sometimes along with *mantra-*

texts in matters of ritualistic injunctions without mentioning a particular *Brāhmaṇa*-text. It is also possible that once there must have been a *Brāhmaṇa*-text of Vādhūlas like other *Brāhmaṇa*-texts of other *Śākhās*, forming a part of its *Saṁhitā*, as is evident from the following references—

1. वेद-शब्दश्च **मन्त्रब्राह्मण**योः प्रसिद्धः। (*Vyā.* 1.1.1.1)
2. **मन्त्रब्राह्मण**योर्विसृतानां पदार्थानामभिप्रेते कर्मण्यभिप्रेते चावकाशे विनियोगः। (*Vyā.* 1.1.1.1)
3. क्वचिन्मन्त्रा एव पठ्यन्ते, न **ब्राह्मण**मस्ति। (*Vyā.* 1.1.1.1)
4. यत्रापि विधिप्रत्ययगन्धोऽस्ति, तत्रापि नाविदितवेदनार्थं, तदपि **ब्राह्मण**वाक्यानुकरणमेव। (*Vyā.* 1.1.1.1)
5. तत्र 'कृत्तिकास्वग्निमादधीत' इत्यादि, 'वसन्ता ब्राह्मणोऽग्निमादधीत' इत्यादि च **ब्राह्मणा**दवगमयितव्यम्। (*Vyā.* 1.1.1.6)
6. **मन्त्रब्राह्मण**पाठक्रमवैलक्षण्येन पाठाच्छतमानाश्वादिभिः सह निर्देशाच्चान्यत्रापि द्रव्यार्जनमात्र एव संभारान् संभरत इति पश्वादिषु दृश्यते। नन्विह **मन्त्रेण** संभरणं नास्तीति **ब्राह्मणो**क्तमिहानुक्तमपि ग्राह्यम्। (*Vyā.* 1.1.1.6)
7. 'असिदमादत्ते' इत्येवमादीनामेतद् **ब्राह्मण**विहितेभ्योऽन्येषां द्रव्याणां दर्शनात्। (*Vyā.* 1.1.1.6)
8. अतो **ब्राह्मणे** मन्त्रे वा यद् दृष्टमिहानुक्तमपि परिग्राह्यम्। (*Vyā.* 1.1.1.6)
9. 'अपोदूह्य भस्माग्निं मन्थती'ति **ब्राह्मणम्**। (*Vyā.* 1.1.3.3)
10. हिरण्यशल्कस्यापि प्रदानं **ब्राह्मणो**क्तम्। (*Vyā.* 1.1.3.27)
11. रथन्तरेणेति सामनामग्रहणात् **ब्राह्मणे** च गानविधानात् **सामवेदे** च विधानात् साम्नोपस्थानम्। (*Vyā.* 1.1.4.4)
12. अग्न्युपस्थानं नाग्निहोत्राङ्गं, शाखान्तरे विहितं संस्कारान्तरं **ब्राह्मणे** तूष्णींग्रहणात्। (*Vyā.* 1.2.3.4)
13. **ब्राह्मण**विरुद्धानां विधानं विकल्पार्थमित्युक्तम्। (*Vyā.* 1.4.2.42)
14. उभयोरपि पक्षयोः **ब्राह्मण**पाठक्रमोऽविरुध्येत। (*Vyā.* 1.5.2.24)
15. स्वाहाकृत्या उद्दिशति 'सप्तर्षीनेव प्रीणाती'ति **ब्राह्मणम्**। (*Vyā.* 1.5.2.24)
16. स्वाध्याय**ब्राह्मणे** यज्ञोपवीतविशेष आम्नातः। (*Vyā.* 1.6.1.7)

17. **ब्राह्मण**ग्रहणम् प्राङ्मुखेनोदङ्मुखेन वा कर्माणि कर्तव्यानीति प्राप्तस्यापवादार्थप्रदर्शनार्थम् एतत् ज्ञापयति। (*Vyā.* 1.6.1.8)

18. अस्य विधानस्य **ब्राह्मणं** 'प्र वा' इत्यादि। (*Vyā.* 1.6.1.27)

19. अस्य विधानस्य विधायकं **ब्राह्मणवाक्यं** 'परि त्वाऽग्ने' इत्याह। (*Vyā.* 1.6.2.9)

20. अस्मिन् पक्षे पूर्वोक्तं **ब्राह्मणवाक्यं** गायत्रीद्विपदाविषयमेव भवति। (*Vyā.* 1.6.2.10-17)

21. अपर आह– **ब्राह्मणे** गार्हपत्ययोनित्वं तस्यास्तीति तदपेक्षं बहुवचनमिति। (*Vyā.* 1.6.4.19-24)

22. अपरे शाखान्तरविहिते अपोद्य **ब्राह्मणे** प्रागुदीची विहिता। (*Vyā.* 2.1.1.7)

23. **ब्राह्मणवाक्य**मपि 'विद्या वै धिषणा विद्ययैवैनदच्छेती'ति बर्हिरामुख्येनायं गच्छतीत्यर्थः। (*Vyā.* 2.1.1.16)

24. परिमाणानि च **ब्राह्मणे** सामान्यशब्देन 'इयन्तम्' इत्युक्तानि। (*Vyā.* 2.1.1.19-20)

24. मेक्षणानुप्रहरणे[1] तूष्णीं ग्रहणं **ब्राह्मणा**नुकरणम्। **ब्राह्मणे**ऽपि सैव तृतीयाऽऽहुतिरिह[2] प्राप्तस्य स्वाहाकारस्य प्रतिषेधः। (*Vyā.* 2.1.2.17-18)

26. गार्हपत्यस्यात्र निर्वपणानन्तरं तमसीव वा एषोऽन्तश्चरति यः परीणही'ति दर्शनाद् अन आरूह्य निर्वपणं **ब्राह्मणे**ऽभिप्रेतम्। (*Vyā.* 2.1.4.34)

27. **ब्राह्मणे** 'परिवेषो वा' इत्यारभ्य 'अप्रतिवादिन एवैनान् कुरुते' इत्यनेनान्यथोपगूहनं विहितम्। (*Vyā.* 2.2.1.1)

28. तमादायोदपात्रञ्चेत्यादिना **ब्राह्मण**विहितेन 'धृष्टिर्वा उपवेष' इत्यादि विधानेन वा प्रतिपादयति। (*Vyā.* 2.2.1.1)

29. आज्यनिर्वपणं **मन्त्रब्राह्मणयोः** स्रुक्संमार्गपत्नीसन्नहनोत्तरकालं विहितम्। (*Vyā.* 2.2.1.51)

30. अथापि **ब्राह्मणे** 'तस्मात् गवि सते' इत्यादिना प्रकरण एव विहितम्। (*Vyā.* 2.2.1.51)

31. **ब्राह्मणे** यद् वैमृधः पूर्णमासेऽनुनिर्वाप्यो भवति पौर्णमास्यां विहितः। (*Vyā.* 2.2.2.5)

32. स्रुक्संमार्गप्रकारा **ब्राह्मणे** विहिता ग्रहीतव्याः 'अग्रतः संमृज्याद्' इत्यादयः। (*Vyā.* 2.2.3.5-22)

33. आज्योत्पवनं त्रिः मन्त्रश्चावर्तते। तद् **ब्राह्मणे** प्रोक्षण्युत्पवनमाम्नातम्। (*Vyā.* 2.2.4.16)

34. तथा च **ब्राह्मणे** 'एकविंशतिरिध्मदारूणि भवन्ति' इति 'पञ्चदशेध्मदारूण्यभ्यादधातीत्युक्तं वचनमि'ति। (*Vyā.* 2.3.1.3)

35. उत्तरेभ्यः समुन्मुखेभ्यो दक्षिणेत्येव तिर्यक्त्वे सिद्धे तिर्यक्त्वमिति **ब्राह्मण**वचनानुकरणम्। (*Vyā.* 2.3.1.6)

36. 'सामि प्राश्नन्ति सामि मार्जयन्ते' इतीडामधिकृत्य **ब्राह्मणे** दर्शनात्। (*Vyā.* 2.3.2.19-20)

37. प्राशित्रस्य चाग्रेण परिहरणं यच्चा**चार्येणो**क्तं **ब्राह्मणे** वा विद्यते तदस्माकं प्रमाणम्। (*Vyā.* 2.3.2.22)

38. **ब्राह्मणे** विहितायाः....पूर्णपात्रेऽन्ततोऽनुष्टुभेति समायुषेत्यस्यास्मिन् काले विस्रंसनमनूद्य सिद्धवदनुवर्तनं विहितम्। (*Vyā.* 2.3.3.101)

39. नान्वाख्याने **ब्राह्मण**मस्ति। विधायकं वाक्यं नास्तीत्यर्थः। **ब्राह्मणेन** विहितं हि कल्पकारैरन्वाख्यायते। (*Vyā.* 3.1.1.24)

40. अथवा तेषां **ब्राह्मणे**ऽप्यभावात् श्रुत्यन्तरे एतेषामविशेषेणोक्तभावोऽनुमीयते। (*Vyā.* 3.1.2.3-8)

41. 'यो वै यज्ञं योग आगते युनक्ति' इति हि **ब्राह्मण**विहितान्यध्वर्युणा युज्यमानानि कर्मणा वा उभयमभिप्रेतमिवा**चार्येण**। (*Vyā.* 3.2.1.6)

42. 'अनवेक्ष्याज्यमुत्पुनन्ती'ति **ब्राह्मणे** चतुर्थस्यानुवाकस्यान्ते आज्योदकयोरुत्पवनमाम्नाय पञ्चमादौ 'स एतमिन्द्र आज्यस्यावकाशमपश्यत्' इत्यादिना आज्यावेक्षणं विहितम्। (*Vyā.* 3.2.2.27-29)

43. 'त्रयो वै गतश्रिय' इत्यारभ्य **ब्राह्मणे** महेन्द्रयागो विहितः। (*Vyā.* 3.2.3.36-37)

40. एतत् ज्ञापयति **ब्राह्मणेन** कल्पेन वा। (*Vyā.* 3.5.1.1)

44. **ब्राह्मणवाक्येन** विहितस्यान्वाख्यानम्। (*Vyā.* 4.3.1.1)

Here Āryadāsa firmly establishes the fact that *Anvakhyāna* is always based upon *Brāhmaṇa*-text. Since the *Anvakhyāna*-text of Vādhūlas exists, it *Brāhmaṇa* must have existed.

45. **ब्राह्मणे**ऽपि द्रव्यदेवतासंबन्धो वाक्य एव। क्वचिद् 'अग्नयेऽनीक=णोद्यते'ति विहितम्। (*Vyā.* 4.3.1.1)

46. पक्षाश्रितत्वमेषां **ब्राह्मणे** कल्पे वा नोपलभ्यते। (*Vyā.* 4.4.1.3)

47. यत् त्रीणि त्रीणीत्यभ्यासो हविःषु न संभवति सर्वाण्यभिप्रेत्य **ब्राह्मणे**ऽभ्यास इति। (*Vyā.* 4.4.1.29)

48. एतावतैव सिद्धेः 'नार्षेयं वृणीते, न होतारमि'ति **ब्राह्मणा**नुकरणम्। (*Vyā.* 4.4.1.39)

49. **ब्राह्मणे** 'अग्नये देवेभ्य पितृभ्य' इति प्रैषं विधाय 'उभये हि देवाश्च पितरश्चेज्यन्ते' इत्याह। (*Vyā.* 4.4.2.18-76)

50. **ब्राह्मणे** तूत्तरवेदिपरिमाणे विहिताः। इह चात्वालपरिमाणे। तत्र विकल्पो वा स्यादभ्यासो वा। (*Vyā.* 5.1.1.36)

51. **ब्राह्मणे** वा उत्तरवेदिग्रहणमुत्तरनाभ्युपलक्षणार्थम्। अथवोभयोर्विकल्पः। (*Vyā.* 5.1.2.12)

52. **ब्राह्मणे** एकवचनं जात्यपेक्षं, समुदायापेक्षं वा। तदिहापि तुल्यमिति। (*Vyā.* 5.2.1.1)

53. उक्तमग्निमन्थनमिह हौत्रवत्। एतावान् विशेषः। किन्तु 'आयुरसि' इत्यभिमन्त्रणमिह नोक्तम्। तस्य चास्मिन्नेव प्रकरणे **मन्त्रब्राह्मणयोः** पठितस्य लोपो नोपपद्यते। (*Vyā.* 5.2.1.4-8)

54. तथा च **ब्राह्मणे** 'उर्वश्यस्यस्यायुरसी'त्याह। (*Vyā.* 5.2.1.4-8)

    Here, I would like to point out that the *'Purūrvā-urvaśī'* Akhyāna has been dealt with in *Vādhūla Anvākhyānam* under two *Paṭala* (1-2) of the first *Prapāṭhaka.*

55. 'यदुपरिष्टात्पशुं समनक्ति 'मेध्यमेवैनं करोति' इत्येतावदेव **ब्राह्मणे** श्रूयते। (*Vyā.* 5.2.1.23)

56. गुदस्योक्तमवदानं **ब्राह्मणे** विहितम्। तदनेन विकल्पते। (*Vyā.* 5.3.1.53)

57. तथा च **ब्राह्मणम्** 'कृष्णाजिनेन दीक्षयती'ति। (*Vyā.* 6.1.2.31)

58. 'मध्यन्दिने मध्यरात्र' इति **ब्राह्मणे** विहितम्। (*Vyā.* 6.1.4.4-6)

59. **ब्राह्मणे** 'ब्रह्मवादिनो वदन्ती'त्युपक्रम्याग्निहोत्रभक्त्यानुग्रहवचनाच्च। (*Vyā.* 6.1.4.4-6)

60. 'अदितिमिष्ट्वा मारुतीमृचमन्वाहे'ति **ब्राह्मणम्**। (*Vyā.* 6.2.3.2)

61. 'निर्वप्स्यन् वा पत्न्यैवानुमतं निर्वपती'ति हि **ब्राह्मणम्**। (*Vyā.* 6.3.2.32)

62. नन्वाज्यहविष्कत्वमुपांशुयाजस्य कल्पे नास्ति। **ब्राह्मणो**क्तमनुक्तमपीष्यत इत्युक्तोत्तरम्। (*Vyā.* 6.4.1.35-36)

63. **ब्राह्मण**कल्पशुल्बोक्तानां पदप्रक्रमकिष्कूनामन्यतमेन वेदिर्मातव्या। (*Vyā.* 6.4.2.4-29)

64. 'अनतिदृश्नं स्तृणाती'ति हि **ब्राह्मणम्**। (*Vyā.* 6.4.3.3-33)

65. उत्तरवेदिसंभारनिवपनोत्तरकालं **ब्राह्मण** आम्नातमपि हविर्धानसंवर्तनमत एव कर्तव्यमिति एवातःशब्दयोरुपयोगः। । (*Vyā.* 6.5.1.1-2)

66. यदि चैवोत्सर्जत्यक्षशब्दो, यदि च न नैमित्तिकवत् **ब्राह्मणे** दृष्टमपि वाचनं नित्यमित्यर्थः। (*Vyā.* 6.5.1.31)

67. **ब्राह्मणे** चाग्नीषोमीयप्रकरण एव हृदयशूलान्तताऽऽम्नाता। (*Vyā.* 6.8.1.21)

68. 'ऋतुपात्रे लभेते=**ब्राह्मणम्**। अस्य वाक्यस्य पूर्वानुवाकान्ते पाठ आनन्तर्यार्थः। (*Vyā.* 6.9.1.16)

69. अथापि **ब्राह्मणे** 'विद्यमानेऽपि व्यपदेश एकादशकपालानेव प्रातःसवने कुर्यादि'ति बहुवचनान्त एव प्रयोगः। (*Vyā.* 6.9.1.17)

70. 'तस्मात् तृतीयसवन ऋजीषमभिषुण्वन्ती'ति (वाधू.अन्वा. ४.३०.३) **ब्राह्मणे**ऽन्वाख्याने च। (*Vyā.* 6.9.4.38)

71. केषां वा विहरणं, कुतो वा विहरणं, विहृतेषु च किं कर्तव्यमिति न ज्ञायते। तत्सर्वं **ब्राह्मणो**क्तमेवानुजानातीत्यध्यवसितुं शक्यते। किञ्च **ब्राह्मणो**क्तं— 'देवा वै यज्ञं पराजयन्ते'त्युपक्रम्याग्नीध्राद्धिष्णियानां विहरणमाम्नातम्। (*Vyā.* 6.10.3.26)

72. इदमृत्विग्वरणमुपवसथे **ब्राह्मणे** विहितम्। (*Vyā.* 6.10.4.57)

73. **ब्राह्मणे** विहितस्य शेषत्वं तत्रतत्रैवानुक्रान्तम्। **ब्राह्मणे** च 'तस्माद्धविर्धाने चर्मन्नधिग्रावभिरभिषुत्याहवनीये हुत्वा प्रत्यञ्चः परेत्य सदसि भक्षयन्ती'ति। (*Vyā.* 6.11.4.5)

74. 'इन्द्राय त्वेन्द्राय त्वा' इति प्रातःसवनोक्तानामादिग्रहणाभ्यासोऽन्तराणि, **ब्राह्मणे**ऽपि 'इन्द्राय त्वेन्द्राय त्वे'ति मिमीत इत्येवैषां ग्रहणम्। (*Vyā.* 6.12.1.51)

75. तथा च **ब्राह्मणे** 'हिरण्यं ददाती'त्यविशेषेणोक्तं सर्वविषयं भवितुमर्हति। (*Vyā.* 6.12.2.27)

76. अथ वा **ब्राह्मणे** कल्पे च पठितानां पाठानामानर्थक्यं मा भूदिति बह्वृच्यविहितेन विकल्पते। याजुर्वेदिकस्यापि प्रकृतौ विकृतिषु च विशेषाभावो वा। (*Vyā.* 6.12.2.50-56)

77. 'तस्मात् तृतीयसवन ऋजीषम् अभिषुण्वन्ती'ति **ब्राह्मणे**ऽन्वाख्याने (*Vādh.Anvā.* 4.30.3) च वचनाद्। (*Vyā.* 6.13.1.2)

78. अनसोऽवेक्षणं 'यन्मे' इति मन्त्रे च **ब्राह्मणे** च विहितम्। (*Vyā.* 6.14.1.57)

79. **ब्राह्मणे** 'यन्मैत्रावरुणीं वशामालभत' इति विधानात्। (*Vyā.* 6.15.3.102)

80. का पुनरुदवसानीया। **ब्राह्मणे** औपानुवाक्ये विहिता। (*Vyā.* 6.15.4.1-6)

81. यद्यपि तावद् **ब्राह्मणा**र्थो न घटते, तथापि त्वाचार्येणाश्रिताया: शाखाया दुर्ज्ञातत्वात्कल्पपदानि मुख्यवृत्त्या व्याख्येयानि। (*Vyā.* 7.1.1.35-36)

82. सहास्तरणपक्षेऽपि कृष्णाजिनस्योपरिष्टादभावे **ब्राह्मणे** द्यावापृथिवी संस्तव:। (*Vyā.* 7.1.3.12-13)

83. षडुद्यामत्वेऽपि **ब्राह्मण**मस्ति। (*Vyā.* 7.4.1.2)

84. 'एकविंशति पृडक: हिरण्योऽमृतं हिरण्यमि'ति **ब्राह्मण**दर्शनात्। (*Vyā.* 7.4.1.2)

85. **ब्राह्मणे** निमित्तसंयोगेन श्रवणात्। (*Vyā.* 7.4.1.2)

86. 'आज्येन संयौतीत्याज्यसंयुतमि'ति च **ब्राह्मणे** कल्पे च दर्शनात्। (*Vyā.* 7.4.1.19)

87. 'उत्तमे' इति **ब्राह्मणा**नुकरणम्। (*Vyā.* 7.4.2.6)

88. 'येन देवा ज्योतिषोर्ध्वा उदायन्' इत्युख्यं समिन्ध' इति च **ब्राह्मणे** दर्शनात्। (*Vyā.* 7.4.3.4)

89. तैत्तिरीयके **ब्राह्मणे** पदैर्मानमाम्नातम्। (*Vyā.* 7.4.4.15)

90. एकस्या एव चितेरुपधानमभिधाय 'तद्वा एतत्पञ्चचितीकं त्रिचितीकमेकचितीकं चिन्वीतेति **ब्राह्मणम्**' इति चाभिधाय 'स यदेवं कुर्यादि'ति संशयवचनाद् गम्यते। (*Vyā.* 7.5.2.7-10)

91. द्वादश षड् वाऽनड्वाहो **ब्राह्मणे** दृष्टत्वात्। (*Vyā.* 7.5.3.9-10)

92. उपधानं च सर्पशिरस: पाक्षिकोऽस्त्येव, **ब्राह्मणे**ऽभिहितत्वात्। (*Vyā.* 7.6.3.18)

93. उपदधतीति उपधातृबहुत्वं **ब्राह्मणे** दृष्टम्। (*Vyā.* 7.6.3.27-28)

94. विशेषश्च यो ब्राह्मणो यस्मिन् कस्मिंश्चिद्**ब्राह्मणे**ऽभिहितामिष्टकाम-निर्ज्ञातक्रमामिष्टकां यदि वेद स चैतामस्मिन्क्रम उपदधातु। (*Vyā.* 7.11.3.102)

95. **ब्राह्मणा**नुकरणाय धारणेऽप्युपहरणं ग्रीवदघ्नादित्वम्। (*Vyā.* 7.13.1.11)

96. 'तमुत्करे न्यस्येदि'ति दीर्घस्य वंशस्य **ब्राह्मणम्**। (*Vyā.* 7.13.3.11)

97. **ब्राह्मणे** च स्तोक्याप्रकरणे 'स्याज्जुहोती'ति श्रुतत्वाद्। (*Vyā.* 10.2.2.49-51)

98. यदा लब्धायामभ्रमित्यादि शेषो **ब्राह्मणो**क्तः। (*Vyā.* 12.2.6)

99. जयाभ्याताना इत्यादि। तेषां **ब्राह्मणे** व्याख्याताः कामाः। (*Vyā.* 12.3.1)

100. स्वत उन्मादिनस्तस्य स एवेध्म इत्यवश्यं नैय्यग्रोधादीनां ग्रहणं विज्ञेयम्, **ब्राह्मणे** प्रत्यक्षश्रुतत्वात्। (*Vyā.* 12.3.2)

101. उन्मादिने 'तस्मै स्वाहा, ताभ्यः स्वाहे'ति जुहोति इति **ब्राह्मणम्**। (*Vyā.* 12.3.3)

102. अन्ये व्याचक्षते—'इदमि'ति **ब्राह्मणं** प्रतिनिर्दिश्यते। (*Vyā.* 13.1.1)

महामेध *(Mahāmedha)*—

1. सर्वेषां यज्ञायुधानामिहोत्पत्तिवचनमिहोत्पन्नान्याहवनीयादिवत् सर्वकर्मार्थानि यथा स्युरिति। तथा **महामेधे** विनियोगो दृश्यते। (*Vyā.* 1.1.1.5)

2. भस्मपुरीषसिकतोषाणां च निवपनं क्रमेण मन्त्रैः कर्तव्यम्। तथा च **महामेधे**—'अग्न्याधेयिकान् संभारान्' इत्येतावदेवोक्त्वा चितानास्थाय भस्मपुरीषयोश्च निवपनं विदधदाचार्य इहापि तयोः संभवमिच्छति। (*Vyā.* 1.1.3.8)

   It may be pointed out that this *Mahāmedha*-text is still unknown to us. It muct have belonged to the *Vādhūla*-tradition.

8. References to शाखान्तर *(Śākhāntara)* and श्रुत्यन्तर *(Śrutyantara)* in *Vyākhyā*—

While dealing with the rituals, Āryadāsa frequently refers to the differences as well as the similarities found in other *Śākhās* by using the word *Śākhāntara* as under—

(a) **शाखान्तर** *(Śākhāntara)*—

1. क्वचिन्मन्त्रा एव पठ्यन्ते, न ब्राह्मणमस्ति। तेषां च विनियोगः यथा 'दैव्य उपस्थानेऽच्छिद्रेषु' इति **शाखान्तरे** पठितानामवश्योपसंहर्तव्यानां वैकल्पिकानां

च पदार्थानामुपसंहार इति, एवमादीनां क्लृप्तिशब्दवाच्यता। सा च क्लृप्तिः कल्पसूत्राण्यन्तरेण न सिध्यति। (*Vyā.* 1.1.1.1)

2. तथा 'अग्निना देवेन' इत्यादीनां चतुर्थ**शाखान्तर**पठितं समस्तं पठित्वा 'इन्द्रेण सयुजो वयम्' इत्यवसानादित्येतच्छाखाधीतमनुज्ञाय 'अपि वा तेजस्वी' इत्यन्यशाखागतं वैकल्पिकं पठति। उदाहरणमात्रं प्रदर्शितम्। अन्यान्यप्येतच्छाखाश्रयणे बहूनि लिङ्गानि सन्ति। अतो ब्राह्मणे मन्त्रे वा यद् दृष्टमिहानुक्तमपि परिग्राह्यम्। (*Vyā.* 1.1.1.6)

3. **शाखान्तरे** विहितायाः पूर्णाहुतेरयमेवावकाशः। (*Vyā.* 1.2.2.25-26)

4. 'उच्च मार्ष्ट्युप च मार्ष्ट्युभयमाप्नोती'ति **शाखान्तर**वचनम्'। (*Vyā.* 1.2.3.1)

5. अग्न्युपस्थानं नाग्निहोत्राङ्गं **शाखान्तरे** विहितं। (*Vyā.* 1.2.3.4)

6. अपरे **शाखान्तर**विहिते अपोह्य ब्राह्मणे प्रागुदीची विहिता। (*Vyā.* 2.1.1.7)

7. **शाखान्तरे** तादृशस्य सादयित्वा संभृतेष्वपि तन्न विरुध्यते। (*Vyā.* 2.1.1.7)

8. 'कौशं बर्हिर्भवति' इति **शाखान्तरे** विद्यते। (*Vyā.* 2.1.1.17)

9. **शाखान्तरे**ऽपि मूलतः शाखां परिवास्योपवेषं करोतीति। (*Vyā.* 2.1.2.2)

10. आकृतयः **शाखान्तरे** पुरुषार्था आम्नाताः 'वत्सज्ञुं पशुकामस्य वेदं कुर्यादि'त्यादि। (*Vyā.* 2.1.2.2)

11. अयमाचार्यः **शाखान्तर**स्थमपि विधानं केनचित्प्रकारेण सूचयति। (*Vyā.* 2.1.2.14)

12. अपि वा **शाखान्तरे**ष्ववघातान्ते कपालोपधानान्ते च प्रातर्दोहमामनन्ति। तद् द्योतनार्थं **शाखान्तर**स्थमपि विधिं केनचित्प्रकारेण सूचयन्तीत्युक्तम्। (*Vyā.* 2.1.3.32-37)

13. **शाखान्तरे** दर्शपूर्णमासप्रकरणे उक्तं वचनं—'व्रीहिभिर्यजेत यवैर्यजेते'ति। समुच्चयासंभवाच्च विकल्पः (*Vyā.* 2.1.4.2)

14. तथा सति **शाखान्तरे**ऽपि तादृशाः पाठा विद्यन्ते इत्यवगन्तव्यम्। (*Vyā.* 2.1.5.6-7)

15. प्रकृताग्रहणे प्रमाणाभावात्। पत्नी पिनष्टीति **शाखान्तरे**। पत्न्यवहन्ति दासी पिनष्ट्येतद्वा विपरीतमिति। (*Vyā.* 2.2.1.25-33)

16. **शाखान्तरे** वचनं 'यच्छीताभिः संयुयादतिवर्षुकः पर्जन्यः, स यदुष्णाभिः संयुयादवर्षुकः। उष्णाभिश्च शीताभिश्च संयौती'ति। (*Vyā.* 2.2.1.40-42)

17. एवं हि 'नाज्यस्थाल्या अध्याहवनीये जुहोति न ध्रुवाया अधीतरयोरि'ति **शाखान्तरे** वचनमस्ति। (*Vyā.* 2.2.4.27)

18. तथा च प्रस्तरप्रहरणे सह शाखयेति **शाखान्तरे** वचनमस्ति। (*Vyā.* 2.2.4.37)

19. उत्तरेभ्यः समुन्मुखेभ्यो दक्षिणेत्येव तिर्यक्त्वे सिद्धे तिर्यक्त्वमिति ब्राह्मणवचनानुकरणम्, 'उत्तरस्मिन्नाघार ऋजुमाघारयती'ति प्राप्तस्य **शाखान्तरे** विहितस्य वैकल्पिकत्वप्रदर्शनार्थम्। (*Vyā.* 2.3.1.6)

20. **शाखान्तरे** च 'अतिहायेडो बर्हिः प्रतिसमानयत इति, बर्हिष्वाज्यं निदधाती'ति वचनात् बहिरर्थं मन्यन्ते। (*Vyā.* 2.3.1.34)

21. 'अङ्गुष्ठपर्वमात्राणि दैवान्यवदानानि भवन्ति। ज्यायान्यैडानि सौविष्टकृतानि चे'ति **शाखान्तरं** पञ्चावत्तिनः। (*Vyā.* 2.3.1.44-47)

22. **शाखान्तरे** च 'प्राशित्रमवद्यति द्वे' इति वचनमस्ति। (*Vyā.* 2.3.1.44-47)

23. 'यानुत्सृज्य दम्पती सह व्रजतः तानुत्सृज्य पुनरादधीयाता'मिति **शाखान्तरे** वचनम्। अत एकपत्नीकस्य सहगमनं नास्त्येव। (*Vyā.* 3.1.1.7)

24. तत्प्रसंगादेव माहाचमसमपि **शाखान्तर**विहितम्। (*Vyā.* 3.1.2.1)

25. एतदपि **शाखान्तर**विहितमपोद्यते। (*Vyā.* 3.2.2.33-36)

26. 'विंशान्याज्यानि भवन्ति, षोडशान्याज्यानि भवन्ती'ति **शाखान्तरे** विहितत्वात्। (*Vyā.* 3.2.3.1-12)

27. अस्मिन् कल्पे **शाखान्तर**विहिता एव मन्त्रा आचार्येण विनियुज्यन्ते। ते विज्ञातुं न शक्यन्ते इमे याजमाना आम्नाता, इमे आध्वर्यवा इति। आचार्य एव प्रमाणमित्यध्यवसाय कर्तव्यः। (*Vyā.* 3.3.1.1)

28. पञ्चवर्षादिप्रयोगा अपि **शाखान्तरे**षु विद्यन्ते। (*Vyā.* 4.1.1.1)

29. एतज्ज्ञापयति इहानुक्तमपि **शाखान्तरे** पठितं ग्रहीतव्यमिति। (*Vyā.* 5.1.3.28-30)

30. समाहोरात्रश्च कालो वसन्तः शरद् वा। तत्र **शाखान्तरे** वसन्त इति दृष्टे सन्देहो निवर्तते। (*Vyā.* 6.1.1.2)

31. 'अग्नीषोमीयस्येध्माबर्हिरि'ति **शाखान्तरे** दर्शनात्। (*Vyā.* 6.4.3.45-47)

32. एवं सत्यन्तमपेक्षे **शाखान्तरीयं** वैकल्पिकं वचनं द्रष्टव्यम्। (*Vyā.* 7.3.3.56-59)

33. 'असञ्चर एव वल्मीकवपायामन्वस्यती'ति **शाखान्तर**स्थो वैकल्पिको विधिः। (*Vyā.* 7.13.2.18-19)

34. 'अश्मन्नूर्जम्' इति परिषिञ्चतीति श्रुतेः। कल्पवचोऽपि तादृशमेव। वाचनमपि **शाखान्तर**विहितं द्रष्टव्यम्। (*Vyā.* 7.13.3.5)

35. यद्यप्यविशेषेण तैत्तिरीयके प्रवचने 'ऋतुस्थाँ यज्ञाज्ञियेन पुच्छ'मित्युक्तम्, तथापि **शाखान्तर**विशेषवचनं दृष्टमित्यवगन्तव्यम्। (*Vyā.* 7.13.3.14-15)

36. 'अप्रतिरथं ब्रह्मे'ति **शाखान्तरे** वचनं द्रष्टव्यम्। तैत्तिरीयके प्रवचने 'द्वितीयो होते'त्युक्तम्। अथवा **शाखान्तरे** विहितस्य 'द्वितीयो होते'त्यनुवादः। (*Vyā.* 7.14.1.27)

37. द्वादशे द्वादशेऽनवानमिति **शाखान्तर**विहितस्यार्थवादमभिधातुमिति ज्ञापयत्याचार्यः। (*Vyā.* 7.14.3.43)

38. अतः **शाखान्तर**स्थोऽयं विधिः 'अञ्जलिना जुहोतीत्यनेन विकल्पत' इति द्रष्टव्यम्। (*Vyā.* 7.14.4.17)

39. तैत्तिरीयके समस्तेन हस्तग्रहणम्। **शाखान्तर**स्थोऽयं विभागविधिर्द्रष्टव्यः। तयोर्विरोधे विकल्पः। (*Vyā.* 7.15.1.54)

40. 'राष्ट्रमेवास्मिन् ध्रुवमकरदि'ति व्यपदेशात्। साऽन्वारभेतेति **शाखान्तरे** वचनं द्रष्टव्यम्। (*Vyā.* 9.2.4.8)

41. एकद्वित्रिचतुष्टादित्यनेन पक्षमित्यस्य स्थाने विनियोगः **शाखान्तरे** द्रष्टव्यः। (*Vyā.* 9.2.4.14)

42. **शाखान्तरे** वाऽवघ्रापणमित्यवगन्तव्यम्। (*Vyā.* 10.6.1.21)

43. मन्त्रब्राह्मणविहिताच्चाधिकोऽवयवः **शाखान्तरस्य** उपाधीयते। (*Vyā.* 12.1.1)

44. नायं गोत्रप्रत्ययान्त इति। अथवा **शाखान्तरविहितं** वैकल्पिकमेतत्। (*Vyā.* 12.3.5)

(b) **श्रुत्यन्तर** (*Śrutyantara)*— Āryadāsa in his commentary very frequently refers to *Śruti* and *Śrutyantara, i.e.* differences from, or similarities to, from one *Śruti*-text, other *Śruti*-texts in the matter of rituals which have come from generation to generation in oral tradition and presved in other *Śruti*-texts as is evident from the following references—

1. नित्यं काम्यं नैमित्तिकं च वर्णविशेषयुक्तं चाविशेषेण **श्रुत्यन्तरे** विहितम्। (*Vyā.* 1.1.1.6)

2. 'पुरोडाशकपालेन तुषानुपवपन्ति' इति **श्रुत्यन्तरम्**। (*Vyā.* 2.1.5.22)

3. तथा च **श्रुत्यन्तरे**—'यजमानपञ्चमा इडां प्राश्नीयुः' इति। (*Vyā.* 2.3.2.19-20)

4. अथवा तेषां ब्राह्मणेऽप्यभावात् **श्रुत्यन्तरे** एतेषामविशेषेणोक्तभावोऽनुमीयते। (*Vyā.* 3.1.2.3-8)

5. 'स तर्हि गत' इति **श्रुत्यन्तर**दर्शनादनुद्धृतमग्निमभ्यस्तमगात्। (*Vyā.* 3.1.4.2)

6. **श्रुत्यन्तरे** आध्वर्यवे विहितमित्यवगन्तव्यम्। (*Vyā.* 3.3.1.1)

7. एवमन्येषां मन्त्राणां याजमानकाण्डे पठितानां कल्प आध्वर्यवे दृष्टानामाध्वर्यवे एव **श्रुत्यन्तरे** पाठोऽनुमेयः। (*Vyā.* 3.3.1.1)

8. अनुकल्पमिति च **श्रुत्यन्तरे** विहितं वदति न स्वमनीषिकया कल्पितम्। (*Vyā.* 3.3.2.4-5)

9. **श्रुत्यन्तरे** विहितानामाचार्येणाम्नातानां सर्वत्र प्रकृतावेव वैकल्पिकत्वमुक्तम्। तदेतेषामपि यथाकामं प्रयोगः। अनुब्राह्मणस्य प्रयोगः। (*Vyā.* 3.3.2.4-5)

10. अथवा तस्याभावः **श्रुत्यन्तराद्** 'याः फालकृष्टयः व्रीहिभिरेव तासामाग्रयणं कृतं भवति। श्यामाकैरारण्यानामि'ति। (*Vyā.* 3.4.1.1)

11. आचार्येण विहितत्वाच्च **श्रुत्यन्तरे** विद्यत इत्यवगन्तव्यम्। (*Vyā.* 3.4.1.1)

12. **श्रुत्यन्तरे** 'उत्करे वाजिनमासादयती'ति वचनमस्ति। (*Vyā.* 4.1.3.49)

13. तथा च **श्रुत्यन्तरेषु** 'अपशुर्वा एष योऽपन्नदत्, मलं वा एष पशूनां यो सिक्तरेता' इत्यादीनि निन्दावचनान्येतमेवार्थमुपोद्बलयन्ति। (*Vyā.* 5.1.1.1-2)

14. 'त्र्यरत्निश्चतुररत्निर्वा पालाशः पशुबन्धयूप' इति **श्रुत्यन्तरे** वचनम्। (*Vyā.* 5.1.1.14)

15. अन्ये वर्णयन्ति ऐन्द्राग्नमारभ्य होत्रस्य कृत्स्नाम्नानादस्यापि धर्मवत्त्वम्। तच्चोदकवाक्यवदेव **श्रुत्यन्तर**स्थमनुमीयते। (*Vyā.* 5.1.2.21)

16. **श्रुत्यन्तरे** विशेषः 'अञ्जनादि यजमानो यूपं नानुसृजत्यापरिव्ययणादि'ति। (*Vyā.* 5.1.3.28-30)

17. **श्रुत्यन्तरे** च 'वसन्ते वसन्ते ज्योतिषा यजेते'ति श्रूयते। तस्माद्यावज्जीविक एवाभ्यास इति केचित्। (*Vyā.* 6.1.1.2)

18. अन्य आह—**श्रुत्यन्तरे** 'ग्रामे दीक्षतेऽरण्ये यजत' इति वचनमस्ति। तस्योपलक्षणं वपनादि। (*Vyā.* 6.1.1.7)

19. **श्रुत्यन्तर** आम्नातं–'हविर्वै दीक्षितः, पात्रं कृष्णाजिनम्। नाधः कृष्णाजिनादासीत। यदधः कृष्णाजिनादासीत यद्धविषः स्कन्नस्य प्रायश्चित्तं तदस्य कार्यं स्यादि'ति। (*Vyā.* 6.1.3.20)

20. तथा च **श्रुत्यन्तरे**—'द्वादशरात्रीर्दीक्षितो भृतिं वन्वीते'ति। (*Vyā.* 6.1.4.7)

21. तथा च **श्रुत्यन्तरे** वचनम्। (*Vyā.* 6.2.2.5)

22. चतुःशरावादि **श्रुत्यन्तर**विहितम्। (*Vyā.* 6.3.1.34)

23. अवान्तरदीक्षैव पूर्वेति ब्रुवताऽऽचार्येण **श्रुत्यन्तरे** बलवता प्रमाणेनावान्तरदीक्षायाः पूर्वकालत्वं दृष्टमित्यवगन्तव्यम्। (*Vyā.* 6.3.4.7-8)

24. तथाग्नीध्रीयमार्जालीययोरन्तःसदसि केषु च धिष्णियेषु सञ्चरेण केनचित् भवितव्यत्वात् **श्रुत्यन्तर**दर्शनाच्च। (*Vyā.* 6.4.2.4-29)

25. 'भूमिगते स्वाहा करोती'ति **श्रुत्यन्तरे** वचनम्। (*Vyā.* 6.5.3.2)

26. नातो राजानं प्रत्याहरेयुः। अशेषमानयतीत्यर्थः। बहुवचनं **श्रुत्यन्तर**वचनत्वप्रदर्शनार्थम्। (*Vyā.* 6.10.1.20)

27. अतः **श्रुत्यन्तरे** तादृशं वचनमनुमेयम्। (*Vyā.* 6.10.4.2-13)

28. **श्रुत्यन्तरे** पठितमवगन्तव्यम्। (*Vyā.* 6.10.4.57)

29. अपि च **श्रुत्यन्तरे**–'वपया प्रातःसवने चरन्ति पुरोडाशेन माध्यन्दिने सवनेऽङ्गैस्तृतीयसवन' इति। (*Vyā.* 6.11.1.1)

30. 'अन्वारम्भयाजमानाः सोमा' इति **श्रुत्यन्तरे** वचनम्। (*Vyā.* 6.11.1.24)

31. पाशुकस्यापि च तस्यैकशतं प्रयाजानूयाजा इति **श्रुत्यन्तरे** सौमिकानां प्रयाजानूयाजानां संख्याश्रवणं विरुध्येत। (*Vyā.* 6.11.1.26)

32. तस्य पूजार्थं **श्रुत्यन्तरे** पाठ इत्यवगन्तव्यम्। (*Vyā.* 6.11.3.19)

33. वषट्कर्तुश्चतुर्ग्रहद्विदेवत्यादिषु दर्शनाद् 'वषट्कर्तुः प्रथमः' इति **श्रुत्यन्तरे** वचनाद्। (*Vyā.* 6.11.4.5)

34. तथा च भगवता जैमिनिना 'गौश्चाश्वश्चेति **श्रुत्यन्तरे** दृष्टस्य बहुद्रव्यस्य वाक्यस्यार्थं विचारयता 'भागित्वाद्वा गवां स्यादि'ति गवामेव प्राधान्यमभ्यधायि। (*Vyā.* 6.12.2.11)

35. तथा च **श्रुत्यन्तरे** 'गौश्चाश्वश्चे'त्युपक्रम्य 'तस्य द्वादशं शतं दक्षिणा' इत्याम्नातम्। (*Vyā.* 6.12.2.27)

36. तथा च **श्रुत्यन्तरे** 'नायुर्दां जुहोति नाध्वगमनमन्त्रं ब्रूत' इति वारुणप्रघासिके वचनमस्ति। (*Vyā.* 6.15.2.1)

37. वैकृतेषु कर्मस्वश्वमेधादिषु प्रवृत्तिदर्शनं च। **श्रुत्यन्तरे** हि 'अनूपसदमग्निं चिन्वीते'ति च। (*Vyā.* 7.1.1.1)

38. इदं **श्रुत्यन्तर**विहितम्। (*Vyā.* 12.1.2)

39. तदापत्तिप्रायश्चित्तविधानयोः **श्रुत्यन्तरे** विधानमनुमेयम्। (*Vyā.* 12.1.2)

40. एकदेशनाशेऽपि हृदयनाशे पुनरालंभः **श्रुत्यन्तर** आम्नातः। इह विशेषानभिधानाद् हृदयनाशेऽपीदमेव प्रभवतीति गम्यते। (*Vyā.* 12.1.2)

41. 'इदं **श्रुत्यन्तर**वचनम्'। (*Vyā.* 12.1.3)

42. 'उक्थं वाचि सुवर्' इति **श्रुत्यन्तरे** विहितं वैकल्पिकम्। (*Vyā.* 12.1.5)

43. 'चित्ताय स्वाहा, चित्त्यै स्वाहा' (तु.तैसं. ३.४.४.१-२) इति संप्रदानविभक्त्या **श्रुत्यन्तरे** समाम्नाता देवताः। प्रथमया यथाऽऽम्नातमपि हूयमाने नास्ति दोषः। (*Vyā.* 12.3.1)

44. **श्रुत्यन्तर**विहितस्य चतुर्थस्यापि परिग्रहार्थं च। (*Vyā.* 12.3.5)

45. 'तेजस्वी त्वमग्न' इत्यादयः **श्रुत्यन्तर**विकल्पमित्यर्थः। (*Vyā.* 12.3.5)

46. इह **श्रुत्यन्तरे** वचनादाचार्येण कल्पितमनुग्रहवचनमिव लक्ष्यते। (*Vyā.* 12.4.3)

47. **श्रुत्यन्तरे**भ्यः सूत्रान्तरेभ्योऽथेतरेषां स्वर्गः फलम्। (*Vyā.* 13.1.2)

48. **श्रुत्यन्तरे** 'सह पशूनालभत' इति सवनीयस्य स्थाने विहितः। (*Vyā.* 14.4.2)

49. अश्वापादानो आशूनां व्रीहीणाम् ईषच्छन्दानां स्थाने देवयजने साद्यस्क्रा इति **श्रुत्यन्तरे** बहुवचनचोदिता एते। (*Vyā.* 14.4.2)

50. तथा च **श्रुत्यन्तरे**—'सर्वा वा ऋचः सर्वाणि यजूंषि सर्वाणि सामानि वाचःस्तोमे शस्यन्त इति। (*Vyā.* 14.4.3)

9. Ācāryas quoted in *Vyākhyā* by name—

Āryadāsa in his *Vyākhyā* very frequently quotes the views of other Ācāryas by name sometimes in favour and somtimes against Vādhūlas.

अगस्त्य *(Agastya)*—

1. **'अगस्त्यो** आलभ्य उक्ष्णः प्रौक्षदि'ति दर्शनान्मरुद्भ्य एव प्रोक्षति। (*Vyā.* 14.5.1)

अग्निवेश्य *(Agniveśya)*— *Agniveśya* was propounder of one of the four sub-*Śākhās* of the Vādhūlas on whose name his *Śākhā* was called *Āgniveśya,* others being *Kauṇḍinya, Gālava* and *Śāṅkha*. It is very important to note that Āryadāsa for the first time pointed out the four sub-branches of Vādhūlas—

1. चतुर्णां वाधूलानामिति। के ते चत्वारो वाधूलाः ? **कौण्डिन्याग्निवेश्यगालवशाङ्खानां**। (*Vyā.* 1.1.1.5)
2. एवं बोधायना**ग्निवेश्या**भ्यामाम्नातम्।। (*Vyā.* 6.1.3.18)
3. 'व्यूह्य बर्हिः स्तम्बयजुर्हरेदि'त्या**ग्निवेश्यः**। (*Vyā.* 6.4.1.4-7)
4. गन्धर्वो नाम पराया अपत्यमा**ग्निवेशगोत्र**स्तेन साकृतं साशिरस्कम्पम् एतैः सर्पन्तीत्युक्ताः प्रत्यूचुः।। (*Vyā.* 14.7.3)

आङ्गिरस *(Āṅgirasa)*—

1. तत्र तदैव क्रमेणार्षेयवरणब्राह्मणभारता**ङ्गिरस**बार्हस्पत्यभारद्वाजवैश्वामित्राघमर्षण-कौशिकेत्येवं। (*Vyā..* 11.1.4)

आपस्तम्ब *(Āpastamba)*—

1. **आपस्तम्ब** आह—'न पत्नीः संयाजयन्ति, न समिष्टयजुर्जुहोति। सर्वमन्यत् क्रियत' इति। (*Vyā.* 4.4.2.18-76)
2. व्यक्तं चा**पस्तम्बा**चाचार्येणाभिहितम्। याजमानाम्नाये समाम्नानात् समिदाधानं याजमानम्। (*Vyā.* 7.4.3.4)
3. **आपस्तम्बस्य** कल्पे वाजो नाम कश्चित्क्रतुराम्नातः। (*Vyā.* 14.13.1)

आरुणि *(Āruṇi)*—

1. **आरुणि**पक्षोऽत्राचार्येणाम्नातम्। (*Vyā.* 1.5.2.13-16)
2. उद्दालको नामा**रुणि**पुत्रः। (*Vyā.* 3.2.2.11)

आश्मरथ्य *(Āśmarathya)*— Āryadāsa has quoted a text from *ĀśvaŚS* (5.13.8-10) in which the name of *Āśmarathya* occurs. According to Kashikar, *Āśmarathya* belonged to the *Ādhvaryava* school and evidently to the *Kṛṣṇa Yajurveda*

Taittirīya recension.[1]

1. ‘क्रियामा**श्मरथ्यो**ऽन्विताऽप्रतिषेधात्’ इति। (*Vyā.* 6.11.1.1)

आर्क्षाकायण (*Ārkṣakāyaṇa*)—

1. ऋक्षाकस्यापत्यमार्क्षाकिः। आर्क्षाकिरपत्यम् युवा **आर्क्षाकायणः**। पर्यस्तो बुद्ध्या श्रान्तः प्रतिपत्तव्यज्ञानाच्चंक्रम्यते स्म। पुनःपुनरन्यं देशं गतवान् किल। (*Vyā.* 3.2.2.10)

आश्वलायन (*Āśvalāyana*)— The word *Āśvalāyana* has been mentioned in both singular and plural, the former for *Ācārya Āśvalāyana* and the latter for the followers of *Āśvalāyana Śākhā,* as under—

(*a*) 1. नित्यं वा पयसा वा स्वयं च पर्वणि जुहुयादित्या**श्वलायनः** (*ĀśvaŚS.* 2.3.1)। (*Vyā.* 1.5.2.25-27)

2. तथा च **आश्वलायने**नोक्तम्—‘अतो देवा अवन्तु नः’ इति जपेदपि वाऽन्यां वैष्णवीमिति’ (*ĀśvaŚS.* 9.11.17-18)। (*Vyā.* 3.5.1.17)

3. तथा चा**श्वलायनेन** ब्रह्मत्व उक्तम् ‘बहिर्वेदि यां दिशं व्रजेयुः सैव तत्रः प्राची’ इति (*ĀśvaŚS.* 1.12.4)। (*Vyā.* 3.6.2.19)

4. **आश्वलायने**नोक्तम् —‘सा शंय्वन्ता’ (*ĀśvaŚS.* 2.19.2) इति। (*Vyā.* 4.4.2.18-76)

5. ‘एकाङ्गवचने दक्षिणं प्रतीयाद्। अनादेशे’ (*ĀśvaŚS.* 1.1.12-13) इत्या**श्वलायनः**। (*Vyā.* 5.1.1.12)

6. ये प्रायणीयमि’त्या**श्वलायने**नोदयनीय उक्तत्वाच्चाध्वर्योरन्यतरमुभयत्र कर्तारमेकमेवेच्छन्ति (*ĀśvaŚS.* 4.3.1)। (*Vyā.* 6.2.1.3)

7. ततश्च प्रयाजादयः प्राप्नुयुः। तच्चानिष्टमुक्तमा**श्वलायनेन** ‘स्विष्टकृदादि लुप्यते। प्रयाजा आज्यभागौ च’ (*ĀśvaŚS.* 4.8.6) इत्यतोऽङ्गमात्रं परिसञ्चष्टे। अतोऽपूर्वा इति। (*Vyā.* 6.4.1.35-36)

8. उक्तमा**श्वलायनेन**—‘औपवसथ्य उभे पूर्वाह्णे’ (*ĀśvaŚS.* 4.8.17) इति। (*Vyā.* 6.4.2.87)

---

1. Kashikar, C.G., ‘The Ritual Teachers : *Āśmarathya* and *Ālekhana*’, published in *Maṇisāgara,* a collection of papers of Dr. Kashikar, published by Mrs Mandakini Kinjawadekar, for private circulation only.

9. तदुक्तमा**श्वलायनेन**—'सवनीयानां पुरस्तादुपरिष्टाद्वा पशुपुरोडाशेन चरन्ति'; 'अक्रियामेकेऽन्यत्र तदर्थवादवदनात्'; 'क्रियामाश्मरथ्योऽन्विताऽप्रतिषेधात्' इति (*ĀśvaŚS.* 5.13.8-10)। (*Vyā.* 6.11.1.1)

(*b*) 1. अध्यर्धामुक्त्वा ह्यवसानमा**श्वलायना** आमनन्ति (*ĀśvaŚS.* 8.1.3)। (*Vyā.* 2.3.1.4)

2. 'आहवनीये षट्षट् शकलान्यभ्यादधाति' (*ĀśvaŚS.* 6.12.3) इत्या**श्वलायने**। (*Vyā.* 6.3.3.13). Here the word 'आश्वलायने' refers to the text *ĀśvaŚS.*

3. **आश्वलायनाः** पठन्ति 'प्रवर्ग्यवांश्चेदि'ति (*ĀśvaŚS.* 5.13.1)। (*Vyā.* 6.8.3.30)

4. **आश्वलायनाः** ऋतुग्रहप्रचारात् पूर्वमामनन्ति (*ĀśvaŚS.* 5.6.9-11)। (*Vyā.* 6.11.4.5)

5. 'प्राचीनावीतिनो दक्षिणामुखाश्च दद्युस्तिस्त्रस्तिस्त्रः पिण्ड्यः' (*cf. ĀśvaŚS.* 2.6.12) इत्या**श्वलायनाः**। (*Vyā.* 6.14.1.1)

6. 'द्रप्सप्राशनसख्यविसर्जने त्वन्त्य एव' (*ĀśvaŚS.* 7.1.6) इत्या**श्वलायना**नाम्। (*Vyā.* 6.15.1.39)

उद्दालक (*Uddālaka*)—

1. **उद्दालको** नामारुणिपुत्रः। (*Vyā.* 3.2.2.11)

औखीय (*Aukhīya*)—

1. भगाय चरुमित्य**ौखीय**के वचनमवेक्ष्यम्। (*Vyā.* 9.1.3.98)

Here the word 'औखीयके' has been used for the text of *Aukhīyas.*

2. तस्यैवमेव धृतीः पत्सु जुहोतीत्याचार्येण विशेषितत्वा**दौखीय**कत्वाच्च। (*Vyā.* 10.2.2.49-51)

कात्यायन (*Kātyāyana*)—

1. अग्निहोत्रस्त्रुक्स्त्रुवस्य वैकङ्कतत्वमुक्तं भगवता **कात्यायने**न (*KātyŚS.* 4.14.7)। (*Vyā.* 1.5.1.2)

Here Āryadāsa has very respectfully used the word *Bhagavān* for *Kātyāyana.*

2. पितृयज्ञस्य दर्शपूर्णमासयोरङ्गत्वानङ्गत्वे विप्रतिपत्तिराचार्याणाम्। 'अङ्गवान् समभिव्याहारादि'ति **कात्यायनः** (*cf KātyŚS.* 1.10.2)। (*Vyā.* 2.1.2.42)

3. अस्य पयसोऽधर्मकत्वं **कात्यायनः** किलाह—'अधर्मकं वा प्रतिधुक् श्रुतेरि'ति (*cf KātyŚS.* 7.11.7)। (*Vyā.* 4.5.1.1)

कापिष्ठल (*Kāpiṣṭhala)*—

1. श्रूयन्ते च—**कापिष्ठला**नां शाखिन ऐन्द्राग्नं निरूढपशुबन्धं प्रकृत्या साकल्येन पशुधर्मा नाम्नातवन्त इति। (*Vyā.* 5.1.2.21)

काप्य (*Kāpya)*—

1. **काप्यो**ऽध्वर्युर्वैतस्मिन् काल इति च समानाधिकरण्यात्। (*Vyā.* 10.6.1.22)

कौण्डिन्य (*Kauṇḍinya)*— Propounder of one of the four sub-*Śākhās* of Vādhūlas.

1. के ते चत्वारो वाधूलाः ? **कौण्डिन्या**ग्निवेश्यगालवशाङ्खानाम्। (*Vyā.* 1.1.1.5)
2. तथा च **कौण्डिन्याः** पठन्ति—'एतावदेवाहः पौर्णमासेन हविषा यजेते'ति। (*Vyā.* 4.1.1.3). Here the word *Kauṇḍinya* in plural refers to the followers *Kauṇḍinya Śākhā.*
3. तत्र च **कौण्डिन्या** एकत्वमपनीय 'रासाथां', 'तयोर्वामि'ति पठन्ति। (*Vyā.* 6.10.4.2-13)

कौशिक (*Kauśika)*—

1. यथा येन क्रमेण दीक्षिष्यमाणा भवन्ति दीक्षामह इत्यवधारयन्ति। तत्र तदैव क्रमेणार्षेयवरणब्राह्मणभारताङ्गिरसबार्हस्पत्यभारद्वाजवैश्वामित्राघमर्षण**कौशिके**त्येवं सकृदाश्रावितेऽध्वर्युरित्याश्रावणादेरनभ्यावृत्तिः। (*Vyā.* 11.1.14)

कौषीतकि (*Kauṣītaki)*—

1. **कौषीतक्या**दीनां तु श्रोत्रियाणां समिध्येव द्वयोराहुत्योर्होमकल्पविहितस्यास्य प्रशंसार्थमाह—'उभौ हि स लोकाववेदिमञ्चामुञ्च' इति। (*Vyā.* 1.5.1.13-16)
2. **कौषीतका**दीन्यग्न्युपस्थानानि याजमानानीच्छतः समुच्चयानि। केचित् **कौषीतका**दीनामेव समुच्चयमिच्छन्ति, ब्राह्मणग्रहणात्। (*Vyā.* 1.6.5.4)
3. तथा **कौषीतकि**नः समामनन्ति–'आहवनीयं पुनरभ्यावृत्त' इति। (*Vyā.* 5.1.1.6)

गालव (*Gālava)*— Propounder of one of the four sub-*Śākhās* of Vādhūlas.

1. के ते चत्वारो वाधूलाः ? कौण्डिन्याग्निवेश्य**गालव**शाङ्खानाम् कल्पाः। (*Vyā.* 1.1.1.5)

जैमिनि *(Jaimini)*—

1. पितृयज्ञस्य दर्शपूर्णमासयोरङ्गत्वानङ्गत्वे विप्रतिपत्तिराचार्याणाम्। 'अनङ्गत्वमि'ति **जैमिनिः**। (*Vyā.* 2.1.2.42)

2. अथातिरात्रस्यापि प्रथमाहरत्वं **जैमिनीया** आमनन्ति। तच्चाग्निष्टोमेनानिष्टवतो नोपपद्येत। (*Vyā.* 5.1.1.1-2). Here the word *Jaiminīya* in plural refers to the followers of *Jaimini* school.

3. तदुक्तं **जैमिनिना**–'तन्त्रमध्ये विधानाद्वा मुख्यतन्त्रेण सिद्धिः स्यात्, तन्त्रार्थस्यावशिष्टत्वादि'ति। (*Vyā.* 5.3.1.3)

4. तथा च भगवता **जैमिनिना** 'गौश्चाश्वश्चेति श्रुत्यन्तरे दृष्टस्य बहुद्रव्यस्य वाक्यस्यार्थं विचारयता 'भागित्वाद्वा गवां स्यादि'ति गवामेव प्राधान्यमभ्यधायि। (*Vyā.* 6.12.2.11)

5. अभ्युपगतं च भगवता **जैमिनिना**। तच्छिष्यैश्च प्रकृतिविकृत्यर्थश्चाग्निरस्तीति यतस्तैरभिहितम् (*Vyā.* 7.1.1.1)

   Here Āryadāsa has very respectfully used the word *Bhagavān* twice for *Jaimini.*

पाणिनि *(Pāṇini)*—

1. स्मर्यन्ते हि कर्तारो यास्क**पाणिनि**वाधूलप्रभृतयः। (*Vyā.* 1.1.1.1)

2. यथा मण्डूका उत्प्लुत्योत्प्लुत्यागच्छन्ति तथा ह्यधिकारगतिर्भवतीति **पाणिन्या**दिभिः स्मर्यते। (*Vyā.* 2.1.2.1)

पिङ्गल *(Piṅgala)*—

1. 'यजुषामपि सर्वेषां छन्द आपादनीयमि'ति एवं हि भगवान् **पिङ्गला**चार्य आह स्म। (*Vyā.* 11.3.1)

   Here Āryadāsa has very respectfully used the word *Bhagavān* for *Piṅgalācārya*, the author of *Chandaḥ-sūtra*

बादरायण *(Bādarāyaṇa)*—

1. 'समास्त्वाऽग्न' इत्येता आगन्तवोऽन्ते स्युः। अन्ते तु **बादरायण**स्येत्येवं सति 'ज्योतिष्मतीमुत्तमामन्वाहे'त्यनुवादोऽर्थवादसंबन्धार्थः। (*Vyā.* 7.3.1.5-6)

2. एकादशिनीविकारे बहुयूपकेऽश्वमेधे द्विस्तावत्वविधानसामर्थ्याद् रथाक्षा–न्तरालसामर्थ्यताऽनुपपत्तेर्यथासंभवमन्तरालानि भवेयुरिति **बादरायण**भिप्रायेण वा वैकल्पिकं वेदिसम्मानमश्वमेधे स्यात्। (*Vyā.* 7.4.4.15)

It may be pointed out that *Bādarāyaṇa* is regarded as the author the *Brahmsūtra* and his name occurs there (1.3.23, 33; 3.2.41; 3.4.8; 4.1.99; 4.3.15; 4.7.12). But here his views have been quoted as a ritualist.

बोधायन *(Bodhāyana* and *Baudhāyana)*—

Here I would like to point out that Āryadāsa has used both the words *Bodhāyana* and *Baudhāyana* in singular, former indicating the name of Ācārya and the latter, always in plural, for the followers of Bodhāyana-school, or sometimes in singular indicating the text or *Śākhā* as under—

(a) 1. तथा च **बोधायनः** 'अन्वारंभं पौर्णमास्याः समानोपवसथं करोती'ति। (*Vyā.* 1.3.4.28)

2. **बोधायना**चार्येणाप्येवं विनियोगः कृतः। (*Vyā.* 2.1.1.16)

3. तदुक्तं **बोधायने**न—'समूलमेव बर्हिर्भवतीति **बोधायनः**'। (*Vyā.* 4.4.1.3)

4. **बोधायने**नाप्युक्तम्—'देवानां पितर्णिां परिषूतमसि। देवपितृबर्हिर्मा त्वान्वङ्मा तिर्यगि'ति। (*Vyā.* 4.4.2.18-76)

5. तथा च **बोधायने**नोक्तम्—'प्रोक्षणीशेषेण पिष्टानि संयुयादेवं सवनीयानामि'ति। (*Vyā.* 5.3.1.3)

6. एवं **बोधायना**ग्निवेश्याभ्यामाम्नातम्। (*Vyā.* 6.1.3.18)

7. **बोधायना**चार्यो निर्वक्ति 'इहा इहा इहेतीन्द्रस्याह्वानं', 'बृहदिहेहि हेति ह वा' एनान्तादूचुरिति। तदन्ते 'बृहदन्तान्युपार्वतस्वेति ह वा' एनं तदूचुरिति। (*Vyā.* 6.12.1.51)

8. **बोधायने**नाप्येवमेवोक्तम्। (*Vyā.* 6.15.2.2-3)

9. **बोधायना**चार्येणाम्नातम्—'चतुर्थे च पक्षे धाय्याशब्दचोदितानां तिसृणामेवावधार्य लोके प्रयोगः सर्वासामागन्तूनां ज्योतिष्मतीं परिहाप्येति विकल्पना तुल्या। (*Vyā.* 7.3.1.5-6)

10. **बोधायना**चार्यस्य आक्रमणेष्टकोपधानं पृथिव्यभिमर्शनमात्रम्। (*Vyā.* 7.6.1.18)

11. व्यक्तं च, **बोधायना**चार्येणाभिहितम्। (*Vyā.* 7.14.4.5)

12. अग्नावपि देवसुवां हविःषु **बोधायना**चार्येणोक्तत्वाद्। (*Vyā.* 7.15.1.52)

13. तथा चोक्तं **बोधायने**न 'स वैव स्याद्' (बौधा.श्रौ. १४.३) इति। (*Vyā.* 12.1.2)

14. **बोधायना**चार्येण व्याख्यातः—'एष ह वै परिस्रजी यः खलतिः परिक्लेश्य' (बौधाश्रौ. १८.१) इति। (*Vyā.* 14.1.1)

15. तथा चोक्तं द्वैधे—'एतानि च नित्यानि च दद्यादि'ति **बोधायनः**। (*Vyā.* 14.9.3)

(*b*) 1. यथा प्रतीचीः स्फ्येन वेदिमिति प्राञ्च उत्तरतः कूर्चे 'ओषधीभ्यः' इति संकल्प्य मन्त्रं च **बौधायनी**याः पठन्ति। (*Vyā.* 1.5.2.17-18)

2. तथा च **बौधायनाः** प्राशने प्रयुञ्जन्ते। (*Vyā.* 1.5.2.20)

3. **बौधायनी**ये उभयथा तयोर्गमनदर्शनादाचार्येणापि इष्यत इति। (*Vyā.* 2.3.2.22)

4. अन्येऽपि **बौधायना**दय एवमेवामनन्ति। (*Vyā.* 5.2.1.4-8)

5. तस्य पश्वाप्यायनं **बौधायनी**ये विहितमिति। नात्र वाचयतीति दर्शनादन्येषु वाचनं गम्यते। (*Vyā.* 5.2.3.12-20)

6. 'तानि सार्धं कुरुतादि'ति **बौधायनाः** पठन्ति। (*Vyā.* 5.3.1.6)

7. 'पदे युगे प्रक्रमेऽरत्नावियति शम्यायां च मानार्थेषु याथाकामी'ति **बौधयानी**ये शुल्ब उक्तम्। (*Vyā.* 6.1.1.3)

8. तथा च **बौधायनाः** 'एवं पत्नीकेशवर्जमि'त्यामनन्ति। (*Vyā.* 6.1.3.18)

9. **बौधायना** आमनन्ति–'अथ यद् ब्राह्मणेनानादिष्टं भवति 'प्राजापत्यमसि मम भोगाय भव' इत्येव तत् प्रतिगृह्णातीति। (*Vyā.* 6.1.4.7)

10. **बौधायना** आमनन्ति 'पुनरुपनह्य सोमोष्णीषेण वाससा समायत्यात्रैव चर्मणि सादयती'ति। (*Vyā.* 6.3.1.13)

11. 'अथैतस्यैव बर्हिषः स्तीर्णस्य पर्यवलोपं स्तम्बयजुर्हरेदि'ति **बौधायनाः**। (*Vyā.* 6.4.1.4-7)

12. द्वादश प्रादेशम् **बौधायनाः** सदोहविर्धानयोः शौल्बिकमेव परिमाणम्। (*Vyā.* 6.4.2.4-29)

13. प्रागाहवनीयप्रणयनाद्वत्सापाकरणं **बौधायना** आमनन्ति। (*Vyā.* 6.8.3.30)

14. **बौधायना** आमनन्ति 'अथाभिषोष्यन्तः सर्वत एव राजानं पर्युपविशन्ति। पश्चात्प्राङ्मुखोऽध्वर्युरुपविशति। तस्य दक्षिणं बाहुमनु यजमानो, दक्षिणतः

प्रतिप्रस्थाता, उत्तरत आग्नीध्रोऽन्तरेण प्रतिप्रस्थातारं चाग्नीध्रं च यश्चतुर्थोऽभिषुणोती'ति। (*Vyā.* 6.10.1.3)

15. उद्वासने स्थानविशेषान् **बौधायनाः** आमनन्ति—'पात्रियां यान् पञ्चधोपस्तृणीते। मध्यतः पुरोडाशमभिघारितमुद्वासयति। पुरस्ताद् धानाः दक्षिणतः करम्भान् पश्चात्परिवापमामिक्षामुत्तरत' इति। (*Vyā.* 6.10.3.26)

16. अध्वर्योरपि **बौधायनै**श्चमसभक्ष आम्नातम्। (*Vyā.* 6.11.4.19)

17. कर्मान्ते **बौधायना** आमनन्ति—'तथेमावध्वर्यू अचमसौ भवतः। (*Vyā.* 6.11.4.19)

18. **बौधायना** अप्येवमामनन्ति। तेषां पुरस्तादुपरिष्टाद्वा निरुप्तक्रमेण पशुपुरोडाशेन चरति। (*Vyā.* 6.12.1.51)

19. तथाहि **बौधायना** आमनन्ति—'क्व उ खलु माध्यन्दिनीया निरुप्यन्त इति क्षुल्लकवैश्वदेवस्य स्तोत्र इत्येव ब्रूयात्। क्व उ खलु तृतीयसवनीया निरुप्यन्त इति माहेन्द्रस्य स्तोत्र इत्येव ब्रूयादि'ति। (*Vyā.* 6.12.2.68-69)

20. अध्वर्योरपि होतृचमसादीनां **बौधायना** आमनन्ति। (*Vyā.* 6.14.1.1)

21. **बौधायन**ीयकल्पे—'सर्वा इष्टकाः ससूददोहसाः 'तयादेवतसूददोहसाभ्यां च सहासपत्नेषूक्ताक्षरसंपदुपपद्यते। (*Vyā.* 7.6.4.20-21)

22. य**द्बौधायनी**यानामिष्टकाजपे च दर्शनान्नदवत्या विषयं परिहाप्यान्यत्र सूददोहसानुचरणमक्षरसंपत्तिलिङ्गादित्येक एव पक्ष इति केचित्। (*Vyā.* 7.6.4.20-21)

21. याः काश्चन विशिष्टा **बौधायनी**ये दृष्टत्वात्। (*Vyā.* 9.4.4.32)

भवस्वामी *(Bhavasvāmi)*—

1. प्रथमः पक्षो भगवता **भवस्वामि**ना परिगृहीतः। (*Vyā.* 12.1.4)

   Here Āryadāsa has very respectfully used the word *Bhagavān* for *Bhavasvāmi.*

भारद्वाज *(Bhāradvāja)*—

1. **भारद्वाजी**येऽपि तादृशं वचनमस्ति 'यथा प्रकृत्येव वर्तेरन्नि'ति। (*Vyā.* 4.4.2.18-76)

2. **भारद्वाजे**न प्रथमसोमेऽप्यग्निष्टोमसंस्थे साद्यस्क्रे लघीयसो

विकल्पानुपादित्सुना दर्शितं यथा 'प्रवर्ग्यताग्निचित्यता नैकयूपते'ति। (*Vyā.* 6.4.1.2)

3. तथा हि **भारद्वाजी**ये सूत्रे अपः प्रवर्ग्यत्वमुक्तम्। (*Vyā.* 14.4.2)

मनु *(Manu)*—

1. उक्तं च भगवता **मनु**ना—

'यस्मिन् कर्मणि यास्तु स्युरुक्ताः प्रत्यङ्गदक्षिणाः।

स एव ता आददीत' (भजेरन् सर्व एव वा) (मनु. ८.२०८) इति। (*Vyā.* 1.1.2.17)

2. **मनु**ना संभूय समुत्थाने पठितः—

सर्वेषामर्धिनो मुख्यास्तदर्धस्यार्धिनोऽर्धिनः।

तृतीयिनस्तृतीयांशाश्चतुर्थांशास्तु पादिनः। (तु.मनु. ८.२१०) इति। (*Vyā.* 6.12.2.27)

3. अथापि च यत्र स्मृतिशास्त्रेष्वनृत**मनु**क्तं तत्तत्परिग्रहार्थम्—

शूद्रविट्क्षत्रविप्राणां यत्रोक्तेऽर्थे भवेद्वधः।

तत्र वक्तव्यमनृतं तद्धि सत्याद्विशिष्यते॥ (मनु. ८.१०४)

इति **मनु**नाभिहितम्। (*Vyā.* 6.12.2.27)

4. उक्तं च भगवता **मन्वाचार्येण** —

सर्वेषामर्धिनो मुख्यास्तदर्धेनार्धिनोऽपरे।

तृतीयिनस्तृतीयांशाश्चतुर्थांशास्तु पादिनः॥ इति (मनु. ८.२१०) (*Vyā.* 6.12.2.27)

Here Āryadāsa has very respectfully used the word *Bhagavān* twice for *Manu.*

यास्क *(Yāska)*—

1. स्मर्यन्ते हि कर्तारो **यास्क**पाणिनिवाधूलप्रभृतयः। (*Vyā.* 1.1.1.1)

2. उक्तं च भगवता **यास्क**मुनिना—'साक्षात्कृतधर्माण ऋषयो बभूवुस्तेऽवरेभ्योऽसाक्षात्कृत-धर्मभ्य उपदेशेन मन्त्रान् संप्रादुः। उपदेशाय ग्लायन्तोऽवरे विल्मग्रहणायेमं ग्रन्थं समाम्नासिषुः' (निरु. १.२०) इति। (*Vyā.* 1.1.1.1)

3. दक्षिणशब्दस्य हस्तप्रकृतित्वं भगवता **यास्के**नाभिहितं 'दिग् हस्तप्रकृतिः' (निरु. १.७) इति। (*Vyā.* 3.6.2.19)

Here Āryadāsa has very respectfully used the word *Bhagavān* twice for *Yāska.*

वसिष्ठ *(Vasiṣṭha)—*

1. **वसिष्ठस्य** सर्व उक्थ्याद् यस्तृतीयसवनाभिवृद्धिरेवेति मन्यमानो न पृथङ् निर्दिशति। अतो दर्शनद्वयमाचार्यस्येति गम्यते।(*Vyā.* 13.3.1)

वासिष्ठः *(Vāsiṣṭha)—*

1. आमुष्यायण इति **वासिष्ठो** भार्गव इति परमप्रकृत्यैव निर्देशः। (*Vyā.* 6.1.3.22-23)

वृषमन्त्र *(Vṛṣaamantra)—*

1. **वृषमन्त्रेण** तावदनूच्याभिमन्त्रणान्तरं दृश्यते। (*Vyā.* 10.6.1.23-26)

शाङ्ख *(Śānkha)—*

1. के ते चत्वारो वाधूलाः ? कौण्डिन्याग्निवेश्यगालव**शाङ्खा**नाम् कल्पाः। (*Vyā.* 1.1.1.5)

शाट्ययन *(Śāṭyāyana)—*

1. अजस्रेष्वग्निषु न प्रवसतीति **शाट्यायनः**। (*Vyā.* 1.5.2.24-27)

शालीकि *(Śālīki)—*

1. तथा च द्वैधे 'आहवनीयादेवैनौ विहरेदिति **शालीकि**रि'ति। (*Vyā.* 1.2.1.1)

2. 'अत्रो ह स्माह **शालीकि**रतिपन्नः खल्वेष भवति' इत्यादिना सद्यस्कालताऽभिहिता। (*Vyā.* 2.1.1.1)

3. तथा च द्वैधे **शालीकि**पक्षः 'प्रातःसवन एव सर्वेभ्य सवनेभ्यः सवनीयान् निर्वपेदि'ति। (*Vyā.* 6.9.1.17)

शौनक *(Śaunaka)—*

1. प्रणवादि उच्चैरूर्ध्वं वा प्रणवादीति **शौनकः**। (*Vyā.* 3.5.1.8)

10. Ācāryas quoted without name by the phrase अन्ये *(Anye)*, **अपरे** *(Apare)*, **एके** *(Eke)* **and केचित्** *(Kecit)***—**

Besides quoting and referring to the views of above Ācāryas by name, Āryadāsa very frequently also mentions the views of some others Ācāryas by using the terms अन्ये, अपरे, एके and केचित्. Here without quoting them I whould like to give only references from *Vyākhyā*—

अन्ये- **१.**१.१.६^{३}, २.१०, २.१.१, ३.४.२९, ४.१.२५-३१, ५.२.१३-१६, २०, २४-२७, ६.१.७, २०-२६; **२.**१.२.१४, २१, ३.३२-३७, ४.१, १३-१४, ५.६-७, ८-१०, २.१.१३, १५, २५-३३, ४.७-८, ४४, ४९, ३.२.१०-१२; **२.**३.२.१८; **३.**१.१.११, २.३१-३३, २.१.१-३, २.९, १५, ३.१.१, ४.१.४८, ६.१.३; **४.**२.१.३७, २.२१-२२, ३.१.३९, ४.१.३^{२}, २.१८-७६, ३.१०; **५.**१.१.४३, २.१.१, ३.१.६, ३.३.३; **६.**१.१.२, १४, ३.१८, ४.२.७८, ८३, ५.१.८, ६.१.९, ८.३.३०, १०.१.७५, ३.३^{२}, २६, ११.१.२८^{२}, ४.१८, १३.२.३५, १५.१.४१; **१२.**१.२, ४, २.२^{२}, ४.१^{२}; **१३.**१.१, २; **१४.**४.२, ६.१, ९.३, १०.१

अपरे- **१.**१.२.६-८, २.२.१४, ३.४.२९, ४.१.११-२१, ९, २.८; **२.**१.१.१^{२}, ६, ७, १४, २०, ४.१०, २.१.२५-३३, २.३१-३२; **३.**२.१.१-३, ५.२.६; **४.**२.३.७०, ३.१.३२, ३३-७३; **५.**१.२.२१; **६.**२.१.३, ४.२, ७८, ५.१.३६, ९.४.१२, १०.२.१-२, ११.१.१, २८, ४.५; **७.**१.१.३६, १३.२.४, १५.१.५२; **१२.**१.३, २.३, ३.२, ५

एके- **४.**२.१.२८; **५.**१.२.४, ३.१.२३; **९.**२.३.४; **१२.**२.५

केचिद्- **१.**१.१.१, ६^{२}, १६, २.६-८, १०, ३.१०-१६, १९-२०, २१-२६, २.१.१, १४, ३.१.४, ४.२८, २९, ४.१.११-२१, २५-३१, ५.१.१०, २.३, ५, ८, ११-१२, १३-१६, १७-१८, २४-२७^{२}, ६.१.७, २०-२६, ४.१-५, १९-२४, ५.४-५; **२.**१.१.१, ९, १६, २३-२६, ३४, २.११-१३, १४, २०^{२}, ३४, ३.१७-२९, ३०-३१, ३२-३७, ४.८, १३-१४, ५.८-१०, २०, २.१.१३, १५, २५-३३^{२}, ३६, ४०-४२, २.२, ५, २६, ३१-३२, ४.७-८, १०, ३७, ४१, ३.१.८४-८५, २.१०-१२, १७, १९-२०^{२}, २३-२९, ३.५७, ५९, १०२-१०४, १०५; **३.**१.२.१८-२०, ३.३१-३३, ६.१-३, २.१.१-३, ९-११, २.१६, ३.१-१२, २१-२४, ३.२.३, ३.२१, ४.१.४८^{२}, २.१, २५, ५.१.८, २.६, ११; **४.**१.१.४४-४७, ४.२६-२८, २.१.३, २३, ३७^{२}, २.९, ३.७०^{२}, ४.४७-४९, ३.१.३१^{२}, ३२^{२}, ३३-७३, २.१, ४.३७^{३}, ४.१.३^{३}, ११, २.१८-७६, ४.१०; **५.**१.१.१-२, ४०, २.२१^{२}, २.१.१, ३.१२-२०, ४.२२, ३.१.२३-२४, ३२-३३, ५७, २.२९-३०, ४६, ३.२, २४-२५; **६.**१.१.२^{४}, ४, १४, २.३१, ३.७-८, २.१.३, २.५, ३.२^{२}, ३.३.१, १३^{२}, ५३, ४.१.३१-३४, ७३, २.४-२९, ७८, ८३,

३.३-३३[२], ३६-३७, ५.१.३२, ३६[२], ४.२१, ३७, ६.१.९, २.४०, ८.१.२१[४], ३.२९, ३०[२], ९.१.१७, २.५, ३.७[२], १४, २४-२५, ४.१३, १०.१.६१-६६[२], ७५, २.१-२, ३.८, १९, ४.१[२], ११.१.१, २४[२], २५, २८, २.११, ४२, ४.१९[२], १२.१.५१[४], २.२७, ६८-५९, ३.१-५, १५-१६, १३.१.२, १४.१.४३, २.३७, १५.१.१९, ४१, ३.१०३, ४.१-६, २५; **७.**१.१.३५-३६, ४.१.२, ५, ५.२.७-१०, ४.३, ६.२.१५, ४.७, २०-२१, ७.५.१, १२, १४.१.२७, ३.१२, ४.२, १५.१.५२[३], ५४; **८.**१.२.१३, १८, २.१.३-४, २.८, १२, ३.१५-१६; **९.**१.२.४३, ३.८०, २.२.१०, ३.४६, ४.११-१३, ४.४.१-३; **१०.**१.१.२, ५.२.१६, ७.२.३६-३७, ४.२०, ८.१.२, २.१४, ९.१.३६, २.१९; **११.**१.२[२], २.२[२]; **१२.**१.३, २.१[२], २, ३, ५, ३.२, ३, ४, ५, ६, ४.१, ३; **१३.**४.१; **१४.**१.१, ५.२[३], १०.१[२], १२.१, १३.१, १५.१[२]

11. Importance of विधि *(Vidhi)* and अर्थवाद *(Arthavāda)* as noticed by Āryadāsa in his *Vyākhyā*—

Vidhi and *Arthavāda*, both play very important role in the treatment of rituals as a main subject of the *Brāhmaṇas*, whereas in the *Kalpasūtras* dealing with the *Śrauta*-rituals, *Arthavāda* has no important role. Mostly it has been excluded from the *Śrauta*-texts. However, Āryadāsa in his *Vyākhyā* refers to both of them as is evident from the following references—

(a) **विधि** *(Vidhi)*—

1. कथं विधास्यतीति यद्युच्येत, नायं **विधिः**। कस्मात्। वाक्यैरभिहितानामर्थानां सन्निवेशविशेषमात्रमेव कल्पसूत्रकारैः क्रियते। यत्रापि विधिप्रत्ययगन्धोऽस्ति, तत्रापि नाविदितवेदनार्थं, तदपि ब्राह्मणवाक्यानुकरणमेव। यथा 'अमावास्यायामेव दीक्षेत' इति। (*Vyā.* 1.1.1.1)

2. 'याज्ञतीर्थ्यादापूर्णां पौर्णमासीमुपवसेद्' इत्यस्माद्विधेरन्योऽयं **विधिः** कृतः। (*Vyā.* 2.1.1.1)

3. यद्यु बह्व्यः स्युस्ता एवमेव दोहयेदित्युक्तानुवादः स्यात् विधिर्वा[२]। **विधि**पक्षे उत्तरास्वप्यावृत्तिः। (*Vyā.* 2.1.3.30-31)

4. अपि वा शाखान्तरेष्ववघातान्ते कपालोपधानान्ते च प्रातर्दोहमामनन्ति। तद् द्योतनार्थं शाखान्तरस्थमपि **विधिं** केनचित्प्रकारेण सूचयन्तीत्युक्तम्। (*Vyā.* 2.1.3.32-37)

5. पक्षान्तर**विधि**त्सयेष्टिपक्षे दोषोद्भावनम्। (*Vyā.* 3.2.1.9-11)

6. श्वोऽषाढाभिरित्याद्युक्तं वैश्वदेवेन प्रसिद्धं प्रज्ञातेन **विधि**ना। (*Vyā.* 4.2.1.3)

7. द्रव्यदेवतासंबन्ध**विधि**वाक्ये श्रूयमाणो गुणो भवत्यत एष कालो यागस्य। (*Vyā.* 4.3.1.1)

8. तद् 'दक्षिणेन गार्हपत्यमिति यज्ञायुधसंसादनस्य देशो **विधीयते**। (*Vyā.* 4.4.1.3)

9. पक्षाश्रितत्वमेषां ब्राह्मणे कल्पे वा नोपलभ्यते। अतो विशेषेण **विधि**रानाय्यः। (*Vyā.* 4.4.1.3)

10. निवृत्तेषु च प्रयाजादयः सगुणा **विधी**यन्ते। (*Vyā.* 4.4.1.3)

11. यथा 'परिश्रयन्ति', 'समूलं बर्हिर्भवति' इत्युत्पत्ति**विधि**पाठक्रमकारणब्राह्मणा–नुसारेणैवेहाप्याम्नातम्। अत एषां प्राकृत एव क्रम इति। (*Vyā.* 4.4.1.3)

12. अथ यजमानो राजानं देवयजनं याचतीति नैदेशिकेन **विधि**ना। तत्र च पक्षद्वयम्। 'राजन् देवयजनं मे देहि' इत्युक्तो राजाऽऽदित्यमुपतिष्ठते 'नमस्त आदित्य' इत्यादिना ददातीत्यन्यः संशिष्टो ब्रूयात्। स्वयमेव वा राजा ददातीति मनसा ध्यायेद्। अथवा 'स त्रीन् हिरण्यशल्कानादाये'त्यादिना विधानेन सोमादीन् याचति। (*Vyā.* 6.1.1.7)

13. नैदेशिकोऽपि **विधिः** 'स्वे दक्ष' इति समारोपणम्। (*Vyā.* 6.3.4.13)

14. 'निमेष एतस्योक्थ्यस्य प्रतिगर' इति। प्रतिगराभावोऽभिहितो न तु न्यासप्रणवयोर्निमेष–करण**विधिः**। (*Vyā.* 6.9.2.32)

15. स्रुक्ष्विति पूर्वं स्थितस्य 'चतुर्होतारं ध्रुवायां व्याचष्टे' इत्यस्य स्थाने विहितस्योपलक्षणं प्राकृतस्य। नापूर्व**विधिः**। (*Vyā.* 6.10.4.20)

16. 'होतरुपह्वयस्व' इत्येवं मैत्रावरुणादीन्। अथवा नैदेशिकेन **विधि**ना अग्निहोत्रा 'होतरुप मा ह्वयस्व'। ऋतवो होत्राशंसिनः। 'होत्राशंसिन उप मा ह्वयध्वमि'ति तन्त्रेणैव। (*Vyā.* 6.11.3.51)

17. ध्रुवमवनयन्नध्वर्युरात्मानं प्रत्यवनयेद्यजमानस्य नाम गृह्णीयात्। 'ध्रुवं ध्रुवेण हविषा तेऽव सोमं नयामस्यसावि'त्यौपानुवाक्ये **विधि**रनेन विकल्पते। (*Vyā.* 6.14.2.24)

18. अस्ति च तैत्तिरीयकप्रवचने पक्षद्वयं 'पञ्चचितयो भवन्ति षट्चितयो भवन्ती'ति। शुल्बे च द्वयोः पक्षयोरिष्टका सहस्रोपधानप्रकारः परिकल्पितः। अथवा नात्र **याज्ञतीर्थिको विधि**रभिप्रेतः। (*Vyā.* 7.7.5.7-10)

19. एवमिष्टकावकाशाः सुष्ठु शोभनीकृता भवन्तीति। एवं च नित्यवच्छ्रुतः प्रैषो याज्ञतीर्थिकस्य **विधे**रनित्यस्यार्थेन प्रवर्तत' इति न्यायो न कल्पितः स्यात्। (*Vyā.* 7.7.5.7-10)

20. 'असञ्चर एव वल्मीकवपायामन्वस्यती'ति शाखान्तरस्थो वैकल्पिको **विधिः**। (*Vyā.* 7.13.2.18-19)

21. अधर्मकत्वमेव प्रायेणाचार्येणाभिप्रेतं दर्वीहोमं करोतीत्येवं **विधि**र्भवितुमर्हतीति। (*Vyā.* 7.14.3.18)

22. तैत्तिरीयके तावत् प्रवचनेऽञ्जलेः करणत्वं समाम्नातम्। इह स्रुवधारणेऽञ्जलिः करणभूतः, न साक्षाद्धोमं प्रति। अतः शाखान्तरस्थोऽयं **विधिः** 'अञ्जलिना जुहोतीत्यनेन विकल्पते' इति द्रष्टव्यम्। (*Vyā.* 7.14.4.17)

23. तैत्तिरीयके समस्तेन हस्तग्रहणम्। शाखान्तरस्थोऽयं विभाग**विधि**र्द्रष्टव्यः। तयोर्विरोधे विकल्पः। (*Vyā.* 7.15.1.54)

24. गुण**विधि**वाक्ये अनेकगुणविधानानुपत्तेः, कर्मान्तरता वा। (*Vyā.* 8.1.2.18)

25. अश्विनोः पूष्णश्च निगमस्थानेषु असमासैश्च वचनम्। **विधि**निगमयोरेकरूप्यां पदशः। समासयोश्च शब्दान्तरत्वात्। (*Vyā.* 9.4.1.16)

26. अतिरात्रग्रहणं नियमार्थमस्मिन् पक्षे। पूर्वस्मिन् पक्षेऽविधिः। (*Vyā.* 9.5.1.13-14)

27. षष्ठमासि परिपूर्णे पर्यावृत्य पुनरानीय देवयजनसमीपं व्रजान्तरेऽश्वं निरुन्धन्ति। अश्वोत्सर्गप्रभृति षण्मासद्वयमभिधायानन्तर**विधिः**। (*Vyā.* 10.4.1.1)

28. त्वमहमनेनेत्युक्तस्य कालविशेष**विधि**त्सया वेद्यै श्रोणिं प्रति यथा जघनेन प्रवस्यः, तथा तद्वदति। (*Vyā.* 10.4.3.41-43)

29. अश्वादिसम्बन्धाद् 'अश्वस्तूपरो गोमृग' इत्ययमनुवाको **विधि**त्सितः। (*Vyā.* 10.5.3.33-40)

30. एतं रथं देवतार्थं च युक्तं मनुष्य आस्थातुं नोत्सहत इति **कल्पान्तरविधि**द्वारेणैत-दश्वसादनधर्मः स्तूयते। (*Vyā.* 10.5.4.14-17)

31. अत एवाचार्येणोक्तं 'यत्र क्व चाहीनो वा सत्रो वैष एवैतासां प्रकृतीनां प्रदेश' इति। प्रदेशः प्रशासनं **विधिः**। (*Vyā.* 11.2.3)

32. रथन्तरपृष्ठता नियम्यते 'रथादीनां प्रस्तरस्य प्रत्याम्नायत्वं प्रस्तरेण चे'ति क्वचित्समुच्चय**विधानात्**। (*Vyā.* 11.2.3)

33. सावित्रग्रहणमन्त्रस्यानुवादो विशेष**विधि**त्सया। (*Vyā.* 11.2.4)

34. प्रदेशप्रकारकथनम् 'एतयैव जुहुयादेतया भक्षयेदि'ति। यया जुहोति तयैव भक्षयेदित्यभिप्रायः। न होमं प्रति **विधिः**, तस्या **विधिः**, प्रकृतितः प्राप्तत्वात्। (*Vyā.* 11.3.2)

35. यत्रापवादः सामर्थ्यं वा नास्ति तत्र सार्वकालिको **विधिः**। (*Vyā.* 12.3.4)

36. तस्माद् **विधि**प्रतिषेधयोर्विकल्पो युक्त इत्यन्ये। (*Vyā.* 12.4.1)

37. ओन्नयनादित्यभि**विधिः**। (*Vyā.* 12.4.1)

38. दीक्षेत व्रतीति वक्ष्यमाणानामेव कर्मणां **विधिः**। (*Vyā.* 14.7.1)

39. कथं वा व्रात्यवादकथाङ्गानि प्रसिद्धानि प्रतोदपाणिः रथारूढश्चरतीति **विधिः**। (*Vyā.* 14.7.1)

40. नामधेयैस्तद्धर्मकाणि कर्माणि **विधी**यन्ते। (*Vyā.* 14.10.1)

41. अहीन**विधि**त्वाद् द्वादशोपसत्त्वम्। (*Vyā.* 14.13.2)

(b) **अर्थवाद** *(Arthavāda)*—

1. 'आयुष्यमि'त्यादयो मन्त्रवर्णा **अर्थवादाः**। (*Vyā.* 1.6.3.23-24)

2. वेदस्य द्रव्यं दर्भाः। वेदपरिवासनानाम् 'आपो वै दर्भाः' इत्य**र्थवादे** दर्शनात्। (*Vyā.*2.1.2.2)

3. तुषधान्यमिति प्राप्ते 'अग्निरमुष्मिँल्लोक आसी'दित्यस्मिन्ननुवाके 'तेऽग्निं पशुभूतमग्नये मेधायालभन्ते'त्यारभ्य 'तस्मात् सीरलाङ्गलेन कृष्ट्वाऽनुसीतं वपन्ति। तौ प्राजायेतामि'त्येवमन्तेन ग्रन्थेना**र्थवाद**रूपेण व्रीहियवौ विहितौ। (*Vyā.*2.1.4.2)

4. न नृम्णेये बलाधानेऽ**र्थवादो**ऽपि नास्तीत्ययं छन्दोब्राह्मणमेवैतन्मन्त्रलिङ्गादेव कल्पित-मित्यर्थः। (*Vyā.*3.1.1.25)

5. शकटद्वयस्योपरि एकं छदिर्निधेयम्। इतरथा तृतीयस्य हविर्धानस्यावरुध्या इत्य**र्थवादो** नोपपद्यत इति। (*Vyā.*6.5.1.8)

6. परिमाणं विकृतौ प्रत्यवरोहणीये **अर्थवाद**संबन्धार्थं द्वादशं शतमनूद्यते 'तस्य द्वादशं शतं दक्षिणा' इति। तत्प्रकृतितः प्राप्तमनुद्यते। (*Vyā.*6.12.2.27)

7. एवं सति यजुरन्तमं कुर्यादिति सावित्राण्येवाष्टावपेक्ष्य यजुषोऽन्ततायां मन्त्रपाठक्रम एव स्तूयत इत्यवगन्तव्यम्। 'ऋचमन्तमां कुर्यादि'ति चास्यैवा**र्थवाद**तां प्रतिपद्यते। (*Vyā.*7.1.1.35-36)

8. ततः पूर्वमष्टावृचो निगद्य नवमेन यजुषा जुहोति। ऋचमन्तमां कुर्यादित्यपि पुनर्वाचनिक एव क्रमः, **अर्थवादो** वा। (*Vyā.*7.1.1.35-36)

9. 'दध्ना पुरस्ताज्जुहोत्याज्येनोपरिष्टादि'त्यनुवादोऽ**र्थवाद**संबन्धार्थः। (*Vyā.*7.14.3.11)

12. References to आगम *(Āgama)* and इतिहासपुराण *(Itihāspurāṇa)* in *Vyākhyā.*

(a) **आगम** *(Āgama)*—

1. अथायमपि वाधूलेनाचार्येण रचितः कल्पः। तस्य सुखज्ञानार्थमस्माभिर्निगदसिद्धवर्जमस्मद् बुद्ध्या**गमा**नुरूपं व्याख्यायते। (*Vyā.* 1.1.1.1)

2. सर्वकर्मापवर्गे यज्ञायुधानां वृक्षनियमप्रमाणाकृतिविशेषा अनुपदादा**गम**यितव्याः। (*Vyā.* 1.1.1.5)

3. सर्वकर्मकर्तृकरणेऽग्न्यगारसंमार्जनोपलेपनसंमार्जनपात्रप्रक्षालनादि स्मृतिशास्त्राद-नुपदादाचाराच्चा**गम**यितव्यम्। (*Vyā.*1.5.1.2)

4. अन्यत्रापि वाचःस्थानान्यनुपदादा**गम**यितव्यानि। (*Vyā.*4.1.1.18-30)

5. हविषां तन्त्राणां चोच्चैरुपांशुता विध्यवशेषादा**गम**यितव्येति। (*Vyā.*4.1.3.29)

6. धनुरिव प्रस्तरो धारयितव्य इत्या**गमः**। (*Vyā.*6.4.1.62)

7. शुल्बकारेण व्यायाममात्रे चयनविधानाद् देवरथचक्रप्रमाणमित्याचार्येणाभिप्रेतमिति केषांचिद्दर्शनम्, तत्प्रमाणं तज्ज्ञेभ्य **आगम**यितव्यम्। (*Vyā.*7.4.4.15)

8. येन अवरोधादिपर उत्करे ज्ञातरूपे त उज्जभ्योऽपहतन्त्या**गम**यितव्यानि। (*Vyā.* 10.3.2.11)

9. न्यूङ्खो बह्वृचेभ्य **आगम**यितव्यः। (*Vyā.*11.2.4)

10. सर्वत्र प्रतिगरो बह्वृचेभ्य **आगम**यितव्यः। (*Vyā.*11.2.4)

Here, it may be pointed out that the word *Āgama* here does not mean a genre of particular text, but acqisition off knowledge handed down and fixed by tradition in the matter if ritualistic injunctions and practices.

(a) **इतिहासपुराण** *(Itihāsapurāṇa)*—

1. ननु लोके**तिहासपुराणे**ष्वन्ये देवा अन्ये पितर इति। सत्यमेवमेतत्। किन्तु पुराणादिप्रसिद्ध्या यज्ञकर्मणि कल्पयितुं न शक्यते। कल्प्यमाने हि

द्रव्यगुणकालानां देवतात्वं व्याहन्येत। तथा सत्यव्यापित्वं स्यात्। के पुनरिह देवाः। ये च सूक्तं भजन्ते येभ्यश्च हविर्निरूप्यते ते देवाः सूक्तभाजो हविर्भाजश्च। तस्मात्तेषामपि देवतात्वम्। देवदेवताशब्दौ च समानार्थौ। (*Vyā.*4.4.2.18-76)

2. ऋषभोत्सर्गः फलवत्कर्म, तस्य महाफलत्वमि**तिहासेषूक्तम्**–

एष्टव्या बहवो पुत्रा यद्येकोऽपि गयां व्रजेत्।

यजेत वाऽश्वमेधेन नीलं वा वृषमुत्सृजेत्॥ (लिखितस्मृति, ९०) इति॥ (*Vyā.*12.2.2)

बह्वृच *(Bahvṛca)*— The term *Bahvṛca* is generally prevalent for the *Ṛgveddins.*

1. तथा च **बह्वृच**ब्राह्मणं—'व्रीहिभिरिष्ट्वा व्रीहिभिरेव यजेत। यवेभ्यो यवैरिष्ट्वा यवैरेव यजेत। व्रीहिभ्योऽपि वा 'व्रीहिभिरिष्ट्वा व्रीहिभिरेव यजेतैते हि सूयवसतरा भवन्ति' इति। (*Vyā.*3.4.1.1)

2. छन्दोग**बह्वृच**विषयाः आध्वर्यवा अपि सूत्रान्तरेषु मार्गणीयाः। (*Vyā.* 9.5.1.13-14)

3. न्यूङ्खो **बह्वृचे**भ्य आगमयितव्यः। (*Vyā.*11.2.4)

4. सर्वत्र प्रतिगरो **बह्वृचे**भ्य आगमयितव्यः। (*Vyā.*11.2.4)

13. References to contemparary Ācāryas—

Besides quoting the views of his predicessors on the ritualistic matters Āryadāsa also quotes his contempary Ācāryas by using the terms इदानीन्तनाः, ऐदंयुगीनाः, and पौरस्त्याः as under—

(a) 1. **इदानीन्तना**स्तु तद्वैपरीत्यादेवं कुर्वन्तीति किमुत एतदन्तो लभ्यते। धर्मनैपुण्यमव-श्यमेषितव्यं यथा पूर्वैः। ततः संवत्सर एव पुरस्तात् समवसानं कार्यमिति। अथवा पूर्वे मन्त्रब्राह्मणत एव प्रयोगं कल्पयन्तो दीर्घकालं परीक्षन्ते। (*Vyā.*11.4.1)

2. **ऐदंयुगीना**स्तु सूत्रकारैः कल्पितं प्रयोगं स्वल्पेनैव कालेन सुन्वाना इत्येवं कुर्वन्तीति। ततः किम् कल्पप्रशंसया कल्पकारप्रशंसया वा, प्रयोक्तुरतिप्ररोचना भवत्येव। (*Vyā.*11.4.1)

(b) 1. **पौरस्त्ये**ऽर्थे रथचक्रविधाने आसंस्कारपरिसमाप्तेर्भवन्ति। (*Vyā.* 1.3.2.30)

2. अनाचान्तेन वा दृष्टार्थं कर्मोद्देशनं कर्तव्यं स्यात्। अतः **पौरस्त्य** एवार्थः। (*Vyā.* 1.5.2.22-24)

3. अतः **पौरस्त्य** एवार्थो न तु श्रुतहानिरश्रुतकल्पना च दोषः। (*Vyā.* 2.1.2.14)

4. द्विवचनं समुदायद्वयापेक्षमिति **पौरस्त्य** उपपद्यते यद्यपि नापिसृज्यते। (*Vyā.* 2.1.4.37)

5. **पौरस्त्याः** प्रोषितेनैव यजमानेनैव। (*Vyā.* 3.3.1.1)

6. आशितश्चातृप्तेर्भुक्तवति प्रसिद्धः सन्न चाबशनमात्रे तृप्त इति नोपपद्यते। अतः **पौरस्त्य** एवार्थः। प्रयाणमन्त्रस्य सामान्येन विधानमस्तीत्यवगन्तव्यम्। (*Vyā.* 6.1.1.7)

7. चोदनालिंगसंयोगाद् अध्वर्योरेवात्र तन्त्रप्रक्रम इति। तदुत्तारतोऽङ्गारान्निरूह्याधिश्रयतीति प्राकृतोऽग्नीदाज्यमधिश्रयेदितीहाधिश्रयणक्रमे चोद्यमाने तन्त्रमेव चोद्यत इति मत्वा **पौरस्त्यं** व्याख्यानं कृतम्। (*Vyā.* 6.6.1.8)

   Here it may be pointed out that Āryadāsa refers to the views of easterners, who were living in the eastern part of the country in his time.

14. References to प्रयोग *(Prayoga)*-type of texts—

Āryadāsa in his *Vyākhyā* frequently refers to the existence and importance of *Prayoga*-texts and at some places he gives *Prayogas*, as is evident from the following references—

1. तत्तत् संस्कारयुक्ता हि मन्त्राः कर्मणो गुणत्वेनाभ्युदयाय भवन्ति। यथा **प्रयोगे** प्रत्यवायो न भवति, तत्तत्संपद्योगे। (*Vyā.* 1.1.1.1)

2. मध्यमं पक्षमाश्रित्यास्माभिः **प्रयोगे** उक्ताः, यद्यत्र क्रियते दर्शपूर्णमासविकारेष्वपि अग्न्याधेयाङ्गेषु तदेव प्रसज्यते। (*Vyā.* 1.1.1.6)

3. किन्तु **प्रयोग**प्राशुभावाय पुनर्मन्त्रेण संभरणमाध्वर्यवम्। (*Vyā.* 1.1.1.6)

4. अथवा 'आशंसायां भूतवच्चे'ति भूतनिर्देश आशु**प्रयोगा**र्थः। (*Vyā.* 1.1.4.8-9)

5. विप्रकर्षसन्निकर्षयोः दुर्ज्ञेयकालत्वात् तेऽत्र **प्रयोगा**संभवात् तत्कालसन्निकृष्टानां तिथीनां तच्छब्दवाच्यता। (*Vyā.* 2.1.1.1)

6. एवं सत्याग्नेये विकृतौ तद्विकारेषु 'वो जुष्टा'निति मन्त्रेऽन्यत्र 'अमुष्मै जुष्टानि'त्येतावदेव श्रवणाद्युष्मत् **प्रयोगो** न भवति। (*Vyā.* 2.1.5.6-7)

7. तत्रापि तस्मिन्नहनि कर्तव्यस्य कर्मकलापस्य महत्त्वात् **प्रयोग**प्राशुभावाय स्यात्। (*Vyā.* 2.2.4.7-8)

8. 'गृणानो हव्यदातये' इत्यत्राभ्यादधाति। आद्याया एव वा कस्मिंश्चिन्न्यासेऽन्येषां **प्रयोगः**। (*Vyā.* 2.3.1.4)

9. एवमभिप्रेत्याचार्येण महेन्द्रयाजीत्यभ्यधायि अथवा गुणविकारसंवत्सर**प्रयोगे** महेन्द्रयागमभिप्रेत्य सौविष्टकृतयागः। (*Vyā.* 3.2.3.36-37)

10. परिधिप्रहरणशंयुवाकयोः समानकालत्वात् क्रमप्रवृत्तित्वाच्च वाचो यथापाठ एव **प्रयोगो** 'वि ते मुञ्चामि', 'विष्णोः शंयोर्' इत्येतयोः। (*Vyā.* 3.3.2.1-2)

11. श्रुत्यन्तरे विहितानामाचार्येणाम्नातानां सर्वत्र प्रकृतावेव वैकल्पिकत्वमुक्तम्। तदेतेषामपि यथाकामं **प्रयोगः** अनुब्राह्मणस्य **प्रयोगः**। (*Vyā.* 3.3.2.4-5)

12. स यज्ञः यज्ञ**प्रयोग**द्वयात् फलापूर्वमुत्पादयति। तस्मिन्नुत्पन्ने सामर्थ्याद् यजमानः फलग्रहणयोग्यो जायते इत्यर्थः। (*Vyā.* 3.3.3.22)

13. अथापि यथा पयो दृतिर्निष्पत्तेः पयः, एवमेष यज्ञः **प्रयोग**द्वयान्ते फलापूर्वमुत्पाद्य स्वरूपेणैवावतिष्ठते। (*Vyā.* 3.3.3.22)

14. आग्रयणं नामेदं कर्म दर्शपूर्णमासवन्नित्यं यावज्जीवं **प्रयोक्त**व्यम्। (*Vyā.* 3.4.1.1)

15. दर्शपूर्णमासवत् तेषां (चातुर्मास्यानां) सकृत्**प्रयोगो** यावज्जीविकत्वं च दृश्यते। (*Vyā.* 4.1.1.1)

16. पुनः **प्रयोगे**ऽपि सत्याप्रथमसंवत्सरपरिसमाप्तेर्व्रतानि नोत्स्रष्टव्यानि। (*Vyā.* 4.1.1.1)

17. पञ्चवर्षादि**प्रयोगा** अपि शाखान्तरेषु विद्यन्ते। (*Vyā.* 4.1.1.1)

18. अस्या इष्टेः पञ्चवर्षादि**प्रयोगे**ष्वनावृत्तिरारम्भनिमित्तत्वात्। (*Vyā.* 4.1.1.44-47)

19. सायं निर्णिक्तै=दुहानाः इति। दोहयोः **प्रयोगः**। (*Vyā.* 4.2.1.12)

20. किन्तु परसम्बोधनार्थाः प्रैषादय एकेनैव **प्रयोक्तव्याः**। (*Vyā.* 4.2.1.28)

21. व्रीहियवयोः प्रकृतितः प्राप्तेस्तुल्यत्वादिह विशेषवचनभावात्**प्रयोग**सौकर्यार्थं यवमयानि सर्वाणि हवींषि स्युः। (*Vyā.* 4.2.1.37)

22. **तत्र प्रयोगः**। आहवनीयकार्यापन्नास्वप्सु वेदोपवाजनं कर्तव्यमिति वेदमुत्पादयन्ति केचित्। उपवाजनस्यावज्वलनार्थत्वादर्थलुप्तमित्यन्ये।

स्फ्यमग्निहोत्रहवणीं स्रुवं जुहूमाज्यस्थालीमिति सादयित्वा पवित्रे आदाय 'यजमान वाचं यच्छे'त्युक्त्वा 'कर्मणे वामि'ति हस्तौ मार्जयित्वा प्रोक्षणीं संस्कृत्य पात्राणि प्रोक्ष्याज्यं निरुप्याधिश्रित्य पर्यग्निकृत्वा स्फ्येनावस्कभ्य संप्रेष्यति-'स्रुवं च स्रुचश्च संमृढ्याज्येनोदेही'ति। प्रैषार्थावाग्नीध्रः करोति। पत्नीमप्यवेक्षयति। ततोऽध्वर्युरुत्पवनान्तं कृत्वा पवित्रे आहवनीयेऽनुप्रहरति। ततो दम्पती ऊर्णासूत्रमये मेखले पर्यस्येते। वासो दशामये इत्यन्ये। ततस्तुषैश्च निष्कासेन चावभृथमवयन्ति। तुषा ऋजीषादीनां प्रत्याम्नायः। निष्कासः पुरोडाशस्य। तुषाणामत्र प्रतिपत्तिविधानात् प्राकृतं तुषोपवपनं न कुर्वन्ति केचित्। अपरे प्रकृतावपि तुषाणामेकदेशस्यैवोपवपनं कुर्वन्ति। तच्छेषैरवभृथावगमनमिति न निवर्तयन्ति। एतत् सर्वमुपादाय यथोक्तमवभृथमव यन्ति। (*Vyā.* 4.2.3.70)

23. तत्र देवाश्च पितरश्चेति व्यपदेशाद्देवेभ्योऽन्ये पितर इति गम्यते। तत्सर्वत्र देवप्रवादेषूभयं **प्रयोक्तव्यम्**। अतः परं परिहाप्य यथा 'देवस्य त्वा सवितुः प्रसवे' इति, तथा। (*Vyā.* 4.4.2.18-76)

24. गृह्या यजमानस्य गार्हपत्योपस्थाने च तेषामेव 'माऽमुत' इत्यभिप्रेतस्य नाम्नः पञ्चम्यन्तस्य **प्रयोगः**। अथवा 'इतः' इत्यत्र कन्याभावादिति स्मरति। 'अमुत' इति वरेण योगादिति। यथाम्नातमेव **प्रयोगः**। (*Vyā.* 4.4.4.18-23)

25. इह 'देवव्रतानि'वचनम् संवत्सर**प्रयोगा**पेक्षम्। अनेकसंवत्सर**प्रयोगे** हि 'इति चातुर्मास्ययाजिनः' इति वचनाद्यावत्**प्रयोगं** व्रतचर्याः। (*Vyā.* 4.5.2.45)

26. अत्र कश्चिदाह—'प्राक् सोमयागात् सान्नाय्यविकाराणाम**प्रयोगः**। (*Vyā.* 5.1.1.1-2)

27. 'पञ्च वै ब्राह्मा' इत्यस्मिन्ननुवाके पक्षत्रयं विहितम्। पञ्चानामनुक्रमेण **प्रयोगः**। (*Vyā.* 5.1.1.1-2)

28. **प्रयोग**प्राशुभावाय बहुतयानि च व्यापन्ननिष्क्रयार्थम्। (*Vyā.* 6.1.1.2)

29. किमस्य यज्ञक्रतोः संस्कृताग्नेः कालं निमित्तीकृत्याग्निहोत्रादिवद् यावज्जीविकोऽभ्यासः, आहोस्वित् सकृत्**प्रयोगः**। (*Vyā.* 6.1.1.2)

30. 'अथातः **प्रयोगा**णामेव यज्ञक्रतूनेतान् प्रयोक्ष्यमाणो भवतीत्युपक्रम्य' 'तस्यैवमेवैते यज्ञक्रतवः परिप्लवेरन्नि'ति तथा विहितत्वात्। (*Vyā.* 6.1.1.2)

31. अन्य आहुः—'अलमस्मि **प्रयोगा**यालमस्मि तस्मै यन्न व्यवच्छिन्द्यामित्यथ प्रयुञ्जीते'ति वचनात्। (*Vyā.* 6.1.1.2)

32. तथा च 'अग्निर्वै दीक्षितस्य देवते'त्यधिकृत्य विहितस्य प्रयाणमन्त्रस्य 'भद्राद्° ' इत्यस्य **प्रयोग**स्तस्मिन्पक्ष उपपद्यत इति। (*Vyā.* 6.1.1.7)

33. तथा चोक्तं 'निष्ठितकर्म**प्रयोग**भेदात्प्रतितन्त्रं क्रियेते'ति। अत्र युक्तं प्रज्ञावद्भिः विचार्याध्यवसेयम्। (*Vyā.* 6.3.4.30)

34. स्रुचावासाद्य प्राकृतात्कर्मणो विरमति। श्रुतः **प्रयोगः**। प्राप्तिरभिधीयताम्। उच्यते। प्रधानानामुपांशुयाजविकारत्वमुक्तम्। (*Vyā.* 6.4.1.35-36)

35. अथापि ब्राह्मणे 'विद्यमानेऽपि व्यपदेश एकादशकपालानेव प्रातःसवने कुर्यादि'ति बहुवचनान्त एव **प्रयोगः**। (*Vyā.* 6.9.1.17)

36. आम्नातेषु **प्रयोगा**दपि तद्वचनं कृतार्थमित्यपरे न प्रयुञ्जते। (*Vyā.* 6.10.3.19)

37. विकारे क्रियमाणेऽनाम्नात**प्रयोगः** स्यात्। तच्च वचनमन्तरेण न न्याय्यम्। (*Vyā.* 6.10.4.2-13)

38. तासां च प्रत्ययविरहितानां **प्रयोगा**नुपपत्तेः। (*Vyā.* 6.10.4.2-13)

39. उखामित्येकवचननिर्देशः प्राधान्यात् प्रवृञ्जनार्थायाः। संभरते उपकल्पयते पूर्वमेव **प्रयोग**प्राशुभावाय। (*Vyā.* 7.1.1.1)

40. 'चतुर्थे च पक्षे धाय्याशब्दचोदितानां तिसृणामेवावधार्य लोके **प्रयोगः** सर्वासामागन्तूनां ज्योतिष्मतीं परिहाप्येति विकल्पना तुल्या। (*Vyā.* 7.3.1.5-6)

41. **तत्र प्रयोगः।** उपवसथात्पूर्वेद्युरेव शाखामाहृत्य वत्सानपाकृत्य शाखापवित्रं कृत्वाऽस्तमिते सायंदोहं दोहयित्वा प्रातर्दोहाय वत्सानपाकृत्योपोष्य प्रातर्दोहं दोहयित्वौपवसथिकं कर्म कृत्वाऽग्नीषोमीयस्य वपायां हुतायां ततः पुरोडाशनिर्वापकाले पात्राणि सादयेत्। त्रयाण्येकादशकपालान्युपधेयानि। द्वयान्यष्टकपालानि। चतुष्ट्यानि द्वादशकपालानि। एकमेककपालमष्टौ चरुस्थाल्यः तावन्ति मेक्षणानि। आमिक्षापात्रं समेक्षणमग्निहोत्रहवणीं चापवृत्तार्थत्वाच्च शूर्पादीनि च सप्तान्यानि षडौषधार्थानि। पवित्रे कृत्वाऽपः प्रणीय वा हवींषि निर्वपेत्। तत्र धूर्मन्त्रं पवित्रनिधानं चावर्तते। निरसनं दशहोता च तन्त्रं निर्वापादीन्यभ्यावपनान्तमावर्तते। इतरसवमापरिधानात् तन्त्रमिदं देवानामिदममुनः सह यथार्थमग्न इति वर्जयित्वा निरुप्य प्रोक्षणीः संस्कृत्य हवींषि प्रोक्ष्य पात्राणि प्रोक्ष्य समस्ताभिः, अथावघातमारभेत। आवपनप्रभृतिहविष्कृदाह्वानयज्ञायुधोद्वादनवर्जं कृत्स्नमवहननं

प्रतिबीजमावर्तते। तुषोपवापस्तन्त्रेणैवान्त्ये बीजे क्रियेतावर्तेत वा। क्रमानुग्रहायेत्यपरे। आशव आशुपाका: षष्टिकादय:। आम्बा आच्छेदनजा:। कपालान्युपधाय चरुस्थालीं पयश्चाधिश्रित्य चरुपुरोडाशीयान्विभज्य पेषणमारभेत। अत्राप्यधिवपनप्रभृत्यावर्तते। संवपनादिपिण्डकरणान्तं चतुरावर्तते। तत्र आद्यं पिण्डं सप्तधा विभजेत्। 'यथाभागं व्यावर्तध्वमि'ति पञ्चकृत्व:। यथाभागं वर्तेथामित्यन्ते। तत आनुपूर्व्याद्धवींषि अधिश्रयेत्। स्वक्रमे चामिक्षां कृत्वा प्रतापे निधायाप्यनिनयनात् कुर्यात्। उद्वासनकाले पात्र्यामसंभवन्ति हवींषि सामर्थ्यात् पात्रान्तर उद्वासनीयानि। (*Vyā.* 7.15.1.49, 52)

It may be pointed out that here a complete *Prayoga*-text of *Devasuvāmhavimsi* under the heading तत्र प्रयोग: has been given.

42. द्वयोर्बहुवचन**प्रयोग**ान्नरापेक्षम् परिवृक्त्याश्च। (*Vyā.* 9.1.2.46)

43. एवं ब्रुवताऽऽचार्येणार्थवादगतस्याप्यर्थजातस्य **प्रयोग**कालेऽभिसम्बन्धितव्यता ज्ञाप्यते। (*Vyā.* 9.2.3.60)

44. आदायमादायादाय विनियुञ्जति। क्रमविपर्यासेन नियोजनादीनामेककर्तृत्वे तस्यापि पृथक्कर्तृत्वं **प्रयोग**प्राशुभावाय। (*Vyā.* 10.6.1.2)

45. ऐदंयुगीनास्तु सूत्रकारै: कल्पितं **प्रयोगं** स्वल्पेनैव कालेन सुन्वाना इत्येवं कुर्वन्तीति। तत: किम्। कल्पप्रशंसया कल्पकारप्रशंसया वा, प्रयोक्तुरतिप्ररोचना भवत्येव। (*Vyā.* 11.4.1)

46. प्रत्यक्ष उदाहरणस्यामन्त्रित**प्रयोग**दर्शनात्। (*Vyā.* 12.1.1)

15. References to Historical places, Kings and Rivers—

(*a*) **कुरु** (*Kuru*)—

1. **कुरूणा**मश्वपाला निघ्नन्ते। अश्वमेधाश्वो वा भोज्यैरश्वपालैरेवं न कर्तव्यमित्यभि-धित्सया। (*Vyā.* 10.2.3.7)

2. **कुरूणां** कुरुविषयवासिनां मध्ये गोऽजाविधनधान्यादिभि: समृद्धो वैश्य आस। (*Vyā.* 13.4.1)

पाञ्चाल (*Pāncāla*)—

1. तत आरभ्यार्वागन्येऽपि जना: **पाञ्चाल**राजानां नामान्यपरिहारेण न वदन्ति। गिरियकपिमर्त्यादिषु शब्देषु **पाञ्चाल**राजानां नामगन्धो विद्यत इति मत्वा न स्यादिति विशेषेणापि नामानि तच्छब्देन न वदन्ति। (*Vyā.* 14.6.1)

पाटलिपुत्र (*Pāṭaliputra*)—

1. यथा **पाटलीपुत्रकं** देवदत्तं निर्ज्ञातपूर्वं मथुरायां दृष्ट्वा न माथुर इति बुद्धिरुत्पद्यते, किन्वस्यागमनमित्याकांक्षा भवति प्रयोजनं प्रति। (*Vyā.* 3.3.1.1)

2. यत्तूक्तं निर्ज्ञात**पाटलीपुत्रकं** मथुरायां दृष्ट्वा न माथुर इति प्रतीतिर्भवति, प्रयोजनाकांक्षा तु भवतीति। (*Vyā.* 3.3.1.1)

मथुरा (*Mathurā*)—

1. यथा पाटलीपुत्रकं देवदत्तं निर्ज्ञातपूर्वं **मथुरा**यां दृष्ट्वा न माथुर इति बुद्धिरुत्पद्यते, किन्वस्यागमनमित्याकांक्षा भवति प्रयोजनं प्रति। (*Vyā.* 3.3.1.1)

2. यत्तूक्तं निर्ज्ञातपाटलीपुत्रकं **मथुरा**यां दृष्ट्वा न माथुर इति प्रतीतिर्भवति, प्रयोजनाकांक्षा तु भवतीति। (*Vyā.* 3.3.1.1)

यवप्रायदेश (*Yavprāyadeśa*)—

1. पाकार्थं पेष्याणां **यवप्राये** देशेऽन्तर्वेद्यादौ ... सक्तुप्राय आहारो नान्यसक्तवः क्रियन्ते। (*Vyā.* 4.2.1.40)

(*b*) **जनक** (*Janaka*)—

1. '**जनको** ह वैदेहः सोमेन यक्ष्यमाणः' इत्याद्यारभ्य दृष्टत्वादग्न्याधेयविषये चादर्शनाच्च। (*Vyā.* 1.1.1.6)

2. स एव विश्वजित् सर्वपृष्ठो **जनकः**। (*Vyā.* 13.6.1)

पुण्डरीक (*Puṇḍarīka*)—

1. षट्त्रिंशत्वभ्यासगत्वन्ते हैतेन क्षेत्रधर्मात्मा सम्यक् पालयिता **पुण्डरीको** नाम विदेहानामीश्वरो राजा इष्टवान् सुदाम्नो नदस्योत्तरे तीरे।

(c) **गैरेयी** (*Gaireyī*)—

1. **गैरेयी** गिरिजानदीकूलादिस्थं वस्त्वशेषं हरन्तीत्येवं मत्स्यवस्तुहरन्नेव क्रतुर्गच्छति। बृहस्पतिसवेनेष्टवताऽवश्यञ्चतुष्टोमेन यष्टव्यं शान्त्यर्थम्। (*Vyā.* 14.1.2)

यमुना (*Yamunā*)—

1. प्लाक्षं प्रस्रवणं प्राप्योत्थितायां **यमुनायां** कारवद्व्रधेऽवभृथम्। (*Vyā.* 13.5.1)

16. Nature of the *Vyākhyā*-texts—

Generally, a commentator while writing a commentary on a *Kalpasūtra*-text confines himself to pointing out applications of the mantras in a particular ritual accompanying the action to be performed, and sometimes giving justification for it, and sometimes pointing out differences from other traditions. Unlike others Āryadāsa does not confine himself only to explain the *sūtras* concerned, in a simple manner. He rather seems to be a critic of each and every aspect of the contents of the *sūtras*. He gives the views of the Ācāryas belonging to other traditions and in matter of contrversies he gives stress on his own *Vādhūla*-tradition, and in such discussions the *Vyākhyā* of some *sūtras* have become very lengthy, sometimes very brief and somtimes many *sūtras* have been left un-explained.

The discussion about the grammatical construction of the words generally form the main part of any commentary, but Āryadāsa does not give much stress on it. However, at many places he has mentioned the grammatical peculiarities of the words and sometimes pointing out *Chāndas-prayogas,* too. He accepts the utility of *Śikśā, Vyākaraṇa, Nirukta, Chandas* and *Jyotiṣa,* too, for successful performance of rituals in Kalpa also—

1. व्याकरणमपि साधुशब्दापशब्दविवेकव्यवस्थया रक्षोहादिनोपकारकम्। (*Vyā.* 1.1.1.1)
2. शब्दः शास्त्रव्यापारत्वात् तस्य अर्थनिर्वचनान्यपि कर्तव्यानि स्युः। वयं तु लोकवेदयोः शब्दप्रसिद्धान् शब्दार्थानुपादाय सन्दिग्धान् वाक्यार्थान् विचारयिष्यामः। (*Vyā.* 1.1.1.1)
3. अश्वत्थादिष्ववयवे विकारे वा तद्धितः। अशन्या हतोऽशनिहतः, स च वानस्पत्यः, वानस्पत्यानिति विशेषणात्। 'शमीगर्भः' षष्ठीसमासः। (*Vyā.* 1.1.1.3)
4. अत्र केचित् 'संभरते' इत्यात्मनेपदनिर्देशात् संभरणं याजमानं वर्णयन्ति। सत्यम्। आत्मनेपदनिर्देशाद्याजमानं भवितुमर्हति। 'भृञो ञित्वात्'।(*Vyā.* 1.1.1.6)
5. स्वयंसम्पन्नः स्वाहाग्निमित्यादिना विभक्तिवचनं सिद्धमित्यर्थः। (*Vyā.* 1.4.3.19)
6. उपलक्षणत्वाद् वत्सशब्दस्य पुंल्लिङ्गत्वाद्वा। स्त्रीवत्सत्वेऽपि न दोष इति स्त्रीवत्सैवापीत्याह। (*Vyā.* 1.6.2.19)
7. पिष्टानि कुर्वन्ति। बहुवचननिर्देशादनियतकर्तृकत्वम्। (*Vyā.* 2.2.1.25-33)

8. अपां पतिं समुद्रस्था आपस्तद्वदुपचर्यन्ते। छान्दसो दीर्घः।(*Vyā.* 9.2.2.3)

9. एकवचनं जात्यपेक्षम्। (*Vyā.* 10.5.2.9)

10. ऐन्द्राग्नायेति कर्मप्रवचनीये द्वितीयार्थे चतुर्थी व्यत्ययेन। ऐन्द्राग्नमित्यर्थ।(*Vyā.* 10.5.3.41)

11. प्रथमस्या इति **छान्दसो** निर्देशः। (*Vyā.* 10.5.4.40-41)

12. अवशब्दो हेत्यवधारणायाम्। हेतीति प्राप्ते हैतीति **छान्दसो** निर्देशः। (*Vyā.* 10.6.1.27)

13. प्रथमाभ्यां चतुर्थीभ्यां षष्ठीभ्यामिति लिङ्गसमवायाद्ध्युदेति विवेकेनागच्छति। (*Vyā.* 10.7.2.31)

14. 'यत्स्विष्टकृद्भ्यो लोहितं जुहोती'ति बहुवचनात्। (*Vyā.* 10.9.1.29)

15. अथवा प्रज्ञावद्भिः प्रयोजनमस्य मृगयितव्यम्। (*Vyā.* 11.2.3)

16. दैव्येकमित्यार्षम्। छन्दोलक्षणमनुद्धरण अभिचिक्रीरथा अभ्यास आचार्य एवं ह्यस्य शब्दस्यार्थं विवृणोति स्म। (*Vyā.* 11.3.2)

17. अनभिभूतमरिन्देशानिवाभिभूय यजेयमिहाग्नेयनित्येष्टिरुपाकरणीययोः प्रत्याम्ना–तयोर्वायव्ययोपाकरोतीत्येकवचनमविवक्षितम्। (*Vyā.* 12.2.6)

The purpose of writing a commentary is to make easily understandible the text of the *sūtras* which were not understandible otherwise. The meaning which is wellknown through both common man and Veda, leaving that, one should explain the rituals according to one's own knowledge or as prescribed in the *Brāhmaṇa*-texts.

(a) 1. अथायमपि वाधूलेनाचार्येण रचितः कल्पः। तस्य सुखज्ञानार्थमस्माभि**र्निगदसिद्ध**–वर्जमस्मद् बुद्ध्यागमानुरूपं व्याख्यायते। (*Vyā.* 1.1.1.1)

2. अन्वीक्षणादि **निगदसिद्धम्**। (*Vyā.* 1.5.2.25-27)

3. स्वतश्च **निगदसिद्धम्**। (*Vyā.* 12.1.4)

4. अन्ये **निगदसिद्धे**ति न व्याख्यातवानिति। (*Vyā.* 12.3.7)

5. तथोपहव्ये विशेषो **निगदसिद्धः**। (*Vyā.* 13.9.1)

6. इन्द्रष्टुतु **निगदसिद्धः**। विशेषोऽग्निष्टुता व्याख्यातः। (*Vyā.* 14.5.3)

7. अमावास्यायां च सुत्या यथा स्यात्तथा पक्षाद् द्विरात्रादीनामेव द्वादशोपसत्त्वमित्यपरे। **निगदसिद्धः** शेषः। (*Vyā.* 14.13.2)

(b) 1. सर्वकर्मणामधिकारलक्षणन्यायशास्त्रे विस्तारोऽधिगन्तव्यः। इह ग्रन्थगौरवभयादस्माभिर्नाभिधीयते। (*Vyā.* 1.1.1.1)

2. 'संभरते' इति लडन्तः। कथं विधास्यतीति यद्युच्येत, नायं विधिः। कस्मात्। वाक्यैरभिहितानामर्थानां सन्निवेशविशेषमात्रमेव कल्पसूत्रकारैः क्रियते। यत्रापि विधिप्रत्ययगन्धोऽस्ति, तत्रापि नाविदितवेदनार्थं, तदपि ब्राह्मणवाक्यानुकरणमेव। यथा 'अमावास्यायामेव दीक्षेत' इति। (*Vyā.* 1.1.1.1)

(c) While prescribing a ritual or mantra, sometimes different options are given, somtimes opposite views are also given. Āryadāsa makes it clear that where the *Sūtrakāra* gives option or options, there one should not take it as opposite, but when he contradicts others views, it means he is opposite to that.

Āryadāsa employs 'प्रवेधस' mantras for euloguising the *Brahmodana* which has been mentioned by Ācārya Vādhūla. Here he explicitely suggests that if a mantra has not been prescribed by Ācārya, any mantra befiting the occaision may be employed—

'प्रवेधस' इति ब्रह्मौदनमुपतिष्ठते, जुहोति वा। अथवा इहाचार्येणाविनियुक्तानां यथालिङ्गं विनियोगः कर्तव्यः। (*Vyā.* 1.1.2.9)

While explaining the text if some word or ritual have been explained before he does not give again. He mentions clearly that the text has been explained before—

'अग्निर्वै दीक्षितस्य देवते'त्याद्यग्निष्टोमे व्याख्यातम्। (*Vyā.* 12.1.2)

17. Personality, works, place and time of Āryadāsa—

Āryadāsa, is the author of the *Kalpāgamsaṅgraha,* a commentary on the *VādhŚS*. But, curiously enough, his name does not occur in any of the texts of Sanskrit literature. None of the dictionaries has included his name under its entries. His name does not appear in any of the Catalogues. Even Āryadāsa himself has not given any information about his personality. He has not mentioned his name anywhere, as found in other texts, where authors generally use to give the names of their family predicessors, teachers, kings and places *etc,* in the beginning, or at the end of their works. His name appears in M Ad T at the end of *Agniṣṭoma Prapāṭhakas* as अग्निष्टोमाख्यं काण्डमार्यदासस्य कृतौ कल्पागमसंग्रहे समाप्तम् (M p.226, Ad p.486, T p.369). T mentions his name also in the beginning of the commentary as under: आर्यदासकृतकल्पागम-संग्रहाख्यव्याख्योपेतम् (p.1). Kashikar[1] and Prof. Ikari[2] refer to his name as the author of the *VādhūlaKalpsūtraVyākhyā.* They always use the title of the text as *VādhūlaKalpasūtraVyākhyā*. In my opinion the *Kalpāgamasaṅgraha* is the correct nomenclature of the *Vyākhyā* and its author is Āryadāsa.

Āryadāsa was a great scholar and that he had a sound knowledge of all branches of Vedic literature, is evident from his commentary where a large number of quotations have been given by him from various texts. In his commentary he has mentioned many Ācāryas and their work by name, as we have seen above.

When and which place he belonged to, is still unknown to us. We do not know anything about it. From his commentary this much is well-proved that he was a follower of *Vādhūla*-tradition, one of the sub-branches of the *Kṛṣṇa Yajurveda*. He was not a follower of *Taittirīya*-tradition. In his time, though the *Śākhā-Saṁhitā* of the Vādhūlas had almost become extinct, but he was well confirmed about its existence. At many places he has given clear evidences to show the existence of the *Śākhā-Saṁhitā* of the Vādhūlas, different from that of the *Taittirīyas.* For the first time he brought to the notice the existence of four sub-branches of Vādhūlas and their several texts like *VādhūlaŚrautsūtra, Vādhūla-Anvākhyāna, Vādhūlaprayogakḷpti, VādhūlaŚulbasūtra, Anupadasūtra, etc.*

From the references to the historical places like *Kuru, Pañcāla, Pāṭaliputra, Mathurā, Videha* and rivers like *Gaṅgā, Yamunā.* one may conjecture that he might have belonged to the northern part of the country, most probably between the region of *Gaṅgā* and *Yamunā*. Once he has referred to *'Yavaprāya-deśa'*[3], the reigion where barley was most popular grain and people generally used its parched flour for food. This land must have been the original homeland of the *Vādhūla-Śākhā.* At the time of ceremonial sacrificial bath like *Avabhṛtha*[4], the sacrificer

1. Kashikar, 'A Survey of *Śrautsūtras*', The University of Bombay, 1986, p.64
2. Yasuke Ikari, 'New Critical Edition of *Vādhūla Śrautsūtra*', 1.1-1.4 [*Agnyādheya*], 1995 Intro. p.16 fn. 45.
3. पाकार्थं पेष्याणां यवप्राये देशेऽन्तर्वेद्यादौ ... सक्तुप्राय आहारो नान्यसक्तवः क्रियन्ते। (*Vyā.* 4.2.1.40)
4. प्लाक्षं प्रस्रवणं प्राप्योत्थितायां यमुनायां कारवद्वधेऽवभृथम्। (*Vyā.* 13.5.1)

(*Yajamāna*) used to go to perform the ritual at the banks of *Yamunā* and *Gaṅgā* rivers.

The *VādhGS* prescribes a ritual of binding a garland of barley-grain in the right hand of his pregnant wife in the fourth month of her pregnancy. Both, the authors of the *VādhūlaGṛhyasūtraVṛtti*-text and the *Vādhūlagṛhyāgamvṛtti-rahasya* prescribe this ritual at the bank of rivers *Yamunā* and *Gaṅgā*[1].

Here on the basis of these references, one may easily notice the similarities of rituals among these two above mentioned texts. But, this similartity is not because of the fact that these author, too, belonged to the same region of *Gaṅga* and *Yamunā* rivers. In one of the three authors, namely Nārāyaṇa Miśra was definitely a resident of Saṅgamagrama, as is evident from the colophons given at the end of each chapter (except 8th) of the *Gṛhyāgamvṛttirahasya*: इति संगमग्रामवासिमिश्रविरचितनारायणीये वाधूलगृह्यागम–वृत्तिरहस्ये प्रथमोऽध्याय:. On the basis of this reference we may conjecture that most probably Āryadāsa, too, might have been a resident of Saṅgamagrama.

Secondly on the basis of script of all MSS being Malayalam and their being found deposited in only two Vādhūla families Iriñjalakuṇḍa, Cochin, Kerala and Kaḍaṅgaśeri Mana, it is obvious that these must have been written by two authors of the

1. अथैतां यवस्रजं 'विवृत्तचक्रा आसीनास्तीरेणासौ तव' इति विस्रस्य गर्भिण्या दक्षिणे हस्ते बध्नाति। (*VādhGS.* 1.3.7)

'असौ' इत्यस्य स्थाने तस्या नद्या नाम गृह्णाति यस्यास्तीरमाश्रिता भवन्ति 'यमुने तव', 'गंगे तव' इत्यादि। (*Vṛtti* on *VādhGSV.* 1.3.7)

'इत्याहु'रिति मन्त्रस्यावयवोऽत्र निगद्यते।
'विवृत्तचक्रास्तीरेण' नदीत्यादि तवान्तिकम्॥
हुत्वाऽपनीय शाखादीन् विस्रस्यैनां स्रजं ततः।
गर्भिण्या दक्षिणे हस्ते तया बध्नाति मन्त्रतः॥
यस्या नद्याः समीपेऽस्य होमस्य करणं भवेत्।
तस्या नद्या नाम मन्त्रे त्वसौ स्थाने विनिर्दिशेत्॥
संबुध्यन्तं यथा 'गंङ्गे तवे'त्यादि प्रयुज्यते।
अक्षरार्थः समासेन गृह्यस्येहाधुनोच्यते॥ (*VādhGVR.* 2.136-139)

same time. Moreover, the existence of *VādhūlaGṛhyasūtraVṛtti*-text and *Kalpāgamsaṅgraha* of Āryadāsa together in one codex, too, proves the composition of one and the same period. Again there are lot of similarities between these texts in matters of use of technical terms in both. These similirities lead us to hold the view that most probably Āryadāsa the author of the *Vyākhyā*-text and Nārāyaṇa the author of *Kalpāgamavṛttirahasya* and the author of *VādhūlagṛhyasūtraVṛtti*-text are contemporary. It may also be possible that the author of *GṛhyasūtraVṛtti*-text and the author of *Kalpāgamsaṅgraha,* might be one and the same personality, *i.e.* Āryadāsa himself. This needs a separate study.

Devarāja Yajvā, the commentator of *Nighaṇṭu*, whose time is 1313 A.D. has mentioned *Skandasvāmi, Bhavasvāmī, Guhadeva, Śrinivāsa Mādhava etc,* in his *Nighaṇṭu-bhāsya*. From this it is obvious that *Bhavasvāmī* is anterier to Devarāja Yajvā. Since *Āryadāsa* refers *Bhavasvāmī* in his *Vyākhyā*, so it is clear that he could not be prior to him *i.e.* 8th century. Āryādasā does not mention the name of Sāyaṇa, who wrote his commentaries on Vedas with his many assistant Panḍṭis. The time of Sāyaṇa is 1315-1387 A.D. Since the time of *Bhavasvāmī* is 8th century[1] and Āryadāsa has mentioned him very respetfully as 'भगवता भवस्वामिना' (*Vyā.* 12.1.4), so the latter must be posterior to him. Since Nārāyaṇa Miśra[2], the author of *VādhūlaGṛhyāgamaVṛttirahasya* and a resident of Saṅgamagrama in south belonged to the 13th century, Āryadāsa may be tentatively placed near about between tenth to twelfth century A.D. It needs further research.

□ □ □

1. Kashikar C. G., 'A Survey of *Śrautsūtras*', The University of Bombay, 1966, p.46
2. For the date of Nārāyaṇa Miśra, see *VādhGVR,* Intro pp.26-27.

॥ श्रीः ॥

अथ आचार्य–आर्यदासप्रणीता

कल्पागमसंग्रहाख्या

वाधूलश्रौतसूत्रव्याख्या[१]

॥ अथ प्रथमः प्रपाठकः ॥

[अग्न्याधेयम्]

[धर्मं जिज्ञास्यमानानां][२] प्रमाणं वेदः । स च पुरुषार्थं चोदयति ।[३] वेद–शब्दश्च मन्त्रब्राह्मणयोः प्रसिद्धः । तस्याङ्गानि षट् । तद्यथा—शीक्षा व्याकरणं[४] निरुक्तं छन्दोविचितिर्ज्योतिषामयनं कल्प इति ।[४] तत्र स्वराक्षरोच्चारणसंपच्छीक्षया क्रियते । तत्तत् संस्कारयुक्ता हि मन्त्राः कर्मणो गुणत्वेनाभ्युदयाय भवन्ति । यथा प्रयोगे प्रत्यवायो न भवति, [५]तत्तत्संपद्योगे । तथा चोक्तम्—'एकः शब्दः सम्यग् ज्ञातः सुष्ठु प्रयुक्तः स्वर्गे लोके कामधुग्भवति', 'मन्त्रो हीनः[६] स्वरतो वर्णतो वा मिथ्याप्रयुक्तो न तमर्थमाह । स वाग्वज्रो यजमानं हिनस्ति यथेन्द्रशत्रुः[७] स्वरतोऽपराधाद्' इति । व्याकरणमपि साधुशब्दापशब्दविवेकव्यवस्थया रक्षोहादिनोपकारकम् । निरुक्तमपि मन्त्रार्थप्रत्यायनादिना । अर्थाभिधानसंयोगाद्धि मन्त्रेषु शेषभावः । 'गायत्र्या तेजस्कामस्य परिदध्या'[–दित्या]दिषु[८] छन्दसां मन्त्राणां विनियोगः श्रूयते । स च विनियोगः छन्दोविचितिमन्तरेण ज्ञातुं न शक्यते, इति छन्दोविचितेरङ्गभावः । 'कृत्तिकास्वग्निमादधीत', 'अमावास्यायाममावास्यया[९] यजेत[१०]' इत्यादिषु कालज्ञानं ज्योतिषामयनेन क्रियते । अतस्तस्याप्यङ्गभावः । कल्पाख्येन चाङ्गेन यज्ञस्य क्लृप्तिरभिधीयते ।

अत्राह—केयं क्लृप्तिर्नाम । उच्यते–मन्त्रब्राह्मणयोर्विसृतानां पदार्थानामभिप्रेते कर्मण्यभिप्रेते [११]चावकाशे विनियोगः । एकस्मिन्नेव काण्डेऽनुष्ठातव्यक्रमेण पठितानामनुष्ठातव्यक्रमेणैव न[१२] विनियोगः । तद्यथा–आग्रयणग्रहणात्पूर्वं शुक्रामन्थिनोर्होमः पठितः । स च होमो गृहीतेष्वाग्रयणो–क्थ्यध्रुवाश्विनेषु प्रस्थितचमसैः सह कर्तव्यः क्वचित् । क्वचिन्मन्त्रा एव पठ्यन्ते, न ब्राह्मणमस्ति । तेषां च विनियोगः[१३] यथा 'दैव्य उपस्थानेऽच्छिद्रेषु'[१४] इति शाखान्तरे पठितानामवश्योपसंहर्तव्यानां

---

१. M begins with ॥ श्रीः ॥ अथ वाधूलकल्पव्याख्या, Ad :॥ श्री॥ श्री गणपतये नमः॥ वाधूलकल्पसूत्रव्याख्या, T : ॥ श्रीः ॥ महागणपतये नमः । श्रीवाधूलमहर्षिप्रणीतं कल्पसूत्रम् : आर्यदासकृत–कल्पागमसंग्रहाख्यव्याख्योपेतम् । २. M Ad broken. ३. Between चोदयति and वेदशब्दश्च T gives the text नारायणाय नमो नमो वाधूलकाय । सिद्धन्याये नित्यो वे... ४–४. T presents the text as — 'शिक्षाव्याकरणं छन्दो निरुक्तं ज्यौतिषं तथा कल्पश्चेति षडङ्गानि वेदस्याहुर्मनीषिणः ।'. ५. M तद्वत्स°, Ad तद्वत्स°. ६. M Ad हिन. ७. M Ad °शत्रुस्व°. ८. M Ad °दध्यादिषुः ९. M Ad °मावास्या. १०. M Ad यजतत. ११. M Ad वावका°. १२. M Ad om; thus T. १३. M Ad विद्विनि°. १४. M Ad छिद्रे स्थिति; thus T.

[संभारसंभरणाग्न्याहरणादिकर्म]

अग्नीनाधास्यमानः संभारान् संभरते ॥ १ ॥ ऊषाश्च सिकताश्चाखूत्करं च सूदं च

वैकल्पिकानां[1] च पदार्थानामुपसंहार इति, एवमादीनां क्लृप्तिशब्दवाच्यता। सा[2] च क्लृप्तिः कल्पसूत्राण्यन्तरेण न सिध्यति।

एभिरङ्गैर्विनर्ग्यजुःसामलक्षणोऽनेकशाखारूपेण भिन्नोऽपि[3] वेदो[3] न शक्नोति पुरुषार्थं साधयितुं यथा देवदत्तः पाण्यादिभिर्विना। एवमङ्गशब्दाभिलप्या[4]न्येतानि। ज्योतिषामयनान्तानामङ्गानां वेदभेदेन शाखाभेदेन च भेदो नास्ति। कल्पस्त्वेकां शाखामारभ्याविरुद्धां[5] वा मिथः[5] काश्चिदारभ्य प्रवर्तते।

अत्राह—किमेतान्यङ्गानि वेदवन्नित्यानि, उत नेति। उच्यते—अनित्यानीति ब्रूमः। कुतः। कर्तृस्मरणात्[6] नित्यत्वकारणानामभावात्। स्मर्यन्ते हि कर्तारो यास्कपाणिनिवाधूलप्रभृतयः। एवं तर्हि पुरुषबुद्धिप्रणीतत्वादप्रमाणानि ? न, फलवन्ति। उच्यते—न ह्येतानि[7] पुरुषैस्तर्कमवलम्ब्य स्वमनीषया[8] वा प्रणीतानि। किं तर्हि। वेदादेव प्रणीतानि, अतीन्द्रियत्वादेषामनादिशिष्टैश्च परिगृहीतत्वात्। अतो नित्यान्येव। उक्तं च भगवता यास्कमुनिना[9]—'साक्षात्कृतधर्माण ऋषयो बभूवुस्तेऽवरेभ्योऽसाक्षात्कृतधर्मभ्य[10] उपदेशेन मन्त्रान् संप्रादुः। [11]उपदेशाय ग्लायन्तोऽवरे विल्मग्रहणायेमं[11] ग्रन्थं [12]समाम्नासिषुः' (निरु. १.२०) इति। अथायमपि वाधूलेनाचार्येण रचितः कल्पः। तस्य सुखज्ञानार्थमस्माभिर्निगदसिद्धवर्जमस्मद् बुद्ध्यागमानुरूपं व्याख्यायते। तत्र 'यदाहवनीये जुह्वति' इत्यादिभिर्वाक्यैराहवनीयादिम् अतः फलवत्कर्मस्वधिकार इति कृत्वाऽऽहवनीयादिशब्दानां[13] च संस्कारनिमित्तत्वादाधानस्य च संस्कारत्वादग्नीनामग्न्याधेयं पूर्वमाम्नातमाचार्येण।

तस्येदमादिवाक्यम्—'अग्नीनाधास्यमानः[14] संभारान् संभरते'[15] इति। इहाग्निशब्देन जातिनिमित्तत्वात् ज्वलनमात्रवचनेऽप्याहवनीयादय[16] एवाभिधीयन्ते। तान् संस्कर्तुं यस्याभिप्रायः स आधास्यमानः। स पुनः कः ? अर्थी समर्थः शास्त्रेणापर्युदस्तः। एतत् सर्वकर्मणामधिकारलक्षणन्यायशास्त्रे विस्तारोऽधिगन्तव्यः। इह ग्रन्थगौरवभयादस्माभिर्नाभिधीयते। संभारशब्दः कर्मसाधनभूतेषु द्रव्येषु वर्तते। संभरते उपकल्पयते। आधानाख्येन संस्कारेणाग्नीन् संस्कर्तुं संभारानात्मसात्करोतीति पिण्डार्थः। केचिदाचार्याः प्रतिपदं संस्कारान् वर्णयन्ति। तथा सति शास्त्रान्तरव्यापारोऽपि वर्णनीयो भवति। [17]शब्दः शास्त्रव्यापारत्वात् तस्य अर्थनिर्वचनान्यपि कर्तव्यानि स्युः। वयं तु लोकवेदयोः शब्दप्रसिद्धान् शब्दार्थानुपादाय सन्दिग्धान् वाक्यार्थान् विचारयिष्यामः।

---

१. M °ल्पितानां. **२.** M Ad स. **३-३.** M Ad °रूपेण [Ad णा] भिन्नो त्रिवेदो; thus T. **४.** M °लव्या°. **५-५.** M Ad °भ्य विरुद्धामिथः; thus T. **६.** M Ad °णादीनां नित्य°; thus T. **७.** M Ad न...पु°; thus T. **८.** T °मनीषिकया. **९.** T °महर्षिणा. **१०.** M Ad °तेपरेभ्यस्साक्षाकृतधर्मे°. **११-११.** M Ad उपदेशेन ग्लायन्ते परेऽखिलग्रह, T उपदेशेन ग्लायन्ते परे। अतोऽखिलग्रह°. **१२.** M Ad ग्रन्थसे मम्ना°. **१३.** M Ad °नीयशब्दा°. **१४.** M Ad अग्निनाधास्य°. **१५.** M Ad °भर इति. **१६.** M Ad नत्वे हव्या हव्या ह व्याहवचनीया°. **१७.** M T शब्दशास्त्र°; thus T.

वराहविहतं च वल्मीकवपां च शर्कराश्च पुष्करपर्णं च षट् च हिरण्यशल्काञ्छतमानं चेति पार्थिवान्॥ २॥ आश्वत्थं चौदुम्बरं चेति वानस्पत्यान् पालाशं च शमीमयं च वैकङ्कतं चाशनिहतं च शमीगर्भं च विंशतिश्च समिध आर्द्राः सपलाशाश्चित्रियस्याश्वत्थस्य॥ ३॥ अश्वं च॥ ४॥ सर्वाणि च यज्ञायुधानि॥ ५॥ त्रीण्युद्धतानि॥ ६॥ अद्योपवसथ इत्यन्नमेव

'संभरते' इति लडन्तः। कथं विधास्यतीति यद्युच्येत[१], नायं विधिः। कस्मात्। वाक्यैरभिहितानामर्थानां सन्निवेशविशेषमात्रमेव कल्पसूत्रकारैः क्रियते। यत्रापि विधिप्रत्ययगन्धोऽस्ति, तत्रापि नाविदितवेदनार्थं, तदपि ब्राह्मणवाक्यानुकरणमेव। यथा 'अमावास्यायामेव दीक्षेत' इति॥ १॥

संभारानिति सामान्येनोक्तानां विशेषा वक्ष्यन्ते 'ऊषाश्चे'त्यादि। ऊषा इति द्वितीयार्थे प्रथमा। आखूत्करवराहविहतयोरारण्यत्वमिष्यते। पार्थिवग्रहणं च तयोः पार्थिवत्वाय। हिरण्यस्य च पार्थिव-त्वख्यापनार्थम्। शतमानमपि हिरण्यमेव॥ २॥

अश्वत्थादिष्ववयवे विकारे वा तद्धितः। अशन्या हतोऽशनिहतः, स च वानस्पत्यः, वानस्पत्यानिति विशेषणात्। 'शमीगर्भः' षष्ठीसमासः। 'अश्वत्थाद्धव्यवाहात्' इति लिङ्गात्। 'यो अश्वत्थः' इति दर्शनात्। अरण्यर्थस्य वृक्षस्य नियमेनाश्वत्थत्वे 'येनाश्वत्थेन किञ्चिद्वस्तु ग्रामादिर्लक्ष्यते स चित्रियोऽश्वत्थः'। इतिकरणस्य प्रकारवाचित्वाद् वानस्पत्यानित्यश्वादिषु[२] न प्रयुज्यते॥ ३॥

सर्वेषां [२]यज्ञायुधानामिहोत्पत्तिवचनमिहोत्पन्नान्याहवनीयादिवत् सर्वकर्मार्थानि यथा स्युरिति तथा महामेधे विनियोगो दृश्यते। सर्वकर्मापवर्गे यज्ञायुधानां वृक्षनियमप्रमाणाकृतिविशेषा[३] अनुपदादागमयितव्याः। [३]विध्यवशेषा हि तत्राभिधीयन्ते। कस्य पुनस्ते विध्यवशेषाः ? चतुर्णां वाधूलानामिति। के ते चत्वारो वाधूलाः ? [४]कौण्डिन्याग्निवेश्यगालवशाङ्खानां[४] कल्पाः। तथा हि शुल्ब उक्तम् —'वाधूलकाः सवाधूलाश्चत्वारो विहिताः क्रमादि'ति। अतोऽनुपद उक्ताः शेषाः। अत्रान्यैर्ये[५] न विरुध्यन्ते, ते वैकल्पिका ग्राह्याः। ये विरुध्यन्ते तेऽन्यकल्पार्था भवन्ति[६]। इहानुक्ता आकाङ्क्षिता नियम्यन्ते[६]। इह च वृक्षप्रमाणाकृतिविशेषा आकाङ्क्षितास्तैर्निराकाङ्क्षीक्रियन्ते[७]॥ ५॥

तत उद्धतादीनां प्रमाणाकृतिविशेषाः। 'त्रीण्युद्धतानी'ति सभ्यावसथीययोरुद्धतनिवृत्त्यर्थम्। तेऽन्यकल्पार्था[८]भवन्ति। अतः परम् 'अद्य उपवसथ' इत्याधानकर्मारभ्यते।[८] तत्र 'कृत्तिकास्वग्निमादधीत' इत्यादि, 'वसन्ता ब्राह्मणोऽग्निमादधीत' इत्यादि च ब्राह्मणादवगमयितव्यम्[९]। नित्यं काम्यं

---

१. M Ad यदु०. २-२. M broken after ०नस्पत्य up to ज्ञायु०, Ad ०त्यनीत्यश्वत्थादिषु युज्यन्ते; thus T. ३-३. M Ad प्रमाणा... ध्यव०; wrongly give the text 'यज्ञायुधानां=महा...पवर्ग' twice. The sequence of the text in M has been inter-changed and broken as well. ४-४. M कौण्डिन्याग्निवे नियोगो दृश्यते सर्वकर्मापवर्गे यज्ञायुधान...क्तं वाधूलकास्सवाधूलाश्चत्वारो विहिता क्रमादिति; Ad कौण्डन्याग्निवेश्यगारवानां: कल्पाः; T कौण्डिन्याग्निवेश्यशङ्खानां, but corrected as ०वेश्यगारवानां. ५. M Ad अन्यैर्न; thus T. ६-६. M भव...न्त. ७. M Ad क्रियते; thus T. ८-८. M broken between भव and रभ्यते. ९. M ०णभाग० ; thus T.

नैमित्तिकं च वर्णविशेषयुक्तं चाविशेषेण[१] श्रुत्यन्तरे विहितम्। 'शिशिरं च यदैवैनं[१] यज्ञ' इत्यादिना सोमाधानकालश्च[२]। तत्र [३]'द्वियहे त्रियहे वे'त्यादि[३] प्रतीतम्। पूर्वमेव संकल्पोपव्याहरणे च कर्तव्ये। 'मनसा संकल्पयत्यग्नीनाधास्ये = स वाचा व्याहरत्याधास्य[४]' इत्यन्वाख्याने (वाधू.अन्वा. १.६.१) दर्शनात्, तयोश्च[४] प्रथमं कर्तव्यत्वात्। तत्र यथाकाममग्न्याहरणम्। तत उपवसथीयेऽहन्यृत्विजा-मर्हणमानमनं[५] चात्रापीच्छन्ति। अन्ये सोम एवानमनं कुर्वन्ति। श्रद्धाह्वानदेवयजमानयाचनयोः सोमविषये[६] दृष्टत्वाद्वरणस्य च। 'जनको[६] ह वैदेहः सोमेन यक्ष्यमाणः' इत्याद्यारभ्य दृष्टत्वादग्न्याधेयविषये चादर्शनाच्च। यदि वरणं न क्रियते ऋत्विक्परिग्रहणादि[७] न कर्तव्यम्। संभारा नानादेशस्थाः पूर्वमेवैकत्र समुपकल्पिता इह [८]धर्मवन्नियमाच्च यावदर्थं च संस्क्रियन्ते। तत्राध्वर्युः [८]प्राण्यापान्य 'प्रजापतिः प्राचीदिगि'ति जपित्वा उद्धननावोक्षणे कृत्वा संभारान् संभरते। केचित् प्राणनापाननजपानां[९] सोमविषयत्वमेव मन्यन्ते। सौमिकार्थप्राये दर्शनं च [१०]विनियोगकारणं मन्यमाना अन्ये प्रकरणात् वाक्यस्य बलीयस्त्वाच्च सर्वविषयत्वं[१०] मन्यन्ते। एवं ब्रुवताममभिप्रायः सर्वकर्मसु सर्वर्त्विग्भिः पदार्थानामारम्भात् पूर्वमेव तत्त्रयं[११] कर्तव्यमिति। अन्ये अनारभ्याधीतानां[१२] प्रकृत्यर्थत्वाद् [१३]यद्यप्यग्न्याधेयाग्निहोत्रादीनामपि स्वैः स्वैर्धर्मैः[१३] क्वचित् क्वचित् प्रकृतित्वमस्ति[१४]। तथा सति दर्शपूर्णमासयोः सोमे चैवानारभ्याधीतानां विशेषभावे प्रवेश इति इतरत्र[१५] न कुर्वन्ति। मध्यमं पक्षमाश्रित्यास्माभिः प्रयोगे उक्ताः, यद्यत्र क्रियते [१६]दर्शपूर्णमासविकारेष्वपि अग्न्याधेयाङ्गेषु तदेव प्रसज्यते[१६] ॥

अत्र केचित् 'संभरते' इत्यात्मनेपदनिर्देशात् संभरणं याजमानं वर्णयन्ति। सत्यम्। आत्मनेपद-निर्देशाद्याजमानं भवितुमर्हति। 'भृञो ञित्वात्'। किन्तु प्रयोगप्राशुभावाय पुनर्मन्त्रेण [१७]संभरणमा-ध्वर्यवम्। कथमवगम्यते तत्र द्रव्यार्जन[१७]मात्रमिति। मन्त्रब्राह्मणपाठक्रमवैलक्षण्येन[१८] पाठाच्छत-मानाश्वादिभिः सह निर्देशाच्चान्यत्रापि द्रव्यार्जनमात्र एव संभारान् संभरत इति पश्वादिषु दृश्यते। नन्विह मन्त्रेण संभरणं[१९] नास्तीति ब्राह्मणोक्तमिहानुक्तमपि ग्राह्यम्[१९]। कुतः नक्षत्राधानाद्यनुक्त्वा 'स यदि नक्षत्र आधत्त' इत्यनुवदति। अतो ज्ञायतेऽनुक्तमपि ग्रहीतव्यमिति। 'वैश्वानरस्य रूपमि'त्यादयश्च मन्त्राः प्रकरणे तल्लिङ्गाः सन्ति। तत्[२०] यथालिङ्गं मन्त्रक्रमेणैव संभरणं [२०]कर्तव्यम्।

१-१. M broken between विशेषे and देवेन; thus T. Ad यते दैवनं. २. M Ad °कालञ्च. ३-३. M Ad ध्यहे वेत्या. ४-४. M broken between व्यवहार... and श्च... ५. M Ad °नमान°. ६-६. M broken between सोम and ह वैदेहः; thus T. ७. M Ad °ग्रहमादिना. ८-८. M broken between धर्मवं and प्राण्यापान्य. ९. M °जपानां broken. १०-१०. M broken between वि° and विषय°. ११. M Ad तत्र यं. १२. M अनार ... प्रकृ°. १३-१३. M °प्यग्नि...स्वधर्मैः. १४. M Ad प्रकृतत्वमतथा; thus T. १५. M Ad तत्र. १६-१६. M broken between दर्शपूर्णमास and प्रसज्यते. Ad wrongly gives the sign of broken text between तदेव and प्रसज्यते. १७-१७. M Ad °न्त्रेण...नमात्र°; thus T. १८. M Ad °लक्ष्येण. १९-१९. M Ad broken between संभरण and ह्यं; thus T. २०-२०. M Ad broken between तत् (M तन्तं, Ad तं तं) and कर्तव्यम्.

कुर्वीत ॥ ७ ॥ अपि ह गां पचेद्वशश्चास्य स्यात् ॥ ८ ॥ अग्न्याधेयस्य मीमांसा ॥ ९ ॥ ब्राह्मणस्य

ननु तैत्तिरीयश्रुत्याऽयं कल्पो न घटते। कस्माद् ? 'देवो वः सविता प्रेरयतु' इत्यादीनां मन्त्राणाम् एकदेशविकृतानां दर्शनात्।'असिदमादत्ते' इत्येवमादीनामेतद्[१] ब्राह्मणविहितेभ्योऽन्येषां द्रव्याणां दर्शनात्[१]। अग्नौ सावित्रकाणां कल्प आदिग्रहणेन लक्षितानामन्वाख्याने 'सुवर्गेयाय शक्त्या इन्द्रं दानाय हूमहे' (वाधू.अन्वा. ५.३.३) इति साधिकदर्शनादित्येवमादि। अतः स्थालीपुलाकन्या-येनान्ये[२]षामप्येतच्छ्रुत्युक्तमनेन कल्पेनासंबद्धम्। [२]उच्यते। इमामेव शाखामारभ्यायं कल्पो रचित आचार्येण। कुतः ? संप्रदायमार्गे[३] अविच्छिन्नपारंपर्यस्य द्रढिम्नो नोपपद्यते च शाखा विनष्टा तत्क्लृप्त्यर्थं[४] कल्पो न विनष्ट इति। [५]उपनयनात्प्रभृति हि गुरवः शाखां पूर्वमध्यापयन्ति[५], पश्चात् कल्पम्।

[६]नन्वेतच्छाखाश्रयणे दोषा उक्ताः। उच्यते। बह्वीरपि शाखा आरभ्य कल्पसूत्राणि प्रथयन्ति, इति पूर्वमुक्तम्[७]। तत्रायमाचार्य एतच्छाखाधीता अवश्यं विकल्पन्त इति [८]मन्यमानोऽन्यशाखागता-नामनति। तद् द्वयोर्वैकल्पिकत्वं भवति[८]। तथा च क्वचित् क्वचिद् दृश्यते। अग्निष्टोमे ग्रहावकाशानाम्नाय पुनरौपानुवाक्ये ग्रहावकाशैश्चरन्ननुवर्तयति। 'त्रिर्देवेभ्योऽववथा' इत्यन्यशाखागतं मन्त्रमाम्नाय[९] [१०]'परिभूरग्निम्' इत्यादि मन्त्रस्यान्तं गृहीत्वा 'तस्य मे रास्वे'ति समानम् इत्यग्निष्टोमोक्तमनुजानाति[१०]। तथा 'अग्निना देवेन' इत्यादीनां[११] चतुर्थशाखान्तरपठितं समस्तं पठित्वा 'इन्द्रेण सयुजो वयम्' [१२]इत्यवसानादित्येतच्छाखाधीतमनुज्ञाय 'अपि वा तेजस्वी' इत्यन्यशाखागतं वैकल्पिकं पठति। उदाहरणमात्रं प्रदर्शितम्[१२]। अन्यान्यप्येतच्छाखाश्रयणे बहूनि लिङ्गानि सन्ति। अतो ब्राह्मणे मन्त्रे वा यद् दृष्टमिहानुक्तमपि परिग्राह्यम्। अतो मन्त्रैः संभरणं [१३]कर्तव्यम्। इहानाम्नानं किमर्थमिति चेदविकल्पार्थम्। तथा च वाजसनेयिनः समामनन्ति 'न संभारान् संभरेद्' इति। तच्च संभाराभावो[१३] न भवतीति इतिकर्तव्यतया संभरणस्य प्रतिषेधार्थः ॥ ६ ॥

'अद्योपवसथ इत्यन्नमेव कुर्वीत'। प्रथमान्त उपवसथ[१४] इति योगादाधारत्वेनापि निवपति। अस्मिन्नहन्यन्नं दद्यादित्यर्थः। प्रभूतत्वख्यापनार्थ एव-शब्दः ॥ ७ ॥

'वशश्चास्य[१४] स्यात्' इति इच्छा च स्यादित्यर्थः ॥ ८ ॥

१-१. M broken between °एतद् [M सेक] ब्राह्मणा and [न]ात्. **२-२.** M °नान्येष ... उच्यते; Ad °नान्येषामप्येतत्सूक्तानामनेन संबन्ध उच्यते. **३.** M Ad संप्रादेय. **४.** M Ad °क्लृप्त्यर्था. **५-५.** M उपनयन ... यन्ति; Ad शाखाः. **६.** Ad ननुते शाखाः. **७.** M Ad °मुक्ता. **८-८.** M °शाखा ... वति; thus Ad T; Ad अद्वयो°. **९.** M Ad °मम्नाय. **१०-१०.** M °ग्निमित्यादि म... इत्यग्निष्टोक्त°; Ad मेरोः स्वाति; thus T. **११.** M Ad °त्यादिनां; thus T. **१२-१२.** M °सानादि ... तमः, Ad °मनुज्ञायामपि वा तेजस्वी ... पठत्युदाहः°; thus T. **१३-१३.** M कत ... च्च संभारभावौ; Ad किमुत...संभाराभावो; thus T. **१४-१४.** M उपवसन ... स्य स्यादि°; Ad उपवसन ... अस्मिन्नहन्यन्नं दद्यादित्यर्थ प्रकृतत्वख्यापनार्थमेव व...स्य स्यादि.

बहुयाजिनो गृहादग्निमाहरेद् ब्रह्मवर्चसकामो राजन्यस्य गृहादाहरेदिन्द्रियकामो वैश्यस्य बहुपुष्टस्य गृहादाहरेत् पुष्टिकाम इति ॥ १० **॥ स यद्येनमेषकामो विन्द्याद् द्व्यहे त्र्यहे वा पुरस्तादग्निमाहृत्य तमामात्यमेवेन्धीत ॥** ११ **॥ तमपराह्ण उद्धृत्यान्वाहार्यपचनस्योद्धतेनिदधाति ॥** १२ **॥ तत् पितृभ्यो ददाति ॥** १३ **॥** '*शृणोत्वग्निः समिधा हवं मे*' **इति चतुर्गृहीतेन गार्हपत्यस्योद्धते दर्भस्तम्बे हिरण्यमुपास्यानुवित्तिं जुहोति ।** '°शृण्वन्त्वापो धिषणाश्च देवीः ।' '°शृ=हवं मे स्वाहा' **इति ॥** १४ **॥ एवमेवाहनीयस्योद्धते जुहोति ॥** १५ **॥ प्रावृत्यैतामाहुतिमायन्ति ॥** १६ **॥ संवपन्त्येत-**

अग्न्याधेयशब्देनाग्न्याधेयार्थोऽग्निरभिधीयते। तस्य विचारः केन निमित्तेन कीदृशोऽग्निः[१] आहर्तव्य इति ॥ ९ ॥

बहुयाजी सोमयाजी। ब्रह्मवर्चसकामः ब्रह्मनिमित्तं तेजो यस्य स ब्रह्मवर्चसकामः।[१] इन्द्रियकामः। इन्द्रियशब्दो बलधीरतापुरुषकारवचनः, तत्कामः[२]। चक्षुरादीनां वा प्रकर्षगतिः। प्रजोत्पादनसामर्थ्यमित्यपरे[३]। बहुभिः पशुहिरण्यादिभिः पुष्टस्य ॥ १० ॥

स इति प्रकृतानामन्यतमकामो यद्येनं विन्द्यात् लभेत[३] प्राप्नुयादित्यर्थः। आमात्यमेवेन्धीत। लोकाग्निमेवेति। यद्यप्यग्न्याधेयशब्दवाच्यस्तथापि समारोप्य मथित्वा[४] हि [५]तस्यानुगमनादिषु प्रायश्चित्तम्। ततोऽर्वाक् लोकाग्निरेवेति ज्ञापनार्थम्। निष्कामस्य क्रत्वर्थमामात्यादिध्ममादीप्येति[५] ॥ ११ ॥

कामादाहृतं[६] समस्तमन्वाहार्यपचनस्योद्धते निदधाति। अन्यदिध्ममादीप्योद्धृत्य निदधाति ॥ १२ ॥

तस्मिन् पितृभ्यो ददाति। [७]पितृदानमुपवसथगवी, न पिण्डपितृयज्ञः। तस्याप्रकरणाम्नातस्यापि नित्यत्वार्थं देशविध्यर्थं[७] चात्र पितृभ्यो ददातीत्यभिहितम्। उपवसथगव्याः पूर्वमाम्नातयोर्द्वयोरनुवाकयोरन्यत्र विनियोगदर्शनादुद्धरणात्[८] पूर्वमामात्यहोम इति समाख्यानात्, सस्वाहाकाराच्च। 'यद्देवा देवहेडनमि'त्यनुवाको होमार्थः[८]। स हूयते पवमान इत्युपस्थानार्थः। सर्वत्रानादेशे आज्यं होमद्रव्यम्। होम उपस्थानं पितृयज्ञश्च याजमानानि ॥ १३ ॥

[९]असित्वैतदसनीयं वासो अन्यत्परिधायेत्यत्र क्षौमं परिधत्ते। पत्नी च। ततोऽध्वर्युरनुवित्तिहोमं जुहोति[९]। उपासनीयम् हिरण्यं शतमानम् ॥ १४ ॥

आयन्तीति बहुवचनदर्शनात्सर्वकर्मसु स्वामिनोः सन्निधानम्। ब्रह्मा च सर्वकर्मणां दक्षिणतः

१-१. M °ऽग्नि...चर्सकाम, Ad °ऽग्निः...बहुयाजी° वर्चसः °यस्य ब्रह्मवर्चसे कामं. **२.** M Ad तत्काम च°; thus T. **३-३.** M °साम ... लभेतः, Ad दित्याभाति परे. **४.** T gives text under bracket on p.16, line 10-16 and in foot-note points out as under : 'चतुर्दशपत्रे 10 पंक्तौ मथित्वा हि त इत्यनन्तरं 16 पंक्तौ °स्य ह्या ददातीत्यारभ्य 18 पंक्तौ नित्यत्वार्थ इत्येतत्पर्यन्तं च लिखितं पुस्तके वर्तते। देश इत्येतत्पूर्वं पितृभ्यो ददातीत्यनन्तरं प्रक्षिप्ताड्क्तस्तत्र निर्दिष्टः'. **५-५.** M हित ... ध्मादीप्येति. **६.** M Ad काममुदाहृतम्. **७-७.** M Ad पितृभ्योददाति... शविध्यर्थञ्च°. **८-८.** M °दर्श ... होमार्थः; Ad °दर्शनात्पूर्वमात्य°; thus T. **९-९.** M अ ... होति; Ad भरसिक्वैतदसनीयवासे स चान्यत्परि साचेत्यत्र.

मग्निः सते ॥ १७ ॥ तं गार्हपत्यस्योद्धते निवपति ॥ १८ ॥ उपनिवपत्यस्मै शल्कान् यैरेनं रात्रिमिन्धे ॥ १९ ॥ अधिवृक्षसूर्ये ब्रह्मौदनं निर्वपति 'देवस्य त्वा' ॥ १.१.१.२० ॥ **[इति प्रथमः पटलः]**

[हविर्निर्वपणम्]

'देवस्य त्वा सवितुः प्रसवेऽश्विनोर्बाहुभ्यां पूष्णो हस्ताभ्यामदित्यै जुष्टमादित्येभ्यो जुष्टं निर्वपामि' **इति चतुरश्चमसान् व्रीहीणाम्** ॥ १ ॥ **तानेव चतुरोऽपामानीय स्थाल्यामधिश्रयति** ॥ २ ॥ **रोहिते चर्मन्नध्यवघ्नन्ति ब्रह्मौदनम्** ॥ ३ ॥ **तं शृतमाह्वारयत्येव स्थाल्यै बिलम्** ॥ ४ ॥ **नाङ्गारेभ्य उच्छिनत्ति** ॥ ५ ॥ **आज्यं च हिरण्यशल्कं च पात्रियामुपस्तृणीते** ॥ ६ ॥ **तिस्रो दर्वीरुपस्तीर्णाभिघारिता उद्धरति** ॥ ७ ॥ **काममूर्ध्वम्** ॥ ८ ॥ **तत उद्धृत्य व्यूह्य**

आस्ते[१] । तत्रस्थ इति केचित् । आहुतिशब्देन हुतप्रदेशो लक्ष्यते ॥ १६ ॥

रात्रिमिन्धे इति । अत्यन्तसंयोगे द्वितीया ॥ १९ ॥

अधिवृक्षसूर्ये[१] । वृक्षाणामुपर्येवातपो[२] यदा दृश्यते स कालोऽधिवृक्षसूर्याख्योऽस्तमयसमीप इत्यर्थः ॥ १.१.१.२० ॥ **[इति प्रथमः पटलः]**

यः पुरुषाहारपरिमाणः संभवति स [३]निर्वापार्थश्चमसः । शूर्पस्थाल्युलूखलमुसलमाज्य× स्थाली-दर्वीपात्रीणां प्रोक्षणीपात्रवद् दर्भेषु न्युब्ज्य सादनम् । तूर्ष्णीं[३] संस्कृताभिरद्भिरुत्तानानि कृत्वा प्रोक्षणञ्च कर्तव्यमेव । परिस्तरणाज्यसंस्कारादि यद्याज्ञिकैः स्मर्यते तत्सर्वं पूर्वेष्व[४]विरुद्धं कर्तव्यम् ॥ १ ॥

चरुस्थाल्यां चमसेन चरुं निर्वपेत् । चतुर्ष्वपि चमसेषु मन्त्र आवर्त्तते 'त्रिर्यजुषे'त्यादेः[४] प्राप्त्यभावात् ॥ २ ॥

रोहितं चर्मानुडुहमिति ब्रह्मौदने कारणे कार्यवदुपचरितम् ॥ ३ ॥

तं शृतम्[५] विदित्वाऽऽह्वारयति[६], [७]आत्मानं प्रति उपनतं करोति ॥ ४ ॥

तिस्रो दर्वीत्यत्र दर्व्यामेवोपस्तरणाभिघारणं केचित् कुर्वन्ति । अपरे पात्र्यामेव[७] । तत[८] ऊर्ध्वमुपस्तरणाभिघारणं संख्यानियमश्च नास्ति ॥ ६-८ ॥

यावदर्थमुद्धृत्य व्यूह्यापानं कृत्वा [९]हिरण्यशल्कमित्यादिप्रकरणपठितमन्त्रग्रहणपक्षे 'प्रवेधस' इति ब्रह्मौदनमुपतिष्ठते, जुहोति[९] वा । [१०]अथवा इहाचार्येणाविनियुक्तानां[१०] यथालिङ्गं विनियोगः

१-१. M आ ... सूर्ये. Ad om आस्ते; Ad इत्यन्त०. Ad om अधिवृक्ष. **२.** M Ad om वृक्षाणामुपर्येः; thus T

३-३. M Ad निर्वापार्थश्च ... तूर्ष्णीं; thus T. **४-४.** M पूर्वेष [षु] भेदः [त्यादेः] Ad पूर्वेषु अपिविरुद्धं; thus T, Ad चासौ for चमसेन Ad ०च्च त्रिष्व० for चतुर्ष्वपि; thus T. **५.** Ad श्रुतम्. **६.** T आहार०. **७-७.** M ०ह्वारयत्यात्मा ... र पात्रियामेव; Ad ०करोतीति सोऽब्रवीत्त्यत्र; thus T. **८.** M कृत. **९-९.** M हिरण्यशल्क ... जुहोति; Ad प्रवेडसर इति; thus T. **१०-१०.** M Ad वा इहाचार्येण विनि० ; thus T.

हिरण्यशल्कं प्रास्य बहूपसिञ्चति ॥ ९ ॥ तं चत्वार आर्षेयाः प्राश्नन्ति ॥ १० ॥ तान् यजमान एव स्वयमवनेजयेदितीदम् ॥ ११ ॥ तानध्वर्युः संशास्ति 'सकृत्प्राश्योत्पिचत' **इति ॥ १२ ॥ ते सकृत्प्राश्योत्पिचन्ति ॥ १३ ॥** 'समिधाऽग्निं दुवस्यत' **इत्यत्रैव ब्रह्मौदने प्रोन्दन् गायत्रीभिः समिधोऽभ्यादधाति ।** '०घृतैर्बोधयतातिथिम् । आस्मिन् हव्या जुहोतन स्वाहा' **इति । स्वाहाकारः सर्वासु समित्सु ।** 'उप त्वाग्ने हविष्म=ती घृताची=समिधो मम स्वाहा', 'तं त्वा समिद्भिरङ्गिरो=

कर्तव्यः ॥ ९ ॥

तं चत्वार आर्षेयाः शुश्रुवांसो ब्राह्मणाः । [१]महर्त्विज इति केचिद् । अश्वमेधे दर्शनात् तत्रापि हि चत्वार आर्षेया इति चोदना । अन्ये च वर्णयन्ति । उद्गातुरनित्यत्वाददर्शनादृत्विज[१] इति नोपपद्यत इति । उद्गातुरभावे त्रयो वा स्युः[२], अन्यो वा कश्चिदुपादातव्यः स्यात् । तथा सति[३] अनवस्थाप्रसंगः । स चान्याय्यः स्यात् । एतद् उद्गातरि अविद्यमाने । तदभावेऽग्नीदिति । तदपि नोपपद्यते । अनेकार्थत्वप्रसंगात्[३] स्वशासनमयुक्तमेवेत्युक्तम् । अश्वमेधे तु 'यन्महर्त्विजः[४] प्राश्नन्ति' इति ब्राह्मणमपि महर्त्विक् चोदनेनैव[५] । इह तु प्राश्नन्ति ब्राह्मणा ओदनमिति । अयमप्याचार्यो यत्रेच्छति तत्र 'तमेत एव चत्वारो महर्त्विजः[५] प्राश्नन्ति' इति वदति । ज्येष्ठबन्धोश्च ब्रह्मौदने दर्वीहोमे[६] सिद्धवचनम् एवं सत्युपपद्यते । अनुपदे पुरस्तात् [७]'प्रत्यङ्ङध्वर्युरुपविशति' इत्यादि यस्मिन् कल्पे विरोधो नास्ति तदर्थं स्यात् ॥ १० ॥

अवनेजनं पादप्रक्षालनम् । इदमिति ब्राह्मणान्तरप्रदर्शनं[७], स्मृतिदर्शनं वा ॥ ११ ॥

तानध्वर्युः संशास्तीत्यादि[८] । उत्पेचनम् अङ्गुलिप्रसारणम् ॥ १२-१३ ॥

अत्रैवेति 'यदाज्यमुच्छिष्यते तेन [९]समिधोऽभ्यज्यादधाती'ति वचनात् प्राशनोत्तरकालं भवितुमर्हती'ति मन्यमानः प्राशनमध्ये विदधद् व्यक्तवचनमस्तीति[९] द्योतयति । प्रोन्दन्[१०] णमुलर्थे शतृप्रत्ययो व्यत्ययेन । 'गायत्रीभिस्त्रिष्टुग्भिर्जगतीभिः' इति ऋग्गादानेनैव [११]सिद्धे छन्दोग्रहणे 'गायत्रीभिर्ब्राह्मणस्यादध्यात्, 'त्रिष्टुग्भी राजन्यस्य' इति पक्षे उपयुज्यः । स च पक्षो विकल्पते 'राजयज्ञे य उ वैको यजते[११] ब्राह्मण एव भूत्वा यजत' इत्यादिना । तथा सति ब्राह्मणविहितपक्षे 'समिध्यमानः [१२]प्रथमः' इत्याद्यास्तिस्र आसु समित्सु स्युः । एताश्च तासां स्थाने भवन्ति[१२] । तथा 'त्वामग्ने समिधानम्' इति वैश्यस्य । 'स्वाहाकारः सर्वासु समित्सु' इयं परिभाषा येषु समिदाधानमन्त्रेषु स्वाहाकारो नास्ति तेषां स्वाहाकारान्तत्वं यथा स्यादिति । 'समिदसि' 'तेजोऽसि तेजो मयि धेहि' इत्यादीनाम् । नन्वस्यां परिभाषायां सत्यां येषु मन्त्रेषु स्वाहाकार आम्नायते तत्राम्नानवैयर्थ्यम् । उच्यते ।

१-१. M महर्त्विज्य ... रित्यत्वाद० ; Ad चोदनाय इति for चोदना उरवातुर० ; for उद्गातुर०. **२.** M Ad स्यरण्यो for स्युः अन्यो. **३-३.** M तथासत्यनव ... कार्थत्व०. **४.** M Ad इयं मह for यन्मह. **५-५.** M चोदनेनै ... त्विजः. **६.** M दर्वि०, Ad हविर्होमे. **७-७.** M प्रत्यय ... ब्राह्मणान्तर०. **८.** M Ad शस्ती०. **९-९.** M समिधो ... ति द्योतपति; Ad समिधो आज्यं ददातीति०. **१०.** M Ad om. **११-११.** M सिद्धो मन्दे ग्रहणे गायत्री ... यजते; Ad सिद्धो मन्दे ग्रहणे गायत्री ब्राह्मणस्यास्य० योवै यजते. **१२-१२.** M प्रथम इ... ने भवन्ति.

बृहच्छोचा यविष्ठ्य स्वाहा' **इति ॥ १४ ॥ पर्युदच्याज्यं निदधाति द्विः ॥ १५ ॥ अत ऊर्ध्वं ब्रह्मौदनप्राशाः प्राश्नन्ति ॥ १६ ॥ मिथुनौ समित्सु ददाति ॥ १७ ॥ आण्डीवलं ब्रह्मौदने ॥ १८ ॥ यथाश्रद्धं स्थालीप्राशाय ॥ १९ ॥** 'सꣳशाधि यजमान' **इत्याह** '°यत्ते सꣳशिष्यम्' **इति ॥ २० ॥ सꣳशास्ति यदस्य सꣳशिष्यं भवति ॥ २१ ॥ पुत्रे वा भ्रातरि वर्णमुपनयति ॥ २२ ॥** 'ऋत्वियवती स्थ' **इत्यस्मै निपदः कालेऽरणी आदधाति ।** '°अग्निरेतसौ गर्भं दधाथां ते वामहं ददे तत्सत्यं यद्वीरं बिभृथो वीरं जनयिष्यथः' **इति ॥ २३ ॥ तदनु वाचं यच्छति ॥ २४ ॥ स वाचंयमोऽनुरात्रं शल्कैरग्निमिन्धे ॥ २५ ॥ जागृयाद्धैव, न सुषुप्सेद्वशश्चास्य स्यात् ॥ २६ ॥** 'जातवेदो भुवनस्य रेतः' **इत्युपव्युषेऽरणी निष्टपति ।** '°इह सिञ्च तपसो यज्जनिष्यते । अग्निमश्वत्थादधि हव्यवाहं शमीगर्भाज्जनयन् यो मयोभूः' **इति ॥ २७ ॥** 'अयं ते योनिर्ऋत्वियः' **इत्यरण्योरग्निꣳ समारोहयते ॥ १.१.२.२८ ॥ [इति द्वितीयः पटलः]**

[अरण्योरग्निसमारोहणादिकर्म]

'अयं ते योनिर्ऋत्वियः' **इत्यरण्योरग्निं समारोहयते ।** '°यतो जातो=आरोहाथा नो वर्धया

सिद्धानुवादः संभवति । अन्यत्रापि सिद्धार्था अनूद्यन्ते 'तिस्र एकाहानामुपसद' इति परिभाषा । तथापि बृहस्पतिसवादिषु क्वचित्क्वचित् 'तिस्र उपसद' इति प्रकरणे तु स्वाहाकारान्तत्वसद्भावादुत्कर्षः ॥ १४ ॥

पर्युदच्य विस्राव्य कस्मिंश्चित्पात्रे ॥ १५ ॥

मिथुनौ गोमिथुनौ तत्कर्त्रेऽध्वर्यवे ददाति । उक्तं च भगवता मनुना[१]—

'यस्मिन् कर्मणि यास्तु स्युरुक्ताः प्रत्यङ्गदक्षिणाः ।

स एव ता आददीत' (भजरेन् सर्व एव वा) (मनु. ८.२०८) इति ॥ १७ ॥

[२]आण्डीवलो मुष्करः ब्रह्मौदनप्राशेभ्यः ॥ १८ ॥

स्थाल्या अनुद्धृतं यः प्राश्नाति स स्थालीप्राशः । तस्मै यथाश्रद्धं ददाति यजमानः । स्वेषु पशुषु[३] यं दातुमिच्छति स यथाश्रद्धमिति चोदिते देयः ॥ १९ ॥

पुत्रे वा भ्रातरि वर्णमुपनयति । ऋणं कालान्तरे देयमवश्यं देयं च भुक्तिदानादि ॥ २२ ॥

निपदःकाले निपदनकाले न्याय्ये शयनकाले रात्रिचतुर्थभागे गत इत्यर्थः ॥ २३ ॥

अनुरात्रं यावती रात्रिस्तावन्तं कालम् ॥ २५ ॥

अनुपरमेण जागृयादेव । जागरणं निद्राभावः । न सुषुप्सेत्, स्वप्तुं नेच्छेत् । न शयीतेत्यभिप्रायः । निद्रेच्छा यदि स्यादित्यर्थः ॥ २६ ॥

उपव्युषे उषः समीपे निष्टपनसमारोपणे याजमाने ॥ १.१.२.२७ ॥ **[इति द्वितीयः पटलः]**

---

१. Ad मुनिना. २. M Ad आण्डि°. ३. M Ad पशुष्कं.

रयिम्' **इति** ॥ १ ॥ **संवपन्त्येतमग्निं सते** ॥ २ ॥ **तस्यैष ज्वाले मथ्यते** ॥ ३ ॥ **जातेऽस्मिन्नन्वाहार्य-पचनस्योद्धतमेतमग्निं हरन्ति** ॥ ४ ॥ **अवोक्ष्य** 'मयि गृह्णाम्यग्रे अग्निम्' **इति द्वाभ्यामात्मन्नग्निं गृह्णीतेऽध्वर्युः** । '○रायस्पोषाय सुप्रजास्त्वाय सुवीर्याय=अवहाय परा गाद्' **इति** ॥ ५ ॥ 'सं या वः प्रियास्तनुवः' **इति संभारान् संयौति** । '○सं प्रिया हृदयानि वः आ=तनुवो मम' **इति** ॥ ६ ॥ **संभारेषु होतर्नि् व्याचष्टे** ॥ ७ ॥ 'ऋतं स्तृणामि पुरीषं पृथिव्याम्' **इति गार्हपत्यस्योद्धते तृतीयं संभाराणां निवपति** ॥ ८ ॥ **वाचयति** 'ऋतेऽधि सत्यमादधे सत्येऽध्यग्निमादधे' **इति** ॥ ९ ॥ **प्रोक्ष्य** 'अग्नेर्जनित्रमसि' **इति शकलमादत्ते** ॥ १० ॥ 'वृषणौ स्थः' **इति वृषणौ** ॥ ११ ॥ 'उर्वश्यसि' **इत्यधरारणिम्** ॥ १२ ॥ 'पुरूरवा' **इत्युत्तरारणिम्** ॥ १३ ॥ 'घृतेनाक्ते' **इत्यनक्ति** ॥ १४ ॥ 'वृषणं दधाथाम्' **इत्यवदधाति** ॥ १५ ॥ 'गायत्रं छन्दोऽनु प्रजायस्व' **इति छन्दोभिरात्मानमभि निवर्तयते** । '○त्रैष्टुभं छन्दोऽनु प्रजायस्व', 'जागतं छन्दोऽनु प्रजायस्व' **इति** ॥ १६ ॥ **दशहोतारमरण्यो-र्व्याचष्टे** ॥ १७ ॥ **मन्थन्त्यग्निम्** ॥ १८ ॥ 'आयुरसि' **इति जातमभिमन्त्रयते** ॥ १९ ॥ **जाते** 'वरं

---

[1]संवपनमनियतकर्तृकम् ॥ २ ॥

तस्याग्नेर्ज्वाले[2] एष उन्मथ्यमानोऽग्निर्मथ्यते। ज्वाले पूर्वज्वलितप्रदेशे गार्हपत्यस्योद्धत इत्यर्थः। 'अपोदूह्य भस्माग्निं [3]मन्थती'ति ब्राह्मणम् ॥ ३ ॥

अथवा 'ज्वालासमीपे जात' इत्यादिदर्शनादग्निग्रहणम् ॥ ४ ॥

अध्वर्योः स्वस्याग्नेरात्मन्येवावस्थापनम्। मन्त्रलिङ्गप्राप्तस्य ग्रहणे क्रमादिह 'अपेतेति'[4] व्युदसनम्[5] ॥ ५ ॥

भस्मपुरीषसिकतोषाणां[6] च निवपनं[7] क्रमेण मन्त्रैः कर्तव्यम्। तथा च महामेधे— 'अग्न्याधेयिकान्[8] संभारान्' इत्येतावदेवोक्त्वा[9] चितानास्थाय[10] भस्मपुरीषयोश्च निवपनं विदधदाचार्य इहापि तयोः[11] संभवमिच्छति। ऊषां निवपंश्चन्द्रमसि कृष्णं ध्यायति ॥ ८ ॥

वृषणावपि शकलौ[12]। एतयोश्च[12] दर्भमयत्वं केचिदामनन्ति[13]। निवर्तनमात्मनेपदनिर्देशाद्याज-मानम्। तच्चाधरारणेः।[14] तथोदीचीं पूर्वां[15] निदधाति। उत्तरारणिमित्यपरे।[16] तथा सति प्राचीप्रत्यग्योनि-देशम्[17] ॥ १०-१६ ॥

होतृव्याख्यानमाध्वर्यवम्[18] ॥ १७ ॥

'आयुरसि' इत्यभिमन्त्रणं याजमानमिति[19] केचित्। 'उर्वश्यसि' इत्याध्वर्यवमध्ये

---

१. M Ad संवनन○, T सवपन○. **२.** M Ad ○ग्ने ज्वाले. **३.** M Ad ○ग्निर्मन्थ○. **४.** M Ad अपोते○. **५.** M Ad व्युदजनं; thus T. **६.** M Ad पुरीषेसिकतोपान. **७.** M Ad ○वपनक्र○. **८.** M Ad ○धेयीका○. **९.** M Ad ○तावतोक्त्वा; thus T. **१०.** M Ad चितास्थाय, T चितास्थाने. **११.** M Ad om; thus T. **१२-१२.** M Ad शकलावेलतयो○. **१३.** M Ad आमन्ति. **१४.** M Ad तच्चाधरणे. **१५.** M Ad पूर्वा○. **१६.** M Ad उत्तरान्निमि○. **१७.** M Ad प्राचि प्रत्यग्र्यो. **१८.** M Ad ○ध्वर्यवत्. **१९.** M Ad व्याज○.

ददामि' **इति वाचं विसृजते** ॥ २० ॥ **तं** 'भूर्भुवः' **इति त्रिभिरक्षैरञ्जलावाधत्ते** ॥ २१ ॥ 'अमीषां त्वा देवानां व्रतपते व्रतेनादधे' **इति यद्देवत्यो भवति** ॥ २२ ॥ 'गायत्रेण छन्दसा' **इति ब्राह्मणः** ॥ २३ ॥ 'त्रैष्टुभेन छन्दसा' **इति राजन्यः** ॥ २४ ॥ 'जागतेन छन्दसा' **इति वैश्यः** ॥ २५ ॥ 'प्रजापतेस्त्वा प्राणेनाभिप्राणिमि' **इत्येनमभिप्राणिति ।** '॰पूष्णः पोषेण मह्यम् । दीर्घायुत्वाय शतशारदाय शतं शरद्भ्य आयुषे वर्चसे' **इति** ॥ २६ ॥ 'मयि धातः श्रियं धेहि' **इत्यस्मै दक्षिणत आसीनोऽध्वर्युरुत्तरतो हिरण्यशल्कमुपास्यति** ॥ २७ ॥ **वाचयति** 'श्रियै माऽधिपतिं कुरु दिशामीशानो मघवानिन्द्रो मा यशसाऽनक्तु', 'जहामि सेदिमनिराममीवां प्रियया तनुवा संभव' **इति** ॥ २८ ॥ 'अहं त्वदस्मि' **इति सन्नमुपतिष्ठते** ॥ १.१.३.२९ ॥ **[इति तृतीयः पटलः]**

[सन्नोपस्थानम्]

'अहं त्वदस्मि' **इति सन्नमुपतिष्ठते ।** '॰मदसि त्वमेतं ममासि योनिस्तन्व योनिरस्मि । यथायथं वह हव्यानि देवान् पुत्रः पित्रे लोककृज्जातवेदः' **इति** ॥ १ ॥ 'आयं गौः पृश्निरक्रमीद्' **इति तिसृभिः सर्पराज्ञीभिरुपतिष्ठते ।** '॰असदन्मातरं पुनः । पितरं च प्रयन्त्सुवः', 'त्रिꣳशद्धाम विराजति वाक् पतङ्गाय धीयते । प्रति वस्तोरह द्युभिः' **इति** ॥ २ ॥ **आहुतिषाहे गार्हपत्ये चतुर्गृहीतेन दशहोतुराहुतिं जुहोति** ॥ ३ ॥ 'अभि त्वा शूर नोनुम' **इति**

पठितोऽर्थक्रमा-दुत्कृष्टो मन्त्र आध्वर्यवो[1] भवितुमर्हति। तथा जाताभिमन्त्रणात्[2] परस्य वाग्विसर्गस्य पुनर्जातग्रहणम्[3] उभयोर्नानाकर्तृत्वं बोधयति । कथम् । क्रमो नारम्भणीयः । जातमात्र एव 'वरं ददामि' इति वाचं विसृजत इति । कस्मात् । नानाकर्तृकत्वात् एकत्वात्कर्तुरनेकत्वाच्च[4] पदार्थानामवश्यंभावी क्रम इति श्रुत्यादिभिः क्रमोऽवगम्यते[5]। यजमानस्य स्वेषु पशुषु यः प्रतिग्रहीतुरिष्टः स वरः ॥ १९-२० ॥

व्याहृतीभ्यामञ्जलावाधाय 'अमीषां त्वा देवानां व्रतपते'[6] इति संभारेष्वादधीत। तूष्णीमञ्जलावाधानम्[7] । संभारेष्वेव[8] मन्त्रवदाधानम् । अनुपदकारस्य 'भृगूणामङ्गिरसामादित्यानाम्-भूणामि 'त्येवमादिषु 'त्वा देवानाम्' इत्यनुषङ्गः । इतरे यथाम्नातम्। रथकारस्य छन्दो नास्ति। वैश्यकर्मसंयोगाद्रथकार इति केचित् । तथा सति 'जागतेने'ति । जात्यन्तरमित्यपरे ।[9] सर्वत्र आधानं याजमानम्[10] ॥ २१-२६ ॥

हिरण्यशल्कस्यापि प्रदानं[11] ब्राह्मणोक्तम् इहावचनाद्वैकल्पिकम्। तच्चार्तिलिङ्गाद् द्वेष्याय ॥ १.१.३.२७ ॥ **[इति तृतीयः पटलः]**

उपस्थानद्वयं याजमानम् ॥ १-२ ॥

'अभि त्वा शूर नोनुमः' इति रथन्तरेणोपतिष्ठते । रथन्तरेणेति सामनामग्रहणाद् ब्राह्मणे च गानविधानात् सामवेदे च विधानात् साम्नोपस्थानम् । ऋग्द्वयस्य[12] साम्नि नित्यत्वादृगनुक्रमणस्या-

---

१. M Ad ॰ध्वर्यवं. २. M ज...गाभि॰. ३. M Ad ॰ण. ४. M Ad कर्तृत्वा॰. ५. M Ad क्रमो गम्यते. ६. T प्रतपते. ७. M Ad ॰ञ्जलिनावा. ८. M Ad ॰भारेष्वव. ९. M Ad जात्या॰. १०. M Ad यज॰. ११. M Ad ॰स्याति प्रधानं. १२. M Ad ॰मृगूव्यस्य, T ऋग्द्रव्य॰.

रथन्तरेणोपतिष्ठते। '०अदुग्धा इव धेनवः। ईशानमस्य जगतः सुवर्दृशमीशानमिन्द्र तस्थुषः', 'न त्वावाँ अन्यो दिव्यो न पार्थिवः न जातो न जनिष्यते। अऽश्वायन्तो मघवन्निन्द्र वाजिनो गव्यन्तस्त्वा हवामहे' **इति** ॥ ४॥ **इध्ममादीपयन्ति** ॥ ५॥ **उपयमनीरुपकल्पयन्ति** ॥ ६॥ **अश्वं पल्पूलितमानयन्ति** ॥ ७॥ **आदित्यमुद्यन्तं प्रतीक्षत आहवनीयेन** ॥ ८॥ **उदित आदित्ये** 'ओजसे बलाय त्वोद्यच्छे' **इति तिसृभिरिध्ममुद्यच्छते।** '०वृषणे शुष्मायायुषे वर्चसे सपत्नतूरसि वृत्रतुः', 'यस्ते देवेषु महिमा सुवर्गो यस्त आत्मा पशुषु प्रविष्टः। पुष्टिर्या ते मनुष्येषु पप्रथे तया नो अग्ने जुषमाण एहि', 'दिवः पृथिव्याः पर्यन्तरिक्षाद्वातात्पर्जन्यादद्भ्य ओषधीभ्यः। यत्र यत्र जातवेदः सं बभूविथ ततो नो अग्ने जुषमाण एहि' **इति** ॥ ९॥ 'प्राचीमनु प्रदिशं प्रेहि विद्वान्' **इत्यश्वप्रथमाः प्रयन्ति।** '०अग्नेरग्ने पुरो अग्निर्भवेह'। 'विश्वा=द्विपदे चतुष्पदे' **इति** ॥ १०॥ **विषुवदागच्छन्ति** ॥ ११॥ **तत् तिष्ठन्नाह** 'निवपान्वाहार्यपचनस्य संभारान्' **इति** ॥ १२॥ 'ऋतꣳ स्तृणामि पुरीषं पृथिव्याम्' **इत्यन्वाहार्यपचनस्योद्धतेऽर्धꣳ संभाराणां निवपति** ॥ १३॥ **वाचयति** 'ऋतेऽधि सत्यमादधे सत्येऽधि मातरिश्वानं वायुमग्निमा दधे' **इति** ॥ १४॥ 'निवपाग्निम्' **इत्याह** ॥ १५॥ **तं** 'भूमिर्भूम्ना' **इत्यभिमन्त्रयते** ॥ १.१.४.१६॥ **[इति चतुर्थः पटलः]**

तं 'भूमिर्भूम्ना' **इत्यभिमन्त्रयते।** '०द्यौर्वरिणाऽन्तरिक्षं महित्वा। उपस्थे ते देव्यदितेऽग्निमन्नादमन्नाद्यायादधे' **इति** ॥ १॥ 'मयि धातः श्रियं धेहि' **इत्येवास्मै दक्षिणत आसीनोऽध्वर्युरुत्तरतो हिरण्यशल्कमुपास्यति** ॥ २॥ **वाचयति** 'श्रियै माऽधिपतिं कुरु दिशामीशानो मघवानिन्द्रो मा यशसाऽनक्तु', 'जहामि सेदिमनिराममिणां प्रियया तनुवा संभव' **इति** ॥ ३॥ 'इमा उ

नर्थक्यप्रसङ्गादृचा साम्ना वेति विकल्पः प्रतिषिद्धः। नह्येतेषां[1] सामानि गायेत्। तदभावेऽपि योनिभिरुपतिष्ठेत। नैतदेवम्। सामश्रवणसामर्थ्याद्धि उद्गाता कल्प्यते। सः कथं तदभावे गृह्येत। दक्षिणादानादिषु न क्वचिच्छ्रूयते। कस्तर्ह्यर्थः। अनुपदकार आह—'यद्युद्गाता न स्यात् तर्हि[2] यजमानः स्वयमेवोत्थायाभिहिंकृत्य योनिभिरुपतिष्ठेते'ति ॥ ४॥

उद्यन्तमादित्यम्[3] आहवनीयेनेति हेतौ तृतीया। आहवनीयाधानहेतोः। अर्धोदित आहवनीयाधानं यथा संभवति तथेत्यर्थः। 'उदित आदित्ये' इति भूतकालनिर्देशो दिवाऽऽहवनीयमादधातीति पक्षान्तरं मन्यमानेनैवमुक्तं स्यात्। अथवा 'आशंसायां भूतवच्चे'ति भूतनिर्देश आशुप्रयोगार्थः। तिसर्णिामन्ते उद्यमनम्[4] ॥ ८-९॥

'प्राचीम्' इति गमनमन्त्रः। अग्निर्ह्यत्राभिधीयते। कालार्थसंबन्धः, यथा 'हविष्कृदेहि' इति। पूर्वः प्रैषो यजमानस्य, उत्तरोऽध्वर्योः ॥ १.१.४.१०॥ **[इति चतुर्थः पटलः]**

प्रेषितो यजमानः पूर्वमेव तत्रस्थमग्निं संभारेष्वाधायाभिमन्त्रयते। ऋक्सामयोर्विकल्प उक्तः ॥ १॥

---

१. M Ad ह्येकेषां. २. M Ad om; thus T. ३. T अपरमित्यादित्यः. ४. M Ad ०मानं; thus T.

मामुपतिष्ठन्तु रायः' **इति विषुवति हिरण्यशल्कं सन्नमुपतिष्ठते।** '०आभिः प्रजाभिरिह सं वसेय। मयीदं तिष्ठतु विश्वरूपं वसोर्मध्ये दीदिहि जातवेदः' **इति** ॥ ४ ॥ 'कया नश्चित्र आ भुवद्' **इति विषुवदति प्रयन्ति वामदेव्येन।** '०ऊती सदावृधः सखा। कया शचिष्ठया वृता', 'कस्त्वा सत्यो मदानां मꣳहिष्ठो मत्सदन्धसः। दृढा चिदारुजे वसु', 'अभी षु णः सखीनामविता जरितॄणाम् शतं भवास्यूतिभिः' **इति** ॥ ५ ॥ **प्राञ्चमश्वमाक्रमयत्युत्तरत आहुत्यै दक्षिणस्येर्मस्य पदा** ॥ ६ ॥ **पुनः प्रत्यञ्चं तेनैव** ॥ ७ ॥ **तमुदञ्चमुत्सृजति** ॥ ८ ॥ 'ऋतꣳ स्तृणामि पुरीषं पृथिव्याम्' **इत्याहुत्याꣳ संभारान् निवपति** ॥ ९ ॥ **वाचयति** 'ऋतेऽधि सत्यमादधे सत्येऽधि मातरिश्वानं सूर्यमग्निमा दधे' **इति समापयति यजुः** ॥ १० ॥ **उपनिवपत्युपयमनीः** ॥ ११ ॥ **सादयत्यग्निम्** ॥ १२ ॥ 'भुर्भुवः सुवः' **इति सर्वैः पञ्चभिराहवनीयम्** ॥ १३ ॥ 'अमीषां त्वा देवानां व्रतपते व्रतेना दधे' **इति यद्देवत्यो भवति** ॥ १४ ॥ 'गायत्रेण छन्दसा' **इति ब्राह्मणः** ॥ १५ ॥ 'त्रैष्टुभेन छन्दसा' **इति राजन्यः** ॥ १६ ॥ 'जागतेन छन्दसा' **इति वैश्यः** ॥ १७ ॥ 'मयि धातः श्रियं धेहि' **इत्येवास्मै दक्षिणत आसीनोऽध्वर्युरुत्तरतो हिरण्यशल्कमुपास्यति** ॥ १८ ॥ **वाचयति** 'श्रियै=संभव' **इति** ॥ १९ ॥ 'यदिदं दिवः' **इति सन्नमुपतिष्ठते।** '०यददः पृथिव्याः संविदाने पयसि संबभूवतुः। तयोः पृष्ठे निहिते जातवेदाः शंभूः प्रजाभ्यस्तनुवे स्योनः' **इति** ॥ २० ॥ 'आज्यमाहर' **इत्याह** ॥ २१ ॥ **द्वयमाज्य-माहरन्ति पर्युदक्तं चाज्यस्थाल्या च** ॥ १.१.५.२२ ॥ **[इति पञ्चमः पटलः]**

॥ इति प्रथमप्रपाठके प्रथमोऽनुवाकः ॥

संबन्धस्य कालार्थता ईर्मस्य पूर्वपादस्य ॥ ६ ॥

आहुत्यां हुतानुवित्तिहोमे प्रदेशे ॥ ९ ॥

'सूर्यमग्निमादधे' इति समापयति यजुः। किमर्थमिदमुच्यते, लिङ्गविरोध इवात्र दृश्यते। मातरि श्वसितीति[1] मातरिश्वा। अन्तरिक्षे गच्छतीत्यर्थः। तथा चोक्तं—'माताऽन्तरिक्षं, निमीयन्तेऽस्मिन् भूतानि' इति। 'सूर्य आदित्यः। स च दिवि गच्छति' इति। तस्माद् विरोधः। मातेति द्यौरप्यभिधातुं शक्यते, 'निमीयन्ते[2]ऽस्मिन् नक्षत्राणी'ति। अतो न[3] विरुध्यत [4]इत्याचार्याभिप्रायः[4]। एतत् ज्ञापयति [5]'लिङ्गाविरोधेन विनियोगः कर्तव्य' इति। ब्राह्मौदनिकं[6] होतृहोमशेषं च ॥ १.१.५.१० ॥ **[इति पञ्चमः पटलः]**

॥ इत्यार्यदासस्य[7] कल्पागमसंग्रहे प्रथमप्रपाठके प्रथमोऽनुवाकः ॥

---

१. Due to displacement of folio. M and Ad wrongly give the text from कर्तव्य (M p.13, line 5, Ad p.32, line 3) up to तस्या हिता (M p.14, line 16, Ad p.35, line 13) between मातरि श्वसितीति and मातरिश्वाऽन्तरिक्षे. This line has been placed at its proper place in T see fn. 2 on p.15. **२.** M Ad ०यते; thus T. **३.** M म, Ad य. **४-४.** M Ad इत्य...यः; thus T. **५.** M Ad लिङ्गवि०. **६.** M ब्राह्मौ०. **७.** M इत्याचार्यपादस्य.

॥ अथ प्रथमप्रपाठके द्वितीयोऽनुवाकः ॥

[समिधोऽभ्याधानादिकर्म]

'समिध्यमानः प्रथमोऽनु धर्मः' **इति त्रिष्टुग्भिः समिधोऽभ्यादधाति पर्युदक्तेनाभ्यज्याहवनीये।** '०समक्तुभिः=देवान् स्वाहा'; 'यास्ते विश्वा=शर्म स्वाहा'; 'सप्त ते अग्ने=घृतेन स्वाहा' **इति** ॥ १ ॥ **चतुर्गृहीतेन सप्तहोतारमाहवनीये जुहोति** ॥ २ ॥ 'त्वामिद्धि हवामहे' **इति बृहतोपतिष्ठते।** '०साता वाजस्य कारवः। त्वां वृत्रेष्विन्द्र सत्पतिं नरस्त्वां काष्ठास्ववर्वतः'; 'स त्वं नश्चित्र वज्रहस्त धृष्णुया मह स्तवानो अद्रिवः। गामश्वꣳ रथ्यमिन्द्र सं किर सत्रा वाजिं न जिग्युषे' **इति** ॥ ३ ॥ 'त्वामग्ने समिधानं यविष्ठ' **इत्यपरेण गार्हपत्यं परीत्य जगतीभिः समिधोऽभ्यादधाति पर्युदक्तेनैवाभ्यज्यान्वाहार्यपचने।** '०देवा दू=यन्वति स्वाहा'; 'त्वामग्ने प्रदिव आहुतं घृतैः सु=ष्ठसे स्वाहा'; 'घृतप्रतीको घृतयोनिः=घृतं पिबन् यजसि देव देवान् स्वाहा' **इति** ॥ ४ ॥ **चतुर्गृहीतेन षड्ढोतारमन्वाहार्यपचने जुहोति** ॥ ५ ॥ 'अश्वं न त्वा वारवन्तम्' **इति वारवन्तीयेनोपतिष्ठते।** '०वन्दध्या अग्निं नमोभिः'; 'सम्राजन्तमध्वराणाम्'; 'स घा नः सुनूः शवसा पृथुप्रगामा सुशेवः। मीढ्वाँ अस्माकं बभूयात्'; 'स नो दूराच्चासाच्च नि मर्त्यादघायोः। पाहि सदमिद्विश्वायुः' **इति** ॥ ६ ॥ **पञ्चहोतारमामात्ये जुहोति चतुर्होतारꣳ सभायाम्** ॥ ७ ॥ **आगत्य** 'अभि प्र वः सुराधसम्' **इति सर्वान् श्यैतेनोपतिष्ठते।** '०इन्द्रमर्च यथाविदे। यो जरितृभ्यो मघवा पुरोवसुः सहस्रेणेव शिक्षति; 'शतानीकेव प्र जिगाति धृष्णुया हन्ति वृत्राणि दाशुषे। गिरेरिव प्र रसा अस्य पिन्विरे दत्राणि पुरुभोजसः' **इति** ॥ ८ ॥ **सशीर्ष्णः करोति** ॥ ९ ॥ 'घर्मशिरः' **इति गार्हपत्यमुपतिष्ठते** ॥ १.२.१.१० ॥ **[इति प्रथमः पटलः** (६)**]**

'घर्मशिरः' **इति गार्हपत्यमुपतिष्ठते।** '०तदयमग्निः संप्रियः पशुभिर्भुवच्छर्दिस्तोकाय तनयाय

समिध्यमाना याज्याऽऽहवनीये। उक्तं छन्दोग्रहणप्रयोजनम्। होमसंबन्धो गार्हपत्यादिभिः [1]शब्दैर्निर्देशस्य प्रयोजनमाहितमात्राणामेवैतेषामनुगमनादिषु विहितं प्रायश्चित्तं कर्तव्यं यथा स्यादिति। अत एवाग्निव्रतान्यपि संस्कारवैकल्यमात्रान्नारंभणीयमिति। अत्रोपस्थानानि[2] याजमानानि[2]। सभ्यावसथ्योराधानं नेष्यते। सतोः कर्मसम्बन्धविधानात् कथं तयोराधानप्राप्तिः[3]। उच्यते। 'यत् [4]त्रेधाग्निराधीयते' इत्याहवनीयाधानगुणवाक्यमध्ये श्रवणादनयोरपि ततो विहरणमिति। तथा च द्वैधे[5] 'आहवनीयादेवैनौ[5] विहरेदिति शालीकिरि'ति[6]। अन्ये 'यत् त्रेधाग्निराधीयत' इति गार्हपत्ययोनित्वं मन्यन्ते। तथा चोक्तम्—'अपि वा गार्हपत्यादेवान्वाहार्यपचनमादधीते'ति। श्यैतेनोपस्थानं प्रत्येकमुपस्थेयम्[7]। प्राधान्यादिति केचिद्[7]। बहुवचनान्तत्वादुपस्थानोपकारकस्य दृष्टार्थत्वाच्च तन्त्रमित्यपरे ॥ १.२.१.१ ॥ **[इति प्रथमः पटलः** (६)**]**

---

१. M Ad शब्दो; thus T. **२-२.** M Ad ०पस्था...नि; thus T. **३.** M Ad ०प्रवृत्तिः; thus T. **४.** M Ad यत्रेधानिराधी०. **५-५.** M Ad द्वे ... देवैनौ; thus T. **६.** M Ad ०किरिति; thus T. **७-७.** M Ad ०स्थेयः ...केचि०; thus T.

यच्छ' **इति** ॥ १ ॥ 'वातः प्राणः ' **इत्यन्वाहार्यपचनम्** । ' °तदयमग्निः संप्रियः पशुभिर्भुवत् स्वदितं तोकाय तनयाय पितुं पच' **इति** ॥ २ ॥ 'अर्कश्चक्षुः ' **इत्याहवनीयम्** । ' °तदसौ सूर्यस्तदयमग्निः संप्रियः पशुभिर्भुवद्' **इति** ॥ ३ ॥ 'यत्ते शुक्र शुक्रं वर्चः ' **इत्याहवनीयमेव** । ' °शुक्रा तनूः शुक्रं ज्योतिरजस्रम् । तेन मे दीदिहि तेन त्वाऽऽदधेऽग्निनाग्ने ब्रह्मणा', 'आनशे व्यानशे सर्वमायुर्व्यानशे' **इति** ॥ ४ ॥ **विराजोऽभ्यादधाति पर्युदक्तेनैवाभ्यज्य** 'ये ते अग्ने शिवे तनुवौ' **इति द्वे गार्हपत्ये** । ' °विराट् च स्वराट् च ते मा विशतां ते मा जिन्वतां ताभ्यां त्वाऽऽदधे स्वाहा' **इति** ॥ ५ ॥ 'ये ते अग्ने शिवे तनुवौ' **इति द्वे अन्वाहार्यपचने** । ' °सम्राट् चाभिभूश्च ते मा विशतां ते मा जिन्वतां ताभ्यां त्वाऽऽदधे स्वाहा' **इति** ॥ ६ ॥ 'ये ते अग्ने शिवे तनुवौ' **इत्याहवनीये** । ' °विभूश्च परिभूश्च ते मा विशतां ते मा जिन्वतां ताभ्यां त्वाऽऽदधे स्वाहा' **इति** ॥ ७ ॥ 'ये ते अग्ने शिवे तनुवौ' **इति द्वे आहवनीय एव** । ' °प्रभ्वी च प्रभूतिश्च ते मा विशतां ते मा जिन्वतां ताभ्यां त्वाऽऽदधे स्वाहा' **इति** ॥ ८ ॥ **पवमानतनूरभ्यादधाति पर्युदक्तेनैवाभ्यज्य** 'या ते अग्ने पवमाना तनूः' **इत्येकां गार्हपत्ये** । ' °पृथिवीमन्वाविवेश या गायत्रे छन्दसि या रथन्तरे सामन् तया त्वाऽऽदधे तस्यास्ते स्वाहा' **इति** ॥ ९ ॥ 'या ते अग्ने पावका तनूः' **इत्येकामन्वाहार्यपचने** । ' °अन्तरिक्षमन्वाविवेश या त्रैष्टुभे छन्दसि या वामदेव्ये सामन् तया त्वाऽऽदधे तस्यास्ते स्वाहा' **इति** ॥ १० ॥ 'या ते अग्ने शुचिस्तनूः' **इत्येकामाहवनीये** । ' °दिवमन्वाविवेश या जागते छन्दसि या बृहति सामन् तया त्वाऽऽदधे तस्यास्ते स्वाहा' **इति** ॥ ११ ॥ **उदपात्रमादायोत्परेत्य इमां दिशं प्राचीमुदीचीमरण्येऽनूच्याभिस्तनूभिरुपस्थाय यं द्वेष्टि यजमानस्तं ध्यायति** ॥ १२ ॥ **अपः परिषिच्याप्रतीक्षमाव्रजते** ॥ १३ ॥ **आगत्य विराजक्रमैरुपतिष्ठते** ॥ १४ ॥ 'नर्य प्रजां मे गोपाय' **इति गार्हपत्यम्** ॥ १५ ॥ 'अथर्व पितुं मे गोपाय' **इत्यन्वाहार्यपचनम्** ॥ १६ ॥ 'शꣳस्य पशून् मे गोपाय' **इत्याहवनीयम्** ॥ १७ ॥ 'सप्रथ सभां मे गोपाय' **इति सभ्यम्** ॥ १८ ॥ 'अहे बुध्निय मन्त्रं मे गोपाय' **इत्यावसथीयम्** ॥ १९ ॥ **पूर्णाहुतिमेवातो जुहोति** ॥ २० ॥ **परिश्रित्याहवनीयं चतुर्गृहीतं गृह्णीते । अभिपूर्य सप्तहोतारं व्याचष्टे** ॥ २१ ॥ 'सप्त ते' **इत्येतामृचं मध्यतो दधाति** ॥ २२ ॥ **समिधमाधाय होतुराहुत्या जुहोति** ॥ २३ ॥ **वरमस्मै ददाति** ॥ २४ ॥ **सन्तिष्ठते पूर्णाहुतिः** ॥ २५ ॥ **अग्निहोत्रमेवातो जुहोति** ॥ १.२.२.२६ ॥ **[इति द्वितीयः पटलः** (७)**]**

अरण्येऽनूच्याभिरुभौ ॥ १२ ॥

विराजक्रमैरिति विराट्शब्दस्याकारान्तत्वमपीष्यते इत्यवगम्यते। अत्र प्रतीकग्रहणमिति[1] केचित्। अपरे निर्दिष्टमात्र[1] एवेति ॥ १४ ॥

पूर्णाहुतिमेवातो जुहोति। शाखान्तरे विहितायाः [2]पूर्णाहुतेरयमेवावकाश इत्येवातः शब्दयोरुपयोगः ॥ १.२.२.२५–२६ ॥ **[इति द्वितीयः पटलः** (७)**]**

१–१. M Ad °ग्रहणमि...निर्दि; thus T. **२.** M Ad पूर्णाहुतोयमे° ; thus T.

[अग्न्युपस्थानम्]

अग्निहोत्रमेवातो जुहोति ॥ १ ॥ **उन्नीते दशहोतारं व्याचष्टे** ॥ २ ॥ 'भूः स्वाहा' **इति पूर्वामाहुतिं जुहोति, होतुराहुत्योत्तराम्** ॥ ३ ॥ **अग्नीनेवात उपतिष्ठते** ॥ ४ ॥ 'उप प्रयन्तो अध्वरम्' **इत्याहवनीयम्**। '○मन्त्रं वोचेमाग्नये आरे अस्मे च शृण्वते' **इति** ॥ ५ ॥ 'अस्य प्रत्नामनुद्युतम्' **इति गार्हपत्यम्**। '○शुक्रं दुदुहे अह्रयः। पयः सहस्रसामृषिम्' **इति** ॥ ६ ॥ 'अग्निर्मूर्धा' इत्याहवनीयम्। '○दिवः ककुत्=रेताꣳसि जिन्वति' **इति** ॥ ७ ॥ 'अयमिह प्रथमो धायि धातृभिः' **इति गार्हपत्यम्**। '○होता यजिष्ठो अध्वरे=विशे विशे' **इति** ॥ ८ ॥ 'उभा वामिन्द्राग्नी आ हुवध्यै' **इत्युभौ सहोपतिष्ठते**। '○उभा राधसः सह मा=सातये हुवे वाम्' **इति** ॥ ९ ॥ 'अयं ते योनिर्ऋत्वियः' **इत्याहवनीयम्**। '○यतो जातो=वर्धया रयिम्' **इति** ॥ १० ॥ 'अग्न आयूꣳषि पवस' **इति द्वाभ्यामाग्निपावमानीभ्यां गार्हपत्यमुपतिष्ठते**। '○आ सुवोर्जमिषं च नः आरे=दधत्पोषं रयिं मयि' **इति** ॥ ११ ॥ 'अग्ने पावक रोचिषा' **इति द्वाभ्यामन्वाहार्यपचनम्**। '○मन्द्रया देव जिह्वया। आ देवा=हविश्च नः' **इति** ॥ १२ ॥ 'अग्निः शुचिव्रततमः' **इति द्वाभ्यामाहवनीयम्**। '○शुचिर्विप्र =तव ज्योतीꣳष्यर्चयः' **इति** ॥ १३ ॥ 'आयुर्दा अग्नेऽस्यायुर्मे देहि' **इत्याहवनीयमेव**। '○वर्चोदा अग्नेऽसि वर्चो मे देहि।' '○तनूपा अ=ऊनं तन्म आ पृण' **इति** ॥ १४ ॥ 'चित्रावसो स्वस्ति ते पारमशीय' **इति रात्रिं मनसा ध्यायति** ॥ १५ ॥ 'इन्धानास्त्वा शतꣳ हिमा' **इति समिधमादधाति**। '○द्युमन्तः समिधीमहि। वयस्वन्तो=वर्षिष्ठे अधि नाके स्वाहा' **इति** ॥ १६ ॥ 'सं त्वमग्ने सूर्यस्य वर्चसाऽगथाः' **इत्युपतिष्ठते**। '○समृषीणाꣳ स्तुतेन=प्रजया सृज' **इति** ॥ १७ ॥ 'सं त आकुर्वन्तु स्वं यजमान' **इत्याह**। '○यदन्यत्र मनसा तद् ध्याय' **इति** ॥ १८ ॥ **तत्समाकृतमभिमन्त्रयते** 'सं पश्यामि' ॥ १.२.३.१९ ॥ **[इति तृतीयः पटलः** (८)**]**

अग्निहोत्रं स्रुगुत्प्रदानान्तं[१] होतृहोमवर्जं तूष्णीं क्रियते। 'तस्मान्नु[२] हैनं जातमेतेन[२] पयसा प्रत्य-वेक्षेत[३]' इति दर्शनात् पयसैव चाहुतिः स्यात्। अग्निहोत्रस्यावृत्त्यभावात् कालसामान्यात् प्रातरग्नि-होत्रधर्मत्वे प्राप्ते 'न ह्येवैषा प्रातराहुतिर्न सायमाहुति'रिति दर्शनान्नान्यतरधर्मत्वम्[४]। अत उन्मार्जनाव[४]मानयोर्विकल्पः। 'उच्च मार्ष्ट्युप[५] च मार्ष्ट्युभ[५]यमाप्नोती'ति[६]शाखान्तरवचनम्' ॥ १ ॥

अग्न्युपस्थानं नाग्निहोत्राङ्गं शाखान्तरे विहितं, संस्कारान्तरं ब्राह्मणे तूष्णींग्रहणात्। इह च मन्त्रपरिसंख्यानात् त्रिवृत्तं च यथोक्तं च क्रियते ॥ १.२.३.४ ॥ **[इति तृतीयः पटलः** (८)**]**

॥ इति व्याख्यायां प्रथमप्रपाठके द्वितीयोऽनुवाकः ॥

---

१. M Ad प्रधाना○. **२-२.** M Ad तस्मा ... न पयसा; thus T. **३.** M Ad पेक्षेति. **४-४.** M Ad न्यतर ... नावमा○; thus T. **५-५.** M Ad मार्ष्युप चमाष्यु. **६.** M Ad om शाखान्तर; thus T.

'सं पश्यामि प्रजा अहमिडाप्रजसो मानवीः सर्वा भवन्तु नो गृहे अम्भ स्थ=बह्वीर्मे भूयास्त' **इति** ॥ १ ॥ 'सꣳहिताऽसि विश्वरूपीः' **इत्यग्निहोत्रियै वत्समभिमृशति।** '○आ मोर्जा विशा गौ=मयि वो रायः श्रयन्ताम्' **इति** ॥ २ ॥ 'उप त्वाऽग्ने दिवेदिवे' **इति तिसृभिर्गायत्रीभिराहवनीय-मुपतिष्ठते।** '○दोषावस्तर्धिया वयं नमो=सचस्वा न स्वस्तये' **इति** ॥ ३ ॥ 'अग्ने त्वं नो अन्तमः' **इति तिसृभिर्द्विपदाभिर्गार्हपत्यमुपतिष्ठते।** '○उत त्राता=रयिं दाः' **इति** ॥ ४ ॥ 'ऊर्जा वः पश्याम्यूर्जा मा पश्यत' **इति गृहान् परेक्षते** ॥ ५ ॥ 'रायस्पोषेण वः पश्यामि रायस्पोषेण मा पश्यत' **इति गाः** ॥ ६ ॥ 'इडा स्थ मधुकृतः' **इति ता एव।** '○स्योना=श्रयन्ताम्' **इति** ॥ ७ ॥ 'तत्सवितुर्वरेण्यम्' **इत्याहवनीयम्।** '○भर्गो देवस्य धीमहि। धि=दयात्' **इति** ॥ ८ ॥ 'सोमानꣳ स्वरणं कृणुहि' **इति गार्हपत्यम्।** '○ब्रह्मणस्पते=य औशिजम्' **इति** ॥ ९ ॥ 'कदा चन स्तरीरसि' **इत्याहवनीयम्।** '○नेन्द्र=पृच्यते' **इति** ॥ १० ॥ 'परि त्वाऽग्ने पुरं वयम्' **इत्यनुष्टुभा गार्हपत्यमभ्येति।** '○विप्रं=रावतः' **इति** ॥ ११ ॥ 'अग्ने गृहपते' **इत्युपतिष्ठते।** '○सुगृहपतिरहं त्वया गृहपतिना भूयासꣳ सुगृहपतिर्मया त्वं गृहपतिना भूयाः' **इति** ॥ १२ ॥ **आशिष आशास्ते** 'शतꣳ हिमास्तामाशिषमाशासे मह्यममुष्मै ज्योतिष्मतीम्' **इति** ॥ १३ ॥ **आत्मनोऽग्रे नाम गृह्णाति** ॥ १४ ॥ 'अमुष्मा अमुष्मै' **इत्यनुपूर्वं पुत्राणां,** 'तन्तवे' **इत्यन्ततः** ॥ १.२.४.१५ ॥ **[इति चतुर्थः पटलः** (९)**]**

॥ इति प्रथमप्रपाठके द्वितीयोऽनुवाकः ॥

॥ अथ प्रथमप्रपाठके तृतीयोऽनुवाकः ॥

[आग्नेयीष्टिः]

हविष्क्लृप्तिरेवातः ॥ १ ॥ यज्ञायुधानि सꣳसाद्यापः प्रणीयाग्नेयमष्टाकपालं निर्वपति ॥ २ ॥ तं तनूभिः परियजति ॥ ३ ॥ निरुप्ते प्राणग्रहाꣳश्च पृश्नीꣳश्च व्याचष्टे ॥ ४ ॥ समासन्नेऽ-

---

हविष्क्लृप्तिरेवातः । हविःशब्देनेष्टिरुपलक्ष्यते । [१]इष्टीनां क्लृप्तिरेवारभ्यते[१] । एतावानेव संस्कारः परिशिष्टः । 'अतः ' इति तत्तदित्यर्थः ॥ १ ॥

अग्निर्देवता अस्याग्नेयः । तद्धितप्रत्ययेन चतुर्थ्या यावद् द्रव्यदेवतासंबन्धे[२] चोदित इति कर्तव्यतार्थित्वे सति तत्सदृशयोर्दर्शपूर्णमासयोर्धर्मा[३] अग्न्याधानादय[३] इति कर्तव्यताकांक्षा निवर्तयति । तथा प्राप्तानां धर्माणां[४] चोदकेन यज्ञायुधानि संसाद्यापः प्रणीयेति प्रदर्शनार्थमाम्नायन्ते नाङ्गेयत्वार्थम् ।[५] अत 'एकविंशतिदारुमिध्मम्'[५] (वाधूश्रौ. २.१.१) इत्यादि प्रतिपद्यते ॥ २ ॥

'तं तनूभिः परियजति '[६] इति । 'पवमानं हविर्भिरुच्छ्रयतो यजती 'ति[६] ॥ ३ ॥

निरुप्ते प्राणग्रहांश्च पृश्नींश्च व्याचष्टे । अत्र केचित् बहुहविष्केषु प्रत्यर्थं व्याचक्षते । [७]संस्कारभेदाद् इतरथा [८]निरुप्त इति लक्षणा स्यात् । [८]कालवाचित्व इत्यन्य आह । तत्र संभव [९]आवृत्त्यनुपपत्तेर्ग्रहसंमार्गवत्[९] संनिपत्योपकारकत्वाभावात् । उक्तिमात्रत्वात् संस्कारस्य । तस्य च तन्त्रेण प्रयोक्तुं शक्यत्वान्न भिद्यत इति ॥ ४ ॥

१–१. M Ad इ ... वारभ्यते; thus T. २. M Ad चतुर्थ्याव द्रव्यदेवतरासंख्य The text beginning with कर्तव्यतार्थत्वे and ending with तस्या हिता in both M and Ad which was given wrongly between मातरिश्वसिति and मातरिश्वाऽन्तरिक्षे has been placed here at its proper place, as also given in T. ३–३. M Ad ०धर्मा ...ादय इति क० ; Ad ०धर्मा आग्न्याधानादु ... य इति. ४. M Ad कर्माणां. ५–५. M नाङ्गेय...शति दारु०. ६–६. M ०यजती...विर्भिरुच्छयतो; thus T. ७. M Ad ०स्कारभे०, T कार्यभे०. ८–८. M निर...काल० ; thus T. ९–९. M आपत्यनुपपत्ते...द्रसं०, Ad आपत्यनुपपत्तेर्ग्रह सममार्ग० ; thus T.

पानग्रहाꣳश्च पृश्नीꣳव्याचष्टे ॥५॥ '**ध्रुवा असदन्**', '**यन्मे अग्ने**' **इति समभिमृश्य दशहोतारं व्याचष्टे** ॥ ६ ॥ **अग्नये समिध्यमानायानुवाच आह** ॥७॥ **सप्तदश सामिधेनीरन्वाह** ॥८॥ **आवाहयन् तनूरप्यावाहयत्यग्निं पवमानमथाग्निं पावकमथाग्निं शुचिम्** ॥ ९ ॥ **अनूक्तासु सामिधेनीषु स्रुवेणाघारमाघार्याह** 'अग्नीदग्नीन् त्रिस्त्रिः समृड्ढि' **इति** ॥ १० ॥ **स्रुग्भ्यामुत्तरमसꣳ-स्पर्शयन्नत्याक्रम्य ध्रुवाꣳ समज्य सादयित्वा प्रवरं प्रवृणीते** ॥ ११ ॥ **सीदति होता** ॥ १२ ॥ **प्रसूतः स्रुचावादत्ते** ॥ १३ ॥ **प्रयाजान् यजति** ॥ १४ ॥ **प्रयाजानिष्ट्वाऽत्याक्रम्य द्विर्ध्रुवामभिघारयति, सकृद्धविः** ॥ १५ ॥ **द्विरेव ध्रुवाम्** ॥ १६ ॥ **उपभृतमन्ततः** ॥ १७ ॥ **आज्यभागौ यजति** ॥ १८ ॥ **वार्त्रघ्नावाज्यभागौ** ॥ १९ ॥ 'अग्नये पवमानायानुब्रूहि' **इत्याहाज्यस्य गृह्णानश्चतुः** ॥ २० ॥ 'अग्न आयूꣳषि पवसे' **इत्यन्वाह** ॥ २१ ॥ 'अग्ने पवस्य' **इति यजति** ॥ २२ ॥ **वषट्कृते जुहोति** ॥ २३ ॥ 'अग्नयेऽनूब्रूहि' **इत्याहोपस्तृणानोऽवद्यन्** ॥ २४ ॥ 'अग्निर्मूधा' **इत्यन्वाह** ॥ २५ ॥ 'त्वमग्ने पुष्करादधि' **इति यजति** ॥ २६ ॥ **वषट्कृते जुहोति** ॥ २७ ॥ 'अग्नये पावकायानुब्रूहि' **इत्याहाज्यस्यैव गृह्णानश्चतुः** ॥ २८ ॥ 'अग्ने पावक रोचिषा' **इत्यन्वाह** ॥ २९ ॥ 'स नः पावक दीदिवः' **इति यजति** ॥ ३० ॥ **वषट्कृते जुहोति** ॥ ३१ ॥ 'अग्नये शुचयेऽनुब्रूहि' **इत्याहाज्यस्यैव गृह्णानश्चतुः** ॥ ३२ ॥ 'अग्निः शुचिव्रततमः' **इत्यन्वाह** ॥ ३३ ॥ 'उदग्ने शुचयस्तव' **इति यजति** ॥ ३४ ॥ **वषट्कृते जुहोति** ॥ ३५ ॥ 'अग्नये स्विष्टकृतेऽनुब्रूहि' **इत्याह द्विरुपस्तृणानः** ॥ ३६ ॥ **सकृदुत्तरार्धात् पुरोडाशस्यावद्यति** ॥ ३७ ॥ **चतुरभिघारयति** ॥ ३८ ॥ **सप्तावत्तः स्विष्टकृत्** ॥ ३९ ॥ **गायत्रियौ संयाज्ये** ॥ ४० ॥ 'अग्निꣳ स्तोमेन बोधय' **इत्यन्वाह** ॥ ४१ ॥ 'स हव्यवाट्' **इति यजति** ॥ ४२ ॥ **वषट्कृते जुहोति** ॥ ४३ ॥ **अत्याक्रम्य यथायतनꣳ स्रुचौ सादयित्वा प्राशित्रमवद्यति** ॥ ४४ ॥ **अप उपस्पृश्य त्रिरिडया उपस्तृणीते, द्विरवद्यति,**

दशहोता चतुर्होता[१] च तत्स्थाने ॥ ६ ॥

अग्निं पवमानमथाग्निमिति क्रमार्थम्[१] । तथा[२] पावकशुच्योः, तथा स्विष्टकृद्विधेः ॥ ९ ॥

अपि तयोः प्रतिपत्तिकर्मत्वादप्रतिपाद्यत्वाद्ध्रुवाज्यस्य सप्तावत्तदशावत्तसंपादनार्थं वचनमिति कथमप्रतिपाद्यत्वम् । *सर्वार्थत्वाद् ध्रौवस्याकृतप्रयोजनत्वात् कृतप्रयोजनं हि प्रतिपाद्यते ॥ ११ ॥

[२]द्विर्ध्रुवामभिघारयति सकृद्धविरिति । किमिदं [३]पवमानार्थं द्वितीयमभिघारणम्, उत वचनमिति । ब्रूमः ।[३] आज्यभागयोरिह प्रकृतौ चाव्यवधानादविवेकाच्च तन्त्रेणाभिघारणं दृष्टम् । [४]अस्याप्याज्यभागाभ्यामव्यवधानमिति एकस्य चतुः स्याद्[५] वचनम् ॥ १५–१८ ॥

१–१. M चतुर्होता...अग्निंव...मार्थम् द्वि०, T ०चतुर्होम तू स्थाने; thus Ad, but om द्वि. **२–२.** M Ad om. T gives this text after line 8 on p.28, line 9-15. Since this text deals with *VādhŚS* 1.3.1.9, I have put here before द्विर्ध्रुवामभिधारयति *etc.* which have been given in all M Ad and T द्विर्ध्रुवामभि धारयति = कथ तस्माद्चवनत्. ***.** M सर्वा...कृति० ; thus T ; T कृत प्रयो०. **३–३.** M पव...ान...ति ब्रूमः ; Ad धारेण...वचमिनति ब्रूम; thus T. **४.** M अस्य...व्यवधानमव...तस्मात् वचनंत, Ad ०भागाभ्याम्यं व्यवधान०. **५.** M Ad give the text after तस्माद्वचनात्; thus T.

पञ्चकृत्वोऽभिघारयति ॥ ४५ ॥ **दशावत्तेडा** ॥ ४६ ॥ **उपहूतायामिडायामग्नीध आदधाति** ॥ ४७ ॥ **प्राश्नन्ति** ॥ ४८ ॥ **मार्जयन्ते** ॥ ४९ ॥ **परिहरन्ति ब्रह्मणे** ॥ ५० ॥ **प्राशिते प्राशित्रेऽग्नीदुदपात्रेणोत्कर उपसीदति** ॥ ५१ ॥ **अत्राग्न्याधेयदक्षिणा ददाति** ॥ ५२ ॥ **सन्ततिमनु होतुराहुतिं जुहोति** ॥ ५३ ॥ **प्रसिध्यति कर्म** ॥ ५४ ॥ **सन्तिष्ठत एषेष्टिः** ॥ ५५ ॥ **यज्ञायुधानि सꣳसाद्याप: प्रणीयैन्द्राग्नं चैकादशकपालं निर्वपति** ॥ १.३.१.५६ ॥ **[इति प्रथमः पटलः** (१०)**]**

[ऐन्द्राग्नेयीष्टिः]

ऐन्द्राग्नं चैकादशकपालं निर्वपत्यादित्यं च चरुम् ॥ १ ॥ **निरुप्ते प्राणग्रहाꣳश्च पृश्नीꣳश्च व्याचष्टे** ॥ २ ॥ **समासन्नेऽपानग्रहाꣳश्च पृश्नीꣳश्च दशहोतारं व्याचष्टे** ॥ ३ ॥ **तस्यै वृधन्वन्तावाज्यभागौ** ॥ ४ ॥ 'इन्द्राग्निभ्यामनुब्रूहि' **इत्याहोपस्तृणानोऽवद्यन्** ॥ ५ ॥ 'इन्द्राग्नी रोचनादिवः' **इत्यन्वाह** ॥ ६ ॥ 'श्नथद्वृत्रम्' **इति यजति** ॥ ७ ॥ **वषट्कृते जुहोति** ॥ ८ ॥ 'अदित्या अनुब्रूहि' **इत्याहोपस्तृणानोऽवद्यन्** ॥ ९ ॥ 'अदितिर्न उरुष्यतु' **इत्यन्वाह** ॥ १० ॥ 'महीमू षु मातरम्' **इति यजति** ॥ ११ ॥ **वषट्कृते जुहोति** ॥ १२ ॥ **त्रिष्टुभौ संयाज्ये** ॥ १३ ॥ **सन्ततिमनु होतुराहुतिं जुहोति** ॥ १४ ॥ **प्रसिध्यति कर्म** ॥ १५ ॥ **सन्तिष्ठत एषेष्टिः** ॥ १६ ॥ **एतन्नु द्विबर्हिः** ॥ १७ ॥ **अथ यदि त्रिबर्हिः कुर्याद् यज्ञायुधानि सꣳसाद्याप: प्रणीयाग्नेयञ्चाष्टाकपालं निर्वपत्यग्नये च पवमानाय पुरोडाशमष्टाकपालम्** ॥ १८ ॥ **तदेतत् सर्वगायत्रं प्रथमं हविः** ॥ १९ ॥ **यज्ञायुधानि सꣳसाद्याप: प्रणीयाग्नये च पावकाय पुरोडाशमष्टाकपालं निर्वपत्यग्नये च शुचये पुरोडाशमष्टाकपालम्** ॥ २० ॥ **तस्यै रयिमन्तावाज्यभागौ यथादेवतꣳ हविषोः** ॥ २१ ॥ **विराजौ संयाज्ये** ॥ २२ ॥ **सन्ततिमनु होतुराहुतिं जुहोति** ॥ २३ ॥ **प्रसिध्यति कर्म** ॥ २४ ॥ **सन्तिष्ठत एषेष्टिः** ॥ २५ ॥ **यज्ञायुधानि सꣳसाद्याप: प्रणीयैन्द्राग्नं चैवैकादशकपालं निर्वपत्यादित्यं च चरुम्** ॥ २६ ॥ **सो एषा तथा क्लृप्तैवेष्टिः** ॥ २७ ॥ **एतदु त्रिबर्हिः** ॥ २८ ॥ **द्विबर्हिस्त्वेवाव-**

अत्राग्न्याधेयदक्षिणा ददाति। अत्रास्मिन् काल इह दीयमानाः सर्वेषामग्निसंस्काराणां भवन्तीत्यग्न्याधेयदक्षिणा[1] इत्युक्तम्। अग्नीध उपबर्हणमित्याद्या[2] ब्राह्मणोक्ताः। आद्वादशभ्य[3] इति धेन्वादीनां [4]वा सौवर्णानां[4] तुल्यजातीयानां संख्या। विद्यमान उद्गातरि धेन्वादीनां तस्य भागः ॥ १.३.१.५२ ॥ **[इति प्रथमः पटलः** (१०)**]**

आदित्यश्चरुर्धृतो[5] भवति। शृतकल्प आज्यमानयति। तच्छेषं चार्षेयाः[6] प्राश्नन्ति ॥ ९-१६ ॥

द्विबर्हिरिरिति[6]। बर्हिःशब्देन[7] इष्टिर्लक्ष्यते ॥ १७ ॥

सर्वगायत्रमिति [8]होतृविषयम् ॥ १९ ॥

यथादैवतं[8] याज्यानुवाक्या विधानार्थमवस्थितवचनम् तं वा एतद्व्यूढमित्यादिनोपोद्बल-

---

१. M Ad °तीत्याग्नेय; thus T. **२.** M बर्हिणमित्य; thus T ... क्ता. **३.** Ad आदा दश. **४-४.** M Ad T वासोपसर्जनां; thus T. **५.** M Ad चरुधृते. **६-६.** M °चार्षेया....रिति. **७.** M Ad बहि°. **८-८.** M °विषयस्तथादे° [Ad दै°].

स्थितम् ॥ २९ ॥

[द्वादशाहव्रतम्]

तस्यैतं द्वादशाहः समिद्धा अग्नयो भवन्ति ॥ ३० ॥ **तस्यैतद् व्रतम्** ॥ ३१ ॥ **नानृतं वदति** ॥ ३२ ॥ **न मांसमश्नाति** ॥ ३३ ॥ **न स्त्रियमुपैति** ॥ ३४ ॥ **नास्य पल्पूलनेन वासः पल्पूलयन्ति** ॥ ३५ ॥ **अधःशाय्यमृन्मयपाय्यशूद्रोच्छिष्टी** ॥ ३६ ॥ **स्वयं पादौ प्रक्षालयते** ॥ ३७ ॥ **भक्ताशी स्यादिति तदेकम्** ॥ ३८ ॥ **अग्निहोत्रोच्छिष्टव्रतः स्यादिति तदेकम्** ॥ ३९ ॥ **यदेव चतुर्णां स्रुवाणामुन्नीतानामुच्छिष्येत तद्व्रतः स्यादिति तदेकम्** ॥ ४० ॥ **यदेवैनं किञ्चागच्छेत् तद्व्रतः स्यादिति तदेकम्** ॥ ४१ ॥ **एतेषां यतमत् कामयेत तत्कुर्यात्** ॥ ४२ ॥ **तस्यैतत् सर्वदोपस्थान-मग्नीनाम्** ॥ ४३ ॥ 'ज्योतिष्मन्तं त्वाऽग्ने' ॥ १.३.२.४४ ॥ **[इति द्वितीयः पटलः (११)]**

यति ॥ २९ ॥

[१]तस्येत्याहिताग्निः प्रतिनिर्दिश्यते[१]। परिसमाप्ताग्निसंस्कारो वा। पौरस्त्येऽर्थे रथचक्रविधाने आसंस्कारपरिसमाप्तेर्भवन्ति। अन्यस्मिन्नगत (?) उत्तरे वा[२] द्वादशाहे [३]सकलसंस्कारान्ते वचनात् तदाशंका। अपरिसमाप्तेष्वग्निसंस्कारेष्वाहितमात्रेष्वाहिताग्निर्भवति[४]। स च प्रकृत इति संशयः। परिसमाप्त्युत्तरकालमिति ज्यायः[५]। तदादिविधानमर्थवद् भवति। समिद्धा अजस्रा[६] उद्धरणपक्षेऽपि यथाऽऽहिता एवावतिष्ठन्ते। अनुपरमेण ज्वलिता धार्यपक्षेऽपि भवन्ति ॥ ३० ॥

तस्याहिताग्नेरेतद् द्वादशाहमित्यनुवर्तते[७] चातुर्मास्यादिषु पुनर्व्रतविधानात् ॥ ३१ ॥

शूद्रायोच्छिष्टं शूद्रोच्छिष्टम्। तदस्यास्तीति शूद्रोच्छिष्टी। न शूद्रोच्छिष्टी अशूद्रोच्छिष्टी[८] ॥ ३६ ॥

भक्ताशी[९] सकृदाशी, हविराकारव्रत इत्यन्ये ॥ ३८ ॥

उन्नीतोच्छेषेण[१०] भक्षनिवृत्तिः स्वयंहोमो वा नियम्यते ॥ ४० ॥

किञ्चागच्छेदयाचितशिष्टभोजनीयं लभेत[११] ॥ ४१ ॥

तस्यैतद् अग्नीनां द्वादशाहानुवृत्तिः सर्वदा अग्निहोत्रे विद्यमानेऽप्यविद्यमानेऽपि। रथचक्रविधाने द्वादशाहमृतुहोमैरियादित्यग्निहोत्राभावः[१२]। अविद्यमानेऽपि[१३] प्रवृत्त्यर्थं सर्वदेत्युक्तम् ॥ १.३.२.४२–४३ ॥ **[इति द्वितीयः पटलः (११)]**

१–१. M तस्येत्याहि...श्यते; Ad °व्याहितानि. **२.** M Ad om; thus T. **३.** M Ad om सकल; thus T. **४.** M आहि...ग्निर्भवति; Ad °हितमातेष्वा°; thus T. **५.** Ad न्याय्यः. **६.** M Ad अजस्र; thus T. **७.** After तस्याहिता the text in both M and Ad has been disturbed by the displacement of the folio M p.14, line 15, Ad p. 35, line 13, after तस्याहिता the text begins from p.16, line 16 in M and from p.40, line 7 in Ad. **८.** M Ad अन्नशू°; thus T. **९.** Ad भवता°. **१०.** M Ad उन्निंतीच्छेषेण; T °न्नीतोच्छेषणे. **११.** M Ad लभते. **१२.** Ad °होमैरित्यात्यग्नि°. **१३.** Ad T °मानेप्यप्र°.

[सर्वदोपस्थानम्]

'ज्योतिष्मन्तं त्वाऽग्ने ज्योतिष्मान् समिन्धे' **इत्याहवनीयꣳ समिन्धे** ॥ १ ॥ 'मनसे त्वा सुवर्गाय लोकाय' **इत्युपतिष्ठते** ॥ २ ॥ 'आयुष्मन्तं त्वाऽग्न आयुष्मान् समिन्धे' **इति गार्हपत्यꣳ समिन्धे** ॥ ३ ॥ 'आयुषे त्वा प्रजननाय' **इत्युपतिष्ठते** ॥ ४ ॥ 'अन्नादं त्वाऽग्नेऽन्नादः समिन्धे' **इत्यन्वाहार्यपचनꣳ समिन्धे** ॥ ५ ॥ 'प्राणाय त्वाऽन्नाद्याय' **इत्युपतिष्ठते** ॥ ६ ॥ 'कामाय वो व्याप्त्यै ज्योतिष्मतः शकेयम्' **इति सर्वान् सहोपतिष्ठते** । '°वित्तं च मे गोपायताशां च' **इति** ॥ ७ ॥ 'अवन्तु मामृषयो देवजाताः' **इति सप्तर्षिभ्यो नमस्करोति** ॥ '°त्रातार उत नस्तनूनां तनूधाः । अमर्त्या मर्त्यमभि मा सचन्तामा मा विशन्तु पितरो दिविष्ठाः' **इति** ॥ ८ ॥ **अथ** 'आपो व्रतभृतो व्रतं मे धारयताप्सु श्रद्धा' **इत्याह** ॥ ९ ॥ **नाचामति** ॥ १० ॥ 'चक्षुरसि', 'श्रोत्रमसि' **इत्यधिवदत्यमृतं ब्राह्मणम्** ॥ ११ ॥ **पञ्चप्रक्रमं वेदिमभिप्रक्रामति** ॥ १२ ॥ 'आपो हि ष्ठा मयोभुवः' **इत्यन्तर्वेदि तृचेन मार्जयन्ते** ॥ १३ ॥ 'इडायै वास्त्वसि' **इतीमामभिमृशति** । '°वास्तुमान् भूयासम्' 'प्रतिष्ठाऽसि प्रतिष्ठेषम्' **इति** ॥ १४ ॥ 'ब्रध्नस्य विष्टपेऽहं माꣳ सादयामि' **इति दक्षिणत आहवनीयस्योपविशति** ॥ १५ ॥ 'कामस्य कामेन वोऽनुवीक्षे' **इत्यग्नीननुवीक्षते** ॥ १६ ॥ 'असौ मे कामः समृध्यताम्' **इति यं कामं कामयते तमाशास्ते** ॥ १७ ॥ **सꣳ हैवास्मै स कामः पद्यते** ॥ १८ ॥ **आरम्भ एवातः** ॥ १.३.३.१९ ॥ **[इति तृतीयः पटलः** (१२)**]**

[उपवसथहोम आरम्भणीयेष्टिश्च]

आरम्भ एवातः ॥ १ ॥ **अद्य पौर्णमास्या उपवसथ इत्यग्नीनां भस्मोद्धरन्ति** ॥ २ ॥ **परि-स्तृणन्त्यग्नीन्** ॥ ३ ॥ **उपवसथरूपं कुर्वन्ति** ॥ ४ ॥ **सायमहुत्वाऽग्निहोत्रं गार्हपत्य आज्यं विला-**

ततो निगद[1]व्याख्यातम् ॥ १.३.३.१-१९ ॥ **[इति तृतीयः पटलः** (१२)**]**

आरम्भ एवातः साधारणाः परिसमाप्ताः । साधारणसंस्कारत्वात् तेषां तंत्रताऽग्निसंस्काराणाम् । अतः परमसाधारणा इत्येवातः शब्दयोरुपयोगः ॥ १ ॥

अस्मिन्नहनि भस्मोद्धरणं नियमेन कर्तव्यम् । तच्च शुचौ प्रदेशे[2] नियमेन नित्यं स्थापयितव्यम् । भस्मोत्करमनूद्य [3]'तस्माल्लोष्टमाददीते'त्यादि दर्शनादुपवसथे उपवसथे च प्रवृद्धं भस्मापनीय तत्रैव न्युप्यते[4] ॥ २ ॥

परिस्तृणन्त्यग्नीनिति पौर्णमास्याङ्गभूतानामभ्याधानान्वाधानादीनां[5] प्रदर्शनार्थम् ॥ ३ ॥

उपवसथरूपं कुर्वन्तीति । 'सयामस्मा=न्यानु[6](?) च ब्राह्मणानि' इत्येवमादीनां प्रदर्शनार्थं सारस्वतादीनां 'दर्शपूर्णमासावालभमान' इत्यादि वाक्येनारंभात् पूर्वमेव कर्तव्यत्वे प्राप्ते तन्त्रमध्ये[7]

---

१. M Ad निगदं; thus T. **२.** M Ad प्रदेशनिय°. **३.** T कस्मा°. **४.** Ad भुञ्जते. **५.** Ad भूतानां अग्न्याथा. **६.** Ad सयामस्मान्या च, सयामस्मा...न्यानु. Here abri text is given. **७.** Ad मन्त्रतन्त्र°; thus T.

प्योत्पूय स्रुवं च स्रुचश्च संमृज्य प्राङेत्याहवनीयस्यार्धं चतुर्गृहीतं गृह्णीते ॥ ५ **॥ तज्जुहोति** 'पूर्णा पश्चात्' **इत्याहवनीये ॥** ६ **॥ अपरं चतुर्गृहीतं गृह्णीते ॥** ७ **॥ तज्जुहोति** 'यत्ते देवा अदधुः' **इत्याहवनीय एव ॥** ८ **॥ प्रत्यङ् परेत्य गार्हपत्यस्यार्धं चतुर्गृहीतं गृह्णीते ॥** ९ **॥ तज्जुहोति** 'यत्ते देवा अदधुः' **इति गार्हपत्ये ॥** १० **॥ अपरं चतुर्गृहीतं गृह्णीते ॥** ११ **॥ तज्जुहोति** 'पूर्णा पश्चात्' **इति गार्हपत्य एव ॥** १२ **॥ गत्वाऽन्वाहार्यपचनस्यार्धं चतुर्गृहीतं गृह्णीते ॥** १३ **॥ तज्जुहोति** 'एकाष्टका' **इत्येकाष्टकाम् ॥** १४ **॥ एकाष्टकाः हुत्वा वसन्ति ॥** १५ **॥ प्रातर्हुत्वाऽग्निहोत्रं गार्हपत्य आज्यं विलाप्य स्रुवं च स्रुचं च संमृज्यात्रैव चतुर्गृहीतं गृह्णीते ॥** १६ **॥ तज्जुहोति** 'यत्ते देवा अदधुः' **इति गार्हपत्ये ॥** १७ **॥ अपरं चतुगृहीतं गृह्णीते ॥** १८ **॥ तज्जुहोति** 'पूर्णा पश्चाद्' **इति गार्हपत्य एव ॥** १९ **॥ गत्वाऽन्वाहार्यस्यार्धं चतुर्गृहीतं गृह्णीते ॥** २० **॥ तज्जुहोति** 'संवत्सरस्य प्रतिमाम्' **इति प्राजापत्यम् ॥** २१ **॥ अपरेण गार्हपत्यं परीत्य प्राङेत्याहवनीयस्यार्धं चतुर्गृहीतं गृह्णीते ॥** २२ **॥ तज्जुहोति** 'पूर्णा पश्चात्' **इत्याहवनीये ॥** २३ **॥ अपरं चतुर्गृहीतं गृह्णीते ॥** २४ **॥ तज्जुहोति** 'यत्ते देवा अदधुः' **इत्याहवनीय एव ॥** २५ **॥ यज्ञायुधानि सꣳसाद्याऽपः प्रणीयारम्भ-णीयामिष्टिं निर्वपति आग्नावैष्णवमेकादशकपालꣳ सरस्वत्यै चरुꣳ सरस्वते द्वादशकपालम् ॥** २६ **॥ निरुप्ते प्राणग्रहाꣳश्च पृश्नीꣳश्च व्याचष्टे ॥** २७ **॥ तस्य हविष्कृता वाचं विसृज्य चतु-र्गृहीतेन चतुर्होतारमाहवनीये जुहोति ॥** २८ **॥ तमेव समासन्ने व्याचष्टे ॥** २९ **॥ तस्यै वार्त्रघ्ना-वाज्यभागौ ॥** ३० **॥** 'अग्नाविष्णू', 'अग्नाविष्णू', 'प्र णो देवी', 'आ नो दिवः', 'पीपिवाꣳसꣳ सरस्वतः स्तनम्', 'यस्य व्रतं पशवो यन्ति सर्वे' **इति हविषाम् ॥** ३१ **॥ त्रिष्टुभौ संयाज्ये ॥** ३२ **॥**

विधानाद्वचनमस्तीति ज्ञायते। अयमप्याचार्यः[१] चातुर्मास्यपशुसोमेष्वप्येमवेवोपदिशति[२] ॥ ४ ॥

हविष्कृता वाचं विसृज्येत्यादि, गार्हपत्य आज्यमित्यादि। एते होमा औपानुवाक्यैर्विकल्पन्ते। विनिवेष इति केचित्। 'अमावास्यायामग्नय आधीयन्त' इत्युपक्रम्य विधानात्। तेषामुपक्रान्ते पौर्णमास्यास्तन्त्रे क्रियमाणाऽन्वारंभणीया सद्यस्काला क्रियेत। आचार्यप्रवृत्त्या ज्ञायते तन्त्रप्रसंगाभावौ न स्त इति। तथाप्युद्धरणं सामर्थ्यात् प्रसज्यते। अभ्याधानं[३] धारणत्वाद्[४] धृतत्वाच्च पुनर्न क्रियते। अग्न्यन्वाधानं देवतापरिग्रहार्थत्वात् क्रियत एव। अनुपदकार आह- संयुक्ततन्त्राणां बर्हिराहरेत्[५]। परिदेशनाद्यावर्तेत। विभवेत्परिदेशनमित्यपरम्, ऊहेनोद्यमनं हरणं सादनमिति तन्त्रत्वं[६] दृष्टम्। तथा सत्यग्न्यन्वाधानमपकृष्यमाणं तन्त्रेण क्रियेत। तथा च बोधायनः[७] 'अन्वारंभं पौर्णमास्याः समानोपवसथं[८] करोती'ति ॥ २८ ॥

तमेव समासन्ने व्याचष्ट इति। दशहोतुर्विकृत्यर्थं केचिदनेन कल्पयन्ति। अपरे अपानग्रहादीन्[९] निवर्तयन्ति, दशहोतुः प्राप्त्यभावात्[१०]। अन्ये नित्यानुवाद इति वर्णयन्ति ॥ २९ ॥

---

१. Ad अयम ... चार्यः. **२.** Ad सोमेप्येव°. **३.** Ad अग्न्या°. **४.** M Ad धारणार्थत्वात्; thus T. **५.** Ad बहिरा°. **६.** M Ad तन्त्रत्वद्°. **७.** M Ad बोधा°; thus T. **८.** M °स्यास्नुमानो, °स्यासुमानो°. **९.** Ad अपानकाहा°. **१०.** M Ad प्राप्त्याभा°.

दक्षिणामुखे मिथुनौ गावौ दत्वा यथाश्रद्धं ददाति ॥ ३३ ॥ **सन्ततिमनु होतुराहुतिं जुहोति** ॥ ३४ ॥ **प्रसिध्यति कर्म** ॥ ३५ ॥ **सन्तिष्ठत आरम्भणीयेष्टिः** ॥ ३६ ॥ **यज्ञायुधानि सꣳसाद्यापः प्रणीय प्रसिद्धं पौर्णमासेन हविषा यजते** ॥ १.३.४.३७ ॥ **[इति चतुर्थः पटलः** (१३)**]**

॥ इति प्रथमप्रपाठके तृतीयोऽनुवाकः ॥

दक्षिणामुखे अन्वाहार्यात् पूर्वमित्यर्थः । ननु अन्वाहार्यस्य दक्षिणार्थत्वादिहाम्नातैर्बाधो युक्तः । सत्यं युक्तः[१] । किन्तु उभयमन्यार्थमनूद्यते । वास्त्वेष्ट्यामतः समुच्चयोऽभिप्रेत इति मत्वैवमभ्यधायि[२] ॥ ३३ ॥

प्रसिद्धं हविषेति । जात्यपेक्षमेकवचनम्[३] ॥ १.३.४.३७ ॥ **[इति चतुर्थः पटलः** (१३)**]**

॥ इति व्याख्यायां प्रथमप्रपाठके तृतीयोऽनुवाकः[४] ॥

---

१. M Ad युक्तम्. **२.** Ad °मग्ध्या°. **३.** M Ad जात्यापे°. **४.** M Ad T तृतीयः.

॥ अथ प्रथमप्रपाठके चतुर्थोऽनुवाकः ॥

[पुनराधेयम्]

प्रसिद्धा आग्न्याधेयिकाः संभाराः ॥ १ ॥ **अथेतरे पुनर्निष्कृतो रथः, पुनरुत्स्यूतं वासः, पुनरुत्सृष्टोऽनड्वान्, दर्भः शतकाण्डः, षड्ढिरण्यशल्कास्तेषां त्रयोऽष्टापृडकाः, द्वे तृण-कलाप्यौ** ॥ २ ॥ **अद्यर्द्धिपुनराधेयस्योपवसथ इत्यग्नीनां भस्मोद्धरन्ति** ॥ ३ ॥ **शल्कैरग्निमिन्धे गार्हपत्यम्** ॥ ४ ॥ **अधिवृक्षसूर्ये ब्रह्मौदनं निर्वपति** ॥ ५ ॥ **तस्मिन् श्रप्यमान एवाध्वर्युरग्निहोत्रं जुहोति** ॥ ६ ॥ **तꣳ शृतमाह्वारयत्येव स्थाल्यै बिलम्** ॥ ७ ॥ **नाङ्गारेभ्य उच्छिनत्ति** ॥ ८ ॥ **आज्यं च हिरण्यशल्कं च पात्रियामुपस्तृणीतेऽनष्टापृडकम्** ॥ ९ ॥ **तिस्रो दर्वीरुपस्तीर्णाभिघारिता उद्ध-रति** ॥ १० ॥ **काममूर्ध्वम्** ॥ ११ ॥ **तत उद्धृत्य व्यूह्य हिरण्यशल्कं प्रास्यानष्टापृडकं बहूप-सिञ्चति** ॥ १२ ॥ **तं चत्वार आर्षेयाः प्राश्नन्ति** ॥ **१३** ॥ **तान् यजमान एव स्वयमवनेजयेद् इतीदम्** ॥ १४ ॥ **तानध्वर्युः सꣳशास्ति** 'सकृत्प्राश्योत्पिचत' **इति** ॥ १५ ॥ **ते सकृत्प्राश्योत्पिचन्ति** ॥ १६ ॥ **नात्र समिधोऽभ्यादधाति** ॥ १७ ॥ **आण्डीवलं ब्रह्मौदने ददाति** ॥ १८ ॥ **यथाश्रद्धं स्थालीप्राशाय** ॥ १९ ॥ **व्यूहन्त्येते अङ्गारपुरीषे आहवनीयस्य चान्वाहार्यपचनस्य च** ॥ २० ॥ **ते यदा सꣳशाम्यतोऽथैनयोर्भस्मोद्धरन्ति** ॥ २१ ॥ 'सꣳशाधि यजमान' **इत्याह**। '०यत्ते सꣳशिष्यम्' **इति** ॥ २२ ॥ **सꣳशास्ति यदस्य सꣳशिष्यं भवति** ॥ २३ ॥ **पुत्रे वा भ्रातरि वर्णमुपनयति** ॥ २४ ॥

---

[१]प्रसिद्धाः प्रज्ञाता अग्न्याधेये भवा आग्न्याधेयिकाः संभाराः। ते तथैवोपकल्पयितव्याः ॥ १ ॥

पौनराधेयिका इदानीं वक्ष्यन्ते। [२]पुनर्निष्कृतो रथः विशिलष्टसन्धिः पुनर्निष्कृतः। पुनरुत्स्यूतं जीर्णं पुनः प्रोतम्। पुनरुत्सृष्टो द्विरुत्सृष्टः। हिरण्यशल्काः प्राकृता एव विशेषार्थम् अनूद्यन्ते। अष्टापृडका[३] अष्टापुलकाः, द्वे शुष्कतृणकलाप्यौ ॥ २ ॥

'अद्यर्द्धिपुनराधेयस्योपवसथ'[४] इति। किमिदं फलार्थम्[५] उत नैमित्तिकमिति। ऋद्ध्यर्थं पुनराधेयम्। 'पुनराधीयन्ते'[६] केवलमि'त्यारभ्य 'य एवं पुनराधेयस्यर्द्धिं'[७] वेदर्ध्नोत्येवे'ति विहितम्। अतः फलार्थम् ॥ ३ ॥

अत ऊर्ध्वं द्विः प्राश्नन्ति। व्यूहनाद्युद्धरणपक्षापेक्षमिति केचित्। कुतः धार्यपक्षे हि अहुतेऽग्निहोत्रे अनुद्धतत्वाच्च पुनर्न क्रियेत। उद्धरणस्याग्निपरिग्रहार्थत्वात् पुनरुद्धृत्य होम इत्यादि बहुकल्प्यम्। अपरे विशेषं मन्यन्ते। यद्यपि हुतेऽनुगमनं तथाप्यनुगमनप्रायश्चित्ताभावयोर्वयं न मुच्यामहे[८]। पुनरुद्धृत्य होममात्रं विशेषः। इतरस्मिन्नपि नित्यवच्छुतस्य पाक्षिकत्वं दोषः। हविःशेषेण हुत्वोद्वासनमभिमर्शनं चाश्रुतं कल्प्येत। अस्मिन् पक्षे तृणकलाप्यावपि नित्ये ॥ ११-२१ ॥

---

१. M Ad T अथ चतुर्थः. २. M पुरं नि०, Ad परं नि०; thus T. ३. M ०पृधका, Ad ०पृथकाः; thus T. ४. M अद्यर्धि, Ad अध्य०. ५. M हलार्थ, Ad फलार्थ. ६. M Ad पुनराधेयं ते. ७. M Ad ०स्यर्धिं. ८. Ad मनुष्यामहे.

'ऋत्वियवती स्थः' **इत्यस्मै निपदः कालेऽरणी आदधाति** ॥ २५ ॥ **तदनु वाचं यच्छति** ॥ २६ ॥ **स वाचंयमोऽनुरात्रꣳ शल्कैरग्निमिन्धे** ॥ २७ ॥ **जागृयाद्धैव, न सुषुप्सेद् वशश्चास्य स्यात्** ॥ २८ ॥ **औषसमेवाध्वर्युरग्निहोत्रमधिश्रयति** ॥ २९ ॥ **अण्वीमिव समिधं कुरुते** ॥ ३० ॥ **अरणी एव धारयन् वाचंयम आस्ते यजमानायतने** ॥ ३१ ॥ **आदीपयन्ति तृणकलाप्यौ** ॥ ३२ ॥ **गार्हपत्य एवाहवनीयायामात्येऽन्वाहार्यपचनाय प्रहरन्ति तृणकलाप्यौ** ॥ ३३ ॥ **ते अध्वर्युरुन्नीतेनाग्नि-होत्रेणानुद्रवति** ॥ ३४ ॥ **सादयन्ति तृणकलाप्यौ** ॥ ३५ ॥ **समिधमाधायाप्तुमिव पूर्वामाहुतिꣳ हुत्वा ज्यायसीमुत्तरामाहुतिं जुहोति** ॥ ३६ ॥ **ते यदा सꣳशाम्यतोऽथैनयोर्भस्म निमृजन्ति** ॥ ३७ ॥ **सिकताभिराखरौ व्यूहन्ति** ॥ ३८ ॥ 'जातवेदो भुवनस्य रेतः' **इत्युपव्युषेऽरणी निष्टपति** ॥ ३९ ॥ 'अयं ते योनिर्ऋत्वियः' **इत्यरण्योरग्निꣳ समारोहयते** ॥ ४० ॥ **संवपन्त्येतमग्निं सते** ॥ ४१ ॥ **अत्रानुवित्तिं जुहोति** ॥ ४२ ॥ **प्रसिध्यति कर्मा यदेनमञ्जलावाधानात्** ॥ १.४.१.४३ ॥ **[इति प्रथमः पटलः** (१४)**]**

प्रसिध्यति कर्मा यदेनमञ्जलावाधानात् ॥ १ ॥ **तं** 'भुवो भूर्' **इति त्रिभिरक्षैररञ्जला-वाधत्ते** ॥ २ ॥ 'अमीषां त्वा देवानां व्रतपते व्रतेनादधे' **इति यद्देवत्यो भवति,** 'गायत्रेण छन्दसा' **इति ब्राह्मणः,** 'त्रैष्टुभेन छन्दसा' **इति राजन्यः,** 'जागतेन छन्दसा' **इति वैश्यः** ॥ ३ ॥ 'प्रजापतेस्त्वा प्राणेनाभि प्राणिमि' **इत्येनमभिप्राणिति** ॥ ४ ॥ 'मयि धातः श्रियं धेहि' **इत्यस्मै दक्षिणत आसीनोऽध्वर्युरुत्तरतो हिरण्यशल्कमुपास्यत्यष्टापृडकम्** ॥ ५ ॥ **वाचयति** 'श्रियै माधिपतिं कुरु=प्रियया तनुवा संभव' **इति** ॥ ६ ॥ 'अहं त्वदस्मि' **इति सन्नमुपतिष्ठते** ॥ ७ ॥ 'आऽयं गौः पृश्निरक्रमीत्' **इति तिसृभिः सर्पराज्ञीभिरुपतिष्ठते** ॥ ८ ॥ **अत्र समिधोऽभ्यादधाति** ॥ ९ ॥ **मिथुनौ समित्सु ददाति** ॥ १० ॥ **आहुतिषाहे गार्हपत्ये चतुर्गृहीतेन दशहोतुराहुतिं जुहोति** ॥ ११ ॥ 'अभि त्वा शूर नोनुमः' **इति रथन्तरेणोपतिष्ठते** ॥ १२ ॥ **दर्भꣳ शतकाण्डमिध्ममुपनह्यति** ॥ १३ ॥ **इध्ममादीपयन्ति** ॥ १४ ॥ **उपयमनीरुपकल्पयन्ति** ॥ १५ ॥ **अनड्वाहं पल्पूलितमानयन्ति** ॥ १६ ॥ **आदित्यमुद्यन्तं प्रतीक्षन्त आहवनीयेन** ॥ १७ ॥ **उदित आदित्ये** 'ओजसे बलाय त्वोद्यच्छे' **इति तिसृभिरिध्ममुद्यच्छते** ॥ १८ ॥ 'प्राचीमनु प्रदिशं प्रेहि विद्वान्' **इत्यनुडुत्प्रथमाः प्रयन्ति** ॥ १९ ॥

अरणी एव धारयन् वाचंयम आस्ते यजमानः। [1]अत्रोपवेशनोपस्पर्शनाचमनानामभावः केचिदिच्छन्ति। अन्ये प्रविश्योपस्पृश्याचम्य यजमानायतने अरणी एव धारयन्नास्त इति वाग्यतोऽ-प्युन्नयनमनुजानाति ॥ २५-३१ ॥

अर्थप्राप्तेष्वेव[2] व्रतः उद्धृत्योपासनमवोक्षणानुसमिन्धनं च न स्तः। सामर्थ्यात् पूर्वस्याहुतेरल्पत्वम् उद्वासनाशंकया विदधौ। अतः समिन्धनाद्यभावः[3] ॥ १.४.१.३६ ॥ **[इति प्रथमः पटलः** (१४)**]**

[4]अनडुत्पद आधानं प्राकृतञ्चेदिह नियमः, इतरथा वचनम् ॥ १६ ॥

---

१. M Ad °त्र वेशनो°. **२.** M Ad अथ. **३.** M Ad °भावं; thus T. **४.** M Ad अनधुत्प°.

विषुवदागच्छन्ति। तत् तिष्ठन्नाह—'निवपान्वाहार्यपचनस्य संभारान्' **इति** ॥ २० ॥ 'ऋतं स्तृणामि पुरीषं पृथिव्याम्' **इत्यन्वाहार्यपचनस्योद्धतेऽर्धꣳ संभाराणां निवपति** ॥ २१ ॥ **वाचयति—** 'ऋतेऽधि सत्यमादधे सत्येऽधि मातरिश्वानं वायुमग्निमादधे' **इति** ॥ २२ ॥ 'निवपाग्निम्' **इत्याह** ॥ २३ ॥ **तं** 'भूमिर्भूम्ना' **इत्येनमभिमन्त्रयते** ॥ २४ ॥ 'मयि धातः श्रियं धेहि' **इत्येवास्मै दक्षिणत आसीनोऽध्वर्युरुत्तरतो हिरण्यशल्कमुपास्यत्यष्टापृडकम्** ॥ २५ ॥ **वाचयति** 'श्रियैमाधिपतिं कुरु=प्रिया तनुवा सं भव' **इति** ॥ २६ ॥ 'इमा उ मामुपतिष्ठन्तु रायः' **इति विषुवति हिरण्यशल्कꣳ सन्नमुपतिष्ठतेऽनष्टापृडकम्** ॥ २७ ॥ 'कया नश्चित्र आ भुवद्' **इति विषुवति प्रयन्ति वामदेव्येन** ॥ २८ ॥ **प्राञ्चमनड्वाहमाक्रमयत्युत्तरत आहुत्यै दक्षिणस्येर्मस्य पदा** ॥ २९ ॥ **पुनः प्रत्यञ्चं तेनैव** ॥ ३० ॥ **तमुदञ्चमत्सृजति** ॥ ३१ ॥ 'ऋतꣳ स्तृणामि पुरीषं पृथिव्याम्' **इत्याहुत्याꣳ संभारान् निवपति** ॥ ३२ ॥ **वाचयति—**'ऋतेऽधि सत्यमादधे सत्येऽधि मातरिश्वानꣳ सूर्यमग्निमादधे' **इति समापयति यजुः** ॥ ३३ ॥ **उपनिवपत्युपयमनीः** ॥ ३४ ॥ **सादयत्यग्निम्** 'सुवर्भुवो भूः' **इति सर्वैः पञ्चभिराहवनीयम्** ॥ ३५ ॥ 'अमीषां त्वा देवानां व्रतपते व्रतेनादधे' **इति यद्देवत्यो भवति।** 'गायत्रेण छन्दसा' **इति ब्राह्मणः;** 'त्रैष्टुभेन छन्दसा' **इति राजन्यः,** 'जागतेन छन्दसा' **इति वैश्यः** ॥ ३६ ॥ 'मयि धातः श्रियं धेहि' **इत्येवास्मै दक्षिणत आसीनोऽध्वर्युरुत्तरतो हिरण्यशल्कम् उपास्यत्यष्टापृडकम्** ॥ ३७ ॥ **वाचयति** 'श्रियै माधिपतिं कुरु=प्रिया तनुवा संभव' **इति** ॥ ३८ ॥ 'यदिदं दिवः' **इति सन्नमुपतिष्ठते** ॥ ३९ ॥ **प्रसिध्यति कर्मा हविष्क्लृप्त्यै** ॥ ४० ॥ **हविष्क्लृप्तिरेवातः** ॥ ४१ ॥ **यज्ञायुधानि सꣳसाद्यापः प्रणीयाग्नेयमष्टाकपालं निर्वपति** ॥ ४२ ॥ **अन्तस्तनूरेष पुरोडाशः** ॥ ४३ ॥ **तं शृतमासन्नमेतेन यजुषाऽभिमृशति** 'या ते अग्ने पवमाना तनूस्तया त्वा समर्धयामि', 'या ते अग्ने पावका तनूस्तया त्वा समर्धयामि', 'या ते अग्ने शुचिस्तनूस्तया त्वा समर्धयामि' **इति सर्वमाग्नेयं भवति** ॥ ४४ ॥ **तस्य सामिधेनीनां मीमाꣳसा।** 'प्र वो वाजा' **इत्युत्सृजत्येताम्, अनिरुक्तैषा** ॥ ४५ ॥ 'वाजयन्निव नू रथान्' **इत्येतामत्र निदधाति।** '०योगानग्नेरुपस्तुहि। यशस्तमस्य मीढ्ढुषः' **इति** ॥ ४६ ॥ 'तं त्वां समिद्भिरङ्गिरः' **इत्युत्सृजत्येताम्, अनिरुक्तैषा** ॥ ४७ ॥ 'अधा ते अङ्गिरस्तम' **इत्येतामत्र निदधाति।** '०अग्ने वेधस्तम

आग्नेयमष्टाकपालं निर्वपति। ननु पञ्चकपालः पौनराधेयिकः। ब्राह्मणविरुद्धानां विधानं[1] विकल्पार्थमित्युक्तम्। अथवा उदवा उदवसानीयायां विकल्प इहापि भवति। 'आग्नेयं पञ्चकपालमुदवसानीय'मित्यारभ्य 'अष्टाकपालः कार्य' इति हि तत्र विकल्पितं पुनराधेयविधेरिति[2] तां व्याहरन्ति ॥ ४२ ॥

[3]अन्तस्तनुर्हविषामभावोऽविमर्शनं च विधीयते। सर्वाग्नेयं[4] यावदुक्तम् ॥ १.४.२.४३-४४ ॥

[इति द्वितीयः पटलः (१५)]

---

१. Ad om. **२.** M Ad ०विधिरि०, T ०विधेरिति. **३.** M Ad अन्तस्तनुस्तनु, T अन्तस्तनुस्तनुस्तनु०. **४.** M Ad ०ग्नेयं यं.

प्रियम्। वोचेम ब्रह्म सानसि' **इति** ॥ ४८ ॥ **प्रसिध्यति कर्मा प्रयाजेभ्यः** ॥ १.४.२.४९ ॥ **[इति द्वितीयः पटलः** (१५)**]**

प्रसिध्यति कर्मा प्रयाजेभ्यः ॥ १ ॥ **विभक्तीरुक्त्वा प्रयाजानां वषट्करोति** ॥ २ ॥ 'ओश्रावय' **इत्याह** 'समिधो यज' **इति** ॥ ३ ॥ 'ये यजामहे', 'अग्न' **इति विभक्तिमाह** ॥ ४ ॥ 'समिधः समिधो अग्न आज्यस्य वियन्तु' **इति वषट्करोति** ॥ ५ ॥ 'आ याहि वीतये' **इत्यनुमन्त्रयते**। '०गृणानो=बर्हिषि' **इति** ॥ ६ ॥ 'ओश्रावय' **इत्याह** 'यज' **इति** ॥ ७ ॥ 'ये यजामहे', 'अग्निम्' **इति विभक्तिमाह** ॥ ८ ॥ 'तनूनपादग्न आज्यस्य वेतु' **इति वषट्करोति** ॥ ९ ॥ 'दूतं वृणीमहे' **इत्यनुमन्त्रयते**। '०होतारं=क्रतुम्' **इति** ॥ १० ॥ 'ओश्रावय' **इत्याह** 'यज' **इति** ॥ ११ ॥ 'ये यजामहे', 'अग्निना' **इति विभक्तिमाह** ॥ १२ ॥ 'इडो अग्न आज्यस्य वियन्तु' **इति वषट्करोति** ॥ १३ ॥ 'अग्निः समिध्यते' **इत्यनुमन्त्रयते**। '०कवि= जुह्वास्यः' **इति** ॥ १४ ॥ 'ओश्रावय' **इत्याह** 'यज' **इति** ॥ १५ ॥ 'ये यजामहे', 'अग्निः' **इति विभक्तिमाह** ॥ १६ ॥ 'बर्हिरग्न आज्यस्य वेतु' **इति वषट्करोति** ॥ १७ ॥ 'वृत्राणि जङ्घनत्' **इत्यनुमन्त्रयते**। '०द्रविण=हुतः' **इति** ॥ १८ ॥ **स्वयंस्सम्पन्न उत्तमः प्रयाजः** ॥ १९ ॥ **आज्यभागौ यजति** ॥ २० ॥ **बुधन्वन्तावाज्यभागौ** ॥ २१ ॥ 'अग्नयेऽनुब्रूहि' **इत्याहाज्यस्य गृह्णानश्चतुः** ॥ २२ ॥ 'उद्बुध्यस्वाग्ने' **इत्यन्वाह** ॥ २३ ॥ **जुषाणेन यजति** ॥ २४ ॥ **वषट्कृते जुहोति** ॥ २५ ॥ 'अग्नये पवमानायानुब्रूहि' **इत्याहाज्यस्यैव गृह्णानश्चतुः** ॥ २६ ॥ 'अग्निर्ऋषिः' **इत्यन्वाह**। '०पवमान=महागयम्' **इति** ॥ २७ ॥ 'एह्यू षु ब्रवाणि ते' **इत्युपशयी**। '०अग्न इत्थेतरा गिरः। एभिर्वर्धास इन्दुभिः' **इति** ॥ २८ ॥ **जुषाणेनैव यजति** ॥ २९ ॥ **वषट्कृते जुहोति** ॥ ३० ॥ 'अग्नयेऽनुब्रूहि' **इत्याहोपस्तृणानोऽवद्यन्** ॥ ३१ ॥ **पङ्क्त्यो याज्यानुवाक्या भवन्ति** ॥ ३२ ॥ 'अग्ने तमद्य' **इत्यन्वाह** ॥ ३३ ॥ 'अधा ह्यग्ने' **इति यजति** ॥ ३४ ॥ **वषट्कृते जुहोति** ॥ ३५ ॥ 'पुनरूर्जा निवर्तस्व' **इति पुरस्तात् पुरोडाशस्य स्रुवाहुतिं जुहोति** ॥ ३६ ॥ 'सह रय्या निवर्तस्व' **इत्युपरिष्टात्** ॥ ३७ ॥ 'अग्नये स्विष्टकृतेऽनुब्रूहि' **इत्याहोपस्तृणानोऽवद्यन्** ॥ ३८ ॥ 'आभिष्टे अद्य गीर्भिः' **इत्यन्वाह** ॥ ३९ ॥ 'एभिर्नो अर्कैः' **इति यजति** ॥ ४० ॥ **वषट्कृते जुहोति** ॥ ४१ ॥ **अत्याक्रम्य यथायतनंस् स्रुचौ**

---

[1]स्वयंसम्पन्नः स्वाहाग्निमित्यादिना[2] विभक्तिवचनं[2] सिद्धमित्यर्थः ॥ १९ ॥

उपशयी समीपे शेते इत्यर्थः। पुरोनुवाक्यां सप्रणवामुक्त्वा अप्रणवामुपशयीमाह ॥ २८ ॥

अक्षरपंक्त्यो याज्यानुवाक्याः ॥ ३२ ॥

प्रधानस्विष्टकृतेः प्रयाजशेषाभिघारणविवृद्धयः पावमानाद्यर्थं[3] च। इह तदभावान्नास्ति विवृद्धिः। इतरथाग्न्याधेयविकारत्वादिहापि प्राप्नोति। तदा स्विष्टकृदादौ शेषकार्यत्वं वाचनिकपक्षयोः ॥ १.४.३.३८ ॥ **[इति तृतीयः पटलः** (१६)**]**

---

१. M Ad द्वयं० ; thus T. **२-२.** M Ad T ० दि न विभवतिवचनं. **३.** M वावमान्यर्थं०.

सादयित्वा प्राशित्रमवद्याप उपस्पृश्येडामवद्यति ॥ ४२ ॥ **उपहूतायामिडायामग्नीध आदधाति** ॥ ४३ ॥ **प्राश्नन्ति** ॥ ४४ ॥ **मार्जयन्ते** ॥ ४५ ॥ **परिहरन्ति ब्रह्मणे** ॥ ४६ ॥ **प्राशिते प्राशित्रेऽग्नीदुदपात्रेणोत्कर उपसीदति** ॥ ४७ ॥ **अत्र पुनराधेयदक्षिणा ददाति पुनर्निष्कृतः रथं, पुनरुत्स्यूतं वासः, पुनरुत्सृष्टमनड्वाहम्** ॥ ४८ ॥ **सन्ततिमनु होतुराहुतिं जुहोति** ॥ ४९ ॥ **प्रसिध्यति कर्माऽनूयाजेभ्यः** ॥ १.४.३.५० ॥ **[इति तृतीयः पटलः (१६)]**

प्रसिध्यति कर्माऽनूयाजेभ्यः ॥ १ ॥ **विभक्तीरुक्त्वाऽनूयाजयोर्वषट्करोति** ॥ २ ॥ 'ओश्रा-वय' **इत्याह** 'देवान् यज' **इति** ॥ ३ ॥ 'ये यजामहे' ॥ ४ ॥ 'अग्नेः' **इति विभक्तिमाह** ॥ ५ ॥ 'देवं बर्हिर्वसुवने वसुधेयस्य वेतु' **इति वषट्करोति** ॥ ६ ॥ 'स्तोमं मनामहे' **इत्यनुमन्त्रयते** । '°सिध्रमद्य दिविस्पृशं देवस्य द्रविणस्यवः' **इति** ॥ ७ ॥ 'ओश्रावय' **इत्याह** ॥ ८ ॥ 'यज' **इति** ॥ ९ ॥ 'ये यजामहे' ॥ १० ॥ 'अग्नौ' **इति विभक्तिमाह** ॥ ११ ॥ 'देवो नाराशꣳसो वसुवने वसुधेयस्य वेतु' **इति वषट्करोति** ॥ १२ ॥ 'यो मर्तो दुवः' **इत्यनुमन्त्रयते** । '°धियं जुजोष धीतिभिः । भसन्नु ष प्रपूर्व्य इषं वुरीतावसे' **इति** ॥ १३ ॥ **स्वयꣳसम्पन्न उत्तमोऽनूयाजः** ॥ १४ ॥ **प्रसिध्यति कर्मा पत्नीसंयाजेभ्यः** ॥ १५ ॥ **अग्निन्यक्ताः पत्नीसंयाजानामृचः कुर्यात्** ॥ १६ ॥ 'अग्ने' **इत्येवोक्त्वाऽनुब्रूयाद्, यजेद्वा** ॥ १७ ॥ **प्रसिध्यति कर्म** ॥ १८ ॥ **सन्तिष्ठत एषेष्टिः** ॥ १९ ॥ **यज्ञायुधानि सꣳसाद्यापः प्रणीयैन्द्राग्नं चैकादशकपालं निर्वपत्यादित्यं च चरुम्** ॥ २० ॥ **सो एषा तथा क्लृप्तैवेष्टिः** ॥ २१ ॥ **एतदु द्विबर्हिर्ऋद्धिपुनराधेयम्** ॥ २२ ॥ **अथ परोप्तपुनराधेयस्य** ॥ २३ ॥ **एत एवोभये संभारा अन्यत्र तृणकलापीभ्याम्** ॥ २४ ॥ **काले समिधोऽभ्यादधाति** ॥ २५ ॥ **प्रसिध्यति कर्मा सर्पराज्ञीभ्यः** ॥ २६ ॥ **सर्पराज्ञीभिरुपस्थाय तिसृभिरुत्तराभिरुपतिष्ठते** 'यत्त्वा क्रुद्धः परोवप', 'यत्ते मन्युपरोप्तस्य', 'मनो ज्योतिर्जुषताम्' **इति** ॥ २७ ॥ **प्रसिध्यति कर्माऽ-ग्निहोत्रात्** ॥ २८ ॥ 'सप्त ते अग्ने समिधः सप्तजिह्वाः' **इत्यग्निहोत्रं जुहोति** ॥ २९ ॥ **प्रसिध्यति कर्मा प्रथमस्या इष्टेः सन्तत्यै** ॥ ३० ॥ **सन्ततिमनु तिस्रः स्रुवाहुतीर्जुहोति** 'लेकः सलेकः सुलेकः',

---

एतद् द्विबर्हिर्ऋद्धिपुनराधेयम् । अस्य त्रिबर्हिः पक्षो नास्ति ॥ २२ ॥

अथ परोप्तपुनराधेयस्य । यदाहिताग्नेः प्रजायां पशुषु वोपद्रवो जायेत तदोद्वासनीयेष्ट्या उद्वास्य[1] उपजातसामर्थ्य आदधीत । भागधेयं वा 'अग्निराहित इच्छमानं[2] 'इत्येवमादिना[3] विहितम् । अथवा अवृत्त्या[3] उपद्रवणं वा परोप्योपजातसामर्थ्य[4] आदधीत तथालिङ्गम् ॥ २३ ॥

'यत्त्वा क्रुद्धः परो वप' इति तन्नैमित्तिकम् । अनुपदकारस्तत्रोपवसिथकायाः[5] नित्यत्वमाह ॥ २७ ॥

'सप्त ते' इति पूर्वस्याहुतेर्मन्त्रः प्रत्याम्नायते ॥ २९ ॥

---

१. M Ad °वास्या. २. M Ad °मान. ३-३. M इत्येव ... अवृत्त्या; Ad इत्येवमानो; thus T. ४. T परोऽप्यो°. ५. M कार तत्रो; Ad °कारसतत्रो.

'केतः सकेतः सुकेतः', 'विवस्वाँ अदितिर्देवजूतिः' **इति** ॥ ३१ ॥ **प्रसिध्यति कर्म** ॥ ३२ ॥ **सन्तिष्ठत एषेष्टिः** ॥ ३३ ॥ **यज्ञायुधानि सꣳसाद्यापः प्रणीयाग्निवारुणमेकादशकपालमनु निर्वपति** ॥ ३४ ॥ **तस्यै रयिमन्तावाज्यभागौ यथादेवतꣳ हविषः** ॥ ३५ ॥ **विराजौ संयाज्ये** ॥ ३६ ॥ **सन्ततिमनु होतुराहुतिं जुहोति** ॥ ३७ ॥ **प्रसिध्यति कर्म** ॥ ३८ ॥ **सन्तिष्ठत एषेष्टिः** ॥ ३९ ॥ **यज्ञायुधानि सꣳसाद्यापः प्रणीयैन्द्राग्नं चैवैकादशकपालं निर्वपत्यादित्यं च चरुम्** ॥ ४० ॥ **सो एषा तथाक्लृप्तैवेष्टिः** ॥ ४१ ॥ **एतदु त्रिबर्हिः परोप्तपुनराधेयम्** ॥ ४२ ॥ **न तु हास्याशां चनेयात्** ॥ ४३ ॥ **स यत्र हाप्येतत् कर्म क्रियमाणमुपाधिगच्छेत् सर्वाह्णꣳ हैव। यदीयात् ततोऽन्यां दिशमियादास्तमयादादित्यस्य** ॥ १.४.४.४४ ॥ **[इति चतुर्थः पटलः** (१७)**]**

॥ इति प्रथमप्रपाठके चतुर्थोऽनुवाकः ॥

तत[1] एतत्त्रिबर्हिः [2]परोप्तपुनराधेम्। अस्यापि[2] द्विबर्हिःपक्षो नास्ति ॥ ४२ ॥

अस्मिन् कर्मणि क्रियमाणे अस्यां दिशि नेयात्। यदि गच्छेदन्यां दिशमास्तमयाद्[3] गच्छेत् ॥ १.४.४.४३-४४ ॥ **[इति चतुर्थः पटलः** (१७)**]**

॥ इति व्याख्यायां प्रथमप्रपाठके चतुर्थोऽनुवाकः ॥

---

१. Ad यत. **२-२.** M प... अस्यापि, Ad ०धेयस्यापि. **३.** Ad ०मस्तम०. Abri text of sūtra.

॥ अथ प्रथमप्रपाठके पञ्चमोऽनुवाकः ॥

[अग्निहोत्रम्]

उद्धृतानग्नीनुपासिष्यमाणोऽन्तरा गार्हपत्यं चान्वाहार्यपचनं च प्रपद्य दक्षिणत आहवनीयस्योपविशति ॥ १ ॥ अथास्मा अग्निहोत्रं होष्यतेऽपः परिहरति ॥ २ ॥ ता उपस्पृशति

'*उद्धृतानग्नीन्*[1] *=उपविशति*'। किमिदमुद्धरणं नाम। अर्थायार्थायाग्निं[2] प्रणयति। अप्रवृत्ते[3] [4]कर्मणि लौकिकः संपद्यते यथा समारूढ[4] इति परसूत्रे दृष्टानुमितं[5] वेदवचनमस्तीति। अस्यां च शाखायामग्निहोत्रप्रकरणे यदग्निमुद्धरतीति दृश्यते[6]। अनुद्धृताग्निनिर्मो[7]चनप्रायश्चित्तविधानं चाह। तथा सति बहुवचनं नोपपद्यते। एकोऽप्याहवनीय उद्धृतः।[8] उच्यते—'यत् त्रेधाऽग्निराधीयत' इत्याहवनीयगुणवाक्ये श्रवणात्[9] सभ्यावसथ्यापेक्षं बहुवचनम्। नैतदेवम्। यत् 'त्रेधाग्निराधीयत' इति गार्हपत्याहवनीयाधानमध्ये स्थानादन्वाहार्यपचनाधानार्थमाम्नातम्। तथापि 'तस्मादेतावन्तोऽग्नय आधीयन्ते' इति पञ्चत्वं विहितं तदपेक्षं स्यात्। तयोराधानं नेष्यते। असतोः कर्म न प्राप्नोति। भवतु। को दोषः? यावज्जीवश्रुतित्वं बाधितं भवति। तथा सति उद्धरणेन कालो लक्ष्यते। अथवाऽवयवप्रसिद्ध्या तथा विधाय ऊर्ध्वहृतानुद्धृतानिति *ज्वलितानित्यर्थः।[10] तथा सति धार्यपक्षेऽन्तर्द्वादशाहे च। उपासिष्यमाणं[11] क्रियमाणं कर्म [12]ज्ञानपूर्वं प्रत्यवेक्षते। विहितं च याजमानं ज्ञानपूर्वं[12] करोति स यजमान इत्यर्थः। [13]स उक्तेन पथा प्रपद्योपविशति[13] ॥ १ ॥

कर्त्रे होष्यते जुहोमीति[14] स्वाम्येवाभिधीयते[15]। तथा च दृश्यते—'सुवर्णरजते[16] हिरण्ये मुखयोः प्रत्यस्य वाचं यच्छत' इत्यारभ्य 'स यत्रास्मै प्रातर्विशत्यस्मै य उपविष्टस्तस्मात् इति गम्यते। प्रोथ इति स्वामिने परिहरणं[17] [18]सर्वकर्मकर्तृकरणेऽग्न्यगारसंमार्जनोपलेपनसंमार्जनपात्र–प्रक्षालनादि[18] स्मृतिशास्त्रादनुपदादाचाराच्चावगमयितव्यम्[19]। उद्धरणपक्षे गार्हपत्यं ज्वलयित्वा आमात्यादन्वाहार्य–

---

१. M उद्धृतोऽग्नि; Ad °तोग्निः. **२.** Ad अर्थायार्थाग्निं. **३.** M °यत्यर्थववृत्ते; Ad °त्यपवृत्ते. **४–४.** M कर्मणि...समारूढ़; Ad लौकिकामपयते. **५.** Ad परसूत्रे दृष्टोऽनुमितं twice; M दृष्टोऽनु°. **६.** Ad om. **७.** M Ad T °तामिनिर्मो°. **८.** Ad उद्धृत्यः. **९.** M Ad श्रवणा अभ्या°. ***.** Due to displacement of folios in the original Malayalam MS a large portion of the text dealing with *Agnihotra* beginning with ज्वलितान् तथा (M p. 288, line 7; Ad p. 605, line 9) and ending with पर्वणि (M p.293, line 7; Ad p.615, line 11) has wrongly been copied under *Rājasūya* Prapāṭhaka. It has rightly been noticed by the scribe in marginalia note in both the MSS : अत्र ग्रन्थपातः अध्यायद्वयस्याभावश्च (M p.288, Ad p.605, line 11). T (p.36, line 5) rightly gives this text here. Vide fn. * on p.444. **१०.** M Ad ज्वलितान त, T तथा वि धार्य... द्वादशाहे च. **११.** M Ad उपासष्यमाण. **१२–१२.** M Ad कर्म यः...यः प्रत्यवेक्षते...मानज्ञानपूर्वं. **१३–१३.** T °नोपवसथावद्योपविशति। अयै उपविष्टपतस्मा इति गम्यः। ऊर्ध्वहृतानुद्धृतानिति ज्वलितानित्यर्थः। होष्यते. **१४.** M Ad जुहोतीति; thus T. **१५.** T °भिधायते. **१६.** T wrongly gives स्वरन्य between रजते and हिरण्ये. **१७.** T °हरणा(?). **१८–१८.** T °कर्मसु कर्तृकरणेत्यग...संमार्ज°, M °लेपनवन सं°, Ad °नो प्रलेपनवन°. **१९.** M °चाराच्छा°.

'विद्युदसि विद्य मे पाप्मानम्' **इति** ॥ ३ ॥ **अथ** 'आपो व्रतभृतो व्रतं मयि धत्त मयि श्रद्धा' **इत्याचामति** ॥ ४ ॥ **अग्निहोत्रीमुपह्वयते** 'इर एहि मयि श्रयस्व', 'इर एहि मयि श्रयस्व', 'श्रद्ध एहि सत्येन त्वाऽऽह्वयामि' **इति** ॥ ५ ॥ 'इयमसि' **इति वेदिमुपदिशन् ब्रूयात्**। '०तस्यास्तेऽग्निर्वत्सः सा मेऽग्निना वत्सेन श्रद्धां तपोऽमुं कामं धुक्ष्व' **इति** ॥ ६ ॥ **यं कामं कामयते तमाशास्ते सः हैवास्मै स कामः पद्यते** ॥ ७ ॥ **वाचंयमोऽग्रेणाहवनीयं परीत्य** 'भूतकृत स्थः' **इति गार्हपत्यादुदीचो**

पचनमा[1]हृत्य ज्वलन्तमाहवनीयमुद्धरेत्। 'वाचा[2] त्वा[2] होत्रेण' इति मन्त्रेण। कुत एतत्। '[3]अमृताहुतिर्ह वा[3] एषा हूयते=[4]हु'ता भवती'तीयमृताहुतिममृतायां जुहोमी'त्यस्य मन्त्रावयवस्यार्थमभिप्रेत्याचार्येणो–क्तमिति मन्यामहे। यद्यपि प्रायश्चित्ते[5] दृष्टोऽयं मन्त्रस्तथापीतः प्राप्तस्यानुवादः। एवं प्रकरणादग्निहोत्र एव मन्त्रेणोद्धरणम्, अन्यत्र तूष्णीमेव। उद्धृत्य [6]उपास्य च[6] बहूनि[7] काष्ठानि प्रक्षिप्य ज्वालयित्वा पूर्वापरौ परिमृज्य परिस्तृणाति। अपराग्निहोमाभावे पूर्वमेव प्रतिपत्तौ कूर्चद्वयस्य दर्शनादुपावहरणीयम्[8]। कूर्चमुत्तरेण गार्हपत्यं निधाय तस्मिन् पात्राण्युपावहरति। स्रुवाग्निहोत्रहवण्यौ स्थालीमभिद्योतनार्था औषधीः समिधमुपवेषमिति[9]। ततो यजमान उक्तेन पथा प्रविश्योपविशति। अग्निहोत्रस्रुक्स्रुवस्य वैकङ्कतत्वमुक्तं[10] भगवता कात्यायनेन। 'वैकङ्कतं स्रुक्स्रुवं निष्टप्ये[11]'त्याचार्येण प्रतिपत्तौ नासिकयोः स्रुचाविति। तस्माद् वैकङ्कतोऽग्निहोत्रः[12] ॥ २ ॥

स्रुव[13] उपस्पृश्याचम्याग्निहोत्रीमुपहूय वेदिमुपदिशन् ब्रूयाद्यजमानः ॥ ३–६ ॥

अस्मै सम्पद्यते पयो[14]होमाभावादुपह्वानं[15] नास्ति। ततो दक्षिणत उपसृजतीत्यादिना विधानेन दोग्धि। पूर्वौ दुह्यादपरौ पूर्वौ दुह्यादिति[15]। तथा 'तस्मान्नु ह सर्वेषामेव स्तनानामग्निहोत्रं दुह्यादि'ति पाक्षिकं वचनं न स्यात्। त्रैवर्णिको[16] दोग्धा। दुग्धमाहृत्यापरेण गार्हपत्यं सादयति। अथाध्वर्युः पूर्वमपः[17] परिहृतवान् ॥ ७ ॥

वाचंयमोऽग्रेणाहवनीयं परीत्य परिस्तीर्णमग्निं परिषिञ्चति 'ऋतं त्वा'[18] इत्यादि। परिषेकाभावोऽपीष्यते आचार्येण। प्राण्यापान्यार्त्विज्यं[19] करिष्यन् ब्रूयात् 'प्रजापतिर्' इति। सर्वकर्मसु

---

१. M Ad ०हार्यवचन०. **२–२.** T वा...त्वा होत्रेण cf *ĀpŚS.* 6.1.6. **३–३.** M Ad अमृता इति र्हवा; T अमुत्राहुतिर्हुत्वा. **४.** Ad हति र्भवन्ती०; M Ad हूयते=भवन्ती० (cf वाधू.अन्वा. १.११.५). **५.** T (प्रा(ग)दृष्टोयं. **६–६.** M Ad om; thus T. **७.** T आहुतिका०. **८.** M Ad ०णीयः; thus T. **९.** T ०दोषधी...समधि०. **१०.** M Ad ०ककत्व०. **११.** M Ad ष्टव्ये०. **१२.** T ०ग्निःहोमाभावात अपह्वान नास्ति ततो दक्षिणत उपसृण तीत्यादिना विधानेन दोग्धि दोग्धि। पूर्वौ दुह्यादपयोत्रध्यपः. **१३.** M स्रुवः, T om. **१४.** T अपः. **१५–१५.** T दुह्यादपयोऽत्रध्यपः उपस्पृश्याचम्याग्निहोत्री नुपहूय वा वेदिमुपरि... रान् ब्रूयाद यजमानम्। अन्ये कामं संपद्यते...वरो ह्यादिति क्रमनियमार्थं ध्यापरौ पूर्वाविति. **१६.** M ०वणको, Ad ०वर्णको. **१७.** M Ad पूर्वपद; thus T. **१८.** M Ad च; thus T. **१९.** M Ad om प्राण्यापान्य; T ऋत्विजयं करिष्या (?).

अङ्गारान्निरूहति ॥ ८ ॥ **व्यन्तान् कृत्वा गृह्णाति** 'अग्नय आदित्यं गृह्णामि रात्रियाऽहः' **इति** ॥ ९ ॥ 'सुभूते श्रयस्व' **इत्यधिश्रयति** ॥ १० ॥ 'उद्यन् सुवर्गो लोकः' **इत्यभिद्योतयति**। '०त्रिषु लोकेषु रोचय' **इति** ॥ ११ ॥ 'उद्भुव आप स्थः' **इति स्रुवेणापः प्रत्यानयति**। '०उदिमं यजमानं भावयत प्रजया पशुभिः' **इति** ॥ १२ ॥ 'उद्यन् सुवर्गो लोकः' **इत्येवाभिद्योतयति**। '०त्रिषु लोकेषु रोचय' **इति** ॥ १३ ॥ 'अन्तरितꣳ रक्षोऽन्तरिता अरातयः' **इति प्रसलैस्त्रिः पर्यग्निकरोति** ॥ १४ ॥ **प्रच्छिद्याभिद्योतनस्य निरस्यति** 'अपहता व्यृद्धिरपहतं दौःष्वप्नियमपहतं पापमपहतं पापस्य पापकृतः पापं कर्म, यो नः पापं कर्म करोति प्रत्यगेनमृच्छतु' **इति** ॥ १५ ॥ **अनुपहत्याभिद्योतन-मुद्वासयति** ॥ १६ ॥ 'विष्णोः क्रमोऽसि', 'विष्णोः क्रान्तमसि', 'विष्णोर्विक्रान्तमसि' **इति त्रिर्भस्मन् सादयित्वा चतुर्थेन प्रतिष्ठापयति** ॥ १७ ॥ **आत्मानमङ्गारानभिप्रकम्प्य** 'सुभूतमकर्त' **इति पराचः प्रत्यूहति** ॥ १८ ॥ **सुप्रत्यूढान् कृत्वा दक्षिणेन हस्तेन स्रुवं च समिधं चादत्ते** ॥ १.५.१.१९ ॥ **[इति प्रथमः पटलः** (१८)**]**

दक्षिणेन हस्तेन स्रुवं च समिधं चादत्ते सव्येन स्रुचम् ॥ १ ॥ **निष्टपति** 'प्रत्युष्टꣳ रक्षः प्रत्युष्टा अरातयः' **इति गार्हपत्ये** ॥ २ ॥ **निष्टप्याह** 'उन्नयामि' **इति** ॥ ३ ॥ 'देवेभ्यो हव्यं

सर्वर्त्विग्भिः स्वव्यापारादौ कर्तव्यं सर्वकर्मविषये[१] ॥ ८ ॥

व्यन्तान्[२] विच्छिन्नान् तानङ्गारान् कृत्वा अग्निहोत्रस्य द्रव्यं गृह्णाति। सोममपि। लतामेव[३] होमयोग्यं कृत्वा जुहोति[४]। सोमशब्दस्याकृतिवचनत्वाद्रसग्रहण[५]स्याश्रवणाच्च। अपरे[६] रसस्यैव होमे दृष्टत्वाद्रसमुपाददते ॥ ९ ॥

अधिश्रयणस्य श्रपणार्थत्वाच्छ्रपणानर्थिनां द्रव्याणामधिश्रयणं नास्ति। दधितण्डुलादीनामधि-श्रयणीयेषु[७] न स्यात्। श्रुतपथे[८] विज्ञानार्थत्वादिति[८] केचित्। तथा च शतपथे ॥ १० ॥

अवद्योतयति। श्रुतं[९] वेदा इति परेऽभिघारणसंस्कृतेः कुर्वन्ति ॥ ११ ॥

तथापः प्रत्यानयनं [१०]वेगोपशमनार्थत्वादनधिश्रयणीयेऽप्याज्ये विलयनार्थत्वाद्[१०] विरोधादपः[११] प्रत्यानयनं नास्ति। आज्ये दर्भाग्रयोः प्रत्यानयनं[१२] सूत्रकार आमनति ॥ १२ ॥

'हरस्ते मा विनीषमिति[१३] द्वे दर्भाग्रे प्रत्यस्यति' पर्यग्निकरणं सर्वेषां क्रियते ॥ १.५.१.१४ ॥ **[इति प्रथमः पटलः** (१८)**]**

'ओमुन्नय'[१४] इत्यनुजानाति यजमानः स्वयंहोमे[१५], प्रवासस्थे च पत्नी। तस्य यावदुक्तन्याय्यत्वात् पत्नी विहिता[१६]। पुत्रादिरिति केचित् ॥ ३ ॥

---

१. M Ad सर्वविषयं कर्मविषयं; thus T. **२.** T विषयेप्यन्तान् विच्छि०. **३.** T लततामेव. **४.** T जुह्वति. **५.** Ad ०ग्रहणस्य श्रव०. **६.** T ०पुरे. **७.** T ०तण्डुलादिनाभिद्योतनमनधिश्रय०. **८–८.** M Ad शृतविज्ञानां, T च्छुतपते विज्ञाना०. **९.** M Ad शृतं. **१०–१०.** T वेगोपशमनार्थत्वाधि ... न्याज्ये ... नार्थत्वात्. **११.** M Ad ०रोधाभावः. **१२.** M Ad प्रत्यासनं, T प्रत्ययनं. **१३.** Ad विन०, M विनिष्टमिति. **१४.** T आमुन्न०. **१५.** T होमो. **१६.** T पत्नीविहितः.

मह्यमभयायो३मुन्नय' **इति ॥ ४ ॥ उन्नयति** 'भुवदिडा' **इति प्रथमः स्रुवम्,** 'जनदिडा' **इति द्वितीयम्,** 'वृधदिडा' **इति तृतीयम्,** 'करदिडा' **इति चतुर्थम्,** 'सुवरिडा' **इति पञ्चमं यदि पञ्चोन्नीती ॥ ५ ॥ उन्नीयाभिमृशति** 'सजूर्देवैः सायंयावभिः' **इति ॥ ६ ॥ उन्नीते दशहोतारं व्याचष्टे ॥ ७ ॥ उपोत्थाय मुखदघ्ने हरति** 'अग्निं वैश्वानरमाप्रीणीहि' **इति ॥ ८ ॥ विषुवत्युद्यच्छते ॥ ९ ॥ कूर्चे स्रुचः सादयित्वा समिधमादधाति** 'रजतां त्वाऽग्निज्योतिषं वायुमतीꣳ सुवर्ग्याꣳ सुवर्गाय लोकाय रात्रिमक्षितिमिष्टकामुपदधेऽमृतं प्राणे दधामि। प्रजापतिस्त्वा सादयतु पृथिव्याः पृष्ठे तया देवतयाऽङ्गिरस्वद् ध्रुवा सीद' **इति ॥ १० ॥ अथैतावन्मात्रे समिधो जुहोति** 'अग्निर्ज्योतिर्ज्योतिरग्निः स्वाहा' **इति ॥ ११ ॥ हुत्वाऽनुप्राणिति** 'अमृतं प्राणं मयि दधाम्या मा प्राणो

---

[1]पूर्णा वाऽनूचो वा[1] चतुरुन्नयति। पञ्चममुन्नयनं [2]पञ्चावत्तिनामिति केचित्। [3]अनवदानत्वान्, पञ्चावत्तीनामेव[3] सूत्रकार आमनति[4] ॥ ५ ॥

'सजूर्देवैः' इत्युन्नीतं[5] स्थालीगतं वा ॥ ६ ॥

उन्नीत एव दशहोता[6] व्याख्येयः। उन्नीयोपसादयतीत्येव[7] पक्ष [8]आचार्येणानभिप्रेतः। अतो अन्नं होष्यन्नुपसादयेदित्येषः[8] पक्ष आश्रितः ॥७॥

'अग्निं वैश्वानरम्' इत्येतं मन्त्रं [9]केचिद्धरणे प्रयुञ्जते[9]। पूर्वप्रतीते अपरे उद्यमने[10]। [11]अनेकादृष्टकल्पनाभयाद् दृष्टार्थस्याहरणस्य[11] गुणत्वे हि मन्त्रेणादृष्टकल्पना, उद्यमने[12] चान्या। उद्यमनगुणत्वे[13] [14]मन्त्रगुणत्वेनोद्यमनेनैकमेवादृष्टम् तच्चावश्यं कल्पयितव्यम् ॥ ८ ॥

उपसादनीये कूर्चे सादयति ॥ १० ॥

'एतावन्मात्रे' इति सामान्येनोक्तमनुपदकारो[15] विशिनष्टि द्व्यङ्गुलमात्रे इति। 'कनीयस्तस्य पूर्वम्'[16] इत्यादि ब्राह्मणविहितं द्रष्टव्यम्। अन्वाख्यानोक्तं च—'तां पुरा दीप्तोरिति[17] [18]परीप्सोर्' इत्यादि (वाधू.अन्वा. २.८.१)। 'अग्निर्ज्योतिर्' इत्यत्र। अनेन 'अग्निर्ज्योतिः सूर्यः स्वाहा' 'सूर्यो[19] ज्योतिरग्निः स्वाहे'ति प्रातरिति[20] विकल्पते। एतौ मन्त्रौ[21] केचिद्विनिवेशयन्ति। 'प्रजापतिरकामयते'त्याद्यनुदितहोमविधाना[22]धिकारे दृष्टः[23]। संसृष्टहोममुदितहोम एव स्थापयन्ति[24]। असंसृष्टहोमं विधायानन्तरमभ्युदिते प्रायश्चित्तविधानात्। तत्रानुदितहोमेऽयं पक्षो युक्त इवाभाति।

१-१. M Ad पूणान्वाना°, T पूर्णा स वानूचो वा. **२.** M Ad °वर्तिना; T °पत्तीना°. **३-३.** M Ad अनवादान पञ्चावर्तिनाम्; T अपादानत्वात् पञ्चापत्तीना°. **४.** T °मनन्ति. **५.** M Ad °देवैरिति तं. **६.** T (वशं (?) होता. **७.** T °यो(या)वसा°. **८-८.** M Ad °णानभिप्रेतना होष्यन्, T आचार्येण नाभिप्रेतान्ना (त) (अन्नं). **९-९.** T नेकदृष्ट°, T कैश्चिद् धरणे उपयुज्यते. **१०.** M Ad उद्यमाना; thus T. **११-११.** M Ad अनेकादृष्टकल्पनाभयद्दृ... ार्थस्य. **१२.** M Ad उच्यमाने. **१३.** M Ad उद्यमान°. **१४.** M Ad मन्त्र मन्त्रगुणत्वेनोद्यमाने, T °मन्त्रगुणः। केनोद्यमनेन. **१५.** M Ad °मनुवदकारो. **१६.** M Ad पूर्वेत्या°. **१७.** T पुरादीरिति. **१८.** M Ad वरीप्सो°. **१९.** Ad T सूर्यज्योति. **२०.** Ad प्रसरि°. **२१.** M Ad मन्त्रे. **२२.** M Ad °द्युदितहोम°, T °दितिहेतोर्होम. **२३.** M Ad दृष्टम्; thus T. **२४.** M Ad एव व्यस्थाप°; T स्थापयति.

विशतु सहामृतेन शान्त्या अप्रदाहाय' **इति** ॥ १२ ॥ **अथैतामाहुतिं प्रत्यवेक्षते यैषा गार्हपत्ये हूयते** ॥ १३ ॥ **तां जुहोति** 'अग्नये गृहपतये स्वाहा' **इति मनसा** ॥ १४ ॥ **होतुराहुतिमनुद्रुत्योत्तरत उत्तरामाहुतिं जुहोति** ॥ १५ ॥ **हुत्वाऽन्वपानिति** 'अमृतमपानं मयि दधाम्या माऽपानो विशतु सहामृतेन शान्त्या अप्रदाहाय' **इति** ॥ १६ ॥ **अतिवाल्य कूर्चे स्रुचः सादयित्वा प्रतीचीः स्रुचमुपमार्ष्टि** ॥ १७ ॥ **प्राञ्चः हस्तं कूर्चे निमार्ष्टि** ॥ १८ ॥ **उत्तरतो द्वितीयमुपमृज्य दक्षिणा**

---

[1]आचार्यस्तु प्रायेणानुदितहोममेवोपदिशन् क्वचिदुदितहोमं[1] स्पृशति । तदभिप्रायेणासंसृष्टहोममेवा-मनतीति मन्यामहे। उदितहोमानुदितहोमावादिविकल्पावेवेष्यते[2]। अनिष्टव्योन्नीय[3] हुत्वेति वचनादेव[3] सिद्धे यत्न आनन्तर्यार्थः[4] । स्रुचमनिधायैवेत्यर्थः ॥ ११-१२ ॥

अथैमताामाहुतिं= हूयते[5] । [6]केचिदपदेनाग्निहोत्रमध्वर्युरेव जुहोतीति वर्णयन्ति[6] । अस्मिन् पक्षे[7] अथैतामाहुतिं प्रत्यवेक्षते[8] । गार्हपत्यमवेक्ष्य[9] गत्वा तां जुहोति । अन्ये[10] यजमानं होतारं मन्यन्ते । तथा सति एतामाहुतिं गार्हपत्ये हूयमानां प्रत्यवेक्षते[11] । कः ? परिशेषाद्यजमानः[12] । गार्हपत्यं प्रतीक्ष्य इत्यत्र गार्हपत्यशब्देन गार्हपत्याहुतिरभिप्रेता। तथा चोक्तम्—'स यस्यैषा हूयेत[13] स एव' (वाधू.अन्वा. २.४.१) इत्यादि। उभयोरपि पक्षयोर्हुत्वोपसादयन्ति 'अग्नये गृहपतये स्वाहा' (वाधू.अन्वा. २.४.१) इत्यन्वाख्यानाम्नातेन[14] विकल्पते। मनसा होतुर्जुहोति[15]। आरुणिपक्षोऽत्राचार्येणाम्नातम्। कौषीतक्यादीनां तु [16]श्रोत्रियाणां समिध्येव[16] द्वयोराहुत्योर्होमकल्पविहितस्यास्य प्रशंसार्थमाह—'उभौ हि स लोकाववेदिमञ्चामुञ्च' इति[17] (वाधू.अन्वा. २.११.५) ॥ १३-१६ ॥

अतिवाल्य कूर्चे स्रुचं[18] सादयित्वा प्रतीचीं स्रुचमुपमार्ष्टि[19] । यथा पयो हस्ते लिख्यते[20] तथा प्रतीचीमिति । प्रत्यङ्मुखं[21] सादयित्वेति केचित् । क्रियावाद इत्यन्ये । यथा प्रतीचीः स्फ्येन वेदिमिति प्राञ्च[22] उत्तरतः[22] कूर्चे[23] 'ओषधीभ्यः' इति संकल्प्य[24] मन्त्रं च बौधायनीयाः पठन्ति 'ओषधीभ्यस्त्वौषधीञ्जिन्व' इति ॥ १७-१८ ॥

तथोत्तरे 'पितृभ्यस्त्वे'त्यादिलोपं [25]स्रुच्युपमृज्य द्वितीयं गृहीत्वा 'पितृभ्यः' इति संकल्प्य बहिर्वेदि निमार्ष्टि प्राचीनावीती[26] ॥ १९ ॥

१-१. M Ad आचार्यस्तत्प्रायेणानुदितहोमेवेच्छति न क्वचिदु दितहोमं°. २. M Ad विकल्पाविष्य°. ३-३. M Ad निष्टव्योऽग्नीय हुत्वेति पाठादेव, T अग्निष्ट°. ४. M Ad °र्यार्थम्. ५. M Ad °माहुतिं हूयते, T °माहुतिर्भूयते. ६-६. M Ad केचिदपराग्निहोममध्वर्युरेव जुहोति हीति वर्णयति. ७. M Ad om अस्मिन् पक्षे; thus T. ८. M Ad प्रत्यपे°. ९. M Ad °पेक्ष्य; T °पत्यावपेक्ष्य. १०. M Ad अन्यैर्यज°. ११. M Ad प्रत्यपेक्षते. १२. M Ad °माना. १३. M Ad यस्यैषा हू=यते. १४. T इत्याख्यानाम्नातेन. १५. T होत्वजु. १६. M Ad यत्नात्समि° ; thus T; Cf *Vādh. Anvā*. 2.11.5. १७. T लोकावपदि°. १८. T om. १९. M Ad स्रुवम°, T स्रुचमु°. २०. T विन्यते. २१. T °मुखीं. २२-२२. M Ad °ञ्च...त्तरत. २३. M Ad om; thus T. २४. M Ad om; thus T. २५. M Ad लोपं स्रुच्युन्मृज्य; T लेशपं ध्रुच्छृपमृज्य. २६. M Ad °वीति; thus T.

बहिर्वेदि द्वितीयं निमार्ष्टि ॥ १९ ॥ **द्विरचुक्कारं प्राश्नाति** ॥ २० ॥ **अत्रैवोदगावृत्तो भक्षयति** 'आग्नेयं ज्योतिः शुक्रं प्रजननमश्वावद्गोमद्धिरण्यवद्रयिमत्पुष्टिमत्क्षत्रवत् तस्य तेऽग्निपीतस्य मधुमत उपहूतस्योपहूतो भक्षयामि' **इति** ॥ २१ ॥ **उत्तिष्ठन्नुद्दिशति** ॥ २२ ॥ **द्विराचम्य द्विः संक्षाल्य स्रुचं निनयति** ॥ २३ ॥ **सुनिर्णिक्ताः स्रुचं कृत्वोत्प्रदाय वाचंयमोऽग्रेणाहवनीयं परीत्याग्नीननुवीक्षते** 'अभयं वोऽभयं मे अभयं मे अभयं वः' **इति** ॥ २४ ॥ 'आयुरसि' **इत्याहवनीयम्** ॥ २५ ॥

द्विरचुक्कारं[१] प्राश्नाति। चुक्कारमिति शब्दानुकरणम्, अशब्द इत्यर्थः। एतत् ज्ञापयत्यमन्त्रं प्राशनमिति। तथापि शब्दः संभवति। तूष्णीमेव प्राशनम्। अन्ये आह—'अग्निर्ज्योतिः सूर्यो[२] ज्योतिः' इत्येतयोर्मध्ये। ब्राह्मणे 'प्रजा ज्योतिः' इति मन्त्र आम्नातः। तस्यानर्थक्यपरिजिहीर्षया स्थानात् प्राशने[३] मन्त्रः प्रयोक्तव्य इति। तथा च बौधायनाः प्राशने प्रयुञ्जन्ते[४] ॥ २० ॥

तत्रैवोदगावृत्तो[५] भक्षयति मन्त्रेण ॥ २१ ॥

उत्तिष्ठन्नुदङ्मुखमाचम्य[६] द्विः प्रक्षाल्य स्रुचमुत्तिष्ठन् द्विरुद्दिशति। अन्य आह—अस्यां वचनव्यक्तौ व्यवहितकल्पना। साऽपि सत्यां गतौ न न्याय्या। अतो भक्षयित्वाऽनाचम्यैवोद्दिशति। ततो द्विः संक्षाल्य स्रुचं[६] निनयति। आचमनद्वित्वे [७]अदृष्टकल्पना प्रसिद्धिविरोधश्चेति[७]। अन्य उत्तिष्ठन्नुद्दिशति द्विरिति वाक्यं कल्पयन्ति। अन्यद्वाक्यं निनयनान्तम्। उभयोरपि पक्षयोः [८]ब्राह्मणपाठक्रमोऽविरुध्येत'। निर्णेनेक्ति[८] शुध्यै निष्टपति। स्वाहाकृत्या[९] उद्दिशति 'सप्तर्षीनेव[१०] प्रीणाती'ति ब्राह्मणम्[११]। अनाचान्तेन वा दृष्टार्थं कर्मोद्देशनं कर्तव्यं स्यात्। अतः पौरस्त्य एवार्थः। उदादि[१२]स्रुचमित्यन्तमेकवाक्यम्। द्विरिति प्रधानक्रियया संबध्यते। निष्टपनमिहानुक्तमपि कर्तव्यम्। निनयतीति पृथग् वाक्यं, तच्च निनयनं सप्तर्षीन् ध्यात्वा द्विरुद्दिश्य ॥ २२–२४ ॥

दक्षिणापर्यावृत्योपसमिन्धनं[१३] कृत्वाऽन्तर्वेदि कर्तव्यम्। तथाहि ब्राह्मणं–'हुत्वोपसमिन्धनम्'[१४] इति। अविशेषवचनात्[१५] त्रयाणामिति केचित्। होमसंयोगाद्[१६] द्वयोरित्यन्ये। ब्राह्मणे पश्चिमे होमाभावादाहवनीयस्यैवेत्यपरे[१७]। स्रुगुत्प्रदानान्तमाध्वर्यवम्[१८]। एवं तर्हि वाचंयमोऽग्रेणाहवनीयं परीत्येत्यादि नोपपद्यते[१९]। अत्र केचिदाहुः–[२०]अनुपदवचनाभिप्रायम् एतदिति। तत्र हि सर्वं[२१] याजमानमग्निहोत्रं भवतीति। अथैक आहुः—अङ्गारनिरूहणप्रभृत्याऽग्निहोत्रस्योपसादनादध्वर्युः कुर्यात्। परिक्रम्याहवनीये यजमानो जुहुयात्। प्रत्युत्क्रम्याध्वर्युः गार्हपत्ये नयति[२२]। तस्मिन् पक्षद्वये भक्षोऽपि याजमान एव। ततो वाचंयम[२३] इत्याद्युपपद्यते इति। अन्ये अन्तर्द्वादशाहे[२४] पर्वणि च

---

१. M Ad द्वरच्चु०. २. M Ad सूर्य. ३. T प्रानौ. ४. M Ad ०युञ्जते, T ०ञ्चन्ते. ५. M Ad ०वृत्ता. ६–६. M Ad after उत्तिष्ठन्नु दि =स्रुचं; thus T. ७–७. M Ad ०द्वित्वे ०प्रसिद्धिः; thus T. ८–८. M Ad ब्राह्मण परिक्रमो निरुध्यते निर्नेक्ति. ९. M Ad स्वगकृत्वा; thus T. १०. M Ad ०र्षीनिति. ११. M Ad ब्राह्मणः; thus T. १२. Ad उददि; thus T. १३. M Ad ०णाचार्या०. १४. M Ad समिन्धा०. १५. M Ad वचनानां त्र०. १६. M Ad ०योग द्वयो०. १७. M Ad ०नीयस्येत्य परे. १८. M Ad स्रुकप्रधाना०. १९. M Ad ०त्यादिना उप०. २०. M Ad अनुवचना०. २१. M Ad om सर्वं; thus T. २२. M Ad ०पत्य इति; thus T. २३. M Ad ०यमेत्या०. २४. M Ad अन्येऽप्यन्त०.

'विश्वायुरसि' **इति गार्हपत्यम्** ॥ २६ ॥ 'विश्वमायुरसि' **इत्यन्वाहार्यपचनम्** ॥ २७ ॥ 'तन्तुरसि' **इत्याहवनीयमेव**। '०ततोऽसि ततस्ते अस्मि ततो मेऽस्त्यनु मा तनुहि' **इति** ॥ २८ ॥ 'प्रजया पशुभिरहमसौ भूयासम्' **इत्यात्मनोऽग्रे नाम गृह्णाति** ॥ २९ ॥ 'असौ भूयाद् असौ भूयाद्' **इत्यनुपूर्वं पुत्राणां**, 'तन्तुर्मे भूयात्' **इत्यन्ततः** ॥ ३० ॥ **ज्योतिष्मन्तं त्वाऽग्ने** ॥ १.५.२.३१ ॥ **[इति द्वितीयः पटलः** (१९)**]**

'ज्योतिष्मन्तं त्वाऽग्ने ज्योतिष्मान् समिन्धे' **इत्याहवनीयं समिन्धे** ॥ १ ॥ 'मनसे त्वा सुवर्गाय लोकाय' **इत्युपतिष्ठते** ॥ २ ॥ 'आयुष्मन्तं त्वाऽग्ने आयुष्मान् समिन्धे' **इति गार्हपत्यꣳ समिन्धे**। '०आयुषे त्वा ***[१]**(प्रजननाय' **इत्युपतिष्ठते** ॥ ३ ॥ 'अन्नादं त्वाऽग्नेऽन्नादः समिन्धे' **इत्यन्वाहार्य-पचनꣳ समिन्धे** ॥ ४ ॥ 'प्राणाय त्वाऽन्नाद्याय' **इत्युपतिष्ठते** ॥ ५ ॥ 'कामाय वो व्याप्त्यै ज्योतिष्मतः शकेयम्' **इति सर्वान् सहोपतिष्ठते**। '०वित्तं च मे गोपायताशां च' **इति** ॥ ६ ॥ 'अवन्तु मामृषयो देवजाताः' **इति सप्तर्षिभ्यो नमस्करोति** ॥ '०त्रातारः उत नस्तनूनां तनूधाः। अमर्त्या मर्त्यमभि मा सचन्तामा मा विशन्तु पितरो दिविष्ठाः' **इति** ॥ ७ ॥ **अथ** 'आपो व्रतभृतो व्रतं मे धारयताप्सु श्रद्धा' **इत्याह** ॥ ८ ॥ **नाचामति** ॥ ९ ॥ 'चक्षुरसि', 'श्रोत्रमसि' **इत्यधिवदत्यमृतं ब्राह्मणम्** ॥ १० ॥ **पञ्चप्रक्रमं वेदिमभिप्रक्रामति** ॥ ११ ॥ 'आपो हि ष्ठा मयोभुवः' **इत्यन्तर्वेदि तृचेन मार्जयन्ते** ॥ १२ ॥ 'इडायै वास्त्वसि' **इतीमामभिमृशति**। '०वास्तुमान् भूयासम्' 'प्रतिष्ठाऽसि प्रतिष्ठेषम्' **इति** ॥ १३ ॥ 'ब्रध्नस्य विष्टपेऽहं माꣳ सादयामि' **इति दक्षिणत आहवनीयस्योप-विशति** ॥ १४ ॥ 'कामस्य कामेन वोऽनुवीक्षे' **इत्यग्नीननुवीक्षते** ॥ १५ ॥ 'असौ मे कामः समृध्यताम्' **इति यं कामं कामयते तमाशास्ते** ॥ १६ ॥ **सꣳ हैवास्मै) स कामः पद्यते** ॥ १७ ॥ 'यत्ते सुशीमे' ॥ १.५.३.१८ ॥ **[इति *[२]तृतीयः पटलः** (२०)**]**

'यत्ते सुसीमे हृदयम्' **इतीमामभिमृशति**। '०आदावन्तः प्रजापतौ। तस्यामृतस्य त्वं वेत्थ माऽहं

---

*[१]. Text abri. आयुषे त्वा=स कामः पद्यते see I.3.3.4-17. *[२]. Vyākhyā of the 3rd Paṭala (sūtras 1-18) is not given in the MSS.

स्वयंहोममामनन्ति। स्वयमहतवासा[१] यजमानोऽग्निहोत्रं जुहुयात्। अजस्रेष्वग्निषु न प्रवसतीति [२]शाट्यायनः। नित्यं वा पयसा वा स्वयं च पर्वणि जुहुयादित्याश्वलायनः[२] (द्र. आश्व. श्रौ. २.३.१)। गमनमन्यत्र। स[३] यदग्निहोत्रं होष्यन्[४] दक्षिणत आहवनीयस्योपविशति [५]तदेवासीना होमाः सायम्, आदित्यस्योदयात् प्रातरितिवचनात्[५] परिगमनं नास्ति। अन्वीक्षणादि[६] निगदसिद्धम् ॥ १.५.२.२५-२७ ॥ **[इति द्वितीयः पटलः** (१९)**]**

---

१. M Ad स्वयं महा तपसा; thus T. २-२. M Ad शाभ्याय निनयन वाग्वां, T शाट्यायन निनय वा (?) पयसा वा स्वयं च पर्वणि जुहुयादित्याश्वालायन... After this, remaining text of Agnihotra due to displacement of folio again begins with गमन° M (p. 21, line 1) and Ad (p.49, line 7). ३. M Ad om; thus T. ४. M होष्यं, Ad होष्यम्. ५-५. M तदेवा सताहोमा, Ad °वासीना होमा साया...दि...त्यस्यो°. ६. M Ad अरवीक्ष°.

पौत्रमघꣳ रुदम्', 'वेद हृदयꣳ सुसीमायै गूढमन्तः प्रजापतौ। [तस्यामृतस्य त्वं वेत्थ] माऽहं पौत्रमघं नि गाम्' **इति** ॥ १ ॥ **उपास्याग्नीनेतेनैव यथेतं निष्क्रम्य गार्हपत्यमुपतिष्ठते** 'अग्ने रक्ष णः', 'इन्द्र त्रायस्व', 'सोम मृडय', 'अदिते नः पाहि', 'वैश्वानरं ज्योतिरसि तन्माऽव', 'मैत्रावरुणं ज्योतिरसि तन्माऽव', 'मा नो विव्याधिनो विदन् मो अभिव्याधिनो विदन्', 'इषूः शरव्या [अस्मद्विषूचीरिन्द्र पातय', 'विष्वञ्चो अस्मच्छरवः पतन्तु या अ]स्ता याश्चास्याः। दैवीर्मानुषीरिषवोऽस्माकं सपत्नान् विविध्यत', 'यो नः सपत्नो योऽसपत्नोऽरातीयति देवास्तान् धूर्वन्तु ब्रह्मवर्म ममान्तरम्' **इति** ॥ २ ॥ **ब्रह्मवर्मणोपस्थाय कामꣳ संविशति** ॥ ३ ॥ **इति नु सायम्** ॥ ४ ॥ **अथ प्रातः** ॥ ५ ॥ **प्रसिध्यति कर्माऽङ्गाराणां निरूहणात्** ॥ ६ ॥ **व्यन्तान् कृत्वा गृह्णाति** 'आदित्यायाग्निं गृह्णाम्यह्ने रात्रिम्' **इति** ॥ ७ ॥ **प्रसिध्यति कर्माऽभिमर्शात्** ॥ ८ ॥ **उन्नीयाभिमृशति** 'सजूर्देवैः प्रातर्यावभिः' **इति** ॥ ९ ॥ **प्रसिध्यति कर्मा समिध आधानात्** ॥ १० ॥ **समिधमादधाति** 'हरिणीं त्वा सूर्यज्योतिषं वायुमतीꣳ सुवर्ग्याꣳ सुवर्गाय लोकायाहरक्षितिमिष्टकामुपदधेऽमृतं प्राणे दधामि प्रजापतिस्त्वा सादयतु दिवः पृष्ठे तया देवतयाऽङ्गिरस्वद् ध्रुवा सीद' **इति** ॥ ११ ॥ **अथैतावन्मात्रे समिधो जुहोति** 'सूर्यो ज्योतिर्ज्योतिः सूर्यः स्वाहा' **इति** ॥ १२ ॥ **प्रसिध्यति कर्मोन्मार्जनात्** ॥ १३ ॥ **प्राचीꣳ स्रुचमुपमार्ष्टि** ॥ १४ ॥ **प्रत्यञ्चꣳ हस्तं कूर्चे निमार्ष्टि** ॥ १५ ॥ **उत्तरतो द्वितीयमुन्मृज्य दक्षिणा बहिर्वेदि द्वितीयं निमार्ष्टि** ॥ १६ ॥ **द्विरचुक्कारं प्राश्नाति** ॥ १७ ॥ **अत्रैवोदगावृत्तो भक्षयति** 'सौर्यं ज्योतिः शुक्रं प्रजननमश्वावद् गोमद्धिरण्यवद्रयिमत्पुष्टिमत्क्षत्रवत्तस्य ते सूर्यपीतस्य मधुमत उपहूतस्योपहूतो भक्षयामि' **इति** ॥ १८ ॥ **प्रसिध्यति कर्म** ॥ १९ ॥ **अनुपस्थायाग्नीननुवीक्षते** 'नमो वोऽस्तु श्रद्धा मे मा वि गात्' **इति** ॥ १.५.४.२० ॥ **[इति चतुर्थः पटलः** (२१)**]**

॥ इति प्रथमप्रपाठके पञ्चमोऽनुवाकः ॥

उपास्याग्नीनिति। पूर्वोक्तस्यैव कर्मकलापस्य परामर्शनम्। अथवा तेन प्रतिपद्यत[१] आपर्वण इत्यत्रानुवाकद्वयस्यावकाशदर्शनार्थः। येन पथा प्रविष्टस्तेनैव निष्क्रम्य[२] ॥ २ ॥

ब्रह्मवर्मणोपस्थाय कामं समाविशति[२]। सायंप्रातयोरग्निहोत्रयोरेका[३] पूर्वनिष्पादकत्वात् कर्ममध्ये व्रतचारिणा भवितव्यमिति मा विज्ञायीत्येवमुक्तम्। अतः प्रातर्विशेषाभिधि-त्सयाऽधिकरोति ॥ ३ ॥

अनुपस्थायेत्यातः सामञ्जस्येन[४] गच्छति। अनुपस्थायेति केचिन्माहाचमसादि वर्णयन्ति। ननु तत्सर्वदोपस्थानमित्युक्तत्वात् प्रातरपीष्यते। नैतत्। तस्यैतं द्वादशाहमित्यनुवृत्तिर्निर्दिश्यत इति तत्रोक्तम्। तथापि रहस्यपरिपठितेषु वैकल्पिकेषु रात्रिं च कृत्वा अहस्त्वकृत्वेति च कालद्वयेऽप्यनपायस्तस्यां विधीयते[५]। अतोऽनुवाकद्वयस्य प्रतिषेधः। तस्यापि तत्रैव प्रतिषिद्धत्वान्न प्रातरिति ब्रह्मवर्मण[६] प्रतिषेधः। तथा चोक्तमनुपदे 'नप्रातर्ब्रह्मवर्मणोपतिष्ठते'[७] ॥ १.५.४.२० ॥ **[इति चतुर्थः पटलः** (२१)**]**

॥ इति व्याख्यायां प्रथमप्रपाठके पञ्चमोऽनुवाकः ॥

---

१. M Ad °पद्यता पर्वण. २-२. M निष्क्रम...सनाविशति, Ad निष्क्रमय ब्रह्मवर्येणो°. ३. M Ad सायंप्रातरग्निहोत्र°. ४. M सामज्ञेन. ५. M Ad व्यवणीते, M Ad व्यवधीयते. ६. M Ad °वर्मस्य. ७. M °वर्मणोऽवति°, Ad °वर्मणोवति°.

॥ अथ प्रथमप्रपाठके षष्ठोऽनुवाकः ॥

[अग्न्युपस्थानम्]

अग्नीनुपस्थास्यमानो भवति ॥ १ ॥ तस्याग्निहोत्र्युपक्लृप्ता भवति पुँवत्सा ॥ २ ॥ यदि न पुँवत्साऽपि स्त्रीवत्सैव ॥ ३ ॥ स यदि नक्षत्र आधत्ते यदस्योपनिशान्तमग्न्युपस्थानं भवति तेन प्रतिपद्यत आ पर्वणः ॥ ४ ॥ अथ यदि पर्वण्याधत्त एतेनैव प्रतिपद्यते ॥ ५ ॥ प्रतिधाप्यैतं वत्सं बध्नन्ति ॥ ६ ॥ स यज्ञोपवीतं कृत्वाऽप आचम्य यजमानायतने तिष्ठन्नाहवनीयमुपतिष्ठते ॥ ७ ॥

अग्नीनुपस्थास्यमानो भवति ॥ १ ॥

तद्वृत्तदर्शनाद् यद्वृत्ताध्याहारः कर्तव्यः। योऽग्नीनुपस्थास्यमानो भवति तस्येति। अग्न्युपस्थानस्य [१]कर्तव्यतानूच्याग्निहोत्रीं च[१] पुंवत्सत्वं विधीयते ॥ २ ॥

तदभावे स्त्रीवत्साऽपि विहिता ॥ ३ ॥

नक्षत्राधानं काम्यं नित्यं चाविशेषेण[२]। नक्षत्रमुपाधायाधाने कृते यदस्योपनिशान्तः पर्वण उपनिशान्तमुपलक्षितमित्यर्थः। [३]सर्वदोपस्थानमित्युक्त्वा माहाचमसम्। ननूक्तं सर्वत्र[३] ग्रहणस्य प्रयोजनमुच्यते। तथापि माहाचमसमेव समीपे लक्षितम्। उपनिशान्तं कस्य समीपे अग्निहोत्रस्याग्निहोमानन्तरं पठितमित्यर्थः। तेन प्रतिपद्यत आ पर्वणः। पूर्वं [४]तेनोपस्थायानुवाकद्वयेनोपतिष्ठति इत्यर्थः[४], नान्यतरनिवृत्तिरुक्ता ॥ ४ ॥

पर्वाधानपक्षेऽनुवाकद्वयेनोपस्थाय [५]माहाचमसेनोपतिष्ठते। अविशेषेण पक्षद्वये पूर्वोत्तरकालमनुवीक्षणान्तेऽनुवाकाभ्यामुपस्थाय माहाचमसेन ॥ ५ ॥

प्रतिधाप्य दोहोत्तरकालं[५] पाययित्वा ॥ ६ ॥

स यज्ञोपवीतं कृत्वाऽप आचम्य स्मृतिशास्त्रस्य शेषत्वाद्यज्ञोपवीताचमनयोर्नित्यत्वाद् यज्ञकर्मसु, इह विधानस्यानर्थक्यं स्मृतिशास्त्रप्राप्तस्य प्रदर्शनार्थं भवति। एवं तर्हि अभावे [६]यज्ञोपवीतिना चान्तेन[६] प्रक्रान्तत्वादनुवाक एवेह वचनम्। अथवा नित्यादाचमनादन्यदाचमनं स्मृतावेव विहितमस्ति। केषाञ्चिद् यज्ञकर्मणि कथमब्धिगामिभि[७]स्त्रिभिः पिबेद् व्याहृतीभिः, त्रिः परिमृजेदिति। तथा [८]स्वाध्यायब्राह्मणे यज्ञोपवीतविशेष[८] आम्नातः। अजिनं वासो वासो वा दक्षिणत उपवीय दक्षिणं बाहुमुद्धरतेऽवधत्ते सव्यमिति यज्ञोपवीतम्। तदुभयं सर्वकर्मसु कर्मादावेव कर्तव्यमिति केचित्। अन्ये

१-१. M om, M wrongly repeats the text: प्रतिषेधस्तस्यापि तत्रैव प्रतिषिद्धत्वान्न प्रातरिति ब्रह्मवर्मस्य प्रतिषेधस्तथा चोक्तमनु... after अग्न्युपस्थानस्य; thus T. २. Ad °विशेषण°. ३-३. M सर्वदोपस्थानम...सर्वत्र°; thus T. ४-४. M °पस्थाय...इत्यर्था. ५-५. M °चमसेन... कालं; thus T. ६-६. M य...चान्ते°. ७. M Ad °ब्धिंगाभिः. ८-८. M °ब्राह्म...शेष.

कवातिर्यङ्ङिवोपतिष्ठेतेति ब्राह्मणम्। कवातिर्यङ्ङिवोपतिष्ठते ॥ ८ ॥ 'उप प्रयन्तोऽध्वरम्' **इत्यनुच्छन्दसं** 'चित्रावसो स्वस्ति ते पारमशीय' **इत्यातः** ॥ ९ ॥ 'चित्रावसो स्वस्ति ते पारमशीय' **इति रात्रिं मनसा ध्यायति** ॥ १० ॥ 'इन्धानास्त्वा शतꣳ हिमाः' **इति समिधमादधाति।** '°द्युमन्तः समिधीमहि वयस्वन्तो=वर्षिष्ठे अधिनाके स्वाहा' **इति** ॥ ११ ॥ **एतयैव तिस्रोऽभ्यादध्यादिति** ॥ १२ ॥ **अथैकमेतामेव तिस्रः कृत्वोऽभ्यादध्याद् ब्राह्मणमु वै भवति** 'एषा वै सूर्मी कर्णकावत्येतया ह स्म वै देवा असुराणाꣳ शततर्हा=स्तृत्या अच्छंबट्कारम्' **इति** ॥ १३ ॥ **एकस्या एवैतद् ब्राह्मणम्** 'एकामभ्यादध्यादिति' ॥ १४ ॥ **एकामेवाभ्यादधात्येषा स्थितिः** ॥ १५ ॥ 'सं त्वमग्ने सूर्यस्य वर्चसाऽगथाः' **इत्युपतिष्ठते।** '°समृषीणाꣳ स्तुतेन=प्रजया सृज' **इति** ॥ १६ ॥ 'सं त आकुर्वन्तु स्वं यजमान' **इत्याह।** '°यदन्यत्र मनसा तद् ध्याये' **ति** ॥ १७ ॥ **तत्समाकृतमभिमन्त्रयते** 'सं पश्यामि प्रजा अहमि=बह्वीर्मे भूयास्त' **इति** ॥ १८ ॥ 'सꣳहितासि विश्वरूपीः' **इत्यग्निहोत्रियै वत्समभिमृश-त्युत्तरेणाग्रेणान्वाहार्यपचनं प्राञ्चं तिष्ठन्तमभीव दक्षिणमक्षिकटम्।** '°आ मोर्जा विशा

यत्रयत्र यज्ञोपवीतं कृत्वाऽप [१]आचम्येति कल्पे विहितम् ॥ ७ ॥

कवातिर्यङ्ङिव[१] ईषत्तिर्यङिव। इवशब्दः[२] सम्प्रत्यर्थे नोपमार्थे। ब्राह्मणग्रहणम् प्राङ्मुखेनोदङ्मुखेन वा कर्माणि कर्तव्यानीति प्राप्तस्यापवादार्थप्रदर्शनार्थम्[३] एतत् ज्ञापयति। यत्र वचनं प्रतिषेधो वा संभवो वा [४]न प्राङ्मुखेन न वोदङ्मुखेन[४] वा कर्तव्यमिति ॥ ८ ॥

अनुच्छन्दसं पाठक्रमेणैवेत्यर्थः ॥ ९ ॥

रात्रिं मनसा ध्यायति। मन्त्रार्थे स्मर्यमाणे 'चित्रावसो' इत्यत्र रात्रिं मनसा ध्यायति ॥ १० ॥

एतयैव[५] तिस्रः कृत्वाऽभ्यादध्यादिति मन्त्रावृत्या। [६]केचिच्छित्वाऽभ्यादधति त्रिभिर्मन्त्रावयवैस्तिस्रः[६]। तेषां तिस्रः कृत्वेति स्त्रीलिङ्गस्य प्राप्तिश्चिन्त्या ॥ १२ ॥

स्थितिवन्तमेव[७] तत् ब्राह्मणापेक्षम्। सूर्मी शतघ्नी कर्णकावती कण्टकवती[८] शतं शतं हिंसितव्यस्य[९] स्तृहन्ति हिंसन्ति। वज्रमायुधम् अच्छंवटकारम् अशेषमित्यर्थः ॥ १३–१५ ॥

'सं त=ध्याये'ति। हे यजमान ते[१०] स्वं धनं समाकुर्वन्तु सह स्थापयन्तु यत्समानेतुं[११] शक्यं, असन्निहितं तन्मनसा ध्यायेति[१२]। अत्र स्वशब्देन प्रजाश्च पशवश्चाभिधीयन्ते। मन्त्रवर्णान्नान्यद्धनं छागो वा मन्त्रवर्णादित्यनेन न्यायेन ॥ १७ ॥

समाकृतं समानीतम्। 'सं[१३] पश्यामीति' ऊर्जं वो भक्षीये'ति एतेन[१४] प्रजानुमन्त्रणम्[१५]। '[१६]रेवती'त्यादि पश्वनुमन्त्रणम् ॥ १८ ॥

'संहितासि विश्वरूपी'रिति पुंल्लिङ्गत्वं दृष्ट्वा पुंवत्सत्वं विहितमाचार्येण। उपलक्षणत्वाद्

१–१. M आचम्ये...त्र वेतिर्यङिवा Ad तत्रतिर्यङिवा. **२.** M Ad उपशब्दः. **३.** M Ad °नार्थ ए°. **४–४.** M Ad न...वादङ्मुखेन. **५.** M Ad एतामे°. **६–६.** M दध... यवै°, Ad दधनि°. **७.** M Ad स्थितिवनमेतत्. **८.** Ad कण्डक°. **९.** M Ad हिंसिवतंस्त्यहन्ति. **१०.** M Ad तं. **११.** Ad °नेतं. **१२.** M ध्याययति. **१३.** M Ad यं. **१४.** M Ad °तदनूं. **१५.** M Ad °मन्त्रेण. **१६.** M Ad रेवतीमित्या°.

गौपत्येन रायस्पोषेण=रायः श्रयन्ताम्' **इति** ॥ १९ ॥ **अथ प्रत्यङ् परेत्य षड्भिः गार्हपत्यमुपतिष्ठते** 'उप त्वाऽग्ने दिवेदिवे', 'राजन्तमध्वराणाम्', 'स नः पितेव सूनवे', 'अग्ने त्वं नो अन्तमः', 'तं त्वा शोचिष्ठ दीदिवः', 'वसुरग्निर्वसुश्रवाः' **इति** ॥ २० ॥ 'ऊर्जा वः पश्याम्यूर्जा मा पश्यत' **इति गृहान् परेक्षते** ॥ २१ ॥ 'रायस्पोषेण वः पश्यामि रायस्पोषेण मा पश्यत' **इति गाः** ॥ २२ ॥ 'इडा स्थ मधुकृतः' **इति ता एव**। '०स्योनामा विशते=रायः श्रयन्ताम्' **इति** ॥ २३ ॥ **अथ प्राङेत्य चतसृभिराहवनीयमुपतिष्ठते** 'तत्सवितुर्वरेण्यम्', 'सोमानꣳ स्वरणम्', 'कदा चन स्तरीरसि', 'परि त्वाऽग्ने पुरं वयम्' **इति** ॥ २४ ॥ **अथ प्रत्यङ् परेत्य गार्हपत्यमुपतिष्ठते** 'अग्ने गृहपते सुगृहपतिरहं=गृहपतिना भूयाः' **इति** ॥ २५ ॥ **आशिष आशास्ते** 'शतꣳ हिमास्तामशिषमाशासे मह्यममुष्मै ज्योतिष्मतीम्' **इत्यात्मनोऽग्रे नाम गृह्णाति,** 'अमुष्मा अमुष्मै' **इत्यनुपूर्वं पुत्राणां,** 'तन्तवे' **इत्यन्ततः** ॥ २६ ॥ **तस्यैतद् ब्राह्मणं** 'प्र वा एषोऽस्माल्लोकाच्च्यवते य आहवनीयमुपतिष्ठते गार्हपत्यमुपतिष्ठतेऽस्मिन्नेव लोके प्रतितिष्ठत्यथो गार्हपत्यायैव निह्नुते' **इति यदेतत्** ॥ २७ ॥ **अथैकꣳ समानमाषड्भ्यः** ॥ १.६.१.२८ ॥ **[इति प्रथमः पटलः** (२२)**]**

अथैकꣳ समानमाषड्भ्यः ॥ १ ॥ **षड्भिर्गार्हपत्यमुपतिष्ठते** ॥ २ ॥ 'ऊर्जा वः पश्याम्यूर्जा मा पश्यत' **इति गृहान् परेक्षते** ॥ ३ ॥ **प्राङेत्य तिसृभिराहवनीयमुपतिष्ठते** 'तत्सवितुर्वरेण्यम्', 'सोमानꣳ स्वरणम्', 'कदा चन स्तरीरसि' **इति** ॥ ४ ॥ 'परि त्वाऽग्ने पुरं वयम्' **इत्येषा परिशेते** ॥ ५ ॥ **अथ प्रत्यङ् परेत्य गार्हपत्यमुपतिष्ठते** 'अग्ने गृहपते' **इति** ॥ ६ ॥ **तथैव आशिष आशास्ते** ॥ ७ ॥

वत्सशब्दस्य पुंल्लिङ्गत्वाद्वा। स्त्रीवत्सत्वेऽपि न दोष इति स्त्रीवत्सैवापीत्याह। दक्षिणमक्षिकटम्[1], अक्ष्णः अन्तं कटाक्षम्[2] ॥ १९ ॥

ततो गार्हपत्यसकाशं गत्वा गायत्रीभिर्द्विपदाभिश्च तमुपस्थाय गृहान् गाश्च परेक्ष्य प्राङेत्य चतसृभिराहवनीयमुपस्थाय पुनरपि गार्हपत्यं गत्वा 'अग्ने गृहपते' इति तमुपस्थाय 'शतꣳ हिमाः' इत्याशिषमाशास्ते। अत्र 'शतं हिमाः' इत्यादि सर्वेषु नामग्रहणेषु अनुषजन्ति केचित्। अन्ये द्वितीयादिषु 'तामाशिषम्' इत्याद्येव पठन्ति ॥ २०–२६ ॥

अस्य विधानस्य ब्राह्मणं 'प्र वा' इत्यादि। कोऽभिप्रायः ? यद्यपि गायत्रीद्विपदाक्रम एतदाम्नातः, तथापि[3] प्रकरणस्य तुल्यत्वात् गार्हपत्यस्योपस्थानेनैव परिसमापयितव्यम्, नाहवनीयोपस्थानेनेति। पाठक्रमेणैव सिद्धे उत्तरविधानापेक्षयोक्तम् ॥ १.६.१.२७ ॥ **[इति प्रथमः पटलः** (२२)**]**

तथाऽन्यविधानमाहवनीयोपस्थानार्थानां चतसर्णां ऋचामन्त्यां स्थापयित्वा गार्हपत्यमुपस्थायाशिष[4] आशास्य शिष्टयाऽऽहवनीयमुपतिष्ठते ॥ १–८ ॥

---

१. T °क्षितटम्. **२.** Ad कटक्षं, T कटाक्षः. **३.** M Ad तथा; thus T. **४.** M Ad आशिषमा° ; thus T.

प्राङेत्यैकयाऽऽहवनीयमुपतिष्ठते 'परि त्वाग्ने पुरं वयम्' **इति** ॥ ८ ॥ **तस्यैतद् ब्राह्मणं** 'परि त्वाऽग्ने पुरं वयम्' **इत्याह परिधिमेवैतं परिदधात्यस्कन्दायेति यदेतत्** ॥ ९ ॥ **अथैकꣳ समानमा-षड्भ्यः** ॥ १० ॥ **षड्भिर्गार्हपत्यमुपस्थायात एवोपतिष्ठते** 'अग्ने गृहपते' **इति** ॥ ११ ॥ **तथैवाशिष आशास्ते** ॥ १२ ॥ 'ऊर्जा वः पश्याम्यूर्जा मा पश्यत' **इति गृहान् परेक्षते** ॥ १३ ॥ **प्राङेत्य चतसृभिराहवनीयमुपतिष्ठते** 'तत्सवितुर्वरेण्यम्', 'सोमानꣳ स्वरणं', 'कदा चन स्तरीरसि', 'परि त्वाऽग्ने पुरं वयम्' **इति** ॥ १४ ॥ **तदेतत्प्राक्सꣳस्थमुपो एतद् ब्राह्मणमाप्नोति** 'परि त्वाऽग्ने पुरं वयम्' **इति यदेतत् प्रथमा वाऽस्त्विति द्वितीया वा** ॥ १५ ॥ **तेन हैतेन सायमेवोपतिष्ठते, न प्रातः** ॥ १६ ॥ 'नक्तमुपतिष्ठते न प्रातः । सꣳ हि नक्तं व्रतानि सृज्यन्ते सह श्रेयाꣳश्च पापीयाꣳ-श्चासाते । ज्योतिर्वा अग्निस्तमो रात्रिर्यन्नक्तमुपतिष्ठते ज्योतिषैव तमस्तरति' **इति हि ब्राह्मणम्** ॥ १७ ॥ **श्वोभूत आग्निपावमानीरुद्धरति** 'अग्न आयूꣳषि पवसे' **इत्येताः षड्टचः** ॥ १८ ॥ **नाग्नि-पावमानिकेन संवत्सरमुपतिष्ठते** ॥ १९ ॥ **संवत्सरस्य परस्तादाग्निपावमानीभिरुपतिष्ठते** ॥ २० ॥ **सोऽत ऊर्ध्वं काममेव साग्निपावमानिकेनोपतिष्ठते, काममुद्धरेत्** ॥ २१ ॥ **तस्यैतद् ब्राह्मणम्** 'यथा वै पुरुषोऽश्वो गौर्जीर्यत्येवमेवाग्निराहितो जीर्यति, संवत्सरस्य परस्ताद् आग्नि-

अस्य विधानस्य विधायकं ब्राह्मणवाक्यं 'परि त्वाऽग्ने' इत्याह । परिधिमेवैतं[१] परिदधातीति । परिधिशब्दः समाप्तिवचनः । अत्रानयर्चा समापयितव्यम् । दृश्यते च परिधिशब्दस्य समाप्तिवचनत्वम् 'समिद्धोऽग्न आहुते'त्याह परिधिमेवैतं परिदधात्यस्कन्दाये'ति । एवमुक्त्वा यदत ऊर्ध्वमु[२] तादृगेव तदिति ब्रुवन् समाप्तिवचनत्वं द्योतयति ॥ ९ ॥

अस्मिन् पक्षे पूर्वोक्तं[३] ब्राह्मणवाक्यं[४] गायत्रीद्विपदाविषयमेव भवति । पाठक्रमाच्छ्रुतिक्रमो बलीयान् । तृतीयविधानं[५] हि गार्हपत्यमुपस्थायात्रैव स्थितो[६] 'अग्ने गृहपते' इत्यादि तत आशिष[७] आशास्य गृहपरेक्षणं कृत्वा 'तत्सवितु'रित्यादिभिश्चतसृभिराहवनीयमुपतिष्ठते । एतत्प्राक्संस्थं परिधिवचनं चेह न विरुध्यते । त्रयः पक्षाः । प्रथमो द्वितीयो वा आचार्येणेष्यते[८] । कुतः ? पाठक्रमं बाधितुं श्रुतिक्रमबलीयस्त्वादेकस्यैव मन्त्रस्योत्कर्षो[९] युक्तः, न बहूनामिति ॥ १४-१५ ॥

श्वोभूते यस्मिन्नहन्यग्निहोत्रमारब्धं[१०] तत उत्तरेद्युराग्नीपावमानीरपनयति ॥ १८ ॥

संवत्सरे पूर्णे अनन्तरं यदहस्तस्मिन् साग्निपावमानिकेन ॥ २० ॥

तत ऊर्ध्वमनियमः साग्निपावमानिकेन वा, [११]अनग्निपावमानिकेन वा[११] ॥ २१-२२ ॥

---

१. M वैकं. **२.** M Ad र्ध्वमु, T ऊर्ध्वम्, correctd as ऊर्ध्वमु. **३.** M Ad पूर्वमेवोक्तम्. **४.** M Ad वाच्यं; thus T. **५.** M Ad विधानमिति; thus T. **६.** Ad °स्थितेग्नि°. **७.** M Ad °माशास्य. **८.** M Ad प्रथमा द्वितीया आचार्येणेष्येते [Ad ष्यते]; thus T. [प्रथमद्वितीयावाचार्येणेष्येते ?]. **९.** M Ad मन्त्रस्युत्क°. **१०.** M Ad ° ब्धः. **११-११.** M Ad om; thus T.

पावमानीभिरुपतिष्ठते पुनर्नवमेवैनमजरं करोत्यथो पुनात्येव' **इति यदेतत्** ॥ २२ ॥ **तद् वा एतद-ग्न्युपस्थानमायुष्यं लोक्यं पुत्रियं पशव्यम्। आयुष्मान् ह वै लोकी पुत्री पशुमान् भवति य एतेनोपतिष्ठते** ॥ २३ ॥ **तस्मिन्वा एतस्मिन्नग्न्युपस्थाने सर्वाणि छन्दाꣳसि सर्वा आशिषः सर्वे कामाः** ॥ २४ ॥ **न ह वा अस्य किञ्चिच्छन्दोऽपराद्धं भवति नाशीर्न कामो य एतेनोपतिष्ठते** ॥ २५ ॥ **स यथा ह वा इदं महायज्ञः सर्वैश्छन्दोभिस्तायत एवꣳ ह वा अस्याग्निहोत्रꣳ सर्वैश्छन्दोभिस्तायते य एतेनोपतिष्ठते** ॥ २६ ॥ **अथ माहाचमसम्** ॥ २७ ॥ **ज्योतिष्मन्तं त्वाऽग्ने** ॥ १.६.२.२८ ॥ **[इति द्वितीयः पटलः (२३)]**

'ज्योतिष्मन्तं त्वाऽग्ने ज्योतिष्मान् समिन्धे' **इत्याहवनीयं समिन्धे**। '॰मनसे त्वा सुवर्गाय *[1](लोकाय' **इत्युपतिष्ठते** ॥ १ ॥ 'आयुष्मन्तं त्वाऽग्न आयुष्मान् समिन्धे' **इति गार्हपत्यꣳ समिन्धे** ॥ २ ॥ 'आयुषे त्वा प्रजननाय' **इत्युपतिष्ठते** ॥ ३ ॥ 'अन्नादं त्वाऽग्नेऽन्नादः समिन्धे' **इत्यन्वाहार्यपचनꣳ समिन्धे** ॥ ४ ॥ 'प्राणाय त्वाऽन्नाद्याय' **इत्युपतिष्ठते** ॥ ५ ॥ 'कामाय वो व्याप्त्यै ज्योतिष्मतः शकेयम्' **इति सर्वान् सहोपतिष्ठते**। '॰वित्तं च मे गोपायताशां च' **इति** ॥ ६ ॥ 'अवन्तु मामृषयो देवजाताः' **इति सप्तर्षिभ्यो नमस्करोति** ॥ '॰त्रातार उत नस्तनूनां तनूधाः। अमर्त्या मर्त्यमभि मा सचन्तामा मा विशन्तु पितरो दिविष्ठाः' **इति** ॥ ७ ॥ **अथ** 'आपो व्रतभृतो व्रतं मे धारयताप्सु श्रद्धा' **इत्याह** ॥ ८ ॥ **नाचामति** ॥ ९ ॥ 'चक्षुरसि', 'श्रोत्रमसि' **इत्यधिवदत्यमृतं ब्राह्मणम्** ॥ १० ॥ **पञ्चप्रक्रमं वेदिमभिप्रक्रामति** ॥ ११ ॥ 'आपो हि ष्ठा मयोभुवः' **इत्यन्तर्वेदि तृचेन मार्जयन्ते** ॥ १२ ॥ 'इडायै वास्त्वसि' **इतीमामभिमृशति**। '॰वास्तुमान् भूयासम्' 'प्रतिष्ठाऽसि प्रतिष्ठेषम्' **इति** ॥ १३ ॥ 'ब्रध्नस्य विष्टपेऽहं माꣳ सादयामि' **इति दक्षिणत आहवनीयस्योप-विशति** ॥ १४ ॥ 'कामस्य कामेन वोऽनुवीक्षे' **इत्यग्नीननुवीक्षते** ॥ **१५** ॥ 'असौ मे कामः समृध्यताम्' **इति यं कामं कामयते तमाशास्ते** ॥ १६ ॥**) सꣳ हैवास्मै स कामः पद्यते य एतेनोपतिष्ठते** ॥ १७ ॥ **अथ प्रवसदुपस्थानम्** ॥ १.६.३.१८ ॥ **[इति तृतीयः पटलः (२४)]**

***[1]**. Text abri. मनसे त्वा सुवगार्य=सꣳ हैवास्मै see I.3.3.2-17.

'आयुष्यमि'त्यादयो मन्त्रवर्णा अर्थवादाः[1] ॥ २३-२४ ॥

अपराद्धं[2] बहिष्कृतम् ॥ २५ ॥

माहाचमसस्यात्र पाठ एतेनैव प्रतिपद्यत इत्यत्र 'तन्तुर्मे भूयादि'ति। अतः परं माहाचमसात्पूर्वमनुवाकद्वयमिति[3] ज्ञापनार्थम् ॥ १.६.२.२७ ॥ **[इति द्वितीयः पटलः (२३)]**

पूर्वस्मिन्नेवानुवाके आम्नातात् सर्वैरुपस्थानविकल्पैः समुच्चीयते 'य एतेनोपतिष्ठते' इति [4]प्राधान्यवचनात्स्वयमेवेति च प्रभवति ॥ १.६.३.१-१७ ॥ **[इति तृतीयः पटलः (२४)]**

१. M Ad T ॰वर्णार्थ॰. **२.** M Ad T अपरार्धं. **३.** M Ad वाचकद्वय॰, T corected as ॰वाचक॰. **४.** M Ad प्रधान॰.

[प्रवसदुपस्थानम्]

अथ प्रवसदुपस्थानम् ॥ १ ॥ **प्रवसन्नग्न्युद्धरणकालमनशनेन प्रतिगोपायति, अग्निहोत्रं वाचोयम्येन** ॥ २ ॥ **स यदाहुतं मन्यते, स यज्ञोपवीतं कृत्वाऽप आचम्य प्राङ्विोदङ् तिष्ठन् जपत्यासीनो वा** 'भूर्भुवः सुवरग्नय आहोष्यमाणा अग्नय आहूयमाना अग्नय आहूताः स्विष्टं च मे हुतं स्वाहुतं च गोपायत', 'ऋतसत्याभ्यां मा पात', 'अहोरात्राभ्यां मा पात', 'प्राणापानाभ्यां मा पात', 'द्विपात् पुषेयं', 'चतुष्पात् पुषेयं', 'अहरशीय रात्रिरशीय' **इति सायम्,** 'रात्रिरशीयाहरशीय' **इति प्रातः, अहर्वा ऋतः रात्रिः सत्यम्** ॥ ३ ॥ **अपि ह वा अस्याहुतः हुतं भवति य एतेनोपतिष्ठते** ॥ ४ ॥ **अथ परोक्षादुपस्थानम्** 'भूर्भुवः सुवर्, इहैव सन् तत्र सतो वो अग्नयः प्राणेन वाचा मनसा बिभर्मि तिरो मा सन्तमायुर्मा प्रहासीज्ज्योतिषा वो वैश्वानरेणोपतिष्ठे' **इति** ॥ ५ ॥ **अथागत्य माहासांपदेनोप-तिष्ठते** 'ओऽम्' **इति गार्हपत्यम्,** 'ओऽम्' **इत्यन्वाहार्यपचनम्,** 'ओऽम्' **इत्याहवनीयम्** ॥ ६ ॥ **ओऽम् इति वै स्तूयते, ओऽम् इति शस्यते ओऽम् इत्याश्राव्यते** ॥ ७ ॥ **अथ तथा हास्य त्रिस्त्रिभिर्वेदैरेकैक उपस्थितो भवति य एतेनोपतिष्ठते** ॥ ८ ॥ **अथ प्रसिद्धं तूष्णीं तृतीयः समिधोऽभ्यादधाति** ॥ ९ ॥ **अथ समारोपणम्** ॥ १० ॥ 'अयं ते योनिर्ऋत्वियः' **इत्यरण्योरग्निः समारोहयते** । '॰यतो जातो=रयिम्' **इति** ॥ ११ ॥ **अथो खल्वाहुः** 'यदरण्योः समारूढो नश्येदुद् अस्याग्निः सीदेत् पुनराधेयः स्यादि' **ति** ॥ १२ ॥ 'या ते अग्ने यज्ञिया तनूस्तयेह्यारोह' **इत्यात्मन्**

प्रवसदुपस्थानम् प्रवसत उपस्थानम्। अतीतव्यतिरेकेणैतेनोपस्थाय नित्येनोपतिष्ठते। तत्र समि-न्धनसमिदाधानादीनि[१] सन्निहितेन केनचित् कर्तव्यानीति। अन्य आह—'तेषां मन्त्राणां प्रत्यगाशीष्ट्वात्[२] स्वयमेव वदति कर्माण्यसंभवादन्यः करोतीति। तथा च केचित् पठन्ति—'अथेमाः समिधः प्रवसतस्तू-ष्णीमभ्यादधाति'[३] इति। प्रत्यगाशिषस्तावदन्यकर्तृकेष्वपि विद्यते। त आत्मनि प्रयुज्यमानाः[४] स्वामिन-मभिदधति यथा स्वामिनि वर्तमानं[५] जयशब्दमात्मनि सैनिका उपचरन्ति 'वयं जितवन्त' इति। समाकृताभिमन्त्रणमसंभवे समिदाधानवत् संप्रयुक्तम्। प्रैषमध्वर्युरेव वदति यथा—'यजमान वाचं यच्छेति'। वत्साभिमर्शनं समिदाधानवत् गोगृहपरेक्षणमग्न्यसन्निधावपि[६]। स्वसन्निधौ यदि विद्यते स्वयमेव परोक्षादुपस्थानमनुपस्थाय प्रव्रजितस्याग्निहोत्रकाल आगते[७] कर्तव्यम्। तत्र प्रवसदुपस्थानम्। ततोऽनित्यमिदम्। प्रथम एवाहनि प्रवसदुपस्थानं सायं प्रातरावर्तते। नित्यम् यथावस्थितमा-प्रयोजनसिद्धेः[८] ॥ १-५ ॥

प्रोष्यागत्य माहासांपदेनेत्यादि[९] ॥ ६-९ ॥

समारोपणम्। अग्निहोत्रहोमकाले[१०] तदर्थमुद्धृतानां ज्वलितानामुद्धृतानां वा कर्मण्यकृते प्रयाण

---

१. M Ad ॰धानादि सन्नि॰; thus T. २. M Ad प्रत्यगाशीष्टात्स्व॰; thus T. ३. M Ad ॰दधति. ४. M Ad ॰माना स्वा॰. ५. M Ad ॰मान. ६. M Ad क्षणमग्निमग्नि स॰; thus T. ७. M Ad ॰काल आह ते. ८. M Ad ॰वसित॰. ९. M Ad माह सां पयोदने॰. १०. M Ad कारके.

समारोपयमाणस्त्रिरपान्यात्। '०आत्मानमच्छा वसूनि कृण्वन्नस्मे नर्या पुरूणि। यज्ञो भूत्वा यज्ञमासीद स्वां योनिं जातवेदो भुव आजायमानः सक्षय एहि' **इति ॥** १३ **॥ अथ प्रत्यवरोहणम्** 'भूर्भुवः सुवराजुह्वानः सुप्रतीकः विश्वे देवा यजमानश्च सीदत' **इति ॥** १४ **॥ अथ द्वितीयम्** 'उपावरोह जातवेदः पुनस्त्वं देवेभ्यो हव्यं वह नः प्रजानन्। आयुः प्रजाः रयिमस्मासु धेह्यजस्रो दीदिहि नो दुरोणे' **इति ॥** १५ **॥ उभाभ्यां वैकेन वा ॥** १६ **॥ अथातोऽग्नीनामेवोद्वातानां प्रायश्चित्तिः ॥** १७ **॥ स यदि सर्व एवोद्वायेयुः** 'अयं ते योनिर्ऋत्वियः' **इत्यायतनानि समारोह्योद्धृत्यैतद् भस्मावोक्ष्य मथित्वाऽग्नीन् विहृत्य सन्ततिः हुत्वाऽथ सिद्धमग्निहोत्रं जुहोति ॥** १८ **॥ अथ द्वितीयम्** 'अयं ते योनिर्ऋत्वियः' **इत्येवायतनानि समारोह्योद्धृत्यैवैतद् भस्मावोक्ष्य मथित्वाऽग्नीन् विहृत्य सन्ततिः सव्याहृतिकाः हुत्वाऽथ सिद्धमेवाग्निहोत्रं जुहोति ॥** १९ **॥ अथ तृतीयम्** 'अयं ते योनिर्ऋत्वियः' **इत्येवायतनानि समाराह्योद्धृत्यैवैतद् भस्मावोक्ष्य मथित्वाऽग्नीन् विहृत्य प्रसिद्धः होतृभिश्चरति पूर्णाहुत्यन्तैः ॥** २० **॥ अथ सिद्धमेवाग्निहोत्रं जुहोति ॥** २१ **॥ अथ चतुर्थम्** 'अयं ते योनिर्ऋत्वियः' **इत्येवायतनानि समारोह्योद्धृत्यैवैतद् भस्मावोक्ष्य मथित्वा गार्हपत्यमष्टाभिरुपतिष्ठते**– 'उदु त्वा विश्वे देवाः', 'उद्बुध्यस्वाग्ने', 'उदेनमुत्तरां नय', 'उद्वयं तमसस्परि', 'उदुत्तमं वरुण पाशमस्मत्',

---

उपस्थिते प्रकरणात्। तथा सत्येकवचनमविवक्षितम्। अर्थित्वादितरयोरविजात्यपेक्षं वा ॥ १०-१३ ॥

आत्मसमारोपणे औपानुवाक्याम्नातेष्वेव द्रव्येषु प्रत्यवरोपणम्[१] ॥ १४-१६ ॥

उद्वातप्रायश्चित्तम्। बहुवचननिर्देशात्पक्षद्वयम्। उद्धरणपक्षे धार्यपक्षेऽग्निहोत्रार्थं ज्वलितेषु सर्वेषूद्वातेषु तत्र वाऽऽम्नातमन्यत्र। केचिदायतनानीत्यादिना[२] बहुवचनमविवक्षितं मन्यन्ते, अन्वाहार्यपचनस्य[३] पृथग्योनित्वात्। तथा चौपानुवाक्ये वास्तोष्पतीयविधाने द्वयोरेव समारोपणं दृश्यते।'अयं ते योनिर्ऋत्वियः' इति च वक्तुं न शक्यते, पृथग्योनित्वात्। अपर आह–ब्राह्मणे गार्हपत्ययोनित्वं तस्यास्तीति तदपेक्षं बहुवचनमिति। इतरथास्मिन् पक्षे[४] द्वयोरेव समारोपणाभिहितस्यामात्यादाहरणमेवेत्यपरे वर्णयन्ति। अनेकयोनित्वपक्षेऽपि [५]वचनात्समारोपणं किमिव वचनं न [५]कुर्यात्। यथाऽऽग्नेयादीनां[६] पृथङ् निरुप्तानां सहितानां[७] च संवपनोत्तरकालं[८] यथा स्वंस्वमेव[९] भागो[१०] भवति।'

---

१. M Ad प्रत्यवरोहण०. २. M Ad ०यतनानित्या०. ३. M Ad अन्वाहार्यस्य; thus T. ४. M इतरथास्मिन् पक्षे मात्यादाहरणमे... वरे, Ad ०रोपणादितस्या० ; thus T. ५-५. M ०पक्षेऽपि वमा...समारोपणं कम...न कुर्यात्, T पक्षे वि पि वच० ; thus Ad. ६. Due to displacement of folios the text after यथाग्नेयादीनां पाठोऽनुमेयः, beginning with 'ऊर्जेत्वे 'ति (M p.26, line 11; Ad p.60, line 8) and ending with उत्तरत्र आहनीय (M p.30, line 1, Ad p.67, line 5) dealing with *Darśapūrṇamāsa*, has wrongly been placed here under *Agnyupasthāna*. The remaining text of *Agnyupasthāna* after यथाग्नेयादीनां in M p.30, line 2 ff, Ad 67, line 5 ff would continue upto the end of Prapāṭhaka I. The text between आग्नेयादीना and वहतानां is broken in M and Ad. This displacement has been noticed by the scribe who has informed in a note there : पाठोऽनुमेयः (M p.26, line 11, Ad p.67, line 7). T gives the entire text in a proper order. ७. M वहताना०, Ad सहावहता०. ८. M Ad संवननो०. ९. M स्वं स्वमेव०. १०. M Ad भागो.

'मनो ज्योतिर्जुषताम्', 'तन्तुं तन्वन्', 'त्वमग्न सप्रथा असि जुष्टो होता वरेण्यः। त्वथा यज्ञं वि तन्वते' **इति** ॥ २२ ॥ **एताभिरुपस्थाय चत्वारि चतुर्गृहीतानि जुहोत्युप वा तिष्ठते** 'अग्नेऽङ्गिरः', 'अग्नेऽभ्यावर्तिन्', 'पुनरूर्जा', 'सह रय्या' **इति** ॥ २३ ॥ **अथैनमुद्धरति** 'भूर्भुवः सुवर्वाचा त्वा' ॥ १.६.४.२४ ॥ **[इति चतुर्थः पटलः** (२५)**]**

'वाचा त्वा होत्रा प्राणेनोद्गात्रा चक्षुषाऽध्वर्युणा मनसा ब्रह्मणा श्रोत्रेणाग्नीधैतैस्त्वा दैव्यैः पञ्चभिर्ऋत्विग्भिरुद्धरामि', 'उद्ध्रियमाण उद्धर पाप्मनो यदविद्वान् यच्च विद्वाꣳश्चकार। अह्ना यदेनः कृतमस्ति पापꣳ सर्वस्मान्मोद्धृतो मुञ्च तस्मात्' **इति सायम्;** '°रात्र्या यदेनः कृतमस्ति पापꣳ सर्वस्मान्मोद्धृतो मुञ्च तस्मात्' **इति प्रातः** ॥ १ ॥ 'सूर्यस्याग्नेः प्रियया तनुवा सङ्गच्छस्व', 'अषाढ उग्रः पृतनाषाढमृध्रः स्योना योनिः स्योना पृथिवी मा त्वा तितीर्षꣳस्तारीत्', 'ओजोऽसि सहोऽसि बलमसि भ्राजोऽसि यशः श्रीरसि वृत्रहा', 'यो नः सनाभिर्यो विनाभिरभिदासति तमग्नेऽहं तया द्विषन्तं भ्रातृव्यं ब्रह्मणो गिरिणाऽभिनिदधामि', 'अमृताहुतिममृतायां जुहोम्यग्निं पृथिव्याममृतस्य जित्यै। तेनामुं काममनन्तं जयानि प्रजापतिर्यं प्रथमो जिगाय। अग्निमग्नौ स्वाहा' **इति सायम्;** 'सूर्यमग्नौ स्वाहा' **इति प्रातः** ॥ २ ॥ **अथ सिद्धमग्निहोत्रं जुहोति** ॥ ३ ॥ **अथ कौषीतकं** 'भूर्भुवः सुवर्वागायुर्वागु विश्वायुर्विश्वमायुः' सर्वायुः सर्वमायुः' **इति** ॥ ४ ॥ **सर्वꣳ हैवायुरेति य एतेनोपतिष्ठते** ॥ ५ ॥ **अथ पाञ्चं** 'भूर्भुवः सुवः, प्र वो देवायाग्नये यच्छानि गुह्यानि नामानि रूपाणि भूतान्याकूतिर्मे समृध्यतां मनसस्पतिर्मे समृद्ध्यताꣳ श्रद्धा मे मा विगात्' **इति सायं;** 'प्र वो देवाय सूर्याय' **इति प्रातः** ॥ ६ ॥ **एतावद्वा अस्ति यावदेतद्यच्छानि गुह्यानि नामानि रूपाणि भूतानि** ॥ ७ ॥ **आकूतिर्हैवास्मै मनसस्पति य एतेनोपतिष्ठते** ॥ ८ ॥ **अथ पैङ्गम्** 'भूर्भुवः सुवः

अयं ते योनिः'रिति च वनस्पतिजात्यपेक्षामिहवती'त्येते[1] चत्वारः पक्षाः। तेषां त्रयो धार्यपक्षे चतुर्थ उद्धरणयोगादुद्धरणपक्षे[2]। सन्ततिः सर्वेषु हूयते[3]। द्वितीये व्याहृतयश्चाविशेषात्[4] ॥ १.६.४.१९-२४ ॥ **[इति चतुर्थः पटलः** (२५)**]**

कौषीतकादीन्यग्न्युपस्थानानि [5]याजमानानीच्छतः समुच्चयानि। केचित् कौषीतकादीनामेव समुच्चयमिच्छन्ति, ब्राह्मणग्रहणात्। न यथाहितादीनामविशेषेण विधानात्। तानि सायं प्रातर्भवन्त्य-विशेषेण विधानात् पाञ्चे[6] च दर्शनात् ॥ ४ ॥

यच्छानि दानानि ॥ ७ ॥

आकूतिस्तर्कः। मनसस्पतिरात्मा। तावदेव लौकिको विद्यत इत्युपस्थानस्य

---

१. M जात्यपेक्षं...तत...चत्वा°; thus Ad, T doubtful. २. T °पक्षो. ३. Ad हयते. ४. M Ad °हृतयत्वा. ५. M Ad यज°. ६. Ad प्राञ्चे.

सुप्रजाः प्रजया भूयासꣳ सुवीरो वीरैः सुवर्चा वर्चसा सुपोषः पोषैः' **इति ॥ ९ ॥ सुप्रजा हैवास्य प्रजया भवति सुवीरो वीरैः सुवर्चा वर्चसा सुपोषः पोषैर्य एतेनोपतिष्ठते** ॥ १० ॥ **अथ वार्कलम्** 'भूर्भुवः सुवर्नमो वोऽस्त्वभयं वोऽस्त्वभयं मे अस्तु महः' **इति** ॥ ११ ॥ **अभयꣳ हैवास्मै महो भवति य एतनोपतिष्ठते** ॥ १२ ॥ **अथ वैश्यस्योपस्थानम्** 'भद्रमस्तु वः सुभद्रमस्तु वो भद्रं वस्यो अस्तु मे' **इति** ॥ १३ ॥ **भद्रꣳ हैवास्मै वस्यो भवति य एतेनोपतिष्ठते** ॥ १४ ॥ **अथ यथाहितं** 'भूर्' **इति गार्हपत्यं,** 'भुवः' **इत्यन्वाहार्यपचनं,** 'सुवः' **इत्याहवनीयं** 'वेदानां रसाः' **इति** ॥ १५ ॥ **अथैकम्** 'भर्तुं वः शकेयम्' **इति** ॥ १६ ॥ **अथैकम्** 'श्रद्धा मे मा वि गात्' **इति** ॥ १७ ॥ **अथैकम्** 'यस्मै कामाय प्रजापतिरग्निहोत्रमजुहोत् तं काममाप्यासयाग्निहोत्रस्याशीः सा म आशीरिदमहमाभ्यामाहुतिभ्यां गायत्रेण छन्दसा त्रिवृता स्तोमेन रथन्तरेण साम्ना वषट्कारेण वज्रेण द्विषन्तं भ्रातृव्यं पाप्मानं मृत्युमतितराणि' **इति** ॥ १८ ॥ **द्विषन्तꣳ हैवास्य भ्रातृव्यं पाप्मानं मृत्युमतितरति य एतेनोपतिष्ठते** ॥१९ ॥ **अथैकं तूष्णीमहरहः संवत्सरमुपतिष्ठते** ॥ २० ॥ **संवत्सरस्य परस्ताद् यं कामं कामयते तमाशास्ते** ॥ २१ ॥ **सꣳ हैवास्मै स कामः पद्यते य एतेनोपतिष्ठते** ॥ २२ ॥ **तस्यैतद् ब्राह्मणम्। मनुष्यायेन्वै योऽहरहराहृत्याथैनं याचति। स इन्वैतमुपार्च्छति। अथ को देवानहरहर्याचिष्यतीति यदेतत्। तस्मान्नोपस्थेयः। अथ खल्वाहुराशिषे वै कं यजमानो यजत इत्येषा खलु वा आहिताग्नेराशीर्यदग्निमुपतिष्ठते। तस्मादुपस्थेयः** ॥ १.६.५.२३ ॥ **[इति पञ्चमः पटलः** (२६)**]**

॥ इति प्रथमप्रपाठके षष्ठोऽनुवाकः ॥

॥ इति अग्न्याधेयाख्यः प्रथमः प्रपाठकः ॥

□ □ □

स्तुत्यर्थः ॥ १.६.५.८ ॥ **[इति पञ्चमः पटलः** (२६)**]**

॥ इति व्याख्यायां प्रथमप्रपाठके षष्ठोऽनुवाकः ॥[1]

॥ इति कल्पागमसंग्रहे अग्न्याधेयाख्यः प्रथमः प्रपाठकः ॥

□ □ □

---

१. M Ad T षष्ठोऽध्यायः.

॥ अथ द्वितीयः प्रपाठकः ॥

[दर्शपूर्णमासौ]

[उपवसथकर्म]

अद्योपवसथ इत्येकविंशति दारुमिध्मं प्रपूतशकलं हुत्वाऽग्निहोत्रमाहवनीयेऽभ्या-

[१]*अद्योपवसथ=दधाति।* कस्योपवसथः[१]। दर्शपूर्णमासयोः। कुत एतत्। सन्तिष्ठेते दर्शपूर्णमासावि'त्युपसंहारे दर्शनात्। अमावास्याया उपवसथ इति। यस्मिन्नहनि यागः ततः पूर्वेद्युरभिधीयते। चन्द्रादित्ययोः परमविप्रकर्षः पौर्णमासीकालः। [२]परमसन्निकर्षोऽमावास्यायाः। [३]विप्रकर्षसन्निकर्षयोः दुर्ज्ञेयकालत्वात् तेऽत्र प्रयोगासंभवात् तत्कालसन्निकृष्टनां तिथीनां[४] तच्छब्दवाच्यता। तथा च सति द्वे तिथी[५] पौर्णमासी, द्वे चामावास्या। तयोरेकस्यां पूर्वेद्युः कर्म[६] अपरेद्युर्यागः[७]। पञ्चदश्यामुपवासः प्रतिपदि याग इत्यर्थः। तथा च 'पूर्वेद्युः कर्मसु 'श्वो यज्ञाय रमतां देवताभ्यः' इति दृश्यते। 'इमामूर्जं पञ्चदशी'मिति च दृश्यते। अयमप्याचार्यः 'आपूर्णां पौर्णमासीमुपवसेत्, यदा न पुरस्तान्न पश्चाच्चन्द्रमसं पश्येदथामावास्यामुपवसे'दिति वक्ष्यति। किं चान्यत् 'न सायमस्ति, देवतयाऽ[८]जुष्ट'मिति लिङ्गदर्शनात्पूर्वाह्णे याग इष्यते। स च यदा पूर्वेद्युः पञ्चदशी, उत्तरेद्युः प्रतिपत्। रात्रौ पूर्वाह्णे वा पर्वसन्धिः तदा पर्वसंपत्[९]। यदा [१०]मध्याह्नप्रभृत्यास्तमयात् पर्वसन्धिर्भवति[११], तदा कस्मिन्नहन्युपव-सथः कस्मिन् याग इति। उच्यते[१२]। यस्मिन्पर्वसन्धिः तस्मिन्नहन्युपवसथ उत्तरेद्युर्यागः। तथा चोक्तं-द्वैधे— 'यत्रैतदुपवसतोऽस्तमित आदित्ये पुरस्ताच्चन्द्रमा लोहितीभवन्निवोदियात्[१३], तमुपवसथं जानीया'दिति। पञ्चदशीमित्यादि विरोधश्च न भवति, प्रातरेव यागश्च भवति[१४]। किन्तु 'पूर्वामेव पौर्ण-मासीं यजेत उत्तराममावास्यामि'ति ब्रुवत आचार्यस्याभिप्रायो ज्ञातव्यः। 'याज्ञतीर्थ्यादापूर्णां[१५] पौर्णमासीमुपवसेद्' इत्यस्माद्विधेरन्योऽयं विधिः कृतः[१६]। 'तत्र ह [१७]यद्वाऽपक्षीय-माणामुपवसे'दित्युक्तत्वात्संपूर्णामित्यर्थाद् गृह्यते। इह 'पूर्वामेव पौर्णमासीं यजेते'ति पञ्चदश्यां याग उपलक्ष्यते। तत्र पौर्णमास्याश्चतुर्दश्यामुपवसथः पञ्चदश्यां यागः। नैतदेवम्। एवंविधेषु पर्वसूभयेद्युः पञ्चदशी यदा भवति तयोः पूर्वस्मिन्नुपोष्य परेद्युर्यागः। नोत्तरस्मिन्नुपोष्य प्रतिपदि याग इति। तथा सति 'आपूर्णां

१-१. M Ad °अद्योपवसथः, T °अद्योपवसथं...पवसथः. **२.** Ad om परम. **३.** M Ad प्रकर्षः° ; thus T. **४.** Ad तीर्थानां. **५.** M तिथे; thus T. **६.** M Ad कर्मणः; thus T. **७.** T र्योगः. **८.** M Ad देवया. **९.** M Ad सर्वसं° ; thus T. **१०.** M Ad मध्यात्; thus T. **११.** M Ad पूर्वसन्धिः; thus T. **१२.** M Ad show the sign (,,) indicating the close of the paragraph, if not the Paṭala. **१३.** Ad भवोदयात्. **१४.** M Ad give न before भवति. **१५.** M Ad °तीर्थिकाराः पूर्णां, T °तीर्थिकादा° :. **१६.** M Ad कृतम्. **१७.** M Ad यद्वाप.

दधाति ॥ १ ॥ एकं दारु गार्हपत्ये ॥ २ ॥ एकमन्वाहार्यपचने ॥ ३ ॥ एकमाहवनीये ॥ ४ ॥ काममूर्ध्वं ततोऽभ्यादध्यात् ॥ ५ ॥ अमावास्याया उपवसथेऽग्निहोत्रोच्छिष्टमातच्य निदधाति हविरातञ्चनाय ॥ ६ ॥ उत्परेत्य शाखामाच्छिनत्ति या प्राची वोदीची वाऽप्रतिशुष्काग्रा भवति

पौर्णमासीमुपवसे 'दित्यनेनाप्येकवाक्यता भवत्येव। भवति[१] हि तस्मिन्नीषत्पूर्णता। अपरेद्युश्च सन्धेरुत्तर–कालमपक्षीयमाणता। तत्र केचिदनेनैव वाक्येन तादृशेषु पर्वसु सद्यस्कालतां पौर्णमास्या इच्छन्ति। कुतः? प्रातरेव देवतापरिग्रहे इमामूर्जं पञ्चदशीमिति सम्यक् संपद्यत इति। 'अत्रो ह स्माह शालीकि–रतिपन्नः खल्वेष भवति' इत्यादिना सद्यस्कालताऽभिहिता। अस्मिन्पक्षे 'श्वो यज्ञाय रमता 'मिति न संबध्यते। तेषां तत्पदलोपः। स च वचनमन्तरेण नोपपद्यते। यदि वचनमस्ति तदन्याम्[२] अमावास्यायां तूत्तरामावास्यामिति वचनात्पूर्वोक्त एव पक्षः। यस्मिन्नहन्यपराह्णे सन्धिः तस्मिन्नहन्युपवसथः, श्वोभूते च याग इति। यस्मिन्नहन्युपवसथस्तस्मिन्नहन्येकविंशति दारुमिध्ममुपनीतव्यम्। किं प्रपूतशकलम–ग्निहोत्रं हुत्वा तमग्निमपनीयोद्धरणपक्षे तूष्णीं दर्शपूर्णमासार्थमुद्धृत्याहवनीयं तस्मिन्नादधाति ॥ १ ॥

तथैकं दार्वित्यादि। अभ्याधानान्वाधानयोर्नानाकर्तृत्वात्[३] क्रमविचारे प्रयोजनं नास्ति। धारणार्थत्वाद्वेदं पूर्वं देवतापरिग्रहार्थत्वात्। पश्चात्तदस्य देवतापरिग्रहार्थमाचार्यो व्यक्तीकरोति 'तथा पूर्वे देवतां परिग्रहीष्यामह इति वदन्त' इति ॥ २–४ ॥

काममूर्ध्वं ततोऽभ्यादध्यात्। शकलनियमः संख्यानियमश्च नास्ति। असमापनादभ्याधानप्रतिषेधः। प्रतिप्रसवश्चानेन वचनेन क्रियते ॥ ५ ॥

'*अमावास्याया= तञ्चनाये*'[४] ति। पूर्वस्य[४] पदार्थस्य [५]पर्वद्वयसाधारण्यादिहामावास्याया इत्यधिकरोति। अग्निहोत्रोच्छिष्टं स्थालीगतं कृतेऽप्यपराग्निहोमे विद्यमानत्वाद्[६]। अपरे तन्निवृत्तिप्रसङ्गाद् गव्यमवशिष्टमिति वर्णयन्ति। हुतेऽपि[७] शिष्यत इत्युक्तम्। हविरातञ्चनाय मूर्तत्वापादानाय ॥ ६ ॥

'*उत्परेत्य*[८] *शा=षे त्वे*' ति[८]। पलाशस्य लोमशकलस्य[९] शाखावृक्षस्य प्राग्गतोदग्गता[१०] वा शाखा। द्वितीयो 'वा'-शब्दस्तृतीयमर्थं गमयति। प्रागुदीची वेति वर्णयन्ति। अन्य आह—'यत्प्राचीं यदुदीचीमि 'ति। प्रागुदीच्यभिधानार्थत्वादिह 'वा'-शब्दश्चार्थे। प्राची चोदीची च प्रागुदीचीत्यर्थः। अपरे शाखान्तरविहिते अपोद्य ब्राह्मणे प्रागुदीची विहिता। तयोरपि ग्रहणं यथा स्यादिति। ते एवाम्नाते, इतरा स्वयमेव सिध्यतीति। 'इषे त्वे 'ति छेदनं सर्वत्र कर्मानुकूल आख्यातशब्दः स्मर्तव्यो, वाक्यपरिपूरणार्थं न प्रयोक्तव्यः। अथवा मन्त्रस्य कर्मणश्च बहुकृत्वः संबन्धदर्शनादन्तरेणापि आख्यातपदं क्रियास्मरणं भवति। 'वसुभ्यस्त्वा युनज्मी[११] 'त्येवमादिषु प्रदर्श्यत[१२] इति चेत्, न।

---

१. M Ad भवत्येव; thus T. २. M Ad T तदनाम. ३. M नाक° Ad नीकर्तृकत्वाः. ४–४. M Ad T °नायं पू°. ५. M Ad T वर्णद्वय°. ६. M Ad °त्वाद्वप°. ७. Ad हु=, T हुते विशि°. ८–८. M Ad T उत्परेत्यपल...षे त्वेति. ९. M Ad लोमशकस्य. १०. M Ad प्रगतोद [Ad ह]गता. ११. M Ad न ज्ञीत्ये°. १२. M Ad प्रदृश्यत; thus T.

'इषे त्वा' **इति** ॥ ७ ॥ 'ऊर्जे त्वा' **इत्येनामनुमार्ष्टि** ॥ ८ ॥ **तयाऽऽगत्य वत्सानपाकरोति** 'वायव स्थ' **इति पुंस:,** 'उपायव स्थ' **इति स्त्री:** ॥ ९ ॥ 'देवो व: सविता प्रेरयतु' **इति गा अनुमन्त्रयते।** '०श्रेष्ठतमाय कर्मण आप्यायध्वमघ्निया इन्द्राय देवेभ्यो=वो वृणुक्तु' **इति** ॥ १० ॥ 'ध्रुवा अस्मिन् गोपतौ स्यात बह्वी:' **इति यजमानं वर्षभं वा गोष्ठं वाऽभिमन्त्रयते** ॥ ११ ॥ 'यजमानस्य पशून् पाहि' **इत्युत्तरार्धेऽग्न्यागारस्य पलाशशाखामुपगूहत्यग्निष्ठस्य वाऽनस:** ॥ १२ ॥ 'देवस्य त्वा

शाखान्तरे तादृशस्य *[सादयित्वा संभृतेष्वपि तन्न विरुध्यते। इतरेतरयुक्तान्येव भवन्ति[१]। तेषां वृक्षनियम: परिमाणञ्च विध्यवशेषेषु संख्याविकल्पनमुक्तम्। तत्रैव वक्ष्याम:। इध्माबर्हिषी सहैव क्षेमं निदधाति] ॥ ७ ॥*

'ऊर्जे त्वे'ति शाखामनुमार्ष्टि॥ ८ ॥

[२]'वायव स्थे'ति पुंवत्सा:, उपायव स्थ' इति स्त्रीवत्सा:[२] अपाकर्तव्या:[३]। त्रयाणां त्रिवृद्दोहं विधाय वाचंयमोऽनन्वारभ्योत्तरा इति विदधत् षडवमान् दर्शयति। अथ षडवमा वत्सा अपाकर्तव्या:। तथाऽपा[४]करणमन्त्रयोर्बहुवचनान्तत्वं युक्तम्। एवं तर्हि त्रय: पुंवत्सा: त्रय: स्त्रीवत्सा: अत्रोपादेया:[५] प्राप्नुवन्ति। एवं सति 'स यद्येकमेव दुग्धं स्यादि'त्यत्रोह: प्राप्नोति। नैतदेवम्, विधानसामान्यान्नोह्यते। तथा सत्यन्यन्तराभावेऽपि नोह:[६]। अतस्तेनैव हेतुनाऽसमर्थनिगमत्वमनयो:[७] मन्त्रयोरध्यवसीयते। एवं सति 'या यजमानस्य व्रतधुगि'त्यादिषु विकृतावप्यविकार एव। अन्यतराभावे तत्संयुक्तस्य लोपं केचिदिच्छन्ति। उभयो: समुच्चयमपरे॥ ९ ॥

'*देवो व: सविता प्रेरयतु*' इति गा अपाकरोति। शाखयैव ततो गच्छन्तीरनुमन्त्रयते 'श्रेष्ठतमाय'[८] इत्यादिना[८] ॥ १० ॥

'*ध्रुवा अस्मिन्नि*'ति यजमानादयस्त्रयोपि वक्तुं शक्यन्ते इति कृत्वा त्रयो विकल्पिता: ॥ ११ ॥

अग्निष्ठस्य[९] यस्मिँश्चक्रचराणामग्नय: स्थाप्यन्ते तदग्निष्ठमन:।[१०] अथवा यज्ञभाण्डपूर्णमनो गार्हपत्यस्योपरि नित्यम्[११] ॥ १२ ॥

अपरेण गार्हपत्यं तृणानि संस्तीर्य[१२] तिष्ठन्नसिदं[१३] वाऽश्वपरशुं वा निधायादत्ते। 'देवस्य त्वा'

***–*.** Due to displacement of folios in both M and Ad the text beginning with सादयित्वा (M p.26, line 11; Ad p.60, line 7) and ending with निदधाति (M p.30, line 1; Ad p.67, line 5) dealing with *Darśapūrṅamāseṣṭi* has wrongly come under *Agnyādhāna*. This has been shifted to here at its proper place; also see fn.6, p.45. T rightly gives the entire text here at its proper place. **१.** M Ad भवति. **२–२.** M Ad T °वायव 'स्थेति.... स्त्रीवत्सा. **३.** M Ad om; thus T. **४.** Ad अपक°. **५.** M Ad °देय:; thus T. **६.** M Ad °नेह; thus T. **७.** Ad °मर्थत्वनिग°. **८–८.** M wrongly repats एवं सति = भावे between श्रेष्ठतमाये and °इत्यदिना. **९.** Ad अग्निष्टोमस्य. **१०.** M Ad °ग्निषुमन:. **११.** M Ad T wronlgy mention the end of the Paṭala here : तत्र पटलच्छेदोऽमावास्याधिकार निवृत्त्यर्थ:। अतो बर्हि:संभरणं द्वयो: साधारणम्॥. **१२.** M Ad स च स्त्रीर्य. **१३.** M तिष्ठन्दसि°, Ad विष्टं दसि°.

सवितुः प्रसवे' **इत्यपरेण गार्हपत्यं तृणानि संस्तीर्य तिष्ठन् असिदं वाऽश्वपरशुं वा निधायादत्ते।** '०अश्विनोर्बाहुभ्यां पूष्णो हस्ताभ्यामाददे' **इति॥** १३॥ 'यज्ञस्य घोषदसि' **इति (अभिमन्त्रयते)॥** १४॥ 'प्रत्युष्टꣳ रक्षः प्रत्युष्टा अरातयः' **इति गार्हपत्ये निष्टपति॥** १५॥ 'उर्वन्तरिक्षमन्विहि' **इति बर्हिषोऽर्धमन्तरा वेदिं चोत्करं च प्रेत्य** 'प्रेयमगात्=रासदे' **इति वेदिं प्रत्यवेक्षते॥** १६॥ 'देवानां परिषुतमसि' **इति यत्र बर्हिर्लोप्स्यन् भवति तत्परिदिशति** '०वर्षवृद्ध-मसि' **इति॥** १७॥ 'देवेभ्यस्त्वोर्ध्वबर्हिभ्यः' **इत्यूर्ध्वं तृणस्तम्बमुन्मार्ष्टि॥** १८॥ 'देवबर्हिर्मा त्वाऽन्वङ् मा तिर्यक्' **इत्यभिपद्यते॥** १९॥ 'पर्व ते राध्यासम्' **इत्यसिदेनाधिनिदधाति॥** २०॥ 'आच्छेत्ता ते मा रिषम्' **इत्याच्छिनत्ति॥** २१॥ 'देवबर्हिः शतवल्शं विरोह' **इत्याच्छेदनान्यभि-**

इत्यादिना सर्वत्र ब्राह्मणोक्तं विकल्पत इत्युक्तम्॥ १३॥

'उर्वन्तरिक्षमन्विहि'[1] इत्यन्तरा वेदिं[2] चोत्करं च [3]वेद्युत्करावन्तरेण ऋत्विग्यजमानानां पत्न्याश्च यज्ञपात्राणां मेधादीनां चायमेव पन्थाः। तत् क्वचित् क्वचित् प्रदर्शयति। 'विसंस्थिते संस्थिते च संचर' इति विध्यवशेषेषु च तथैवाम्नातम्। 'प्रेयम्' इत्यादेर्मन्त्रस्य समस्तस्य वेदिप्रत्यवेक्षणे विनियोग इति केचित्। मध्य इति करणाभावात्तदयुक्तमिव लिङ्गविरोधात्। 'प्रेयम्' इत्यादेर्मन्त्रस्य समस्तस्य गमनप्रकाशकत्वात्। ब्राह्मणवाक्यमपि 'विद्या वै धिषणा विद्ययैवैनदच्छेती'ति बर्हिरामुख्येनायं गच्छतीत्यर्थः। उक्तमिति करणाभावे यथालिङ्गं विनियोगः कर्तव्य इति। अतो जुष्यन्तो गमनमन्त्रः, शेषो वेदिप्रत्यवेक्षणे। बोधायनाचार्येणाप्येवं विनियोगः कृतः॥ १६॥

यत्र बर्हिः परिदिशति[4] किंजातीयं बर्हिर्गृहीतव्यम्। 'कौशं बर्हिर्भवति'इति शाखान्तरे विद्यते। विध्यवशेषेषु सप्तबर्हिर्जातयस्तुल्यविकल्पा[5] इवाम्नायन्ते कुशाश्च दर्भाश्च क्षीरदर्भाश्च मुञ्जाश्चाश्ववालाश्चैक्षवाश्चेति[6]। परिदेशनं[7] सर्वतो मर्यादाग्रहणम्। यावद्भिभवति नातिरिच्यते चेति मन्यते तावत्परिदिशति॥ १७॥

परिदिष्टस्यैवोन्मार्जनमभिपद्यते॥ १८॥

सव्येन हस्तेन गृह्णाति यावता मुष्टिः परिपूर्यते तावत्। अथवा अस्य मुष्टेः प्रस्तरार्थत्वात् प्रस्तरपरिमाणानामन्यतरपरिमाणानि। परिमाणानि च ब्राह्मणे सामान्यशब्देन 'इयन्तम्' इत्युक्तानि, विध्यवशेषे[8] विशेषितानि '[9]स्रुग्दण्डमात्रः स्रुवदण्डमात्र ऊर्वस्थिमात्र' इति[9]। अपरिमित इत्युक्तपरिमाणविकल्पः॥ १९-२०॥

---

१. M Ad ०मन्वेमीत्य०. **२.** M Ad T चोत्तरं. **३.** M Ad वेद्यु; thus T. **४.** M Ad om परि; thus T. **५.** Ad ०जातीय. **६.** M Ad ०वालश्च. **७.** T ०देशानम्. **८.** M Ad ०शेष वि०. **९-९.** M Ad स्रुगूण्डमात्र ऊर्वस्थि....इति; thus T.

मृशति ॥ २२ **॥ सव्ये हस्तेऽसिदं समस्य** 'सहस्रवल्शा वि वयं रुहेम' **इत्यात्मानं प्रत्यभि-मृशते ॥** २३ **॥ अप उपस्पृश्य** 'पृथिव्याः संपृचः पाहि' **इति प्रथममुष्टिं निदधाति ॥** २४ **॥ तं प्रस्तराय संचष्टे ॥** २५ **॥ तूष्णीमत ऊर्ध्वम् अयुजो मुष्टीन् लुनाति सप्त वा नव वैकादश वा त्रयोदश वा यथाप्तं मन्यते ॥** २६ **॥ अथ** 'अदित्यै रास्नासि' **इति त्रिरन्वाहितं प्रसलैः सन्नहनं प्रवेष्टयति ॥** २७ **॥ तदुदीचीनाग्रं वितत्य** 'सुसंभृता त्वा संभरामि' **इत्यस्मिन् संभरति ॥** २८ **॥** 'इन्द्राण्यै सन्नहनमसि' **इति समुत्पारयति ॥** २९ **॥** 'पूषा ते ग्रन्थिं ग्रथ्नातु' **इति व्यत्ययमावेष्ट-यति ॥** ३० **॥** 'स ते माऽस्थात्' **इत्यनुलोममुपगूहति ॥** ३१ **॥** 'इन्द्रस्य त्वा बाहुभ्यामुद्यच्छे'

सव्ये हस्तेऽसिदं[1] समस्य तेन मुष्टिना सह निधायाच्छेदनानि छेदनशिष्यानि मूलानि। आत्मानं प्रति हृदयदेश इत्यर्थोऽभिमृश्यते। उपग्रहव्यत्ययः प्रथममुष्टिं निदधातीत्यत्र तूष्णीमत ऊर्ध्वमयुजो मुष्टिं लुनातीति[1]। [2]अथवा द्वितीयादीनामपि[3] तुल्यत्वख्यापनार्थं कथं तुल्यत्वं सर्वेषां तुल्यसंस्कारत्वमुपपद्यते च प्रकरणस्य तुल्यत्वादामनन्ति च केचित्। तुल्यत्वात् संस्कारभेदाच्च संस्कारानुवृत्तिर्न्याय्या। 'सव्ये हस्तेऽसिदं समस्ये'ति ब्रुवत आचार्यस्याप्ययमेवाभिप्रायः। संभवति ह्यसिदादीनामुन्मार्जनान्तानां[4] तत्रत्वम्। अतः प्रमादादनिधानार्थं समासवचनम्। प्रमादान्निहिते पुनरपि मन्त्रेणादानं प्रस्तरस्य जात्यन्तरत्वे परिदेशनोन्मार्जने त्वावर्तेते। परिदिष्टस्याविभवे च [5]सर्वमुष्टिवदभिपदनाद्यावर्तते। आत्माभिमर्शनस्यानावृत्तिः। [6]सप्ताद्यानुक्रमणादर्वाक् सप्तभ्यो न गृह्णाति। त्रयोदशभ्य ऊर्ध्वमपि गृह्णाति यदि तावद्भिः प्रयोजनं न सिध्यति। उक्तसंख्यापेक्षमेव हस्तग्रहणमिति चेत् तथा सति अयुग्ग्रहणमेवास्य प्रयोजनं मृग्यम्॥ २३-२६ ॥

त्रिरन्वाहितं प्रसलैः सन्नहनं प्रवेष्टयति ॥ २७ ॥

यथा रज्जुर्भवति तथाऽस्मिन्संभरति ॥ २८ ॥

अस्मिन्त्सन्नहने सह स्थापयति सर्वमुष्टीन् समुत्पूरयति[7]। संहितौ सन्नहननान्तावूर्ध्वं गमयित्वा मुष्टिभिः सन्नहनं पूरयति। सन्नहनमश्लथं करोतीत्यर्थः ॥ २९ ॥

व्यत्ययमावेष्टयति[8]। व्यतिगमय्यान्ते[9] मूलमग्रेण वेष्टयति[10] ॥ ३० ॥

अनुलोममुप गूहति। वेष्टिशेषमग्रं[11] सन्नहने प्रागग्रमुपगूहति ॥ ३१ ॥

१-१. M Ad हस्ते सिदं समस्यते न मुष्टिना सह न...आत्मानं प्रति...देश इत्यर्थ...अभिमृशते उपग्रहव्य...मुष्टीनां आमनन्ति च केचित् तूष्णीमत ऊर्ध्वमयुजो मुष्टिं लुनोतिति, T सम(स्य ? स्ये) ते। न मुष्टिं तानर्तस...निधाय. **२.** अथवा द्वितीयादीनामपि तुल्यत्वख्या...तुल्यत्वं सर्वेषां तुल्यसंस्कारत्वमुप्पद्यते च प्रकरणस्य तुल्यत्वादामनन्ति च केचित् तृष्णीमत ऊर्ध्वसयुजौ मुष्टिं लुनोतीति। M Ad लुनो°. **३.** M Ad Text beginning with अथवा and ending with लुनातीति repeated. **३.** M Ad द्वीना°. **४.** M Ad ह्यसि दादानादीना°. **५.** M Ad °मुष्टिष्वभि°; thus T. **६.** M Ad सप्राद्यनु°. **७.** M °मुत्पार°; Ad °मुत्पाद°. **८.** M Ad वृत्यावे°. **९.** M Ad °गमस्या°; thus T. **१०.** M Ad °यन्ति. **११.** M Ad शेषग्रं; thus T.

इत्युद्यच्छते ॥ ३२ ॥ 'बृहस्पतेर्मूर्ध्ना हरामि' **इति शीर्षन्नधिनिधत्ते** ॥ ३३ ॥ 'उर्वन्तरिक्षमन्विहि' **इत्यन्तरा वेदिं चोत्करं च हृत्वोत्तरत आहवनीयस्य सादयति** 'देवंगममसि' **इति** ॥ ३४ ॥ **यत्र गुप्तं मन्यते तन्निदधात्यनधः** ॥ २.१.१.३५ ॥ **[इति प्रथमः पटलः]**

[पितृयज्ञः]

त्रिवृच्छाखापवित्रं करोति ॥ १ ॥ **वेदं करोति** ॥ २ ॥ **वेदिं करोति** ॥ ३ ॥ **द्वे मेक्षणे करोति** ॥

अन्तरा वेदिञ्चोत्करं च हृत्वोत्तरस्य श्रोणेर्हृत्वा विहाराभिमुख्येनावृत्य उत्तरत आहवनीयस्य किञ्चिदन्तर्धाय सादयति 'देवंगमम्' इत्यादिना। सन्नहनोत्तरकालमेव यद्यत्प्रयोजनं बर्हिस्तद् गृह्णाति परिस्तरणवेदशाखापृष्ठ्याद्यर्थम्। सकृदाच्छिन्नं च पितृयज्ञार्थम्, तत्सर्वं सह बर्हिषाऽऽहर्तव्यम्। केचिदिध्मकाष्ठान्यपि तत्रैव [१]ग्रहीतव्यानि मन्यन्ते। तत्प्रायेण न शक्यते। ओषधिवनस्पतीनां सह न्यासस्यावश्यंभावित्वाभावात्। संभरणं च तेषां चोद्यते न छेदनम्। अतो पूर्वमेवाहृतान्यस्मिन्काले संभ्रियन्ते। [२]अत्र पटलच्छेदोऽमावास्याया अधिकारनिवृत्यर्थः। अतः बर्हिसंभरणं द्वयोः साधारणम्।[२] ननु पूर्वेद्युरिध्माबर्हिः करोतीति द्वन्द्वेन समासेन इतरेतरयुक्तानां समाहृतानां वा विधानम्। उच्यते उत्तरत आहवनीयस्य सादयित्वा संभृतेष्वपि तन्न विरुध्यते। इतरेतरयुक्तान्येव भवन्ति[३]। तेषां वृक्षनियमः परिमाणं च विध्यवशेषेषु संख्याविकल्पनमुक्तम्। तत्रैव वक्ष्यामः ॥ ३४ ॥

इध्माबर्हिषी सहैव क्षेमे निदधाति ॥ २.१.१.३५ ॥ **[इति प्रथमः पटलः]**

इध्मसंवृश्चनानि शाकलं चेध्मं त्रिवृच्छाखापवित्रं करोति। पटलावसानेन साधारण्ये निवर्तिते पुनरमावास्याया उपवसथ इत्यधिक्रियते[४]। कुत एतत्। भवतु साधारण्यनिवृत्तिः पटलावसानेन, मा वा[५]। एतन्न मृष्यामहे। पूर्वनिवृत्तस्यामावास्याधिकारस्य पुनरिहाधिकार इति[६]। उच्यते। शाखापवित्र-करणममावास्यविषयमेवावश्यं [७]विज्ञेयम्, सांनाय्योत्पवनार्थत्वात्, पौर्णमास्यां च तदभावात्। निवृत्ते च साधारणाधिकारे शाखापवित्रकरणेनामावास्याया उपवसथ इति प्रतीयमाने तन्निवृत्तिलक्षणाभावात् उत्तरेऽपि पदार्था अमावास्याया उपवसथ एव भवन्ति। अथवाऽमावास्याधिकारः पटलावसानेन निवर्तितः। स पुनः साधारणाधिकारे निवृत्ते उत्तरे पदार्थाः क्व निवेशितार इत्याकाङ्क्षा[८] मण्डूक-प्लुत्याऽमावास्याधिकार आगच्छति। यथा मण्डूका उत्प्लुत्योत्प्लुत्यागच्छन्ति[९] तथा [१०]ह्यधिकार-गतिर्भवतीति पाणिन्यादिभिः स्मर्यते ॥ १ ॥

ननु वेदकरणं पर्वद्वय इष्यते। सत्यमिष्यते। श्वोभूते वेदिकरणममावास्यायां[११] वेदिकरणेनाप-कृष्टं[१२] पुरस्तात् स्तम्बयजुषो वेदेन वेदिं संमार्ष्टीति विहितं, तथा श्वोभूते वेदिकरणं विज्ञायते। अच्छिद्रकल्पे 'परिस्तरणानन्तरकालं निष्ठितं वेदमभिमन्त्रयते' इत्याह। निष्ठितग्रहणं पर्वद्वयकाल-

---

१. Ad गृही°. २-२. M Ad T om. This text has been wrongly given at the end of the Vyākhyā on *VādhŚS* 2.1.1.12. see fn. 5-5 on p.45. ३. M Ad भवति. ४. M Ad इत्यधीति सते. ५. M Ad om; thus T. ६. Ad om. ७. M Ad after text between °पवित्रकरणम्...भावास्थाया; thus T. ८. M Ad °क्षायां; thus T. ९. T om आ. १०. M Ad व्यधि°. ११. M Ad °करणामा°. १२. M Ad °नावकृ°.

४॥ तयोरन्यतरेणाधिवृक्षसूर्ये पितृभ्यो निदधाति॥५॥ निधत्त अन्यतरः॥६॥ उदकुम्भम् आहरन्त्युलूखलमुसलꣳ शूर्पꣳ स्फ्यꣳ स्थालीमिति॥७॥ एकैकं तानि दक्षिणेनान्वाहार्यपचनꣳ सꣳसादयति॥८॥ अर्धपात्रं व्रीहीणां मनसा निरुप्य दक्षिणेनान्वाहार्यपचनमविवेकमवघ्नन्ति॥

वेदापेक्षमिति मन्यामहे। इतरथा[१] वेदमभिमन्त्रयत इत्येवावक्ष्यत्। तच्च प्रातर्यज्ञायुधानां संसादनात्पूर्वं भवति। सादनप्रोक्षणलाभाय शाखापवित्रमपाकरणार्थायां दर्भमयं भवति। 'त्रिवृत्पलाशशाखायां दर्भमयं भवती'त्याधारत्वेन हि शाखा श्रूयते। 'इयान्प्रादेशसंमित'[२] इति लिङ्गात् प्रमाणमध्यवसीयते[३]। अनुपदकार आह—'शाखापवित्रस्यौषधानां[४] त्रिवृतं पृथ्वीं[५] रज्जुं वाऽपाकृत्य[६] ग्रन्थ्यासंज्यात्[७]। समान्यग्राणि[८] च मूलानि चेति। अत्र सांनाय्यार्थाङ्गारनिरूहणार्थम्[९] उपवेषो दृश्यते। मन्त्रे 'उपवेषोऽसी'त्यादौ। शाखान्तरेऽपि मूलतः शाखां परिवास्योपवेषं करोतीति। अतः शाखां परिवास्य मूलमुपधाय[१०] निधत्ते। वेदस्य द्रव्यं दर्भाः। वेदपरिवासनानाम् 'आपो वै दर्भाः' इत्यर्थवादे[११] दर्शनात्। आकृतयः शाखान्तरे पुरुषार्था आम्नाताः 'वत्सज्ञुं[१२] पशुकामस्य वेदं कुर्यादि'त्यादि। क्रत्वर्थाभावे च पुरुषार्थस्य ग्रहणं न्याय्यं दर्शयति च आचार्यः। उखायां त्र्युद्धिं नवाश्रिमिति। [१३]तासामाकृतीनाम-विशेषेणान्यतमो[१३] [१४]गृह्यते। प्राथम्याद् वत्सज्ञुर्वा[१५] प्रसलैरोषधीरावेष्ट्य[१६] मूलेष्वग्राण्यवस्येत्। तमेतं वत्सज्ञुम्[१७] इत्याचक्षते॥ २॥

वेदिं करोति प्रागुत्तरस्मात्परिग्रहात् आम्नातक्रम एव॥ ३॥

पौर्णमास्यां मेक्षणयोरवतक्षणानि[१८] शाकल इध्म उपसन्नह्यति॥ ४॥

इतरं निधत्ते चरुमेक्षणार्थम्, अन्यतरेणाधिवृक्षसूर्य[१९] इत्यादि॥ ५–६॥

'उदकुम्भमाहरन्ति' इति[२०]। इति-शब्दः प्रकारवाची॥ ७॥

यान्यत्रोपयुज्यन्ते तानि सर्वाण्येकैकमाहृत्य सादयति। प्राचीनावीतं कृत्वा दक्षिणाग्रैर्दक्षिणा[२१] प्रागग्रैर्वान्वाहार्यपचनं[२२] परिस्तीर्य दक्षिणेनान्वाहार्यपचनं तृणानि संस्तीर्य तेषूदकुम्भादि सादयेत्॥ ८॥

अर्धपात्रं व्रीहीणां मनसा निरुप्य (इति)। पात्रशब्दः पुरुषाहारपरिमाणवाची। यथा द्विकुडवमात्राः[२३] तण्डुला भवन्ति तावतो[२४] व्रीहीन्निर्वपेदित्यर्थः। प्रायोवृत्या प्रस्थभुजो हि मनुष्या भवन्ति। मनसा निरुप्य। निर्वपणे हि मन्त्रो वाऽनुश्रूयते[२५]। अतः 'पितृभ्य' इति मनसा संकल्प्य

---

१. M Ad इतरथा, T तथा. **२.** M Ad समित. **३.** M °सीय...अनु°; Ad सीय अनु°. **४.** M Ad पवित्र ओषाधीना°, T °पवित्रस्यौषधानां. **५.** M Ad पृथ्वी. **६.** M वापार्क्त्वा, Ad वापकृत्वा. **७.** M Ad सज्यात्. **८.** M Ad T सामान्या°. **९.** M Ad °र्थउप°; thus T. **१०.** M °मुप...धय, Ad °मुप...य, T °मु...षाय. **११.** M Ad इत्यष्व्यर्थवादे; thus T. **१२.** M Ad वत्सञ्जुं. **१३–१३.** M Ad तासाम...तीनां, T तासा(म)न्यतरं निधत्ते. T om the remaining text before निधत्ते in the fn. 5 (T p.65) T Informs : 'तासामित्यनन्तरं अत्र नास्ति। तत् लिखित्वा संयोजितम्'. This text is found in M and Ad. **१४.** T om. **१५.** M Ad वत्सञ्जु°. **१६.** Ad T प्रसले शेषधी°. **१७.** M Ad वत्सञ्जुं. **१८.** Ad °क्षणायो. **१९.** M Ad °तरणातिवृ°. **२०.** M Ad इति once. **२१.** M Ad दक्षिणा प्रागग्रैः. **२२.** M Ad °हार्यवच°. **२३.** M Ad कुटुम्ब, T कुडुष. **२४.** M Ad तावन्तः. **२५.** M Ad मन्त्रो नश्रू°.

९ ॥ **तान् सकृत् फलीकृतान् कृत्वा न्यूनान् स्थालीमधिश्रित्यावपति** ॥ १० ॥ **दक्षिणावृत्तः श्रपयति** ॥ ११ ॥ **न पुराऽऽज्यस्यानयनात् प्रतिष्ठापयति** ॥ १२ ॥ **यदाऽस्मिन्नाज्यमानयत्यथ प्रतिष्ठापयति** ॥ १३ ॥ 'ये पितर्णिां प्रतिरूपा भवन्तः' **इति दक्षिणेनान्वाहार्यपचनः स्फ्येनोद्धन्ति।** '०असुरा उपासते यज्ञमेतम्। परापुरो निपुरो ये हरन्त्यग्निस्तानस्मात् प्रणुनोतु यज्ञात्' **इति** ॥ १४ ॥

एकपवित्रान्तर्हितायां[१] स्थाल्यां सकृदेव निरुप्य पवित्रान्तर्हित एव शूर्पे निर्वपति। ततस्तेनैव पवित्रेण तूर्ष्णीं प्रोक्षणीः[२] संस्कृत्य [३]कामण्डलुकाभिर्वोत्तानानि पात्राणि कृत्वा व्रीहीन् पात्राणि च प्रोक्षेत्। तत उक्तप्रदेशे व्रीहीणां तण्डुलानां च विवेकं कुर्वीत[४]। आतण्डुलभावादवघ्नन्ति। बहुवचन-मनियतकर्तृकत्वार्थम्॥ ९ ॥

फलीकरणविप्रमोकं सकृदेव कुर्वन्ति। व्रीहिपरिमाणादीषन्न्यूनपरिमाणोदकां स्थालीमधिश्रित्य तिरः पवित्रमावपति ॥ १० ॥

एरकोपबर्हणाञ्जनाभ्यञ्जनाज्यानां भावे अत्राज्यमपि तूर्ष्णीं संस्करोति। तेनैव पवित्रेण [५]क्वैषामस्तित्वमुपलब्धम्[६]। उपवसथगव्यामाह[७]। सर्वानिवान्यान्[८] स्थालीपाकान्[९] सूत्रमिति कथमविद्यमानत्वम्। इह संभरणविनियोगाभावाद्वैकल्पिकत्वं तत्रैव वक्ष्यामः। स्रुवमेक्षणदर्वीणां तूर्ष्णीं संमार्गः। 'मस्तु पितर्णिामि'ति दर्शनादाज्यं मस्तु केचिदिच्छन्ति। स्वयंविलीनमाज्यं मस्तु, विलयनमिश्रमित्यन्ये। [१०]आज्याभावेऽन्यदाज्यमानीयावतारयन्ति ॥ ११-१३ ॥

[११]दक्षिणत उद्धन्ति[११] दक्षिणत उद्धनने[१२] सकृदेवेति नियमो नास्ति[१३]। अत्र केचिदाहुः—उद्धननं भूप्रदेशसंस्कारः। संस्कृतेन च भूप्रदेशेनान्यार्थेन भवितव्यम्। तस्मिन् प्रदेशे पिण्डदाने क्रियमाणे तत् संस्कारः[१४] प्रयोजनवान् भवति। इतरथाऽदृष्टं कल्पनीयम्। अतो दक्षिणतोऽपि पिण्डदानमस्ति। अपरेणान्वाहार्यपचनं[१५] दीयमानेषु तत्रैवोद्धननादि कर्तव्यमिति। अन्ये आह। सर्वत्र दक्षिणत उद्धननं श्रूयते, पश्चात् पिण्डदानं च। एवं क्रियमाणे[१६] श्रुतहान्यश्रुतकल्पने स्याताम्। अतो यथाश्रुतमेव कर्तव्यमिति। नैतदेवम्। उपवसथगव्यान्न दक्षिणेन, नापरेणाम्नातम्। दक्षिणेत्युत्तरत उपक्रम्य दक्षिणापवर्गमुद्धननमात्रं बौधायनादिभिश्च दक्षिणत आम्नातम्। अतः पौरस्त्य एवार्थो न तु श्रुतहानिरश्रुतकल्पना च दोषः। अयमाचार्यः शाखान्तरस्थमपि विधानं केनचित्प्रकारेण सूचयति। अतो नास्ति दोषो वचनस्य विद्यमानत्वात्। एकोपबर्हणे पिण्डदानस्य दक्षिणतः सादयति। विद्यमानयोः एतावदेव प्रयोजनम्॥ १४ ॥

---

१. M हिकायां. **२.** M Ad °स संस्कृ. **३.** M Ad °डुलु°. **४.** M Ad विवेकमकुर्वत. **५.** M त्वैषां. Ad कैषा°. **६.** M Ad लब्धः. **७.** Here some text related to उपवसथगव्य seems to be omitted or broken. **८.** M Ad °न्यात्. **९.** M Ad °पाकात् ... सूत्र°, T give reading of MS रव as त् वैत्राय सू° .... **१०.** M Ad °भावेस्थाल्यादाज्य°. **११-११.** M Ad om; thus T. **१२.** M Ad °नेन; thus T. **१३.** M Ad om; thus T. **१४.** M Ad °कारं. **१५.** M Ad °र्यवच°. **१६.** M Ad श्रूयभाणे; thus T.

उल्मुकमादाय प्राङभितपति ॥ १५ ॥ 'उदीरतामवर उत्परासः' **इत्युदपात्रेणावोक्षति**। 'उन्मध्यमाः पितरः=हवेषु' **इति** ॥ १६ ॥ **यज्ञोपवीतं कृत्वा मेक्षणेन तिस्र आहुतीर्जुहोति** 'सोमाय पितृमते स्वधा नमः', 'यमायाङ्गिरस्वते पितृमते स्वधा नमः', 'अग्नये कव्यवाहनाय स्वधा नमः' **इति** ॥ १७ ॥ **तूष्णीं मेक्षणमनुप्रहरति** ॥ १८ ॥ **प्रसव्यमन्वाहार्यपचनं दक्षिणाग्रैः सःस्तीर्य** 'मार्जयन्तां पितरः' **इति त्रीण्युदपात्राणि निनयति**। '°मार्जयन्तां पितामहाः', 'मार्जयन्तां प्रपितामहाः' **इति** ॥ १९ ॥ 'एतत्ते तत' **इति तिस्रो दर्वीर्ददाति**। '°याःश्च त्वमन्वसि ये च त्वामभितो ये च त्वया सह स्वधाक्षिति', 'एतत्ते पितामह याःश्च त्वमन्वसि ये च त्वामनु=क्षितिः', 'एतत्ते प्रपितामह याःश्च त्वमन्वसि ये च त्वामनु=क्षितिः' **इति** ॥ २० ॥ 'एतद्वः पितामहाः' **इति हैव जीवत्पिता दद्यात्** ॥ २१ ॥ 'अत्र पितरो यथाभागं मन्दध्वम्' **इत्युक्त्वोदगावर्तते** ॥ २२ ॥ **आतमितोरास्ते** ॥ २३ ॥ 'सुसंदृशं त्वा वयम्' **इत्याहवनीयमभिव्यनिति**। '°मघवन मन्दिषीमहि। प्र नून° पूर्णबन्धुरः

ततो यज्ञोपवीतमित्यादि। मेक्षणानुप्रहरणे[१] तूष्णीं ग्रहणं ब्राह्मणानुकरणम्। ब्राह्मणेऽपि सैव तृतीयाऽऽहुतिरिह[२] प्राप्तस्य स्वाहाकारस्य प्रतिषेधः ॥ १७–१८ ॥

तिस्रो दर्वीर्ददाति। दर्व्येव[३] च केचिद्[४] ददति[४]। अपरे दर्व्योद्धृत्य [५]कस्मिंश्चित् पात्रे पिण्डान् कृत्वा ददति। पिण्डानामावृतेति[५] दर्शनात् पिण्डशब्दस्य वृत्तेषु प्रसिद्धेः। आज्यस्य विद्यमानत्वे [६]पिण्डानामुपस्तरणाभिघारणार्थता। अन्यत्र विनियोगाश्रवणादामनन्ति च केचित्[६] स्रुवेणोपस्तीर्णाभि-घारितान् पिण्डान् ददाति[७] ॥ २० ॥

'एतद्वः पितामहाः प्रपितामहाः' इति हैव जीवत्पिता[७] दद्यात्। 'एतद्वः'[८] इत्यादिमन्त्रः आद्यपदद्वयमनुषज्य द्वौ मन्त्रौ कृत्वा द्वौ पिण्डौ जीवत्पिता[८] ददाति। देवताद्वित्वाच्छन्द वा[९] द्वित्वम्। नन्वनुषङ्गस्य [१०]वाक्यसामर्थ्यत्वादेकवाक्यगतस्योक्तानुषङ्गो न युक्तः। सत्यम्। आचार्येण क्वचित् क्वचित्[११] प्रदर्श्यते[१२]। 'ये देवा यज्ञहनो यज्ञमुषः[१२] पृथिव्यामध्यासते'[१३] इत्यत्र यज्ञहनयज्ञमुषशब्दयोरन्यानि पदान्यनुषज्य मन्त्रद्वयं करोति। तथाऽत्रापि। नन्वेवं क्रियमाणे[१४] 'त्रिर्निदधाती'ति[१४] श्रुतिः पक्षाश्रिता भवति। उक्तं देवताद्रव्यद्वित्वं कल्पयति। अन्ये आहुः–एक एव यथाम्नातो मन्त्रः त्रयः[१५] पिण्डाः। प्रतिपिण्डं मन्त्रावृत्तिः। एवं त्रिर्निदधातीत्यपाक्षिकं भवति। युक्तम्। प्रज्ञावद्भिर्विचार्याध्यवसेयम् ॥ २१ ॥

व्यनिति प्राण्यापानिति[१६]। ऊष्मणो व्यावृत उपास्ते पिण्डगतोष्मा यावन्नोपरमति तावदुदङ्मुख

---

१. Ad °णात् प्रकरणे; thus T. **२.** Ad °तिरिति प्रा. **३.** M दर्व्ये, Ad द्रव्ये. **४–४.** Ad केचिदिति; thus T

५–५. M क....मावृते; Ad कृत्वा दद...मावृत्तेति; thus T. **६–६.** M पिण्डदानामुपवसथ...अन्यत्र–. ात् आमन्ति; Ad उपस्तरणाभिधारणार्थता...अन्यत्र विनियोगश्रवणादामनन्ति केचित्. स्रुवेणो ददति...; thus T. **७–७.** M ददाति...पिता दद्यात्, Ad ददाति...इति हवै जीवपिता; thus T. **८–८.** M एतद्व...ादिर्मन्त्र आद्यवद्वयम...°ङ्गस्य; °आद्यवद्वयमनुषज्य द्वेन मन्त्रौ कृत्वा द्वेन पिण्डेन जीवपिता. **९.** छन्द वा. **१०.** Ad वाक्यसमाप्तत्वा. **११.** T क्वचित् once. **१२–१२.** M प्रदृश्यते...ना यज्ञमुषं; Ad °हने यज्ञमृष्टं. **१३.** M °ध्यासत; Ad °ध्यास्तं. **१४–१४.** M Ad °माणं निद°. **१५.** M Ad मन्त्र[Ad °न्त्रत्रय]पिण्डा मन्त्रपिण्डा. **१६.** M Ad °पानीति.

स्तुतो यासि वशाँ अनु। योजा न्विन्द्र ते हरी'॥ २४॥ 'अक्षन्नमीमदन्त हि' **इति गार्हपत्यम्।** '०अव=हरी' **इति** ॥ २५ ॥ 'स घा तं वृषणꣳ रथम्' **इत्यन्वाहार्यपचनम्।** '०अधि=हरी' **इति** ॥ २६ ॥ 'अमीमदन्त पितरः सोम्याः' **इत्यभिपर्यावर्तते** ॥ २७ ॥ **यः स्थाल्यामतिशिष्यते तं त्रिरवजिघ्रति** 'ये सजाताः समनसो=शतꣳ समाः' **इति** ॥ २८ ॥ 'नमो वः पितरो रसाय' **इति नमस्कारैरुपतिष्ठते।** '०नमो वः पितरः शुष्माय=वसिष्ठो भूयासम्' **इति** ॥ २९ ॥ 'मार्जयन्तां पितरः' **इति त्रीण्युदपात्राणि निनयति।** '०मार्जयन्तां पितामहाः', 'मार्जयन्तां प्रपितामहाः' **इति** ॥ ३० ॥ **दशाञ्छिनत्ति** 'एतद्वः पितरो वासो वीरं मह्यं दत्त' **इति** ॥ ३१ ॥ 'उत्तर आयुषि लोम छिनीत' **इति ब्राह्मणम्** ॥ ३२ ॥ **दशामेव छिनत्ति** ॥ ३३ ॥ 'अक्षन्पितरः' **इत्युपतिष्ठते।** 'अमीमदन्त पितरोऽतीतृपन्त पितरोऽमीमृजन्त पितरः' **इति** ॥ ३४ ॥ 'परेत पितरः सोम्याः' **इति सꣳसादयति।** '०गम्भीरै=मदन्ति' **इति** ॥ ३५ ॥ 'मनो न्वा हुवामहे' **इति तिसृभिर्मन आह्वयते।** '०नाराशꣳसेन स्तोमेन सचेमहि' **इति** ॥ ३६ ॥ 'यदन्तरिक्षं पृथिवीमुत द्याम्' **इत्यात एव गार्हपत्यमुपतिष्ठते।** '०यन्मा=नसम्' **इति** ॥ ३७ ॥ 'प्रजापते न त्वदेतान्यन्यः' **इति यज्ञोपवीतं कृत्वाऽऽहवनीय-स्यार्धमेति।** '०विश्वा=रयीणाम्' **इति** ॥ ३८ ॥ **आगत्यैता दर्वीः पात्रे समस्यति** ॥ ३९ ॥ **उपनिनय-त्युदकुम्भम्** ॥ ४० ॥ **अनुप्रहरति बर्हिः** ॥ ४१ ॥ **सन्तिष्ठते पितृयज्ञः** ॥ २.१.२.४२ ॥ **[इति द्वितीयः पटलः]**

आस्ते॥ २४॥

दशाया[१] [२]उत्तर आयुषि लोम्ना विकल्पः[२]। उत्तरमायुः पञ्चाशतः परम्। षष्टेरित्यन्ये॥ ३१-३३॥

ततो 'अमीमदन्त पितरः' इत्यादि षड्भिर्नमस्कारैरनुषज्यानुषज्य केचिदुपतिष्ठन्ते। अकर्मकरणत्वात् सकृदुच्चारणेनैव सर्वेषां शेषत्वं प्रतिपत्तुमुत्सहन्त इत्यन्ये नानुषजन्ति।[३] अस्मिन्पक्षे व्यत्यासं निह्नुते इति यत्र वचनं तत्रानुषङ्गः। अन्यस्मिन्पक्षे प्रदर्शनम्। विद्यमानयोरञ्जनाभ्यञ्जन-योर्वासो दानात्पूर्वम्॥ ३४॥

संसादयति गमनायानुजानाति॥ ३५॥

तिसृभिर्मन आह्वयते। पितृगतं मनो निवर्तयति॥ ३६॥

आहवनीयसकाशादागत्यैता दर्वीः पात्रे समस्यति सह स्थापयति॥ ३८-३९॥

उदकुम्भशेषं च समीपे निनयति॥ ४०॥

अन्वाहार्यपचने[४] बर्हिश्चानुप्रहरति॥ ४१॥

अत्र पटलावसानम्। याजमानत्वात् पितृयज्ञस्योत्तरेषु कर्मसु परिस्तरणादिषु तन्निवृत्त्यर्थम्।

---

१. M Ad दशाया. **२-२.** M Ad om, T gives the text दशाया...रिन्तन्ये between दनात्पूर्वं and संसादयति [T धयति]. **३.** M Ad इत्यनेनानु; thus T. **४.** M Ad °वचने.

[सायंदोहः]

परिस्तृणन्त्यग्नीन् ॥ १ ॥ **उपावहरति पात्राणि सायं** ॥ २ ॥ **निर्णिक्तैः पात्रैर्गा आयतीः**

कथमवगम्यते पितृयज्ञस्य याजमानत्वम्। 'तिसृभिर्मन आह्वयत' इत्यात्मनेपददर्शनात्। अन्यत्र च[१] महापितृयज्ञादौ पितृदानस्य याजमानत्वदर्शनादनुपदे च सर्वपितृयज्ञस्य याजमानत्वम्। आहुतिपर्यन्तस्याध्वर्यवत्वम्[२]। परस्य याजमानत्वं[३] विकल्प्याम्नातम्। यद्येवं याजमान एव कस्मान्न पठ्यते। पाठेनैव हि सिद्धं भवति। उच्यते। पितृयज्ञस्य दर्शपूर्णमासयोरङ्गत्वानङ्गत्वे[४] विप्रतिपत्तिराचार्याणाम्। 'अनङ्गत्वमि'ति जैमिनिः। 'अङ्गवान् समभिव्याहारादि'ति कात्यायनः। तत्र प्रयाजादिवदाग्नेयादिविकृतिषु[५] गच्छति। आग्नेयादिसमुदायो[६] यत्र गच्छति [७]कुण्डपेयादिषु प्रवर्तत इत्याचार्याणामुपदेश इत्याग्नेयादिसमुदायमध्ये पठितः। आचार्येणोक्तं पटलावसानम्॥ २.१.२.४२ ॥ **[इति द्वितीयः पटलः]**

परिस्तृणन्त्यग्नीनुपावरोहति पात्राणि। अस्य पदार्थद्वयस्य सायमिति शेषः। ननु पिण्ड[७]पितृयज्ञोत्तरकालत्वात् सायंकालता सिद्धा सिध्यति। किन्तु [८]अमावास्याकालत्वात्परिस्तरणपात्रोपावहरणे[९] पौर्णमास्यामनभिहिते स्याताम्। अतः पौर्णमास्यर्थं सायंग्रहणम्। पदार्थद्वयं सायं-कालमात्रे यथा स्यादिति। परिस्तरणे बहुवचननिर्देशो नियतकर्तृकत्वार्थम्[१०]। अथवाऽच्छिद्रकल्पे मन्त्रेण परिस्तरणेऽपि तथा दृष्टत्वात् तत्रानियतकर्तृत्वस्यान्याय्यत्वादविवक्षितत्वम्। अन्य आह—'परिस्तृणीते'ति। न परिस्तरणस्य करणमन्त्रः। आत्मनि मध्यमपुरुषबहुवचनस्य चायुक्तत्वादस्मिन् मन्त्रेऽध्वर्युणा प्रैषवदुक्तेऽन्ये परिस्तृणन्ति। अत्रान्यस्याभावादाग्नीध्रो वेति। तथाऽनुपदकार आह। अथ परिस्तरणम्। परिस्तृणीत परिधत्ताग्निम्। परिहितोऽग्निरित्यध्वर्युः संप्रेष्येत्। अथाग्नीध्रः[११] परिस्तरणार्थं बर्हिरादाय प्राचीनाग्रैश्चोदीचीनाग्रैश्च[१२] परिस्तृणुयात्। सर्वैः प्राचीनाग्रैरित्यपरं पूर्वपक्षं प्रथमं स्तृणुयात्। अथ दक्षिणमथापरमथोत्तरम्। पूर्वापरयोर्दक्षिणोत्तरयोस्तयोरधर उत्तरः। पूर्वस्मात् पूर्वस्मान्न कनीयांस इतरे ब्रह्मयजमानयोरग्नीध[१३] इत्यायतनानि संस्तीर्योदगपवर्गं करोतीति। तथा परिस्तृणन्त्यग्नीनिति। संपरिस्तरणमात्रमिहाग्नीनां कुर्यादित्युक्त्वा प्रातः परिस्तरणं विहितवान्। तत्र वचनं न्यायो वा मृग्यम्[१४] ॥ १ ॥

पात्रोपावहरणम् प्रक्षालनार्थम्। सर्वयज्ञपात्राणां प्रक्षालनं कर्तव्यम्। तत्र स्मृतिशास्त्रस्य शेषत्वमुक्तम्। तद्यथा मनुना विहितम्—

मार्जनं यज्ञपात्राणां पाणिना यज्ञकर्मणि।

चमसानां ग्रहाणां च शुद्धिः प्रक्षालनेन तु॥ (मनु. ५.११६)

---

१. M Ad om; thus T. २. M पर्यन्तन्याध्व, Ad पर्यन्तस्यविपर्यत्वं. ३. M Ad मानवत्वं. ४. M Ad ङ्गत्वान्नङ्ग. ५. M Ad दायान्तं ग° ; thus T. ६. M Ad समुदायान्तं; thus T. ७-७. M Ad text traceable ?; thus T. ८. M Ad वास्यका. ९. M पात्रोपावरोहणे, Ad पात्रोपहरणे. १०. M कर्तृत्वा. ११. M Ad °ग्नीध्रं. १२. M Ad °श्चोदीना°. १३. M इतरे... ारग्नीध. १४. M Ad मृग्यः; thus T.

प्रतीक्षते 'एता आचरन्ति' **इति** ॥ ३ ॥ 'इह व इन्द्रो रमयतु गावः' **इति यजमानं वर्षभं वा गोष्ठं वाऽभिमन्त्रयते** ॥ ४ ॥ **हुत्वाऽग्निहोत्रꣳ सांनाय्यं दोहयति** ॥ ५ ॥ 'उपसृष्टां प्रब्रूताद्' **इत्याह** ॥ ६ ॥ **यथोपसृष्टां प्राह** ॥ ७ ॥ **अथाभिमन्त्रयते** 'अयक्ष्मा वः=घृतं च' **इति** ॥ ८ ॥ 'जीवा जीवन्तीरुप वः

कमण्डलूनां[१] च तथा विप्राणां ब्रह्मचारिणाम्।

[२]हस्तोऽग्निर्ब्राह्मणस्येति तथा[३] हि श्रूयते श्रुतिः ॥

चरूणां स्रुक्स्रुवाणां च शुद्धिरुष्णेन वारिणा। (मनु. ५.११७)

स्फ्यशूर्पशकटानां[४] च मुसलोलूखलस्य च ॥

इति। चरुशब्देन चरुस्थाल्यभिधीयते ॥ २ ॥

निर्णिक्तैः पात्रैरिति। इत्थंभूतलक्षणा तृतीया। प्रतीक्षत अभिमुखमीक्षते ॥ ३ ॥

'इह वः' इत्यादि यजमानाद्यभिमन्त्रणम् ॥ ४ ॥

अग्निहोत्रं हुत्वा सांनाय्यस्थालीं पुरीषैर्गोमयेन वा परिलिप्यापरेण गार्हपत्यं सादयति। ओषधीः संस्तीर्य अरिक्तं हि मृण्मयमग्नावधिश्रितं भिद्येत दीर्येत वा, तन्मा भूदिति परिलेपनम्। दोहनपात्रं संदाननियोजने उपवेषमपिधानचमसं शाखापवित्रमिति सन्निधायोत्तानानि कृत्वा कामण्डलुकाभिरद्भिः[५] प्रोक्षेत् 'शुन्धध्वं दैव्याय कर्मणे देवयज्यायै' इति ॥ ५ ॥

तत उपसृष्टामित्यादि[६] ॥ ६ ॥

तत एकस्या वत्समुत्सृज्य[७] 'उपसृष्टे'ति प्राह दोग्धा। शूद्रे दोग्धर्याग्नीध्रः प्राह। तथा [८]प्रश्नप्रतिवचनम् ॥ ७ ॥

'अयक्ष्मा वः' इत्यादिनाऽध्वर्युरभिमन्त्रयते। तत्र मन्त्रस्य बहुवचनान्तत्वात् सर्वासां गवां तन्त्रेणाभिमन्त्रणम्। नैतदेवम्। उपसृष्टगोसंस्कारत्वाद् वत्सोपसर्गस्य पर्ययेण कर्तव्यत्वात् सर्वगवीषु[९] प्रत्येकमावृत्तिः। तथा [१०]सत्यकिञ्चित्करत्वं बहुवचनस्य। अन्य आह–कर्मकरणेषूपरवमन्त्रादिषु[११] तद्युज्यते। क्रियमाणानुवादिषु दूरात्कर्माभिदधत्सु तन्त्रता युज्यत इति। क्रियमाणानुवादिनोऽपि क्रियमाणमेव कर्मानुवदन्ति, न करिष्यमाणमित्यपरे ॥ ८ ॥

'जीवा [१२]जीवन्ती'रिति। गोधुक्संस्कारत्वात्संस्कृतस्य तेनैव पुनः संस्कारस्य

---

१. Verse 'कमण्डलूना = श्रूयते श्रुतिः' is not found in the *Manusmṛti*. 'चमसानां = कमण्डलूना=श्रूयते श्रुतिः' from the 2nd hemistitch of the verse मार्जनं *etc.* in the *Manusmṛti*. Thus there is a difference in the order of Pādas here in comparison to *Manusmṛti* text. २. M Ad हस्तोग्नि. ३. T तथा हि, M Ad तत्राग्नि. ४. M Ad शर्पूकटा°. ५. M Ad काभिः; thus T. ६. M °सृष्टमीत्या°; Ad °सृष्टमि°. ७. M Ad वात्समु°. ८. T प्रति°. ९. M Ad गवि°; thus T. १०. M Ad तस्य कि° (Ad अकि°). ११. M Ad °णेषु परमन्त्रा°. १२. T जीवन्त.

सदेम' **इति गोदुहमुपसीदन्ताम्** ॥ ९ ॥ 'मातारिश्वनो घर्मोऽसि' **इति गार्हपत्यादुदीचोऽङ्गारान्निरूहति** ॥ १० ॥ 'द्यौरसि पृथिव्यसि' **इति स्थालीमादत्ते** ॥ ११ ॥ 'विश्वधाया अस्युत्तरेण धाम्ना' **इत्यधिश्रयति** ॥ १२ ॥ 'दृꣳहस्व मा ह्वारिषीः' **इत्येनामङ्गारेषु दृꣳहति** ॥ १३ ॥ 'वसूनां पवित्रमसि' **इत्यस्यै बिले प्राचीनाग्रꣳ शाखापवित्रमुपदधाति।** '°शतधारं=सहस्रधारम्' **इति** ॥ १४ ॥ **वाचंयमः स्थालीमन्वारभ्यास्ते** ॥ १५ ॥ **आहरन्त्यस्मै दुग्धम्** ॥ १६ ॥ **पृच्छति** 'कामधुक्षः' **इति** ॥ १७ ॥ 'अमूम्' **इति** ॥ १८ ॥ 'सा विश्वायुः' **इति** ॥ १९ ॥ **आहरन्त्येवास्मै दुग्धम्** ॥ २० ॥ **आनयन्तं पृच्छति** 'कामधुक्षः' **इत्येव** ॥ २१ ॥ 'अमूम्' **इति** ॥ २२ ॥ 'सा विश्वव्यचाः' **इति** ॥ २३ ॥ **आहरन्त्येवास्मै दुग्धम्** ॥ २४ ॥ **आनयन्तं पृच्छति** 'कामधुक्षः' **इत्येव** ॥ २५ ॥ 'अमूम्' **इति** ॥ २६ ॥ 'सा विश्वधायाः' **इति** ॥ २७ ॥ 'बहु दुग्धीन्द्राय हविः' **इति त्रिरुक्त्वा** 'वत्सेभ्यो देहि' **इति वाचं विसृजते** ॥ २८ ॥ **सा यद्येकैव दुग्धा स्यात्तदेवमेव त्रिर्विगृह्णीयात्** ॥ २९ ॥ **यद्यु बह्व्यः स्युस्ता एवमेव दोहयेत्** ॥ ३० ॥ 'हुतः स्तोको हुतो द्रप्सः' **इति विप्रुषोऽनुमन्त्रयते यत्र गोदुङ् मार्जयते।**

प्रयोजनाभावादनावृत्तिः ॥ ९ ॥

अङ्गारान् निरूहति शाखामूलेनोपवेषेण ॥ १० ॥

'कामधुक्षः' इत्येतावानेव केचित्। प्रतिवचनार्थवादे 'भद्रमेवासां कर्माविष्करोती'ति दर्शनाद् द्वयोर्मन्त्रयोरादिग्रहणमिति युक्तम्। यस्यां देवानां मनुष्याणां पयो हितमिति हि भद्रं कर्म। द्वितीयाद्यास्वप्युपसृष्टाद्यावर्तते। तन्त्रपक्षे नास्ति। अन्यस्मिन्नपि पक्षे सकृदेव वा प्रैषः। पुरुषसंस्कारत्वात् वत्सोपसर्गाभिमन्त्रणयोरेवावृत्तिः। दुग्धैकत्वे नास्त्यावृत्तिः। तत्रापि प्रश्नादीनामावृत्तिः पूर्वोक्तानामेवेति[१] वदन्ति ॥ १७–२९ ॥

यद्यु बह्व्यः स्युस्ता एवमेव दोहयेदित्युक्तानुवादः स्यात् विधिर्वा[२]। विधिपक्षे उत्तरास्वप्यावृत्तिः। मन्त्राणामनुवादकत्वे 'वाचंयमोऽनन्वारभ्ये[३]'त्यत्र तूष्णीकत्वं, चतुर्थादिषु[४] दोहेषु 'सा विश्वधाया' [५]इत्यस्यैवावृत्तिः। 'कामधुक्ष[६]' इत्याह तृतीयस्या[७]' इति वचनाद्। अबुद्धिरप्रवृत्तिरशेषकरत्वाद् विध्यतिदेशबुद्धिः। दुग्धद्वित्वे न्याय्यः[८]। गृह्यानयेद्दृजुरागुप्तनिधानात्[९]। निधाय परिभोजनीया बर्हिरादायोपस्तृणाति। पूर्वापरावग्नी प्रातर्दोहः। एवमेव[१०] वत्सापाकरणाद्यतिदिष्यते[११]। शाखया[१२] चोदितस्य[१३] शाखापवित्रेणापाकरणस्यायुक्तत्वादुद्गृह्य तयैव शाखयापाकृत्य[१४] तत्रैव पुनरुपगूहन्ति केचित्। तदानीमेवान्यां शाखामाहृत्य दर्भैर्वा प्रातर्दोहाय वत्सानपाकृत्य प्रातर्दोहाय संविशेदिति विध्यवशेषः। मातर्णीमपि संसृष्टानामपाकरणं कर्तव्यम्। यद्यत्रैव स्थितिः, अनुमन्त्रणं नास्ति। अथ चेद् गोष्ठं गच्छन्ति विद्यत एवापाकरणद्रव्यस्योद्गूहनम्। शाखापवित्र एव अभिद्योतनादीनां प्रतिषेधं विधाय पुनः

---

१. M Ad पूर्वोक्तमेव नाम°. **२.** M र्वा पि विधि°. **३.** M Ad अवाचम् यमोनन्वा°. **४.** M Ad चतुर्थ्यादि°. **५.** M Ad इत्यास्यैवा°. **६.** M Ad कम°. **७.** M Ad तृतीयस्य. **८.** T न्यायः. **९.** T गृह्यान°. **१०.** M एव मे व° Ad एवमेवेति. **११.** M वत्सा चाकरणा°, Ad वसा पकर°; thus T. **१२.** Ad शाखाया. **१३.** M चोदितत्वास्य. **१४.** M Ad °यावाकृ°.

'०स्वाहाग्नये बृहते नाकाय द्यावापृथिवी अग्नये पाहि विप्रुषः' **इति** ॥ ३१ ॥ **दोहनेऽप आनीय** 'संपृच्यध्वमृतावरीः' **इति संक्षालनमानयति।** '०वृण्वतीः पयसा पय ऊर्मिणीर्मधुमत्तमाः। मन्द्रा धनस्य सातये' **इति** ॥ ३२ ॥ 'उद्यन् सुवर्गो लोकः' **इत्यभिद्योतयति।** '०त्रिषु लोकेषु ***१**(रोचय' **इति** ॥ ३३ ॥ 'अन्तरितꣳ रक्षोऽन्तरिता अरातयः' **इति प्रसलैस्त्रिः पर्य)ग्निकरोति** ॥ ३४ ॥ **अनुपहत्याभिद्योतनम्** 'इन्द्रस्त्वा श्रीणातु' **इत्येनान् प्रतिष्ठापयति** ॥ ३५ ॥ **तन्न पुरा शीतादतिसृजेत्** ॥ ३६ ॥ **यदा शीतं मन्यतेऽथ** 'इन्द्रस्य त्वा भागꣳ सोमेनातनच्मि' **इति हविरातञ्चनेनातनक्ति** ॥ २.१.३.३७ ॥ **[इति तृतीयः पटलः]**

[व्रीहिनिर्वापः]

हविरातच्याग्निहोत्रहवणीं च शूर्पं च स्फ्यं च कपालानि च शम्यां चोलूखलमुसलं च

***१**. Text abri. त्रिषु लोकेषु=अग्नि see I.5.1.13-14.

संक्षालनान्तमित्याह ॥ ३०-३१ ॥

यदि संक्षालनान्तं विधानं ततोऽभिद्योतनादीनां प्रतिषेधानर्थक्यम्। यदि प्रतिषिद्धवर्जं[१] क्रियेत ततः संक्षालनान्तता नोपपद्यते। ततः प्रतिषेधवचनं नित्यानुवाद इति केचित्। यथा इडान्त आतिथ्यः[२] सन्तिष्ठतेऽनूयाजान्[३]यजति इति। अन्ये प्रतिषिद्धं संक्षालनिनयनवर्जं कृत्वाऽन्ते संक्षालनमानयन्ति। तदुभयमयुक्तं नित्यानुवादश्च[४]। अथ 'शृतमि'ति पर्यग्निकरणे उपनिधानवचनम् अनर्थकमत्रैव स्थितत्वात्। इतरस्मिन् पक्षे पक्तिवैषम्यमशृतं[५] चोदकं च तद् भवति। प्रसिद्धिश्च तादृशी नैव[६]लोके न वेदे। किं युक्तं परस्पर[६]विरोधाद्विकल्प[७] इति। वा-शब्दादीनामन्तरेणापि मिथो विरुध्यमानयोर्विकल्प[८] आश्रयणीयः[९] यथा 'उदिते होतव्यमनुदिते[१०] होतव्यमि'ति।

अपि वा शाखान्तरेष्ववघातान्ते कपालोपधानान्ते च प्रातर्दोहमामनन्ति[११]। तद् द्योतनार्थं शाखान्तरस्थमपि[१२] [१३]विधिं केनचित्प्रकारेण सूचयन्तीत्युक्तम्। प्रतिषिद्धवच्च करणपक्षे दध्नोऽधस्तान्निदधाति। एकस्यैवापिधानचमसस्य[१३] प्रतिपत्तौ दर्शनादपिधानं सान्नाय्यस्येत्येतत्पक्षमाश्रित्योपनिधानवचनम्। इतरस्मिन् पक्षे [१४]तत्रैवाप्रतापे निदधाति। प्रातर्दोहे[१४] शाखाया उदगग्रत्वं विशेषः। अत्रापि पटलावसानेनामावस्याधिकारो निवृत्तः ॥ २.१.३.३२-३७ ॥ **[इति तृतीयः पटलः]**

निर्वप्स्यन्[१५] यज्ञायुधानि संसादयति[१६]। अनेन वाक्येन सर्वेषां यज्ञायुधानां संसादनं चोद्यते। तत् स्फ्यादीनि दशानुक्रमन्ति[१७]। तत् किमिति। 'द्वेद्वे संभरती'त्युपक्रम्य दशानामेवानुक्रमणात्तेष्वेवावश्यं

---

१. M Ad °वर्णं. **२.** M Ad आदित्यः. **३.** M °ते नारूयाजान्, Ad नानूयाजात्य°. **४.** M Ad °वादञ्च. **५.** M Ad पङ्क्तिवैषम्यमादृतञ्चो° ; thus T. **६-६.** M लोके न वे.... रा विरोधात्, Ad नैर्लोकेन. **७.** Ad कलप°. **८.** Ad °कल्प्य. **९.** M आन्तणीय. **१०.** M होतव्य...तव्यमनु°. **११.** M प्रा...नद्यो, Ad °न द्यो. **१२.** M शाखान्तरम°. **१३-१३.** M वि...प्रकारेण...ापि विधानवमसस्य, Ad प्रकारेण...वर्जम्; thus T. **१४-१४.** M Ad तत्रैवा...प्रात°. **१५.** M °र्वप्स्यज्ञ, Ad °र्वप्स्य; thus T. **१६.** M Ad साध°. **१७.** M Ad दर्शानुक्रा[M क्र]मति.

द्रुपदं चोपलां चात्राहरन्ति ॥ १ ॥ पुरोडाशीयाꣳश्च ॥ २ ॥ तानपरेण गार्हपत्यं निधाय 'वैष्णवी

द्वन्द्वनियमः। अन्येष्ववश्यंभावित्वं मा विज्ञायीति। यज्ञायुधानां संसादनात्पूर्वं[1] पौर्णमास्यां वेदकरणं[2] परिस्तरणस्य गतिः पूर्वमेवोक्ता। यदि प्रातर्वेदकरणात् पूर्वं, क्व यज्ञायुधानां सादनप्रोक्षणे। उलूखल-मुसलकपालानां पुनः श्रवणाद् देशपृथक्त्वं विज्ञायते। तानि यत्र प्रयोजनवन्ति तत्र साद्यन्ते। कपालानि जघनेन गार्हपत्यम्[3]। उलूखलमुसले चावहननस्थाने। शूर्पादाने चाग्रहणात्। 'स्फ्यं च पुरोडाशीयां-श्चादाये'त्युत्तरत्र दर्शनात् कपालैः सह द्वन्द्वनियमाच्च कपालैरेव स्फ्यः साद्यते। युगपत्साद्यमानयोर्द्वयोः प्राथम्यादाद्यं दक्षिणेन पाणिनाऽविरोधाद्। इतरत्[4] सव्येनोत्तरेण वाऽग्रेण गार्हपत्यम् इतराणि। 'स्फ्येन पुरोडाशीयान् सादये'दिति विध्यवशेषेषूक्तम्। तथा चोदयनीये अपरेण गार्हपत्यसादनं[5] दृष्टम्। तच्च पूर्वेण शालामुखीयं प्राप्तस्य निवृत्यर्थम्। [6]तस्यैवाहवनीयत्वादपरेणाहवनीयमिति प्राप्तं नियम्यते। अतोऽन्तरा गार्हपत्यं चाहवनीयं च सादनमिष्यत इवाचार्येण स्फ्यादीनि वर्जयित्वा। ऊर्ध्वं दशभ्यः कानि साद्यन्ते। जुहूं चोपभृतं च स्रुवं च ध्रुवां चाज्यस्थालीं चेडापात्रं[7] च पात्रीं च द्वे च मेक्षणे वेदं च प्राशित्रप्रहरणं च प्रणीतापात्रीं[8] चाज्यस्थालीं चोपवेषं च शृतावदानं च मदन्तीस्थालीं च पिष्टसंयवनीं[9] चान्वाहार्यस्थालीं[10] च चरुस्थालीं च पत्नीसन्नहनं च वृषारवं च काश्चित्समिधः पृष्ट्याद्यर्थं[11] च बर्हिरन्यान्यपि च यान्युपयुज्यन्ते तानि च। द्वन्द्वेन[12] यथासंभवं वा सादयति। संसादनं[13] च सम्यक् सादनम्। तृणानि संस्तीर्य तेषूपरि न्युब्ज्य सादयतीत्यर्थः ॥ १ ॥

[14]आहरन्ति पुरोडाशीयान्[14]। यस्य कार्यं पुरोडाशस्तत्करणं पुरोडाशीयशब्दाभिलप्यम्। तद् ग्रहणेन चरव्या अप्युपलक्ष्यन्ते। तच्चावघातादिदर्शनादप्रतिषिद्धम्। तुषधान्यमिति प्राप्ते 'अग्निरमुष्मिँल्लोक आसी'दित्यस्मिन्ननुवाके 'तेऽग्निं [15]पशुभूतमग्नये मेधायालभन्ते'त्यारभ्य 'तस्मात् सीरलाङ्गलेन कृष्ट्वाऽनुसीतं वपन्ति। तौ प्राजायेतामि'त्येवमन्तेन ग्रन्थेनार्थवादरूपेण व्रीहियवौ विहितौ।

ननु सोमप्रकरणमेतत्[16]। सत्यम्। सोमाङ्गेषु न संभवतीत्येवमभिहितम्। कथमसंभव उदव-सानीयायाम्। उच्यते। [17]अष्टाकपालस्य याज्यानुवाक्ये विधीयेते[17]। तस्य चाष्टाकपालस्य पङ्क्त्यौ याज्यानुवाक्ये भवत इति। अथापि दीक्षणीयान्वाख्यान इदमुक्तम्। उदवसानीयासमाप्ते सोमे कथं पुनः प्रकृतस्याष्टाकपालस्येह प्रवेशः। प्रकृतमष्टाकपालं स्तुत्वोत्तरस्मिन्ननुवाक्येऽष्टाकपालस्य दीक्षा-प्रयोजनसाधकत्वं[18] दर्शयित्वा पुनर्दीक्षणीयमेकादशकपालानि स्तौति।

[19]नन्ववयुत्यवादेऽष्टाकपालस्य स्तुतिः। नैतदेवम् आग्नेय्यौ हि याज्यानुवाक्येऽत्र[20] दृश्येते।

---

१. M Ad संभारात्° ; thus T. २. M देवकरणं, T °करणपरि°. ३. M Ad °पत्य उलू°. ४. M Ad इतर स°. ५. M °पत्यं सादरं. ६. M रस्यै°. ७. M Ad °लीञ्चे...पत्रं. ८. M Ad °पात्रं°. ९. M Ad °सार्थयवनीं°. १०. M Ad om स्थालीञ्च. ११. M Ad वृष्ट्या°. १२. M द्वन्द्वौ. १३. M Ad सादरम्. १४-१४. M आहर = शीयान्, Ad आहरन्ति यान्, T आहार + शीयान्. १५. M पशुं भूतम°. १६. M Ad सामप्र°. १७-१७. M Ad om; thus T [° यते]. १८. T °जनासाध°. १९. T °नन्वयुत्यवादो°. २०. M Ad om अत्र.

स्थः' **इति पवित्रे आदत्ते** ॥ ३ ॥ **यस्मिन्काले्ऽग्निहोत्रमुद्वासयति तस्मिन् कालेऽग्निहोत्रस्थालीः सादयित्वा तिरःपवित्रमस्यामप आनीय ता उपोत्थाय मुखेन सम्मिता अन्तर्वेदि निदधात्यनतिनता इव** ॥ ४ ॥ **पवित्रे आहरन्नेति** ॥ ५ ॥ **दक्षिणमंसमभिनिवर्तते** ॥ ६ ॥ 'कर्मणे वां देवेभ्यः शकेयम्' **इति सपवित्रौ हस्तौ मार्जयते** ॥ ७ ॥ 'वेषाय त्वा' **इत्यग्निहोत्रहवणीं चरु-स्थालीः शूर्पं चादत्ते** ॥ ८ ॥ 'प्रत्युष्टꣳ रक्षः प्रत्युष्टा अरातयः' **इति गार्हपत्ये निष्टपति** ॥ ९ ॥ 'उर्वन्तरिक्षमन्विहि' **इत्यन्तरा वेदिं चोत्करं च हृत्वोत्तरतः प्रागावृत्त उपस्थं कृत्वोपविशति** ॥ १० ॥ 'धूरसि धूर्व धूर्वन्तम्' **इति पुरोडाशीयान् मुष्टीन् वाचयति पवित्रे अधिनिधाय**। '०धूर्व तं=स्त्वं देवानामसि स=मा ह्वरिषीर्विष्णुस्त्वा क्रमताम्, मित्रस्य=हिꣳसिषम्' **इति** ॥ ११ ॥ 'उरु

'अग्निर्मूर्धा भुव' इति आग्नावैष्णवस्य[१] आग्नावैष्णवीभ्यां भवितव्यम्। अथापि 'तदाहुः—यदाग्नेय्यौ याज्यानुवाक्ये 'अग्नयेऽनुब्रूहि' 'अग्निं यजे'ति यजन्तीत्यनूद्य[२] क्वास्यैता देवताः प्राश्नन्तीति परि-चोदयति। अतः प्रकृतस्यैवाष्टाकपालस्यान्वाख्यानमिदम्[३]। अतः व्रीहियवयोरन्यतरस्य[४] पुरोडाशी-यत्वमाग्नेयान्वाख्यानत्वमग्नीषोमीयादीनामपि प्रदर्शनमध्यवदानीयस्तुतौ च। 'अथ यत्पुमांसं निन्युस्ते व्रीहियवा अभवन्' इत्यस्मिन्नर्थे दृश्यते। शाखान्तरे दर्शपूर्णमासप्रकरणे उक्तं[५] वचनं—'व्रीहिभिर्यजेत यवैर्यजेते'ति। समुच्चयासंभवाच्च विकल्पः ॥ २ ॥

तानपरेण गार्हपत्यं निधाय। ब्रह्मणि स्वायतन आसीने पृष्ठ्यास्तीर्त्वा[६] पवित्रे आदत्ते[७]। कथम्[८]। पृष्ठ्यास्तरणं परिभोजनीयादादाय बर्हिर्गार्हपत्यादारभ्याहवनीयाद्[९] 'यज्ञस्ये'ति स्तृणाति। पवित्रे[१०] प्रादेशमात्रे दर्भाग्रे परिभोजनीयादेव ग्रहीतव्ये, पृष्ठ्याया इत्येके ॥ ३ ॥

यस्मिन्काले। कालशब्दः **स्थानवाची** 'औदुम्बर्यै कालः', 'उपरवकालः' इति यथा। तच्च **स्थानमुत्तरेण** गार्हपत्यम्। प्रतिपत्तौ दृश्यमानश्चमसोऽग्निहोत्रस्थाल्या विकल्पते[११]। अपः प्रणेष्यन् 'ब्रह्मन्नपः प्रणेष्यामि, यजमान वाचं यच्छे'ति प्रेष्यति ॥ ४ ॥

दक्षिणमंसमभिनिवर्तत इति विहाराभिमुख्यस्य प्रदर्शनार्थम्। तस्मादुत्तरत उपचारोऽध्वर्युः स्याद्दक्षिणा पर्यावर्तन इति। सर्वविषया हि परिभाषा ॥ ६ ॥

अग्निहोत्रहवण्यादीनि प्रत्येकमादत्ते। शूर्पादानार्थे[१२] एव मन्त्रद्वयम्। इतरदन्वाच्य[१३] शिष्टमिति केचित्। तथा च 'वेषाय' ह्येनदादत्ते' इति नपुंसकलिङ्गमुपपद्यते। तथा सति विकृतावपि शूर्पा-भावेऽन्ययो[१४]र्मन्त्राभावः। इहापि सहैवादानम्[१४] ॥ ८ ॥

अपरेण गार्हपत्यमुपविश्य उपस्थं करोति ॥ १० ॥

पुरोडाशीयेषु पवित्रे निधाय दशहोतारं संग्रहं[१५] व्याख्याय शकटमन्त्रं वाचयति 'धूरसी'ति ॥ ११ ॥

---

१. M अग्ना° वस्या. २. M °त्यरूद्य. ३. M °ख्यानम्. ४. M °यवोरन्य°. ५. M Ad °व्यक्तं; thus T. ६. M Ad पृष्ट्या°. ७. Ad अदत्ते. ८. M Ad om, T gives it in fn. ९. M Ad °नीयाज्ञस्येति. १०. Ad पवित्रे twice. ११. Ad °कल्प्यते. १२. M Ad शूर्पदा°. १३. M Ad न्वाचयशि°. १४-१४. M मन्त्राभा...हवादानम्. १५. M Ad सग्रहं; thus T.

वाताय' **इति किञ्चित् पुरोडाशीयेभ्यो निरस्यति** ॥ १२ ॥ **दशहोतारं व्याख्याय शूर्पे पवित्रे अधिनिधाय पुरोडाशीयान्निर्वपति सपवित्रायामग्निहोत्रहवण्याम्** ॥ १३ ॥ 'देवस्य त्वा सवितुः प्रसवे' **इति चतुरो मुष्टीन् निर्वपति**। '०अश्विनोर्बाहुभ्यां पूष्णो हस्ताभ्यामग्नये जुष्टं निर्वपामि' **इति त्रिर्यजुषा तूष्णीं चतुर्थम्** ॥ १४ ॥ 'यच्छन्तु त्वा पञ्च' **इति निर्वपति** ॥ १५ ॥ **सपवित्रं चरुस्थालीमादत्ते** ॥ १६ ॥ **तस्यां** 'देवस्य त्वा सवितुः प्रसवे' **इत्येव चतुरो मुष्टीन्निर्वपति**। '०अश्विनोर्बाहुभ्यां पूष्णो हस्ताभ्यामिन्द्राग्निभ्यां जुष्टं निर्वपामि' **इत्यमावास्यायामनीजानस्य**, 'इन्द्राय' **इतीजानस्य, त्रिरेव यजुषा तूष्णीं चतुर्थम्** ॥ १७ ॥ 'यच्छन्तु त्वा पञ्च' **इत्येव निर्वपति** ॥ १८ ॥ **सपवित्रमेव स्रुचमादत्ते** ॥ १९ ॥ **तस्यां** 'देवस्य त्वा सवितुः प्रसवे' **इत्येव चतुरो मुष्टीन् निर्वपति**। '०अश्विनोर्बाहुभ्यां पूष्णो हस्ताभ्यामग्नीषोमाभ्यां जुष्टं निर्वपामि' **इति पौर्णमास्यामनीजानस्य**, 'इन्द्राय' **इतीजानस्य, त्रिरेव यजुषा तूष्णीं चतुर्थम्** ॥ २० ॥ **चतुर्थे भूयसोऽभ्यावपति** ॥ २१ ॥ **यावतोऽत्रातिशिनष्टि** 'यच्छन्तु त्वा पञ्च' **इत्येव निर्वपति** ॥ २२ ॥ 'अग्निꣳ होतारमिह तꣳ हुवे' **इति निरुप्तेषु वाचयति**। '०देवान् यज्ञिया =अस्य' **इति** ॥ २३ ॥ 'कस्त्वा युनक्ति स त्वा युनक्ति' **इत्युलूखल आवपति** ॥ २४ ॥ 'यानि घर्मे' **इति कपालान्युपचिनोति**। '०कपालान्युपचिन्वन्ति= इन्द्रवायू युङ्क्ताम्' **इति** ॥ २५ ॥ 'इदं देवानाम्' **इति निरुप्तानभिमृशति** ॥ २६ ॥ 'इदमु नः सह' **इति यतो निर्वपति** ॥ २७ ॥ 'रक्षायै त्वा नारात्यै' **इति स्फ्यं च पुरोडाशीयाꣳश्चादायोत्तिष्ठति** ॥ २८ ॥ 'सुवरभि विख्येषम्' **इत्यनुवीक्षते** ॥ २९ ॥ 'वैश्वानरं ज्योतिः' **इत्याहवनीयम्** ॥ ३० ॥ **अथ गृहानन्वीक्षते** 'दृꣳहन्तां दुर्या द्यावापृथिव्योः' **इति** ॥ ३१ ॥ **प्रक्रामति** 'उर्वन्तरिक्षमन्विहि' **इति** ॥ ३२ ॥ 'अदित्यास्त्वोपस्थे सादयामि' **इत्युत्तरेण**

किञ्चिदपनेतव्यम्[१]। तृणादि निरस्यति ॥ १२ ॥

[२]सपवित्रायामग्निहोत्रहवण्यां[२] निरुप्य तदेव पवित्रमन्तर्धाय शूर्पे निर्वपति[३]। तथा स्थाल्यां चतुर्थे भूयसोऽभ्यावपति। अभ्यावापोऽग्नीषोमीयादिधर्मश्चतुर्थ इति। तन्निर्वापादिविधानादिति केचित्। तथा सत्युत्तरस्य [४]पुरोडाशस्य महत्त्वं तदनुरोधाद् गम्यते। अन्ये वर्णयन्ति 'चतुर्मुष्टिमात्रेण पुरोडाशपरिमाणप्रयोजने सिध्यत' इति। तत्पर्याप्त्यर्थमभ्यावापो विहितः। तस्याग्नीषोमीयादिधर्ममध्ये विधानं स्थानसंबन्धमात्रमिति दक्षिणस्य पुरोडाशस्य ज्यायस्त्वम् प्रयोजनापेक्षयाऽनुपदकारो वदति। पूर्वस्मिन्नपि पक्षे [५]विकृतावग्नीषोमीयादिविकारेऽभ्यावापो बहुष्वपि तद्विकारेषु प्रत्येकम् इतरस्मिन्ननेकेषु ॥ १३-१४ ॥

अन्त्यस्य चतुर्थे निर्वापेऽभ्यावपति। तथैकस्मिन्नपि। निरुप्तेषु वाचयतीत्यस्यार्थं याजमाने वक्ष्यामः। उलूखलमुसलग्रहणं दृषदुपलस्यापि प्रदर्शनार्थमिति व्याचक्षते ॥ २४ ॥

'अदित्यास्त्वोपस्थे सादयामी'ति सादनमन्त्रः ॥ ३३ ॥

---

१. T ञ्चिदुप°. २-२. M Ad °मग्नि...निरुप्य; thus T. ३. M निवपति, Ad T निपतति. ४. M Ad °त्तरपुरो°; thus T. ५. M Ad प्रकृता°; thus T.

गार्हपत्यं पुरोडाशीयान् सादयति ॥ ३३ ॥ 'अग्ने हव्यꣳ रक्ष' **इति गार्हपत्यमभिमन्त्रयते** ॥ २.१.४.३४ ॥ **[इति चतुर्थः पटलः]**

[व्रीह्यवघातः]

परिक्षाल्य स्रुचं तिरः पवित्रमस्यामप आनयति ॥ १ ॥ 'विष्णोर्मनसा पूते स्थः' **इति पवित्रे अनुमार्ष्टि** ॥ २ ॥ 'देवो वः सवितोत्पुनातु' **इत्युदीचीनाग्राभ्यां पवित्राभ्यामप उत्पुनाति।** '°अच्छिद्रेण पवित्रेण=रश्मिभिः' **इति** ॥ ३ ॥ 'आपो देवीः' **इति त्रिरुदिङ्गयति।** '°अग्रेगुवोऽग्र इमं यज्ञं नयताग्रे यज्ञपतिं धत्त देवायुवं युष्मानिन्द्रोऽवृणीत वृत्रतूर्ये' **इति** ॥ ४ ॥ 'प्रोक्षिताः स्थ' **इति**

'अग्ने हव्यं रक्षे'ति[१] परिदधाति। गार्हपत्यस्यात्र निर्वपणानन्तरं तमसीव[२] वा एषोऽन्तश्चरति यः परीणही'ति दर्शनाद् अन आरूह्य निर्वपणं ब्राह्मणेऽभिप्रेतम्[३]। तथा 'धूरसी'ति मन्त्रो हि शकटाभिधायी तथाऽग्निष्ठस्य वाऽनस इति। कल्पेऽपि[४] शकटस्य विद्यमानत्वे लिङ्गम्। तदभावेऽप्याचार्येण 'धू'र्मन्त्रस्य विहितत्वात् निवृत्तिः[५]। तद्भावे च यथालिंगं विभागः कर्तव्यः॥ २.१.४.३४॥ **[इति चतुर्थः पटलः]**

परिक्षाल्य स्रुचं [६]प्रकृतामग्निहोत्रहवणीम्॥ १॥

'देवो वः' इति मन्त्रः पच्छो विभज्य त्रीन्मन्त्रान् कृत्वा[७] तैस्त्रिरुत्पुनाति॥ ३॥

उदिङ्गयति ऊर्ध्वं स्तोकयति। अस्यापि[८] मन्त्रस्य त्रेधा विभागः। 'नयत देवायुवं वृत्रतूर्य' इति मन्त्रान्ताः[९]। सर्वस्यैकमन्त्रत्वमपरे। तथा सति सकृन्मन्त्रमुक्त्वा त्रिरुदिङ्गयति, अद्भिरप इत्यन्याभिः मन्त्रावृत्तिरत्रेष्यते॥ ४॥

'अग्नये वो जुष्टा=त्या भवन्ति'। अत्र सन्देहः किं पृथक् पृथक् प्रोक्षणम् उत तन्त्रेणेति। पृथक् पृथग् देवेभ्यो निरुप्तानां मन्त्रेषु च भिन्नेषु पृथगेव प्रोक्षणं युक्तम्। एवं सत्याग्नेये[१०] विकृतौ तद्विकारेषु 'वो जुष्टा'निति मन्त्रेऽन्यत्र[११] 'अमुष्मै जुष्टानि'त्येतावदेव श्रवणाद्युष्मत् प्रयोगो न भवति। अन्येऽवहननपेषणयोः[१२] साहित्यश्रवणाद् अर्वाचीनप्रोक्षणस्यापि सहत्वमेव युक्तम्, मिश्रणस्यावश्यं-भावित्वात्। अपि च तन्त्रेण कर्तुं शक्यानामावृत्तेरन्याय्यत्वात् तन्त्रेणैव प्रोक्षणं कर्तव्यम्[१३]। एवं सतीह युष्मद[१३]स्तन्त्रोच्चारणं विकृतावपि मुख्येन तन्त्रेण प्रयोक्तव्यम्। एवमाह—'अग्नीषोमादितन्त्रताम-भि[१४]प्रेक्ष्य 'अमुष्मा अमुष्मा' इत्येवावक्ष्यत्। 'वो जुष्टान्प्रोक्षामी[१४]'ति पदत्रयस्य तन्त्रोच्चारणसंभवादतो भेदनैव प्रोक्षणमाचार्येणाभिप्रेतमित्युच्यते। संवपनसंयवनयोः प्रकृत्या तन्त्रत्वमवश्यमभ्युपगन्तव्यम्[१५]।

---

१. T रक्षस्व. २. M Ad °न्तरमसीव. ३. M °प्रेति, Ad ब्राह्मणोभिप्रैति; thus T. ४. M Ad कल्पेवि. ५. M Ad °त्तिम्; thus T. ६. M Ad प्रकृतम°. ७. M Ad om. ८. M Ad अन्यस्या°; thus T. ९. M Ad °त्रान्ताम्; thus T. १०. M Ad °ग्नेय विकृ°; thus T. ११. M Ad मन्त्रो°; thus T. १२. Ad पोष°. १३-१३. M मेव...तीहय...दस्यन्त्रो°. १४-१४. M प्रेक्ष्या...इत्ये°; वो ज...ति पद°.; उच्यते...तन्त्रमव°; अनूष...वा जुष्टं. T, वो जुष्टान्-क्षान् प्रोक्षा°. १५. M Ad भ्युपगम्य; thus T. १६. M Ad षक्त°; thus T.

त्रिरञ्जिरपः प्रोक्षति ॥ ५ ॥ 'अग्नये वो जुष्टान् प्रोक्षामि' **इति पुरोडाशीयान् प्रोक्षति** ॥ ६ ॥ 'अमुष्मै जुष्टानमुष्मै जुष्टान्' **इति यद्देवत्या भवन्ति** ॥ ७ ॥ 'शुद्धन्तां दैव्याय कर्मणे' **इत्युत्तानानि पात्राणि प्रोक्षति**। '०देवयज्यायै' **इति** ॥ ८ ॥ **उलूखलमुसलं प्रोक्षति** ॥ ९ ॥ **कपालानि प्रोक्षति** ॥ १० ॥ **पूर्वेण गार्हपत्यं प्रोक्षणीः सादयित्वा स्फ्यं च पुरोडाशीयाꣳश्चादायोलूखलस्यार्धमेति** ॥ ११ ॥ **निधाय पुरोडाशीयान्** 'अदित्यास्त्वगसि' **इति कृष्णाजिनमादत्ते** ॥ १२ ॥ 'अवधूतं रक्षोऽवधूता अरातयः' **इत्यवधूनोति** ॥ १३ ॥ 'प्रति त्वा पृथिवी वेत्तु' **इति प्रतीचीनग्रीवमुत्तरलोमोपस्तृणाति** ॥ १४ ॥ **अप उपस्पृश्य** 'अधिषवणमसि वानस्पत्यम्' **इत्यस्मिन्नुलूखलमुपदधाति**। '०प्रति त्वाऽदित्यास्त्वग्वेत्तु पृथिवीं दृꣳह' **इति** ॥ १५ ॥ 'अग्नेस्तनूरसि वाचो विसर्जनम्' **इत्यस्मिꣳश्चतुरो मुष्टीनावपति**। '०देव=गृह्णामि' **इति** ॥ १६ ॥ 'बृहद्ग्रावासि (वानस्पत्यः)' **इति मुसलमादत्ते** ॥ १७ ॥ **ऊर्ध्वꣳ हत्वाऽवदधाति** 'स इदं देवभ्यो हव्यꣳ शमिष्व सुशमि शमिष्व' **इति** ॥ १८ ॥ 'हविष्कृदेहि' **इति त्रिः प्रहरति**। '०हविष्कृदेहि हविष्कृदेहि' **इति** ॥ १९ ॥ **हविष्कृता वाचं विसृज्य दक्षिणतः प्राचीꣳ शम्यां निधाय** 'इषमा वदोर्जमावद' **इति त्रिः स्फ्येनोद्वादयति**।

तत्रापि जुष्टशब्दोऽनुषङ्ग[१६] एव। तथा सति शाखान्तरेऽपि तादृशाः पाठा विद्यन्त इत्यवगन्तव्यम्। अस्यां हि शाखायां 'अग्नये वो जुष्टं प्रोक्षाम्यग्नीषोमाभ्या'मिति पाठः ॥ ६–७ ॥

पुरोडाशीयानां पात्राणां च त्रिस्त्रिः प्रोक्षणम्। उलूखलमुसलकपालानां पृथक् प्रोक्षणं केचिन्मन्यन्ते। अन्ये देशपृथक्त्वाद् द्विःस्मरणं[१] कदाचित् [२]स्यादित्यविस्मरणार्थमुक्तम्। तन्त्रेणैव प्रोक्षणं कर्तव्यम् ॥ ८–१० ॥

संभवादिति उत्तरप्रतीचीं[३] दिशं[४] प्रत्यवधूननम्[४] ॥ १३ ॥

'[५]अग्नेस्तनूरसी'त्यादि एको मन्त्रः। कुतः[६]। मन्त्रचतुष्ट्यत्वाशंकानिवृत्यर्थम्[७] इह[८] वाक्यद्वयमतीत्य कर्मविहितं प्रतिमुष्ट्यावर्तते च ॥ १६ ॥

'हविष्कृदेही'ति[९] न प्रहरणमन्त्रः कालार्थे संबन्धेन। अत उच्चैष्ट्वं बीजभेदे[१०]नावृत्तिश्च भवति। उलूखलभेदे तन्त्रत्वे तु हविष्कृदध्रिगुपुरोनुवाक्यामन्त्रो[११] तस्यावृत्तिर्भिन्नकालेष्विति सूत्रकार[१२]परिभाषा ॥ १९ ॥

शम्यामुलूखलेन[१३] संस्पृष्यन्[१४] निधायोद्वादयति[१५]। तत्र[१६] 'इषमावदे'ति दृषदं समाहन्ति, 'ऊर्जमा वदे'त्युपलाम्[१७]। 'द्युमद्वदत[१८]'इत्यादिना शम्यामुलूखलेन संस्पृष्यम्[१९]। कुत एतत्। अव च[२०] हन्ति। दृषदौ च समाहन्तीति द्वन्द्वसम्पादने दर्शनान्मन्त्रयोश्चैकवचनान्तत्वात् सति संभवे एकस्य कर्मणो

---

१. M ०त्वाद्विस्म०, Ad क्त्वादिद्वस्म० ; thus T. २. M Ad ०दित्यपिस्मर०. ३. M Ad उत्तरा प्रतीचीं; thus T. ४–४. M दिशि०...विधून० ; thus T. ५. Ad अग्नस्त०. ६. M T om. ७. M Ad ०ष्टयशङ्का० ; thus T. ८. M Ad इव. ९. M ०कृद्दे०. १०. M Ad भेदेनोवृ०. ११. M Ad ०ध्रिगुपुरो०, T ०गुपरोऽनु०, M Ad ०मनो. १२. M Ad ०काल० ; thus T. १३. M Ad T ०खले. १४. M Ad ससृष्टं; thus T. १५. Ad ०योद्दाद० ; thus M T. १६. M Ad T तन्त्रेष०. १७. Ad ०वहेत्यु०. १८. M Ad ०वदेत्या०. १९. M Ad संसृष्टाम्; thus T. २०. Ad om च.

'°द्युमद्वदत वयः संघातःसंघातं जेष्म' **इति** ॥ २० ॥ **उच्चैः समाहन्तवा इति संप्रेष्यति** ॥ २१ ॥ **उत्तुषान् कृत्वा** 'वर्षवृद्धमसि' **इति शूर्पमादत्ते** ॥ २२ ॥ 'प्रति त्वा वर्षवृद्धं वेत्तु' **इति पुरोडाशीयानुद्वपति** ॥ २३ ॥ **उपविश्योदगावृत्तः परापुनाति** 'परापूतं रक्षः परापूता अरातयः' **इति** ॥ २४ ॥ **अवहत्य तुषानपरेणोलूखलमधस्तात् कृष्णाजिनस्योपवपति** 'रक्षसां भागोऽसीदं=नयाति' **इति** ॥ २५ ॥ **अप उपस्पृश्य विविनक्ति** 'वायुर्वो विविनक्तु' **इति** ॥ २६ ॥ 'देवेभ्यः शुन्धध्वम्' **इति विविक्तानभिमृशति** ॥ २७ ॥ **आवपन्नाह** 'त्रिष्फलीकृतान् प्रब्रूताद्' **इति** ॥ २.१.५.२८ ॥ **[इति पञ्चमः पटलः]**

॥ इति द्वितीयप्रपाठके प्रथमोऽनुवाकः ॥

बहुमन्त्रत्वानुपपत्तेः। बहुवचनान्तस्य मन्त्रस्य स्फ्यशम्योलूखलेषु[१] सामर्थ्यं भवति। पठन्ति च[२] केचित्— 'द्विर्दृषदि सकृदुपलायामि[३]'ति ॥ २० ॥

तत 'उच्चैः समाहन्तवा'[४] इति संप्रेष्यति। आग्नीध्रो वृषारवयादायोच्चैः[५] सर्वाणि यज्ञायुधानि उद्वादयति ॥ २१ ॥

उत्तुषाः[६] उपरि तुषा एव यथा भवन्ति तथाऽवहत्य[७] तुषान्। विशेषाश्रवणाद्धस्तेनेति[८]। 'पुरोडाशकपालेन तुषानुपवपन्ति' इति श्रुत्यन्तरम्। क्वचिद्विशेषं चामनन्ति। अष्टाकपालस्य मध्यमकपालेनेति[९] ॥ २२ ॥

विविक्तानभिमृशति[१०] ॥ २६ ॥

द्वयं त्रिष्फलीकर्तवै 'त्रिष्फलीकृतान् प्रब्रूताद्' इति प्रैषः[११] ॥ २.१.५.२७ ॥ **[इति पञ्चमः पटलः]**

॥ इति व्याख्यायां द्वितीयप्रपाठके[१२] प्रथमोऽनुवाकः ॥

---

१. M Ad स्फ्यशम्यामुलू°. **२.** Ad om च. **३.** T उपलया°. **४.** T समाहन्त वा. **५.** M Ad वृषारमा°. **६.** M Ad उक्तषा. **७.** Ad तथोपवहत्य, T °वहूय. **८.** Ad °णाद्वस्ते°. **९.** Ad कपालेति. **१०.** M Ad विवक्ता°. **११.** Ad शेषः. **१२.** M Ad पुरोडाश्यां°.

॥ अथ द्वितीयप्रपाठके द्वितीयोऽनुवाकः ॥

[कपालोपधानम्]

'धृष्टिरसि ब्रह्म यच्छ' **इत्युपवेषमादत्ते** ॥ १ ॥ 'अपाग्नेऽग्निमामादं जहि' **इति द्वावङ्गारौ निवर्तयति** ॥ २ ॥ **तयोरन्यतरं** 'निष्क्रव्यादꣳ सेध' **इति दक्षिणा प्रतिनुदते** ॥ ३ ॥ 'आ देवयजं वह' **इत्यन्यतरमावर्तयति** ॥ ४ ॥ **तस्मिन्नुपरि** 'ध्रुवमसि पृथिवीं दृꣳह' **इति मध्यमं कपालमुपदधाति**। '°ब्रह्म दृꣳह क्षत्रं दृꣳह प्रजां दृꣳह रयिं दृꣳह रायस्पोषं दृꣳह सजातान् यजमानाय दृꣳह' **इति** ॥ ५ ॥ **तन्न पुराऽङ्गारस्योद्धानादतिसृजेत्** ॥ ६ ॥ **तूष्णीमस्मिनङ्गारमुपदधाति** ॥ ७ ॥ 'पृथिव्यै मूर्धानं मा निर्धाक्षीः' **इति वा** ॥ ८ ॥ 'धर्त्रमस्यन्तरिक्षं दृꣳह' **इति पुरस्तादुपदधाति**। '°ब्रह्म=दृꣳह' **इति** ॥ ९ ॥ 'धरुणमसि दिवं दृꣳह' **इति पश्चादुपदधाति**। '°ब्रह्म=दृꣳह' **इति** ॥ १० ॥ 'धर्मासि दिशो दृꣳह' **इति पूर्वेण पर्याहृत्य दक्षिणत उपदधाति**। '°ब्रह्म=दृꣳह' **इति** ॥ ११ ॥ 'विश्वा आशा दिशो दृꣳह' **इत्युत्तरतः प्रधिकमुपदधाति**। '°ब्रह्म=दृꣳह' **इति** ॥ १२ ॥ 'परिचितम्' **इतीतरं कुर्यात्**। '°ब्रह्म=दृꣳह' **इति** ॥ १३ ॥ 'चितः स्थ' **इति द्वे उत्तरतः सꣳस्पृष्टे उपदधाति**। '°ब्रह्म दृꣳहतं क्षत्रं दृꣳहतं प्रजां दृꣳहतं रयिं दृꣳहतं रायस्पोषं दृꣳहतं सजातान् यजमानाय दृꣳहतम्' **इति** ॥ १४ ॥

धृष्टिः=आदत्ते। उपवेषमितरयज्ञायुधवन्नित्यप्रकारः प्रादेशमात्र[1] आपितृमेधान्नित्यः। पितृमेधे प्रतिपाद्यते 'सव्य उपभृदुपवेषावि'ति। तस्य 'यो नः कनीय' इत्युत्करे उपगूहनं प्रतिपत्तिः। स्रुगुलूखलादिविमोकवत् संस्कारः। स एव गुणाधिकोऽच्छिद्रकल्पे विहितः[2]। ब्राह्मणे 'परिवेषो वा'[2] इत्यारभ्य '[3]अप्रतिवादिन एवैनान् कुरुते' इत्यनेनान्यथोपगूहनं विहितम्। त्रयाणामपि वैकल्पिकत्वं 'यः पुनः शाखामूलमयं तेन[4] सान्नायार्थमङ्गारानिरूह्य तमच्छिद्रकेण वा तमादायोद[5]पात्रञ्चेत्यादिना ब्राह्मणविहितेन 'धृष्टिर्वा उपवेष' इत्यादि विधानेन वा प्रतिपादयति ॥ १ ॥

उत्तरां प्राञ्च[6] प्रधिकमुपदधाति। प्रधावुपधेयं प्रधिकम्। इतरत्प्रागुदीच्यामुपधेयं प्रधिकम् ॥ १२ ॥

परिचित्सु विप्रतिपद्यते। केचित्तैरवकाशान् [7]पूरयित्वा आरभ्य मन्त्रान्[7] वदन्ति। यथा अग्निचित्यायां तथा बहुवचनान्तो मन्त्रः समर्थितो भवतीति। तथा चानुपदकारः 'षट्कपालसप्तकपालेष्विति परिचिन्मन्त्रमूहेदि'त्याह। अन्ये 'परिचित उपदधातीति' करणमन्त्रेण[8] चोदितत्वान्मन्त्रावृत्या सर्वाण्युपधेयानि सन्निपातिष्वकिञ्चित्करत्वात् बहुवचनस्येति। एवं सति षट्कपालसप्तकपालयोरविकारत्वम्[9] ॥ १३ ॥

अववृत्य, अवतार्य यावद्भिः पाकसिद्धिस्तावद्भिरभिवासयति ॥ १४ ॥

---

१. M Ad प्रदेश°. २–२. M विहितो...षो वा, Ad ब्राह्मणोपनिवे°; thus T. ३. M Ad प्रति; thus T. ४. M Ad °मयतेन. ५. M °दपा....ह्मण; Ad °पात्रत्वेत्यादिना; thus T. ६. M Ad प्रतीचीं. ७–७. M परयि...न्त्रान्. ८. M Ad मन्त्रत्वेन; thus T. ९. M Ad °वितारम्; thus T.

त्रिरावृत्याङ्गारान् ‘भृगूणामङ्गिरसां तपसा तप्यध्वम्’ **इत्यङ्गारैरभिवासयति** ॥ १५ ॥ **उत्तरतोऽङ्गारान्निरूह्य चरुस्थालीमधिश्रित्य तिरःपवित्रमप आनयति** ॥ १६ ॥ **एवमेवैकादशकपालस्य कपालान्युपदधाति** ॥ १७ ॥

[व्रीहिपेषणं पिष्टसंवपनञ्च]

विस्राव्य तण्डुलाꣳश्चरव्यानपयच्छति ॥ १८ ॥ ‘अदित्यास्त्वगसि’ **इति कृष्णाजिनमादत्ते** ॥ १९ ॥ ‘अवधूतꣳ रक्षोऽवधूता अरातयः’ **इत्यवधुनोति** ॥ २० ॥ ‘प्रति त्वा पृथिवी वेत्तु’ **इति प्रतीचीनग्रीवमुत्तरलोमोपस्तृणाति** ॥ २१ ॥ **अप उपस्पृश्य** ‘धिषणाऽसि पर्वत्याः’ **इत्यस्मिन् दृषदमुपदधाति**। ‘॰प्रति त्वाऽदित्यास्त्वग्वेत्तु पृथिवीं दृꣳह’ **इति** ॥ २२ ॥ ‘दिवः स्कम्भनीरस्यन्तरिक्षं दृꣳह’ **इति पश्चादुदीचं शम्यामुपोहति** ॥ २३ ॥ ‘धिषणाऽसि पार्वतेयी प्रति त्वा पर्वतिर्वेत्तु दिवं दृꣳह’ **इति दृषद्युपलामुपदधाति** ॥ २४ ॥ ‘धान्यमसि धिनुहि देवान्’ **इति चतुरो मुष्टीनधिवपति**। ‘॰धिनुहि यज्ञं धिनुहि यज्ञपतिं धिनुहि मा यज्ञन्यम्’ **इति** ॥ २५ ॥ ‘प्राणाय त्वा’ **इति प्राचीं प्रमृणति** ॥ २६ ॥ ‘व्यानाय त्वा’ **इति दक्षिणा** ॥ २७ ॥ ‘अपानाय त्वा’ **इत्यात्मानं प्रति** ॥ २८ ॥ ‘उदानाय त्वा’ **इत्युदङ्** ॥ २९ ॥ **पिनष्टि** ‘दीर्घामनु प्रसितिꣳ सꣳसचेथाम्’ **इति** ॥ ३० ॥ ‘आयुषे धाम्’ **इति बाहू अन्ववेक्षते** ॥ ३१ ॥ ‘देवो वः सविता हिरण्यपाणिः प्रति गृह्णातु’ **इति प्रपतिताꣳस्तण्डुलानन्ववेक्षते**। ‘॰अदब्धेन वश्चक्षुषाऽवेक्षे सुप्रजास्त्वाय’ **इति** ॥ ३२ ॥ **पिष्टानि कुर्वन्ति** ॥ ३३ ॥ **तानि**

---

[१]एवमेवोपदधाति। अत्र केचिदङ्गारद्वयनिर्वर्तनाद्यारभन्ते[२]। निर्वर्त्यमानाङ्गारसंस्कारत्वं प्रतिनोदनस्य युक्तम्। कुतः। तथा हि साक्षात्कपालोपधानेन[३] संबन्ध इति। अन्ये निर्वर्तनप्रतिनोदन[४]संस्कृतस्य[५] गार्हपत्यादावर्त्यमानस्याङ्गारस्य तत्संस्कार[६]संस्कृतस्यावयवत्वात् साक्षादेव[६] संबन्ध इति ‘आ देवयजं वह’ इत्याद्यावर्तत इति ॥ १५ ॥

अथ मदन्तीरधिश्रयति ॥ १६ ॥

‘धान्यमसी’त्यादयश्चत्वारो मन्त्राः। तेषु ‘देवस्य त्वा सवितुः प्रसवेऽश्विनोर्बाहुभ्यां पूष्णो हस्ताभ्यामधिवपामी’त्यनुषजन्ति केचित्। अपरे[७] ‘धान्यमसी’त्येव। अन्ये यथापाठमेव कुर्वन्ति। केचित् प्रथममेव[८] ‘देवस्य त्वा’ इत्यादिम्[९], इतरान्[९] यथापाठमेव [१०]संवपन्तिः ‘पींषाणूनि[११] कुरुताद्’ इति प्रेष्यति। पिष्यानि[१२] कुर्वन्ति। बहुवचननिर्देशादनियतकर्तृकत्वम्[१३]। संवपन्तीति[१४] स्त्रीलिंगनिर्देशात् प्रकृतां पत्नीमन्तरेण स्त्री नास्ति। प्रकृताग्रहणे प्रमाणाभावात्। पत्नी पिनष्टीति[१५] शाखान्तरे। पत्यवहन्ति दासी पिनष्य्येतद्वा[१६] विपरीतमिति ॥ २५–३३ ॥

---

१. M Ad add स before एव. **२.** M Ad निवर्त्य॰; thus T. **३.** M कपालोवधा॰. **४.** M Ad निव॰. **५.** M Ad ॰ताद्; thus T. **६–६.** M ॰स्या..साक्षादेव; Ad स्यावयवा सा॰. **७.** M Ad अपरो. **८.** M Ad ॰प्रथम एव [M ए..]; thus T. **९–९.** M Ad इत्यादि...मितरान्. **१०.** M Ad असंवपन्ती. **११.** M Ad विंषोणूनि. **१२.** M Ad विष्टा॰. **१३.** M कतृत्वम्, Ad कर्तृत्वम्; thus T. **१४.** M Ad असंव॰; thus T. **१५.** M Ad विन॰. **१६.** M Ad विनष्टीतीत्येत॰.

पात्रियाः संवपति ॥ ३४ ॥ **पवित्रे आददान आह** 'प्रणीताभ्योऽध्याहर वेदं परिवासय' **इति** ॥ ३५ ॥ **एतत् कुर्वन्ति** ॥ ३६ ॥ **स्रुवेण प्रणीताभ्योऽध्याहरति** ॥ ३७ ॥ **उपयम्य वेदं परिवास्य मार्जयति** ॥ ३८ ॥ 'देवस्य त्वा सवितुः प्रसवे' **इत्यपरेण गार्हपत्यं प्रागावृत उपविश्योदीचीनाग्राभ्यां पवित्राभ्यां पिष्टानि संवपति।** '°अश्विनो=भ्यामग्नये जुष्टानि संवपामि, अमुष्मै जुष्टान्यमुष्मै जुष्टानि' **इति यद्देवत्यानि भवन्ति** ॥ ३९ ॥ 'समाप ओषधीभिरग्मत' **इति तिरःपवित्रं स्रुवेणाप आनयति।** '°समोषधयो रसेन सꣳ रेवतीर्जगतीभिर्मधुमतीर्मधुमतीभिः सृजध्वम्' **इति** ॥ ४० ॥ **भूयसीरप आनीय** 'अद्भ्यः परिप्रजाताः स्थ' **इति त्रिरब्जिः परिप्रजनयति।** '°समद्भिः पृच्यध्वम्' **इति** ॥ ४१ ॥ 'जनवीतये त्वा संयौमि' **इति संयौति।** '°अग्नये जुष्टान्यमुष्मै जुष्टान्यमुष्मै जुष्टानि' **इति यद्देवत्यानि भवन्ति** ॥ ४२ ॥ **प्रम्णाय पिष्टानि** 'मखस्य शिरोऽसि' **इति पिण्डं करोति** ॥ ४३ ॥ 'यथाभागं व्यावर्तेथाम्' **इति व्यावर्तयति** ॥ ४४ ॥

[पुरोडाशश्रपणम्]

'इदमहꣳ सेनाया अभित्वर्यै मुखमपोहामि' **इति वेदेनाष्टाकपालस्य प्राचोऽङ्गारानपोहति,**

तानि पात्र्यां संवपति। पात्रीपिष्टसंयवनीसमाख्यानात् प्रतिपत्तौ दर्शनाच्च ॥ ३४ ॥

एतत्कुर्वन्तीति बहुवचनं कर्तृनियमार्थमिति केचित्। प्रकृतत्वादाग्नीध्र एव। अविवक्षितं बहुवचनमित्यन्ये ॥ ३६ ॥

स्रुवेण प्रणीताभ्योऽध्याहरति समर्थेनोपयत्य केनचित्पात्रेण 'अमुष्मै जुष्टान्यमुष्मै जुष्टानी'ति। द्विर्वचनं पर्वद्वयापेक्षम् ॥ ३७–३९ ॥

स्रुवेणाप आनयतीति अप इति वर्तमाने पुनरब्ग्रहणं भूयसीरप आनीयेत्यन्यत्वं गमयतीत्यतः प्रणीताभ्योऽन्या आनीय परिप्लावयति। शाखान्तरे वचनं 'यच्छीताभिः[१] संयुयादतिवर्षुकः[२] पर्जन्यः[३], स यदुष्णाभिः[३] संयुयादवर्षुकः[४]। उष्णाभिश्च शीताभिश्च संयौती'ति। अतः कपालद्वि[५]कस्योपधानोत्तरकालं मदन्तीस्थाल्यां[६] तिरःपवित्रमप आनीय मदन्तीरधिश्रयति। तथा चास्यां शाखायां लिङ्गं[७] 'समापो अद्भिरग्मते'ति[८] उदकद्वयस्य दर्शनम्। अतः प्रणीताभिश्च मदन्तिकाभिश्च[९] संयवनपरिप्लावने[१०] प्रणीताभ्य एवानीय मदन्तीरधिश्रयन्ति केचित्। तथा सति पवित्रान्तर्धानाभावः। उत्पूतत्वात्तासां संयवनं पुरोडाशमेक्षणेन ॥ ४०–४२ ॥

प्रम्णाय[११] बहुशः संयुत्य प्रमृज्य ॥ ४३ ॥

व्यावर्तनोत्तरकालम् 'अग्नये त्वा' 'अग्नीषोमाभ्यां त्वा' इत्यादिभिर्व्यादिशति[१२] ॥ ४४ ॥

---

१. M Ad यच्छती°. २. M Ad वर्षकः; thus T. ३–३. M पर्ज...स्य द्यदु, Ad °न्यस्सद्यदु°. ४. Ad °वर्षक. ५. M Ad °द्वितयो°, T °कयो. ६. M Ad °दन्ति°. ७. M Ad द्विगं; thus T. ८. M Ad द्भिरश्मते. ९. M Ad मदन्तीभिः. १०. M Ad संवपन°. ११. Ad प्रेम्णाय. १२. M °दिभि...दशति.

नात्मानं प्रत्यपोहेत् ॥ ४५ ॥ 'घर्मोऽसि विश्वायुः' **इत्यधिश्रयति** ॥ ४६ ॥ 'उरु प्रथस्वोरु ते यज्ञपतिः प्रथताम्' **इति सर्वाणि कपालान्यभिप्रथयति** ॥ ४७ ॥ **तिरःपवित्रं चरुमावपति** ॥ ४८ ॥ **एवमेवैकादशकपालमधिश्रयति** ॥ ४९ ॥ **पात्रियामप आनीय** 'त्वचं गृह्णीष्व' **इति त्रिरद्भिस्त्वचं ग्राहयति।** '०अग्निस्ते त्वचं मा हिꣳसीत्' **इति** ॥ ५० ॥ 'महीनां पयोऽसि' **इति तिरः पवित्रमाज्यं निर्वपति।** '०अपामोषधीनाꣳ रसस्तस्य ते पयसः पिबमानस्याक्षितस्याक्षीयमाणस्य निर्वपामि देवयज्यायै' **इति** ॥ ५१ ॥ **तदुत्तरतोऽङ्गारान्निरूह्याधिश्रयति** ॥ ५२ ॥ **उपनिदधात्यस्मै दधिसान्नाय्यम्, अथ शृतम्** ॥ ५३ ॥ **अथ दर्व्योपवेषेण वाऽङ्गारमादाय** 'अन्तरितꣳ रक्षोऽन्तरिता अरातयः' **इति प्रसलैस्त्रिः पर्यग्निकरोति** ॥ ५४ ॥ **अपिसृज्याङ्गारम्** 'अविदहन्तः श्रपयत' **इति वाचं विसृजते** ॥ २.२.१.५५ ॥ **[इति प्रथमः पटलः (६)]**

[वेदिकरणम्]

'अविदहन्त श्रपयत' **इति वाचं विसृजते।** '०मेक्षय चरुम्' **इति** ॥ १ ॥ 'देवस्त्वा सविता श्रपयतु' **इत्यनुपूर्वꣳ हवीꣳष्यभिमृशति।** '०वर्षिष्ठे अधिनाके' **इति** ॥ २ ॥ 'अग्निस्ते तनुवं माऽति

सर्वाणि कपालान्यभिप्रथयति। अत्र पुरोडाशसंस्थानविशेषोत्तुंगमित्याद्यनुपदे द्रष्टव्यम्। उत्तुंगमश्वशफमात्रं, कूर्माकृतिं पुरोडाशं त्र्यङ्गुलोत्सेध[1]मपरिमितोत्सेधं वा ॥ ४७ ॥

पात्र्यामप आनीय तासां पुरोडाशमानीय[2] परिमृज्य त्वचं करोति[2] ॥ ५० ॥

आज्यनिर्वपणं मन्त्रब्राह्मणयोः स्रुक्संमार्गपत्नीसन्नहनोत्तरकालं विहितम्। इह पुरोडाशं चाधिश्रयत्याज्यं चेति द्वन्द्वसंपादने दर्शनाद्विहितमाचार्येण। आज्यशब्दो यद्यप्यजादीनामपि तुल्यः तथापि 'महीनां पयोसी'ति मन्त्रलिंगाच्छागो वा मन्त्रवर्णादित्यनेनैव न्यायेन गव्यस्यैव ग्रहणम्। मही इति गोनाम, पय इति प्रकृतिशब्दो विकारस्य निरुप्यमाणस्योपलक्षणार्थः। गवामाज्यमसीत्यर्थः। अथापि ब्राह्मणे 'तस्माद् गवि सते' इत्यादिना प्रकरण एव विहितम्॥ ५१ ॥

'धर्मो[3] वा एष' इत्यादिना पुरोडाशस्य विहितं सत् पर्यग्निकरणं सान्नाय्योपनिधानदर्शनात्सर्वविषयमित्यनुमीयते। अन्य आह—श्रुतिवाक्यस्य पुरोडाशविषयत्वे ज्ञात[4] उपनिधानदर्शनमात्रेण सर्वविषयता न कल्पयितव्येति॥ २.२.१.५४॥ **[इति प्रथमः पटलः (६)]**

'हवींषी'ति बहुवचननिर्देशादविशेषेण सर्वहविर्विषयमभिदर्शनम्। अथवा [5]श्रपणलिंगादौषधहविर्विषयं केचिदाहुः। पुरोडाशं वाऽधिश्रितमित्यारभ्य विहितत्वात् पुरोडाशविषयमेव। अविवक्षितं बहुवचनमिति। युक्तमध्यवसेयम्॥ २ ॥

अवज्वलनाभिवासने पुरोडाशविषये प्रत्येकं च स्याताम्। इह वाग्विसर्गदर्शनात्संवपनप्रभृतिवाग्यमत्वमवगम्यते।[6] पवित्रादानात्पूर्वं प्रेषणे[7] क्रियमाणे[8] विश्वस्ताः कुशलाः श्रपयन्ति। आग्नीध्रश्चरुं

---

१. M Ad ०लोत्वेधम०. **२-२.** M परिमृज्य...करोति; Ad ०मृज्य निर्वपणं करोति; T ०ज्यात्वचं करोति. **३.** M Ad घर्मो. **४.** M Ad जात. **५.** M Ad श्रवण०. **६.** M Ad वाग्यम्यत्व०. **७.** M Ad पेषणे; thus T. **८.** M Ad om; thus T.

धाक्' **इति तृणैरवज्वालयति** ॥ ३ ॥ 'अग्ने ब्रह्म गृह्णीष्व' **इति भस्मनाऽभिवासयति।** '°अतमेरुर्यज्ञोऽतमेरुर्यजमानोऽतमेरवो यजमानस्य पशवः' **इति** ॥ ४ ॥ **तूष्णीं पात्रीं च बर्हिश्च स्फ्यं च संक्षालनं चादायाहवनीयस्यार्धमेति** ॥ ५ ॥ **अन्तर्वेद्येकां लेखां लिखत्युत्तरेंऽसे, बहिर्वेदि द्वे** ॥ ६ ॥ 'एकताय स्वाहा' **इत्यन्तर्वेदि निनयति;** 'द्विताय स्वाहा', 'त्रिताय स्वाहा' **इति बहिर्वेदि** ॥ ७ ॥ **तूष्णीमुल्मुकेनाभितप्य निर्णिज्य पात्रीं मार्जयित्वा प्रक्षाल्य स्फ्यं च बर्हिश्चान्तर्वेदि निनयति** ॥ ८ ॥ **वेद्यामग्नीच्चाध्वर्युश्चोपविशतः** ॥ ९ ॥ **पश्चात्प्रागावृत्तोऽग्नीद् दक्षिणं जान्वाच्योत्कर उपसीदति** ॥ १० ॥ 'देवस्य त्वा सवितुः प्रसवे' **इति स्फ्यमादत्ते।** '°अश्विनो=माददे' **इति** ॥ ११ ॥ 'शतभृष्टिरसि वानस्पत्यः' **इत्येनं बर्हिषा संमार्ष्टि।** '°द्विषतो वधः। इन्द्रस्य बाहुरसि दक्षिणः सहस्रभृष्टिः = तेजा मा मा हिꣳसीः' **इति** ॥ १२ ॥ 'देवस्य सवितुः सवे' **इत्यन्तर्वेद्युदीचीनाग्रं बर्हिर्निदधाति** ॥ १३ ॥ 'पृथिवि देवयजन्योषध्यास्ते मूलं मा हिꣳसिषम्' **इति स्फ्येन प्रहरति** ॥ १४ ॥ 'व्रजं गच्छ गोस्थानम्' **इत्युत्करस्यार्धꣳ हरति** ॥ १५ ॥ 'वर्षतु ते द्यौः' **इति वेदिं प्रत्यवेक्षते** ॥ १६ ॥ 'बधान देव सवितः' **इत्युत्करे निबाधते।** '°परमस्यां परावति शतेन

मेक्षयति। भस्मना साङ्गारेणाभिवासनं यथा सम्यक् श्रपणार्थं[1] भवति। [2]वेदसंस्पर्शनं वेदेनाभिवासनम्[2] ॥ ३–४ ॥

[3]श्रुतिमुत्सृज्यान्यग्रहणस्यान्याय्यत्वात् तूष्णीं ग्रहणस्य च[3] 'सं ब्रह्मणा पृच्यस्वे'त्यस्य प्रतिषेधार्थत्वात् बहुवचनमविवक्षितम्। केचिदन्यथा[4] बहुवचनं परिहरन्ति वैमृधापेक्षमिति। किमिदं [5]वैमृधं नाम। ब्राह्मणे[5] यद् वैमृधः पूर्णमासेऽनुनिर्वाप्यो भवति पौर्णमास्यां विहितः[6]। ननु तस्य संस्थाप्य पौर्णमासीं वैमृधमनु निर्वपतीति नानातन्त्रता[7] विहिता। सत्यम्। विहिता वैमृधः पौर्णमासेऽनु[8]। निर्वास्या[9] सेन्द्रेति दध्ना [10]तुल्यवत्प्रसंख्यानात्[10]समानतन्त्रतापीष्यत इति मन्यामहे। अतस्तदपेक्षं बहुवचनमिति ॥ ५ ॥

अभिग्रहणे उल्मुको गार्हपत्याद् गृह्यते [11]श्रपणलिंगात् 'देवस्त्वे'ति [12]श्रपणमन्त्रप्राप्त्याशंका- निवृत्त्यर्थं तूष्णीं ग्रहणं पूर्वमेव [13]तत्रोपविष्टयोर्ब्रह्मयजमानयोर्दक्षिणत[13] इति विधानं कालान्तरेऽपि[14] क्रियमाणे तत्रैवानयोरुपवेशनार्थम्[15]। आग्नीध्र [16]उत्करमभिगृह्योत्करसमीप उपविशति ॥ ८–१० ॥

वेदेन[16] वेदिं संमृज्य स्फ्यं च बर्हिश्च सादयति। बर्हिः परिभोजनीयाद् ग्रहीतव्यम्[17] ॥ ११–१३ ॥

'स्फ्येन [18]प्रहरतीति' बर्हिषो मूलं वेद्या एकदेशं च। तदुभयमुत्तरस्यार्धं हरति[18] ॥ १४–१५ ॥

---

१. M Ad श्रवणा°. २–२. M वेदस...वेदेना° ; thus T. ३–३. T takes it as additional and gives in fn. a. ४. T takes केचिदन्यथा as additional. ५–५. M वैमृधापे....यद्वैमृधः, Ad om ब्राह्मणं. ६. M Ad विहितम्. ७. M Ad °तनूता; thus T. ८. M Ad °पूर्णमासे. ९. M Ad नि=वास्या. १०–१०. M दध्ना ...नात् सामन; Ad वत संख्यानात् सामनः. ११. M Ad श्रवण°. १२. M Ad श्रवण°. १३–१३. M तन्त्रोपतिष्टये ... दक्षिणत; Ad तन्त्रो°. १४. M Ad °न्तरेविक्रिय°. १५. M Ad °नार्थः. १६–१६. M उत् ...गृह्यो°. उप विश...देन वेदीन्; thus T. १७. M Ad °तव्या. १८–१८. M प्रहरतीति...तदुभयमुद्गरस्याध्व. गरति; Ad बर्हिषोतमूलं वेद्य एक° मुद्गरस्य° ; thus T.

पाशैर्योऽस्मान् द्वेष्टि यं च वयं द्विष्मस्तमतो मा मौक्' **इति**॥ १७॥ **द्वितीयं प्रहरति** 'देवयजनात्पृथिव्याः पृथिवि देवयजन्योषध्यास्ते मूलं मा हिꣳसिषम्' **इति**॥ १८॥ 'व्रजं गच्छ गोस्थानम्' **इत्येवोत्करस्यार्धꣳ हरति**॥ १९॥ 'वर्षतु ते द्यौः' **इत्येव वेदिं प्रत्यवेक्षते**॥ २०॥ 'बधान देव सवितः' **इत्येवोत्करे निबाधते**। '°परमस्यां=मा मौक्' **इति**॥ २१॥ **तृतीयं प्रहरति** 'देवयजनात् पृथिव्याः पृथिवि देवयजन्योषध्यास्ते मूलं मा हिꣳसिषम्' **इति**॥ २२॥ 'व्रजं गच्छ गोस्थानम्' **इत्येवोत्करस्यार्धꣳ हरति**॥ २३॥ 'वर्षतु ते द्यौः' **इत्येव वेदिं प्रत्यवेक्षते**॥ २४॥ 'बधान देव सवितः' **इत्येवोत्करे निबाधते**। '°परमस्यां=मा मौग् अररुस्ते दिवं मा स्कान्' **इति**॥ २५॥ **तूष्णीं चतुर्थꣳ हरति सबर्हिषा**॥ २६॥ 'वसवस्त्वा परिगृह्णन्तु गायत्रेण छन्दसा' **इति दक्षिणतः प्राचीꣳ स्फ्येन वेदिं परिगृह्णाति**॥ २७॥ 'रुद्रास्त्वा परिगृह्णन्तु त्रैष्टुभेन छन्दसा' **इति पश्चादुदीचीम्**॥ २८॥ 'आदित्यास्त्वा परिगृह्णन्तु जागतेन छन्दसा' **इत्युत्तरतः प्राचीम्**॥ २९॥ 'इमां नराः कृणुत वेदिमेत्य' **इति करणं जपति**। '°वसुमतीं=रिष्येत्' **इति**॥ ३०॥ 'अग्नीदितस्त्रिर्हर' **इत्याहाग्नीध्रम्**॥ ३१॥ **समुद्धतस्य त्रिरग्नीद्धृत्वा हस्तेन संमार्ष्टि**॥ ३२॥ **अथाह** 'ब्रह्मन्नुत्तरं परिग्राहं परिग्रहीष्यामि' **इति**॥ ३३॥ 'ऋतसदसि' **इति दक्षिणतः प्राचीं स्फ्येन वेदिं परिगृह्णाति**॥ ३४॥ 'सत्यसदसि' **इति पश्चादुदीचीम्**॥ ३५॥ 'घर्मसदसि' **इत्युत्तरतः प्राचीम्**॥ ३६॥ 'धा असि स्वधा असि' **इति प्रतीचीꣳ स्फ्येन वेदिं योयुप्यते**॥ ३७॥ **समुद्धन्ति**॥ ॥ २.२.२.३८॥ **[इति द्वितीयः पटलः** (७)**]**

ननु चतुर्थे [1]हरणे बर्हिषेति वक्ष्यति तद्वैधर्म्येण चात्र भवितव्यम्। उच्यते। छेदस्य विहरणार्थत्वे प्रयोजनवत्त्वम्[1]। इतरथाऽदृष्टार्थं छेदनं[2] स्यात्। अपि च केचिदति[3]शिष्टेन बर्हिषेति[3] चतुर्थे [4]हरणे पठन्ति॥ २६॥

'इमां नरा' इति मन्त्रो न कर्मकरणम्[4]। [5]विकृतिषु करणं वा[5] जपतीति *दर्शनात्॥ ३०॥

उद्धनने [6]तस्माच्चतुरङ्गुलं खननमित्यादि[6] द्रष्टव्यम्। आग्नीध्रस्य हरणे हस्तेनेति केचित्। अपरे हस्तसंमार्गसाधनत्वेन। श्रूयते हरणं तु पूर्वं येन दृष्टं तेनैवेति॥ ३१–३२॥

[7]अथ शब्दः कालान्तरे[7] क्रियमाणस्य वेदिकरणस्यैतावत्वसूचकः। प्राचीमुदीचीं प्रवणां करोति।* दक्षिणतो वर्षीयसीं[8] करोतीत्यादि द्रष्टव्यम्॥ ३३–३६॥

योयुपनं[9] समीकरणम्॥ २.२.२.३७–३८॥ **[इति द्वितीयः पटलः** (७)**]**

१–१. M हरणे...याजन°, Ad हरणे...वक्ष्यति; ° धानम्येन चान्त्रतव्यम् उच्यते छेतस्य ग्रहणा°. **२.** M Ad दृष्टार्था देनं. **३–३.** M शिष्टेन ... षेति. **४–४.** M हरणेति...मन्त्रो न कर्मकरणः करणः Ad चतुर्थेहरणे इमां न दा इति° करणः; thus T. **५–५.** M °षु करं, Ad °पुष्करं वा. T takes the text विकृतिषुकरं as additional not a part of the text. ***–***. T wrongly gives the text in fn, not in the body of the text. M Ad rightly give the text under the body of the text as the part of comm. on sūtra 30-36. **६–६.** M तस्माच्च...नु...लंघेयेत्या°; thus T. **७–७.** M Ad अथ...काला°. **८.** T °यसी. **९.** T यायोपवनं; M Ad योयोपनं.

[प्रोक्षणीरासादनं स्फ्यप्रक्षालनं स्रुक्संमार्जनञ्च]

'अग्नीत् प्रोक्षणीरासादयेध्माबर्हिरुपसादय स्रुवं च स्रुचश्च संमृड्ढि पत्नीं सन्नह्याज्येनोदेहि' **इति** ॥ १ ॥ **मार्जयित्वाऽग्नीत् स्फ्यस्य वर्त्मन्नुपनिनीय प्रोक्षणीः सादयति** 'अमुष्य त्वा प्राणे सादयामि' **इति** ॥ २ ॥ **उत्तरेणोत्करं स्फ्यं निहन्ति** ॥ ३ ॥ **यं देष्टि यजमानस्तं ध्यायति** ॥ ४ ॥ **अप उपस्पृश्य मार्जयित्वा प्रक्षाल्य स्फ्यमागत्य वेदपरिवासनैः स्रुचः संमार्ष्टि** ॥ ५ ॥ 'स्रुवोऽस्यनाधृष्टः सपत्नसाहः' **इति स्रुवमादत्ते** ॥ ६ ॥ 'प्रत्युष्टꣳ रक्षः प्रत्युष्टा अरातयः' **इति गार्हपत्ये निष्टपति** ॥ ७ ॥ 'आयुः प्राणं मा निर्मृक्षम्' **इति संमार्ष्टि**। '°वाजिनं त्वा सपत्नसाहꣳ संमार्ज्मि' **इति त्रिरन्तरतः सकृदधस्तात्** ॥ ८ ॥ **तं निष्टप्य प्रयच्छति** ॥ ९ ॥ 'जुहूरस्यनाधृष्टा सपत्नसाही' **इति जुहूमादत्ते** ॥ १० ॥ 'प्रत्युष्टꣳ रक्षः प्रत्युष्टा अरातयः' **इत्येव गार्हपत्ये निष्टपति** ॥ ११ ॥ 'चक्षुः श्रोत्रं मा निर्मृक्षम्' **इति संमार्ष्टि**। '°वाजिनीं त्वा सपत्नसाहीꣳ संमार्ज्मि' **इति त्रिरेवान्तरतः सकृदधस्तात्** ॥ १२ ॥ **तां निष्टप्यैव प्रयच्छति** ॥ १३ ॥ 'उपभृदस्यनाधृष्टा सपत्नसाही' **इत्युपभृतमादत्ते** ॥ १४ ॥ 'प्रत्युष्टꣳ रक्षः प्रत्युष्टा अरातयः' **इत्येव गार्हपत्ये निष्टपति** ॥ १५ ॥ 'प्रजां योनिं मा निर्मृक्षम्' **इति संमार्ष्टि**। '°वाजिनीं त्वा सपत्नसाहीꣳ संमार्ज्मि' **इति त्रिरेवान्तरतः सकृदधस्तात्** ॥ १६ ॥ **तां निष्टप्यैव प्रयच्छति** ॥ १७ ॥ 'ध्रुवाऽस्यनाधृष्टा सपत्नसाही' **इति**

'*अग्नीत् प्रोक्षणीरा=देही*'ति। प्रैषपदार्थानां प्रथमस्याग्नीत् कर्ता[१] दर्शितः। अतः सर्वेषामाग्नीध्र[२] एव कर्ता।[२] अन्य आह–स्फ्यनिहननमाध्वर्यवम्। तस्य हि हस्ते स्फ्यः। तत्कृतवतश्चाप[३] उपस्पर्शनमार्जन[४] स्फ्यप्रक्षालनसंमार्जनानि ॥ १–३ ॥

प्रक्षाल्य स्फ्यम् आगत्य वेदपरिवासनैः स्रुचः संमार्ष्टीति समानकर्तृत्वं गम्यते। अतः संमार्गादीनामाध्वर्यवत्वमपि [५]वरुणप्रघासेषु 'यदेवाध्वर्युः[६] करोति तत्प्रतिप्रस्थाता करोति' इति चोदितेन प्रतिप्रस्थात्रा[७] कर्तव्यः स्रुक्संमार्गो दृश्यते। 'स्रुवौ स्रुचः संमृष्ट आज्यानि गृह्णीत' इति संमार्गाज्यग्रहणयोः समानकर्तृकता दृश्यते। [८]तस्मादाध्वर्यवा इत्युच्यन्ते[८]। आत्मनि प्रेषणस्य[९] विप्रतिषेधात् प्रेषितेनान्येन भवितव्यम्। स च पारिशेष्यात्प्रदर्शितत्वाच्चाग्नीत् स्यात्। [१०]यदुक्तम् अप उपस्पर्शनादीनां समानकर्तृकत्वमि'ति। प्रक्षाल्य स्फ्यमित्युक्ते चावश्यमन्यदध्याहर्तव्यं सादयतीत्यादि। तेन [११]विरहितत्वात्समानकर्तृकता न भवति। अवश्यमिध्माबर्हिषोः सादनम्। प्रैषचोदितं प्रक्षालनोत्तरकालं कर्तव्यमस्ति। तच्चाध्याहार्यम्। इध्माबर्हिरुपसाद्यागत्य संमार्ष्टीत्यवगन्तव्यम्। यदुक्तं वरुणप्रघासेषु प्रतिप्रस्थातृदर्शनं तत् परिहर्तव्यम्[१२]। इह विप्रतिषेधादाचार्येणाग्नीच्चोदितो न वचनाद्यश्चार्थादर्थो न तच्चोदकः प्रापयतीति

---

१. M Ad °ग्नीत्, T °ग्नीध्रः. **२–२.** M °षामा...व कर्ता, Ad °ग्नीध. **३.** M Ad T ततु तपतश्च. **४.** M Ad °मार्जने. **५.** T add तद्; before वरुण°. **६.** M Ad °ध्वर्यः. **७.** Ad °प्रस्थाता. **८–८.** M तस्मदध्वर्यवा इ...हन्ते; Ad तस्मादध्व°; T उच्यते. **९.** M Ad प्रश्नस्य. **१०.** M तदु°. **११.** M Ad विहित°, T रहित°. **१२.** M प...र्तव्यम्.

ध्रुवामादत्ते ॥ १८ ॥ 'प्रत्युष्टꣳ रक्षः प्रत्युष्टा अरातयः' **इत्येव गार्हपत्ये निष्टपति** ॥ १९ ॥ 'गोष्ठाद्रयिं मा निर्मृक्षम्' **इति संमार्ष्टि**। '°वाजिनीं त्वा सपत्नसाहीꣳ संमार्ज्मि' **इति त्रिरेवान्तरतः सकृदधस्तात्** ॥ २० ॥ **तां निष्टप्यैव प्रयच्छति** ॥ २१ ॥ **तूष्णीं प्राशित्रहरणमादाय** 'प्रत्युष्टꣳ रक्षः प्रत्युष्टा अरातयः' **इत्येव गार्हपत्ये निष्टपति** ॥ २२ ॥ 'रूपाद्वर्णं मा निर्मृक्षम्' **इति संमार्ष्टि**। '°वाजिनं त्वा सपत्नसाहꣳ संमार्ज्मि' **इति त्रिरेवान्तरतः सकृदधस्तात्** ॥ २३ ॥ **तन्निष्टप्यैव प्रयच्छति** ॥ २४॥ **अद्भिर्वेदपरिवासनानि सꣳस्पृश्य सञ्चर उदस्यति** ॥ २५ ॥ **हृत्वा स्रुचोऽपरे-णोत्करं तृणानि संस्तीर्योदगावृत्तान्यनुपूर्वꣳ सꣳसादयति** ॥ २.२.३.२६ ॥ **[इति तृतीयः पटलः** (८)**]**

[पत्नीसन्नहनं बर्हिरादिप्रोक्षणं वेद्यां हविरासादनञ्च]

आगत्यापरेण गार्हपत्यमासीनां पत्नीꣳ सन्नह्यति 'आशासाना=सुकृताय कम्' **इति** ॥ १ ॥ 'सुप्रजसस्त्वा वयम्' **इत्येनामुपनिषदं वाचयति**। '°सुपत्नीरुप सेदिम=अदब्धासो अदाभ्यम्' **इति** ॥ २ ॥ 'इन्द्राणीवाविधवा भूयासम्' **इत्युपनिषदम्**। '°अदितिरिव सुपुत्रा अस्थूरि त्वाग्ने गार्ह-पत्युपनिषदम्' **इति** ॥ ३ ॥ 'पयस्वतीरोषधयः' **इति तिरःपवित्रमप आशयति**। '°पयस्वद्वीरुधां प=सृज' **इति** ॥ ४ ॥ 'अग्ने व्रतपते' **इति मार्जयित्वा समिधमाधापयति**। '°व्रतं च=ध्यताꣳ स्वाहा' **इति** ॥ ५ ॥ 'आज्यमसि' **इत्येनामाज्ये वाचयति**। '°अदब्धेन त्वा चक्षुषाऽवेक्षे प्रजायै मे निकामधारणमसि सुप्रजास्त्वाय' **इति** ॥ ६ ॥ 'तेजोऽसि तेजोऽनुप्रेहि' **इत्यादायाज्यꣳ हरति** ॥ ७ ॥

न्यायविदां दर्शनम्। तत्र च विप्रतिषेधो नास्ति चोदकप्राप्तेश्चाभाव उक्तः। यच्च 'स्रुचः समृष्ट आज्यानि गृह्णीत' [1]इति समानकर्तृकता[1] दृश्यत इति। अनुवादत्वान्नास्ति दोषः। यथासंभवश्चानुवादो व्याख्येयः। अत एषामनाध्वर्यवत्वं मन्यामहे। पश्चात्प्रागुपसादयति। दक्षिणमिध्ममुत्तरं बर्हिरुत्तरत आहवनीयस्य। स्रुक्संमार्गप्रकारा [2]ब्राह्मणे विहिता ग्रहीतव्याः[2] 'अग्रतः संमृज्यादि'त्यादयः ॥ ५-२५ ॥

यस्य हस्ते स्रुचः प्रयच्छति स एव स्रुचस्तृणेषु सादयति तत्सूचनार्थमत्र पटलावसानम् ॥ २.२.३.२६ ॥ **[इति तृतीयः पटलः** (८)**]**

'आगत्या[3]=सन्नह्यति'। अत्र पत्न्या आगमनचोदनात् पूर्वेषु कर्मसु स्वामिन्याऽपि नावश्यं सन्नि-हितया भवितव्यमिति बोधयति[4]। अथ[5] 'यजमान[6] वाचं यच्छे'त्यादिषु तस्या व्रतं नास्ति। 'अपरेण गार्हपत्यमि'त्युक्तापि सन्नहनकाले 'देशाद्दक्षिणत उदीच्यन्वास्ते'। सन्नह्यति सन्नाहयतीत्यर्थः ॥ १ ॥

व्रतमुपेत्य पश्चात् प्राच्यासीना[7] आज्यमवेक्षेत। आज्यमवतार्य वेदे प्रतिष्ठाप्य तदीक्षमाणां वाचयति ॥ ६ ॥

पुनर्गार्हपत्येऽधिश्रित्य 'तेजोऽसि तेजोऽनुप्रेही'त्यादाय[8] 'वायुस्त्वा' इत्यादिना हरति यदि

१-१. M इति...ाकर्तृ°. **२-२.** M ब्राह्मण वि...ग्रही°; thus Ad T. **३.** T °आगत्याः. **४.** M °मिति...धयति. **५.** M Ad अतो; thus T. **६.** T °यजमानवाचं यच्छेदिति. **७.** M Ad °सीन आ; thus T. **८.** M Ad °त्यादयाः.

'वायुस्त्वाऽन्तरिक्षात्पातु सूर्यो दिवः' **इति।** 'अग्निस्ते हरो मा प्रतिधाक्षीत्' **इत्याहवनीयेऽधिश्रयति, यदि पत्न्यन्वास्ते ॥** ८ ॥ 'देवेभ्य ऊर्जे सीद' **इत्युत्तरेण प्रोक्षणीः सादयति ॥** ९ ॥ 'अग्नेर्जिह्वासि' **इत्येनदेवान्तरावकाशेनावेक्षते।** '०सुभूर्देवानां धाम्नेधाम्ने देवेभ्यो यजुषेयजुषे भव' **इति ॥** १० **॥** 'एहि यजमान' **इत्याह ॥** ११ **॥ पूर्वेणाहवनीयं यजमानः परिक्रामति ॥** १२ **॥ उत्तरेण प्रणीता दक्षिणेनोत्करमुत्तरेण स्रुचोऽपरेण वेदिमत्याक्रम्य दक्षिणा उदगावृत्त उपविशति ॥** १३ **॥** 'आज्यमसि' **इत्येनमाज्ये वाचयति।** '०सत्यमसि=तस्य ते भक्षीय' **इति ॥** १४ **॥** 'असवे तन्मे गोपाय' **इत्यात्मनश्छायामवेक्षते ॥** १५ **॥** 'तेजोऽसि' **इत्येनदुदीचीनाग्राभ्यां पवित्राभ्यामाज्यं पुनाति।** '०शुक्रमसि ज्योतिरस्यमृतमस्युद्धूतशुष्मः सत्यौजाः' **इति ॥** १६ **॥ स्रुवं च जुहूं चादत्ते ॥**

पत्न्यान्वास्त[१] इति। सन्नहनादीनामधिश्रयणान्तानां शेषः। अनालंभुकायां[२] सर्वं निवर्तते। अथवाऽनन्तरस्यैव शेषः। तथा[३] सति 'तेजोऽसी'त्यादेरनिवृत्तिः। सन्नहनादीनां 'तामवरुध्य यजेते'त्यनेनैव हि[४] निवृत्तिः। क्रत्वर्थमप्याज्यावेक्षणान्निवर्तते। अनेकपत्नीकस्यैकयैवाज्यावेक्षणम् क्रत्वर्थत्वाद्। अन्ये आह—'सा यदि द्वयोर्वा तिसर्णां वैका स्यादि'त्यारभ्य 'ययाऽस्यै[५] कुशलं स्यात् सास्यैश्वरात् पत्नीकर्म कुर्यादि'ति। कयाचित्कर्तव्यं कर्म तदनुज्ञयाऽन्यया[६] कर्तव्यं विदधत्। क्रत्वर्थानामपि सर्वाभिः कर्तव्यतां ज्ञापयति[७]। तस्मात्सर्वाः कुर्युरिति। सत्रे यजमानानामात्मनः पत्न्या क्रत्वर्थेष्वप्यकृतेषु पत्न्या कृतं न भवति। पत्नी शब्दस्य संबन्धशब्दत्वादिति सत्रिविषयत्वं केचिन्मन्यन्ते। तत्र 'द्वयोर्वा तिसर्णां वे'ति परिगणनमनर्थकमिति चेत्, प्रदर्शनार्थं भवति। तथापि[८] अश्वमेधे 'त्रिभिरत्रायन्ती'ति सर्वासां पान्नेजनार्थं हरणदर्शनाद् 'एत्य प्रसिद्धमेव पशूनामाप्याययन्ती'ति बहुवचनदर्शनाच्च[९] क्रत्वर्थानामपि सर्वाभिः कर्तव्यता ज्ञायते। तत्रापि तस्मिन्नहनि कर्तव्यस्य कर्मकलापस्य महत्त्वात् प्रयोगप्राशुभावाय[१०] स्यात्॥ ७–८ ॥

यथा 'येऽग्निष्ठे तानध्वर्युः प्रतिप्रस्थाता चे'त्यादि अवान्तरावकाशेनावेक्षेते[११]। तत्को[१२] द्वितीयः प्रकृतत्वादाग्नीध्र इति केचित्। प्रैषचोदितेष्वेव कर्मसु तस्याधिकारः। अतो यजमान[१३] इत्यन्ये॥ १० ॥

[१४]आत्मनश्छायामवेक्षतेऽध्वर्युः 'असवे तन्मे[१४] गोपाये'ति एतावानेव मन्त्रः ॥ १५ ॥

आज्योत्पवनं त्रिः मन्त्रश्चावर्तते। तद् ब्राह्मणे प्रोक्षण्युत्पवनमाम्नातम्[१५] ॥ १६ ॥

अथाज्यवतीभ्यामप इत्युत्तरत्र[१६] चोदिङ्गनादि[१६] तद्धविःपात्रप्रोक्षणशेषानिधानपक्षे[१७]। तद्धि[१८] तत्र नास्ति। अतो[१८] यत्र शेषनिधानं तस्मिन्पक्षे तास्वेव बह्वीरानीय सादयति। इह चोत्पवनाद्यभावः। इतरस्मिन्

---

१. M Ad पल्यान्वा०. २. M Ad ०लम्भूका०; thus T. ३. M शेषः...सति. ४. M Ad om; thus T. ५. M यया...कुश०. ६. M Ad ०नुज्ञाय; thus T. ७. M Ad आपय०; thus T. ८. M ०वति...मश्व०. ९. T ०वचनाच्च, M ०वचनः...नाच्च. १०. M प्र...यस्यात्; Ad प्राशुभाय; thus T. ११. T वेक्षते. १२. M Ad को. १३. M यजान. १४–१४. M ०च्छाया...वेतन्मे; Ad ०वक्ष्यताध्वर्युः स वे तन्मे. १५. M Ad ०नमम्नातम्. १६–१६. M इत्युत्तर ...चोदिगङ्गनादि, T ०ज्यवतीभ्याम...कक्ष्यामप०. १७. M ०क्षण शेषनिधा०. १८–१८. M तद्धि...अतो; Ad तद्धि तन्त्रं०.

१७॥ **तस्यां गृह्णाति** 'तेजोऽसि धामासि प्रियं देवानामनाधृष्टं देवयजनम्' **इति चतुरः स्रुवान्**॥ १८॥ **ताꣳ संमृज्य प्रयच्छति**॥ १९॥ **उपभृतमादत्ते**॥ २०॥ **तस्यां गृह्णाति** 'शुक्रमसि धामासि प्रियं देवानामनाधृष्टं देवयजनम्' **इति चतुरः स्रुवान्**॥ २१॥ **तूष्णीमपराꣳश्चतुरोऽर्धस्रुवान्**॥ २२॥ **ताꣳ समृज्यैव प्रयच्छति**॥ २३॥ **ध्रुवामादत्ते**॥ २४॥ **तस्यां गृह्णाति** 'अमृतमसि धामासि प्रियं देवानामनाधृष्टं देवयजनम्' **इति चतुरः स्रुवान्**॥ २५॥ **चतुर्थे भूयोऽभ्यानयति**॥ २६॥ **पत्नीसंयाजेभ्योऽतिशिनष्टि**॥ २७॥ **ताꣳ संमृज्यैव प्रयच्छति**॥ २८॥ **अपरेण वेदिꣳ सस्रुवामाज्यस्थालीं निधाय तूष्णीं स्रुवेणावोक्षति**॥ २९॥ **उपोत्थाय** 'कृष्णोऽस्याखरेष्ठोऽग्नये त्वा जुष्टं प्रोक्षामि' **इति विस्रस्येध्मं प्रोक्षति**॥ ३०॥ 'वेदिरसि बर्हिषे त्वा जुष्टां प्रोक्षामि' **इति वेदिम्**॥ ३१॥ 'बर्हिरसि स्रुग्भ्यस्त्वा जुष्टं प्रोक्षामि' **इति बर्हिः**॥ ३२॥ 'प्रोक्षिताः स्थ' **इत्यद्भिरेवापः प्रोक्षति**॥ ३३॥ **अन्तर्वेदि पुरोग्रन्थि बर्हिरासाद्य** 'दिवे त्वा', 'अन्तरिक्षाय त्वा', 'पृथिव्यै त्वा' **इति प्रोक्षति**॥ ३४॥ **तूष्णीं पुरस्ताद् ग्रन्थिमभिषिञ्चति, तूष्णीं पश्चात्**॥ ३५॥ 'शुन्धतां लोकः पितृषदनः' **इति दक्षिणायाꣳ श्रोण्यां निनयति**॥ ३६॥ 'ऊर्जं पृथिवीं गच्छत स्वधा पितृभ्य ऊर्ग् भव बर्हिषद्भ्यः' **इति सन्ततमेवोत्तरस्यै श्रोण्यै निनीयापरेणात्मानं पूर्वेणोत्कर उदूह्य**

पक्षे रिक्तायां स्रुचि बह्वीरानीय सादयति। इह चोत्पवनादि[1] कर्तव्यम्[1]। इतरस्मिन्[2] पक्षद्वयेऽप्याज्यवती। पवित्रे तासु प्रक्षिपति। आज्यग्रहणे पञ्चगृहीतिनो[3]ऽन्त्यानां मन्त्राणामावृत्तिः॥ १७-२६॥

पत्नीसंयाज्येभ्य उच्छिनष्टि। पत्नीसंयाजग्रहणमपराग्न्योः कर्तव्यानां होमानां[4] प्रदर्शनार्थमाहवनीयकर्तव्यानां निवृत्यर्थं च। [5]इतरदपि ध्रुवाप्रत्यञ्जनादि[5] क्रियते। एवं हि[6] 'नाज्यस्थाल्या अध्याहवनीये[7] जुहोति न ध्रुवाया[8] अधीतरयोरि'ति शाखान्तरे वचनमस्ति। तद्धोममात्रं निवर्तयति, न प्रत्यञ्जनादि। यत्राज्यग्रहणे स्रुग्धारणं[9] क्रियते स धरुणप्रदेशः॥ २७॥

'दिवे त्वा' 'अन्तरिक्षाय त्वा' [10]'पृथिव्यै त्वा' इति त्रिः प्रोक्षति।[10] मन्त्रत्रित्वात् प्रोक्षणमप्यावर्तते। अथवा सर्वैर्मन्त्रैः सकृदेव प्रोक्षणम्। तथा चानुपदकार आह—'दिवे त्वा' इत्यग्राणि, 'अन्तरिक्षाय त्वा' इति मध्यानि, 'पृथिव्यै त्वा' इति मूलानि, 'समस्तैरित्यपरमि'ति॥ ३४॥

ऊर्ध्वाग्रं शुल्बाग्रं प्रत्यञ्चमायम्य[11] [12]विस्रस्य बर्हिरित्यादि[12]। पुरस्तात् सपवित्रं प्रस्तरं गृह्णाति। सपवित्रमित्यविशेषवचनात् शाखापवित्रमपि विसृजन्ति[13] केचित्। तथा च प्रस्तरप्रहरणे सह शाखयेति शाखान्तरे वचनमस्ति। तच्चानुगृहीतं भवति। तस्मिन् पवित्रे अपि सृजतीति[14]। 'अथ प्रस्तरे पवित्रं

१-१. M °नादि क...पक्ष, T °नाद्यभावः. २. M Ad om; thus T. ३. T पञ्चगृहीतोऽन्त्या°. ४. M Ad om; thus T. ५-५. M इतरदपि ...त्यञ्ज°. T इतरदपि इत्यञ्जनादि; thus Ad. ६. M Ad om; thus T. ७. Ad om अधि. ८. M Ad ध्रुवाय; thus T. ९. M Ad °धरणं; thus T. १०-१०. M पृथिव्यै...मन्त्र° Ad om इति, T om त्रिः. ११. M Ad व्यत्यञ्चमया°; thus T. १२-१२. M विस..रित्या°; thus Ad T. १३. M Ad T °प्यविसृजति. १४. M Ad °पवित्रे अविसृजतीति; thus T.

प्रोक्षणीधानं बर्हिर्विस्रस्य 'विष्णोः स्तूपोऽसि' **इति पुरस्तात् प्रस्तरं गृह्णाति ॥** ३७ **॥ तं यजमानाय प्रयच्छति, ब्रह्मणे वा ॥** ३८ **॥ सव्ये वा हस्ते कुरुते ॥** ३९ **॥ साग्रं सन्नहनं कृत्वा दक्षिणायाः श्रोण्यां निदधाति ॥** ४० **॥** 'देवबर्हिः' **इत्येतद् बर्हिर्मुष्टिनाऽभिच्छादयति।** '०ऊर्णाम्रद=देवेभ्यः' **इति ॥** ४१ **॥** 'उरु यज्ञाय' **इति त्रीन् प्राचो मुष्टीन् प्रकिरति।** '०उरु यजमानायोरु ते यज्ञपतिः प्रथताम्' **इति ॥** ४२ **॥** 'स्तृणीत बर्हि' **इति वाचं विसृजते ॥** ४३ **॥ अथ पश्चात् त्रिवृद् बर्हिः स्तृणन्त्यनतिदृश्नम् ॥** ४४ **॥ प्रस्तरमादाय प्राङुत्सृप्य परिधीन् परिदधाति ॥** ४५ **॥** 'गन्धर्वोऽसि विश्वावसुः' **इति मध्यमं परिधिम्।** '०विश्वस्मान्नेत्राद् यजमानस्य परिधिरसीड ईडितः' **इति ॥** ४६ **॥** 'इन्द्रस्य बाहुरसि दक्षिणतः' **इति दक्षिणार्ध्यम्।** '०विश्वस्मा=डितः' **इति ॥** ४७ **॥** 'मित्रावरुणौ त्वोत्तरतः परिधत्ताम्' **इत्युत्तरार्ध्यम्।** '०ध्रुवेण धर्मणा विश्वस्मा=ईडितः' **इति ॥** ४८ **॥** 'सूर्यस्त्वा पुरस्तात्पातु' **इति दक्षिणतः समिधमा दधाति।** '०कस्याश्चिदभिशस्त्या=मध्वरे वर्षिष्ठेऽधिनाके स्वाहा' **इति ॥** ४९ **॥ तूष्णीमुत्तरत आदधाति ॥** ५० **॥** 'ध्रुवोऽसि ध्रुवोऽहꣳ सजातेषु भूयासम्' **इति मध्यमे परिधौ वाचयति।** '०धीरश्चेता वसुविद्' **इति ॥** ५१ **॥** 'उग्रोऽस्युग्रोऽहꣳ सजातेषु भूयासम्'

विसृजती'ति[१] दर्शनादनयोरेव दर्भाग्रयोरविसर्गः[२]। द्विवचनं समुदायद्वयापेक्षमिति पौरस्त्य उपपद्यते यद्यपि नापिसृज्यते। प्रस्तरसादनकाले शाखापवित्रमपि[३] सादयति ॥ ३७ ॥

यदि सादयति पुरस्तादितरेभ्यो मुष्टिभ्यः पूर्वं साग्रं सन्नहनं कृत्वा [४]समाग्रमित्यर्थः ॥ ४० ॥

प्राचो[४] मुष्टीन् प्रकिरति। प्रकिरणे त्रीभिर्मुष्टिभिः [५]समस्ता वेदिर्व्याप्यते[५] ॥ ४२ ॥

ततः 'स्तृणीत बर्हि'रित्युक्ते तथैव द्विः समस्ता वेदिः स्तीर्यते ॥ ४३ ॥

तथा त्रिवृद् भवति पुरस्तादेवाग्रेऽथ पश्चात्। अथ पश्चादिति सूत्रकारवचनम्। तथा सति प्राग्गताः पूर्वं [६]पूर्वभाग इत्यर्थः[६]। त्रीन्मुष्टीनुदगपवर्गं[७] स्तीर्त्वा 'स्तृणीते'ति प्रेष्यति। प्रेषितो मध्यमभागं स्तीर्त्वाऽपरभागं स्तृणाति तथा त्रिवृद् भवति। अनुपदकारेणाम्नातम्—'दक्षिणं पक्षं प्राञ्चं स्तृणुयात्, प्रत्यञ्चं मध्यमं, प्राञ्चमुत्तमम्। सर्वा वा प्राचीं स्वर्गकामस्य[८], सर्वा वा प्रतीचीमायुष्कामस्य[९], प्रतिषजन् धातूनुभयकामस्य। प्राचीं स्तीर्त्वा प्रतीचीं स्तीर्त्वा प्राचीं स्तृणुयादपवर्गं करोती'ति। अस्मिन्पक्षे दक्षिणत एव पक्षत्रये कार्यः। स्तृणीतेत्यादि तथा यथोक्तं स्तृणुयात्। तथा च त्रिवृद् भवति स्तृणीतेति। स्तृणन्तीति बहुवचननिर्देशादनियतः[१०] कर्ता। अन्ये परिशेष्यादाग्नीध्र इति ॥ ४४ ॥

'सूर्यस्त्वा पुरस्तात् पात्वि'ति समिदाधानमन्त्रावयमेव [११]केचिदिच्छन्ति। अन्ये लिङ्गादाह[११]वनीयाभिमन्त्रणम् ॥ ४९ ॥

मध्यमे परिधौ वाचयति। एवं तर्हि[१२] ऊर्ध्वं समिदाधानात्पूर्वं[१३] वक्तव्यम्। किमर्थम्।

---

१. M Ad जति द० ; thus T. **२.** M Ad ०ग्रयोरपि सर्गः. **३.** M Ad ०त्रः यदि साद० ; thus T. **४-४.** M समाग्रमि...प्राचो. **५-५.** M Ad ०स्तां वेदिं व्यप्यते; thus T. **६-६.** M पूर्वभाग...र्थः. **७.** M Ad ०वर्गः; thus T. **८.** M Ad ०कामन्यः; thus T. **९.** M म...मस्य. **१०.** M ०र्देश...नियं०. **११-११.** M केचिदि...अ...दाह० ; thus Ad T. **१२.** T तत्. **१३.** Ad समिधानात्.

इति दक्षिणार्ध्ये। '०उग्रश्चेत्ता वसुविद्' **इति** ॥ ५२ ॥ 'अभिभूरस्यभिभूरहꣳ सजातेषु भूयासम्' **इत्युत्तरार्ध्ये**। '०अभिभूश्चेता वसुविद्' **इति** ॥ ५३ ॥ 'युनज्मि त्वा ब्रह्मणा दैव्येन' **इति मध्यमे परिधौ स्पर्शयित्वा समिधमादधाति**। '०हव्याया=ते अग्नये स्वाहा' **इति** ॥ ५४ ॥ **आगत्यापरेण वेदिं प्रागावृत्त उपविश्य** 'विशो यन्त्रे स्थः' **इत्यन्तर्वेद्युदीचीनाग्रे तिरश्ची सादयति** ॥ ५५ ॥ **तयोरुपरि** 'वसूनाꣳ रुद्राणामादित्यानाꣳ सदोऽसि' **इत्युत्तरपवित्रं प्रस्तरꣳ सादयति** ॥ ५६ ॥ **तꣳ सव्येनानुव्रजेत्** ॥ ५७ ॥ 'घृताच्यसि' **इति जुहूमादत्ते** ॥ ५८ ॥ 'द्यौर्जन्मना जुहूर्नाम्ना प्रिया देवानां प्रियेण नाम्ना प्रिये सदसि सीद' **इत्युपरि प्रस्तरे जुहूꣳ सादयति** ॥ ५९ ॥ **तां दक्षिणेनानुव्रजेत्** ॥ ६० ॥ 'घृताच्यसि' **इत्युपभृतमादत्ते** ॥ ६१ ॥ 'अन्तरिक्षं जन्मनोपभृन्नाम्ना प्रिया देवानां प्रियेण नाम्ना प्रिये सदसि सीद' **इत्युत्तरेण जुहूमुपभृतꣳ सादयति मनाक् प्रत्यूढामिव** ॥ ६२ ॥ **ताꣳ सव्येनैवानुव्रजेत्** ॥ ६३ ॥ 'घृताच्यसि' **इति ध्रुवामादत्ते** ॥ ६४ ॥ 'पृथिवी जन्मना ध्रुवा नाम्ना प्रिया देवानां प्रिये=सीद' **इत्युत्तरेणोपभृतं ध्रुवाꣳ सादयति मनाक् प्रत्यूढतरामिव** ॥ ६५ ॥ **सस्रुवामाज्यस्थालीमादायागत्यापरेण गार्हपत्यं प्रागावृत्त उपविश्योपस्तीर्णाभिघारितान्यनुपूर्वं हवीꣳष्युद्वासयति** ॥ ६६ ॥ **प्रत्यनक्ति कपालनि** ॥ ६७ ॥ **तानि संख्यायोद्वासयति** ॥ ६८ ॥ **समभिघार्य हवीꣳष्याहरन्ति** ॥ ६९ ॥ **पूर्वेण जुहूमष्टाकपालमासादयति, तमुत्तरेण चरुम्, तमुत्तरेणैकादशकपालम्, दक्षिणायाꣳ श्रोण्यां**

अव्यवधानार्थम्। व्यवहितपाठे [1]हि सन्देहः स्यात्। अध्याहर्तव्यं वा परिधीयमान इति[1]। यजमानस्य विहितेनाविभागार्थत्वाद् व्यवहितपाठे[2]ऽप्यध्याहर्तव्यमेव। यद्येवमध्याहृतस्य परिधीयमानानीत्यस्य च लक्षणावृत्तिः। कथम्। मन्त्रेण परिधाय हि वाचयितुं शक्यम्। परिधानमन्त्रान्तेन हि कर्मादिविहितम्। नैतदेवम्। परिधिपरिधानं नामैकं कर्म द्रव्यभेदाद्विहितम्[2]। तन्मध्ये क्रियमाणे वर्तमानकालता न[3] विहन्यते। ननु समिधावादधाति परिधिषु वाचयित्वाग्नी युनक्तीति विकृतिषु दृश्यते। उच्यते। परिधिषु वाचयित्वा समिधावादधातीति तत्र संबन्धः कर्तव्यः। आह–यत्र क्त्वाप्रत्ययस्तत्रैवं शक्यते। यत्र तु समिधावादधाति यजमानं यजुर्भिर्वाचयतीति तत्र न शक्यते। अतो वर्तमानसामीप्ये वर्तमानवद्वेति[3] वत्-[4]प्रत्ययस्य ग्रहणम् ॥ ५१–५४ ॥

तिरश्ची[5] परिभोजनीयाद् गृह्येते[6] ॥ ५५ ॥

उपभृदादानसादने सव्येन। समभिघारणं सर्वप्रदेशसमञ्जनम्। पुरोडाशयोरितरेषु भूयस्त्वम् ॥ ६१–६३ ॥

[7]'पूर्वेण जुहूमि'त्यादिना[7] उद्वासने सादने[8] चोदगपवर्गता विधीयते। एकस्यामेव हि पात्र्यां

१–१. M हि स...स्याद... ध्याहर्तव्य...ति; thus T. **२–२.** M Ad ०पाठेऽप्य...व्यमेदाद्विः, Ad only, sign of broken text between लक्षणावृत्या and कथं though the entire text is given. **३–३.** M न...मानसा...मानवश्चेति. **४.** Ad ल प्रत्य०. **५.** M त्रिरश्मी; thus Ad T. **६.** M गृह्यते; thus Ad T. **७–७.** पूर्वौ जुहोमीत्या. **८.** M Ad सदने.

दधिसान्नाय्यम्, उत्तरस्याः शृतम् ॥ ७० ॥ **दक्षिणतस्तिष्ठन् व्रतमुपैति** ॥ ७१ ॥ 'पयस्वतीरोषधयः' **इति तिरः पवित्रमप आचामति।** '°पयस्वद्वीरुधां पयः=सꣳसृज' **इति** ॥ ७२ ॥ 'अग्ने व्रतपते' **इति मार्जयित्वा समिधमादधाति।** '°व्रतं चरिष्यामि=स्वाहा' **इति** ॥ ७३ ॥ **आगत्य** 'ध्रुवा असदन्' **इति ध्रुवा अभिमृशति।** '°ऋतस्य योनौ सुकृतस्य लोके ता विष्णो पाहि (पाहि) यज्ञं पाहि यज्ञपतिं पाहि मां यज्ञनियम्' **इति** ॥ ७४ ॥ 'यन्मे अग्ने अस्य यज्ञस्य रिष्यात्' **इत्यनुपूर्वꣳ हवीꣳष्यभिमृशति।** '°यद्वा स्कन्दा=स्थे भूर्भुवः सुवरों वाग्' **इति** ॥ ७५ ॥ **चतुर्होतारं ध्रुवायां व्याचष्टे** ॥ २.२.४.७६ ॥ **[इति चतुर्थः पटलः** (९)**]**

॥ इति द्वितीयप्रपाठके द्वितीयोऽनुवाकः ॥

उद्वास्यासादनम्[1] ॥ ७० ॥

व्रतोपायनमध्वर्योरेव ॥ ७१ ॥

हविषामानुपूर्व्यं यागक्रमेण। अतो ध्रुवामभिमृश्य जुहूमुपभृतम् आग्नेयादीꣳश्चानुपूर्वमभिमृशति[2] ॥ २.२.४.७४–७५ ॥ **[इति चतुर्थः पटलः** (९)**]**

॥ इति व्याख्यायां द्वितीयप्रपाठके द्वितीयोऽनुवाकः ॥

---

१. मलास्यासदनं. २. M °श्चाभिमृ° Ad °श्चनपूर्वाभि° ; thus T.

॥ अथ द्वितीयप्रपाठके तृतीयोऽनुवाकः ॥

[समिधोऽभ्याधानमाघाराघारणञ्च]

'अग्नये समिध्यमानायानुब्रूहि' **इत्याह** ॥ १ ॥ **प्रणवे प्रणवे तिस्रः समिधोऽभ्यादधाति, न्यासे चैव प्रणवे चैवात ऊर्ध्वम्** ॥ २ ॥ 'समिद्धो अग्न आहुत' **इत्येतामध्वर्युरिध्मौ परीप्सति** ॥ ३ ॥ **अतिशिनष्टि समिधः** ॥ ४ ॥ **यदा जानाति** 'आजुहोत दुवस्यत' **इत्यथ वेदेन त्रिरुपवाजयति**

अग्नये=त्याह। होतरि प्रविश्य स्वस्थाने स्थित इध्मात् समिधमादधानः प्रेष्यति ॥ १ ॥

प्रणवे=दधाति। तिसृभ्य ऊर्ध्वं न्यासे च प्रणवे चादधाति। एव-शब्द उक्तस्यैवार्थस्य संवृत्यर्थ आचार्येण प्रयुज्यते प्रायेण ॥ २ ॥

समिद्धो अग्न आ=परीप्सति। पर्याप्तुमिच्छति। किमुक्तं भवति। 'पञ्चदशानुब्रूयादि'त्यादिष्वप्येतयैव समिदाधानं परिसमापयितुमिच्छेदित्यर्थः। समिध्यमानः समिद्धो अग्न इत्यनयोर्मध्ये आगन्तूनां धाय्यादीनां[१] निवेशोऽयमिति परिशब्दं प्रयुक्तवत आचार्यस्याभिप्रायः। एवमेकविंशति समिधोऽभ्याधेयाः संपद्यन्ते। एवं व्याख्यायमाने कल्पवाक्यस्यार्थः सामञ्जस्येन गच्छति। 'पञ्चदशेध्मदारूण्यभ्यादधाति' इत्यनया[२] श्रुत्या विरोधः। कल्पविहितानामेतच्छाखाविरुद्धानां[३] गतिः पूर्वमेवोक्ता[३] विकल्पा इति। अथाप्यस्य विधानस्य लिङ्गमस्ति [४]'ततस्तामेकविंशतिधा संभरामि सुसंभृते'ति[५]। ननु परिध्यूर्ध्वसमिधोऽनूयाजसमिद्भिः[६] सहैकविंशतिः। तथा च ब्राह्मणे 'एकविंशतिरिध्मदारूणि[७] भवन्ति' इति[८] [९]'पञ्चदशेध्मदारूण्यभ्यादधातीत्युक्तं वचनमि'ति[९]। परिध्यादिभिः सहैकविंशतिः। त्रीन् परिधीन् तिस्रस्तिस्रः[१०] समिध इति [११]पृथगनुक्रमणं नोपपद्यते[११]। अवयुत्ववाद[१२] इति चेदृच एकवाक्यत्वं गम्यमानं विहन्यते। उपवेषाद्यनुक्रमणात् समस्ताया[१३] ऋचोऽवयुत्ववादत्वं नोपपद्यते। [१४]अथवा 'प्रणवे प्रणवे[१४] तिस्रः[१५] समिधोऽभ्यादधाति' इति गतम्। न्यासे चैवेति पुनरेतदेकं वाक्यम्। तिस्र इत्याद्यनुवर्तते[१५] वाक्यसमाप्त्यर्थम्। एकस्मिन् न्यासे तिस्रः सहाभ्यादधातीत्यर्थः। [१६]प्रणवो चाऽत [१६]ऊर्ध्वम्। च-शब्द एव शब्दस्यार्थे प्रणवन्यासयोः प्रकृतयोरत ऊर्ध्वं प्रणव एवेति नियम्यते। एवं पञ्चदशैवाभ्याधेयाः[१७] ॥ ३ ॥

सामिधेनीभ्योऽतिरिच्य[१८]मानानां तिसृणां समिधाम[१८]भ्याधानं देशविधाने[१९] न्यासे चैव तिस्र इति। 'गृणानो हव्यदातये' इत्यत्राभ्यादधाति। आद्याया एव वा कस्मिंश्चिन्न्यासेऽन्येषां प्रयोगः। आद्याया

---

१. M Ad धार्यादी° ; thus T. **२.** M Ad इत्यादिना. **३-३.** M विरुद्ध ... वोक्ता. **४.** M Ad ततस्त्वामे° ; thus T. **५.** M om ति. **६.** M Ad °समित्सहैक°. **७.** M Ad °तिमिध्म°. **८.** M Ad om इति; thus T. **९-९.** M °दारू...वचन°. **१०.** M Ad तिस्रः once; thus T. **११-११.** M °क्रमण...पठ्यते. **१२.** M अवयित्ववाद, Ad अवयिवत्व°. **१३.** Ad °क्रमणायात्. **१४-१४.** M अथवा...वे. **१५-१५.** M ति...वर्तत. **१६-१६.** M Ad प्रणवेत ऊ° ; thus T. **१७.** M Ad °धेयः; thus T. **१८-१८.** M °मानान्ति...धाम°. **१९.** M Ad °धानदेश विधानं [Ad ना]; thus T.

'○उच्छुष्मो अग्ने=दासते' **इति** ॥ ५ ॥ **स्रुवेणाघारमाघारयत्युत्तरेभ्यः समुन्मुखेभ्यो दक्षिणा तिर्यञ्चं** 'प्रजापतये स्वाहा' **इति मनसा** ॥ ६ ॥ **अथाह** 'अग्नीत् परिधीꣳश्चाग्निं च त्रिस्त्रिः समृड्ढि' **इति** ॥ ७ ॥ **इध्मसन्नहनानि स्फ्य उपसंगृह्य त्रिरग्नीन्मध्यमं परिधिꣳ संमार्ष्टि, त्रिर्दक्षिणार्ध्यम्, त्रिरुत्तरार्ध्यम्, त्रिरग्निम्** ॥ ८ ॥ 'भुवनमसि विप्रथस्व' **इति स्रुच उपतिष्ठते**। '○अग्ने यष्टरिदं नमः' **इति** ॥ ९ ॥ 'जुह्वेह्यग्निस्त्वा ह्वयति देवयज्यायै' **इति जुहुमादत्ते** ॥ १० ॥ 'उपभृदेहि देवस्त्वा सविता ह्वयति देवयज्यायै' **इत्युपभृतमादत्ते** ॥ ११ ॥ 'सुयमे मे अद्य घृताची भूयास्तम्' **इति स्रुचौ संदधाति** ॥ १२ ॥ 'अग्नाविष्णू मा वामवक्रमिषम्' **इत्याक्रामति**। '○विजिहाथां=णुतम्' **इति** ॥ १३ ॥ **आक्रम्य जपति** 'विष्णोः स्थाने तिष्ठानि यत इन्द्रस्तिष्ठन् वीर्यमकृणोत्ततो वीर्यं क्रियासम्' **इति** ॥ १४ ॥ 'सꣳरभ्योर्ध्वो अध्वरो दिविस्पृग्' **इति मध्यमे परिधौ सꣳस्पृश्यर्जुमाघारमाघारयति**। '○अह्रुतो यज्ञो यज्ञपतेरिन्द्रावान्त्स्वाहा' **इति** ॥ १५ ॥ **सन्ततमेवोत्तरमाघारमाघारयति दक्षिणेभ्यः समुन्मुखेभ्य उदञ्चं तिर्यञ्चम्** ॥ १६ ॥ **असꣳस्पर्शयन् स्रुचावत्याक्रामयति** 'पाहि माग्ने' **इति** ॥ १७ ॥ **अत्याक्रम्य** 'सं ज्योतिषा ज्योतिरङ्क्ताम्' **इति जुह्वा ध्रुवाꣳ समनक्ति**। '○सꣳ हविषा

एव प्रणवेषु न्यासेषु च षडभ्यादधाति। ननु आद्याया एक एव न्यासः[1]। [2]अध्यर्धामुक्त्वा ह्यवसानमाश्वलायना[2] आमनन्ति। अस्मच्छ्रुत्यपेक्षमाचार्येणाम्नातमिति किमत्रायुक्तम्। अस्माकं तु सर्वास्वर्धर्चेन सन्दधातीत्येव। अस्मिन् व्याख्याने पूर्वेण समाने विशेषो न्यासशब्दाभ्यासो[3] श्रुतः कल्पयितव्यः। आद्ये कल्पवाक्यस्योत्तरयोः [4]श्रुतिवाक्येनाविगीतिः ॥ ४ ॥

'आजुहोते'त्युपलक्षणम्[4]। 'त्वं वरुण' इत्यस्या अपि। तथा जगत्यादीनामपि ॥ ५ ॥

स्रुवेणाघारमाघारयति वेदेनोपयत्य। पूर्वः [5]समुन्मुखशब्दोऽपरपर्यन्तवाचीत्येवं व्याचक्षते। उत्तरेभ्यः समुन्मुखेभ्यो[6] दक्षिणेत्येव तिर्यक्त्वे सिद्धे तिर्यक्त्वमिति ब्राह्मणवचनानुकरणम्[7], 'उत्तरस्मिन्नाघार ऋजुमाघारयती'ति प्राप्तस्य शाखान्तरे विहितस्य वैकल्पिकत्वप्रदर्शनार्थम्[8] ॥ ६ ॥

'अग्ने यष्टरिदं नम' इत्याहवनीयमिति। शेषो दिविस्पृगन्तं परिधिस्पर्शन आघारमन्त्रावयव इत एवेत्यन्ये ॥ ९ ॥

आघार्यमाणं यजमानोऽन्वारभते[9] ॥ १५–१६ ॥

[10]असंस्पर्शयन्नत्याक्रामति[10]। अत्याक्रामन् 'पाहि माग्न' इति जपति ॥ १७ ॥

द्विः समनक्ति। त्रिरेव समज्यादिति विकल्पः श्रूयते। तत्र द्वित्वे समस्तं मन्त्रमुक्त्वा [11]द्विः समनक्ति त्रित्वे 'सं ज्योतिषा ज्योतिरङ्क्ताम्' इत्यनुषज्य त्रीन् मन्त्रान् कृत्वा[11] त्रिः समनक्ति। अथवा तत्राप्येक एव

---

१. M Ad एकवन्न्यास; thus T. **२–२.** M °मुक्त्वा ह...लायना, Ad मुक्ता° ; thus T. **३.** M Ad शब्दोऽभ्यासे; thus T. **४–४.** M नापि... होतेत्यु° ; Ad °पिगीतिराज्ञे होतेत्युपलक्षणत्वम्; thus T. **५.** M Ad सन्मुख°, T पूर्वस्मिन् मुखशब्दो. **६.** M Ad समिन्यु°. **७.** M ब्राह्मणा...नुकरणम्; Ad ब्राह्मणानुक° ; thus T. **८.** M Ad °शनमात्रम्; thus T. **९.** Ad °रभेत. **१०–१०.** M °न्नत्य...मति, Ad °त्याश्रवमति; thus T. **११–११.** M द्विः समनक्ति। त्रि...त्वङ्क्ताभि°, T °त्रित्वे त्वङ्क्तामि°.

हविः सं यज्ञपतिराशिषा' **इति** ॥ १८ ॥ **यथायतनः स्रुचौ सादयित्वोत्तिष्ठन् प्रवराया-श्रावयति** ॥ १९ ॥ **स्फ्यमादायाग्नीत्पश्चादन्वारभते** ॥ २० ॥ **इध्मसन्नहनानि स्फ्य उप-संगृह्याश्रावयति** ॥ २१ ॥ 'ओ श्रावये'**त्याह** ॥ २२ ॥ 'अग्निर्देवो होता देवान् यक्षद्विद्वाꣳश्चिकि-त्वान्मनुष्वद् भरतवदमुवदमुवद्ब्रह्मण्वदेह वक्षद् ब्राह्मणा अस्य यज्ञस्य प्राविताऽर इत्यसौ मानुषः' **इत्याहवनीये शकलं प्रास्यति यथा होतुर्नाम भवति** ॥ २३ ॥ 'सीद होतर्' **इत्याह** ॥ २४ ॥ **बर्हिष्येव बर्हिरुपगूहति** ॥ २५ ॥ **सीदति होता** ॥ २६ ॥ **यदाऽऽजानाति** 'घृतवतीमध्वर्यो स्रुच-मास्यस्व' **इत्यथाञ्जलिं करोति** । '°अश्विनाध्वर्यू ब्राह्मणा प्र णः शास्त नमो वो अस्तु' **इति** ॥ २७ ॥ **स्रुचावादायाध्वर्युरत्याक्रामति** ॥ २८ ॥ **अत्याक्रम्याश्राव्याह** 'समिधो यज' **इति** ॥ २९ ॥ **वषट्कृते पश्चात् समिन्मुखे जुहोति** ॥ ३० ॥ 'यज यजे'**ति** ॥ ३१ ॥ **पञ्च प्राचः प्रयाजान् यजति** ॥ ३२ ॥ **चतुर्थेऽर्धः समानयते** ॥ ३३ ॥ **उपभृतोऽधि सर्वं प्रयजति** ॥ ३४ ॥ **प्रयाजानिष्ट्वा-**

मन्त्रः । एवं पक्षान्तरेणावैलक्षण्यं भवति ॥ १८ ॥

बर्हिस्तीर्णाद् [1]गृह्यते। उत्तरत्र[1] 'बर्हिष्येव बर्हिरुपगूहति' इति दर्शनात्। आश्रावणादीनां प्लुतं[2] लक्षणशास्त्रादनुपदाद्वा ग्राह्यम् ॥ १९ ॥

आश्रावणानन्तरमाग्नीध्रः सर्वत्रेध्मसन्नहनानि स्फ्य उपसंगृह्य[3] प्राङ्मुखो 'अस्तु श्रौषडि'ति प्रत्याश्रावयेत्। उत्करदेशे तिष्ठन् सन्नहनोपसंग्रहणमाप्रतिपत्तेः[4] ॥ २०-२२ ॥

अमुवदमुवदित्यत्र[5] यजमानस्यार्षेयांस्त्रीन्परान्[6] [6]यथा पराशरवत्[7] शक्तिवद् वसिष्ठवदिति। सवेदोवद्वीतहव्यवद्[8] भृगुवदिति च। परस्तादर्वाचोऽवृणीत इति होतुर्विधानम्[9] ॥ २३ ॥

अञ्जलिकरणम् ऋत्विग्यजमानेभ्यः ॥ २७ ॥

'प्रयाजानि'ति संज्ञानिर्देशो व्यवहारार्थो धर्मग्रहणार्थश्च। तद्यथा 'अभिक्रामं जुहोती'ति। अथ स्रुचोरादान[10]मित्यस्मिन्ननुवाके ये यस्य धर्मा विहिताः ते तस्य शेषभूता उपक्लृप्ता विज्ञेयाः। तत्र यतो मन्येत 'अनभिक्रम्य होष्यामी'ति तत्स्थानं कल्पयेत्। अस्पृष्टमिव[11] दक्षिणं वेद्यन्तमि'त्युक्तम्। तत्र [12]प्रयाजेषु 'अभिक्रामन् जुहोती'ति [13]वचनादाश्रावणात्पूर्वमभिक्रम्याभिक्रम्य[13] जुह्वदाश्रावयति। ततोऽनभिक्रम्य जुहोति ॥ २८-३२ ॥

अत्रोपभृतस्य समानयनं बर्हिरर्थम् उभयार्थमिति वदन्ते[14]। समानीतेनोभयोर्यागयोः क्रियमाणयोः कुतः संशयः। समानयत उपभृतम्[15] इति। 'तेजो[15] वा आज्यं प्रजा बर्हिः [16]प्रजास्वेव तेजो दधाती'ति दर्शनात्[16]। शाखान्तरे च 'अतिहायेडो बर्हिः प्रतिसमानयत इति, बर्हिष्वाज्यं निदधाती'ति वचनात् बर्हिरर्थं

१-१. M गृह...त उत्त; thus Ad T. **२.** M Ad प्लुतिं; thus T. **३.** M Ad °संग्राह्य; thus T. **४.** T gives a text from MS ख M as संहरण. **५.** M अमु...वदि°, Ad अमुपद उवदि°. **६-६.** M °परान् ...यथा, Ad °त्रीन्परार्थ°. **७.** M Ad °शरवक्तिवद्व°; thus T. **८.** M Ad °वेदोपद्वीत°. **९.** M Ad होतृवि°; thus T. **१०.** M स्रु...दान; Ad स्रुचोदान°. **११.** M Ad °दास्पृष्ट°. **१२.** Ad प्रयोजे°. **१३-१३.** M °श्रवणात्पूर्व ...त्याभिक्राम्य; thus Ad T. **१४.** M Ad पद°. **१५-१५.** M Ad भृतस्तेजो; thus T. **१६-१६.** M Ad प्रजा...नो दर्श°; thus T.

ऽत्याक्रम्य ध्रुवामभिघारयति। अथाष्टाकपालमथ चरुमथैकादशकपालमथ दधिसान्नाय्यमथ शृतमुपभृतमन्ततः ॥ ३५ ॥ 'अग्नयेऽनुब्रूहि' **इत्याहाज्यस्य गृह्णानश्चतुः** ॥ ३६ ॥ **ध्रुवां प्रत्यज्य प्रस्तरः समज्योत्तिष्ठति** ॥ ३७ ॥ **अत्याक्रम्याश्राव्याह** 'अग्निं यज' **इति** ॥ ३८ ॥ **वषट्कृत उत्तरार्धे जुहोति** ॥ ३९ ॥ 'सोमायानुब्रूहि' **इत्याहाज्यस्यैव गृह्णानश्चतुः** ॥ ४० ॥ **ध्रुवां प्रत्यज्य प्रस्तरः समज्यैवोत्तिष्ठति** ॥ ४१ ॥ **अत्याक्रम्याश्राव्याह** 'सोमं यज' **इति** ॥ ४२ ॥ **वषट्कृते दक्षिणार्धे जुहोति** ॥ ४३ ॥ **उपस्तीर्याप उपस्पृश्यावद्यन्नाह** 'अग्नयेऽनुब्रूहि' **इति** ॥ ४४ ॥

मन्यन्ते। तेनैव द्रव्येणोभयोः क्रियमाणयोरुभयार्थत्वम्[१] कथं पुनर्बर्हिरर्थत्वे [२]तेनैवोत्तरस्य यागः। उच्यते[२]। परद्रव्यैकदेशवृत्तित्वं तस्य पूर्वस्मिन्पक्षेऽप्रवृत्ते बर्हिर्यागे द्रव्यापचारे नोत्तम[३] औपभृतग्रहणं[४] प्रयोजयेद्[५] द्विदेवत्यानिवाऽऽदित्यग्रहः। पितृयज्ञे च समानयनमुत्तरस्मिन्विपरीतम् शृतस्य [६]पूर्वस्यावदेयत्वे शृतं पूर्वं[६] दध्नोऽभिघारयति[७] ॥ ३४ ॥

ध्रुवाऽऽज्यादुपस्तरणाभिघारणं प्रत्यञ्जनमाज्यस्थाल्याज्यादुपांशुयाजा[८]...यागयोर्मध्य इत्यनु-वर्तते। मध्येऽग्नेः प्राची प्रधानाहुतीः संस्थापयति ॥ ३५ ॥

अवदानानां बदरीपलाश[९]मात्रत्वं रहस्येषु दृश्यते 'बदरीपलाशमात्रेणावदानेने'ति[९]। 'अङ्गुष्ठ-पर्वमात्राणि दैवान्यवदानानि भवन्ति[१०]। ज्यायान्यैडानि[११] सौविष्टकृतानि चे'ति शाखान्तरं पञ्चा-वत्तिनः[१२]। प्रधानानां त्रिस्त्रिरवद्यति[१३]। नित्यमेवोपस्तरणाभिघारणम् तथाहि[१४] श्रियमिष्टौ दृश्यते। नैकेषाम्। एकदेवत्यानां प्रत्येकं त्रिस्त्रिः 'इन्द्रं यजे'ति प्रदर्शनम्। अग्नीषोमादीनामपि शृतावदानेन दध्ना शृतेन वाऽभिपूरणं प्राशित्रावदानेऽतोऽष्टाकपालस्येत्यादि। तस्याविद्धनिरकृन्तन्यवेन संमितमित्य-विशेषवचनात्सर्वेभ्यः[१४]। कर्तव्यस्य प्रदर्शनार्थं 'निरकृन्तन्नि'ति छेदनप्रदर्शनादनौषधीनां[१५] नास्ति। इहैकस्मादेवावदानदर्शनात्[१६] संवत्सरविधेयेष्टौ[१७] च प्रथमस्य प्राशित्रदर्शनादेकस्मादेव मुख्यादवदान-मित्याचार्यस्याभिप्रायः।[१८] कथं प्रतिपत्तौ प्राशित्रहरणे द्वित्वदर्शनम्। द्वित्वदर्शनादेवाज्यस्य ज्ञास्यन्ति। अथवा पुरोडाशधर्मत्वं [१९]प्रतिप्राशित्रमाधारभेदं च मत्वोक्तम्[१९]। अथवा द्वित्वं प्रदर्शनार्थमनेकस्यापि। ननु प्रायणीयादौ चरोः प्राशित्रं दृश्यते। विकृतौ चरोः पुरोडाशविकारत्वं वक्ष्यामः। तदभिप्रायं तत् स्यात्। भित्वा वैकमिति मुख्यधर्मत्वाभिप्रायम्। यद्येवं विकृतिषु [२०]बहुहविष्कासु बहुभिर्भवितव्यम्। भवन्तु। [२०]तत्रोत्पन्नानि तत्रैव प्रतिपाद्यन्ते[२१]। शाखान्तरे च 'प्राशित्रमवद्यति द्वे' इति वचनमस्ति। स्रुवदण्डप्रक्षालनदर्शनात् स्रुवदण्डेनाभिघारणम् 'पूर्वेण स्रुचोऽपरेण परिधीनि'ति दर्शनादपरेणापि स्रुचो

---

१. M Ad °यार्थं; thus T. **२-२.** M तेनैवो...उच्यते. **३.** T नौत्तम°. **४.** M ओपभृ°. **५.** M प्रयोनये, Ad प्रयोनयो. **६-६.** M °स्याव ...पूर्वं, Ad om शृतं; thus T. **७.** Ad दध्नोरभि°. **८.** M Ad T °याजा... यागयोर्म°. **९-९.** M °मात्र ...ननेति, T °दानेति. **१०.** T °न्तीज्या°. **११.** M Ad °धोनि; thus T. **१२.** M पञ्चव° पञ्चावर्तिनः. **१३.** M Ad °रपद्यति. **१४-१४.** T takes it as additional text, hence gives it under fn. **१५.** M Ad °दनौषधी. **१६.** M इहैक...दानदर्शनात्; thus T. **१७.** M Ad विधेष्टौ; thus T. **१८.** M Ad चार्याभि; thus T. **१९-१९.** M प्राशित्रम...क्तम्. **२०-२०.** M बहुहविष्कार...तत्रो°; Ad तव्यं अभवन्. **२१.** M Ad तत्रैव पाद्यन्ते; thus T.

पश्चाच्च पुरस्ताच्चाष्टाकपालस्यावद्यति ॥ ४५ ॥ अभिघारयति ॥ ४६ ॥ प्रत्यनक्ति ॥ ४७ ॥ ध्रुवां प्रत्यज्य प्रस्तरꣳ समज्योत्तिष्ठति ॥ ४८ ॥ अत्याक्रम्याश्राव्याह 'अग्निं यज' **इति ॥ ४९ ॥ वषट्कृते मध्ये जुहोति ॥ ५० ॥ उपस्तीर्याप उपस्पृश्यावद्यन्नाह** 'सोमायानुब्रूहि' **इत्युपाꣳशु पौर्णमास्याम्,** 'विष्णवे' **इत्यमावास्यायाम् ॥ ५१ ॥ पश्चाच्च पुरस्ताच्च चरोरवद्यति ॥ ५२ ॥ अभिघार-यति ॥ ५३ ॥ प्रत्यनक्ति ॥ ५४ ॥ ध्रुवां प्रत्यज्य प्रस्तरꣳ समज्यैवोत्तिष्ठति ॥ ५५ ॥ अत्याक्रम्या-श्राव्याह** 'अमुं यज' **इति ॥ ५६ ॥ वषट्कृते पूर्वार्धे जुहोति ॥ ५७ ॥ उपस्तीर्यैवाप उपस्पृश्यावद्यन्नाह** 'अग्नीषोमाभ्यामनुब्रूहि' **इति पौर्णमास्याम्,** 'इन्द्राग्निभ्याम्' **इत्यमावास्या-यामनीजानस्य,** 'इन्द्राय' **इतीजानस्य ॥ ५८ ॥ पश्चाच्च पुरस्ताच्चैकादशकपालस्या-वद्यति ॥ ५९ ॥ पश्चाच्च पुरस्ताच्च दध्नः स्रुवेणावद्यति ॥ ६० ॥ पश्चाच्च पुरस्ताच्च शृतस्य स्रुवेणावद्यति ॥ ६१ ॥ दध्नोऽभिपूरयति ॥ ६२ ॥ अभिघारयति ॥ ६३ ॥ प्रत्यनक्ति ॥ ६४ ॥ ध्रुवां प्रत्यज्य प्रस्तरꣳ समज्योत्तिष्ठति ॥ ६५ ॥ अत्याक्रम्याश्राव्याह** 'इन्द्रं यज' **इति ॥ ६६ ॥ वषट्कृतेऽपरार्धे जुहोति ॥ ६७ ॥** 'अग्नये स्विष्टकृतेऽनुब्रूहि' **इत्याहोपस्तृणानोऽवद्यन् ॥ ६८ ॥ सकृदुत्तरार्धादष्टाकपालस्यावद्यति ॥ ६९ ॥ सकृदुत्तरार्धान् मेक्षणेन चरोरवद्यति ॥ ७० ॥ तदवदायाधोऽधः स्रुचावग्नीधे प्रयच्छति ॥ ७१ ॥ सकृदुत्तरार्धादेकादशकपालस्या-वद्यति ॥ ७२ ॥ सकृदुत्तरार्धाद् दध्नः स्रुवेणावद्यति ॥ ७३ ॥ सकृदुत्तरार्धाच्छृतस्य स्रुवेणाव-द्यति ॥ ७४ ॥ शृतस्याभिपूरयति ॥ ७५ ॥ अभिघारयति ॥ ७६ ॥ प्रत्यनक्ति ॥ ७७ ॥ ध्रुवां प्रत्यज्य प्रस्तरꣳ समज्यैवोत्तिष्ठति ॥ ७८ ॥ अत्याक्रम्याश्राव्याह** 'अग्निꣳ स्विष्टकृतं यज' **इति ॥ ७९ ॥ वषट्कृते उत्तरार्धेऽतिहाय पूर्वा आहुतीर्जुहोति ॥ ८० ॥ अनुप्रहरत्यग्नीन्मेक्षणम् ॥ ८१ ॥ तत् सꣳस्रावेणाभिजुहोति ॥ ८२ ॥ अत्याक्रम्य यथायतनꣳ स्रुचौ सादयित्वा यतोऽष्टाकपालस्य सौविष्टकृतमवद्यति ततो यवमात्रं प्राशित्रमवद्यति ॥ ८३ ॥ तत्पूर्वेण स्रुचोऽपरेण परिधीनतिहृत्य**

हविषां सादनमस्तीति गम्यते। [1]प्राशित्राभिघारणमिडोपस्पर्शनाभिघारणं चाज्यस्थाल्या[1] अयागार्थ-त्वात्। सर्वस्मै वा एतद्यज्ञाय गृह्यते ॥ ४४-४७ ॥

'यद् ध्रौवमाज्यमि'ति[2] हि वचनम्। यज्ञाय यागायेत्यर्थः। अत एवात्र ध्रुवायां प्रत्यञ्जनमनाम्नातम्[3] ॥ ४८-४९ ॥

अवदानान्यनपक्तप्रदेशानि[4] संभिद्य [5]सग्धाभिघार्य होत्र इडामादधाति[5]। पूर्वेण होतारमननुसृजन्निति [6]वाक्यम्। पूर्वेण होतारमिति[6] [7]प्रतिमुखं ददाति न पार्श्वयोः। अन्यतरत्प्रत्यननुसृजन्निडापात्रमत्याक्रम्य[7] दक्षिणत उदगावृत्त[8] उपविशति यजमानः। केचिदध्वर्योरेव

१-१. M °मिडे... रणञ्चाज्य, Ad °मिडोपस्तरणाभि°. २. M यध्रुवायाज्य°; thus T. ३. T gives in fn the text of a MS ख as तवदव. ४. M Ad °नवक्तुप्रदे°. ५-५. M सन्धा...होत्रमिडा°; Ad सन्धायाभि° होत्रमि°, T सग्धाभि°. ६-६. M वाक्य...होता°. ७-७. M प्रतिमुखं... प्रत्यनु...क्रम्य; Ad परत्वयोरन्ततरत्प्रत्यनुसृन्वानुसृजन्. ८. M Ad उदावृत्त; thus T.

दक्षिणतो वेद्यै सादयित्वाऽभिघारयति ॥ ८४ **॥ अप उपस्पृश्य मार्जयित्वा प्रक्षाल्य स्रुवदण्डं प्रक्षाल्येडापात्रमुपस्तृणीते ॥** २.३.१.८५ **॥ [इति प्रथमः पटलः** (१०)**]**

[इडोपाह्वानम्]

दक्षिणार्धादष्टाकपालस्य पुरोडाशशकलमवद्यति ॥ १ **॥ तच्चमसेऽवदधाति ॥** २ **॥ अवदानानि संभिद्य पूर्वार्धादष्टाकपालस्य चतुरङ्गुलं यजमानभागमवद्यति ॥** ३ **॥ संभेदनान्यवदायाज्येनाभ्यज्य द्वितीयमवद्यति ॥** ४ **॥ दक्षिणार्धाच्चरोरवदायावदानानि संभिद्य द्वितीयमवद्यति ॥** ५ **॥ दक्षिणार्धादेकादशकपालस्यावदायावदानानि संभिद्यैव द्वितीयमवद्यति ॥** ६ **॥ दक्षिणार्धाद्दध्नः स्रुवेणावदायावदानानि संक्षुभ्य द्वितीयमवद्यति ॥ ७ ॥ दक्षिणार्धाच्छृतस्य स्रुवेणावदायावदानानि संभिद्यैव द्वितीयमवद्यति ॥** ८ **॥ दध्नो वा शृतस्य वाऽभिपूरयति ॥** ९ **॥ उभयोर्वाऽभिघार्य होत्र इडामादधाति ॥** १० **॥ पूर्वेण होतारमनुत्सृजन्नत्याक्रामति ॥** ११ **॥ होतुरङ्गुलिमाज्येनाक्त्वा होतुः पाणावुपस्तृणीते ॥** १२ **॥ द्विरवद्यति ॥** १३ **॥ सकृदभिघारयति ॥** १४ **॥ चतुरवत्तावान्तरेडा ॥** १५ **॥ अन्वारभेते अध्वर्युश्च यजमानश्च ॥** १६ **॥ यदाऽऽजानाति**

---

[१]स्थानान्तरगमनचोदनेति ब्रुवते। तदयुक्तम् 'पुरस्तात्प्रत्यङ्ङासीन[१] इडाया[२] इडामादधातीत्यनेन विरोधात्। दक्षिणत उपविष्टः[३] [४]पुनरागत्यावद्यतीति चेद् गमनमुदङ्मुखता चादृष्टार्थे स्याताम्। अत्याक्रामणं[४] च वेदिलंघन[५] एव [६]दृश्यते, न स्थानान्तरगमनमात्रे[६]। तस्मादन्तरेणापि यजमानग्रहणं [७]वेदिमत्याक्रम्य दक्षिणत[७] उपविष्टः पुनरागत्याक्रम्येडाया दक्षिणत उदगावृत्त उपविशति'॥ २.३.१.८४–८५ ॥ **[इति प्रथमः पटलः** (१०)**]**

होतुः प्रदेशिन्याः पर्वणी उत्तमे आज्यस्थाल्या आज्यमादायानक्ति[८]। ततो [९]होतुः पाणावुपस्तृणीते[९]। केचि'दिडाया इडामादधाती'त्यस्यार्थं[१०] निर्वर्णयन्तो [११]लेपादेवोपस्तरणाभिघारणं कुर्वन्ति। अन्येऽवदानविषयमेव। तदुपस्तरणाभिघारणमाज्यस्थाल्या एवेति वर्णयन्ति ॥ १०–१२ ॥

यदाऽऽजानातीडोपहूतेति=उपहवन्तेऽशीयेति। अत्र केचिद्विकल्पमिच्छन्ति[१२]। यजमानेन यथा विहितं तथा विभागेन वाचयेत्। अत्र वा[१३] 'सुरूपा'दिसमस्तमित इडामाहूयमानामित्यादिषु[१४] यथाविहितमवयवमेवार्वाक्[१५] यजमानो वदति। अत्र 'सुरूपादिसमस्तं वाच्यमाने [१६]'सा मे सत्याशीः'[१६] इत्यादि तन्त्रमिति विकल्पकल्पनाया बहुदोषादावृत्तेश्चादृष्टकल्पनाभयाद्। यदा जानाति[१७] 'इडोपहूते'ति

१–१. M स्थानान्तर ...पुरस्ता°, Ad °नान्तरे ग°; thus T. **२.** M इधाय, Ad इडाय; thus T. **३.** M °दधातीत्यनेन वि...उपविष्टं; Ad °विष्टं. **४–४.** M पुनरागम्य...त्याक्रामणं; Ad °गम्या°; गनमुद°; त्याक्रम°; T gives a text from MS ख as °त्युत्क्रमणं. **५.** M Ad वेदलं; thus T. **६–६.** M दृश्यते...नन्तरा...गत्र; Ad स्थानान्तरायनक्तितो होतुः. **७–७.** M Ad वेदिम...दक्षिणत; thus T. **८.** M Ad °मुपादाया°; thus T. **९–९.** M होतुः वा...त्वुप°. **१०.** T gives a text from MS ख as इत्यस्य वचनस्यार्थं. **११.** Ad लोपा°; thus M T. **१२.** M Ad चित्कल्प°; thus T. **१३.** M Ad वसुरूपा°. **१४.** M Ad इडामाप्रियमाणां; thus T. **१५.** M Ad °मेव वाक्. **१६–१६.** M Ad सासोत्याशी; thus T. **१७.** M Ad °भयाद्य भाजनातीडो°; thus T.

'इडोपहूता' **इत्यथाध्वर्युर्युजमानं वाचयति** 'सुरूपवर्षवर्ण=मघोनी; जुष्टिरसि=तेऽशीय' **इति ॥ १७ ॥ बर्हिषदमष्टाकपालं कृत्वा** 'ब्रध्न पिन्वस्व' **इत्यध्वर्युर्यजमानं वाचयति ।** '°ददतो मे मा क्षायि कुर्वतो मे मोपदसत्', 'दिशां क्लृप्तिरसि दिशो मे कल्पन्तां कल्पन्तां मे दिशः', 'आशानां त्वाऽऽशापालेभ्यश्चतुर्भ्यो अमृतेभ्यः। इदं भूतस्याध्यक्षेभ्यो विधेम हविषा वयम्', 'अपस्पिन्व ओषधीर्जिन्व द्विपात्पाहि चतुष्पादव दिवो वृष्टिमेरय' **इति ॥ १८ ॥ पात्रियां पुरोडाशं समवधाय पुरस्तात् प्रत्यगावृत्ताय द्विरुपस्तीर्णाभिघारितमग्नीध आदधाति ॥ १९ ॥** 'अग्निर्मा दुरिष्टात्पातु' **इति पूर्वस्मिन्नवदाने वाचयति।** '°सविताऽघशꣳसात्' **इति ॥ २० ॥ उत्तरस्मिन्** 'यो मेऽन्ति

शब्दपदार्थकत्वं परित्यज्यार्थपदार्थकत्वमेवास्य कल्पयन्ति। यदिडोपहूता होत्राकाङ्क्षितेति जानाति, तदा वाचयति इडाहरणकाल इत्यर्थः। अस्मिन्पक्षे [१]याजमानविहितेन विभागेन वाचयतीत्येवं क्रियमाणे विकल्पावृत्तिदोषो[२] न भवति।[२] यत्र दैव्या[३] अध्वर्यव उपहूता उपहूता मनुष्या इति जानाति, तदाध्वर्युरुपहूतः 'पशुमानसानी'त्याह। तथा यजमान 'उपहूतोऽयं यजमानः' इति ॥ १७ ॥

अत्र यदि न समवैति 'सा मे सत्याशी'रित्यादेर्मन्त्रात्परस्ताद्बर्हिषदमष्टाकपालं चतुर्धा कृत्वा [४]'ब्रध्ने'त्यादि वाचयति। अन्ये चतुर्धाकरणस्याभावं मन्यन्ते। आचार्येणाभि[५]हितत्वात् चतुर्धाकरणमेव युक्तम्। श्रुत्युक्तस्याप्रतिषेधात्। 'दिशां क्लृप्तिरसी'ति लिङ्गात् समवधायेति ब्रुवत आचार्यस्याप्यय-मेवाभिप्रायः ॥ १८ ॥

समवधाय सन्धाय अवधायेत्यर्थः। पृथग्भूतानां हि सन्धानमुपपद्यते[६]। अस्मिन्पक्षे [७]व्यादेशोऽपि कर्तव्यः। 'इदं ब्रह्मणे' इत्यादिभिः पात्रियां समवधायेडां[८] प्राश्नन्ति। कुत एतत्। 'सामि प्राश्नन्ति सामि मार्जयन्ते'[९] इतीडामधिकृत्य ब्राह्मणे दर्शनात्। के पुनः प्राश्नन्ति। अविशेषात् सर्वर्त्विग्यजमानाः। तथा च श्रुत्यन्तरे—'यजमानपञ्चमा इडां[१०] प्राश्नीयुः' इति[१०]। अच्छिद्रकल्पेऽध्वर्योर्भक्षाभावो दृश्यते। तत्प्रश्नोऽस्ति 'अध्वर्यो [११]प्राशीदग्नीदि'त्यादीति। [१२]अतस्तद्वर्जानामिडाप्राशनमित्येकः पक्षः। इहाचार्येणाविहितत्वाद्धोत्रे दत्ता, दत्तैवेडेत्यन्येषामभागित्वम्। तथा च [१३]'केचिदामनन्ति धित्सेद्वा निधित्सेद् वा' इति[१३]। यजमानादिभ्योऽवदातुमात्मार्थं निधातुं वेच्छेदित्यर्थः। तथा सति अस्मिन्नेव काले चतुर्धाकृतस्य स्वं भागं द्विरुपस्तीर्णाभिघारितमादधाति। 'षट् संपद्यन्ते' इति दर्शनात्। प्रत्येकं [१४]द्वयोरवदानयोरुपस्तरणाभिघारणम्।'सविताघशंसात्पात्वि'ति[१४] केचिदनुषजन्ति ॥ १९-२० ॥

---

१. Ad यज°. २-२. T दोषा°...न्ति. ३. M Ad दैव्य. ४. Ad प्रध्ने°. ५. M Ad °णानभि°; thus T. ६. M Ad सन्धानामु°. ७. M Ad प्यदेशो°. ८. M Ad °धायेधां. ९. M Ad °यत. १०-१०. M इडां...ति. ११. M Ad प्राश्नी°; thus T. १२. M °वर्ज्जा°. १३-१३. M केचि...निधित्सेद्वे; Ad धित्से सेडामुपहूय इड इति T धित्सेद्धा. १४-१४. M °रुपस्त...विताघशंशात्पत्विति.

दूरेऽरातीयति तमेतेन जेषम्' **इति** ॥ २१ ॥ **प्राशित्रं परेक्षते** ॥ २२ । **प्राश्नन्ति** ॥ २३ ॥ **एतस्मिन् काले त्रिरध्वर्युर्हस्तात् प्राणेन प्राश्नाति** ॥ २४ ॥ **मार्जयन्ते** ॥ २५ ॥ 'मनो ज्योतिर्जुषताम्' **इति जपति**। '०आज्यं विच्छिन्नं यज्ञꣳ समिमं दधातु बृहस्पतिस्तनुतामिमं नो यज्ञं विश्वे देवा इह मादयन्ताम्' **इति सन्ततमा ब्रह्मणः** ॥ २६ ॥ **वेदेनाष्टाकपालस्य पुरोडाशशकलं पूर्वेणाहवनीयꣳ सहाद्भिर्ब्रह्मणे परिहरति** ॥ २७ ॥ **प्राश्नाति ब्रह्मा** ॥ २८ ॥ **मार्जयते** ॥ २९ ॥ **अद्भिर्वेदꣳ सꣳस्पृश्यैतेनैव यथैतमेत्याध्वर्यवे प्रयच्छति** ॥ ३० ॥ **चरौ यजमानभागं प्रास्यापरेणात्मानं पूर्वेणोत्करमुदगावृत्तान्यनुपूर्वꣳ हवीꣳष्युद्वासयति** ॥ ३१ ॥ **आहरन्त्यन्वाहार्यम्** ॥ ३२ ॥ **स यद्यन्यत्र पक्वः स्यादन्वाहार्यपचनेऽधिश्रयेत्** ॥ ३३ ॥ **यद्यनुपसिक्तः स्यादाज्यस्योपसिञ्चेत्** ॥ ३४ ॥ **तस्मिन्**

प्राशित्रं परेक्ष्य परिहरति इह परिहरणवचनात्। ब्रह्मत्वे च 'यत्तिरश्चीनमतिहरेदित्यस्यापोदितस्य[१] पक्षस्य विहितेन विकल्पत्वं मन्यन्ते। उभयोरपि पक्षयोर्व्यामिश्रत्वमन्य इच्छन्ति। कथम्। [२]ब्रह्मयजमानयोर्वेदिमत्याक्रम्योपविष्टयोरुभयोर्हरणपरिहरणदर्शनात्। अग्रेणाहवनीयं गत्वो-पविष्टयोरग्रेण परिहरणमिति एवमव्यवायो[३] भवतीति। कथं पुनरग्रेण गमनं तयोरुपलक्ष्यते। बौधायनीये उभयथा [४]तयोर्गमनदर्शनादाचार्येणापि इष्यत इति। अन्य आह-अस्मिन्कल्पे व्यवेत्योपवेशनं दृष्टम्। प्राशित्रस्य चाग्रेण परिहरणं यच्चाचार्येणोक्तं ब्राह्मणे वा विद्यते तदस्माकं प्रमाणम्[५]। इहावचनादपरिहरणं च कल्पयितुं न शक्यते। यथा ब्रह्मत्वे दृष्टस्य[६] 'ब्रह्मन्नप'[६] इत्यस्य प्रैषस्य नित्यत्वम्। यत्तूक्तम्-'एवमव्यवायो भविष्यती'ति किमिव वचनान्न लभ्यम्। अत्र युक्तं विचारणीयम्। [७]व्यवायपरिहरणपक्षे गार्हपत्यसमीपादागतानां हविरादीनां द्रव्याणां परिहरणं कर्तव्यम्। तच्च दृश्यते—'पूर्वेण ब्रह्माणं च यजमानं[८] चातिहृत्यान्तर्वेद्यासादयती'त्याचार्यस्यायमभिप्राय इव लक्ष्यते॥ २२ ॥

प्राशिते प्राशिते सर्वेषां मार्जनं 'सन्ततमा ब्रह्मण'[९] इत्यस्य शेषो विध्यवशेषोऽथापः संप्रयच्छेयुरग्नीदध्वर्यवेऽध्वर्युर्होत्रे होता यजमानाय सन्ततमाब्रह्मण इति, 'व्यस्तमिव वा। एतद्यज्ञस्ये'-त्यारभ्य विहितत्वादिडाङ्गत्वं मार्जनस्य मन्वाना इडाप्राशनं कृतवतामेव मार्जनं केचिदिच्छन्ति। इहाविशेषेण वचनादविशेषेणेत्यन्ये॥ २३-२९ ॥

ब्रह्मभागं परिहृत्य होत्रेऽध्वर्यवे च स्वं स्वं भागं ददाति। तौ च प्राश्नीतः ॥ ३० ॥

यजमानभागं चरौ प्रास्य [१०]चर्वादीनि सान्नाय्यान्तानि[१०] [११]हवींष्यनुक्रमेणोक्तेन पथोद्वासयति॥ ३१ ॥

अन्वाहार्यं चतुर्णामशितुं भवति समर्थं दक्षिणार्थत्वात्॥ ३२ ॥

स च यद्बीजीय आवापस्तद्बीजीयो भवति। तस्मिन्नपूर्वमाज्यमुपसिञ्चति॥ ३३-३४॥

---

१. M Ad दित्यस्योपोदि°. २. M ब्र...यार्वेदि. ३. M Ad °मप्यवायो. ४. M Ad त...र्शनादा°; thus T. ५. M Ad ब्राह्मणं; thus T. ६-६. M Ad दृष्टस्य...प. ७. M Ad व्यपायं°. ८. M यजमा...ति हत्या°. ९. M Ad T ब्राह्मण. १०-१०. M चर्वादीनि सा...नि. ११. M Ad हविष्यनु°.

'प्रजापतेर्भागोऽसि' **इति पत्नीं वाचयति।** '०ऊर्जस्वान् पयस्वान् प्राणापानौ मे पाहि समानव्यानौ मे पाह्युदानव्यानौ मे पाह्यक्षितोऽस्यक्षित्यै त्वा मे मेक्षेष्ठा अमुत्रामुष्मिन् लोक इह च' **इति**॥ ३५ ॥ **तं पूर्वेणाज्यं यजमानं चातिहृत्यान्तर्वेद्यासादयति**॥ ३६ ॥ **तस्मिन्नेवाध्वर्युर्यजमानं वाचयति**॥ ३७ ॥ **तमपरेणात्मानं पूर्वेणोत्करमुदञ्चमुद्वासयत्यग्नीधे ब्रह्मणे होत्रेऽध्वर्यव इति**॥ ३८ ॥ 'मनो ज्योतिर्जुषताम्' **इति स्रुवेण सन्ततिं जुहोति।** '०आज्य=मादयन्ताꣳ स्वाहा' **इति**॥ ३९ ॥ 'एहि यजमान' **इत्युक्त्वाऽऽन्वारब्धे यजमाने होतुराहुतिं द्वितीयां जुहोति**॥ ४० ॥ **अथाह**– 'ब्रह्मन् प्रस्थास्यामः, समिधमाधायाग्नीत् परिधीꣳश्चाग्निं च सकृत्सकृत् संमृड्ढि' **इति**॥ ४१ ॥ **इध्मसन्नहनानि स्फ्य उपसंगृह्य सकृदग्नीन्मध्यमं परिधिं संमार्ष्टि, सकृद् दक्षिणार्ध्यम्, सकृदुत्तरार्ध्यम्, सकृदग्निम्**॥ ४२ ॥ **संमृज्यासञ्चरे तृणान्युदस्यति**॥ ४३ ॥ **स्रुचावादा–याध्वर्युरत्याक्रामति**॥ ४४ ॥ **अत्याक्रम्याश्राव्याह** 'देवान् यज' **इति**॥ ४५ ॥ **वषट्कृते मध्ये समिधो जुहोति**॥ ४६ ॥ 'यज यज' **इति त्रीन् प्रतीचोऽनूयाजान् यजति**॥ ४७ ॥ **उत्तमꣳ हुत्वा प्राचीराहुतीः सꣳस्रावेण संभिनत्ति**॥ ४८ ॥ **अत्याक्रम्य यथायतनꣳ स्रुचौ सादयित्वा** 'वाजस्य मा'॥ २.३.२.४९ ॥ **[इति द्वितीयः पटलः (११)]**

[स्रुग्व्यूहनाद्युत्तरतन्त्रम्]

'वाजस्य मा प्रसवेनोद्ग्राभेणोद्गृभीद्' **इति दक्षिणेनोत्तानेन प्रस्तरं च जुहूञ्चोद्गृह्णाति**॥ १ ॥ 'अथा सपत्नाँ इन्द्रो मे निग्राभेणाधराँ अकः' **इति सव्येनोपभृतं निबाधते**॥ २ ॥ 'उद्ग्राभं च निग्राभं च = व्यस्यताम्' **इति प्राचीं जुहूमुदूहति प्रतीचीमुपभृतमपोहति**॥ ३ ॥ **सव्ये हस्ते प्रस्तरꣳ समस्य** 'वसुभ्यस्त्वाऽनज्मि' **इति स्रुचा मध्यमं परिधिमनक्ति**॥ ४ ॥ 'रुद्रेभ्यस्त्वाऽनज्मि' **इति**

पत्नीं वाचयित्वा तमादायापरेण गार्हपत्यं परिहृत्य [1]दक्षिणेन पूर्वेण च ब्रह्मयजमानावतिहृत्यान्तर्वेद्यासादयति[1] ॥ ३५–३६ ॥

यजमानं वाचयित्वोक्तेन पथोद्वासयित्वाऽध्वर्युरुद्वासनात्पूर्वमुद्वास्यमानं व्यादिशति यजमानो–'ऽग्नीधे ब्रह्मणे' होत्रे'त्यादिना। यथादेवतं यथाद्रव्यं च प्रतिगृह्णन्ति। 'ब्रह्मण ओदनमि'ति [2]सर्वत्रैवं दक्षिणाप्रतिग्रहे। प्रधानदक्षिणास्वेव[2], नाङ्गदक्षिणास्वित्यन्ये। होतुराहुतिं द्वितीयामित्याच्छिद्रकाणाम–नित्यत्वप्रदर्शनार्थम्। नित्येषु हि तेषु सन्ततिमन्विति विहितानामनाज्ञातानामन्ते स्यात्। तथा सति पञ्चमी भवति। 'सन्ततिमनुहोतुराहुति'मिति च विकृतिषु दर्शनादभाव एव [3]भवति॥ ३८–३९ ॥

संस्रावेण संभिनत्ति, अविच्छिन्नाहुतीः[3] करोति॥ २.३.२.४८ ॥ **[इति द्वितीयः पटलः (११)]**

'उद्ग्राभं चे'ति प्राच्यां जुह्वा उदूहनेऽथा सपत्नानिति प्रतीच्योपभृतोपोहने॥ ३ ॥

१–१. M दक्षिण...नावतिः. **२–२.** M सर्वत्रैवन्द...स्वेव; Ad दक्षिणाति स्वग्रहे प्रस्थानदक्षिणास्वेव, T प्रधानं. **३–३.** M भवन्ति...विच्छिन्नाहुतीः.

दक्षिणार्ध्यम् ॥ ५ ॥ 'आदित्येभ्यस्त्वाऽनज्मि' **इत्युत्तरार्ध्यम्** ॥ ६ ॥ **यथायतनः स्रुचौ सादयित्वा मध्यमं परिधिमन्वारभ्याश्रावयति** ॥ ७ ॥ 'ओ श्रावय' **इत्याह** ॥ ८ ॥ 'इषिता दैव्या होतारो भद्र-वाच्याय प्रेषितो मानुषः सूक्तवाकाय सूक्ता ब्रूहि' **इति** ॥ ९ ॥ **अनुप्रहृत्य शकलं निधाय जुहूमाहृत्योपभृतं प्रस्तरं स्रुक्ष्वनक्ति** 'अक्तं रिहाणाः' **इत्यग्राणि जुह्वाम्,** 'वियन्तु वयः' **इति मध्यान्युपभृति,** 'प्रजां योनिं मा निमृक्षमा प्यायन्तामाप ओषधयः' **इति मूलानि ध्रुवायाम्** ॥ १० ॥ **त्रिभिरक्त्वा** 'मरुतां पृषत्यसि' **इति प्रस्तरमनु प्रहरति** ॥ ११ ॥ 'वशा पृश्निर्भूत्वा दिवं गच्छ' **इति धूममुद्यन्तमुदीक्षते**। '°ततो नो वृष्टिमेरय' **इति** ॥ १२ ॥ 'रयिं गच्छ' **इत्यपरेण मुष्टिं प्रस्तरात्तृणमपयच्छति** ॥ १३ ॥ **तज्जुह्वामवदधाति** ॥ १४ ॥ **अथ सर्वं प्रस्तरमनुप्रहरति** ॥ १५ ॥ **यत् प्रस्तरात्तृणमपयच्छति तज्जुह्वामक्त्वा** 'इदं ब्रूहि' **इत्याहाग्नीधम्** ॥ १६ ॥ 'अनुप्रहर संवदस्व' **इत्याहाग्नीत्** ॥ १७ ॥ 'अगानग्नीत्' **इत्याहाध्वर्युः** ॥ १८ ॥ 'अगन्' **इत्याहाग्नीत्** ॥ १९ ॥ 'श्रावय' **इत्याहाध्वर्युः** ॥ २० ॥ 'श्रौषट्' **इत्याहाग्नीत्** ॥ २१ ॥ **अनुप्रहरति** ॥ २२ ॥ 'स्वगा दैव्या होतृभ्यः स्वस्तिर्मानुषेभ्यः शंयोर्ब्रूहि' **इति** ॥ २३ ॥ 'स्वस्तिवचनो भूयासम्' **इत्यात्मानं प्रत्यभिमृशते** ॥ २४ ॥ **अप उपस्पृश्य** 'आयुष्पा अग्नेऽस्यायुर्मे पाहि' **इति प्राणान् संमृशते**। '°चक्षुष्पा=पाहि' **इति** ॥ २५ ॥ 'य परिधिं पर्यधत्थाः' **इति मध्यमं परिधिमनुप्रहरति**। '°अग्ने देव पणिभिः= चेतयातै' **इति** ॥ २६ ॥ 'अग्नेः प्रियं पाथोऽपीतम्' **इत्यभितः परिधीन् प्रहरति** ॥ २७ ॥ **यदा जानाति** 'ऊर्ध्वं जिगातु भेषजम्' **इत्यपः स्रुचौ संप्रगृह्णाति**। '°सꣳस्रावभागाः स्थेषा=मादयध्वम्' **इति** ॥ २८ ॥ 'घृताचीः स्थः' **इति ध्रुवायाः सꣳस्रावं प्रश्चोत्य** 'धुरि धुर्यौ पातम्' **इत्यभितः स्रुग्भ्यां ध्रुवाः**

स्रुचा मध्यमं परिधिम् अन्वारभ्य प्रह्वस्तिष्ठन्नाश्रावयति ॥ ७ ॥

प्रस्तरस्याग्राणि सकृन्मन्त्रमुक्त्वा त्रिरनक्ति। अतिग्रहणम्। तथा मध्यमूलानि प्रस्तरप्रहरणेनाक्त्वाग्रं[१] प्रहरेदित्यादि द्रष्टव्यम् ॥ १०-१४ ॥

अथ सर्वं प्रस्तरमनुप्रहरति। नामग्रहणादूर्ध्वं[२] प्रहरति। सर्वं ततो नापहरतीत्यर्थः। न च नामग्रहणमात्रे। तत ऊर्ध्वमनियमः। सूक्तवाकान्ते अपयतं बर्हिरक्त्वा 'इदं ब्रूहि' इत्यादि प्रेषितोऽध्वर्युणा होता मुहूर्तमात्रं[३] विलम्ब्य यथा शंयुवाकेन[३] यथा परिधिप्रहरणं संगच्छते तथा ब्रवीति ॥ १५-२३ ॥

इमां भूमिम् आत्मानं प्रति हृदयदेशं प्रत्यभिमृशते ॥ २४ ॥

'आयुष्पा' इत्यादिषु यथालिङ्गं संमर्शनम् ॥ २५ ॥

स्रुक्संग्रहणे दक्षिणेन जुहूं सव्येनोपभृतमाहवनीयस्योपरि जुहूं जुह्वामुपभृतं, यथा संस्रावो[४] जुह्वां

---

१. M प्रहरप्रहरे° ; Ad प्रहरेणेनात्यग्रं प्रहरे° ; thus T. २. M Ad °ग्रहणमूर्ध्वं. ३-३. M मुहूर्तम...शंयु° ; Ad °मात्रं अवि° ; thus T. ४. M Ad संस्रापो; thus T.

समनक्ति ॥ २९ ॥ 'अग्नेर्वामपन्नगृहस्य सदसि सादयामि' **इति स्फ्ये जुहूः सादयति, नोपभृतः सःस्पर्शयति** ॥ ३० ॥ 'सुम्नाय (सुम्निनीः सुम्ने मा) धत्तम्' **इति स्रुवं च जुहूं चादत्ते** ॥ ३१ ॥ **होत्रे वेदं प्रयच्छति** ॥ ३२ ॥ **दक्षिणेन गार्हपत्यमध्वर्युश्च यजमानश्च प्रपद्येते, उत्तरेण होता चाग्नीच्च** ॥ ३३ ॥ **आज्यस्य सःस्पृश्याग्नीच्छाकलमिध्मं गार्हपत्येऽभ्यादधाति** ॥ ३४ ॥ **अपरेण गार्हपत्यं प्रागावृत्त उपविश्य पत्नीः संयाजयति** ॥ ३५ ॥ 'सोमायानुब्रूहि' **इत्याहाज्यस्य गृह्णानश्चतुः** ॥ ३६ ॥ 'ओ श्रावय' **इत्याह** ॥ ३७ ॥ 'सोमं यज' **इति** ॥ ३८ ॥ **वषट्कृते मध्ये जुहोति** ॥ ३९ ॥ 'त्वष्ट्रेऽनुब्रूहि' **इत्याहाज्यस्यैव गृह्णानश्चतुः** ॥ ४० ॥ 'ओ श्रावय' **इत्याह** ॥ ४१ ॥ 'त्वष्टारं यज' **इति** ॥ ४२ ॥ **वषट्कृते जुहोति** ॥ ४३ ॥ 'राकाया अनुब्रूहि' **इत्याहाज्यस्यैव गृह्णानश्चतुः** ॥ ४४ ॥ 'ओ श्रावय' **इत्याह** ॥ ४५ ॥ 'राकां यज' **इति** ॥ ४६ ॥ **वषट्कृते जुहोति** ॥ ४७ ॥ 'देवानां पत्नीभ्योऽनुब्रूहि' **इत्याहाज्यस्यैव गृह्णानश्चतुः** ॥ ४८ ॥ 'ओ श्रावय' **इत्याह** ॥ ४९ ॥ 'देवानां पत्नीर्यज' **इति** ॥ ५० ॥ **वषट्कृते जुहोति** ॥ ५१ ॥ 'अग्नये गृहपतयेऽनुब्रूहि' **इत्याहाज्यस्यैव गृह्णानश्चतुः** ॥ ५२ ॥ 'ओ श्रावय' **इत्याह** ॥ ५३ ॥ 'अग्निं गृहपतिं यज' **इति** ॥ ५४ ॥ **वषट्कृत उत्तरार्धेऽतिहाय पूर्वा आहुतीर्जुहोति** ॥ ५५ ॥ **वेदे स्रुचः सादयित्वा होतुरङ्गुष्ठमाज्येनाक्त्वा होतुः पाणौ चतुरवत्तामिडामादधाति** ॥ ५६ ॥ **अन्वारभन्तेऽध्वर्युर्यजमानः पत्नी च** ॥ ५७ ॥ **उपहूताया-**

पतति, जुह्वाश्चाहवनीये तथा[१] मन्त्रेण संप्रगृह्णाति। उभयोः संस्रावं[२] ध्रुवायां[३] प्रश्चोत्य उभाभ्यामभितः समनक्ति ॥ २९ ॥

'अग्नेर्वामि'ति मन्त्रेण [४]स्फ्ये सादयति जुहूं संस्पर्शयति नोपभृतम्[४] ॥ ३० ॥

तान्न सादयति ॥ ३१ ॥

यजमानेनाभिमन्त्रितं वेदं होत्रे प्रयच्छति ॥ ३२ ॥

यदा यजमानो यजमानायतन एवासीनोऽनुमन्त्रयते तदा न गच्छति। उत्तरेण होताग्नीदाज्यं च गच्छति[५]। यथा सूत्रकारेणाम्नातं– 'स्फ्यमाज्यस्थालीमुदकमण्डलुमाग्नीध्र'[६] इति। अन्य आमनन्ति दक्षिणेनाज्यस्थालीं सस्रुवां सव्येन जुहूमिति[७]। अतो दक्षिणेनाप्याज्यस्य मार्गः[८] ॥ ३३ ॥

मेक्षणयोरवतक्षणानि सप्त चान्ये च शाकलाः[९]। शाकल इध्मः। वेद उपभृत्स्थानीयः ॥ ३४ ॥

स्फ्यहस्तः प्रत्याश्रावयति। पूर्वोक्तसूत्रकारवचनादर्शनादिह चाप्रतिषेधात् कामसंयोगेन वैकल्पिकी राका। तथा कर्मसंयोगेनाम्नायते। 'नित्यवदेके समामनन्ती'ति ॥ ४४–४७ ॥

केचिदामनन्ति आपन्नोऽपि[१०] गत्वान्वारभते यजमानः ॥ ५७ ॥

---

१. M Ad ऽथो; thus T. **२.** M Ad संस्राव. **३.** M Ad स्रुवा° ; thus T. **४–४.** M Ad स्फ्ये सादयति। जुहूं संस्पर्शयति चोपभृतं. This text is not according to the purport of the *sūtra*-text. **५.** M Ad गच्छन्ति; thus T. **६.** M °मण्डुलु°. **७.** M Ad जुहोमीति. **८.** M Ad मार्गं; thus T. **९.** M Ad शकलाः; thus T. **१०.** M Ad अव्यपन्नोऽपि [Ad न्नोपि], T प्रप°.

मिडायामुत्तरतः प्रागावृत्ताय द्विरग्नीध आदधाति ॥ ५८ ॥ **प्राश्नन्ति** ॥ ५९ ॥ **मार्जयन्ते** ॥ ६० ॥ 'मनो ज्योतिर्जुषताम्' **इति जपति**। '०आज्यं विच्छिन्नं यज्ञꣳ समिमं दधातु। बृहस्पतिस्तनुतामिमम्=दयन्ताम्' **इति सन्ततमा पत्नियै** ॥ ६१ ॥ 'सं पत्नी पत्या सुकृतेषु गच्छताम्' **इति स्रुवेण पत्नीहोमं जुहोत्यन्वारब्धायां पत्न्याम्**। '०यज्ञस्य युक्तौ धुर्यावभूताम्। संक्रामन्तौ विजहतामरातिमुत्तमं ज्योतिर्दिव्यारभेताꣳ स्वाहा' **इति** ॥ ६२ ॥ **वेदस्य तृणं प्रच्छिद्यते** ॥ ६३ ॥ **जुह्वाञ्चाज्यस्थाल्यां चाक्त्वा** 'इदं ब्रूहि' **इत्याहाग्नीधम्** ॥ ६४ ॥ 'अनुप्रहर संवदस्व' **इत्याहाग्नीत्** ॥ ६५ ॥ 'अगानग्नीत्' **इत्याहाध्वर्युः** ॥ ६६ ॥ 'अगन्' **इत्याहाग्नीत्** ॥ ६७ ॥ 'श्रावय' **इत्याहाध्वर्युः** ॥ ६८ ॥ 'श्रौषट्' **इत्याहाग्नीत्** ॥ ६९ ॥ **अनुप्रहरति** ॥ ७० ॥ 'स्वगा दैव्या होतृभ्यः स्वस्तिर्मानुषेभ्यः शंयोर्ब्रूहि' **इति** ॥ ७१ ॥ **यदा जानाति** 'ऊर्ध्वं जिगातु भेषजम्' **इत्यथ स्रुवं च स्रुचं च संप्रगृह्णाति** ॥ ७२ ॥ **चतुर्गृहीतं गृह्णीते** ॥ ७३ ॥ **फलीकरणानावपति** ॥ ७४ ॥ **तान् जुहोति** ॥ ७५ ॥ **वेदेनोपयच्छत्यन्वाहार्यपचने फलीकरणहोमम्** 'अग्नेऽदब्धायोऽशीततनो पाहि=योनिꣳ स्वाहा' **इति** ॥ ७६ ॥ **स्रुवं च जुहूं चादत्ते** ॥ ७७ ॥ **होत्रे वेदं प्रयच्छति** ॥ ७८ ॥ **प्राडेत्य ध्रुवामाप्याययति** 'आप्यायतां ध्रुवा घृतेन=यज्ञे अस्मिन्' **इति** ॥ ७९ ॥ **वेदस्य तृणानि बर्हिषोपसंगृह्य** 'देवा गातुविदः' **इति स्रुचा जुहोति**। '०गातुं वित्त्वा=यज्ञꣳ स्वाहा वाचि' **इति** ॥ ८० ॥ 'समक्तं बर्हिर्हविषा घृतेन' **इति ध्रुवायां बर्हिरक्त्वाऽनु प्रास्यति**। '०समादित्यैर्वसुभि सं मरुद्भिः। समिन्द्रो विश्वदेवेभिरक्ता दिव्यं नभो गच्छतु यत्स्वाहा' **इति** ॥ ८१ ॥ 'स्वाहा वाते धाः' **इत्युपरिष्टात् सꣳस्रावेणाभि जुहोति** ॥ ८२ ॥ **निधाय स्रुचं पूर्वेणाहवनीयं प्रणीता**

प्राश्नन्तीति बहुवचनं ब्रह्मयजमानाध्वर्यूणां भक्षं प्रापयति सन्निधानात्[१]। तेन विनापि चरितार्थत्वात्। न ब्रह्मण[२] इत्यन्ये। केचित्पत्नीमपि प्राशयन्ति। तदयुक्तम्—

सह ब्रह्मौदनं कुर्यात् सहाग्न्याधानमेव च।
सह यज्ञक्रियाः सर्वा हविषां भक्षणाद्विना ॥

इति मनुवचनम्[३]। प्रत्यक्षवचनमन्तरेण तद्बाधस्यान्याय्यत्वात् ॥ ५९ ॥

मार्जनदर्शनादिति चेत् भक्षमन्तरेणापि मार्जनमुपपद्यते 'उपस्पृश्य मार्जयित्वे'ति[४]। 'बृहस्पतिस्तनुतामि'त्यस्येडाङ्गत्वमिति[५] चेत्, होतुः पाणावक्त्वैत्रेडा[६], [७]सा च नान्यैः[७] प्राश्यते[८] ॥ ६०–६१ ॥

[९]इध्मसंव्रश्चनान्यभ्याधाय फलीकरणहोमं[९] जुहोति[१०] ॥ ७४–७६ ॥

---

१. M Ad असन्नि°. २. M Ad ब्राह्मण. ३. The verse quoted in the name of Manu is not found in the *Manusmṛti*. ४. M Ad °मार्जनीयत्वेति; thus T. ५. M Ad °मित्यैंडांग°; thus T. ६. M °वत्तैडा, Ad °वत्रैडा, T वक्तैवा. ७–७. M Ad सा वचनान्यैः. ८. M Ad प्रश्यते, T प्राश्यन्त न...इध्म°. ९–९. M Ad °सप्रश्चनान्यमाडा...ण होमं. १०. Ad जुहोतीति.

आहृत्यार्धमन्तर्वेदि यजमानस्याञ्जलावानयति ॥ ८३ ॥ **अभिपूर्य पूर्णपात्रे वाचयति** 'सदसि सन्मे भूयाः सर्वमसि=क्षेष्ठाः' **इति** ॥ ८४ ॥ 'प्राच्यां दिशि देवा ऋत्विजो मार्जयन्ताम्' **इति यजमानस्याञ्जलावानयति**। '°दक्षिणायां दिशि मासाः पितरो=मार्जयन्ताम्' **इति** ॥ ८५ ॥ **निधाय स्थालीमुपोत्थाय दक्षिणं वेद्यन्तमनु विष्णुक्रमान् क्रमते** 'विष्णोः क्रमोऽस्यभिमातिहा=दिशोऽनु-विक्रमे निर्भक्तः स यं द्विष्मः' **इति** ॥ ८६ ॥ 'अगन्म सुवः सुवरगन्म' **इति प्राङ् प्रक्रामति** ॥ ८७ ॥ 'संदृशस्ते मा च्छित्सि' **इत्यादित्यमुपतिष्ठते**। '°यत्ते=पृथिव्या अस्मादन्नाद्यान्निर्भजानि=सं ज्योतिषाऽभूवम्' **इति** ॥ ८८ ॥ 'ऐन्द्रीमावृतमन्वावर्ते' **इति दक्षिणा पर्यावर्तते** ॥ ८९ ॥ **तदानीमेवोपावर्तते** 'समहं= रायस्पोषः' **इति** ॥ ९० ॥ 'समिद्धो अग्ने मे दीदिहि' **इत्युप वा समिन्धे समिधं वाऽभ्यादधाति**। '°समेद्धा ते अग्ने दीद्यासꣳ स्वाहा' **इति** ॥ ९१ ॥ 'वसुमान् यज्ञो वसीयान् भूयासम्' **इत्युपतिष्ठते** ॥ ९२ ॥ 'अग्न आयूꣳषि पवसे' **इति द्वाभ्यामाग्निपावमानीभ्यां गार्हपत्यमभ्येति**। '°आ सुवोर्जं=मयि' **इति** ॥ ९३ ॥ 'अग्ने गृहपते' **इत्युपतिष्ठते**। '°सुगृहपति=तन्तवे' **इत्यन्ततः** ॥ ९४ ॥ 'कस्त्वा युनक्ति स त्वा विमुञ्चतु' **इत्युलूखलमुसलं परेक्षते** ॥ ९५ ॥ 'यानि घर्मे कपालानि' **इति कपालानि**। '°उपचिन्वन्ति=ञ्चताम्' **इति** ॥ ९६ ॥ 'यज्ञो बभूव स आ बभूव' **इति यज्ञस्य पुनरालम्भं प्राडेति**। '°स प्र यज्ञे स वावृधे स देवानां=रयीणाम्' **इति** ॥ ९७ ॥ 'सोमाँ अग्नेऽविमाँ अश्वी यज्ञः' **इति प्राङुत्क्रम्य जपति**। '°नृवत्सखा=सभावान्' **इति** ॥ ९८ ॥ 'पयस्वतीरोषधयः' **इति तिरःपवित्रमप आचामति**। '°पयस्वद्वीरु=सꣳसृज' **इति** ॥ ९९ ॥ 'अग्ने व्रतपते' **इति मार्जयित्वा समिधमादधाति**। '°व्रतमचारिषं तदशकं तन्मेऽराधि स्वाहा' **इति** ॥ १०० ॥ **आगत्यापरेण गार्हपत्यमासीनां पत्नीं विस्रꣳसयति** 'इमं विष्यामि=तनुवा मम' **इति** ॥ १०१ ॥ 'पयस्वतीरोषधयः' **इति तिरःपवित्रमप आशयति**। '°पयस्व=सृज' **इति** ॥ १०२ ॥ 'अग्ने व्रतपते' **इति मार्जयित्वा समिधमाधापयति**।

अयञ्च कालः पत्न्या योक्त्रविस्रंसनस्य[1]। [2]तथा अच्छिद्रकल्पे[2] विधानात्। तत्रापि यत्र पत्नीं[3] विस्रंसयति[4]। ब्राह्मणे [5]विहितायाः....पूर्णपात्रेऽन्ततोऽनुष्टुभेति[5] समायुषेत्यस्यास्मिन् काले विस्रंसनमनूद्य [6]सिद्धवदनुवर्तनं विहितम्॥ १०१ ॥

तथाऽञ्जलौ योक्त्राधानपूर्णपात्रनिनयनमुखविमार्जनानि[6] वेदस्य तृणानि बर्हिषो[7]...गृह्यन्ते ('समङ्क्तां बर्हिर्हविषा घृतेन समादित्यैर्वसुभिः सं मरुद्भिः। समिन्देण विश्वेभि)र्देवे-भिरङ्क्तामि'त्यन्तो मन्त्रो(मार्ज)ने[7]। 'दिव्यं नभः' इत्यादिरनुप्रासने[8] प्रणीताभ्योऽर्धमञ्जलावानी-यान्तर्वेद्यामासाद्याभिपूर्य यजमानभागप्राशनोत्तरकाले[8] पूर्णपात्रे वाचयति। यदि कालान्तरे यजमानभागप्राशनमप्राशितमेव वाचयति। येषामुत्तरपदार्था यजमानकर्तृकास्तेषां निधाय स्थालीमिति निहितायां स्थाल्यामिति

---

१. M Ad योक्तवि°. **२–२.** M तथा ...कल्पे. **३.** M यत्र...श्नीं. **४.** M Ad ° यतीति. **५.** M Ad या...र्ण पात्रेऽन्ततो° [Ad पात्रेन्त], Ad योक्त्राधाना°. **६–६.** M ° वदनुप...पात्रनि°; thus Ad T. **७–७.** M Ad बर्हित...त्राञ्जने [Ad प्राञ्जने]; T बहिषो...गृह्यन्ते... रक्तामित्यन्तो मन्त्रोऽञ्जने. Doubtful reading. **८–८.** M Ad ° प्रासने [T ° साने] प्रणीत...भिर्य यज...नोत्तर; thus T.

'°व्रतमचारिषं तदशकं तन्मेऽराधि स्वाहा' **इति** ॥ १०३ ॥ **प्रतिपरैति पत्नी दक्षिणतः** ॥ १०४ ॥ **उपविश्य यजमानभागं प्राश्नाति** 'प्रजापतेर्विभान्नाम=मानेन' **इति** ॥ १०५ ॥ **सन्तिष्ठेते दर्शपूर्णमासौ सन्तिष्ठेते दर्शपूर्णमासौ** ॥ २.३.३.१०६ ॥ **[इति तृतीयः पटलः** (१२)**]**

॥ इति द्वितीयप्रपाठके तृतीयोऽनुवाकः ॥

॥ इति दर्शपूर्णमासाख्यो द्वितीयः प्रपाठकः ॥

□ □ □

व्याख्येयम्। आध्वर्यवत्वे[१] नास्ति वक्तव्यम्[२]। [३]किन्त्वाशीराशासनेऽध्वर्युर्यजमानस्य[३] तत्पुत्राणां च नामानि[४] गृह्णाति। नैतदेवम्। आत्मनोऽग्रे नाम गह्णातीत्युक्तम्। यद्येवमभिप्रेप्स्येद् यजमानस्येत्येवावक्ष्यत्[५]। उच्यते। एवं कर्तव्यमिति[६] अस्माभिर्न शक्यते वक्तुम्। एवमुक्ते कोऽर्थ इति विचारणीयम्। आशिषां[७] च यजमानार्थत्वम्। [८]युक्तम्। तत्र कथमर्थोऽवगम्यत इति चेदात्मनः स्वामिन[८] इत्यध्याहर्तव्यम्। एवं सर्वत्र प्रत्यगाशीःषु येषां याजमानत्वं[९] तेषां नास्ति विचारणीयम्। व्रतसर्ग[१०] आध्वर्यवः। तत्र चेन्न कृतो योक्त्रविमोक इह क्रियते। व्रतविसर्गोऽत्रैव। तत्र योक्त्रविमोके व्रतसर्गमपि तत्रैव कारयन्ति केचित्। [११]मुखं विमृष्टेऽवभृथस्यैव[११] रूपं कृत्वोत्तिष्ठतीति[१२] ॥ १०२–१०४ ॥

उक्तवचनाद्यजमानभागप्राशनस्यायमप्येकः[१३] कालः। वरुणपाशविमोकं[१४] सौमिके यागे केचित्कुर्वन्ति। सर्वकर्मसु सर्वर्त्विग्विषयमित्यपरे॥ १०५ ॥

अभ्यासो मङ्गलार्थः[१५]। सन्तिष्ठेते[१६] दर्शपूणमासौ॥ २.३.३.१०६ ॥ **[इति तृतीयः पटलः** (१२)**]**

॥ इति व्याख्यायां द्वितीयप्रपाठके तृतीयोऽनुवाकः ॥[१७]

॥ इति कल्पागमसंग्रहे दर्शपूर्णमासाख्यो द्वितीयः प्रपाठकः ॥[१८]

□ □ □

---

१. M Ad आध्वर्युवत्वे; thus T. **२.** T प्रक्तव्यम्. **३–३.** M Ad °शीराशासे...नस्य, T °राशने°. **४.** M Ad नामा न; thus T. **५.** T यजमानं योत्येवावक्ष्यत्. **६.** M gives the text व्याख्येयम् also between कर्तव्यम् and अस्माभिः. **७.** Ad आव्रिषां. **८–८.** M युक्तन्तु कथमते....दात्मनन्तामिन°, Ad °चोदात्मन°. **९.** M Ad यज°; thus T. **१०.** M Ad वतस्सर्ग. **११–११.** M मु...भृतस्यैव, T °भृत°. **१२.** M कृतोत्ति°. **१३.** M Ad प्राश्नंन्यायम°; thus T. **१४.** M Ad °मोकः. **१५.** T मङ्गलात्. **१६.** M Ad सन्तिष्ठते. **१७.** M इति तृतीयः। समाप्तश्च।, Ad इति तृतीयः समाप्तः।, T इति तृतीय प्रपाठः समाप्तः।. **१८.** M Ad T No mention of Prapāṭhaka.

॥ अथ तृतीयः प्रपाठकः ॥

[याजमानम्]

[प्रवत्स्यदुपस्थानम्]

प्रवसथमेष्यन् भवति ॥ १ ॥ **स पुरस्तादेव सꣳशास्ति यदस्य सꣳशिष्यं भवति** ॥ २ ॥ **स यज्ञोपवीतं कृत्वाऽप आचम्य यजमानायतने तिष्ठन्नाहवनीयमुपतिष्ठते** 'मम नाम प्रथमं जातवेदः=बिभराष्यग्ने' **इति** ॥ ३ ॥ **अथ वाचंयमः प्रव्रजति** ॥ ४ ॥ **स यदा वै वाचं यच्छति मनस्तर्हि वाक् समारोहति। यदु वै मनः स प्राणः, साऽनार्ता देवता; सोऽनार्तां देवताꣳ समारोह्य प्रवसति** ॥ ५ ॥ **सोऽगारेण वा वृक्षेण वाऽन्तर्धाय वाचं विसृजते** ॥ ६ ॥ **तस्य प्रवसतो व्रतम्** ॥ ७ ॥

---

[१]*प्रवसथमेष्यन् भवति ।* प्रकृष्टे[२] देशे वस्तुमेष्यन् भवति। यं देशं गत्वा तस्मिन्नेवाहनि समीपमागन्तुमग्नीनां न शक्यते तं देशं गमिष्यन्नित्यर्थः ॥ १ ॥

मनस्तर्हि वाक्[३] समारोहति। वाचाऽभिधित्सितोऽर्थो[४] मनसि वर्तते। नियमिता यदा[५] वाङ्न प्रवर्तते मनः [६]समारूढेव तदा भवति[६]। यदु वै[७] मनः स प्राणः। शरीरान्तर्गतो वायुः प्राण इत्युच्यते। कर्मबुद्धीन्द्रियाणां दशानामेकादशं मन[८]आख्यमुभयात्मकमिन्द्रियम्। तयोः पुरुषार्थं प्रवर्तमानयोरात्मलाभोपक्रान्तिः[९] तुल्यकाले। [१०]अन्यतरादर्शनेऽ[११]न्यतरस्याप्यदर्शनमिति। मन एव प्राण[११] इत्यभेदोपचारः। प्राणस्य च न कदाचित् [१२]स्वव्यापारनिवृत्तिः, अतोऽनार्तेत्युच्यते[१२] ॥ ५ ॥

अग्न्यगारमगारादिनान्तर्धाय पत्न्या[१३] प्रवासविधानाभावादविधाने च सान्निध्यस्यावश्यकर्तव्यत्वादप्रवासे प्राप्तेऽनेकपत्नीकस्यैकया[१४] क्रत्वर्थेषु[१४] क्रियमाणेष्वितरासां प्रवासोऽनुज्ञायते इति गम्यते[१५]। स्त्र्युपगमनप्रतिषेधादेवैकपत्नीकस्यापि[१५] पत्न्या प्रवासोऽनुज्ञायत इति कस्मान्न ज्ञायते। उच्यते। 'यानुत्सृज्य दम्पती सह व्रजतः[१६] तानुत्सृज्य पुनरादधीयाता'मिति [१७]शाखान्तरे वचनम्। अत [१७]एकपत्नीकस्य सहगमनं नास्त्येव ॥ ७ ॥

---

१. M Ad do not mention the title of the Prapāṭhaka. Ad starts with श्रीः अथ प्रथमः, a reference to first Anuvāka. T begins with the title ॥ याजमानम् ॥. **२.** M Ad प्रकृष्टदे° ; thus T. **३.** Ad प्राक्. **४.** T °भिनिर्णीतोऽर्थो. **५.** M Ad यदि; thus T. **६–६.** M मन... भवति, Ad मनसा मा गूढेव; thus T. **७.** M य दुवै. **८.** M Ad आद्यमु° ; thus T. **९.** M Ad °लाभाप क्रान्ती; thus T. **१०.** M Ad अन्यतरादर्शना° ; thus T. **११–११.** M °न्यतर...व प्राण; thus Ad T. **१२–१२.** M स्वव्यापार...र्तेत्यु°, Ad स्वव्र्या° ; thus T. **१३.** M Ad पत्न्यां; thus T. **१४–१४.** M °पत्नीकै ...षु; thus Ad T. **१५–१५.** M °गम्यते ...देवैक°. **१६.** M Ad व्रजीवः; thus T. **१७–१७.** M श...त एकत्नी° ; thus Ad.

नानृतं वदति। अनत्यधःशायी प्राकृछयिता वा॥८॥ (प्रपथात्) प्रागुच्चारः समिधमाहरति॥९॥ इडाऽग्निर्भवति॥१०॥ न द्वादशीमति प्रवसति॥११॥ यथा दैव्ये विपरिधायैवं प्रोष्य गृहानुपावर्तते॥१२॥ प्रपथात्समिधं कुरुते॥१३॥ अग्नीन् पराख्याय वाचं यच्छति मनस्तर्हि वाक् समारोहति। सोऽनार्तामेव देवतां समारोह्य गृहानुपावर्तते॥१४॥ स यज्ञोपवीतं कृत्वाऽप आचम्य यजमानायतने तिष्ठन्नाहवनीये विपरिधत्ते 'मम नाम तव च=गन्धर्वः' **इति॥१५॥ तूष्णीं तृतीयं समिधोऽभ्यादधाति॥१६॥ अन्वाहार्यपचनमेत्य तूष्णीं तृतीयꣳ समिधोऽभ्यादधाति॥१७॥ अभिप्रपद्य गार्हपत्यमुपतिष्ठते** 'त्वत्पितारो अग्ने=सुहिते मा धाः' **इति॥१८॥ तूष्णीं तृतीयꣳ समिधोऽभ्यादधाति॥१९॥ उपचिनोति परि वा समूहयति** 'अयमग्निः श्रेष्ठतमोऽयं=सुवीर्यम्' **इति॥२०॥ अथ यजमानायतने तृणेषु कूर्चे वोपविश्यामन्त्रयते** 'यो नाभिवदत्यभिवदितव्यान् संवदते यैरस्य संवदितव्यं भवति' **इति नु दैव्यमुपस्थानम्॥२१॥ एवं ह देवा उपतस्थुरेवमृषय एवं ये पूर्वे श्रोत्रिया ऋतायव आसुः॥२२॥ तदेतद् ह्युत्सन्नं व्रतस्य गरिम्णाऽविद्यया वाऽन्येन वा॥२३॥ नान्वाख्याने**

न द्वादशीमतिप्रवसति[१]। [२]प्रस्थानतिथिमारभ्य। अन्ये पक्षद्वयोर्द्वादशीं[२] तिथिमिति व्याचक्षते। दर्शपूर्णमासाः [३]सान्निध्यनिवृत्यर्थमिति॥११॥

देवैर्वस्त्रपरिधानमिव कृत्वा प्रोषित इत्यर्थवादोऽस्मिन् [४]पक्ष उपपद्यतेतराम्॥१२॥

प्रकृष्टः[४] पन्थाः[५] प्रपथः, दूरत एवेत्यर्थः॥१३॥

पराख्याय दृष्ट्वाऽऽहवनीयेन विपरिधत्ते। यथायथं नामधेयविपरिधानं करोत्यग्निनाऽऽहवनीयेन॥१४–१५॥

समिधं त्रिप्रादेशां[६] त्रिधा[७] कृत्वा तूष्णीं[८] तृतीयमादधाति॥१६–२०॥

आमन्त्रणादि यथाप्राप्तं वयः[९] संबन्धापेक्षया[९]॥२१॥

[१०]ऋतायवः सत्यकामा[१०] यज्ञकामा वा॥२२॥

गरिम्णा गुरुत्वेन [११]वाऽविद्यया वाऽज्ञानेन वा[११]॥२३॥

नान्वाख्याने ब्राह्मणमस्ति। विधायकं वाक्यं नास्तीत्यर्थः। ब्राह्मणेन[१२] विहितं हि

---

१. M Ad °शीमिति. **२–२.** M प्रस्थान...न्ये पक्षयो°. **३.** T न्निध्या [...] ना, T has misunderstood the text. T also mentions in fn. about the loss of some text between निवृत्ति अतो° (इह कियांश्चिद् ग्रन्थो लुप्त इव भाति). **४–४.** M पक्ष...प्रकृष्टः. **५.** M Ad पान्थाः. **६.** M Ad °प्रादेशं; thus T. **७.** M Ad om; thus T. **८.** M Ad T तृतीयं. **९–९.** T रवय सं...नीयेन विपरि...वन्धा°. **१०–१०.** M ऋ...ामा, Ad ऋतायाव, T ऋताय वा. **११–११.** M Ad वा विद्यया वा अनेन वा, T विद्यया वा ज्ञानेन वा. **१२.** M Ad ब्राह्मणे; thus T.

ब्राह्मणमस्ति ॥ २४ ॥ न नृम्णेये, छन्दोब्राह्मणमेवैतत् ॥ २५ ॥ तदेतदप्येकरात्रेणोपेप्सेद् दैव्यस्योपेप्सेद् ॥ २६ ॥ इति नु दैव्यमुपस्थानम् ॥ ३.१.१.२७ ॥ [इति प्रथमः पटलः]

[विराजक्रमोपस्थानम्]

अथातो विराजक्रमाः ॥ १ ॥ स पुरस्तादेव सꣳशास्तीति समानम् ॥ २ ॥ स यज्ञोपवीतं कृत्वाऽप आचम्य पश्चात्तिष्ठन् गार्हपत्यमुपतिष्ठते 'नर्य प्रजां मे गोपाय' **इति ॥ ३ ॥** 'अथर्व पितुं मे गोपाय' **इत्यन्वाहार्यपचनम् ॥ ४ ॥** 'शꣳस्य पशून् मे गोपाय' **इत्याहवनीयम् ॥ ५ ॥** 'सप्रथ सभां मे गोपाय' **इति सभ्यम् ॥ ६ ॥** 'अहे बुध्निय मन्त्रं मे गोपाय' **इत्यावसथीयम् ॥ ७ ॥** 'नमो वोऽस्तु गोपायत मा' **इति सर्वान् समस्तान् ॥ ८ ॥ अथ वाचंयमः प्रव्रजति ॥ ९ ॥ स यदा वै वाचं यच्छतीति समानम् ॥ १० ॥ सोऽगारेण वा वृक्षेण वाऽन्तर्धाय वाचं विसृजते ॥ ११ ॥ तस्य**

कल्पकारैरन्वाख्यायते ॥ २४ ॥

न नृम्णेये बलाधानेऽर्थवादोऽपि[1] नास्तीत्ययं छन्दोब्राह्मणमेवैतन्मन्त्रलिङ्गादेव[1] कल्पित-मित्यर्थः ॥ २५ ॥

[2]तद् एतद् एकरात्रेणापि[2] यत्र गत्वा निवृत्तिः कर्तुं न शक्यते तस्यामपि यात्रायामिदमुपस्थानमाप्तुमिच्छेत। दैव्यस्य देवत्वस्य[3] दैव्यं नामैतदुपस्थानम् ॥ ३.१.१.२६-२७ ॥ **[इति प्रथमः पटलः]**

अथातो[3] *विराजक्रमाः*[4] ।विहितमेतदुपस्थानम्। प्रवसथमेष्यन्नेवमुपतिष्ठेतैकमेकमिति[5] सर्वं[6] याजमानकाण्डे[7] पठितम्। [8]तत्प्रसंगादिदमत्रान्वाख्यायते। तत्प्रसंगादेव माहाचमसमपि शाखान्तर-विहितम्। एतादृशं संबन्धं प्रयोजनं वाऽभिप्रेत्य[9]। अथातः शब्दं क्वचित्प्रयुङ्क्तेऽयमाचार्यः[10]। तत्र[11] व्याख्यातृभिस्तदन्वेषणीयम् ॥ १ ॥

[12]नात्रादिग्रहणम् एतावत्परिमाणा एव मन्त्राः। पुनरागत्योपस्थानेऽजूगुप[13] इति दर्शनात् तस्य[13] च मन्त्रपाठेऽभावात्। अथवा तेषां ब्राह्मणेऽप्यभावात्[14] श्रुत्यन्तरे [15]एतेषामविशेषेणोक्त-भावोऽनुमीयते[15] ॥ ३-८ ॥

१-१. T Wrongly takes the text between °र्थवा and °देव additional and gives the same in the fn. as '°दोऽपि नास्तीत्ययं छन्दोब्राह्मणमेवैतन्मन्त्रलिङ्गा' इति मध्ये वर्तते. Actually this text is commentary on sūtra 3.1.1.25. २-२. M एत...ापि. ३-३. M Ad देवकत्वस्य; thus T. T wrongly takes the text between देवत्वस्य and ता as additional and gives the same in the fn. as : 'दैव्यं नामैतदुपस्थानं। अथा' इति मध्येऽस्ति. Actually it is the text of commentary on sūtra 26-27. ४. M Ad °विराजक्रमात्; thus T. ५. M Ad तिष्ठेतैकमक; T °तिष्ठन्नैकमे°. ६. T पूर्वं. ७. M Ad °कारण्डे, T यज°. ८. M त...गादि°. ९. M Ad वापिप्रे°. १०. M Ad °युङ्क्तोऽ; thus T. ११. M Ad अत्रत्य; thus T. १२. M Ad नात्रदिग्ग्र, T नात्रादि°. १३-१३. M स्थाने...दर्शना°; Ad °जुगूपदर्श°; T जुहुव इति द°. १४. M Ad °भावः; thus T. १५-१५. M Ad °रेतेषामविशेषणोक्ता भावानुमीयन्ते, T °मपि शेषे°.

प्रवसतो व्रतम् ॥ १२ ॥ **कामाशनं कामशयनं कामालङ्कारोऽपरिमितं प्रवसतः** ॥ १३ ॥ **यथा दैव्ये विपरिधायैवं प्रोष्य गृहानुपावर्तते** ॥ १४ ॥ **प्रपथात् समिधं कुरुते** ॥ १५ ॥ **अग्नीन् पराख्याय वाचं यच्छति** ॥ १६ ॥ **स यदा वै वाचं यच्छतीति समानम्** ॥ १७ ॥ **स यज्ञोपवीतं कृत्वाऽप आचम्य पश्चात्तिष्ठन् गार्हपत्यमुपतिष्ठते** 'नर्य प्रजां मेऽजुगूपस्तां मे गोपाय' **इति** ॥ १८ ॥ **तूष्णीं तृतीयः समिधोऽभ्यादधाति** ॥ १९ ॥ 'अथर्व पितुं मेऽजुगुपस्तं मे गोपाय' **इत्यन्वाहार्यपचनम्** ॥ २० ॥ **तूष्णीं तृतीयं समिधोऽभ्यादधात्युप वा निदधाति** ॥ २१ ॥ 'शꣳस्य पशून् मेऽजुगुपस्तान् मे गोपाय' **इत्याहवनीयम्** ॥ २२ ॥ **तूष्णीं तृतीयः समिधोऽभ्यादधात्युप वा निदधाति** ॥ २३ ॥ 'सप्रथ सभां मेऽजुगुपस्तां मे गोपाय' **इति सभ्यम्** ॥ २४ ॥ 'अहे बुध्निय मन्त्रं मेऽजुगुपस्तं मे गोपाय' **इत्यावसथीयम्** ॥ २५ ॥ 'नमो वोऽस्त्वजुगुपत मा गोपायत' **इति सर्वान् समस्तान्** ॥ २६ ॥ **अथ यजमानायतने तृणेषु कूर्चे वोपविश्येति समानम्** ॥ २७ ॥ **स यद्** 'अजूगुपोऽजूगुपः' **इत्युपतिष्ठेत प्रवसतो गोप्तारो मन्येरन्, न सार्धं वसतः** ॥ २८ ॥ **स यद्** 'अजूगुपो गोपाय' **इत्युपतिष्ठेत यथा हैवास्य प्रवसतो गोप्तारो मन्यन्त एवꣳ सार्धं वसतः** ॥ २९ ॥ **तस्माद्** 'अजुगुपस्तान् मे गोपाय' **इत्येवोपतिष्ठेत** ॥ ३० ॥ **इत्युवेव विराजक्रमाः** ॥ ३.१.२.३१ ॥ **[इति द्वितीयः पटलः]**

[माहाचमसोपस्थानम्]

अथातो माहाचमसम् ॥ १ ॥ **माहाचमसेनोपस्थास्यमानो भवति** ॥ २ ॥ **स पुरस्तादेव सꣳशास्तीति समानम्** ॥ ३ ॥ **स यज्ञोपवीतं कृत्वाऽप आचम्य पश्चात्तिष्ठन् गार्हपत्यमुपतिष्ठते** 'अभयं ते अभयं मे मानुषान्मा भयाद् गोपाय' **इति** ॥ ४ ॥ 'अभयं ते अभयं मे' **इत्यन्वा-हार्यपचनम्**। '°पित्रियान्मा भयाद् गोपाय' **इति** ॥ ५ ॥ 'अभयं ते अभयं मे' **इत्याहवनीयम्**। '°दैव्यान्मा भयाद् गोपाय' **इति** ॥ ६ ॥ 'नमो वो अस्तु गोपायत मा' **इति सर्वान् समस्तान्** ॥ ७ ॥ **अथ वाचंयमः प्रव्रजति** ॥ ८ ॥ **स यदा वै वाचं यच्छतीति समानम्** ॥ ९ ॥ **सोऽगारेण वा वृक्षेण वाऽन्तर्धाय वाचं विसृजते** ॥ १० ॥ **तस्य प्रवसतो व्रतं यथा विराजक्रमेषु** ॥ ११ ॥ **यथा दैव्ये विपरिधायैवं प्रोष्य गृहानुपावर्तते** ॥ १२ ॥ **प्रपथात् समिधं कुरुते** ॥ १३ ॥ **अग्नीन् पराख्याय वाचं यच्छति** ॥ १४ ॥ **स यदा वै वाचं यच्छतीति समानम्** ॥ १५ ॥ **स यज्ञोपवीतं कृत्वाऽप आचम्य**

तस्य प्रवसतो [१]व्रतमेतत् प्रदर्श्यते कामाशनादि। तच्च व्रतमपरिमितं कालं प्रवसतो यावत्काममध्वानं प्रवसति। यद्यप्यपरिमितं विज्ञातं तथापि [२]तत्संवत्सरादर्वागेवेष्यते। तत ऊर्ध्वं प्रायश्चित्तं विदधति ॥ १२-१३ ॥

केचिद् 'अजुगुपोऽजुगुप'[३] इति। 'नर्य प्रजां मेऽजूगुपः[४]', 'अथर्व पितुं मेऽजूगुपः' इत्युपतिष्ठेत[५]। तस्माद् 'अजुगुपो गोपाये'त्येवोपतिष्ठेत इति ॥ ३.१.२.१८-२० ॥ **[इति द्वितीयः पटलः]**[६]

---

१. M Ad व्रतं तत्प्र° ; thus T. २. M तत्सव...तेष्यते, Ad तत्सव°. ३. M Ad अजुगूप इति. ४. T °वजुगुपः. ५. M Ad °तिष्ठते. ६. M Ad T do not mention the end of the Paṭala.

यजमानायतने तिष्ठन्नाहवनीयमुपतिष्ठते 'अभयं तेऽभयं मे दैव्यान्मा भयादजुगुपस्तस्मान्मा भयाद् गोपाय' **इति** ॥ १६ ॥ **तूष्णीं तृतीयः समिधोऽभ्यादधात्युप वा निदधाति** ॥ १७ ॥ 'अभयं ते अभयं मे' **इत्यन्वाहार्यपचनम्**। '°पित्रियान्मा भयादजूगुपस्तस्मान्मा भयाद् गोपाय' **इति** ॥ १८ ॥ **तूष्णीं तृतीयः समिधोऽभ्यादधात्युप वा निदधाति** ॥ १९ ॥ 'अभयं ते अभयं मे' **इति गार्हपत्यम्**। '°मानुषान्मा भयादजूगुपस्तस्मान्मा भयाद् गोपाय' **इति** ॥ २० ॥ **तूष्णीं तृतीयः समिधोऽभ्यादधात्युप वा निदधाति** ॥ २१ ॥ 'नमो वो अस्त्वजुगुपस्तस्मादु गोपायत मा' **इति सर्वान् समस्तान्** ॥ २२ ॥ **अथ यजमानायतने तृणेषु कूर्चे वोपविश्येति समानम्** ॥ २३ ॥ **अयमु ह वै लोको गार्हपत्योऽन्तरिक्षलोको ऽन्वाहार्यपचनः सुवर्गो आहवनीयः** ॥ २४ ॥ **स यत् प्रवत्स्यन्नितः पराच उपतिष्ठत इमानेव लोकानाप्नोति न काचनार्तिर्भवति, न रिष्टिः** ॥ २५ ॥ **स यत्पुनरेत्यैवमेवोपतिष्ठेत प्रैभ्यो लोकेभ्यश्च्यवेत, क्षिप्रे हैवास्माल्लोकात् प्रेयात्** ॥ २६ ॥ **स पुनरेत्यामुतोऽर्वाच उपतिष्ठत एष्वेव लोकेषु प्रतितिष्ठति, नार्तिमर्च्छति, सर्वमायुरेति** ॥ २७ ॥ **अहरहर्वा...पाप्मनो बिभ्य...वेत्स्यति। स नो श्रद्धावित्। तं परा वावप्स्यन्न्यगेवाभ्यवहरिष्यतीति** ॥ २८ ॥ **स यद्** 'अभयं ते अभयं' **मे इत्युपतिष्ठतेऽभयमेवैभ्यो दधाति, तेऽस्मा** 'अभये दत्ते अभयं' **ददति** ॥ २९ ॥ **त्रीण्यु ह वै भयानि, दैव्यं पित्रियं मानुषमिति** ॥ ३० ॥ **एतद्वै दैव्यं योऽलोकतायै बिभेत्यथ हैतत् पित्रियं योऽप्रजाताया अथ हैतन्मानुषं योऽपशुतायै** ॥ ३१ ॥ **न ह वा एनं देवतो न पितृतो न मनुष्यतो भयमागच्छति य एतेनोपतिष्ठते** ॥ ३२ ॥ **इत्युवेव माहाचमसम्** ॥ ३.१.३.३३ ॥ **[इति तृतीयः पटलः]**

[विच्छिन्नप्रायश्चित्तिः]

अथातो विच्छन्नप्रायश्चित्तिः ॥ १ ॥ **स यद्यस्मै प्रोषुषे काञ्चिद् यज्ञार्तिमाचक्षीरन्नभि**

---

[1]विहितानुवाद एव ॥ १–२५ ॥

अलोकतायाः[1] पञ्चम्यर्थे चतुर्थी। न विद्यन्तेऽस्य[2] लोका इत्यलोकः। अलोकस्य भावोऽलोकता[3]। यद्यप्यविशेषेणोक्तस्तथापि[4] पुण्यकृद्भोग्यो[5] लोकोऽत्र गृह्यते। आहवनीयान्वाहार्य[6]पचनयोरुपनिधानवचनमुद्धरणपक्षापेक्षमिति केचित्। अन्ये तत्राप्युपस्थान[7]कर्मोद्धारणं प्रयोजयन्ति[8]। ततोऽविशेषेण[9] वाचनिकमित्याह[10]। ज्ञापकमेतदप्रयोजकत्वस्येति। अरणिगतेष्वरण्य उपस्थानयोग्या आमनन्ति किल। अस्मिन्पक्षे आयतनोपस्थानं यथासमारोपणं गार्हपत्यस्यैव वा[11] पश्चात्॥ ३.१.३.३१–३३ ॥ **[इति तृतीयः पटलः]**

'स तर्हि गत' इति श्रुत्यन्तरदर्शनादनुद्धृतमग्निमभ्यस्तमगात्[11], [12]तथाभ्युदियादग्नावग्निमध्यु–

१–१. M Ad विहित एवालोक° ; thus T. **२.** M न विद्यतेऽस्य लोक इत्य...स्य भावः, Ad न विद्यतेऽस्य°. **३.** M Ad आलो° ; thus T. **४.** M Ad °णोक्ता. **५.** M Ad °कृद्भ्यो; thus T. **६.** M Ad °र्यवच°. **७.** M Ad तत्र उपस्था° द्धरणं. **८.** M Ad °यति. **९.** M ततोवि...ाह; Ad ततो विशे°. **१०.** M Ad वाचकमि°. **११.** M Ad om; thus T. **११.** T °गाम्. **१२.** M ...ग्नावग्नि°, T तथाज्युदगात्.

वाऽस्तमयादभि वोदगादभि वोदहार्षुरुद्धृतो वोदवासीद् अनो वा रथो वा व्यवासीद् अग्नि-होत्री वा न्यसदद् अग्निहोत्रे वाऽधिश्रिते चान्तरेणागादिति, अन्यां वैवंरूपां काञ्चिद् यज्ञार्ति-माचक्षीरन् गार्हपत्य आज्यं विलाप्योत्पूय स्रुवं च स्रुचं च संमृज्य प्राङेत्याहवनीयस्यार्धं चतुर्गृहीतं गृह्णीते ॥ २ ॥ **तज्जुहोति** 'मनो ज्योतिर्जुषतामाज्यं विच्छिन्नं यज्ञꣳ समिमं दधातु। या इष्टा उषसो निम्रुचश्च ताः संदधामि हविषा घृतेन स्वाहा' **इति** ॥ ३ ॥ **स यथाऽऽत्मनाऽऽत्मानं सन्दध्यात् पर्वणा पर्व श्लेष्मणा चर्मण्यं वाऽन्यद्वा श्लेषयेद् एवमेतद्यज्ञस्य विलिष्टं संदधाति, संस्करोति** ॥ ४ ॥ **न ह वै तत्र काचनार्तिर्भवति न रिष्टिर्यत्रैषा प्रायश्चित्तिः क्रियते** ॥ ५ ॥ **तन्नु ह स्मैतत् पूर्वे श्रोत्रिया यत्र क्व च दशतꣳ रात्रीरतिप्रोषुस्तद् विच्छिन्नरूपमेव मेनिरे, ते ह स्मैतां जुह्वति** ॥ ६ ॥ **तदाहुर्नानाख्याते जहुयात्** ॥ ७ ॥ **यथाऽनार्तम् आर्तरूपं कुर्वीत यथाऽनुपतापिनं भिषज्येत्तादृक् तत्** ॥ ८ ॥ **तस्मान्नानाख्याते जुहूयादिति** ॥ ९ ॥ **नानाख्याते जुहोत्येषा स्थितिः** ॥ १० ॥ **इत्युवेव विच्छिन्नप्रायश्चित्तिः** ॥ ११ ॥ **अथातोऽन्वाधानस्यैव** ॥ ३.१.४.१२ ॥ **[इति चतुर्थः पटलः]**

[अन्वाधानम्]

अथातोऽन्वाधानस्यैव ॥ १ ॥ **तन्नु हैतदेके महारात्र एवाग्निहोत्रꣳ हुत्वाऽग्नीनन्वादधति** 'अग्निहोत्राद्धि यज्ञास्तायन्ते तथाऽग्निहोत्रेण यज्ञꣳ संतꣳस्यामहे' **इति वदन्तः** ॥ २ ॥ **ब्राह्मणमु वै भवति** 'यथा वै समृतसोमा एवं वा एते=श्वोभूते यजते' **इति** 'यथा पूर्वे देवताः परिग्रहीष्यामहे' **इति**

द्धृतवन्तः। उद्धृतो वा हुतेऽग्निहोत्रे उदवासीदनो वा रथो[1] वाऽन्तराश्नीयायात्[1]। अग्निहोत्र्युप-सृष्टा[2] न्यसददिति शेषम्[3]। 'अन्यां वैवंरूपामि'ति[4] वचनात् प्रायोदर्शनाच्चाग्निहोत्रविषयाण्येव प्रायश्चित्तनिमित्तानि[5]।'अग्निहोत्रं [6]तेनाहौषुरित्यादीनि विष्यन्दनिकावपनाभिवर्षणान्यपि[7]' ॥ २ ॥

स यथाऽऽत्मनाऽऽत्मानं[8] तुल्यजातीयेन तुल्यजातीयं श्लेष्मणा श्लेषणसमर्थेन[9]। विलिष्टं विश्लिष्टम् ॥ ४ ॥

रिष्टिर्विनाशः। प्रायश्चित्ते कृतेऽप्यकृतेऽपि यदि तत्रस्था आचक्षते[10] हविःषु होतव्यम्। यदि न, न होतव्यम्[10] ॥ ३.१.४.५–११ ॥ **[इति चतुर्थः पटलः]**

अतः परं दर्शपूर्णमासयोर्याजमानमन्वाधानादि ॥ १ ॥

समृतसोमाः[11] संगतसोमाः[12]। ये नद्यादिनाऽनन्तर्हिताः[13] समानेऽहनि सोमैर्यजन्ते ते

१–१. M Ad रथो [Ad रथे] वान्तराग्नीयायात्; thus T. **२.** M Ad त्र्युपस्पृष्टा, T °त्र्युपसृष्टान्यष°. **३.** M Ad शेषः; thus T. **४.** M Ad °रूपमिति. **५.** M °श्चित्त...त्रं; Ad °श्चित्तानि° ; thus T. **६.** M Ad तेन गौरित्या°. **७.** M विष्यन्दन किटा [Ad °क्रिय] वचनाभिः. **८.** T °त्मानस्तु°. **९.** M Ad om श्लेषण; thus T. **१०–१०.** M आच...होतव्यम्; Ad हविषु होतव्यम्. **११.** M Ad °सोमः°. **१२.** M Ad °संगतास्सोमाः; thus T. **१३.** M येन द्यादिनानंतहीतः, Ad येन द्यादिनातर्हीतः.

वदन्तः ॥ ३ ॥ **स यदेवं कुर्याद्यथाऽनागतायातिथ्यं कुर्याद् यथाऽनागतं जिगृहीषेत् तादृक् तत्** ॥ ४ ॥ **अथ हैक उदितेऽन्वादधति** 'तथा पश्यन्तो देवताः परिग्रहीष्यामहे' **इति वदन्तः** ॥ ५ ॥ **स यदेवं कुर्याद् यथाऽतीतायातिथ्यं कुर्याद्, यथाऽतीतं जिगृहीषेत् तादृक् तत्** ॥ ६ ॥ **विरश्मावादित्येऽन्वादध्यात्** ॥ ७ ॥ **पूर्वो वा अग्निरर्चिषाऽधूमेन तपत्यमुत आदित्यस्तेजसा रश्मिभिः। तावत्र संगेच्छेते। स यथा समागतौ परिगृह्णीयात् समागतौ प्रीणीयात् तादृक् तत्** ॥ ८ ॥ **तस्माद्विरश्मावेवादित्येऽन्वादध्यादिति** ॥ ९ ॥ **विरश्मावेवादित्येऽन्वादधात्येषा स्थितिः** ॥ १० ॥ **विहव्यानां प्रथमयाऽऽहवनीय एकां, द्वे तूष्णीम्** ॥ ११ ॥ **तूष्णीं गार्हपत्ये तिस्रः** ॥ १२ ॥ **तूष्णीमन्वाहार्यपचने तिस्रः** ॥ १३ ॥ **प्राङेत्याहवनीये चतुर्थीमभ्यादधाति प्राक्सꣳस्थतायै** ॥ १४ ॥ **अथ यजमा–नायतने तिष्ठन् द्विरुत्तराभिरुपतिष्ठते** ॥ १५ ॥ **अथैकमेवान्वाधाय नोपतिष्ठते** ॥ १६ ॥ **अथैकं विहव्यानामेव प्रथमाऽऽहवनीय एकां द्वे तूष्णीम्** ॥ १७ ॥ 'अग्ने जातान्' **इति गार्हपत्य एकां द्वे तूष्णीम्** ॥ १८ ॥ **प्राङेत्याहवनीये चतुर्थीमभ्यादधाति प्राक्सꣳस्थतायै** 'अर्वाञ्चमिन्द्रममुतो हवामहे यो गोजिद्धनजिदश्वजिद्यः। इमं नो यज्ञं विहवे जुषस्वास्य कुर्मो हरिवो मेदिनं त्वा स्वाहा' **इति** ॥ १९ ॥ **अथ यजमानायतने तिष्ठन् सप्तभिरेवोत्तराभिरुपतिष्ठते** ॥ २० ॥ **अथैकमेवान्वाधाय नोपतिष्ठते** ॥ २१ ॥ **अथासन्नमित्याचक्षते** ॥ २२ ॥ **अथैकं विहव्यानामेव प्रथमयाऽऽहवनीय एकां द्वे तूष्णीम्** ॥ २३ ॥ **द्वितीयया गार्हपत्य एकां द्वे तूष्णीम्** ॥ २४ ॥ **तृतीययाऽन्वाहार्यपचन एकां द्वे तूष्णीम्** ॥ २५ ॥ **प्राङेत्याहवनीये चतुर्थीमभ्यादधाति प्राक्सꣳस्थतायै** ॥ २६ ॥ **अथ यजमानायतने तिष्ठन् द्विरुत्तराभिरुपतिष्ठते** ॥ २७ ॥ **अथैकमेवमेवान्वाधाय नोपतिष्ठते** ॥ २८ ॥ **अथैकं द्वाभ्यामाहवनीये द्वे, एकां तूष्णीम्** ॥ २९ ॥ **द्वाभ्यां गार्हपत्ये द्वे, एकां तूष्णीम्** ॥ ३० ॥ **द्वाभ्यामन्वाहार्यपचने द्वे, एकां तूष्णीम्** ॥ ३१ ॥ **प्राङेत्याहवनीये चतुर्थीमभ्यादधाति प्राक्सꣳस्थतायै** ॥ ३२ ॥ **अथ यजमानायतने तिष्ठन् द्वाभ्यामुत्तराभ्यामुपतिष्ठते** ॥ ३३ ॥ **अथैकमेवान्वाधाय नोपतिष्ठते** ॥ ३४ ॥ **अथैकं तिसृभिराहवनीये तिस्रः** ॥ ३५ ॥ **तिसृभिर्गार्हपत्ये तिस्रः** ॥ ३६ ॥ **द्वाभ्यामन्वाहार्यपचने द्वे एकां तूष्णीम्** ॥ ३७ ॥ **प्राङेत्याहवनीये चतुर्थीमभ्यादधाति प्राक्सꣳस्थतायै** ॥ ३८ ॥ **नात्रोपतिष्ठते** ॥ ३९ ॥ **अथ यथाऽऽहितम्** ॥ ४० ॥ 'भूः' **इति गार्हपत्ये तिस्रः** ॥ ४१ ॥ 'भुवः' **इत्यन्वाहार्यपचने तिस्रः** ॥ ४२ ॥ 'सुवः' **इत्याहवनीये तिस्रः** ॥ ४३ ॥ **एतन्नु ह यथाऽऽहितमित्याचक्षते** ॥ ४४ ॥ **एतेषां यतमत् कामयेत तत्कुर्यात्** ॥ ४५ ॥ **इत्यु वेवान्वाधानस्य** ॥ ३.१.३.४६ ॥ **[इति पञ्चमः पटलः]**

समृतसोमाः। अथवा संगतसोमाः[1] समृतसोमाः[2] ॥ ३ ॥

विहव्या 'ममाग्ने वर्च' इत्याद्याः। दशस्वप्यन्वाधानविकल्पेषु पृथक् पृथगेकैकां[3] [4]समिधमादधाति यथाहिते प्रतिसमिधं मन्त्रावृत्तिः ॥ ३.१.५.११–४४ ॥ **[इति पञ्चमः पटलः]**

---

१. M Ad अथवा between समृतसोमा and संगतसोमाः; thus T. **२.** M समृता...इत्याद्याः; thus T. **३.** M °गेकैकं. **४.** M Ad समधमा°.

[व्रतोपायनम्]

अथातो व्रतोपायनस्यैव ॥ १ ॥ **तन्नु हैतद् एकेऽग्नीनेवान्वाधाय व्रतमुपयन्ति** ॥ २ ॥ **तथा नो व्रतोपेतानाम्** ॥ ३ ॥ **यद्यजुषा कृत्यं तत् करिष्यन्ति, यजुषा शाखामाहृत्य यजुषा वत्सानपाकरिष्यन्ति इति** ॥ ४ ॥ **अथ दक्षिणतस्तिष्ठन् व्रतमुपैति** 'विक्रम्य विक्रम्य हीन्द्रो वृत्रमहन् समृद्ध्यै' **इति ब्राह्मणम्** ॥ ५ ॥ 'पयस्वतीरोषधयः' **इति तिरःपविमप आचामति।** '°पयस्व=सꣳसृज' **इति** ॥ ६ ॥ 'अग्ने व्रतपते' **इति मार्जयित्वा समिधमादधाति।** '°व्रतं चरिष्यामि=ताꣳ स्वाहा' **इति** ॥ ७ ॥ **प्राण्यापानिति** ॥ ८ ॥ **प्राणैरात्मानमन्तरतः पूरयित्वाऽऽह** 'इदमहमनृतात् सत्यमुपैमि' **इति** ॥ ९ ॥ **अनृतं वै मनुष्याः सत्यं देवा मनुष्येभ्यस्तद्देवानुपैति** ॥ १० ॥ **एवꣳ ह देवा व्रतमुपेयुरेवमृषय एवं ये पूर्वे श्रोत्रिया ऋतायव आसुः** ॥ ११ ॥ **अथो इदमाहुः** 'यदि गावो यजुषाऽपाकृतानां धयेयुर्वा

योऽग्नीनन्वाधाय[१] व्रतमुपैतीत्यविशेषेण पर्वद्वये व्रतकालः। बर्हिषा पूर्णमासे व्रतमुपैति[२], [३]वत्सैरमावास्यायामिति विशेषविधानम्[३]। [४]तत्रानन्वाधानानन्तरस्यैव व्रतकालस्य[४] गुणवत्वं मन्यमानास्तदेव कुर्वन्ति केचित्। तस्य गुणवत्वाभिधित्सयाऽग्नीनेवान्वाधाय व्रतमुपयन्तीत्याह। गुणवत्त्वं वाऽदस्तथा[५] न इत्यादि। व्रतेतिकर्तव्यता दक्षिणत इत्याद्याह। [६]शाखाहरणान्तमपाकरणकर्म। तथाऽसिदादानादिगुप्तनिधानान्तं संभरणकर्म[६]। अतस्तयोरपि कालयोः क्रियमाणं भवत्येव ॥ १-३ ॥

सगुणं बर्हिः तस्य[७] याजुषस्य कर्मणोऽत्राभावादिति[८] तस्योत्तरम्। अथो इत्याहुरित्यादि गुरुप्रायश्चित्तप्रसंगभयात्[९] सायमपाकरणे क्रियमाणे वत्सैरमावास्यायामिति[९] व्रतमुपेयुषः[१०] सामर्थ्यात् कृतबर्हिःसंभरणवेदिकरणपितृयज्ञस्य प्राप्नोति। [११]अतोऽन्वाधायैव व्रतं गुणवदिति स्तुतिः[११]। कथं

---

१. M Ad योगीनन्वा°. **२.** T gives the text in fn. **३-३.** M °मावास्याम...धानम्, Ad विशेषैर्विधा°, T वत्सेष्वमावा°. **४-४.** M Ad तत्रान्वाधानान्तरस्यैव व्रतकालस्यागुण°. **५.** M Ad T गुणवत्वं वादस्तथा°. **६-६.** M शाखाहरण...न्तन्तमुपा°, Ad °हरण...न्तमुपा; thus T. **७.** M गुणात्वबहिभू°, Ad सगुणबहिर्भू°, T सगुणं बर्हि तस्य. **८.** M Ad कर्मणोऽर्थभा°; thus T. **९-९.** M प्रसङ्गभय...णे क्रि...पवायायमित व्रतमुपेयुषे; T वत्सेष्वमावा°. **१०.** Ad वृत्रमुपेयुषे. **११-११.** M °धायैवदतिस्तु°.

नंश्येयुर्वा प्रायश्चित्तिः कार्या स्यादि**'ति** ॥ १२ ॥ **सायमेव यजुषा शाखामाहृत्य यजुषा वत्सानपाकरोति** ॥ १३ ॥ **प्रातर्ह स्मैवम्** ॥ १४ ॥ **आ दक्षिणायै व्रतमुपैति** ॥ १५ ॥ **स ह स्म वाचंयमो भवत्या सꣳस्थायै** ॥ १६ ॥ **तदाहुः** 'कोऽर्हति व्रतोपेतो वाचंयमो बहु वदन् सत्यं वदन्नि**'ति** ॥ १७ ॥ **स यदव्रतोपेतस्य यद्यजुषा कुर्याद् यथाऽदीक्षितं वाऽव्रतोपेतं वा याजयेत्तादृक् तत्** ॥ १८ ॥ **त्रीण्यु ह वै दर्शपूर्णमासयोर्व्रतोपायनानि—अन्वाधाय बर्हिषा वत्सैः** ॥ १९ ॥ **अथैकमासन्नेष्विति** ॥ २० ॥ **स यथा ह वा अनसोऽपरीणत्का व्रीहियवा शीर्यन्त एवं ह वाऽव्रतोपेतस्य यद्यजुषा क्रियते तच्छीर्यते** ॥ २१ ॥ **इष्टैरेवावृता प्रणेष्यमाणा न शीर्येतेष्टिः** ॥ २२ ॥ **नेष्टिरुपवसथ इवास्ति** ॥ २३ ॥ **उत्सीदति तद् यदासन्नेषु हविःष्विति** ॥ ३.१.६.२४ ॥ **[इति षष्ठः पटलः]**

॥ इति तृतीयप्रपाठके प्रथमोऽनुवाकः ॥

पुनरुपलभ्यते [१]सायमपाकरणमस्तीति। तत्र [२]गुरुप्रायश्चित्तप्रसंगभयादित्युक्तम्। सत्यमुक्तम्[(क)]। न तावता [(ख)]संकल्पकालप्राप्तस्यापाकरणस्योत्कर्षो युक्तः। स्यादेतदेवम्[(ग)]। तर्ह्यस्मादेवानुवादाद्वचनमस्तीत्यनुमेयम्[२]। अस्मिन्पक्षे गा आयतीः प्रतीक्ष्य[३] वत्सान् मातृभिः संसृज्य तत्कृताधानानपाकरोति ॥ ११-१२ ॥

[(च)]अदीक्षितं वा अव्रतोपेतं[(छ)] वा व्रतोपायनानि व्रतोपायनकालाः ॥ १८ ॥

अपरीणत्काः[(ज)] न विद्यते येषां परीणत्कः ते अपरीणत्काः[३]। [४]अस्रवणार्थं निधेयमाधारं परीणत् कृतधानादेषा निन्दा दक्षिणायी[४] पक्षस्य। तथापि विहितत्वादानर्थक्यपरिजिहीर्षया विकृतौ तस्यात्मलाभ[५] इति ॥ २१ ॥

स [६]इष्टैरेवापः प्रणेष्यन्नित्याह[६]। मानसीनेष्टिरिति। सर्वा[७] उपांश्विति विहितानामनुवादः[८] ॥ २२ ॥

नेष्टिरुपवसथ[८] इवास्ति[९]। सद्यस्कालत्वात् सद्यस्कालोत्तरा[९] ततिरिति। सति[१०] सम्भवेऽप्यहः[११]कालता न्याय्येति[११] ज्ञापयितुम् इवशब्दः प्रयुक्तः ॥ २३ ॥

उत्सीदति तद्यदासन्नेषु हविःष्विति। नायं यजमानकालोऽनवकाशत्वादानर्थक्याच्चाध्वर्यवः स काल[१२] इति तत्राम्नातं याजमाने ॥ ३.१.६.२४ ॥ **[इति षष्ठः पटलः]**

॥ इति व्याख्यायां तृतीयप्रपाठके प्रथमोऽनुवाकः ॥[१३]

---

१. M साय वोकरणमिति, Ad °मपाकरणमिति; thus T. **२-२.** M ∴ °भय...णेक्रि...पवा...स्यादेतदेवन्तर्ह...नुवादवचन°; (क) Ad उक्तं सत्य; (ख) Ad संगवकालस्यापा°; (ग) Ad स्यादेवन्तर्हि. **३-३.** M प्रतीक्ष्य...रणात्काः, Ad प्रतीक्ष्येव जा मातृभिः ससृज्यत कृतवानानापा°; (च) Ad आदी°; (छ) Ad आवृतीपेतं; (ज) Ad आपरीणत्काः, येषां परीणत्के आपरीणत्के, T अपरीणका. **४-४.** M अस्रवणं...रं परिणद्देषा नि...णायी; Ad अस्रवणार्थं निधेयमारः परिणेर्द्देशानिन्यनक्षीणायी; thus T. **५.** M Ad °त्मलाभि. **६-६.** M इष्टेः णेष्य°, Ad पमेष्य°; thus T. **७.** M सर्वा...वाश्विति. **८-८.** M Ad °मनुवादनेष्टेरूप°, T °मनुपादा°. **९-९.** M इवास्ति...सद्य..लोत्तराः. **१०.** M Ad om; thus T. **११-११.** M संभवव्य... कन्याय्येति; Ad संभवेप्याह—कालकन्याय्येति. **१२.** M Ad सकला. **१३.** M इति प्रथमः; Ad इति प्रथमः समाप्तः.

॥ अथ तृतीयप्रपाठके द्वितीयोऽनुवाकः ॥

[निरुप्यमाणहविरभिमन्त्रणं, पात्राणां भिन्ने तत्कृते प्रायश्चित्तविधानञ्च]

अथातो हविर्निरुप्यमाणमभिमन्त्रयते 'अग्निं होतारमिह=अस्य' **इति** ॥ १ ॥ **तदाहुः— हविरेव निरुप्यमाणमभिमन्त्रयेत,** 'अग्निं होतारमिह तं हुवे' **इत्यृत्विज आयतः** ।' °आयन्तु देवाः सुमनस्यमानाः' **इति** ॥ २ ॥ **तानेव पुनर्वियतः** 'वि यन्तु देवा हविषो मे अस्य' **इति** ॥ ३ ॥ **मीमांसैषा** ॥ ४ ॥ **समस्तेन हविरेव निरुप्यमाणमभिमन्त्रयेत** ॥ ५ ॥ **उलूखलमुसलं दृषदुपलं**

उपस्तीर्य[१] पूर्वश्चाग्निरपरश्चेति वैकल्पिकत्वाभिप्रायेणेह[२] नोक्तम् प्रातरशनम्। [३]सायमस्मा औपवसथिकां स्वयं च ब्राह्मणानिति[३]। स्वयं च भुञ्जीतेत्यस्मा इति संबन्धाद् गम्यते। सायमशनं पय- आदीन्यपोह्याथाधिवृक्षसूर्य इत्यादिना विहितम्। तेन च ब्राह्मणविहितान्यारण्याशनादीनि विकल्पन्ते। 'यो वै श्रद्धा'मित्यनुवाके 'यो वै देवेभ्य' इत्यतोऽर्वाङ्[४] न याजमानम्। आध्वर्यवमित्यभिप्रेत्या-ध्वर्यवम् आम्नातम्। अतो व्रतोपायनादनन्तरं हविर्निरूप्यमाणमित्यारब्धव्यम्।

[५]*अथातो हविर्निरूप्यमाणमभिमन्त्रयते।* अत्र केचित् प्रत्येकं[५] हविर्निरूप्यमाणमभिमन्त्र्य [६]निरुप्तेषु वाच्यमानो ब्रवीतीति[६] वर्णयन्ति[७]। तत्रानेकादृष्टकल्पनाः[८]। अपरे वर्तमानकालसामीप्ये वर्तमानकालप्रत्ययं[९] लक्षणया परिकल्प्य निरुप्तेषु वाच्यमानेन सकृदेव पक्तव्यमिति[१०]। तत्र तन्त्रत्व-मनुगृहीतं भवति। किन्तु शक्तस्य लक्षणाऽऽश्रयणीया। सा चान्याय्या। अन्ये वर्णयन्ति स्रुचि निरुप्ते प्राङ्निवपनात्[११] प्रत्येकं वाच्यमानोऽभिमन्त्रयते। तथा निरुप्यमाणं निरुप्तं च भवति। निवपनान्तो[१२] हि निर्वापः।'संस्कार्यभेदाच्च संस्कारानिवृत्तिर्न्याय्ये'ति ॥ १-३ ॥

मीमांसा विचार इत्यर्थः। लिंगसामर्थ्यादादिग्रहणे[१३] [१४]लक्षणावृत्तित्वं चावेक्ष्यम्[१४]। पूर्वपक्षं लिङ्गमत्रापि च विरुध्यते। देवेभ्य एव प्रतिप्रोच्येति नोपपद्येत[१५]। 'देवान्यज्ञियानायन्तु देवा' इति एकमन्त्रः स्यात्[१६]। तत्र लक्षणाभ्युपगन्तव्येति सिद्धान्तः। एतेन ज्ञायते। अन्यत्रापि लिङ्गेन विभागः कर्तव्य इति ॥ ४-५ ॥

उलूखलमुसलयोरध्वर्युणा युज्यमानयोर्योगः। दृषदुपलयोः[१७] कर्मणि युज्यमानयोर्विमुच्य-मानयोश्च योगविमोकौ। [१८]अथवाऽऽध्वर्यवम् उलूखलमुसलग्रहणं प्रदर्शनार्थम्। इह दर्शनाद् विमोचनादर्शनाच्च। अथवा [१८]दृषदुपलग्रहणमपि प्रदर्शनार्थमेव। सर्वस्य यज्ञसाधनस्य।'यो वै यज्ञं

---

१. M ... पूर्वश्चा° ; thus Ad T. २. M Ad °प्रायेण; thus T. ३-३. M Ad सयामस्मा=ब्राह्मणानिति; thus T. ४. M Ad इत्यतोर्वा=ङ्न. ५-५. T om text between अथातो and प्रत्येकं. ६-६. M निरुप्तेषु...नो ब्रुव°. ७. M Ad om; thus T. ८. M Ad तत्रानेका दृष्ट कल्पना, T °नेकादृष्टकल्पना. ९. M Ad प्रत्यय; thus T. १०. M Ad वक्तव्य°. ११. M Ad प्रवचनात्, T प्रार्दन्नि°. १२. M Ad निवनान्तो; thus T. १३. M Ad सामर्थ्याद्वादिग्र° ; thus T. १४-१४. M Ad लक्षणावृत्तित्वापेक्ष्यं; thus T. १५. Ad °पद्येते. १६. M यद्येकमन्त्रस्यान्नत्र, Ad मन्त्रस्यां; thus T. १७. M दृषदुपल...कर्मणि. १८-१८. M ध्वर्यव उलू. Ad om text between विमोकौ and अथवा दृषदु°.

युज्यमानं 'कस्त्वा युनक्ति' **इति** ॥ ६ ॥ 'यानि घर्मे कपालानि' **इति कपालानि।** '°उपचिन्वन्ति वेधसः। पूष्णस्तान्यपि व्रत इन्द्रवायू युङ्क्ताम्' **इति** ॥ ७ ॥ **एतदेवानुद्रुत्य विमोचनकाले** 'इन्द्रवायू विमुञ्चताम्' **इति** ॥ ८ ॥ **अथातः कपालस्यैव नष्टस्य** ॥ ९ ॥ **तद्वै ब्राह्मणं भवति** 'यद्येकं कपालं=मेककपालम्' **इति** ॥ १० ॥ **तदाहुः** 'यदेतस्यै प्रायश्चित्तीया इष्टेर्नश्येन ततः प्रायश्चित्तिश्च नातिशिष्येत' **इति** ॥ ११ ॥ **गार्हपत्ये स्रुवाहुतिं जुहुयात्** 'त्रयस्त्रिंशत्तन्तवो ये=एतद्धामि स्वाहा' **इति** ॥ १२ ॥ **अथान्यत् प्रतिनिदधाति** 'घर्मो देवाँ अप्येतु' **इति नु यद्युपहितानाम्** ॥ १३ ॥ **अथ यद्युद्वास्यमानानामेतामेव जुहुयात्** 'त्रयस्त्रिंश=अप्येतु स्वाहा' **इति** ॥ १४ ॥ **अथातः कपालस्यैव भिन्नस्य** ॥ १५ ॥ **स यद्यप्रोक्षितानां भिद्येतान्यदाहृत्याथ चेष्टेत्** ॥ १६ ॥ **अथ यदि प्रोक्षितानां भिद्येत गार्हपत्ये स्रुवाहुतिं जुहूयात्** 'अभिन्नो घर्मो=रन्ति स्वाहा' **इति** ॥ १७ ॥ **अथान्यत् प्रतिनिदधाति** 'यदृते चिदभिश्रिषः=पुनः' **इति** ॥ १८ ॥ **अथैनद् भस्मन्नुपोहति** ॥ १९ ॥ **अथातः पात्राणामेव दीर्णानाम्** ॥ २० ॥ **स यद्यप्रोक्षितानां दीर्येतान्यदाहृत्याथ चेष्टेत्** ॥ २१ ॥ **अथ यदि प्रोक्षितानां दीर्येत तस्या नेदीयो वा दीर्येत गार्हपत्ये स्रुवाहुतिं जुहुयाद्** 'विधुं दद्राणं समने बहूनां

योग आगते युनक्ति' इति[१] हि ब्राह्मण[विहिता-]न्यध्वर्युणा[२] युज्यमानानि कर्मणा वा, उभयमभिप्रेतमिवाचार्येण। तथा ह्यत्र एतदेवानुद्रुत्येति[३] विधत्ते पुनश्च[४] ॥ ६ ॥

'*यानि घर्मे कपालानी*'ति। कपालानीति मन्त्रपाठक्रममनूपाद्य[५] प्रसंगाच्चाम्नातानि प्रायश्चित्तानि तानि न याजमानानि। अनवेतमप्राप्तम्[६] ॥ ७–८ ॥

[७]ततः प्रायश्चित्तिश्च नातिशिष्येतेति[७]। प्रायश्चित्तिश्चातिशिष्येतैव[८]। विनाशे निमित्ते अधिकमङ्गं भवत्येव। तत्सहितं हि कर्म फलापूर्वमुत्पादयति[९]। अथवा प्रायश्चित्तिश्च[१०] नातिशिष्येत [११]नातिरिच्येत। फलमुभयोः पक्षयोस्तुल्यम्। पक्षान्तरविधित्सयेष्टिपक्षे[१२] दोषोद्भावनम्। कपालनाशेऽष्टौ यदि नश्येत्स्रुवाहुतिमिति केचित्, अनवस्थाप्रसंगवचनात्[१३] ॥ ९–११ ॥

उद्वास्यमानानां विनाशे तस्या एव विधानाद् विकल्प्याभावगौरवलाघवं वचनापेक्षमेव वैकल्पिकत्वम्। यथा 'एका देया सहस्रं देया' इति ॥ १४ ॥

[१४]अथैनद् भस्मन्नुपोहति[१४]। भस्मोत्कर इत्यर्थः ॥ १९ ॥

इतरस्य[१५] नेदीयो अन्तिकतरम्। नेदीयो द्वेधा कर्मणा स्थानेन[१६] वा। येन यस्मिन्प्राचुर्येण कर्म क्रियते तत्तस्य कर्मणो नेदीयः स्थानादासन्ने[१७]। आसन्ने[१८] गृह्यमाणेऽनवस्था प्रसंगः ॥ ३.२.१.२२ ॥

[इति प्रथमः पटलः (७)]

---

१. M Ad °नक्तोहि. **२.** M Ad ब्राह्मण...न्यध्वर्युणा [T ...न्य]. **३.** M Ad °नुभूत्येति. **४.** M Ad पुनरपि; thus T. **५.** M Ad °क्रमानुपोद्य. **६.** T अनवेतः अप्राप्तः. **७–७.** M न तत...शिष्येतेति; thus Ad T. **८.** M Ad °शिष्येतेति. **९.** T कर्मकलापूर्व° ; thus T. **१०.** M Ad °तिश्चानाति; thus T. **११.** M Ad तानति. **१२.** M पक्षान्तर...क्षे. **१३.** Ad इति between प्रसङ्ग and वच°. **१४–१४.** M ...न्युपोहति; Ad भस्मन्यु. **१५.** M Ad यत°. **१६.** M Ad स्थाने वा. **१७.** M Ad स्थानादासने. **१८.** M Ad आसन्नेन.

युवानꣳ सन्तं पलितो जगार। देवस्य पश्य काव्यं महित्वाऽद्या ममार स ह्यः समानः स्वाहा' **इति** ॥ २२ ॥ **अथान्यत् प्रतिनिदधाति** 'यदूते चिदभिश्रिषः=पुनः' **इति** ॥ २३ ॥ **यदि दारुमयम् अन्वेनत् प्रहरति, अथ यदि मृन्मयं भस्मन्नेवैनदुपोहति** ॥ २४ ॥ **अथातः सान्नाय्यस्य स्कन्नस्य** ॥ ३.२.१.२५ ॥ **[इति प्रथमः पटलः** (७)**]**

[सान्नाय्यस्कन्ने प्रायश्चित्तवधानम्]

अथातः सान्नाय्यस्य स्कन्नस्य ॥ १ ॥ **तन्नु हैतदेके स्वधाꣳ समिव सिञ्चन्ति** 'सं त्वा सिञ्चामि यजुषा' **इति** ॥ २ ॥ **मीमाꣳसैषा** ॥ ३ ॥ **उदपात्रमुपनिनीयानुमन्त्रयेत** 'भूपतये स्वाहा', 'भुवनपतये स्वाहा', 'भूतानां पतये स्वाहा' **इति** ॥ ४ ॥ **यद्यलं प्रचरणाय स्यात् प्रचरेत्** ॥ ५ ॥ **यदि सन्ततिरतिशिष्येत तूष्णीं भूयोऽभ्यानीय प्रचरेत्** ॥ ६ ॥ **अथ यदि सर्वमेव स्कन्देत् सान्ना-य्यावृता सान्नाय्यं दोहयेत्** ॥ ७ ॥ **अथ यदि सर्वमेव भिद्येत** 'विधुं दद्राणम्' **इत्येताꣳ हुत्वा** 'यदूते चिदभिश्रिषः' **इत्येतया प्रतिनिधाय सान्नाय्यावृतैव सान्नाय्यं दोहयेत्** ॥ ८ ॥ **अथ यद्यमेध्यतां नीयाच्छ्वा वा पिबेत् कृष्णशकुनो वा कीटो वा प्रपतेदप एनदभ्यवहृत्य निर्णिज्य स्थालीं मार्जयित्वा सान्नाय्यावृतैव सान्नाय्यं दोहयेत्** ॥ ९ ॥ **गथुनसो हार्क्षाकायणस्य हस्ती सान्नाय्यं पपौ। स ह स्म पर्यस्तश्चङ्क्रम्यते, यन्मर्या इत्थमवेदिष्यामो हस्ती नः सान्नाय्यं पातेत्यन्वस्य प्रायश्चित्तिमवक्ष्यामहीति** ॥ १० ॥ **तदु होवाचानुबुध्योद्दालक आरुणिः। अल्पो मर्या गग्लना आस, स एतावन्न विदाञ्चकार। यज्ञो वै यज्ञस्य प्रायश्चित्तिः, सान्नाय्यावृत् सान्नाय्यस्या-ग्निहोत्रावृदग्निहोत्रस्येति** ॥ ११ ॥ **सान्नाय्यावृता सान्नाय्यं दोहयेदिति** ॥ १२ ॥ **सान्नाय्यावृतैव सान्नाय्यं दोहयति** ॥ १३ ॥ **अथात आज्यस्यैव स्कन्नस्य** ॥ १४ ॥ **तन्नु हैतदेके स्वधाꣳ समिव**

अथ यदि सर्वमेव भिद्येतेति। अत्र सर्वग्रहणम्[1] कर्मसंयुक्तस्य[1] कर्मण्यसमर्थस्यैव परित्यागः ॥ ८ ॥

अमेध्यता अयज्ञार्हता। श्वा वा पिबेदित्यादि [2]हविर्दोषप्रदर्शनम्। अन्येष्वपि[2] हविर्दोषेषु परित्यागार्हेष्वेवं कर्तव्यम्। अत्र कीटग्रहणेन पिण्डकारी गृह्यते। स्थाल्या अपरित्यागो वाचनिकः ॥ ९ ॥

ऋक्षाकस्यापत्यमार्क्षाकिः[3]। आर्क्षाकेरपत्यम्[4] युवा आर्क्षाकायणः[4]। पर्यस्तो बुद्ध्या श्रान्तः प्रतिपत्तव्य[5]ज्ञानाच्चंक्रम्यते स्म। पुनःपुनरन्यं देशं गतवान् किल ॥ १० ॥

तदु होवाच [6]तस्मिन्नधिकारे उक्तवान् अनुबुध्य ज्ञात्वा। उद्दालको नामारुणिपुत्रः[7] अल्प[8] अज्ञान इत्यर्थः ॥ ११ ॥

१–१. M सर्वग्रह... युक्तस्य Ad °ग्रहणकर्मसंयु°. २–२. M Ad om; thus T. ३. M Ad आक्षाकिः. ४–४. M Ad आक्षाके°, M °रपत्य...ा कायणः. Ad om युवा; thus T. ५. M Ad °पत्तव्या ज्ञाना°; thus T. ६. M Ad अस्मि°; thus T. ७. M °नामाकणिपु°, T °नामारुणपु°. ८. M Ad T अपः; thus *VadhŚS*. T gives the reading अल्प of a MS ख. in the fn.

सिञ्चन्ति 'संत्वा सिञ्चामि यजुषा' **इति ॥** १५ **॥ मीमाꣳसैषा ॥** १६ **॥ उदपात्रमुपनिनीयान्वेवैतेन मन्त्रयेत** 'भूपतये=स्वाहा' **इति ॥** १७ **॥ यद्यलं प्रचरणाय स्यात् प्रचरेत् ॥** १८ **॥ यदि सन्ततिरतिशिष्येत तूष्णीं भूयोऽभ्यानीय प्रचरेत् ॥** १९ **॥ अथ यदि सर्वमेव स्कन्देदन्यदाहृत्य निरुप्याथ चेष्टेत् ॥** २० **॥ अथ यदि सर्वमेव भिद्येत** 'विधुं दद्राणम्' **इत्येताꣳ हुत्वा** 'यदृते चिदभिश्रिषः' **इत्येतया प्रतिनिधायान्यदाहृत्य निरुप्यैवाथ चेष्टेत् ॥** २१ **॥ अथ यदि गृहीतानां स्कन्देदुदपात्रमुपनिनीयान्वेवैतेन मन्त्रयेत** 'भूपतये=स्वाहा' **इति ॥** २२ **॥ यद्यलं प्रचरणाय स्यात् प्रचरेत् ॥** २३ **॥ यदि सन्ततिरतिशिष्येत तूष्णीं भूयोऽभ्यानीय प्रचरेत् ॥** २४ **॥ अथ यदि सर्वमेव स्कन्देद्यस्या अभिस्कन्देत्तस्या यजुर्भिर्गृह्णीयात् ॥** २५ **॥ अथ यदि सर्वमेव भिद्येत** 'विधुं दद्राणम्' **इत्येताꣳ हुत्वा** 'यदृते चिदभिश्रिषः' **इत्येतया प्रतिनिधाय तस्या एव यजुर्भिर्गृह्णीयात् ॥** २६ **॥ अथात आज्यावकाशस्यैव ॥** २७ **॥ तदवेक्षेत** 'आज्यमसि सत्यमसि' **इति ॥** २८ **॥ तन्नु हैतदेकेऽनवेक्ष्याज्यमुत्पुनन्ति ॥** २९ **॥ स यदेवं कुर्यादाज्यमेव पुनीयान्नात्मानम् ॥** ३० **॥ अथ यद्यवेक्ष्योत्पुनात्याज्येनैवात्मानं पुनीते, पवित्राभ्यामाज्यम् ॥** ३१ **॥ तस्मादवेक्ष्यैवोत्पुनीयात् ॥** ३२ **॥ अथात आज्यग्रहाणामेव ॥** ३३ **॥ तन्नु हैतदेके उदस्य पौरोडाशिकानाज्यग्रहान् यजमानयजूꣳषिकैरनुमन्त्रयन्ते ॥** ३४ **॥ योनिर्वै पौरोडाशिका आज्यग्रहा आत्मा यजमानयजूꣳषिकाः । स यदेवं**

स्वधां समिव सिञ्चन्ति। स्वधा रसः[1] संसेचनबुध्या मन्त्र ब्रुवत [2]इत्यर्थः। अन्ये [2]स्कन्नमाज्यमेव मन्त्रेणोपाददते। तस्मिन् पक्षे [3]स्वधाशब्दश्चानर्थको भवति ॥ १५ ॥

यद्यपि मीमांसैषेत्युक्तं क्रमप्राप्तत्वादन्यत्र विनियोगादर्शनाच्च न पूर्वपक्षतो विकल्पः। अत्रान्यानेतव्यस्य तूष्णीकत्वमुक्तविषयमेवान्यत्र संस्कृत्यानेतव्यमिति केचित्। कृतस्य[4] संस्कारस्य[5] पूर्वशेषे [5]विद्यमानत्वान्न [6]संस्कारस्तद्द्वारेणापूर्वेण संबध्यते। अतोऽन्याय्यमेव तूष्णीमानयनमित्यन्ये॥ १६ ॥

आज्यावकाशस्य आज्यावेक्षणस्य[7] विधानं वक्ष्यत इत्यर्थः। अध्वर्युणा वाच्यमानो मन्त्रमुक्त्वाऽवेक्षते। 'अनवेक्ष्याज्यमुत्पुनन्ती'ति ब्राह्मणे चतुर्थस्यानुवाकस्यान्ते आज्योदकयोरुत्पवनमाम्नाय[8] पञ्चमादौ 'स [9]एतमिन्द्र आज्यस्यावकाशमपश्यत्'[9] इत्यादिना आज्यावेक्षणं[10] विहितम्। [11]क्रमं पाठात्प्राप्तमपोह्य[11] पौरोडाशिके अवान्तरावकाशादनन्तरं कल्प आम्नातमेतं क्रमं [12]स्तौति ॥ २७–२९ ॥

तस्मादवेक्ष्यैवोत्पुनीयादिति[13] ब्रुवता तस्यैव [14]बलवत्त्वमभिप्रेतम्॥ ३२ ॥

---

१. T रसं; thus M Ad. २–२. M इत्य...न्य स्कन्न° ; thus Ad T. ३. T स्वधा शब्द इवशब्दश्चान° ; thus M Ad. ४. M Ad कृत्यस्य; thus T. ५–५. M संस्कार...षे विद्य° ; thus Ad T. ६. M T °रस्तद्वारे°, Ad °कारद्वारे°. ७. M Ad आज्यापेक्ष° ; thus T. ८. M आ...रुत्पवनमा; thus Ad T. ९–९. M एत...स्थावका°, Ad एतमिन्द्रमाज्य°. १०. M Ad आज्यापे°. ११–११. M Ad क्रम पाठात्प्राप्तमेवोपाह्य°. १२. Ad प्रस्तौति; thus M T. १३. M Ad तस्मादेवे क्षयैवो. १४–१४. M बल...ब्दो यजुश्शब्दा°, Ad बलवतामभिप्रेतं...दो यजुःश्शब्दा° ; thus T.

कुर्यादन्यत्र योनेरात्मानं दध्यात्तादृक् तत् ॥ ३५ ॥ **पौरोडाशिकैरेवाध्वर्युर्गृह्णीते यजमानयजूꣳषि-कैर्यजमानोऽनुमन्त्रयेत। यथा योनौ रेतः सिञ्च्याद्योनावात्मानं दध्यात्तादृक् तत्** ॥ ३६ ॥ **स जुह्वामाज्यं गृह्णाति** 'पञ्चानां त्वा' **इति** ॥ ३.२.२.३७ ॥ **[इति द्वितीयः पटलः** (८)**]**

[पञ्चगृहीतीनामाज्यग्रहणविधानम्]

'पञ्चानां त्वा=जनानां यन्त्राय धर्त्राय गृह्णामि' **इति** ॥ १ ॥ 'कामाय त्वा' **इति पञ्चमीं, यदि पञ्चगृहीती** ॥ २ ॥ **चतुर्थे वा काममनुवर्तयति** ॥ ३ ॥ **अथोपभृति** 'चरोस्त्वा पञ्चबि=विशे त्वा यन्त्राय धर्त्राय गृह्णामि' **इति** ॥ ४ ॥ 'कामाय त्वा' **इत्येव पञ्चमीं, यदि पञ्चगृहीती** ॥ ५ ॥ **चतुर्थे वा काममनुवर्तयति** ॥ ६ ॥ **अथोपभृत्येव** 'सुवीर्याय त्वा=गृह्णामि' **इति** ॥ ७ ॥ **कामाय त्वा इत्येव पञ्चमीं, यदि पञ्चगृहीती** ॥ ८ ॥ **चतुर्थे वा काममनुवर्तयति** ॥ ९ ॥ **अथ ध्रुवायां** 'भूरस्माकꣳ ह=ताभ्यो गृह्णामि' **इति** ॥ १० ॥ 'कामाय त्वा' **इत्येव पञ्चमीं, यदि पञ्चगृहीती** ॥ ११ ॥ **चतुर्थे वा काममनुवर्तयति** ॥ १२ ॥ **अथ परिधीन् परिधीयमानानभिमन्त्रयते** ॥ १३ ॥ 'ध्रुवोऽसि=भूयासम्' **इति मध्यमम्।** '०धीरश्चेत्ता वसुविद्' **इति** ॥ १४ ॥ 'उग्रोऽसि=भूयासम्' **इति दक्षिणार्ध्यम्।** '०उग्रश्चेत्ता वसुविद्' **इति** ॥ १५ ॥ 'अभिभूरस्य=भूयासम्' **इत्युत्तरार्ध्यम्।** '०अभिभूश्चेत्ता वसुविद्' **इति** ॥ १६ ॥ **अथ मध्यमं परिधिमन्वारभ्य जपति** 'युनज्मि त्वा=ते' **इति** ॥ १७ ॥ 'यन्म अग्न' **इति प्रस्तरं साद्यमानम्।** '०अस्य=उपस्थ' **इति** ॥ १८ ॥ **भूर्भुवः सुवः इति स्रुचः सन्नाः** ॥ १९ ॥ **अथो आसन्नानि हवीꣳषि** ॥ २० ॥ **इध्ममाधीयमानमभिमन्त्रयते** 'अग्ने देवेद्ध=मन्द्रजिह्व' **इति** ॥ २१ ॥ **तदाहुः** 'अग्ने देवेद्ध मन्द्रजिह्व' **इति इध्मम्,** 'अग्ने मन्विद्ध मन्द्रजिह्व' **इति होतारमीक्षेतेति** ॥ २२ ॥ **मीमाꣳसैषा** ॥ २३ ॥ **समस्तेनेध्ममेवाधीयमानमभिमन्त्रयते** ॥ २४ ॥ **वेदेनोपवाज्यमानम्** 'उच्छुष्मो अग्ने=सते' **इति** ॥ २५ ॥ **स्रुवेणाघारमाघार्यमाणम्**

यजूँषिकशब्दो यजुः[१४] शब्दार्थाभिधायी। प्रातिपदिकान्तरम्। एतदपि शाखान्तरविहितम-पोद्यते ॥ ३.२.२.३३-३६ ॥ **[इति द्वितीयः पटलः** (८)**]**

पञ्चगृहीतीति। पञ्चावत्तिविषयमेतदिति केचित्। 'विंशान्याज्यानि भवन्ति, षोडशान्याज्यानि भवन्ती'ति शाखान्तरे विहितत्वात्। सर्वेषां[१] वैकल्पिकमित्यन्ये ॥ १-१२ ॥

परिध्यभिमन्त्रणं चानयोरुक्तम् ॥ १३-१६ ॥

प्रस्तरं[१] साद्यमानमन्वारभ्य जपतीत्यनुवर्तते ॥ १७-१८ ॥

इध्ममाधीयमानमित्यतस्ततः[२] प्रभृति प्रवराभिमन्त्रणादभिमन्त्रयत इति। 'अग्ने देवेद्धे'ति मन्त्रोऽर्थाद्विपर्यस्तः। 'अमर्त्यस्ये'ति क्रमाद्धोतृप्रवरे प्राप्ते [३]आचार्येणाध्वर्युप्रवरे विनियुक्तः[३]। केचिदाहुः-[४]क्रमादेव होतृप्रवराभिमन्त्रणं[४] प्राप्तम्। अप्राप्तप्रापणार्थमध्वर्युप्रवरे विहितमिति। तथा च सूत्रकारेणाम्नातम् 'होतृप्रवरे चाध्वर्युप्रवरे च जपती'ति ॥ २१-२४ ॥

१-१. M सर्वेषां वै... द्व्यभिमन्त्रणञ्च ... प्रस्तरं; thus Ad T. **२.** M °मित्यातस्तत. **३-३.** M आचार्येण...विनियुक्तः; Ad° ध्वर्युः प्र°. **४-४.** M क्रमादेव...मन्त्रेण, Ad° मन्त्रेण.

'मनोऽसि प्राजापत्यं मनसा मा भूतेनाऽऽविश' **इति** ॥ २६ ॥ **स्रुग्भ्यामुत्तरम्** 'वागस्यैन्द्री सपत्नक्षयणी=विश' **इति** ॥ २७ ॥ **प्रवरं प्रव्रियमाणम्** 'अमर्त्यस्य ते होतर्मूर्धन्नाजिघर्मि रायस्पोषाय=र्याय' **इति** ॥ २८ ॥ **प्रयाजमिष्टमिष्टमनुमन्त्रयते** 'वसन्तमृतूनां=प्रीणीताम्' **इति** ॥ २९ ॥ **उभाविष्टावाज्यभागौ** 'अग्नीषोमयोरहं देवयज्यया चक्षुष्मान् भूयासम्' **इति** ॥ ३० ॥ 'अग्नेरहं देवयज्ययाऽन्नादो भूयासम्' **इत्याग्नेयः हविः** ॥ ३१ ॥ 'दब्धिरस्यदब्धो भूयासममुं दभेयम्' **इत्युपांशुयाजम्** ॥ ३२ ॥ 'अग्नीषोमयोरहं देवयज्यया वृत्रहा भूयासम्' **इत्यग्नीषोमीयम्** ॥ ३३ ॥ 'इन्द्राग्नियोरहं देवयज्ययेन्द्रियाव्यन्नादो भूयासम्' **इत्यैन्द्राग्नम्** ॥ ३४ ॥ 'इन्द्रस्याहं देवयज्ययेन्द्रियावी भूयासम्' **इत्यैन्द्रम्** ॥ ३५ ॥ 'महेन्द्रस्याहं देवयज्यया जेमानं महिमानं गमेयम्' **इति यदि महेन्द्रयाजी** ॥ ३६ ॥ 'अग्नेः स्विष्टकृतोऽहं देवयज्ययाऽऽयुष्मान् यज्ञेन प्रतिष्ठां गमेयम्' **इति सौविष्टकृतम्** ॥ ३.२.३.३७ ॥ **[इति तृतीयः पटलः** (९)**]**

॥ इति तृतीयप्रपाठके द्वितीयोऽनुवाकः ॥

उत्तरमाघारमाघार्यमाणं यजमानोऽन्वारभते। लिंगादाज्यभागयोस्तन्त्रेणानुमन्त्रणवचनाच्च ॥ २७ ॥

'महेन्द्रस्याहं [१]देवयज्यया जेमानं महिमानं [१]गमेयमि'ति महेन्द्रयाजीति। कोऽसौ महेन्द्रयाजी नाम। उच्यते–अनागतश्रीर्महेन्द्रं यजेत। 'त्रयो वै गतश्रिय' इत्यारभ्य ब्राह्मणे महेन्द्रयागो विहितः। तस्यानुमन्त्रणमगतश्रियाणां प्रतिषिध्यते, गतश्रियां विधानार्थम्। त्रयो वै गतश्रियः। शुश्रूवान् बहुश्रुतः, [२][ग्रामणीर्ग्राम]कूटः, राजन्यः क्षत्रियः, तेषां महेन्द्रो देवता। ते महेन्द्रं[३] यजेरन्। यस्य हविष इन्द्रो देवता स[४] महेन्द्रः[५]। त्रयो[६] वै स्वां देवतामित्यादि गतश्रियः। तेषां महेन्द्रो देवतेति वचनादगतश्रियमिदं[७] दोषवचनमिति गम्यते। त्रयो वै स्वां देवतामतीत्यान्यां[८] यजते[८] स्वाया इन्द्रात्प्रच्यवते। न परां महेन्द्रं प्राप्नोति। पापीयान् भवति। तस्मात्स आद्यं संवत्सरमिन्द्रं यजेत। संवत्सरं हि व्रतं नात्येति स्वैवेन्द्राख्या इज्यमाना भूत्यर्थं दीपयन्ती[९] वसीयान् भवति। ततः संवत्सरस्य परस्ताद् अग्नये व्रतपतये निर्वपति। संवत्सरादेनं[१०] यजमानं[११] [१२]स्वदेवतायागेन हुतपावकमग्निर्व्रतपतिः स्वदेवतानिमित्तव्रतमालंभयति। तत ऊर्ध्वं काममिन्द्रं वा महेन्द्रं वा यजेत। गतश्रियां नित्यं महेन्द्रः। एवमभिप्रेत्याचार्येण महेन्द्रयाजीत्यभ्यधायि[१३] अथवा गुणविकारसंवत्सरप्रयोगे महेन्द्रयागमभिप्रेत्य सौविष्टकृतयागः[१४] ॥ ३.२.३.३६–३७ ॥ **[इति तृतीयः पटलः** (९)**]**

॥ इति व्याख्यायां तृतीयप्रपाठके द्वितीयोऽनुवाकः ॥[१५]

१–१. M Ad T यज्यया...नं गमेय° ; thus *VādhŚS* 3.7.28. **२.** M Ad कूटं; thus T. cf *ŚānkhŚS* 2.6.6. **३.** M Ad महेन्द्र; thus T. **४.** M Ad तस्य; thus T. **५.** M Ad महेन्द्रं; thus T. **६.** M यो वैवस्वान्, Ad यो वै स्वां. **७.** M Ad °श्रियामि°. **८–८.** M मतीत्य...ते स्वाया, Ad न्या जते. **९.** M Ad न्ति; thus T. **१०.** M Ad °वत्सरदानं. **११.** M Ad याज°. **१२.** M Ad स्वे°. **१३.** M Ad °त्यभिधायी. **१४.** M Ad संविष्टकृद्यागः, T सौविष्टकृत्याह. **१५.** M इति द्वितीयः, Ad इति वाधूलकल्प सूत्रव्याख्यायां द्वितीयः समाप्तः ॥.

॥ अथ तृतीयप्रपाठके तृतीयोऽनुवाकः ॥

[प्राशित्रेडादीनामभिमन्त्रणम्]

'अग्निर्मा दुरिष्टात्पातु' **इति प्राशित्रमवदीयमानमभिमन्त्रयते।** '°अग्निर्मा दुरिष्टात्=जेषम्'

अथातः प्राशित्रमभिमन्त्रयते[१]। स्विष्टकृदनुमन्त्रणमन्त्रात्परस्य 'अग्निर्मा दुरिष्टात् पातु' इत्यस्य मन्त्रस्यान्यत्र विनियोगो नास्ति। तस्य स्थानात् प्राशित्रावदानाभिमन्त्रणत्वमिष्यते। पूर्वत्रैवाध्वर्यवे कल्पे [२]षडवत्तप्राशित्रपरेक्षणयोर्विनियुक्तस्तदन्यविधानमध्य एवोत्कर्षो मा विज्ञायीति पूर्वोक्तेन न्यायेन प्राशित्रावदानाभिमन्त्रणार्थ एवेति प्रत्याययितुम्। आनन्तर्यार्थम् अथशब्दं, हेत्वर्थं चातःशब्दं प्रयुक्तवानाचार्यः। मा च पौनरुक्त्याशंका भूत्, विकल्पत्वं च मा विज्ञायीति। कथं पुनस्तत्र विधानम्। श्रुत्यन्तरे आध्वर्यवे विहितमित्यवगन्तव्यम्। एवमन्येषां मन्त्राणां याजमानकाण्डे पठितानां कल्प आध्वर्यवे दृष्टानामाध्वर्यव एव श्रुत्यन्तरे पाठोऽनुमेयः। अन्य आह—याजमाने पठिता यद्यप्याध्वर्यवे दृश्यन्ते तथापि याजमानत्वं[३] न जहति[३]। किन्तु तत्र पाठे किन्नु प्रयोजनमिति प्रयोजनाकांक्षा भवति। यथा [४]पाटलीपुत्रकं देवदत्तं[४] निर्ज्ञातपूर्वं[५] मथुरायां दृष्ट्वा न माथुर[५] इति बुद्धिरुत्पद्यते, [६]किन्वस्यागमनमित्याकांक्षा भवति प्रयोजनं[७] प्रति। एवमाध्वर्यवे दर्शनमाध्वर्यवत्वं न प्रतिपादयति[८], प्रयोजनम् अन्वेषणीयमिति। तत्र प्रयोजनममिधीयते। समुच्चयासंभवाद्विकल्पो भवति। पुरोडाशीये दृष्टं[९] याजमानम् अन्यत्र विनिवेशयन्ति[९]। पृथग्याजमानं[१०] प्रकृत्यर्थमाध्वर्यवे दृष्टं[११] दर्शपूर्णमासिकैः[११] सह विकृतिं गच्छतीति। [१२]तदुभयमनुपपन्नम्। विकल्पनायां किं प्रमाणम्। [१३]अन्यत्राम्नातानामन्यत्र कतिपयान्येव दृश्यन्ते। अथ परिसंख्यानमिति[१३] चेत्। अभिन्नगुणानां पुनः श्रवणं परिसंख्यार्थं भवति। इहत्यानां[१४] तत्रत्यानां[१४] च पदार्थानां गुणभेदो दृश्यते। निरुप्यमाणाभिमन्त्रणादिषु वचनेषु वाच्यमानो ब्रवीतीति। तत्र इहाभिमन्त्रयत इति। अस्मत्पक्षे वाच्यमानानामभिमन्त्रयत इति नास्ति विरोधः[१५]। एवमन्येष्वपि तत्रतत्र द्रष्टव्यम्। अन्ये वर्णयन्ति दिङ्मार्जनान्तानां पदार्थानां बहुभिर्लिङ्गैराध्वर्यवत्वमप्युपगम्यते। इदं न मृष्यामहे विष्णुक्रमादयोऽपि तत्र दर्शनादाध्वर्यवा इति। अतस्ते पदार्थाः प्रोषिते[१६] यजमानेऽध्वर्युणा पुत्रादिना वा सन्निहिते कर्तव्याः[१७]। पौरस्त्याः[१८] प्रोषितेनैव यजमानेनैव। अवश्यं चैतदेवं विज्ञेयं यजमानभागप्राशनप्रदर्शनात्[१९]। नह्यध्वर्युणा निमित्तमन्तरेण यजमानभागः प्राशितव्य इति। तदप्ययुक्तम्। विष्णुक्रमादिष्वपि गुणभेदो दृश्यत एव। इहोत्तरं वेद्या अंसमभिप्रच्यवमान इति। तथोत्तरेष्वपि द्रष्टव्यः। तथा च लिङ्गमाध्वर्यवत्वे निधाय स्थालीमुपस्थायेति[२०]। प्रणीता यजमानस्या–

---

१. M Ad °मनुम°. २. M Ad षधव°. ३–३. M मानत्वं...ति. ४–४. M पटली...कन्देव. ५–५. M निज्ञा [Ad निर्ज्ञाय] ...न माधुर. ६. M Ad किन्त्वस्यागमनप्रयोजनमित्याकांक्षा भवति; thus T. ७. M °क्षां...योजनं. ८. M प्रति...दयति. ९–९. M Ad दृष्टं वा भवतः... न्येविनिवेशयन्ति, T दृष्टं वा पतिः, T om अन्यत्र विनिवेशयनित. १०. T °मानः. ११–११. M दृष्ट...र्णमसि°; thus T. १२. M गच्छतः...तदु°. १३–१३. T कल्पनायां (कं...) नमिति चेत्. T takes the text as given in both M and Ad as additional and gives the same in fn. as किं प्रमाणं। अन्यत्राम्नातानामन्यत्र कतिपयान्येव दृश्यन्ते। अथ परिसंख्या इति मध्ये वर्तते. १४–१४. M इहत्या...नाञ्च. १५. M Ad विरोधं; thus T. १६. M Ad प्रेषिते; thus T. १७. M Ad °तव्या. १८. M Ad °रस्त्या प्रेषि°. १९. M Ad °प्राशप्रद°. २०. M मुपोर्थायो, Ad °मुपोस्थायेति.

इति ॥ १ ॥ **इडामाह्रियमाणाम्** 'सुरूपवर्षवर्ण=स्वत्येहि' **इति** ॥ २ ॥ **अवान्तरेडामवदीयमानाम्** 'रन्तिरसि रमतिरसि सूनर्यसि' **इति** ॥ ३ ॥ **तामेवोपाꣳशूपहूयमानाम्** 'जुष्टे जुष्टिं तेऽशीयोपहूत उपहवं तेऽशीय' **इति** ॥ ४ ॥ **उच्चैरुपहूयमानाम्** 'सा मे सत्याऽऽशीरस्य=गमेयम्' **(इति)** ॥ ५ ॥ **तद्वै ब्राह्मणं भवति**—'यर्हि होतेडामुपह्वयेत तर्हि यजमानो=सृजति' **इति** ॥ ६ ॥ **स यत्राभिजानाति** 'इडोपहूता' **इति तद् वायुं मनसा ध्यायति** '°वायुष्टे वत्सस्तमुपावसृजामि, सा मे वायुना वत्सेन श्रद्धा तपोऽमुं कामं धुक्ष्व' **इति यं कामं** *[१]**(कामयते तमाशास्ते** ॥ ७ ॥ **सꣳ हैवास्मै स कामः) पद्यते** ॥ ८ ॥ **बर्हिषदमष्टाकपालं कृत्वा** 'ब्रध्न पिन्वस्व' **इति** ॥ ९ ॥ **अन्वाहार्यम्** 'प्रजापतेर्भागोऽसि' **इति** ॥ १० ॥ **सन्ततिꣳ हूयमानम्** 'मनो ज्योतिर्जुषताम्' **इति** ॥ ११ ॥ **अनुयाजमिष्टमिष्टमभिमन्त्रयते** 'बर्हिषोऽहं देवयज्यया प्रतिष्ठां गमेयम्' **इति** ॥ १२ ॥ **अथ**

*[१]. Text abri. कामं=पद्यते see I.3.3.17-18.

ज्जलावानीय[१] स्थालीं निधायोपोत्थाय[२]दक्षिणं वेद्यन्त=क्रमत इति। यत्र यजमानभागप्राशनमुक्तं[३] तत्र कथम्। विकल्प इत्युक्तमेव। अतः पूर्वोक्तेन न्यायेनाध्वर्यवा एवैते पदार्थाः। आह—निधाय स्थाली-मित्यस्मत्[४] पक्षेऽपि[५] युज्यत एव। प्रोषितेऽपि यजमाने प्रणीतानिनयनमध्वर्युः करोत्येव हि। तत्राध्वर्युणैव कर्तव्यता गम्यते। नान्येन प्रत्यासन्नेन। उच्यते। तथाप्युपवेषोदसनस्य तत्राम्नानं भिन्नगुणत्वं[६] च नोपपद्यते एव। यत्तूक्तं[६] निर्ज्ञातपाटलीपुत्रकं मथुरायां दृष्ट्वा न माथुर इति प्रतीतिर्भवति, प्रयोजनाकांक्षा तु भवतीति।

अस्मिन् कल्पे शाखान्तरविहिता[७] एव मन्त्रा आचार्येण विनियुज्यन्ते। ते विज्ञातुं न शक्यन्ते इमे याजमाना[८] आम्नाता, इमे आध्वर्यवा[९] इति। आचार्यं[९] एव प्रमाणमित्यध्यवसाय कर्तव्यः। तथा सत्युभयत्राम्नानमेषामस्तीति[१०] अवगन्तव्यम्[१०]। तथा सत्युभाभ्यां कर्तव्यम्। यथा 'वाजपस्त्य'मादयः[११]। तथा चोक्तम्—'द्विराम्नातेषूभौ द्विराम्नातस्यार्थवत्वा'दिति ॥ १ ॥

इडामाह्रियमाणामित्यादिषूक्त एव[१२] प्रयोगः ॥ २ ॥

वायुष्टे[१२] वत्स' इत्यस्य कोऽवकाशः। 'सा मे सत्याऽऽशीरस्य यज्ञस्य भूयाद्' इत्याह[१३]। 'एष वै यज्ञस्य दोह'[१३] इत्युक्त्वा वायोर्वत्सस्योपावसर्गस्य प्रदानार्थत्वमुक्तम्। तथा च 'इडोपहूता' इत्येतेषां स्तनभक्तित्वमुक्तम्। तस्मादिडोपहूतेत्याहूते यजमानो 'वायुष्टे वत्स' इति मनसा चिन्तयितव्यो होतारमीक्षमाणेन। तथा सति 'सा[१४] मे सत्याशीः' इत्यादिना[१४] दोग्धि। तस्मान्नु हेडायामेवोपहूयमानायाम् 'ओमोमोम्' इति त्रिः ब्रूयादिति वायुध्यानात् प्राग्भवति ॥ ५-८ ॥

'ब्रध्न पिन्वस्व' इत्यादयो मन्त्रा यथाऽऽध्वर्यवे पठितास्तथैव यजमानेनापि प्रयोक्तव्याः ॥ ९ ॥

उभौ बर्हिषदं कुरुतः तथा स्रुग्व्यूहनम् ॥ १३ ॥

---

१. M Ad °लापानीय. **२.** M Ad °योपत्थाव्य. **३.** M Ad °मान प्रा°; thus T. **४.** M Ad °स्मात्. **५.** T पक्षे. **६-६.** M °त्वञ्च...चूक्तम्. **७.** M Ad °न्तरे विहि°; thus T. **८.** T °माना. **९-९.** M आ...एव प्र...णमि, Ad °आचायमेव, T °ध्वर्यवा. **१०-१०.** M °मेषा...°व्यम्; thus Ad T. **११.** M Ad वाजस्यमा°. **१२-१२.** M एव...युष्टे. **१३-१३.** M °दिव्याहै...दाह°; Ad इत्यापवै य°. **१४-१४.** M सा...ना; thus Ad T.

वाजवतीभ्याः स्रुचौ व्यूहति 'वाजस्य मा प्रसवेन', 'उद्ग्राभं च निग्राभं च' **इति** ॥ १३ ॥ **अथ यत्रोज्जितीर्होता प्रतिपद्यते तद्यथादेवतमनुमन्त्रयते** 'अग्नेरहमुज्जितिमनूज्जेषः सोमस्य=स्विष्टकृतोऽहमुज्जितिमनूज्जेषम्' **इति** ॥ १४ ॥ **ब्राह्मणमु वै भवति—**'एष वा अन्यो यज्ञस्य दोह इडायामन्यः। यर्हि=तर्हि ब्रूयाद् 'एमा अग्मन्नाशिषो' दोहकामाः' **इति** ॥ १५ ॥ **स यत्राभिजानात्याशास्ते** 'अयं यजमानोऽसौ' **इति, तत् जपति** 'एमा अग्मन्नाशिषो=मिषम्' **इति** ॥ १६ ॥ **प्रस्तरं प्रह्रियमाणम्** 'रोहितेन त्वाऽग्निर्देवतां=गमयतु' **इति** ॥ १७ ॥ **अत्र प्रस्तरेण सह यजमानभागमनुप्रहरेत्** ॥ १८ ॥ **यदि यजमानः प्रसवेत्** 'प्रजापतेर्विभान्नाम=सह यजमानेन' **इति** ॥ १९ ॥ **स यत्** 'सह यजमानेन' **इति ब्रूयात् प्रमायुको यजमानः स्यात्** ॥ २० ॥ **ब्राह्मणमु वै भवति** 'अयं वै प्रजापतेर्विभान्नामलोकस्तस्मिन्नेवैनं दधाति सह यजमानेन' **इति** ॥ २१ ॥ **तस्मादु काममेव** 'सह यजमानेन' **इति ब्रूयात् कामम्** 'अमुं यजमानस्य लोकः' **इति** ॥ २२ ॥ **अथ परिधीन् प्रह्रियमाणान्** 'वि ते मुञ्चामि' **इति** ॥ ३.३.१.२३ ॥ **[इति प्रथमः पटलः** (१०)**]**

[शंयुवाक-पत्नीसंयाजादिविधानम्]

'वि ते मुञ्चामि रशना=देवतासु' **इति** ॥ १ ॥ **शंयुवाके** 'विष्णोः शंयोरहं देवयज्यया यज्ञेन प्रतिष्ठां गमेयम्' **इत्याह** ॥ २ ॥ **अथ वेदे** 'वेदोऽसि वित्तिरसि=वाजिनम्' **इत्यनुच्छन्दसम्** ॥ ३ ॥ **वेदे** 'वेदोऽसि वित्तिरसि=विदेय' **इत्याह। वेदेन वै देवा असुराणां वित्तं वेद्यमविन्दन्त तद् वेदस्य**

---

[१]उज्जित्यभिमन्त्रणं यथोक्तमेव[१] ॥ १४ ॥

उपांशुयाजदेवताया मन्त्रब्राह्मणकल्पेष्वभावात् 'एमा अग्मन्', 'रोहितेन त्वा' इत्यनयोर्यथापाठ एव प्रयोगः ॥ १५–१७ ॥

'तस्मिंस्त्वा दधामि सह यजमानेन', 'तस्मिंस्त्वा दधामि यजमानस्य लोक' इति वाऽनुप्रहरणमन्त्रं समापयेत् ॥ ३.३.१.२१–२२ ॥ **[इति प्रथमः पटलः** (८)**]**

परिधिप्रहरणशंयुवाकयोः[२] समानकालत्वात् क्रमप्रवृत्तित्वाच्च वाचो यथापाठ एव प्रयोगो 'वि[३] ते मुञ्चामि', 'विष्णोः शंयोर्' इत्येतयोः ॥ १–२ ॥

वेदाभिमन्त्रणमन्त्राणां ब्राह्मणविहितस्य प्रकृत्यर्थत्वमनुच्छन्दसस्य विकृत्यर्थत्वमनुकल्पस्यानवकाशत्वं च वर्णयन्ति केचित्। एवं[४] सति, अस्य पाठ[४] एव नोपपद्यते। इहाम्नातानां प्रकृतौ विकृतौ[५] वा विनियोगः। उभयविरहितेऽन्यस्मिन् प्रकरणे वेदवति वाचने[६]....विनियोक्तुमस्माकं नास्ति शक्तिः ॥ ३ ॥

अनुकल्पमिति च श्रुत्यन्तरे[७] विहितं वदति न स्वमनीषिकया कल्पितम्। श्रुत्यन्तरे विहितानामाचार्येणाम्नातानां[८] सर्वत्र प्रकृतावेव[८] वैकल्पिकत्वमुक्तम्। तदेतेषामपि यथाकामं प्रयोगः

१–१. M ऊर्ज्जि...थोक्त° ; Ad ऊर्ज्जि°. **२.** M °रणशं...स्समा° ; thus T. **३.** T गोऽपि°. **४–४.** M एव...पाठ; Ad सति...पाठ; thus T. **५.** M सुकृतौ. **६.** M Ad T वाचन...विनि°. **७.** M Ad °त्यन्तरके; thus T. **८–८.** M °तानां...प्रकृ°.

वेदत्वमिति। यद्यद् भ्रातृव्यस्याभिध्यायेत् तस्य नाम गृह्णीयात्। तदेवास्य सर्वं वृङ्क्ते॥ ४॥ 'घृतवन्तं कुलायिनꣳ रायस्पोषꣳ सहस्रिणं वेदो ददातु वाजिनम्' **इत्यनुब्राह्मणम्॥** ५॥ **वेदे** 'वेदोऽसि वित्तिरसि विदेयाहम्', 'साधुसनिरसि सनिताऽसि सनेयाहम् प्रजां पशून सुवर्गं लोकम्', 'कर्मासि करुणमसि=जिनम्' **इति॥** ६॥ **अथात्रैव वाऽऽसीनो दक्षिणतोऽनु समेत्य वा पत्नीसंयाजमिष्टमिष्टमनुमन्त्रयते॥** ७॥ 'सोमस्याहं=धिषीय' **इति सौम्यम्॥** ८॥ 'त्वष्टुरहं देव =पुषेयम्' **इति त्वाष्ट्रम्॥** ९॥ 'उभाविष्यावुत्तरौ देवानां पत्नीरग्निर्गृहपति=प्र भूयासम्' **इति॥** १०॥ **अथ प्राङेत्य ध्रुवामाप्याययति** 'आप्यायतां ध्रुवा घृतेन' **इति॥** ११॥ **अथ समिष्टयजूꣳषि जुहोति** 'देवा गातुविदः' **इति॥** १२॥ **अथ यजमानभागमनुप्रहरेद् यद्यमुत्र प्रहरेयुः** 'प्रजापतेर्विभान्नाम लोकः' **इति॥** १३॥ **अथान्तर्वेदि प्रणीता आसाद्य दक्षिणत उपविश्य यजमानभागं प्राश्नाति॥** १४॥ **व्रतोपेतस्यैषोऽवदीयत इत्याहुस्तथा हास्यान्तर्यज्ञं प्राशितो भवतीति॥** १५॥ **अथाप आचम्यापो न्युप्य पूर्णपात्रमभिमृशति** 'सदसि सन्मे भूयाः' **इति॥** १६॥ **अथ दिशो मार्जयते** 'प्राच्यां दिशि देवा ऋत्विजो=मार्जयन्ताम्' **इति॥** १७॥ **तृचेनाञ्जलौ निनयते** 'आपो हि ष्ठा मयोभुवः' **इति॥** १८॥ **अथ द्वाभ्यामात्मानं विमृष्टे** 'समिन्द्र णः', 'सं वर्चसा' **इति॥** १९॥ **अथोपोत्थाय दक्षिणं वेद्यन्तमनु विष्णुक्रमान् क्रमते॥** २०॥ **उत्तरं वेद्या अꣳसमभि प्रच्यवमानो दक्षिणं पादं पूर्वं प्रहरति॥** २१॥ **सव्येनानु निक्रामति** 'विष्णोः क्रमोऽस्यभिमातिहा' **इति॥** २२॥ **तन्नु हैतदेके चतुर्थेन पर्यायेण वेदिमभि प्रच्यवन्ते। यजमानायतनं वै वेदिः। य एनं तत्र ब्रूयात्**

अनुब्राह्मणस्य प्रयोगः॥ ४-५॥

'वेदोऽसि[1] वित्तिरसि विदेय अदः' इत्यस्य स्थाने द्वेष्यस्य स्वजन्मना[2] यदीप्सितं द्वितीयया वदति। ततः परम् 'अहमित्युक्त्वा द्वेष्यनाम षष्ठ्यन्तं गृह्णात्यन्तरा[3] राकाया 'अहं देवयज्ज्यया[4] प्रजावान्[4] भूयासम्' इति विद्यते किल॥ ६॥

ध्रुवाऽऽप्यायनसमिष्टयजुर्होमावुभाभ्यां क्रियेते[5]। प्रोषिते यजमाने पूर्वोक्तकाले यदि विस्मरेयुः वेदवेदितृणैः सह प्रहरेत्॥ १०-१३॥

प्रणीताभिरध्वर्युणाहृत्यानीताभिर्हस्तौ प्रक्षाल्य यजमानभागं प्राश्नाति॥ १४॥

[6]व्रतोपेतस्येत्यादिनाऽत्र प्राशने गुणत्वमभिधीयते[7] प्रशंसार्थम्॥ १५॥

अध्वर्युणाऽऽनीताभिर्दिशो मार्जयन्ते[8]॥ १६-१७॥

उभे[9] यथालिंगमुभौ[9] यजमानस्याञ्जलौ तृचेन निनयनम्[10]। तिस्र ऋचस्तृचः[11]॥ १८॥

वेद्या उत्तरमंसमभिप्रच्यवमानो गच्छन् सर्वत्रानुव्याहरणस्वभावतयाऽनुव्याहरति दोषो भवति।

---

१. M वेदासि. २. M Ad स्वजनायदी°; thus T. ३. M Ad गृह्णाद्व्यन्तराकाया; thus T. ४-४. M °या...वान्, T gives a text (वाप्यायसमिष्टयजुर्होमावुभाभ्यां) under bracket between प्रजा and वान्. ५. M Ad क्रियते; thus T. ६. Ad व्रतोपस्येत्या°. ७. M Ad मभिप्रशं; thus T. ८. M Ad ° यन्ति; thus T. ९-९. M A उभयथालिङ्गमुभे. १०. M नि...त, Ad नियत, T नियतम्. ११. M Ad तिस्रऋचसूचः.

प्रायतनाद् च्योष्टाऽप्रतिष्ठितो भवतीति ॥ २३ ॥ **अथ हैव स्यात्। तस्मात् तृतीय एव स पर्याये चतुर्थमनुवर्तयेत, प्रपदे वा विकर्षेद्** 'विष्णोः क्रमोऽसि शत्रूयतो हन्ता' **इति** ॥ २४ ॥ **अथोपतिष्ठते** ॥ २५ ॥ **प्राङ् प्रक्रामति** 'अगन्म सुवः सुवरगन्म' **इति** ॥ २६ ॥ **अथादित्यमुपतिष्ठते** ॥ ३.३.२.२७ ॥ **[इति द्वितीयः पटलः (११)]**

[व्रतविसर्गः]

अथादित्यमुपतिष्ठते 'संदृशस्ते मा छित्सि=सं ज्योतिषाऽभुवम्' **इति** ॥ १ ॥ 'ऐन्द्रीमावृतमन्वावर्ते' **इति दक्षिणा पर्यावर्तते** ॥ २ ॥ **तदानीमेवोपावर्तते** 'समहं प्रजया सं मया प्रजा' **इति** ॥ ३ ॥ **अथोपसमिन्धे** 'समिद्धो अग्ने मे दीदिहि' **इति** ॥ ४ ॥ **अथोपतिष्ठते** 'वसुमान् यज्ञो वसीयान् भूयासम्' **इति** ॥ ५ ॥ **अथ द्वाभ्यामाग्निपावमानीभ्यां गार्हपत्यमभ्येति** 'अग्न आयूꣳषि पवसे', 'अग्ने पवस्य' **इति** ॥ ६ ॥ **अथोपतिष्ठते** 'अग्ने गृहपते' **इति** ॥ ७ ॥ **आशिष आशास्ते** 'शतꣳ हिमा=तन्तवे' **इत्यन्ततः** ॥ ८ ॥ 'कस्त्वा युनक्ति स त्वा विमुञ्चतु' **इत्युलूखलमुसलं परेक्षते** ॥ ९ ॥ 'यानि घर्मे कपालानि' **इति कपालानि।** '°उप चिन्वन्ति वेधस=विमुञ्चताम्' **इति** ॥ १० ॥ **अथ यज्ञस्य पुनरालम्भेन प्राङेति** 'यज्ञो बभूव स आ बभूव' **इति** ॥ ११ ॥ **अथ प्राङुत्क्रम्य जपति** 'गोमाँ अग्नेऽविमाँ अश्वी यज्ञः' **इति** ॥ १२ ॥ **अथोपवेषमादत्ते** ॥ १३ ॥ **तं पुरस्तात्प्रत्यञ्चꣳ स्थविमत उत्तर उपगूहति** 'यो नः कनीय=वीरवतीं विदेय' **इति** ॥ १४ ॥ **अथ दक्षिणतस्तिष्ठन् व्रतं विसृजते।** 'विक्रम्य विक्रम्य हीन्द्रो वृत्रमहन् समृद्ध्यै' **इति ब्राह्मणम्** ॥ १५ ॥ 'पयस्वतीरोषधयः' **इति तिरःपवित्रमप आचामति।** '°पयस्व=सꣳसृज' **इति** ॥ १६ ॥ 'अग्ने व्रतपते' **इति मार्जयित्वा**

यदि नानुव्याहरति दोषो नास्ति ॥ २१–२३ ॥

प्रपदे अग्रपदे। [१]पार्ष्णौ तृतीयेन निधाय प्रपदे[१] चतुर्थं प्रयोजेयत्। ब्रह्मयजमानयोर्व्यपेत्योपविष्टयोर्यथा[२] प्रपन्नमेव पन्थाः स्यात्। यद्यपि चतुर्थेन पर्यायेण नातिगच्छति, तथापि तूष्णीमेवातिगच्छति। तत उत्तरकालं न व्यवाय इति। यद्यन्यथेडान्वारम्भार्थं[३] निष्क्रान्तः[४] पुनर्न व्यवैति, इहापि [५]प्रतिनिवृत्य दक्षिणे[५]नाहवनीयं गच्छति। उभयथाप्याचार्या [६]व्याचक्षते। अयमप्याचार्यस्तं पूर्वेण ब्रह्माणं[७] च यजमानं चातिहृत्येत्यन्वाहार्यस्य परिहृत्य सादनं ब्रुवन् पुनरपि तथैव प्रविष्टत्वं दर्शयति ॥ ३.३.२.२४ ॥ **[इति द्वितीयः पटलः (११)]**

तदानीमेवोपावर्तत[८] इति विहारापर्यावर्तननिवृत्यर्थं वदन् दक्षिणेन गमनं [९]दर्शयति। 'संदृशस्ते मा छित्सि[९] = सं ज्योतिषाभुवम्' इत्यातः मन्त्रबहुत्वशंकया विकल्पो मा भूदित्येवमुक्तम्। ऐन्द्रीमावृतमित्यादि ॥ १–३ ॥

उपवेषोपगूहनम्। नित्यस्यैवोपवेषस्य ॥ १३–१४ ॥

१–१. M Ad पार्ष्णीन्तृतीयप्रपदे; thus T. २. M Ad ° र्वेवेत्यो; thus T. ३. M Ad ° न्यथा अन्वाश्म्भार्थ. ४. T निष्क्रान्तं; thus M Ad. ५–५. M Ad om निवृत्य दक्षिणे; thus T. ६. M Ad ° व्याच° ; thus T. ७. M Ad ब्राह्मणं. ८. M Ad ° मेवोपात्तत; thus T. ९–९. M द...ाच्छित्सिः; thus T.

समिधमादधाति। '०व्रतमचारिषं=अराधि स्वाहा' **इति॥ १७॥ प्राण्यापानिति॥१८॥ प्राणैरात्मानमन्तरतः पूरयित्वाऽऽह** 'इदमहꣳ सत्यादमृतमुपैमि' **इति॥१९॥ सत्यं वै देवा अमृतꣳ सुवर्गो लोको, देवेभ्य एव तत् सुवर्गं लोकमुपैति॥२०॥ अथ दक्षिणत उपविश्य पयोऽनुपिबति** 'इदं हविः प्रजननं मे अस्तु दशवीरꣳ सर्वगणꣳ स्वस्तये। आत्मसनि प्रजासनि पशुसन्यभयसनि लोकसनि वृष्टिसनि। अग्निः प्रजां बहुलां मे करोतु। अन्नं पयो रेतो अस्मासु धेहि' **इतीन्वावृत्॥२१॥ अथातो ब्राह्मणमेव यज्ञाद्वा एतद्यजमानो जायते यद्यजते। तमेतं जातं यज्ञमयं लोकमयं प्राणमयममृतमयꣳ सꣳस्कुर्वन्ति। पयोभार्यो वै जातो भवति। नो वै जातायौदनं न सक्तूनुपहरति। पयो वै जाताय प्रतिदधाति। स यथा ह वै दृतिः शुष्को निष्पीत एवꣳ ह वा एष एतर्हि; यज्ञो हैनमतिशुष्कं निष्पीतमाप्याययति। स यत्पयोऽनुपिबत्यात्मानमेव तच्चन्द्रमसमाप्यायन् मन्यते तस्मात्पयोऽनुपिबेत्, पयोऽनुपिबेत्॥** ३.३.३.२२॥ **[इति तृतीयः पटलः** (१२)**]**

॥ इति तृतीयप्रपाठके तृतीयोऽनुवाकः ॥

दक्षिणत उपविश्य पयोऽनु पिबतीत्यत्र सान्नाय्यशेषं पयः पिबतीति व्याचक्षते केचित्। पौर्णमास्यां[1] विकृतिषु चान्यत्पय[1] आहृत्य पिबति। यदि प्रमाणमस्ति तथा अस्तु[2] नाम। वयं तु 'यो वै सोमं भ=संवत्सरं सोमं न पिबती 'त्यारभ्य विहितस्य ग्रहणं मन्यामहे॥ २१॥

पयःपानस्य स्तुत्यर्थं ब्राह्मणम्। पौर्णमास्युपक्रमाद्[3] अमावास्यापवर्गाद्यज्ञादेतस्मिन्काले यजमानो [4]जायते। कथम्। स यज्ञः यज्ञप्रयोग[4]द्वयात् फलापूर्वमुत्पादयति। तस्मिन्नुत्पन्ने सामर्थ्याद् यजमानः फलग्रहणयोग्यो जायते इत्यर्थः। यत्र विद्यते[5] प्राणस्थितिहेतुना यजमानभागप्राशनादिना तन्मयं 'सत्यादमृतमुपैमी 'त्यादिनाऽमृतमयं तैर्वर्धमानस्तन्मयाद्[6] यजमानः पय उच्यते। 'स वा एष [6]पुरुषोऽन्नरसमयः' इति यज्ञाज्जातेन बालसदृशेन पयःपानं कर्तव्यम्। अथापि यथा पयो दृतिर्निष्पत्तेः पयः, एवमेष यज्ञः प्रयोगद्वयान्ते फलापूर्वमुत्पाद्य स्वरूपेणैवावतिष्ठते। यज्ञस्य यजमानार्थत्वाद्यज्ञो यजमानः। चन्द्रमा अपि यजमानः [7]पुनर्नवीभूतः। अनेनैतत्त्रयमाप्यायितं भवति[7]। तस्मात्पयोऽनुपिबेत्[8]। तस्मात् 'कनीयोऽवदानहेत्वा भूयो ब्राह्मणायाहरेदि 'ति वचनाद् ऋत्विजोऽन्यांश्च ब्राह्मणान् यथाशक्त्यन्नेन तर्पयेत्। 'ब्राह्मणांस्तर्पयत वा' इति प्रैषं चानुपदकार आमनति। समाप्तिसूचकोऽभ्यासः[9]॥ ३.३.३.२२॥ **[इति तृतीयः पटलः** (१२)**]**

॥ इति व्याख्यायां तृतीयप्रपाठके तृतीयोऽनुवाकः ॥[10]

१-१. M मास्या...त्पय, Ad ° मास्यां क्वेतिषु°. **२.** M Ad om; thus T. **३.** M Ad ° मासोपक्र°. **४-४.** M जायते।...प्रयोग°. **५.** M Ad विद्यन्ते; thus T. **६-६.** M तन्मय...पुरुषो; Ad ° तन्मय...उच्यतेः°; thus T. **७-७.** M पुन...विभूत अनेनैतत्त्रयमाप्य...ति, Ad अनेनैव तत्र यमाप्ययि°. **८.** M Ad पिबत्. **९.** M समाप्तिसूच...; thus Ad T. In the sūtra-text after तस्मात्पयोऽनुपिबेत the text is पयो न विसृजेत् in M[1]. From the statement समाप्तिसूचकोऽभ्यास it is clear that the text पयो न विसृजेत् is corrupt text of M[1]. **१०.** M Ad T इति तृतीयः.

॥ अथ तृतीयप्रपाठके चतुर्थोऽनुवाकः ॥

[आग्रयणम्]

आग्रयणेष्ट्या यक्ष्यमाणो नवाꣳश्च व्रीहीनुपकल्पयते श्यामाकाꣳश्च ॥ १ ॥ आमावास्येन हविषेष्ट्वा निर्वपति—आग्नेयमष्टाकपालं, सौम्यꣳ श्यामाकं चरुम्, ऐन्द्राग्नं

आग्रयणे=श्यामाकांश्च । आग्रयणं नामेदं कर्म दर्शपूर्णमासवन्नित्यं यावज्जीवं प्रयोक्तव्यम्। एतदर्थमेव दर्शपूर्णमासविधानानन्तरमाम्नायते। तस्य पक्षद्वयं श्रुतावाम्नातं[१] 'वर्षासु श्यामाकैर्यजेत, [२]सर्वैर्यजेते'ति। सार्धक्रियाकालो[२] नाभिहितः। तत्रापि श्रुतेष्वेव त्रिषु कालेष्वनियमेन प्राप्तेषु भूयस्त्वानुग्रहाय श्यामाककालेन भवितव्यम्[३]। इदं व्रीहिश्यामाकयोर्द्वयोरेव समुच्चित्याग्रयणमामनति। तस्यापि शरदेवकालो युक्तः। अस्मिन्पक्षे यवाग्रयणं वसन्तकाल एव[४] कर्तव्यम्। अथवा तस्याभावः श्रुत्यन्तराद् 'याः फालकृष्टाः व्रीहिभिरेव तासामाग्रयणं कृतं भवति। श्यामाकैरारण्यानामि'ति। तथा च बह्वृचब्राह्मणं—'व्रीहिभिरिष्ट्वा व्रीहिभिरेव यजेत। यवेभ्यो यवैरिष्ट्वा यवैरेव यजेत। व्रीहिभ्योऽपि वा 'व्रीहिभिरिष्ट्वा व्रीहिभिरेव यजेतैते हि सूयवसतरा भवन्ति' इति। [५]पृथक् क्रियायां प्रयोगः। श्यामाकेण[५] यक्ष्यमाण इत्यत्रोक्तः। सार्धक्रियायां बीजभेदात् प्रतिदैवतं हवींष्यभ्यस्यन्ते[६]। प्रदाने साहित्यं संभवति। तन्त्रत्व आवृत्तेरन्याय्यत्वात्। आग्रयणं[७] भवतीत्यत्र ऐन्द्राग्नवैश्व-देवसोम्यानां[८] दर्शनात्तेषां याज्यानुवाक्याभिः सह [९]द्यावापृथिव्यस्य च याज्यानुवाक्ययोः समाम्नानात्[९] तासां [१०]देवतानामाग्रयणदेवतात्वं ज्ञायते। क्व पुनराग्नेयस्यात्रोत्पत्तिः। आचार्येण विहितत्वाच्च[११] श्रुत्यन्तरे विद्यत इत्यवगन्तव्यम्। पुराणानामाग्नेयं[१२] निर्वपेद्यथा दन्तेनादान्तं[१२] संयुज्यात्तादृक् तदित्यपि चेदं विधानम्। तथा च सति नवांश्च व्रीहीनित्यत्र[१३] पुराणांश्चेत्यध्याहर्तव्यः। तस्य [१४]'श्यामाकेन यक्ष्यमाण' इत्यत्रादर्शनादनित्यत्वम्[१४]। अत्र च नित्यत्वमिच्छन्ति। [१५]पुरोडाशमुखत्वानुजिघृक्षयाऽपि वा नवानामेवाग्नेयं निर्वपेदित्यनुपदम्॥ १ ॥

आमावास्येन हविषेष्ट्वेति[१५] । [१६]वर्षान्त्येनामावास्येन। यज्ञायुधानीत्यादि [१७]तन्त्रप्रक्रमप्रदर्शनम् इत्युक्तम्। आग्रयणेष्टिमिति नामधेयेन[१८] विधानमाग्रयणेष्टिर्हविरिदमपीत्यूहेन[१८] प्रयोक्तव्यम्[१९]।

---

१. M ततावाम्ना°, Ad ततावदाम्ना° ; thus T. २–२. M सर्वै... ाकालो. ३. M Ad °तव्यः; thus T. ४. M Ad °काल...कर्त°, Ad वसन्त एव कालं...कर्त; thus T. ५. T पृथक्क्रियं [...]केन. T wrongly gives the text प्रयोगः श्यामाक° under fn. ६. M हविष्येभ्यस्स्य°, Ad हविष्येभ्यः स्यः; thus T. ७. M Ad ऐन्द्राग्नं भव° ; thus T. ८. M Ad °देवसौम्या°. ९–९. T takes the text as additional and gives the same in fn. १०. M °माग्रा...त्वं, by showing it सह[...]तासां. ११. M Ad °त्वाच्छु° ; thus T. १२–१२. T °दानादा° ; cf *ApŚS.* 6.29.7-8. १३. M Ad °निति. १४–१४. M तस्य...त्यत्वम्; Ad तस्य श्यामाकौ °यक्ष्य°. १५–१५. M पुरोडाशनुखत्वानुजिघृक्ष...विषेषट्वेति; Ad °विवा°. १६. M Ad वर्षात्ये° ; thus T. १७. T तत्र प्र°. १८–१८. M नाम...विधानमाग्रयणेष्टि...मयीत्यूहेन; Ad °ष्टिहविर्दिनमित्यूहेन. १९. M Ad प्रयोक्तुम्.

द्वादशकपालं, वैश्वदेवं चरुं, द्यावापृथिव्यमेककपालम् ॥ २ ॥ निरुप्ते प्राणग्रहाꣳश्च पृश्नीꣳश्च व्याचष्टे ॥ ३ ॥ तस्य हविष्कृता वाचं विसृज्य चतुर्गृहीतेन सप्तहोतर्निंहवनीये जुहोति 'अग्नये स्वाहा' इत्येतान् ॥ ४ ॥ 'ऊर्ध्वा अस्य समिधो भवन्ति' इति द्वादशाप्रीः ॥ ५ ॥ 'शतायुधाय शतवीर्याय' इति पञ्चाज्यानीर्होतैव ॥ ६ ॥ वैतसात्रिꣳशत्तमः ॥ ७ ॥ शृतेषु हविःषु स्तम्बयजुर्हरति ॥ ८ ॥ वेदिं परिगृह्णाति ॥ ९ ॥ करणं जपति ॥ १० ॥ प्रसिध्यति कर्माऽऽसमासादनात् ॥ ११ ॥ समासन्नेऽ-पानग्रहाꣳश्च पृश्नीꣳश्च व्याचष्टे ॥ १२ ॥ 'ध्रुवा असदन्', 'यन्मे अग्ने' इति समभिमृश्य दशहोतारं व्याचष्टे ॥ १३ ॥ 'अग्नये समिध्यमानायानु वाच' आह ॥ १४ ॥ सप्तदश सामिधेनीरन्वाह ॥ १५ ॥ प्रसिध्यति कर्माऽऽप्रयाजेभ्यः ॥ १६ ॥ 'यज्ञं च मे प्रजां च' इति प्रयाजानिष्टाननुमन्त्रयते । '°सर्वं चायुः सुवर्गं च लोकं च मे क्षत्रं च कामदावत्' इति ॥ १७ ॥ आज्यभागौ यजति ॥ १८ ॥ रयिमन्तावाज्यभागौ ॥ १९ ॥ 'अग्नयेऽनुब्रूहि' इत्याहाऽऽज्यस्य गृह्णानश्चतुः ॥ २० ॥ 'अग्निना रयिमश्नवत्' इत्यन्वाह ॥ २१ ॥ जुषाणेन यजति ॥ २२ ॥ वषट्कृते जुहोति ॥ २३ ॥ 'सोमायानुब्रूहि' इत्याहाज्यस्यैव गृह्णानश्चतुः ॥ २४ ॥ 'गयस्फानो अमीवहा' इत्यन्वाह ॥ २५ ॥ जुषाणेनैव यजति ॥ २६ ॥ वषट्कृते जुहोति ॥ २७ ॥ 'अग्नयेऽनुब्रूहि' इत्याहोपस्तृणानोऽवद्यन् ॥ २८ ॥ 'अग्निर्मूर्धा' इत्यन्वाह ॥ २९ ॥ 'भुवः' इति यजति ॥ ३० ॥ वषट्कृते जुहोति ॥ ३१ ॥ 'सोमायानुब्रूहि' इत्याहोपस्तृणानोऽवद्यन् ॥ ३२ ॥ 'त्वं नः सोम विश्वतः' इत्यन्वाह ॥ ३३ ॥ 'या ते धामानि' इति यजति ॥ ३४ ॥ वषट्कृते जुहोति ॥ ३५ ॥ 'इन्द्राग्निभ्यामनुब्रूहि' इत्याहोपस्तृणानोऽवद्यन् ॥ ३६ ॥ 'इन्द्राग्नी रोचना दिवः' इत्यन्वाह ॥ ३७ ॥ 'श्नथद्वृत्रम्' इति यजति ॥ ३८ ॥ वषट्कृते जुहोति ॥ ३९ ॥ 'विश्वेभ्यो देवेभ्योऽनुब्रूहि' इत्याहोपस्तृणानोऽवद्यन् ॥ ४० ॥ 'विश्वे देवा ऋतावृधः' इत्यन्वाह ॥ ४१ ॥ 'विश्वे देवाः शृणुतेमꣳ हवं मे' इति यजति ॥ ४२ ॥ वषट्कृते जुहोति ॥ ४३ ॥ 'द्यावापृथिवीभ्यामनुब्रूहि' इत्याहोपस्तीर्णाभिघारितमेककपालमादधानः ॥ ४४ ॥ 'द्यावा नः पृथिवी इमम्' इत्यन्वाह ॥ ४५ ॥ 'प्र पूर्वजे' इति यजति ॥ ४६ ॥ वषट्कृते जुहोति ॥ ४७ ॥ 'अनुयजैः' इत्येककपालꣳ

आग्रयणं भवतीति दर्शनादाग्रयणं हविरित्यपि भवति ॥ २ ॥

तस्य हविष्कृता वाचं विसृज्येति ।[1] अवघातपदार्थं परिसमाप्य तण्डुलप्रक्षालनान्ते होतव्यम् । तथा च दृश्यते—'तस्य हविष्कृता वाचं विसृज्य द्वादशोत्तानानि कपालान्युपदधाती'ति । एककपालमुद्वास्य [2]समभिघारणे [3]बह्वाज्यमानीय हविःपृष्ठं[3] कुर्यात् । 'आशयादेककपालस्ये'ति दर्शनात् ॥ ४ ॥

प्रयाजानुमन्त्रणं प्रत्येकं [4]प्राकृतानुमन्त्रणनिवृत्तिश्च चोदनालिङ्गसंयोगात् । तथैककपालेऽपि प्राकृतानुमन्त्रणनिवृत्तिः । तस्य चतुरवत्तसंपादनार्थमाशयाद्[5] द्वितीयमवदानमिच्छन्ति[6] केचित् । अन्ये

---

१. M Ad °विसृजेत्येवघात° . २. M Ad समभि twice. ३–३. M Ad °नीयाहविःपृष्ठं, T °नीयाविःपृष्ठं. ४. M Ad प्रकृता° . ५. M Ad शया द्वि° . ६. Ad °नीयमवदानभवदा° .

हुतमनुमन्त्रयते ॥ ३.४.१.४८ ॥ **[इति प्रथमः पटलः** (१३)**]**

'अनुयज्ञैः' **इत्येककपालꣳ हुतमनुमन्त्रयते।** '°अनु राध्याम गोभिरन्वश्वैरनु विश्वैरनुपुष्टैरनु प्रजयाऽन्विन्द्रियेण देवा न यज्ञमृजुधा नयन्तु' **इति** ॥ १ ॥ **स यदि पर्यावर्तेतर्जुꣳ स्थापयित्वा याज्यापुरोऽनुवाक्याभ्यामभिहृत्य द्वाभ्यामुत्तराभ्यामभि जुहुयात्** 'प्रति यज्ञैः प्रतिष्ठा धनेन प्रत्यश्वैः प्रति विश्वेन पुष्टेन प्रति प्रजया प्रतीन्द्रियेण वैश्वानरो नो अदब्ध स्वस्त्यन्तरा पातु दुरितानि विश्वा स्वाहा', 'सं ते तराꣳसि सं ते वचाꣳसि सं ते पयाꣳसि सं ते वपूꣳषि सं ते पर्वाणि पर्व नो यज्ञियं तु स्वाहा' **इति** ॥ २ ॥ 'अग्नये स्विष्टकृतेऽनुब्रूहि' **इत्याहोपस्तृणानोऽवद्यन्** ॥ ३ ॥ **सकृत्सकृदुत्तरार्धात् सर्वेषाꣳ हविषामवद्यति** ॥ ४ ॥ **आशयादेककपालस्यावदाय द्विरभिघारयति** ॥ ५ ॥ **न प्रत्यानक्ति** ॥ ६ ॥ **गायत्रियौ संयाज्ये** ॥ ७ ॥ 'अग्निꣳ स्तोमेन बोधय' **इत्यन्वाह** ॥ ८ ॥ 'स हव्यवाट्' **इति यजति** ॥ ९ ॥ **वषट्कृते जुहोति** ॥ १० ॥ **अत्याक्रम्य यथाऽऽयतनꣳ स्रुचौ सादयित्वा प्राशित्रमवद्यति** ॥ ११ ॥ **अप उपस्पृश्येडामवद्यति** ॥ १२ ॥ **उपहूतायामिडायामग्नीध आदधाति** ॥ १३ ॥ **प्राश्नन्ति** ॥ १४ ॥ **मार्जयन्ते** ॥ १५ ॥ **परिहरन्ति ब्रह्मणे** ॥ १६ ॥ **प्राशिते प्राशित्रेऽग्नीदुदपात्रेणोत्कर उपसीदति** ॥ १७ ॥ **वासो ददाति** ॥ १८ ॥ **प्रथमजं वत्सं ददाति** ॥ १९ ॥ **यस्य श्रपणं तस्य खारी ददाति** ॥ २० ॥ **सन्ततिमनु होतुराहुतिं जुहोति** ॥ २१ ॥ **प्रसिध्यति कर्माऽऽपत्नीहोमात्** ॥ २२ ॥ **पत्नीहोममनु द्वे स्रुवाहुती जुहोति** 'त्वं दूतः', 'संवत्सरस्य प्रतिमाम्' **इति** ॥ २३ ॥ **प्रसिध्यति कर्माऽऽसौम्यात्** ॥ २४ ॥ **इतरेषाꣳ हविषाꣳ समवदाय** 'भद्रान्नः श्रेयः समनैष्ट

यथोक्तं कुर्वन्ति। आशयादवदानमुक्तविषयं चेति केचित्। अवश्यमिडाया[1] अवदेयम्। ज्ञापयति ह्याचार्यो 'वारुण्याश्च कायस्य चोत्तरस्यामध्वर्युरि'ति ब्रुवन्॥ ३.४.१.४८॥ **[इति प्रथमः पटलः** (१३)**]**

एककपालस्य [2]सकृद्धोमापरिवृद्धि दर्शनाद्वैश्वदेविकस्यैककपालस्य धर्मा इहेष्यन्ते। तत्रैककपालस्य ये विशेषधर्मा बह्वाज्यमानीय[3] हविःपृष्ठं कुर्यादित्यादयस्तानेव कुर्वन्ति केचिद्। एवमाचार्याभिप्राय[4] इति मन्यमाना अप्रतिषेधात् प्रसूमयादीनामप्राप्तिमपरे मन्यन्ते। यस्याग्रयणं व्रीहिश्यामाकादीनां[5] पृथक् पृथगित्यर्थः। अन्य आह—श्यामाकानामारण्यत्वादारण्यस्यादानयोग्यत्वात्पृथक्[6] क्रियायामपि श्यामाकेन[7] यक्ष्यमाण इत्यत्रानुक्तापि[8] ॥ १ ॥

खारी देयेति। खारीशब्दः परिमाणवाची। 'षोडशद्रोणयुक्त[9] खारी, द्रोणं तु चतुराढकमि'ति भाजनविशेषवाची वा। तेन परिमितः खारीशब्दवाच्यः ॥ २० ॥

समवाहितशेषेण सह यजमानभागं त्रिः प्राश्नाति। समवदानस्य[10] दृष्टार्थत्वाय इडायां

---

१. M °डाया मव°, Ad °डायां अव°. **२.** M Ad °द्धोमापरिवृत्ति°. **३.** M Ad बह्वानीय हविः°; T बह्वाज्यमानीयाविः पृष्ठं. **४.** M Ad °प्रायम्. **५.** T °का. **६.** M Ad °यस्यादानं यो°. **७.** M Ad °माकानेव; thus T. **८.** T इत्यस्य...ति; thus T. **९.** M °युक्तारी; Ad °युक्ताखारी; T °युक्. **१०.** M Ad T °मवधान°.

देवाः' **इति दक्षिणत उपविश्य त्रिर्यजमानभागं प्राश्नाति।** '०त्वयाऽवसेन=स्योनः' **इति** ॥ २५ ॥ **प्रसिध्यति कर्म** ॥ २६ ॥ **सन्तिष्ठत एषेष्टिः** ॥ ३.४.२.२७ ॥ **[इति द्वितीयः पटलः** (१४)**]**

॥ इति तृतीयप्रपाठके चतुर्थोऽनुवाकः ॥

यजमानस्य भागे विद्यमाने तत्प्राशनेऽपि मन्त्रं केचिदिच्छन्ति। नवप्राशननिमित्तत्वान्मन्त्रस्य॥ ३.४.२.२५ ॥ **[इति द्वितीयः पटलः** (१४)**]**

॥ इति व्याख्यायां तृतीयप्रपाठके चतुर्थोऽनुवाकः ॥[१]

---

१. M इति चतुर्थेः, Ad इति चतुर्थः समाप्त.

॥ अथ तृतीयप्रपाठके पञ्चमोऽनुवाकः ॥

[ब्रह्मत्वम्]

ब्रह्मा वृतो भवति ॥ १ ॥ **स यज्ञोपवीतं कृत्वाऽप आचम्य द्वाभ्यामात्मन्नग्निं गृह्णीते** 'मयि गृह्णाम्यग्रे अग्निꣳ रायस्पोषाय', 'यो नो अग्निः पितरो हृत्स्वन्तः' **इति** ॥ २ ॥ **हस्तौ संमृशते** 'कर्मणे वां देवेभ्यः शकेयम्', 'शक्त्यै वाꣳ सुकृताय वाम्' **इति** ॥ ३ ॥ 'बृहस्पतिर्ब्रह्मा' **इत्यन्तरा वेदिं चोत्करं च प्रपद्यते** । '°स यज्ञं पातु स यज्ञपतिं पातु स मां पातु स यज्ञन्यम्' **इति** ॥ ४ ॥ **अपरेण वेदिमत्याक्रम्य** 'अहे दैधिषव्य' **इत्युपतिष्ठते यत्रोपवेक्ष्यन् भवति** । '°उदत-स्तिष्ठान्यस्य=योऽस्मत्पाकतरः' **इति** ॥ ५ ॥ 'निरस्तः परावसु' **इति तृणं निरस्यति** ॥ ६ ॥ 'इदमहमायुषः सदने सीदामि' **इत्युपस्थं कृत्वोपविशति** ॥ ७ ॥ **उपविश्य जपति** 'देव सवितरेतं त्वा वृणुते बृहस्पतिं दैव्यं ब्रह्माणं तत् त्वं मनसे प्रब्रूहि मनो गायत्रियै गायत्री त्रिष्टुभे त्रिष्टुब् जगत्यै जगत्यनुष्टुभेऽनुष्टुप् पङ्क्त्यै पङ्क्तिर्वसुभ्यो वसवो रुद्रेभ्यो रुद्रा आदित्येभ्य आदित्या विश्वेभ्यो

---

[1]*ब्रह्मा वृतो*[1] *भवति* ।'भूपते भुवनपते' इत्यनेन मन्त्रेण लिङ्गात् ब्रह्मणो वरणं प्राप्तमविधायै-वानुवदत्याचार्यः । एतत् ज्ञापयति ब्राह्मणेन कल्पेन वाऽविनियुक्तानामपि मन्त्राणां लिङ्गेन विनियोगः कर्तव्य इति । पूर्वेणार्धर्चेन यजमानो वृणीत इति ॥ [2]उत्तरं वृतो जपतीति[2] । एतद् ब्रह्मवरणमित्यपि[3] याज्ञिकानां व्यवहारः प्रसिद्धः । अथापि 'देव सवितरि'त्यस्माज्जपात्पूर्वमाम्नातत्वाच्चान्यस्य वरणस्या-भावाद् गम्यते ॥ १ ॥

उक्तं यज्ञोपवीतमाचमनम्[4] ॥ २ ॥

अन्तरा वेदिं चोत्करं च प्रत्यङ्मुखः[5] प्रविशति । वेदमाञ्जसं विध्यवशेषेषु पथ्यन्तरमुक्तम्[6] । तथागमने प्राङ्मुखः प्रपद्यते...वेद्यै[6] भवति ॥ ४ ॥

तस्याहवनीयप्रणीतादीनामनुपदसमत्ववचनाद् 'दक्षिणमाहवनीयं ब्रह्मायतनम् उत्तरवेद्यै दक्षिणे-नाग्निमि'ति विकृतिषु दर्शनाच्च । स्तम्बयजुःस्थानाद्दक्षिणतो यजमानस्य । अन्य आह—'[7]अग्निहोत्रे दक्षिणत[7] आहवनीयस्योपविशती'ति दर्शनात्सर्वत्र तदेव यजमानायतनम् । तदपरेण ब्रह्मायतनम् । तदु-भयमभिप्रेत्य 'यत्रोपवेक्ष्यन्[8] भवती'त्युक्तमित्यपरे । यत्रेति प्रवर्ग्याद्यर्थम् इत्यन्ये ॥ ५ ॥

प्रसवार्थानां मन्त्राणामादित आरभ्योच्चैष्ट्वं[9] केचिदिच्छन्ति[10] । दृष्टार्थत्वाय[10] उपांशुजपं जपित्वोच्चैः प्रसूयोपांशु कर्म निर्दिशेदिति अनुपदम् । प्रणवादि उच्चैरूर्ध्वं वाऽऽप्रणवादिति[11] शौनकः । तथाऽयमप्याचार्यः 'इन्द्रवन्तः स्तुतेति निराह' इति[12] पठति[12] । तत्प्रदर्शनार्थं भवति ॥ ८ ॥

१–१. M ब्रह्माव...ते; Ad ब्रह्मावुतो°, T ब्रह्माहूतो°. **२–२.** M उ...ति; Ad उत्तरं वृतौ; T om उत्तरं. **३.** M Ad ब्राह्म°. **४.** M Ad यज्ञोपवीतमन्तरा; thus T. **५.** M Ad °मुखं. **६–६.** M °न्तरमु...प्राङ्मुखं प्रपद्यते...वेद्यै; Ad प्राङ्मुखं प्रपद्यते...वेद्यै°. **७–७.** M अग्निहो...त आह°. **८.** M Ad °क्ष्यद्भव°; thus T. **९.** M Ad °रब्धोच्चै°; thus T. **१०–१०.** M केचिदिति... त्वाय; Ad कष्टार्थ°; thus T. **११.** T °वादीति; thus M Ad. **१२–१२.** M स्तुतेति ...पठन्ति.

देवेभ्यो विश्वे देवा बृहस्पतये बृहस्पतिर्ब्रह्मणे ब्रह्म भूर्भुवः सुवर्बृहस्पतिर्देवानां ब्रह्माऽहं मनुष्याणां तꣳ स ऋच्छताद् यो मेऽन्ववापदादुप वा मीमाꣳसातै भूर्भुवः सुवरोऽऽमहमसौ मानुषः' **इति ॥ ८ ॥ प्रणीतासु प्रणीयमानासु वाचं यच्छत्या हविष्कृतः ॥** ९ **॥ स यत्राह** 'ब्रह्मन्नपः प्रणयिष्यामि यजमान वाचं यच्छ' **इति तत्प्रसुवति** 'प्रणय यज्ञं देवता वर्धयैता नाकस्य पृष्ठे यजमानो अस्तु। सप्तर्षीणाꣳ सुकृतां यज्ञं लोकस्तत्रेमं यज्ञं यजमानं च धेह्योऽऽम् प्रणय' **इति ॥** १० **॥ स्तम्बयजुषि ह्रियमाणे वाचं यच्छत्योत्तरस्मात्परिग्राहात् ॥** ११ **॥ स यत्राह** 'ब्रह्मन्नुत्तरं परिग्राहं परिग्रहीष्यामि' **इति तत्प्रसुवति** 'बृहस्पते परिगृहाण वेदिं प्रिया देवानाꣳ स्योना नो अस्तु। स्तृणीत बर्हिरन्तरस्या उपस्थे शिवो नो अस्त्वदित्या उपस्थ ओऽऽम् परिगृहाण' **इति ॥** १२ **॥ सामिधेनीष्वनूच्यमानासु वाचं यच्छत्यापरिधानात् ॥** १३ **॥ अनूच्यमानायां पुरोनुवाक्यायामावषट्कारात् ॥** १४ **॥ स यत्रर्चा वा यजुषा वा करोति तद्वाचं यच्छत्यापरिधानात् ॥** १५ **॥ स यदन्तरेण वाचं विसृजेत यज्ञं विच्छिन्द्यात् ॥** १६ **॥ अथ यदि प्रमत्तो विसृजेत वैष्णवीमृचमनुब्रूयात्** 'विष्णो त्वं नो अन्तमः शर्म यच्छ सहन्त्य। प्र ते धारा मधुश्चुत उत्सन्दुह्रते अक्षितम्' **इति ॥** १७ **॥ प्राशित्रेऽवदीयमाने वाचं यच्छति ॥** ३.५.१.१८ **॥ [इति प्रथमः पटलः** (१५)**]**

प्राशित्रेऽवदीयमाने वाचं यच्छत्या प्रसवात् ॥ १ **॥ स यत्रास्मै प्राशित्रं परिहरति तदप उपस्पृश्य प्रतीक्षते** 'सूर्यस्य त्वा चक्षुषा प्रति पश्यामि' **इति ॥** २ **॥** 'देवस्य त्वा सवितुः= हस्ताभ्यां प्रतिगृह्णामि' **इति परिगृह्णाति ॥** ३ **॥** 'पृथिव्यास्त्वोपस्थे सादयामि' **इति सादयति ॥** ४ **॥ आभ्याꣳ हैके प्राश्नन्ति, आभ्यामेके ॥** ५ **॥ तदनादृत्याभ्यामेव प्राश्नीयात्** 'अग्नेस्त्वाऽऽस्येन प्राश्नामि'

तुल्यन्यायत्वादुत्तरस्मिन् परिग्रहाद्वाचं यच्छतीत्यनुवर्तते ॥ ११-१२ ॥

[१]अनुवर्तमाने सामिधेनीषु[२] वाचं यच्छतीति[२] किमर्थमभिधीयते। क्वचिदनुवर्तयति क्वचित् स्वरशब्देनैव वदति। एतदाचार्यस्य शीलम् ॥ १३ ॥

[३]'वैष्णवीमृचमि'ति सामान्येनोक्त्वा[३] 'विष्णो त्वम्' इत्यृग्ग्रहणं करोति तत्प्रदर्शनार्थम्। इतरथा ऋचमेवावक्ष्यद् वैष्णवीमिति नावक्ष्यत्। तथा च [४]'आश्वलायनेनोक्तम्—'अतो देवा अवन्तु नः' इति जपेदपि वाऽन्यां[५] वैष्णवीमिति' ॥ ३.५.१.१७ ॥ **[इति प्रथमः पटलः** (१५)**]**

अङ्गुष्ठप्रदेशिनीभ्यामेके[६]। अङ्गुष्ठमध्यमाभ्यामेके[६] ॥ ५ ॥

[७]तदनादृत्याङ्गुष्ठोपकनिष्ठिकाभ्यामेव प्राश्नीयात्। अद्भिरभिश्चोत्येति। प्राशित्रहरणस्थमेवाद्भिरभिश्चोतयन्ति केचित्। अपरे प्राशित्रहरणकाल एव पाणितलेनोदकं[८] गृहीत्वा तत्काल एवाभिश्चोतयन्ति ॥ ६ ॥

---

१. M ...र्तमाने. **२-२.** M Ad °धेनीष्वाद्यच्छ° [M ष्वाय]. **३-३.** M वैष्णव...नोक्त्वा; thus T. **४.** M चाश्व...नोक्तम्. **५.** M Ad °विवान्यां. **६-६.** M °मेके...के; thus Ad T. **७.** M तदाना, Ad °दृत्यानाङ्गु°; T °दृत्योङ्गु°. **८.** M पाणि...ादकं.

इत्यद्भिरभिश्च्योत्यातिहायैव दन्तान्। '○ब्राह्मणस्योदरेण बृहस्पतेर्ब्रह्मणा' **इति ॥ ६ ॥ अग्रेण दक्षिणं जान्वेतां दिशꣳ संक्षालं निनीय, निर्णिज्य प्राशित्रहरणं, ब्रह्मभागमस्मिन्नवधाया–द्भिर्मार्जयित्वा प्राणान् संमृशते** 'वाङ्‌ म आसन् नसोः=ऊरुवोरोजोऽरिष्टा विश्वान्यङ्गानि =मा मा हिꣳसीः' **इति ॥ ७ ॥ स यत्राह** 'ब्रह्मन् प्रस्थास्यामः समिधमाधायाग्नीदग्निꣳ सकृत्सकृत् समृड्ढि' **इति तत्प्रसुवति** 'देव सवितरेतत्ते प्राह तत् प्र च सुव प्र च यज बृहस्पतिर्ब्रह्मा स यज्ञं पाहि यज्ञपतिं पाहि स मां पाहि यज्ञन्यं भूर्भुवः सुवरोऽऽम् प्रतिष्ठ' **इति ॥ ८ ॥ स यदभक्तं वाचंयमः स्यात् पितृदेवत्यो भवेद्, बहु भाषेत यज्ञं विच्छिन्द्यात् ॥ ९ ॥ स यत्तीर्थेतीर्थे वाचं यच्छति तन्न पितृदेवत्यो भवति, न यज्ञं विच्छिनत्ति ॥ १० ॥ समिष्टयजुषि हुत एतेनैव यथैतं निष्क्रम्य द्वौ शकलावाहवनीये प्रास्यति** 'यन्म आत्मनो मिन्दाऽभूत्', 'पुनरग्निश्चक्षुरदात्' **इति ॥ ११ ॥ एतेनैव ब्रह्मा भवति दर्शपूर्णमासयोरिष्टीनां चातुर्मास्यानां पशुबन्धस्य ॥ १२ ॥ स यत्रास्मै पुरोडाशं परिहरति तदप उपस्पृश्यैव मनसा प्रतीक्षते ॥ १३ ॥ एवं मनसा प्रतिगृह्णाति ॥ १४ ॥ एवं मनसा प्राणेन प्राश्नाति ॥ १५ ॥ एवमप उपस्पृश्य मनसा प्राणान् संमृशते ॥ ३.५.२.१६ ॥ [इति द्वितीयः पटलः (१६)]**

॥ इति तृतीयप्रपाठके पञ्चमोऽनुवाकः ॥

एतां दिशं प्राच्यां दिशि प्राणान् संमृश्य ब्रह्मभागं[1] प्राश्य पुनरपि मार्जयते ॥ ७ ॥

अभक्तमविभागेन सर्वकालमित्यर्थः ॥ ९ ॥

आयतमनुपरमेण[2] तीर्थेतीर्थे अत्र वाचं यच्छतीति विहिते काले ॥ १० ॥

एतेनैवेत्यादि समानविध्यर्थमिति केचित्। अन्य उत्तरविवक्षार्थं[3] स्तुत्यर्थं वेति भवति[3]। पूर्वस्मिन् पक्षे यथाम्नायं[4] मन्त्रप्रयोगः। इतरस्मिन् तस्य प्रकृत्यर्थत्वाद्विकृतौ यथार्थमूहः ॥ ११ ॥

प्राशित्रस्य विद्यमानपक्षे[5] प्रतीक्षणादीनां मानसत्वं प्राशनं च तुल्यम्। इतरथा भिद्येत हि वाक्यम्। मनसा प्रतिग्रहणादि करोति। तच्च समस्तं पुरोडाशमित्यन्ये प्राशित्रपक्षे[6] यथाप्रकृति कुर्वन्ति[6] ॥ ३.५.२.१३–१६ ॥ **[इति द्वितीयः पटलः (१६)]**

॥ इति व्याख्यायां तृतीयप्रपाठके पञ्चमोऽनुवाकः ॥[7]

---

१. M ब्र...गं. **२.** M Ad अयत°. **३–३.** M °विवक्षा...भवति; Ad °क्षार्थं स्तुत्यर्थं वेति; T takes वेति as additional and adds इति after भवति. **४.** M Ad °म्नात°. **५.** T records one reading पक्षेऽपि in fn. **६–६.** M प्राशित्रप...ति कुर्वन्ति, Ad प्राशित्रपक्षेप्रति° ; thus T. **७.** M इति पञ्चम, Ad इति पञ्चमः समाप्तः ॥, T पञ्चमः.

॥ अथ तृतीयप्रपाठके षष्ठोऽनुवाकः ॥

एतेनैव दीक्षणीयस्य ब्रह्मा भवति ॥ १ ॥ **स यत्राह** 'ब्रह्मन् प्रचरिष्यामो होतर्घर्ममभिष्टुहि' **इति तद्दिवाकीर्त्यामृचमभिव्याहृत्य ब्रह्मा प्रसुवति** ॥ २ ॥ **अथ यत्र प्राञ्चं महावीरः हरति तद्दक्षिणतोऽनुसमेत्य प्रचरतां दक्षिणतस्तिष्ठति** ॥ ३ ॥ **एतेनैवोपसदां ब्रह्मा भवति** ॥ ४ ॥ **महावेद्यै स्तम्बयजुषि ह्रियमाणे दक्षिणत आस्ते** ॥ ५ ॥ **राज्ञो आसाद्यमानस्य दक्षिणत आस्ते** ॥ ६ ॥ **अग्रे ह्रियमाणस्य दक्षिणत इति** ॥ ७ ॥ **उत्तरस्य परिग्राहस्य दक्षिणत आस्ते** ॥ ८ ॥ **हविर्धानयोः प्रोह्यमाणयोर्दक्षिणत एति** ॥ ९ ॥ **औदुम्बर्या उच्छ्रियमाणायै दक्षिणतस्तिष्ठति** ॥ १० ॥ **उपरवाणां**

एतेनैवेत्यादिषु पक्षद्वयमुक्तम्। अनुवादपक्षेऽपि प्रवर्ग्यस्य ब्रह्मत्वमतिदेशेन प्रापयति। तत्र यत्प्रयो-जनवत् तदतिदिश्यते ॥ १ ॥

प्रणयनप्रसवादीनां पदार्थैः संयुज्यते तेषां विधानात्। इह तेषामभावान्निवृत्तिः। वाग्यमनं[1] तदावर्ति[2]प्रायश्चित्तमप्यतिदिश्यते। [2]दिवाकीर्त्यमितीह[3] विहितायाः प्रवर्ग्ये[4] पुनर्वचनं समस्तायाः प्रणवकर्मसंयोजनार्थम्[5] ॥ २ ॥

दक्षिणतोऽनुसमेत्येतिवचनात् महावीरगार्हपत्ययोर्दक्षिणत उपवेशनम्। अन्ये प्रवर्ग्यस्य[6] ब्रह्मत्वं वक्ष्यत इति वाक्यशेषमध्याहरन्ति। तथा यावदत्रोक्तं तत्तत्[7] पदेपदे कुर्वन्ति। तेषामभिप्रायोऽ[7]पूर्वत्वात्प्र-वर्ग्यस्य दर्शपूर्णमासधर्मा न प्रवर्तन्त इति। सत्यम्। चोदकेन[8] नातिदिश्यते। वचनेन त्वतिदिश्यते[9]। वचनातिदेशो हि चोदकादबलीयान्[10]। एतद् ब्राह्मणान्येव पञ्चहवींषीति[11]। वरुणप्रघासादिषु [12]दार्शपौर्णमासांश्चोदकप्राप्तानपनुद्य वैश्वदेविका भवन्ति। एतेन प्रवर्ग्यस्य ब्रह्मा भवतीति श्रुतस्यैवानुषंगो भवति ॥ ३ ॥

यथान्येषु ब्रह्मत्वं वक्ष्यत इत्यध्याहार्यमाणे श्रुतकल्पना। सा च गरीयसी। उपसदादिष्वपि प्राप्तिमन्त एव प्रवर्तन्ते ॥ ४ ॥

'महावेद्यैः=त आस्ते'[13]। तूष्णीमेव। [13]उत्तरस्मिन्परिग्राहे मन्त्रेणोपविश्य 'बृहस्पत' इति आग्नीध्रीयमार्जालीययोस्तत्र तत्र दक्षिणत आस्ते ॥ ५ ॥

सदसि तेषां[14] सर्वेषां तन्त्रेण दक्षिणतः पूर्वेण शालामुखीयं प्रविश्योपस्थे राजानं कृत्वाऽऽ-हुत्योर्दक्षिणत आस्ते। आग्नीध्रे साद्यमाने स्थितेऽपि[15] नयवत्यां[16] हूयमानायामास्ते। उत्थाय पूर्वं गत्वा पूर्वेणाहवनीयं गत्वा प्रदक्षिणमावृत्य वैष्णव्यां हूयमानायां दक्षिणत आस्ते ॥ ८ ॥

---

१. T यमनतदापत्तिप्राय°. २-२. M प्रायश्चि...तदिवा°, Ad ते दिवा. ३. M Ad °कीर्त्यमिति वि°; thus T. ४. M Ad प्रवर्ग्यो. ५. M Ad °योजनां योजनार्थं. ६. M Ad प्रवर्गस्य. ७-७. M तत्त...तेषामभिप्रायोपूर्वा°, Ad तत्तत्तावदेव कुर्वन्ति ते प्रायोर्वा°. ८. M Ad चोदकेनाति°; thus T. ९. M Ad °दिश्यन्ते. १०. M Ad चोदकत्वाद्बली°. ११. M °हवींष्विति. १२. M °पौर्णमा...प्राप्तानप°, Ad °पौर्णमास्यां°. १३-१३. M त आ...वोत्तरस्मिन्. १४. M Ad तेषु; thus T. १५. M Ad स्त्रितोऽ°. १६. M नययत्यां, Ad नवत्यां.

चेष्यमाणानां दक्षिणत आस्ते ॥ ११ ॥ उपस्थे राजानं कृत्वा वैसर्जनानाꣳ हूयमानानां दक्षिणत आस्ते ॥ १२ ॥ अग्नीषोमयोः प्रणीयमानयोर्दक्षिणत एति ॥ १३ ॥ पुराऽग्नेः सादनादुत्तरेणाग्नी–ध्रीयं धिष्णियं परीत्य दक्षिणतस्तिष्ठति ॥ १४ ॥ सन्नेऽग्नौ प्राञ्च आयन्ति ॥ १५ ॥ अध्वर्यवे राजानꣳ संप्रदाय (यथेतमागत्य अग्रेण) प्रदक्षिणꣳ हविर्धानमुपविश्याग्नीषोमीयस्य पशोर्द–क्षिणत आस्ते ॥ १६ ॥ वसतीवरीणां परिह्रियमाणानां दक्षिणतस्तिष्ठति ॥ १७ ॥ आग्नीध्रे संवसन्ते ॥ १८ ॥ स यत्रैनं प्रातरनुवाकाय बोधयन्ति स यज्ञोपवीतं कृत्वाऽप आचम्य द्वाभ्यामा–त्मन्नग्निं गृहीत्वैवमेवान्तरे वेदिं चोत्करं च प्रपद्य पूर्वेण हविर्धाने अपरेणाहवनीयं गत्वाऽग्रेण दक्षिणꣳ हविर्धानमुपविश्योपाकृते प्रातरनुवाके वाचं यच्छत्या परिधानात् ॥ १९ ॥ परिहिते प्रातरनुवाके पूर्वया द्वारा हविर्धानं प्रपद्योत्तरेण ध्रुवस्थालीं परीत्यापरेणाभिषूयमाणस्य दक्षिणत आस्ते ॥ २० ॥ ग्रहाणां गृह्यमाणानां दक्षिणत आस्ते ॥ २१ ॥ स यत्र ग्रहान् गृहीत्वा बहिष्पवमानाय सर्पन्ति तदुद्गातर्निन्वारभ्य ब्रह्मा स्रुवाहुतिं जुहोति 'बृहस्पते' ॥ ३.६.१.२२ ॥
[इति प्रथमः पटलः (१७)]

'बृहस्पते अति यदर्यो अर्हा=चित्रꣳ स्वाहा' **इति ॥ १ ॥ अथोदञ्चꣳ स्तुत्वा बहिष्पवमाना–योपविश्य स यत्राह** 'ब्रह्मन् स्तोष्याम', 'प्रशास्तः' **इत्याह प्रस्तोता,** 'देव सवितरेतत्ते प्राह' **इति प्रसवं जपति ब्रह्मा।** '°तत् प्र च सुव प्र च यज बृहस्पतिर्ब्रह्माऽऽयुष्मत्यात=स्तुत देवस्य सवितुः प्रसव इन्द्रवन्त स्तुत' **इति ॥ २ ॥ त्रिराह** 'रश्मिरसि क्षयाय त्वा क्षयं जिन्व' **इति ॥ ३ ॥ मनसा स्तुते**

अध्वर्यवे राजानं संप्रदाय यथेतं गत्वा यथोक्तं करोति। अग्रेण दक्षिणं हविर्धानमिति ब्रह्मायतने महावेद्या दक्षिणतः। अत्रापि निरसनोपवेशने कर्तव्ये ॥ १६ ॥

स्थानान्तरत्वाद्वसतीवरीणां परिहरणेऽपि महावेद्या दक्षिणत आसनम् ॥ १७ ॥

प्रातरनुवाकाय बोधितः [१]सवनीयपात्रसादनोत्तरकालं यथोक्तं प्रविश्य यथाप्रकृत्युपविशति[२]। आप्रातरनुवाकस्य परिधानादग्निग्रहणादेरिह दर्शनात् प्रत्येकं दीक्षणीयादिषु सोमाङ्गेषु प्राप्तिरनुमीयते। वरणं[३] तु निवर्तते। सामर्थ्येनैव वरणेन[४] [५]साधितत्वात्। अथवा ब्रह्मवरणस्यानमनार्थत्वात्[५] तस्य [६]चानमनार्थत्वान्नानार्थयोश्च बाध्यबाधकत्वाभावादग्निग्रह[७]...च्याभूः प्रपद्य[७] इत्यनुवाको योऽयं तत्रावाम्नातः[८] ॥ १९ ॥

परिहिते प्रातरनुवाके पूर्वया द्वारा हविर्धानं प्रपद्य यथोक्तं करोति। यद्यपि परिहिते[९] प्रातरनुवाक इत्युक्तं तथापि हुते दधिग्रहे प्रविशति ॥ ३.६.१.२० ॥ **[इति प्रथमः पटलः** (१७)**]**

'रश्मिरसी'त्यनुवाकोपलक्षणम्[१०]। इह सर्वमनुवाकं मनसा ध्यात्वा पुनरौपानुवाक्येन विधानेन[११] यथाविभागं[११] यजमानं वाचयति। अथवा तत्र वाचनं विहितम्, इह तेनैव विभागेन

---

१. M Ad सविनय° ; thus T. **२.** M Ad विश्याप्रात°. **३.** M Ad वरुणं. **४.** M Ad वरुणेन. **५–५.** M Ad साधितत्व...नागमना° ; thus T. **६.** M Ad वागमना°. **७–७.** M Ad °दग्निग्र ...च्याभूः प्रपद्य, T °दग्निग्रह...पद्य. **८.** M Ad T ततावाम्नातः. **९.** T takes it as additional. **१०.** T °वाक उप°. **११–११.** M विधाने ...भागं.

बहिष्पवमान एतेनैव यथेतमागत्याग्रेण दक्षिणꣳ हविर्धानमुपविश्य सवनीयस्य पशोर्दक्षिणत आस्ते ॥ ४ ॥ तस्य वपाꣳ हुत्वा मार्जयित्वा सं प्रसर्पन्ति ॥ ५ ॥ प्रसिद्धꣳ संप्रसर्पणम् ॥ ६ ॥ उत्तरेण हविर्धाने दक्षिणेनाग्नीध्रमुत्तरेणाग्नीध्रीयमग्निं गत्वोत्तरेण सदः परीत्यापरया द्वारा सदः प्रस्रप्स्यन् 'देवी द्वारौ मा मा सं ताप्तम्' **इति सदसो द्वारौ समीक्षते ॥ ७ ॥** 'नमः सदसे' **इति सदः प्रेक्षते ॥ ८ ॥** 'नमः सदसस्पतये' **इति यजमानम् ॥ ९ ॥** 'नमः सखीनां पुरोगाणां चक्षुषे' **इति पूर्वप्रसृप्तानामक्षीणीक्षते ॥ १० ॥** 'नमो दिवे नमः पृथिव्यै' **इत्यपरेणौदुम्बरीं गत्वैवमेव सदसो दक्षिणार्धात् तृणमुदस्यति ॥ ११ ॥ एवमुपविशति ॥ १२ ॥ एवमुपविश्य जपति ॥ १३ ॥ उपाकृतेषु पवमानेषु वाचं यच्छत्यापरिधानाद्, आवषट्कारादितरेषाꣳ स्तुतशस्त्राणम् ॥ १४ ॥ स यत्रर्चा वा यजुषा वा करोति तद्वाचं यच्छति इति समानी मीमाꣳसा ॥ १५ ॥ एतेनैव प्रातः-सवनस्य ब्रह्मा भवति ॥ १६ ॥ एतेन माध्यन्दिनस्य सवनस्य ॥ १७ ॥ एतेन तृतीयसवनस्य ॥ १८ ॥ स यत्रावभृथमवयन्ति तद्दक्षिणतोऽनुसमेत्य प्रचरतां दक्षिणतस्तिष्ठति ॥ १९ ॥ एतेनैवोदयनी-**

मानसत्वम्। मानसवाचनयोर्विकल्पः ॥ ३-४ ॥

प्रसिद्धं संप्रसर्पणमिति स्फ्यः[१] स्वस्तिरित्यादि दक्षिणं[२] चमसमित्येतदन्तस्यातिदेशः ॥ ६ ॥

तस्योत्तरेण हविर्धानमित्यादि प्रस्तौति ॥ ७-१० ॥

'नमो दिवे नमः पृथिव्या' इत्यादि द्यावापृथिव्योर्नमस्कारो लिङ्गात् ॥ ११ ॥

सदसो दक्षिणार्ध उद्गातुर्दक्षिणत[३] उदङ्मुख उपविशति। 'तस्मादुद्गातारमभ्यावृत्यास्ते यथा स्वं धिष्णियमि'त्यन्वाख्याने (वाधूअन्वा.४.४०.४) उक्तत्वात् ॥ १२ ॥

एवमुपविश्य जपतीत्युन्निवत इत्यस्य ग्रहणेन[४] 'देव सवितरि'त्यादौ[५] प्रसिद्धग्रहणेन प्राप्तस्यैवानुवादः ॥ १३ ॥

समानी मीमांसा विकल्पना। का पुनरसौ। वाग्यमकाले[६] वाग्विसर्गे प्रायश्चित्तं विभागेन वाग्यमे निन्दा। सर्वकालमनियमे दोष इत्यादि ॥ १५ ॥

स यत्रावभृथः[७]=तिष्ठति। इह दक्षिणत इति न दिग्ग्रहणं, हस्तभागो गृह्यते। कुतो न। अवश्यंभावि[८]प्राग्गमनमवभृथस्य यस्यां दिशि समर्थमुदकं विद्यते तत्र गतं दिशि। दक्षिणशब्दस्य हस्तप्रकृतित्वं भगवता [९]यास्केनाभिहितं 'दिग्[१०] हस्तप्रकृतिः' (निरु. १.७) इति। तथा चाश्वलायनेन ब्रह्मत्व उक्तम् 'बहिर्वेदि[११] यां दिशं व्रजेयुः सैव तत्र[१२] प्राची'ति (आश्वश्रौ.१.१२.४)। अथवा प्राङ्मुखैरेवावभृथो गन्तव्य इत्याचार्याभिप्रायः[१३] ॥ १९ ॥

---

१. T स्फ्यस्व°. **२.** M दक्षिणन्यञ्चमित्येतदन्त°, Ad दक्षिणन्यञ्चमित्यनेतदन्त°; thus T. **३.** M Ad दक्षिणार्ध. **४.** M ग्रहणन्न, Ad ग्रहणं न; thus T. **५.** Ad सवितु°, M सवितरित्य...प्रसिद्ध°, T सवितुरित्यनुप्र°. **६.** M Ad वाग्यकाले. **७.** M Ad भृथः तिष्ठ, T भृथस्तिष्ठ. **८.** M Ad वर्ग्यं हाविः; thus T. **९.** M Ad यास्केनाहितं [M यस्के]. **१०.** M Ad दीर्घ. **११.** M बर्हि. **१२.** T ततः. **१३.** M Ad °चार्योऽभि°.

यस्य ब्रह्मा भवति ॥ २० ॥ **एतेनानूबन्ध्यस्योदवसानीयस्य** ॥ २१ ॥ **स यदि यज्ञ ऋक्तो भ्रेषं नीयात्** 'ब्रह्मणे प्रब्रूत' **इति ब्रूयात्** ॥ २२ ॥ **यदि यजुष्टो यदि सामतो** 'ब्रह्मणे प्रब्रूत' **इत्येव ब्रूयात्** ॥ २३ ॥ **स यदि यज्ञ ऋक्तो भ्रेषं नीयात्** 'भूः स्वाहा' **इति स्रुवाहुतिमाग्नीध्रे जुहुयात्** ॥ २४ ॥ **यदि यजुष्टो** 'भुवः स्वाहा' **इति स्रुवाहुतिमाग्नीध्र एव जुहुयात्** ॥ २५ ॥ **यदि सामतः** 'सुवः स्वाहा' **इति स्रुवाहुतिमाग्नीध्र एव जुहुयात्** ॥ २६ ॥ **अथ यदि सर्वत एव यज्ञो भ्रेषं नीयादविज्ञाताद्वा** 'कुत इदमजनि' **इति गार्हपत्य आज्यं विलाप्योत्पूय स्रुवं च स्रुचं च संमृज्यात्रैव समिधं निगृह्य ब्रह्माणं दक्षिणतो निषाद्य प्राङेत्य तृणेषु कूर्चे वोपसाद्य समिध-माधायाहवनीये जुहुयात्** 'मनो ज्योतिर्जुषतामाज्यमरिष्टं यज्ञꣳ समिमं दधातु। बृहस्पतिस्तनुतामिमं नो विश्वे देवा इह मादयन्तां भूर्भुवः सुवः स्वाहा' **इति** ॥ २७ ॥ **सैषा सर्वप्रायश्चित्तिः** ॥ २८ ॥ **स ह वाव ब्रह्मा य एवं वेद** ॥ २९ ॥ **तस्मादेवंविदमेव ब्रह्माणं कुर्वीत** ॥ ३० ॥ **एतेनैवात्यग्निष्टोमस्य ब्रह्मा भवति** ॥ ३१ ॥ **एतेनैवोक्थ्यस्य** ॥ ३२ ॥ **एतेन षोडशिनः** ॥ ३३ ॥ **एतेनातिरात्रस्य** ॥ ३४ ॥ **एतेनाप्तोर्यामस्य** ॥ ३५ ॥ **एतेन वाजपेयस्य** ॥ ३६ ॥ **एतेन राजसूयस्य** ॥ ३७ ॥ **एतेनार्काश्व-**

ऋक्तो[१] यजुष्टः सामत[२] इति [३]वेदाख्यानम् ऋग्यजुःसाममात्रम्[३]। तस्मिन्तस्मिन्वेद[४] उत्पन्नानां मन्त्रादीनां भ्रेषप्रायश्चित्तं विधीयते ॥ २१-२६ ॥

विज्ञातशब्देन स्मृतिरभिप्रेता। इदमस्मिन् वेद उत्पन्नमिति यन्न ज्ञायत इत्यर्थः। ...ष्टापसर एवानन्तरं[४] प्रायश्चित्तं नेष्यते। 'ब्रह्मणे प्रब्रूतेति[५] भ्रेषकर्ता[६] ब्रवीति स्वामी वा। गार्हपत्य आज्यं [७]विलाप्योत्पूयेति प्रत्येकं भ्रेषप्रायश्चित्ते[८] च तुल्यं तुल्यन्यायत्वात्। एतद्[८] ज्ञापयति। [९]तत्रोक्तानामाहूतीनां[९] तूष्णीं संस्कृतमाज्यं साधनं, न प्राकृतं प्रसज्यत इति। युज्यते च तत् [१०]प्राकृतः संस्कारः[१०] नास्मा अर्थाय विहितः[११]। स्रुक्स्रुवसंमार्ग[१२]प्राकृतसंस्कारात्[१३] पूर्वकालेषूत्तरेषु स एव प्रसज्यते। जुह्वां व्यावृतायां स्रुक्[१४]प्रचररणी गृह्यते[१४] ॥ २७-२८ ॥

अत्यग्निष्टोमः संस्थाविशेषोऽग्निष्टोमोक्थ्ययोर्मध्येऽन्तरेण त्रयोदशं स्तोत्रमत्यग्निष्टोमस्येति।

---

१. Ad उक्तो. **२.** M Ad समत; thus T. **३-३.** M Ad वेदाख्यानयजुस्सा समात्रं; thus T. **४-४.** M Ad तस्मिन्वेद उत्पन्नमिति यन्न... एवानन्तरं, T ...ष्टापसर...ए...वान°. **५.** M Ad °ब्रूतेत. **६.** M Ad भ्रेषकणा; thus T. **७.** M Ad विलोप्यास्तूयेत; thus T. **८-८.** M Ad om text between °श्चिते and °तद्; thus T. **९-९.** M Ad T तत्रो...क्तिकानामा°. **१०-१०.** M Ad प्राकृतं संस्कारं. **११.** M Ad °विहितं. **१२.** M Ad स्रुध्रुव°; thus T. **१३.** M Ad °कारां. **१४-१४.** M Ad °प्रचरन्निगृह्यते, T स्रुक्प्रच...रणिगृ°.

मेधयोः ॥ ३८ ॥ **एतेन सर्वेषां यज्ञक्रतूनाम्** ॥ ३.६.२.३९ ॥ **[इति द्वितीयः पटलः** (१८)**]**

॥ इति तृतीयप्रपाठके षष्ठोऽनुवाकः ॥

॥ इति याजमानाख्यस्तृतीयः प्रपाठकः ॥

□ □ □

अविकृत एव वाऽग्निष्टोमषोडशीस्तोत्राधिको भवति ॥ ३.६.२.३१-३३ ॥ **[इति द्वितीयः पटलः** (१८)**]**

॥ इति व्याख्यायां तृतीयप्रपाठके षष्ठोऽनुवाकः ॥

॥ इति कल्पागमसंग्रहे याजमानाख्यस्तृतीयः प्रपाठकः ॥

□ □ □

॥ अथ चतुर्थः प्रपाठकः ॥

[चातुर्मास्यानि]

[वैश्वदेवपर्व]

शिशिरेऽर्धकक्षमुपोषति ॥ १ ॥ ता वसन्ता प्रसुवो भवन्ति ॥ २ ॥ श्वः फल्गुभिः पौर्ण–

'शिशि = षति'। अथ[१] चातुर्मास्यान्यारभ्यन्ते। 'देवव्रतानि विधाय[२] चातुर्मास्ययाजिन' इति समापनात्समाख्यानाच्च तानि समुदितान्येकफलापूर्वमुत्पादयन्ति[३]। दर्शपूर्णमासवत् तेषां सकृत्प्रयोगो यावज्जीविकत्वं च दृश्यते[४]। अग्निहोत्रादिभिः सहैतान्यप्याम्नाय 'तस्यैवमेवैते यज्ञक्रतवः परिप्लवेरन्नि'ति दर्शनाद्यावज्जीविकता। तथा मार्गशीर्ष्यां शुनासीरीयं विधाय पूर्वेषु पर्वसु विहितानां[५] देवव्रतानामवचनमुत्सर्गाभिप्रायतः[६]। पुनः प्रयोगेऽपि सत्याप्रथमसंवत्सरपरिसमाप्तेर्व्रतानि[७] नोत्स्रष्टव्यानि[८]। तत ऊर्ध्वं संवत्सरं हि व्रतं नातीत्येत्यन्यार्थानुवाददर्शनाद्[९] व्रताभावः। अथवा [१०]नान्यार्थदर्शनमात्रमेव। 'य एवं विद्वान्' संवत्सरं व्रतं चरती'त्यनारभ्याधीतस्य यत्र यत्र व्रतं तत्र तत्र प्राप्तिरित्येवं[११] प्राप्तस्यैत–द्दर्शनम्। तथा यदि पुनः प्रयोक्ष्यमाणः स्यादथ यद्युत्स्रक्ष्यन्निति पक्षद्वयं दृश्यते। पञ्चवर्षादिप्रयोगा अपि शाखान्तरेषु विद्यन्ते। तैष्यां पौर्णमास्यां यजनीयादह्न आरभ्य शिशिराभ्य ऋतुः। 'ता[१२] वसन्ता प्रसुवो[१३] भवन्ति' इत्युक्त्वा 'फल्गुनी[१४] पूर्णमासे वै वैश्वदेवमि'ति विदधत आचार्यस्यायमभिप्रायः शिशिरादेव कक्षं[१५] दर्भस्तम्बं[१६] दहति ॥ १ ॥

सामर्थ्यात्[१७]। ता वसन्ते[१७] लवनसमर्थाः प्रसुवो भवन्ति ॥ २ ॥

[१८]*श्वः फल्गुभिः = तञ्चनाय* इति[१९]। प्रतिपत्पञ्चदश्योः पौर्णमासित्वमुक्तम्। तत्रोत्तराभिः फल्गुनीभिर्यजनीयमहः संपद्यत[२०] इति। ततः पूर्वस्मिन्नहन्यातञ्चनविधानं[२१], श्वोभूते वैश्वदेवयागः[२२]। कुतः। 'अथो वसन्तो वै संवत्सरस्य मुखं मुखं [२३]वा एतत्[२३] संवत्सरस्य यत्फल्गुनी पूर्णमास' इत्युक्ते अपरपक्षादित्वमृतूनां गमिष्यते। 'ता वसन्ता[२४] प्रसुवो भवन्ति'[२५] इति वसन्ते वैश्वदेवं तां[२५] दर्शयति।

---

१. T अत्र. **२.** M Ad विधिनाय. **३.** M Ad °यति; thus T. **४.** M Ad गृह्यते; thus T. **५.** M Ad °हितां [M तान्]; thus T. **६.** M °मुसर्गाभिप्रायता, Ad मुपसर्गाभिप्रायता; thus T. **७.** M Ad °प्ते व्रता°; thus T. **८.** M °ज्ञृष्ट°. **९.** M Ad नातीत्यन्यार्थानुवाददर्शाद्. **१०.** M Ad अथ वान्यार्थ°; thus T. **११.** M °प्तिस्त्ये°, Ad प्राप्तिरस्त्येवं; thus T. **१२.** T अता. **१३.** M Ad प्रसवो, T प्रवसवो (?). **१४.** M Ad फलाहि; thus T. **१५.** M Ad पक्षं, T शिशिरादेवेव. **१६.** M °स्तम्भं. **१७–१७.** M Ad सामर्थ्या चा वसन्तो. **१८.** M Ad T om, thus in sūtra text. **१९.** M Ad T om. **२०.** M Ad संवद्य. **२१.** M Ad T °तञ्च निधानम्. **२२.** M Ad °देवे...वयागः. **२३–२३.** M Ad वोहि. **२४.** T वसन्ताः. **२५–२५.** M Ad °न्ति वसन्त...तान्दः.

मासीत्यग्निहोत्रोच्छिष्टमातच्य निदधाति हविरातञ्चनाय ॥ ३ ॥ **उत्परेत्य पलाशशाखामाच्छिनत्ति** 'इषे त्वोर्जे त्वा' **इति** ॥ ४ ॥ **तयाऽऽगत्य वत्सानपाकरोति** 'वायवः स्थोपायवः स्थ' **इति** ॥ ५ ॥ 'देवो वः सविता प्रेरयतु' **इति गा अनुमन्त्रयते** । '०श्रेष्ठतमाय कर्मण आप्यायध्वमघ्निया विश्वेभ्यो देवेभ्यो भागमूर्जस्वतीः पयस्वतीः' **इति** ॥ ६ ॥ **प्रसिध्यति कर्म** ॥ ७ ॥ 'देवस्य त्वा सवितुः प्रसवे' **इत्यसिदमादायोत्परैति** ॥ ८ ॥ **कक्षस्यार्धमुपोषति** ॥ ९ ॥ **प्रसुवो लुनाति** ॥ १० ॥ **प्रस्तरमापूर्य निदधाति** ॥ ११ ॥ **बर्हिर्लुनाति** ॥ १२ ॥ **तत् त्रेधा सन्नह्यति** ॥ १३ ॥ **एकस्मिन् प्रस्तरमुपनह्यति** ॥ १४ ॥ **तदेकधा पुनः सन्नह्यति** ॥ १५ ॥ **प्रसिद्धमितरत्** ॥ १६ ॥ **बर्हिर्लुनाति** ॥ १७ ॥ **आरम्भणीयाया इष्ट्या आहरन्नैति** ॥ १८ ॥ **यज्ञायुधानि सꣳसाद्यापः प्रणीयारम्भणीयामिष्टिं**

अथातः सन्धीनामेवेत्यत्र द्व्यहकालानां[१] पर्वणां[२] फल्गुनीपूर्णमासादिकालं विदधत्। स यत्[३] पुरस्तान्यजेत हेमन्तमित्यादि वदन्नेतमेवार्थमुपोद्बलयति। तथा च कौण्डिन्याः पठन्ति—'एतावदेवाहः पौर्णमासेन हविषा यजेते'ति। अथवा निवृताधिमासे संवत्सरे प्रायेणोत्तराभिः पञ्चदशी संपद्यते[३]इति कृत्वा पञ्चदश्यां[४] वैश्वदेवस्य यागः तत्प्रकृते द्व्यहकालता[५] न बाधिता भवति। तथा च राजसूये–'वसन्ति[६]। प्रातर्वैश्वदेवेन यजते'।'वसन्ति[७]। प्रातः पौर्णमासेन यजते' (वाधूश्रौ. ९.१.१.६२–६४) इत्युभयोः समानदिवसत्वं दृश्यते। पक्षद्वये गतिश्चिन्त्या ॥ ३ ॥

[८]'इषे त्वा' आदिमन्त्राणां समस्य वचनं प्राकृतस्य प्रदर्शनार्थम् ॥ ४ ॥

अनुमन्त्रणम्। अनुमन्त्रणे[९] 'विश्वेभ्यो देवेभ्यो भागम्' इति मन्त्रान्तरं, न प्राकृतस्योहः। ऊहत्वे 'देवेभ्यो[१०] देवेभ्यो भाग' इति भवितव्यम् ॥ ६ ॥

प्रस्तरमापूर्य निदधाति ॥ ११ ॥

'बर्हिर्लुनाती'ति[११] व्यपदेशाद्राजसूये च[१२] 'ता वैश्वदेवस्य प्रस्तराय संचष्ट' इति दर्शनाच्च। प्रस्तर एव प्रसूमयो[१३], न सर्वं बर्हिः ॥ १२ ॥

त्रेधा सन्नहनम्। तूष्णीमप्राकृतकार्यत्वादेकधा सन्नहनम् ॥ १३–१७ ॥

मन्त्रवत्सन्नहनान्ते वैश्वदेवबर्हिष्यारंभणीया[१४]। बर्हिषः परिदेशनादिकर्मारभ्यते। तथा प्रस्तरबर्हिषोरपि जात्यन्तरत्वाद् वैश्वदेवे पृथक् परिदेशनोन्मार्जने। उभयोः [१५]सहोन्नमनहरणसादनानि। तन्मन्त्रा ऊह्यन्ते[१५]। 'इन्द्रस्य वां बाहुभ्यामुर्वन्तरिक्षमन्वितं देवंगमे स्थः'। पृथग्गुप्तं[१६] निधानं [१७]यज्ञायुधानीत्याद्यारंभणीयायास्तन्त्रप्रक्रमप्रदर्शनार्थम्। आरम्भणीयोत्तरकालं[१७] वैश्वदेवस्य तन्त्रप्रक्रमो[१८]

---

१. M Ad द्व्यहः का° . २. M Ad पर्वाणां; thus T. ३–३. T takes the text as additional स यत् इत्थनन्तरं 'पुरस्तान्यजेत=सम्प'– इति मध्ये अधिकं वर्तते।. ४. M Ad दश्या° ; thus T. ५. M Ad द्व्यहःका° . ६. T wrongly suggests it as वसन्ते. ७. M °वन्ति, Ad °ऽवन्ति for वसन्ति. ८. M Ad इषेत्यादि. ९. T मन्त्रे. १०. M Ad देभ्यो. ११. M Ad लुनो° ; thus T. १२. M Ad broken. १३. T प्रस्तर°. १४. M Ad °देव...बर्हि° ; thus T. १५–१५. M Ad सहोऽन्यमनह... ऊह्यन्त; thus T. १६. M Ad पृथगुप्तं. १७–१७. M Ad °युधाहीत्याद्यरम्भणीयोत्तरकालं; thus T. १८. M Ad तन्त्रव्रतमो.

निर्वपति प्राजापत्यं द्वादशकपालम् ऋतव्यं चरुं वैश्वानरं द्वादशकपालं पार्जन्यं चरुं वैष्णवं त्रिकपालम् ॥ १९ ॥ **निरुप्ते प्राणग्रहांश्च पृश्नींश्च व्याचष्टे** ॥ २० ॥ **समासन्नेऽपानग्रहांश्च पृश्नींश्च (व्याचष्टे।** 'ध्रुवा असदन्', 'यन्मे अग्ने' **इति समभिमृश्य) दशहोतारं व्याचष्टे** ॥ २१ ॥ **तस्यै वार्त्रघ्नावाज्यभागौ** ॥ २२ ॥ 'प्रजापतयेऽनुब्रूहि' **इत्याहोपस्तृणानोऽवद्यन्** ॥ २३ ॥ 'प्रजापते न त्वदेतान्यन्यः' **इत्यन्वाह** ॥ २४ ॥ 'स वेद' **इति यजति** ॥ २५ ॥ **वषट्कृते जुहोति** ॥ २६ ॥ 'ऋतुभ्योऽनुब्रूहि' **इत्याहोपस्तृणानोऽवद्यन्** ॥ २७ ॥ 'ग्रीष्मो हेमन्तः' **इत्यन्वाह** ॥ २८ ॥ 'इदुवत्सराय' **इति यजति** ॥ २९ ॥ **वषट्कृते जुहोति** ॥ ३० ॥ 'वैश्वानरायानुब्रूहि' **इत्याहोपस्तृणानोऽवद्यन्** ॥ ३१ ॥ 'वैश्वानराय पृथुपाजसे' **इत्यन्वाह**। '°विपो रत्ना विधन्त धरुणेषु गातवे। अग्निर्हि देवाँ अमृतो दुवस्यत्यथा धर्माणि सनता न दूदुषत्' **इति** ॥ ३२ ॥ 'त्वमग्ने' **इति यजति**। '°शोचिषा शोशुचान आ रोदसी अपृणा जायमानः। त्वं देवाँ अभिशस्तेरमुञ्चो वैश्वानर जातवेदो महित्वा' **इति** ॥ ३३ ॥ **वषट्कृते जुहोति** ॥ ३४ ॥ 'पर्जन्यायानुब्रूहि' **इत्याहोपस्तृणानोऽवद्यन्** ॥ ३५ ॥ 'पर्जन्याय प्र गायत' **इत्यन्वाह**। '°दिवस्पुत्राय मीढुषे। स नो यवसमिच्छतु' **इति** ॥ ३६ ॥ 'अच्छा वद तवसम्' **इति यजति**। '°गीर्भिरुक्थैः स्तुहि पर्जन्यं नमसा विवास। अभिक्रन्दन् वृषभो वाजिनीवान्रेतो दधात्वोषधीषु गर्भम्' **इति** ॥ ३७ ॥ **वषट्कृते जुहोति** ॥ ३८ ॥ 'विष्णवेऽनुब्रूहि' **इत्याहोपस्तृणानोऽवद्यन्** ॥ ३९ ॥ 'इदं विष्णुर्विचक्रमे' **इत्यन्वाह** ॥ ४० ॥ 'तदस्य प्रियमभि पाथो अश्याम्' **इति यजति**। '°नरो यत्र देवयवो मदन्ति=उत्सः'

युक्तः। आरम्भसंयोगादारम्भो नामाद्यो वा पदार्थ औदासीन्यनिवृत्तिर्वा। तदुभयं वैश्वदेवारंभादेव सिद्ध्यति। तथाप्येतावति गते कर्तव्यमिति वचनमनुमीयते[1]। [मध्ये...न्नस्यापि तन्त्रप्रसङ्गयोरभावो बर्हिर्लवनमात्रं वचनात् तन्त्रेण क्रियते। अभ्याधानान्वाधाने अपि क्रमानुग्रहार्थमपकृष्येते। तथा सति कालैक्यात् तयोरपि तन्त्रता। अग्निं गृह्णामीति विरोधादावर्तते। यथा[1] यज्ञपार्श्व उक्तम्—'श्वः परिग्रहणं लुम्पेदन्यश्चेति[2] वा वदेदि'ति[2]। 'मामूर्जम्'[3] इत्यारंभणीयम्। वैश्वदेवमितीतराणि पदानि तन्त्रेण। गुप्तनिधानोत्तरकालं [4]परिस्तरणाद्यारभन्ते[4]। अथेमानि सर्वत्रोपांशूनि। अन्यत्र ग्रहेभ्यः प्राजापत्यं वायव्यं सावित्रं सारस्वतं द्यावापृथिव्यं वैश्वकर्मणमादित्यं सौर्यमिति विध्यवशेषेषु। अन्यत्रापि[5] [6]वाचःस्थानान्यनुपदादागमयितव्यानि। अस्याचार्यस्याभिप्रायः सर्वत्र वैश्वानरचोदनायां तावत[7] एव देवतात्वमिति ॥ १८–३० ॥

तथाहीह 'वैश्वानरायानुब्रूही'त्यादि। तथा पवित्रेष्ट्यामावहनेन[8] न्यासगुणान्[9] निर्दिश्य 'वैश्वानरमावहे'ति तावत एव ग्रहणात् ॥ ३१–३४ ॥

तस्यै दक्षिणा अनड्वा'निति। अत्र 'पञ्चारम्भणीयायामिष्ट्यां दद्यादि'त्यस्य गुणविधानमिति केचित्[1]। तन्नोपपद्यते। सर्वत्र हि धेनुचोदनायां[2] विना वत्सेन संख्यां न पश्यामः। [3]सोमक्रयणादितोऽत्र न दक्षिणानां[4] नित्यत्वमवगम्यते। दक्षिणावत्पक्षे च नैता नियता संख्या विरोधादनड्वानादयः[5] प्रसिद्धा [6]एव। अस्या इष्टेः[6] पञ्चवर्षादिप्रयोगेष्वनावृत्तिरारम्भनिमित्तत्वात्। अन्य आह– 'राजसूये पवित्रेणारब्धे दिवा

१–१. M Ad °मीयमेव...प्रसङ्गयोरभाव...यज्ञपार्श्वं; thus T. २–२. M Ad न्यश्च वा वदेति; thus T. ३. M °मूर्ज इत्या°. ४–४. M Ad °कालपरिस्तरणान्यारभते. ५. M Ad om अपि. ६. M Ad °न्यन्युपादादा°. ७. M Ad तावदत. ८. M Ad °मावाहनेन. ९. M Ad °गुणा नि°.

इति ॥ ४१ ॥ **वषट्कृते जुहोति** ॥ ४२ ॥ **त्रिष्टुभौ संयाज्ये** ॥ ४३ ॥ **तस्यै दक्षिणा अनड्वान् वत्सतर्यृषभो धेनुर्वामनः** ॥ ४४ ॥ **सन्ततिमनु होतुराहुतिं जुहोति** ॥ ४५ ॥ **प्रसिध्यति कर्म** ॥ ४६ ॥ **सन्तिष्ठत आरम्भणीयेष्टिः** ॥ ४७ ॥ **सायं निर्णिक्तैः पात्रैर्गा आयतीः प्रतीक्षते** 'एता आचरन्ति मधुमद्दुहानाः' **इति** ॥ ४८ ॥ **हुत्वाऽग्निहोत्रꣳ सान्नाय्यं दोहयति** 'बहु दुग्धि विश्वेभ्यो देवेभ्यो हविः' **इति** ॥ ४९ ॥ 'विश्वे त्वा देवा वैश्वानराः श्रीणन्तु' **इत्येनत्प्रतिष्ठापयति** ॥ ५० ॥ 'विश्वेषां त्वा देवानां भागꣳ सोमेनातनच्मि' **इति हविरातञ्चनेनातनक्ति** ॥ ५१ ॥ 'अदस्तमसि विश्वेभ्यस्त्वा देवेभ्यः' **इत्युदन्वता पात्रेणापिदधाति** ॥ ५२ ॥ 'अग्ने हव्यꣳ रक्ष' **इति तद् यत्र गुप्तं मन्यते**

पशुमालभते तस्य पशुपुरोडाशेन सहारम्भणीयेष्टि'रितिवदावृत्तिं[७] दर्शयति। [८]'तत्र वचनमिति[८] चेन्न[९]। आरम्भणीया तत्र विधीयते। आरम्भणीयामनूद्य पशुपुरोडाशेन सह[१०] निर्वापश्चोद्यते। अथवा अर्थान्तरेणास्या अनुवृत्तिस्तेन ज्ञायते न चातुर्मास्यावृत्तावावृत्तिः तथा चोक्तम्—'सकृद्वाऽऽरम्भसंयोगादि'त्यत्र ॥ ४४-४७ ॥

सायं[११] *निर्णिक्तै'रित्यादि*। अत्रानुपदकार आह—'अन्यदेवत्ये सान्नाय्य[१२] ऊहोपाकरणान्तं[१२] च न प्रश्नवाग्विसर्गमन्त्रेषु तथा वोपवेषयोः[१३] सदेनवकालावधो (?) न[१४] इतीह। 'इह वा इन्द्रो रमयतु गाव' इत्येतन्न गणितम्। तत्रैतच्चिन्त्यम्। इहेन्द्रशब्दस्यासमवेताभिधायित्वं मन्यमानेनैवाभिहितमुत प्रदर्शनमथ परिगणनमथवा वचनमिति। तत्र युक्तमत्रार्थन्यायविद्भिरध्यवसेयम् ॥ ४८-४९ ॥

प्रतिष्ठापनान्तत्वं[१५] च नापिधानमन्त्रेषु[१६]। वैश्वदेवप्रकरण एवायं नात्रेत्यनुमानं[१६] कर्तव्यम् [१७]अनूहत्वात्। 'विश्वे[१७] त्वा देवा = श्रीणन्तु[१८]' 'विश्वेषां त्वा देवानां भागम्' इत्यूहत्वे भवितव्यम् ॥ ५०-५१ ॥

अपिधानमन्त्रे प्रकृतेन[१९] विष्णुशब्दस्य असमवेताभिधायित्वादनूहः। ननु विष्णुशब्दस्य [२०]व्याप्तिक्रियायोगादिन्द्राभिधायित्वमुच्यते[२१]। तथा सति देवतानामैश्वर्यात्सर्वशब्दानां सर्वदेवताभिधायित्वं प्राप्नोति। तथा च सति न व्यवतिष्ठेत[२२]। आमिक्षायाः कालसामान्यात् पयोविकारार्थत्वे[२३] दध्नो मन्त्रत्वं प्राप्नोति। तदुक्तम्—'पयो वा कालसामान्यादि'ति। आचार्येण तूभयोर्दोहयोर्मन्त्रवत्वमाम्नातम्। तद्

---

१. M Ad के; thus T. **२.** M Ad हि also after °नायां. **३.** M Ad सामक्र°. **४.** M Ad दक्षिणान्यत्व°. **५.** M Ad °नादाय. **६-६.** M Ad वेवास्येष्टे. **७.** M Ad °पदवृत्तिं. **८-८.** M Ad तत्र नमिति. **९.** M Ad om न. **१०.** T takes सह as additiional. **११.** Ad निर्मिक्तै°. **१२-१२.** M °य्योहोपक°, Ad °य्योवहोप°. **१३.** M Ad तथोपवेषयोः; thus T. **१४.** M Ad °धान. **१५.** M Ad °पनान्तं च. **१६-१६.** M नामानोत्यनु°, Ad नामाप्रेत्यनु°. **१७-१७.** M Ad अनूहत्व द्वित्वे. **१८.** T श्रयणंतु. **१९.** M Ad प्रकृतौ; thus T. **२०.** M Ad व्याप्तक्रि°. **२१.** M Ad °धायित्वान्मु°. **२२.** M Ad °ष्ठेतामामि°. **२३.** M Ad °विकारत्वे; thus T.

तन्निदधाति॥ ५३॥ एवमेव प्रातरग्निहोत्रꣳ हुत्वा सान्नाय्यं दोहयति॥५४॥ नात्र प्रतीक्षते॥५५॥ नाभिद्योतयति॥५६॥ नापः प्रत्यानयति॥ ५७॥ नातनक्ति संक्षालनान्तम्॥५८॥ यज्ञायुधानि संसाद्यापः प्रणीय वैश्वदेवं हविर्निर्वपत्याग्नेयमष्टा-कपालम्॥ ४.१.१.५९॥ [इति प्रथमः पटलः]

आग्नेयमष्टाकपालꣳ निर्वपति सौम्यं चरुꣳ सावित्रं द्वादशकपालं सारस्वतं चरुं पौष्णं चरुं मारुतꣳ सप्तकपालं वैश्वदेवीमामिक्षां द्यावापृथिव्यमेककपालम्॥ १॥ निरुप्ते प्राण-ग्रहाꣳश्च पृश्नीꣳश्च व्याचष्टे॥ २॥ तस्य हविष्कृता वाचं विसृज्य चतुर्गृहीतेन पञ्चहोतार-माहवनीये जुहुयात्॥ ३॥ शृते वा दध्यानयति दधनि वा शृतम्॥४॥ शृतेषु हविःषु स्तम्बयजुर्हरति॥५॥ वेदिं परिगृह्णाति॥ ६॥ करणं जपति॥७॥ प्रसूत उत्तरं परिग्राहं परिगृह्णाति॥ ८॥ योयुपित्वाऽवस्कभ्य संप्रेष्यति 'प्रोक्षणीरासादयेध्मा=धेहि पृषदाज्याय दध्याहरेहि

वाचनिकन्यायाद्धि[1] वचनं बलीयः। सर्वत्रामिक्षाणाम्[2] अस्या आमिक्षाया धर्मप्राप्तिः॥५२॥

यज्ञायुधानि संसा=निर्वपति। यज्ञायुधानीत्यादि तत्रोपलक्षणमित्युक्तम्॥ ४.१.१.५९॥ **[इति प्रथमः पटलः]**

वैश्वदेवं[3] हविर्निर्वपति। वैश्वदेवाख्यामिष्टिं निर्वपतीत्यर्थः। आग्नेयमित्यारभ्य[4] वैश्वदेव्या अनुक्रमणं[5] क्रमार्थम्। पूर्वमेव हि दधिपयसोर्दोहो विहितः। उत्तरत्र च संसर्गो विधीयते। 'दर्शपूर्णमासावालभमान' इत्यादिभिर्वाक्यैस्तस्य[5] तस्य कर्मण आरम्भात् प्राग्विहितानां होतर्णिां कालान्तराणि वदत्ययमाचार्यः। तत्राम्नायानुमानं कर्तव्यं प्रतिपर्वणामस्य अथवाऽवयवेषु[6] समुदायशब्दः चातुर्मास्यानीति। तथा प्रत्यवयवं भिद्यते। पौष्णस्य पेषणस्य विकृत्यर्थत्वाच्चरव्याप[7]नयनकाले तदर्थानपयच्छति। संवपनकाले तदीयानां[8] विभागः॥ १॥

[9]हविःष्वधिश्रित्य क्रियमाणेषु[9] पय उष्णीकृत्यान्यतरदन्यस्मिन्नानयति। तत्कुशलेन श्रपयित्वा प्रतापे निदधाति। प्रवृत्त अमावस्यातन्त्रत्वादस्य कर्मणः पूर्वेद्युः प्राप्तं वेदिकरणमिह वचनात्क्रियते। [10]अथवोत्तरविवक्षार्थत्वादनुवादस्य यथाप्राप्तमेवानुवादः। [11]स्तम्बयजुरुत्तरवेदिवत् स्वग्निप्रणयनार्थं पूर्वं क्रियते[12]। संस्कृतायां हि वेद्यामग्निर्निधातव्यः॥ ५-७॥

प्रोक्षणादिप्रैष 'एहि यजमाने'ति। पृषदाज्यपाचनार्थं[13] कृत आमन्त्रणे संस्कारः आज्यावेक्षणे प्रयुज्यते। अतस्तत्र पुनर्न [14]पक्तव्येत्यन्ये वदन्ति[15]। एवं 'पृषदाज्याय दध्याहर' 'एहि यजमाने'ति

---

१. M Ad °न्याया हि. २. M Ad सवत्रामि° ; thus T. ३. T °देवहवि°. ४. T °मित्यन्यत्र वैश्व°. ५-५. M °क्रमणं...क्रमार्थं पूर्वमेव हि द..विहित उत्तरत्र च स..विधियते दर्शपूर्णमास..भिर्वाक्यै°. ६. M Ad °स्यावयवसमुदाय-च्छन्दश्चा° ; thus T. ७. M Ad °चरज्या° ; thus T. ८. Ad प्रदी°. ९-९. M Ad हविववधिश्रम[Ad य]मा° ; thus T. १०. M Ad अथोत्तर°. ११. T °यजुषी. १२. T क्रियेते. १३. M Ad °ज्ये वाच°. १४. M Ad वक्तव्यतेत्य°, T पक्तव्यतेत्यन्ये. १५. T takes वदन्ति as additional.

यजमान' **इति** ॥ ९ ॥ **एतत् कुर्वन्ति** ॥ १० ॥ **स्रुवं च स्रुचश्च संमार्ष्टि** ॥ ११ ॥ **आज्यानि गृह्णीतेऽध्वर्युः पृषदाज्यवन्ति** ॥ १२ ॥ **इध्माबर्हिः प्रोक्षति** ॥ १३ ॥ **वेदिं प्रोक्षति** ॥ १४ ॥ **आसन्नं प्रोक्षति** ॥ १५ ॥ **अपो निनीय प्रस्तरं गृह्णाति** ॥ १६ ॥ **स्तृणाति बर्हिः** ॥ १७ ॥ **प्राङुत्सृप्य परिधीन् परिदधाति** ॥ १८ ॥ **समिधावादधाति** ॥ १९ ॥ **परिधिषु वाचयित्वाऽग्निं युनक्ति** ॥ २० ॥ **आगत्य तिरश्ची सादयति** ॥ २१ ॥ **तिरश्च्योः प्रस्तरम्** ॥ २२ ॥ **प्रस्तरे जुहूम्** ॥ २३ ॥ **बहिर्षीतरे** ॥ २४ ॥ **अलङ्कुर्वन्ति** ॥ २५ ॥ **उपस्तीर्णाभिघारितेषु हविःषु पात्रे निदधाति** ॥ २६ ॥ **समभिघार्य हवीꣳष्याहरन्ति** ॥ २७ ॥ **समासन्नेऽपानग्रहाꣳश्च पृश्नीꣳश्च व्याचष्टे** ॥ २८ ॥ 'ध्रुवा असदन्', 'यन्मे अग्ने' **इति समभिमृश्य पञ्चहोतारं व्याचष्टे** ॥ २९ ॥ **निर्मन्थ्येन चरति** ॥ ३० ॥ 'अग्नये समिध्यमानायानु वाच' **आह** ॥ ३१ ॥ **सप्तदश सामिधेनीरन्वाह** ॥ ३२ ॥ **आवाहयन् वाजिनोऽप्यावाहयति** ॥ ३३ ॥ **अनूक्तासु सामिधेनीषु स्रुवेणाघारमाघार्याह** 'अग्नीदग्निं त्रिस्त्रिः समृड्ढि' **इति** ॥ ३४ ॥ **स्रुग्भ्यामुत्तरम्** ॥ ३५ ॥ **असꣳस्पर्शयन्नत्याक्रम्य ध्रुवाꣳ समज्य सादयित्वा प्रवरं प्रवृणीते** ॥ ३६ ॥ **सीदति होता** ॥ ३७ ॥ **प्रसूतः स्रुचावादत्ते** ॥ ३८ ॥ **नव प्रयाजान् यजति** ॥ ३९ ॥ **ओ श्रावय इत्याह** ॥ ४० ॥ 'समिधो यज' **इति** ॥ ४१ ॥ 'यज यज' **इति** ॥ ४२ ॥ **चतुर्थेऽर्धं समानीयाष्टमे सर्वꣳ समानयते** ॥ ४३ ॥ **उपभृतोऽधि सर्वं प्र यजति** ॥ ४४ ॥ **प्रयाजानिष्ट्वा-**

पृषदाज्यसंबन्ध एवावतिष्ठते। पृषदाज्यसंबन्धात्कालान्तरे विस्मर्यन्ते ॥ ९ ॥

आज्यावेक्षणे तिरोहितत्वात् पुनरपि पक्तव्यमित्यन्ये[1] वदन्ति। आज्यानि[1] गृह्णीते पृषदाज्यवन्ति। पशुवद्बर्हिषः पञ्चवृत्त्वमनुपद[2] आम्नातम् ॥ १२ ॥

अलंकुर्वन्तोऽनुपूर्वं[3] हवींषि। 'कुर्वन्ति'[4] इति छान्दसो वचनव्यत्ययः। अलंकारो भस्मोदूहनादि ॥ २५ ॥

समभिघारणान्तं संस्कारं कुर्वन्नामिक्षाया अप्युपस्तरणोद्धरणा[5]भिघारणानि करोति। प्रकृतौ समभिघारणमात्रमेव सान्नाय्यस्य क्रियते। अतो[6] विशेषेण वदति ॥ २६–२७ ॥

निर्मन्थ्येन चरति[7]। शकलादानादेरभिहोमान्तस्य[8] पाशुकस्याग्निमन्थनस्य निर्मन्थ्याख्या ॥ ३० ॥

इह पञ्चमप्रभृतयश्चत्वार आगन्तवः प्रयाजाः। तेषां चतुर्थविकारत्वमुक्तमविकारत्वम्[9]। तथानूयाजेषु प्रथमयोर्मध्ये षडागन्तवः। तेषां त्रयस्त्रयः प्रथममध्यमविकाराः। तथा द्वितीयादीनां त्रयाणां प्रथमविकारत्वमनूदितम्। यज्ञपार्श्वे न वक्तव्यो 'यजे'ति। एष द्वारप्रभृतिषु त्रिषु साधारणेन सिद्धो हि, यद्युच्येताधिको भवेत्। कालभेदाद्यजेत्येतमिच्छन्त्येके ॥ ४.१.२.३९ ॥ **[इति द्वितीयः पटलः]**

१–१. M Ad °व्याज्यानि° ; thus T. **२.** M Ad °पदमाम्ना°. **३.** T °कुर्वन्तो पूर्वं°. **४.** M Ad T कुर्वन्त. **५.** T °णोद्धार°. **६.** M Ad अतोऽपि, [Ad °तोपि विशे° न]. **७.** M Ad चरित. **८.** M Ad शकलदानाद° [Ad नोद]रभिरभिहो°. **९.** M Ad °मुत्तमपि° ; thus T.

ऽत्याक्रम्य ध्रुवामभिघारयत्यनुपूर्वꣳ हवीꣳषि ॥ ४५ ॥ **पृषदाज्यमन्ततः** ॥ ४६ ॥ **नोपभृतꣳ रिक्ता हि सा भवति** ॥ ४७ ॥ **आज्यभागौ यजति** ॥ ४८ ॥ **वार्त्रघ्नावाज्यभागौ** ॥ ४९ ॥ 'अग्नयेऽनुब्रूहि' **इत्याहोपस्तृणानोऽवद्यन्** ॥ ४.१.२.५० ॥ **[इति द्वितीयः पटलः]**

'अग्नयेऽनुब्रूहि' **इत्याहोपस्तृणानोऽवद्यन्** ॥ १ ॥ 'अग्निमूर्धा' **इत्यन्वाह** ॥ २ ॥ 'भुवः' **इति यजति** ॥ ३ ॥ **वषट्कृते जुहोति** ॥ ४ ॥ 'सोमायानुब्रूहि' **इत्याहोपस्तृणानोऽवद्यन्** ॥ ५ ॥ 'त्वं नः सोम विश्वतः' **इत्यन्वाह** ॥ ६ ॥ 'या ते धामानि' **इति यजति** ॥ ७ ॥ **वषट्कृते जुहोति** ॥ ८ ॥ 'सवित्रेऽनुब्रूहि' **इत्याहोपस्तृणानोऽवद्यन्** ॥ ९ ॥ 'तत्सवितुर्वरेण्यम्' **इत्यन्वाह** ॥ १० ॥ 'अचित्ती' **इति यजति** ॥ ११ ॥ **वषट्कृते जुहोति** ॥ १२ ॥ 'सरस्वत्या अनुब्रूहि' **इत्याहोपस्तृणानोऽवद्यन्** ॥ १३ ॥ 'चोदयित्री सूनृतानाम्' **इत्यन्वाह** ॥ १४ ॥ 'पावीरवी' **इति यजति** ॥ १५ ॥ **वषट्कृते जुहोति** ॥ १६ ॥ 'पूष्णेऽनुब्रूहि' **इत्याहोपस्तृणानोऽवद्यन्** ॥ १७ ॥ 'पूषा गा अन्वेतु नः' **इत्यन्वाह** ॥ १८ ॥ 'शुक्रं ते अन्यद्' **इति यजति** ॥ १९ ॥ **वषट्कृते जुहोति** ॥ २० ॥ 'मरुद्भ्योऽनुब्रूहि' **इत्याहोपस्तृणानोऽवद्यन्** ॥ २१ ॥ 'मरुतो यद्धवो दिवः' **इत्यन्वाह** ॥ २२ ॥ 'या वः शर्म' **इति यजति** ॥ २३ ॥ **वषट्कृते जुहोति** ॥ २४ ॥ 'विश्वेभ्यो देवेभ्योऽनुब्रूहि' **इत्याहोपस्तृणानो-ऽवद्यन्** ॥ २५ ॥ 'विश्वे देवा ऋतावृधः' **इत्यन्वाह** ॥ २६ ॥ 'विश्वे देवाः शृणुतेमꣳ हवं मे' **इति यजति** ॥ २७ ॥ **वषट्कृते जुहोति** ॥ २८ ॥ 'द्यावापृथिवीभ्यामनुब्रूहि' **इत्याहोपस्तीर्णाभिघारित-मेककपालमादधानः** ॥ २९ ॥ 'द्यावा नः पृथिवी इमम्' **इत्यन्वाह** ॥ ३० ॥ 'प्र पूर्वजे' **इति यजति** ॥ ३१ ॥ **वषट्कृते जुहोति** ॥ ३२ ॥ 'अग्नये स्विष्टकृतेऽनूब्रूहि' **इत्याहोपस्तृणानो-ऽवद्यन्** ॥ ३३ ॥ **सकृत्सकृदुत्तरार्धात् सर्वेषाꣳ हविषामवद्यति** ॥ ३४ ॥ **आशयादेककपालस्या-वदाय द्विरभिघारयति** ॥ ३५ ॥ **न प्रत्यनक्ति** ॥ ३६ ॥ **गायत्रियौ संयाज्ये** ॥ ३७ ॥ 'अग्निꣳ स्तोमेन बोधय' **इत्यन्वाह** ॥ ३८ ॥ 'स हव्यवाड्' **इति यजति** ॥ ३९ ॥ **वषट्कृते जुहोति** ॥ ४० ॥ **अत्याक्रम्य यथायतनꣳ स्रुचौ सादयित्वा प्राशित्रमवद्यति** ॥ ४१ ॥ **अप उपस्पृश्येडामवद्यति** ॥ ४२ ॥ **उपहूतायामिडायामग्नीध आदधाति** ॥ ४३ ॥ **प्राश्नन्ति** ॥ ४४ ॥ **मार्जयन्ते** ॥ ४५ ॥ **परिहरन्ति ब्रह्मणे** ॥ ४६ ॥ **प्राशिते प्राशित्रे चरौ यजमानभागं प्रास्योद्वासयन्ति हवीꣳषि** ॥ ४७ ॥ **अन्वाहार्ये वाचयति** ॥ ४८ ॥ **आसादयन्ति वाजिनम्** ॥ ४९ ॥ **सन्ततिमन्वष्टौ विष्टम्भान्वारोहान् जुहोति**

विकल्पिता एककपालधर्मा आग्रयणेष्ट्यां दृष्ट्य इहापि तुल्याः । तथाह्यनुमन्त्रणमत्र । मिथो हि तेषां तन्त्रे प्राप्तिरुक्ता । हविषां तन्त्राणां चोच्चैरुपांशुता[१] विध्यवशेषादागमयितव्येति ॥ २९ ॥

सान्नाय्यविकारत्वाद्वाजिनस्य श्रोण्योरन्यतरस्यामासादनम् । श्रुत्यन्तरे 'उत्करे वाजिनमासादयती'ति वचनमस्ति ॥ ४९ ॥

विष्टम्भान्वारोहाः स्रुवेण हूयन्ते । प्रसंगाद्धवनद्रव्यमाज्यं सर्वत्रानादेशे[२] । तत्रोत्पन्नेष्वपूर्व[२]मि-

---

१. M °चोच्चै...शुता. **२-२.** M सर्वत्रानादे...पन्ने.

'असवे स्वाहा' **इति** ॥ ४.१.३.५० ॥ **[इति तृतीयः पटलः]**

'असवे' **स्वाहा,** 'वसवे' **स्वाहा,** 'विभुवे' **स्वाहा,** 'विवस्वते' **स्वाहा इति विष्टभ्भाः,** 'मधवे' **स्वाहा,** 'माधवाय' **स्वाहा,** 'शुक्राय' **स्वाहा,** 'शुचये' **स्वाहा इत्यन्वारोहाः** ॥ १ ॥ 'एहि यजमान' **इत्युक्त्वाऽन्वारब्धे यजमाने होतुराहुतिं नवमीं जुहोति** ॥ २ ॥ 'ब्रह्मन् प्रस्थास्यामः' **इति** ॥ ३ ॥ **पृषदाज्येन नवानूयाजान् यजति** ॥ ४ ॥ **आगत्य वाजवतीभ्याꣳ स्रुचौ व्यूहति** ॥ ५ ॥ **शंयुना प्रस्तरपरिधि संप्रकिरति** ॥ ६ ॥ **अप उपस्पृश्यानाज्यलिप्तायाꣳ स्रुचि बर्हिषि विषिञ्चन् वाजिनमानयति** ॥ ७ ॥ **वाजिभ्योऽनुब्रूहि इत्याहोपतिष्ठन्नध्वर्युः** ॥ ८ ॥ 'वाजेवाजेऽवत वाजिनो नः' **इत्यन्वाह** ॥ ९ ॥ 'शन्नो भवन्तु वाजिनः' **इति यजति** ॥ १० ॥ **वषट्कृते जुहोति** ॥ ११ ॥ **ऊर्ध्वज्ञुरेतस्यानुवषट्करोति** ॥ १२ ॥ 'वाजिनस्याग्ने वीहि' **इति दिशो जुहोति** ॥ १३ ॥ **भक्षमुच्छिनष्टि** ॥ १४ ॥ 'तस्य भक्षस्य स्वादोरभक्षि=सञ्चरन्ति' **इति होता प्रथमो भक्षयत्यथाध्वर्युरथ ब्रह्माऽथाग्नीदथ यजमानः** ॥ १५ ॥ **प्राणैस्ते भक्षयन्ति** ॥ १६ ॥ **प्रत्यक्षाद् भक्षो यजमानस्य** ॥ १७ ॥ **प्रेत्य पत्नीः संयाजयन्ति** ॥ १८ ॥ **फलीकरणहोमं हुत्वा प्राडेत्य त्रीणि समिष्टयजूꣳषि जुहोति** ॥ १९ ॥ 'यज्ञ यज्ञं गच्छ=सुवीरः स्वाहा' **इति स्रुवेण हुत्वा ध्रुवामाप्याय्य** 'देवा गातुविदो' **इति स्रुचा जुहोति।** '°गातुं वित्त्वा=वाते धाः' **इति** ॥ २० ॥ **सꣳस्थामनु हविषो निवर्तयते** ॥ २१ ॥ **तस्यैते संभारा उपक्लृप्ता भवन्ति त्रेणी च शलली लोहितायसं च क्षुरः कंसश्च हिरण्यं च शराश्चापश्च** ॥ २२ ॥ **यजमानायतने शरानुपस्तृणीते** ॥ २३ ॥ **तेषूपविशति यजमानः प्रागावृत्त उपस्थं कृत्वा** ॥ २४ ॥ **कꣳसे हिरण्यमवधायाप आनयति** ॥ २५ ॥ **शलल्योपसंगृह्य लोहितायसेन क्षुरेण प्रवपति** ॥ २६ ॥ 'ऋतमेव परमेष्ठी' **इति वाचयति।** '°ऋतं नात्येति

त्युक्तम्। अच्छिद्रिकोपादानेऽनाज्ञाताहुत्यनन्तरं[1] हूयते अत्याक्रम्य ॥ ४.१.३.५० ॥ **[इति तृतीयः पटलः]**

वाजिनचर्याशेषं कंसादावानीय भक्षयितृक्रमेण समुपहूय भक्षयन्ति ॥ १५ ॥

उत्तमे समिष्टयजुषि यथाप्रकृति बर्हिरक्त्वाऽनुप्रास्यति[2] ॥ १९ ॥

त्रिसंख्ययापि[3] संस्रावाभिहोमं निवर्तयति[3] ॥ २१ ॥

अतुल्यत्वात् त्रिषु प्रदेशेषु[4] यस्याः श्वैत्यं[5] सा त्रेणी[6]। शलली श्वाविड्लोम[7]। लोहितायसस्ताम्रमयः[8]। तासामपामेकदेशेनान्ते क्लेदयति ॥ २२ ॥

शलल्या विभज्य तया सह गृहीत्वा वपते[9] वापयति च[9]। पुरस्तादग्रे[10] वपते श्मश्रूणि। अथ दक्षिणतो दक्षिणमुपपक्षमथ पश्चादधस्ताच्छीर्षण्यानामथोत्तरमुपपक्षमथ मध्ये शिरोऽथवा शिरोलिङ्ग

---

१. M Ad °हुत्यान°. २. M प्रस्यति. ३–३. M त्रिस्संख्या वि संस्रभिहे...तर्यति, Ad त्रिस्संख्यवि सं° भिहोमं न नि°, T त्रिसंख्यापि. ४. M Ad प्रादेश°; thus T. ५. M Ad; thus T यस्याश्चैत्यं. ६. Ad श्रोणी, T त्र्ये°; thus M. ७. M Ad श्चाविड्लोम; thus T. ८. M Ad °तायस्ताम्र°. ९–९. M Ad om; thus T. १०. M Ad om.

किञ्चन ऋतेन पृथिवी दृढा उष्णिहा शिर आक्रान्तमुष्णिहा शिर आक्रमीत्। अग्निस्तिग्मेन शोचिषा वैश्वानरस्य तेजसा। ऋतेन त्वा निवर्तये सत्येन परिवर्तये शिवेन त्वोपवर्तये। तदृतं तत्सत्यं तद्व्रतं तच्छकेयं तेन शकेयं तेन राध्यासम्' **इति** ॥ २७ ॥ **पुरस्तादग्रे वपतेऽथ दक्षिणतोऽथ पश्चादथोत्तरतोऽथ मध्ये** ॥ २८ ॥ **सꣳस्थामनु हविषः प्रसिद्धम्** ॥ २९ ॥ **पौर्णमासेन हविषा यजते** ॥ ३० ॥ **देवव्रतानि चरति** ॥ ३१ ॥ **नानृतं वदति** ॥ ३२ ॥ **न माꣳसमश्नाति** ॥ ३३ ॥ **न स्त्रियमुपैति** ॥ ३४॥ **नास्य पल्पूलनेन वासः पप्पूलयन्ति** ॥ ३५ ॥ **अधःशाय्यमृन्मयपाय्यशूद्रोच्छिष्टी** ॥ ३६ ॥ **स्वयं पादौ प्रक्षालयते** ॥ ३७॥ **भक्ताशी स्यात्** ॥ ३८ ॥ **इति चातुर्मास्ययाजिनः** ॥ ४.१.४.३९ ॥ **[इति चतुर्थः पटलः]**

॥ इति चतुर्थप्रपाठके प्रथमोऽनुवाकः ॥

तूष्णीमेव। पूर्वं श्मश्रूण्युपपक्षौ च प्रोप्य शिरस्येव दिग्विभागेन वपनम्। देशभेदात् प्रतिदिशं मन्त्रावृत्तिरिति केचित्। पुरुषसंस्कारत्वादनावृत्तिर्युक्ता[१]। क्षुद्रहोतर्निंनुवर्तयेद्[२] द्वौ द्वौ प्रतिदिशमित्यनुपदम्॥ २६-२८॥

पौर्णमासनिवर्तनयोः संस्थामनु हविष इति विधानात् समुच्चयासंभवाद्विकल्पः। व्यूहेषु पौर्णमास्यन्ते निवर्तनं वपनम्। अथ समस्ते यथादेशं[३] निवर्तनमन्ते वपनमिति विध्यवशेषः[४] ॥ ३० ॥

इति चातुर्मास्ययाजिनः[५]। इतिशब्दः प्रकारवाची। अन्यान्यपि चातुर्मास्ययाजिनो व्रतानि प्राङ्शेत इत्यादीनि विद्यन्ते॥ ४.१.४.३९ ॥ **[इति चतुर्थः पटलः]**

॥ इति व्याख्यायां चतुर्थप्रपाठके प्रथमोऽनुवाकः ॥

---

१. M °त्वादना...क्षुद्र, Ad °वृत्तिरूक्ता. **२.** M Ad T वर्तये. **३.** M Ad °देशनि°. **४.** M Ad इति after °शेषः. **५.** M चातुर्मास्य...इति.

॥ अथ चतुर्थप्रपाठके द्वितीयोऽनुवाकः ॥

[वरुणप्रघासपर्व]

वरुणप्रघासा एवातः ॥ १ ॥ **तेषाꣳ संभाराश्चतस्रश्च स्थाल्यो द्वयानि च यज्ञायुधानि द्वे च बर्हिर्षी चत्वार इध्मा द्वे च वेदी उत्तरवेदिश्च व्रीहियवाश्चैषीकं च शूर्पꣳ शमीपर्णानि च करीरसक्तवश्च मेष्यै च लोमानि मेषस्य च** ॥ २ ॥ **श्वोऽषाढाभिः पौर्णमासीत्यग्निहोत्रो- च्छिष्टमातच्य निदधाति हविरातञ्चनाय** ॥ ३ ॥ **उत्परेत्य पलाशशाखामाच्छिनत्ति** 'इषे त्वोर्जे

वरुणप्रघासा एवातः। वरुणप्रघासानां साकमेधानां च बहुवचनेनैव चोदना। साकमेधेषु तावदिष्टिबहुत्वाद् युज्यते। अत्रापि करम्भपात्रावभृथापेक्षया[1] स्यात्। नैतदेवं[1], तन्निरपेक्षमेव वचनम्। यद् 'वरुणप्रघासा निरुप्यन्ते', 'वरुणप्रघासान्निर्वपन्ति' इत्यतो नित्यं बहुवचनान्त एष शब्दः, यथा दारादिशब्दाः। एवातः शब्दयोः प्रयोजनं वक्तव्यम्। उच्यते। राजसूयावयवभूतानि चातुर्मास्यानि स्वैर्वैर्धर्मैः सहोत्पन्नानि। तानि पुनः 'प्रजा वै [2]सत्रमासते'त्यनुवाकद्वयेन[2] फलवन्ति निरूह्य विहितानि। तत्र [3]सौत्रामण्यꣳहोमुचयोश्चातुर्मास्यान्तरालेषु[3] क्रियमाणयोः तदवयवत्वात् तदङ्गता मा विज्ञायि। राजसूयावयवा एव तौ। अतो निरूह्येषु वैश्वदेवानन्तरं वरुणप्रघासा एवेति ॥ १ ॥

तेषां वरुणप्रघासानां संभारा वक्ष्यन्ते। चतस्रः[4] स्थाल्यः सान्नाय्यतपन्यः[4]। प्राकृतीभ्यां वैकृत्योः सहाम्नानम्। इमे मारुत्यर्थे, इमे वारुण्यर्थे इति विशेषाश्रयणार्थम्। अथवा प्राकृत्योस्तुल्यजातिभ्यां[5] वैकृत्योस्तुल्यत्वख्यापनार्थम्। किं प्रयोजनम्। पञ्चवर्षादिप्रयोगेष्वाधानोत्पन्नयज्ञायुधवदत्रोत्पन्नानि[6] पदार्थानि[6] नित्यं धार्याणि। तथा यज्ञायुधेषु इध्मानां द्वावग्निप्रहरणार्थौ वेद्योः[7] संभारेषु पाठः पूर्वमेव मानशङ्कूनिहननरज्जुपरिवेष्टनानि कर्तव्यानीति। ऐषीकं शरमयं [8]मुञ्जमयमिषीकामयमित्यन्ये। [9]करीरफलमयाः सक्तवः ॥ २ ॥

[9]श्वोऽषाढाभिरित्याद्युक्तं [10]वैश्वदेवेन प्रसिद्धं प्रज्ञातेन विधिना। केचित् परमप्रकृतिप्रज्ञातं मन्यन्ते। कक्षोपोषणाद्यवचनाद्बर्हिषोऽर्धमिति वाचो [11]युक्तिभेदाच्च। अन्य आह- एतद्ब्राह्मणानीत्यादेर्धर्मातिदेशार्थत्वात्सर्वस्य[12] वैश्वदेवधर्मस्य [13]प्राप्तेर्निर्मन्थ्यपृषदाज्येनेव प्रयाजादीनां[13] दर्शनाच्च वैश्वदेवप्रज्ञातत्वं युक्तम्। तथा[14] दक्षिणस्यापि विहारस्यामिक्षाणां[15] वैश्वदेव्यधर्मप्राप्तेः। अतः प्रसूमयत्रेधासन्नहनादि ग्राह्यमिति। तथा सति ग्रीष्मे कक्षमुपोषति[16]। तथा

१-१. M स्या...न तदेवं, T ° क्षया स्यात् तदेवम्. **२-२.** M सत्र...त्यनुवादकद्वेन. **३-३.** M ° मण्यांहोमुपयो°, Ad ° मण्यां अगुं च होमयो°, T ° मण्यां होमुच उभयोश्चा°. **४-४.** M चतस्रश्च...न्याय्य°, T च। तत्र स्थ्याल्याः. **५.** M Ad ° जातीभ्यां; thus T. **६-६.** M Ad T ° त्पन्नानि...र्थानि[T रार्था°]. **७.** M Ad वेद्याः. **८.** M Ad मुञ्ज[Ad जा]यिषी°. **९-९.** M ° फलमया...ढाभिरि°, Ad शरी°. **१०.** M वैश्व°. **११.** M Ad युक्तिं. **१२.** M ° देश...स...वैश्व. **१३-१३.** M ° र्निर्मन्थ्य...तवप्रयाजादीन्, ° नवप्रयादीन° ; thus T. **१४.** M Ad तथापि. **१५.** Ad विहारः समीक्षा° ; T gives a text from MS ख as क्षान्तराणां. **१६.** M Ad ° मुपौष° ; thus T.

त्वा' **इति** ॥ ४ ॥ **तयाऽऽगत्य** '०वत्सानपाकरोति 'वायवः स्थोपायवः स्थ' **इति** ॥ ५ ॥ 'देवो वः साविता प्रेरयतु' **इति गा अनुमन्त्रयते।** '०श्रेष्ठतमाय=मघ्निया मरुद्भ्यो वरुणाय भागमूर्जस्वतीः पयस्वतीः' **इति** ॥ ६ ॥ **प्रसिध्यति कर्म** ॥ ७ ॥ 'देवस्य त्वा सवितुः प्रसवे' **इत्यसिद-मादायोत्परैति** ॥ ८ ॥ **बर्हिषोऽर्ध्वं प्रसिद्धम्** ॥ ९ ॥ **द्वे बर्हिषी लुनाति यजुषाऽन्यत् तूष्णीमन्यत्** ॥ १० ॥ **ते आहरन्नैति** ॥ ११ ॥ **सायं निर्णिक्तैः पात्रैर्गा प्रतीक्षते** 'एता आचरन्ति मधुमद्दुहानाः' **इति** ॥ १२ ॥ **हुत्वाऽग्निहोत्रꣳ सान्नाय्यं दोहयति** 'बहु दुग्धि मरुद्भ्यो वरुणाय हविः' **इति** ॥ १३ ॥ 'मरुतो वां वरुणः श्रीणन्तु' **इत्येनत् प्रतिष्ठापयति** ॥ १४ ॥ 'मरुतो वां वरुणस्य भागं सोमेनातनच्मि' **इति हविरातञ्चनेनातनक्ति** ॥ १५ ॥ 'अदस्ते स्थो मरुद्भ्यो वां वरुणाय' **इत्युदन्वद्भ्यां पात्राभ्यामपिदधाति** ॥ १६ ॥ 'अग्ने हव्यꣳ रक्ष' **इति ते यत्र गुप्ते मन्यते तन्निदधाति** ॥ १७ ॥ **एवमेव प्रातरग्निहोत्रꣳ हुत्वा सान्नाय्ये दोहयति** ॥ १८ ॥ **नात्र प्रतीक्षते** ॥ १९ ॥

महाहविरादिषु[१]न्यायः ॥ ३ ॥

स्तूष्णीमस्य तातिः । इदं न दक्षिणविहारार्थम्[१] । तथा हि क्वचित् क्वचित् दृश्यते । 'तूष्णीं कर्म प्रतिप्रस्थातुरि'ति। 'प्रसिद्धानि तूष्णीं प्रतिप्रस्थाते'ति। अन्यस्योपगूहनान्तं कृत्वा परिदेशनादि प्रागुद्यमनात्तूष्णीं[२] करोति। उद्यमनाद्यूहेन[३] । अन्य आह–प्रसिद्धमित्युक्त्वा पुनस्तूष्णीमिति वचनात्प्रसिद्धं[४] वान्यतरस्य[४] तूष्णीकत्वं वा इति[५] विकल्पः । अनयैव दृष्ट्या दक्षिणविहारार्थानां सर्वकर्मणां याजुषत्वं [६]तूष्णीकत्वं वा विकल्पत इति। तन्नोपपद्यते। यत्रेच्छति तत्र तूष्णीकत्वं[६] विदधाति। तूष्णीं कर्म प्रतिप्रस्थातुः प्रसिद्धानि। तूष्णीमितीह प्रसिद्धं[७], तूष्णीमन्यदिति विरोधाद्विकल्प इति चेदुत्सर्गापवादन्यायो भविष्यति। अथवा तत्रापि प्रसूमयादिविधानार्थं[८] प्रसिद्धग्रहणम्॥ ९–१० ॥

सायं निर्णिक्तैः[९]=दुहानाः[१०] इति दोहयोः प्रयोगः । आतञ्चननिधानम्। अध्वर्युरेव शाखामाहृत्य वत्सानपाकरोति। कुतः । तन्त्रेण गवानुमन्त्रणवाग्विसर्गप्रतिष्ठापनातञ्चनादीनां दर्शनात्प्रधानकर्त्रैवाङ्ग-न्यपि कर्तव्यानीति वचनादेव क्रियेत। तन्त्रेणैव प्रतीक्ष्याग्निहोत्रं हुत्वा मनसा[११] विभज्य [११]मारुत्यर्थाः पूर्वं दोहयेत्। अङ्गारनिरूहणमनुसमयात्स्थाल्यादानाधिश्रयणदूंहणानि पाणिद्वयेन युगपत् क्रियन्ते[१२], तथा प्रतिष्ठापनादिषु दर्शनात्। पवित्रोद्धानादि प्राग् बहुदुग्धेर्मारुत्याः करोति। तिस्रो दोहयित्वा तदेव पवित्रमादाय तदुद्धानादि। वारुण्या[१३] अपि तिस्रो दोहयति। ततो 'बहु दुग्धी'त्याद्या वाचंयमोऽनन्वारभ्योत्तरा[१४] उभयोर्दोहयति। विप्रुडनुमन्त्रणं तन्त्रम्। संक्षालनं मन्त्रं[१५] विभज्य पाणिद्वयेनानयति। प्रत्येकम् [१६]अपां प्रत्यानयनम्[१६] । आतञ्चनं विभज्यातनक्ति[१७] । प्रातर्दोहान्तमध्वर्युणा

१–१. M न्यायस्तू...ण विहारा°, Ad तूष्णीं दक्षिण°. **२.** M Ad °द्यमाना°. **३.** M Ad °मननाद्यू°. **४–४.** M प्रसिद्ध...न्यतरस्य. **५.** M Ad om. **६–६.** Ad om. **७.** M Ad प्रसिद्धः [M द्ध]. **८.** M Ad °मयाविधा°. **९.** M निर्णी°. **१०.** M Ad दुहना; thus T. **११–११.** M मनसापीह...मारु°. **१२.** M Ad क्रियते. **१३.** M Ad आरुण्या. **१४.** M Ad °त्तरं; thus T. **१५.** M Ad om; thus T. **१६–१६.** M Ad अपो[Ad पां] प्रत्यायनं. **१७.** T °ज्यानक्ति; thus M Ad.

नाभिद्योतयति ॥ २० ॥ नापः प्रत्यानयति ॥ २१ ॥ नातनक्ति संक्षालनान्तम् ॥ २२ ॥ पूर्वेणा-हवनीयं वेदी क्लृप्ते भवतः प्रथमात्रादसंभिन्ने ॥ २३ ॥ उत्तरस्यामुत्तरवेदिः ॥ २४ ॥ तयोः स्तम्ब-यजुषी हरत उत्तरस्या अध्वर्युर्दक्षिणायै प्रतिप्रस्थाता ॥ २५ ॥ नानैव स्फ्यावाददाते ॥ २६ ॥ तूष्णीं

तन्त्रेण क्रियते। अतः परं प्रतिप्रस्थातापि[१] स्वानि[१] कर्माणि करोति ॥ १२-२२ ॥

पूर्वेणाहवनीयं=संभिन्ने। अत्र केचित् पूर्वेणाहवनीयमुत्तरां कल्पयित्वा तां दक्षिणेनान्यां कल्पयन्ति। 'यद् द्वितीयां दक्षिणतो वेदिमुद्धन्ती'त्यस्यार्थमेवं मन्यमानाः तथा सति 'पूर्वेणाहवनीयं वेदी' इति कल्पवचनं विरुध्येत[२]। *श्रुतिवाक्ये तु बाहुसंस्तुतिर्नोपपद्येत। वेद्योरुभयतोभावे बाहु-संस्तुतिरुत्पन्ना भवति। तस्माद् यथासम्भवं पूर्वेणाहवनीयं भवतः। प्रथमात्रं त्रयोदशाङ्गुलम्। तत्तूक्तं— 'प्रथोत्तरयुगे त्रयोदशके' इति। मिथस्त्रयोदशाङ्गुलापसृते। उभयोर्विशेषानाश्रवणाद् दक्षिणापि पाशुक्येव। अनुपदकारस्तु सन्नतां दक्षिणामाह। तथा यज्ञपार्श्वे—

[३]दार्शिकी दक्षिणा वेदिः पाशुकी चोत्तरोच्यते।
आयामतः समे च[४] स्तां वेदी[५] बाहू इति श्रुतेः॥' इति

सा यदि सन्नता स्याच्छ्रोण्योरंसयोरिति प्रथमात्रादसम्भेदः ॥ २३ ॥

स्तम्बयजुषोर्हरणे प्रतिप्रस्थातोत्तरां वेदिमग्रेण। सरस्वत्या चोक्तम्—

'अग्रेणैवोत्तरामग्निं प्रतिप्रस्थातृसञ्चरः।
अपरेणापि वा वेदिं हविषां चापि सञ्चरः ॥' इति ॥[६]

समान उत्करो यद्यग्रेण स्यात् प्रदक्षिणमावृत्योत्करे निबाधते। अथवाऽपसलैरावृत्य निबाधते। तमध्वर्युः परिगृह्णाति। यद्यपरेणाध्वर्युः परिगृह्णाति, तयोर्वेद्योः स्तम्बयजुषी हरतस्तूष्णीं कर्म प्रति-प्रस्थातुरिति ॥ २५ ॥

किं स्फ्यादानमात्रस्य तूष्णीकत्वं विधीयते, नेत्याह। तथा हि कर्मग्रहणानर्थक्यं स्यात्। अतः स्तम्बयजुर्हरणस्य। अन्य आह—अस्मिन् प्रकरणे सर्वस्य प्रतिप्रस्थातृविषयस्य कर्मण इति। तूष्णीं कर्म

१-१. M Ad विन्धानि. **२.** M ° ध्येते, Ad ° ध्यते. ***.** The text beginning with श्रुतिवाक्ये तु [comm. on ४.२.१.२३] and ending with जातीयानि कर्त... [comm. on ४.२.१.२८] missing in M and Ad both. However, this missing text has been given in T from p.162, line.17 to p.164, line.12. T notices this in the fn 5 as : '162 पु. 17 पं श्रुतिवाक्ये +164 पु. 12 पं जातीयानि कर्त° इति पर्यन्तं नास्ति'. But the text at the end is repeated. As a matter of fact, the text at the end is missing upto (तुल्यजाती)यानि not (कर्तव्)यानि as given in T. Because of this misunderstanding the text has been repeated at the end. **३.** T ...दाशी दक्षि°. **४.** T gives a reading of MS क as 'चा'. **५.** T ख वेदि. **६.** T om इति.

कर्म प्रतिप्रस्थातुः ॥ २७ ॥ **यदेवाध्वर्युः करोति तत्प्रतिप्रस्थाता करोतीति ब्राह्मणम्** ॥ २८ ॥ **वेदी परिगृह्णीतः** ॥ २९ ॥ **करणं जपति** ॥ ३० ॥ **योयुपित्वाऽवस्कभ्य संप्रेष्यति** 'प्रोक्षणीरासादयत-मिध्माबर्हिषी उपसादयतः स्रुवौ च स्रुचश्च संमृष्टं पत्नीः सन्नह्याज्याभ्यामुदेतं पृषदाज्याय दध्याहरेहि यजमानाग्नीदुत्तरवेद्या उप सीद' **इति** ॥ ३१ ॥ **उत्तरवेदिं निवपति** ॥ ३२ ॥ **इध्मा-**

प्रतिप्रस्थातुरिति। तस्माद्यत्र वचनं तत्र तूष्णीम्' अन्यत्र समन्त्रकम्॥ २७॥

तथा 'यदेवाध्वर्युः करो=ब्राह्मणमि'ति ब्रुवत आचार्यस्याभिप्रायः। उभाभ्यां क्रियमाणं कर्म कालैक्यादेकेनाप्युच्चारितो मन्त्रः प्रकाशयितुं शक्नोति। अतस्तूष्णीकत्वमुपपद्यत इति। तथा च बर्हिःसंभरणाज्यग्रहणयोः प्रसिद्धग्रहणेन प्राप्तानां मन्त्राणां प्रतिषेधार्थं तूष्णीं ग्रहणं करोति। तथा सति 'विमिमित्वा' इत्यादिषु वेद्याद्यभिधायकेषु द्विवत् प्रयोगः प्राप्नोति। स च नोपपद्यते। असम्भवे हि प्रकृतिपाठोपमर्दः। अत्र पुनरुभाभ्यां मन्त्रे प्रयुज्यमाने स्वानि स्वानि द्रव्यादीनि प्रकाश्यन्ते। अत ऊहानुपपत्तिः। किन्तु परसम्बोधनार्थाः प्रैषादय एकेनैव प्रयोक्तव्याः। तथा च 'स्रुवौ स्रुचः संमृड्ढि। अग्नीदग्नी त्रिस्त्रिः संमृड्ढि' इति दृश्यते। तथा [1]चानुपदकार आह—'अध्वर्योरेव[1] प्रतिवचना-श्रावणसंवादसंप्रैषा यौगपद्य एव[2] तूष्णीं कर्म प्रतिप्रस्थातु'रिति। तस्माद् यत्र वचनं तत्र तूष्णीम्, अन्यत्र समन्त्रकम्। ब्राह्मणग्रहणं प्रदर्शनं चोभाभ्यां युगपत् तुल्यजातीयानि *कर्तव्यानि। न पर्यायेणेति बोधयितुम्॥ २८॥

वेदिपरिग्रहणादि मन्त्रवदेव॥ २९॥

तस्याप्यध्वर्युरेव करणं जपति। ऊहेन पृथगग्नीप्रणयतोऽनुख्यातिहोमोऽध्वर्योरेव[3]। तेनैव संप्रैष ऊहेन वक्तव्यः[4]। अन्य आह—अग्निविषय ऊहो नोपपद्यते। एको ह्ययमाहवनीयो विभज्याहितः। नह्येकं कपित्थं द्विधा त्रिधा वा विभक्तमेकत्वं[5] जहात्येकं फलवदित्येव व्यवहरन्ति। तदभिधीयते विभक्तस्यैकस्मिन् सर्षपमात्रेऽप्यवयवेऽग्निशब्दः परिसमाप्यते। प्रत्येकतो ह्याहवनीयकार्यापत्तिः। इतरथाऽऽहवनीये यागः कृतो न भवति। कपित्थावयवत् समस्तस्य कार्यं कर्तुं न शक्नोति। कपित्थाकृतिश्चावयवेन परिसमाप्यते। अत उपपन्नानां[6] वैषम्याच्चोह एवोपपद्यते। तथा चाचार्यप्रवृत्तिः 'अग्नीदग्नी त्रिस्त्रि'रिति। अग्निप्रणयनीयाग्निमन्थनीयसामिधेनीनामनूहत्वं यज्ञपार्श्वेषूक्तम्—

'सामिधेन्यस्त्वनूह्याः स्युर्नर्चमूहेदिति श्रुतेः।

अग्नेः प्रणयनीयाश्च मन्थनीयास्तथैव च॥' इति।

[7]कविर्यज्ञस्ये'त्यध्वर्युरेव वाचयत्यूहेन। [8]व्याघारणाद्युत्तरवेदिसंयुक्तं प्रतिप्रस्थातुर्नास्ति॥ ३०॥

१-१. M Ad तथा...हाध्वर्यो°. **२.** M Ad एतेष्वेव. **३.** M Ad °ध्वर्युं ; thus T. **४.** M Ad वक्तव्यम् **५.** M Ad °मेकं. **६.** M उप...ना...वषभ्या°, Ad उपवर्णनावै°. **७.** M कविर्यज्ञ..ध्वयुरेव; thus Ad T. **८.** M Ad व्याघर°.

वादीपयतः ॥ ३३ ॥ उपयमनीरुपकल्पयतः ॥ ३४ ॥ अग्नेरावृताऽग्नी प्रहरतः ॥ ३५ ॥ प्रसिध्यति कर्माऽतिमुक्तिभ्यः ॥ ३६ ॥ अतिमुक्तीर्हुत्वा यज्ञायुधानि संसाद्यापः प्रणीय वरुणप्रघासान् निर्वपति, आग्नेयमष्टाकपालम् ऐन्द्राग्नमेकादशकपालं मारुतीमामिक्षां वारुणीमामिक्षां

उभयोरतिमुक्तिहोमः ॥ ३६ ॥

यज्ञायुधानीत्यादि तन्त्रप्रक्रमः । अत्र केचिदातञ्चननिधानात्पूर्वमेवाभ्याधानान्वाधाने त्रिषु कृत्वोत्पन्न औत्तरवेदिके[१] तस्मिन् कुर्वन्ति । अन्य एकं कर्माऽन्वाधानात्[२] । तस्यान्यैर्व्यवधानं नोपपद्यते । उत्पन्न एवौत्तरवेदिके सर्वेषु कर्तव्येन पूर्वमिति । अन्ये शालामुखीये कृतं [३]विधारणं देवतापरिग्रहणं च । तस्मादुत्पन्नयोरपि कृतो भवतीति वर्णयन्ति । मध्यमः पक्षो युक्त इवाभाति । दक्षिणाग्नौ [४]प्रतिप्रस्थाताऽभ्यादधातीतरेष्वध्वर्युः । परिस्तीर्य यथोक्तं यज्ञायुधानि संसादयतः[५] । मेषयोर्धर्मत्वे[६] प्रतिप्रस्थात्रा यवयुक्तानि कृष्णाजिनशम्योलूखलदृषदुपलवर्जानि[७] साद्यन्ते । तेषां हि तन्त्रताविभवात् । वरुणप्रघासशब्दवाच्येष्वनुक्रमणादुत्पत्तिवाक्ये[८] मेषी च मेषश्च भवत इति । देवतासंबन्धविरहितयोः श्रवणात् कल्पे च मेषं च मेषीं च करोतीति । करंभपात्रैस्तुल्यवन्निर्देशादपूर्वतां मन्यते । प्रदाने देवतासम्बन्धदर्शनान्मारुत्यामिक्षा भवति वारुण्यामिक्षेति । अतो देवतासंबन्धं यथासम्भवं[९] यथासंख्येनानुवर्त्य[१०] मारुती मेषी वारुणो मेष इति देवतासंबन्धं कृत्वा सधर्मकत्वं कल्पयन्ति । अयं पक्ष आचार्यस्यानभिप्रेतइव लक्ष्यते । सधर्मकत्वे ऐन्द्राग्नविकारत्वादेकादशकपालानि सादयति[११] प्रतिप्रस्थाता, अध्वर्युरप्यष्टौ वारुणस्य । उभयार्थं यवान्[१२] पृथङ् निधत्तः । व्रीहियवयोः[१३] प्रकृतितः [१३]प्राप्तेस्तुल्यत्वादिह विशेष-वचनभावात्प्रयोगसौकर्यार्थं यवमयानि सर्वाणि हवींषि स्युः । उक्तं च यज्ञपार्श्वे—

'करंभपात्राणि तु मेषमेष्यौ धानाश्च मन्थश्च[१४] यवैः क्रियन्ते ।
यावानि सर्वाणि हवींषि वा स्युर्यानि प्रघासे पितृयज्ञ एव' ॥ इति ।

प्रतिप्रस्थाता [१५]मेष्यर्थं प्रणीताः[१५] प्रणयति । ब्रह्मन्निति प्रैषमध्वर्युरेवोहेन वदति । सर्वत्रैवमेव यौगपद्येषु प्रैषेषु न्यायः । धूर्मन्त्रमध्वर्युरेव वाचयति । इतरोऽपि स्वेषु पवित्रमधिनिदध्यात् । उभौ वाचयतः यजमानस्तन्त्रेण वदति । एष एव [१६]सर्वेषु न्यायो यौगपद्येषु[१६] वाचनेषु । ऐन्द्राग्ने निरुप्ते मेष्यर्थं यवान्[१७] प्रतिप्रस्थाता निर्वपति, ततोऽध्वर्युर्वरुणाय । तत एककपालाय व्रीहीन् । शमीपर्णकरीराणि च केचिन्निर्वापादिना संस्कुर्वन्ति, न कथंचित्तेषां देवतासंबन्धो लभ्यते । 'शमीपर्णान्युपवपती'ति[१८] हि चोद्यन्ते । सौम्यानि वै करीराणीत्यपि भक्तिवादः । आमिक्षा देवताभ्यां हि प्रदीयन्ते । प्राणग्रहादीन्[१९]

---

१. M Ad उत्तर° ; thus T. २. M एकं...ाधानात्; T ° धानम् ३. T हि धार° . ४. M Ad प्र...ाभ्या° . ५. M Ad ° यन्तो. ६. M Ad T ° मेषयोधर्म. ७. Ad ° वर्ज्यानि. ८. M Ad ° मणामुत्प° . ९. M Ad om. १०. M ° सं...नुवर्त्य; thus T. ११. M सायन्ति Ad ° यन्ति. १२. T यथापृ° . १३-१३. M व्रीहियवोः प्र...प्राप्ते° . १४. M Ad मन्थय° . १५-१५. M प्रस्थाता...र्थं प्रणीताः. १६-१६. M सर्वेऽन्य...यौग° ; Ad सर्वे न्याय्यो. १७. M Ad यावत् १८. M शमी...वप° . १९. M Ad ° ग्रहादिना; thus T.

कायमेककपालम् ॥ ३७ ॥ निरुप्ते प्राणग्रहाꣳश्च पृश्नीꣳश्च व्याचष्टे ॥ ३८ ॥ तस्य हविष्कृता वाचं विसृज्य पञ्चहोतारमाहवनीये जुहोति ॥ ३९ ॥ यवानां पाकपेष्याणां प्रतिपूरुषं करंभपात्राणि करोत्येकमतिरिक्तम् ॥ ४० ॥ एषु पञ्चमेषु कुशोर्णानि श्लेषयति मेष्यै च लोमानि ॥ ४१ ॥ मेषे कुर्वन्ति ॥ ४२ ॥ इषीकꣳ शूर्पꣳ श्रयन्ते हवीꣳषि ॥ ४३ ॥ आमिक्षे कुरुतः ॥ ४४ ॥ शृतयोर्वा दधिनी आनयतो दध्न्योर्वा शृते ॥ ४५ ॥ शृतेषु हविःषु स्फ्यावाददाते ॥ ४६ ॥ 'ब्रह्मन्नुत्तरौ परिग्राहौ परिग्रहीष्यावः' इति प्रसूतावुत्तरौ परिग्राहौ परिगृह्णीतः ॥ ४७ ॥ योयुपित्वाऽवस्कभ्य संप्रेष्यति 'प्रोक्षणीरासादयतमिध्माबर्हिषी उपसादयतꣳ स्रुचौ च स्रुचश्च संमृष्टं

अध्वर्युरेव । कपालयोगादिभेदेन यवानामवहननादिव्यावर्तनान्तमेकेन सह क्रियते । कर्तृभेदाद्भेदेनेत्येके । ये [१]पुनः कृष्णाजिनादीनां [१]भेदमिच्छन्ति तेषां वक्तव्यं नास्ति । अधर्मकपक्षे परिस्तीर्य स्वमग्निं वेदस्य वेदिकरणात्पूर्वमेव कृतत्वात् प्रतिप्रस्थाता[२] स्फ्यमग्निहोत्रहवण्याकृतिकं[३] प्रोक्षणीपात्रं[३] स्रुवं चाज्यस्थालीमामिक्षापात्रं वेदमिति संसाद्य पवित्रे आदाय हस्तौ[४] मार्जयित्वा [५]प्रोक्षणीपात्रमादाय प्रोक्षणीः संस्कृत्य स्वानि[६] पात्राणि प्रोक्ष्य स्वक्रमे पयोऽधिश्रित्य तप्ते दध्यानीयामिक्षां कृत्वाऽऽज्यं निरुप्याधिश्रित्य पर्यग्निकरोति ॥ ३७ ॥

पञ्चहोतारमध्वर्युरेव जुहोति ॥ ३९ ॥

यवानां पाकपेष्याणा=रिक्तम्[७] । पाकार्थं पेष्याणां यवप्राये देशेऽन्तर्वेद्यादौ[८] ... सक्तुप्राय आहारो नान्यसक्तवः क्रियन्ते । तदपेक्षया पेष्याणां पिष्यानां । कृत्वेत्यत्र कथं कुर्वन्ति । त एव प्रष्टव्याः । प्रतिपूरुषं यावन्तो गृह्यास्तेषामेकैकमित्यर्थः । के पुनर्गृह्याः गृहे भवाः गृह्याः । यजमानस्तत्पुत्राश्चाविभक्तदायादा भ्रातरश्च । अनुपद उक्तम्—'यावन्तो गृह्या अविच्छिन्नपिण्डास्तेषां[९] प्रतिपूरुषं [९]करम्भपात्राणि कुर्यात् । अस्त्रीणमित्येके'[१०] इति । पाकार्थं पेषणमिति वचनात् तानि कृत्वा पचन्ति । करम्भपात्राणीत्यामिक्षावत्[११] संज्ञा । अतः सक्तुभिरतिरिक्तानि[१२] तानि च[१३] कुर्वन्ति ॥ ४० ॥

मेषयोर्धर्मवत्वे अधिश्रयणकाले[१४] तदाकृती[१४] कृत्वाऽधिश्रयतः धर्मकत्वेऽपि तदाकृतिकौ पचतः । ततोऽभिघार्य लोमान्याश्लेषयति ॥ ४१–४४ ॥

आप्य निनयनान्ते स्फ्यावाददाते ॥ ४५–४६ ॥

प्रोक्षण्यादि प्रैषो मन्त्रान्तरं नोहः । अध्वर्युरेव प्रेष्यति[१५] । प्रतिप्रस्थाता स्फ्यमवस्कभ्य[१६] स्थित्वा[१७]

१–१. M पुन...नादीना. **२.** M Ad om प्रतिप्रस्थाता; thus T. **३–३.** M हवण्या...कं प्रोक्ष°. **४.** M Ad मास्तौ. **५.** M मार्जयित्वा...न्नीपात्र°. **६.** T स्वामिनि; thus M Ad. **७.** M Ad °रिक्तः; thus T. **८.** M देशेऽन्तर्वेद्या ...सक्तुप्रा°, Ad देशोन्त°. **९–९.** M तेषां...करंभ°. **१०.** M Ad T दनिस्त्रीणमि°. **११.** M करंभपात्राणिमित्यमीक्षा–संज्ञा, T °मिक्षासंज्ञा; thus Ad. **१२.** M Ad °भिरितिरिक्ता°. **१३.** M Ad च तानि; thus T. **१४–१४.** M का...कृत्वा°, Ad °कृति कृ°. **१५.** T पेष्यति; thus M Ad. **१६.** M Ad °स्तभ्य; thus T. **१७.** M स्स्थि°, Ad स्थिवा.

पत्नीं सन्नह्याज्याभ्यामुदेतं पृषदाज्याय दध्याहरेहि यजमान' **इति ॥ ४८ ॥ एतत् कुर्वन्ति ॥ ४९ ॥ स्रुवौ च स्रुचश्च संमृष्टः ॥ ५० ॥ आज्यानि गृह्णीतोऽध्वर्युः पृषदाज्यवन्ति प्रसिद्धानि, तूष्णीं प्रतिप्रस्थाता ॥ ५१ ॥ इध्माबर्हिषी प्रोक्षतः ॥ ५२ ॥ वेदी प्रोक्षतः ॥ ५३ ॥ आसन्ने प्रोक्षतः ॥ ५४ ॥ अपो निनीय प्रस्तरौ गृह्णीतः ॥ ५५ ॥ स्तृणीतो बर्हिषी ॥ ५६ ॥ प्राञ्चावुत्सृप्य परिधीन् परिधत्तः ॥ ५७ ॥ समिध आधत्तः ॥ ५८ ॥ परिधिषु वाचयित्वाऽग्नी युङ्क्तः ॥ ५९ ॥ आगत्य तिरश्चीः सादयतः ॥ ६० ॥ तिरश्चीषु प्रस्तरौ ॥ ६१ ॥ प्रस्तरयोः जुह्वौ ॥ ६२ ॥ बर्हिषो-रितरौ ॥ ६३ ॥ अलङ्कुर्वन्त्यनुपूर्वꣳ हवीꣳषि ॥ ६४ ॥ उपस्तीर्णाभिघारिते आमिक्षे उद्धरतः ॥ ६५ ॥ मारुत्यां मेषमवदधाति ॥ ४.२.१.६६ ॥ [इति प्रथमः पटलः (५)]**

मारुत्यां मेषमवदधाति, वारुण्यां मेषीम् ॥ १ ॥ ताभ्याꣳ शमीपर्णानि च करीरसक्तूꣳ-श्चोपकिरतः, परःशतानीतरस्मा एवमितरस्यै ॥ २ ॥ अभिघार्य वाजिनं निदधाति ॥ ३ ॥ समभि-घार्य हवीꣳष्याहरन्ति ॥ ४ ॥ ऐन्द्राग्नादध्वर्युरुत्तरस्यां वेद्याꣳ हवीꣳष्यासादयति ॥ ५ ॥ दक्षिणायां मारुतीं प्रतिप्रस्थाता, वारुणीं च कायं चोत्तरस्यामध्वर्युः ॥ ६ ॥ समासन्नेऽपानग्रहाँश्च पृश्नीꣳश्च व्याचष्टे ॥ ७ ॥ 'ध्रुवा असदन्', 'यन्मे अग्ने' **इति समभिमृश्य पञ्चहोतारं व्याचष्टे ॥ ८ ॥ निर्मन्थ्येन चरति ॥ ९ ॥ अग्नये समिध्यमानायानु वाच आह ॥ १० ॥ सप्तदश सामिधेनी-**

स्फ्यवर्त्मोऽपनिनीय प्रोक्षणीः सादयति। स्फ्योदसनादि च[1] करोत्युत्तरस्याम्। आग्नीध्र एव प्रैषार्थानां[2] कर्ता[2]। तत्प्रकृतावेव व्याख्यातम्। पत्नीसन्नहनादि समिदाधानान्तं पत्नीमन्यतरः कारयति। आज्यावेक्षणं पर्यायेण। तथैव यजमानोऽप्युत्तरस्यामवेक्ष्य दक्षिणायामवेक्षते। सर्वं चैवं पर्यायकार्येषु क्रमः। प्रतिप्रस्थातुः शुद्धाज्यग्रहणं तूष्णीकत्वं च ॥ ४८–४९ ॥

वाचनिकं परिधिष्वध्वर्युरेवोहेन वाचयति ॥ ४.२.१.५९ ॥ **[इति प्रथमः पटलः (५)]**

प्राणग्रहादिना अपानग्रहादि व्याख्यातम् ॥ ७ ॥

उभौ पञ्चहोतारम्। एवमादिष्वेकवचनमविवक्षितम्[3] ॥ ८ ॥

निर्मन्थ्येनाध्वर्युरेव चरति। निर्मथितं विभज्य प्रहृत्याभिजुहुतः[4]। उक्तं तु यज्ञपार्श्वे—

'निर्मन्थ्यञ्चातिमुक्त्याश्च संभाराः पृषदाज्यकम्।

वाजिनञ्चोभयत्र[5] स्युराचार्यास्तूत्तरे विदुः ॥

केचिन्निर्मथितस्याग्नेः विभज्य चरन्ति च' ॥ इति ॥ ९ ॥

अग्नये समिध्यमानायानु[6] वाच आह। योऽग्नये समिध्यमानायानुवक्ता[6] तस्मै होत्र आह। प्राकृतं

---

१. M Ad om; thus T. **२–२.** M Ad °र्थानामकर्त्रा; thus T. **३.** M Ad °ष्वेववचनं वि° ; thus T. **४.** M Ad प्रवृत्याभिजुहो° [M हु]ति; thus T. **५.** Ad °यन्त°; thus M T. **६–६.** M Ad om, T समिध्यमानायानुयाज आह—योऽग्नये समिध्य°.

रन्वाह ॥ ११ ॥ आवाहयन् वाजिनोऽप्यावाहयति ॥ १२ ॥ अनूक्तासु सामिधेनीषु स्रुवाभ्यामाघारावाघारयतः ॥ १३ ॥ अथाह 'अग्नीदग्नी त्रिस्त्रिः संमृड्ढि' **इति ॥ १४ ॥ संमृष्ट उत्तरोऽग्निर्भवत्यसंमृष्टो दक्षिणः ॥ १५ ॥ अथ गत्वा प्रतिप्रस्थाता पत्नीं पृच्छति** 'पत्नि कति ते जाराः' **इति ॥ १६ ॥**'इयन्तः' **इति ह ब्रूयाद्यावन्तः स्युः ॥ १७ ॥ यद्यु न स्युः** 'न सन्ति' **इति ब्रूयात् ॥ १८ ॥ यद्यसंख्येया स्युः इयन्तः कनीयांसः इति पांसूनुद्गृह्णीयात् ॥ १९ ॥ सा यत्सन्तं जारं न प्रब्रूयात् प्रियान् ज्ञातीन् रुध्यात् ॥ २० ॥**'असौ मे जार' **इति निर्दिशेद् यं द्विष्यात् ॥ २१ ॥**'तं वरुणो गृह्णातु' **इति यं द्वेष्टि यजमानस्तं ध्यायति ॥ २२ ॥ तां** 'प्रघास्यान् हवामहे' **इति दक्षिणे–नान्वाहार्यपचनं प्रतिप्रस्थाता पत्नीं नयत्यैषीकेण शूर्पेण करम्भपात्राणि बिभ्रतीम्।** '°मरुतो =सजोषसः' **इति ॥ २३ ॥ आगच्छतो दक्षिणमग्निम् ॥ २४ ॥ उपोत्थायास्या अधि यजमानः करम्भपात्राण्यादत्ते ॥ २५ ॥ शीर्षन्नधि निधाय पुरस्तात् प्रत्यङ् तिष्ठन् पुरोनुवाक्यामन्वाह** 'मो

प्रैषमिति शेषः। होतुरुपलक्षणार्थत्वादेकवचनमविवक्षितम्[१]। तस्मात्संप्रैष[१] ऊह्यत[२] एव। यद्यप्यग्नये समिध्यमानायानुवाचः सामिधेनीरन्वाह होत्र[३] इति संबन्धः स्यात्, तथापि न्यायतः प्राप्तमूहं[४] न निवर्तयितुं शक्नोति[५] ॥ १० ॥

प्रतिप्रस्थाता पत्नीं पृच्छति 'पत्नि कति ते जारा' इति। कति पतयस्ते[६] त्वत्[७]संबन्धिनो जाराः पारदारिकाः। प्रश्नेऽत्र प्लुतिः[८]। प्रश्नेन त्वयं विचार्यत इति। प्रतिवचनेन ज्ञायते किं विद्यन्ते जाराः। विद्यमानेषु[९] तेषां संख्या। अथवा[१०] संख्या विस्मृतेति[१०]। तस्याः[११] प्रतिवचनमुत्तरम् 'इयन्त' इत्यादि ॥ १६–१९ ॥

सा यदि विद्यमानं न ब्रूयात् पतिपुत्रादीनामन्यतमं रुन्ध्यात्। ग्राहयेद् वरुणनेति गम्यते ॥ २० ॥

ततो[१२] विद्यमानेषु संख्यापरिमाणे च ज्ञायेत[१३]। परिमाणं निर्दिश्यामुक इति तेषां नामानि च निर्दिशेत्। ततो यं द्विष्यादिति ब्रुवन् प्रतिप्रस्थाता 'तम्' इत्यस्य पदस्यार्थस्मरणे यजमानस्य द्वेष्यं जारं[१४] स्मरति। अपि वा 'असौ मे जारः' इति निर्दिशेद् यं द्विष्यादिति द्वेष्यं [१४]जारशब्दवाच्यं स्मरति। उपमानादवयवप्रसिद्ध्या वा द्वेष्यो 'जार' इत्युच्यते। अस्मिन् पक्षे तं वरुणो गृह्णात्वित्येतावदेव प्रतिप्रस्थातुः। अन्ये वर्णयन्ति जाराणां मध्ये यं द्विष्यात्तमसौ मे जार इति निर्दिशेदिति ॥ २१–२२ ॥

दक्षिणविहारभवैरिध्मसंनहनैर्दक्षिणमग्निं संमार्ष्टि। यौगपद्येषूत्तरविहारिकानेव धारयन् प्रत्याश्रावयति। अयौगपद्येषु यथास्वम्। अथवा युगपदुभयैः। उभयत्र प्रवरमध्वर्युरेवोहेन वृणीते। तथा होतारं अश्विनाध्वर्यू इत्युभौ। प्रयाजशेषेणाभिघारणे प्रतिप्रस्थातोपभृतमन्तत उपविशति। प्रतिप्रस्थाता

१–१. M °नम...स्मात्सं, Ad कस्मात्सं° ; thus T. **२.** M ऊष्यत. **३.** Ad होतेति. **४.** T ऊहयन्. **५.** M Ad शक्येति. **६.** M Ad पय°. **७.** M Ad om; thus T. **८.** M Ad ऽत्रिप्लुति [M त्वय], T तृप्सति. **९.** M विद्या...षु तोषां. **१०–१०.** M अथवा...तस्य; Ad पि स्मृ°. **११.** M Ad तस्य. **१२.** M Ad ते. **१३.** M Ad ज्ञायते; thus T. **१४–१४.** Ad om; जारं for जारं

षु ण इन्द्र पृत्सु=वन्दते गी:' **इति** ॥ २६ ॥ **उभौ याज्यामिति ब्राह्मणम्** ॥ २७ ॥ 'यद् ग्रामे यदरण्ये' **इति प्रतिप्रस्थाता वाचयति**। '०यत् सभायां=अवयजनमसि स्वाहा' **इति** ॥ २८ ॥ **अनुप्रास्यत्यैषीकꣳ शूर्पम्** ॥ २९ ॥ **तौ** 'अक्रन् कर्म कर्मकृत:' **इति प्रतिप्रस्थाता नयति**। '०सह वाचा=सुदानव:' **इति** ॥ ३० ॥ **प्रतिपरैति पत्नी** ॥ ३१ ॥ **दक्षिणत उपविशति यजमान:** ॥ ३२ ॥ **संमार्ष्ट्यग्नीद्दक्षिणमग्निम्** ॥ ३३ ॥ **स्रुग्भिरुत्तरावाघारावाघारयतोऽसꣳस्पर्शयन्तौ स्रुच:** ॥ ३४ ॥ **अत्याक्रम्य ध्रुवे समज्य सादयित्वा प्रवरं प्रवृणीते** ॥ ३५ ॥ **सीदति होता** ॥ ३६ ॥ **प्रसूतौ स्रुच आददाते** ॥ ३७ ॥ **प्रयाजान् यजतो नवेतरो नवेतर:** ॥ ३८ ॥ 'ओ श्रावय' **इत्याह** ॥ ३९ ॥ 'समिधो यज' **इति** ॥ ४० ॥ 'यज यज' **इति** ॥ ४१ ॥ **चतुर्थेऽर्धꣳ समानीयाष्टमे सर्वꣳ समानयत उपभृत्यध्वर्यु:** ॥ ४२ ॥ **उच्छिनष्टि प्रतिप्रस्थाताऽनुयाजेभ्य:** ॥ ४३ ॥ **प्रयाजानिष्ट्वाऽत्याक्रम्य ध्रुवे अभिघारयत:** ॥ ४४ ॥ **ऐन्द्राग्नादध्वर्युरुत्तरस्यां वेद्याꣳ हवीꣳष्यासादयति** ॥ ४५ ॥ **मारुत्यां मेषम–वदधाति वारुण्यां मेषीम्** ॥ ४६ ॥ **दक्षिणायां मारुतीं प्रतिप्रस्थाताऽभिघारयति, वारुणीं च कायं चोत्तरस्यामध्वर्यु:** ॥ ४७ ॥ **पृषदाज्यमन्तत:** ॥ ४८ ॥ **नोपभृतꣳ रिक्ता हि सा भवति** ॥ ४९ ॥ **आज्यभागौ यजति** ॥ ५० ॥ **वार्त्रघ्नावाज्यभागौ** ॥ ५१ ॥ **उपविशति प्रतिप्रस्थातैन्द्राग्नात्** ॥ ५२ ॥ 'अग्नयेऽनुब्रूहि' **इत्याहोपस्तृणानोऽवद्यन्** ॥ ४.२.२.५३ ॥ **[इति द्वितीय: पटल:** (६)**]**

'अग्नयेऽनुब्रूहि' **इत्याहोपस्तृणानोऽवद्यन्** ॥ १ ॥ **प्रसिद्धा: पञ्चानाꣳ हविषां याज्यापुरोनुवाक्या:** ॥ २ ॥ 'इन्द्राग्निभ्यामनुब्रूहि' **इत्याहोपस्तृणानोऽवद्यन्** ॥ ३ ॥ 'इन्द्राग्नी रोचना दिव:' **इत्यन्वाह** ॥ ४ ॥ 'श्नथद्वृत्रम्' **इति यजति** ॥ ५ ॥ **वषट्कृते जुहोति** ॥ ६ ॥ **दक्षिणायां मारुत्यां प्रतिप्रस्थाता प्रचरति** ॥ ७ ॥ 'मरुद्भ्योऽनुब्रूहि' **इत्याहोपस्तृणानोऽवद्यन्** ॥ ८ ॥ **सकृत् पश्चान्मेष्या अवद्यति सकृदामिक्षायै सकृच्छमीपर्णानाꣳ सकृत् करीरसक्तूनाम्** ॥ ९ ॥ **सर्वां च मेषीमुत्तरेणावदानेनावदत्ते** ॥ १० ॥ **सर्वेषां चैतेषामवद्यति** ॥ ११ ॥ **अभिघारयति** ॥ १२ ॥ **प्रत्यनक्ति** ॥ १३ ॥ 'मरुतो यद्' **इत्यन्वाह** ॥ १४ ॥ 'या व: शर्म' **इति यजति** ॥ १५ ॥ **वषट्कृते जुहोति** ॥ १६ ॥ **उपविशति प्रतिप्रस्थाता** ॥ १७ ॥ **सꣳसर्पति होता** ॥ १८ ॥ **वारुण्या च कायेन चोत्तरस्यामध्वर्यु: प्रचरति** ॥ १९ ॥ 'वरुणायानुब्रूहि' **इत्याहोपस्तृणानोऽवद्यन्** ॥ २० ॥ **एवमेवैतेषामवद्यत्यभि–घारयति प्रत्यनक्ति** ॥ २१ ॥ 'अव ते हेड' **इत्यन्वाह** ॥ २२ ॥ 'उदुत्तमम्' **इति यजति** ॥ २३ ॥ **वषट्कृते जुहोति** ॥ २४ ॥ 'कायानुब्रूहि' **इत्याहोपस्तीर्णाभिघारितमेककपालमादधान:** ॥ २५ ॥ 'कया नश्चित्र आ भुवद्' **इत्यन्वाह** ॥ २६ ॥ 'को अद्य युङ्क्ते' **इति यजति** ॥ २७ ॥ **वषट्कृते जुहोति** ॥ २८ ॥ 'अग्नये स्विष्टकृतेऽनुब्रूहि' **इत्याहोपस्तृणानोऽवद्यन्** ॥ २९ ॥ **ऐन्द्राग्नादध्वर्यु–**

कर्मण उपरमतीत्यर्थ:[१]। वेदिश्रोण्यां संसृप्य होता वेदिश्रोण्यां मध्य उपविशति। 'सीद होतरि'ति नावर्तते। निरसनोपवेशने [२]देशभेदादावर्तते। उत्तरस्यां पुनरुपवेशने नावृत्ति:। शेषकार्याणां साहित्यं वाचनिकम् ॥ ४.२.२.२३–३३ ॥ **[इति द्वितीय: पटल:** (६)**]**

---

१. M Ad °त्यर्थं. **२.** M Ad देशेभे°.

रुत्तरस्यां वेद्याः हविषाः स्विष्टकृतमवद्यति ॥ ३० ॥ **अथ प्रतिगृह्णाति प्रतिप्रस्थात्रे** ॥ ३१ ॥ **तमु स उत्तरां वेदिमाहृत्य मारुत्याः स्विष्टकृतमवद्यति** ॥ ३२ ॥ **वारुण्याश्च कायस्य चोत्तरस्यामध्वर्युः** ॥ ३३ ॥ **आशयादेककपालस्यावदाय द्विरभिघारयति** ॥ ३४ ॥ **न प्रत्यनक्ति** ॥ ३५ ॥ **त्रिष्टुभौ संयाज्ये** ॥ ३६ ॥ 'पिप्रीहि' **इत्यन्वाह** ॥ ३७ ॥ 'अग्ने यदद्य विशो अध्वरस्य होतः' **इति यजति** ॥ ३८ ॥ **वषट्कृते जुहोति** ॥ ३९ ॥ **अत्याक्रम्य यथायतनः स्रुचौ सादयित्वा प्राशित्रमवद्यति** ॥ ४० ॥ **तदुभे वेदी अत्यूह्य सादयति** ॥ ४१ ॥ **अप उपस्पृश्यैन्द्राग्नादध्वर्युरुत्तरस्यां वेद्याः हविषामिडामवद्यति** ॥ ४२ ॥ **अथ प्रतिगृह्णाति प्रतिप्रस्थात्रे** ॥ ४३ ॥ **तमु स उत्तरां वेदिमाहृत्य मारुत्या इडामवद्यति** ॥ ४४ ॥ **वारुण्याश्च कायस्य चोत्तरस्यामध्वर्युः** ॥ ४५ ॥ **उपहूतायामिडायामग्नीध आदधाति** ॥ ४६ ॥ **प्राश्नन्ति** ॥ ४७ ॥ **मार्जयन्ते** ॥ ४८ ॥ **परिहरन्ति ब्रह्मणे** ॥ ४९ ॥ **प्राशिते प्राशित्रे चरौ यजमानभागं प्रास्योद्वासयन्ति हवींःषि** ॥ ५० ॥ **अन्वाहार्ये वाचयति** ॥ ५१ ॥ **आसादयन्ति वाजिनम्** ॥ ५२ ॥ **सन्ततिमन्वष्टौ विष्टम्भान्वारोहान् जुहोति** 'मलिम्लुचाय स्वाहा', 'सागराय स्वाहा', 'गणश्रिये स्वाहा', 'अभिभुवे स्वाहा' **इति विष्टम्भाः**; 'नभसे स्वाहा', 'नभस्याय स्वाहा', 'इषाय स्वाहा', 'ऊर्जाय स्वाहा' **इत्यन्वारोहाः** ॥ ५३ ॥ 'एहि यजमान' **इत्युक्त्वाऽन्वारब्धे यजमाने होतुराहुतिं नवमीं जुहोति** ॥ ५४ ॥ 'ब्रह्मन् प्रस्थास्यामः' **इति** ॥ ५५ ॥ **पृषदाज्येन नवानूयाजान् यजत्यध्वर्युर्यदुच्छिनष्टि तेन प्रतिप्रस्थाता** ॥ ५६ ॥ **आगत्य वाजवतीभ्याःस्रुचौ व्यूहतः** ॥ ५७ ॥ **शंयुना प्रस्तरपरिधि संप्रकिरतः** ॥ ५८ ॥ **अप उपस्पृश्यानाज्यलिप्तायां स्रुचि बर्हिषि विषिञ्चन् वाजिनमानयति** ॥ ५९ ॥ 'वाजिभ्योऽनुब्रूहि' **इत्याहोपत्तिष्ठन्नध्वर्युः** ॥ ६० ॥ **प्रसिद्धं वाजिनेन चरति** ॥ ६१ ॥ **दिशो जुहोति** ॥ ६२ ॥ **भक्षमुच्छिनष्टि** ॥ ६३ ॥ **तस्य भक्षस्य** '°सूर्यवर्चा भगभक्तो न आविश विश्वविन्मनसस्पतिरनेहसो मा जागृविः' **इति होता प्रथमो भक्षयत्यथाध्वर्युरथ ब्रह्माऽथाग्नीदथ यजमानः** ॥ ६४ ॥ **प्राणैस्ते भक्षयन्ति** ॥ ६५ ॥ **प्रत्यक्षाद् भक्षो यजमानस्य** ॥ ६६ ॥ **परेत्य पत्नीः संयाजयन्ति** ॥ ६७ ॥ **फलीकरणहोमं हुत्वा प्राङेत्य समिष्टयजूंषि जुहुतस्त्रीणीतरस्त्रीणीतरः** ॥ ६८ ॥ **वारुण्यै निष्कासमितरेषाः हविषां निष्कासान्**

विष्टम्भान्वारोहानध्वर्युरेव जुहोति। उभौ होतृशेषं जुहुतः ॥ ५३ ॥

यथासंभवं यजमानोऽन्वारभते। असंभवे पर्यायेण स्रुग्व्यूहनम्। संभवात् पर्यायेणैव। सूक्तवाक आश्रावणप्रेषणे अध्वर्योरेव। सर्वत्रैवं यौगपद्येष्वनुब्रूह्याश्रवणेषु। [1]वाजिनचर्योभयत्रोत्तरस्मिन्नेव इति पूर्वमेवोक्तम्। पृथक् क्रियायामपि समानीय भक्षयन्ति ॥ ५४–६६ ॥

पत्नीसंयाजानां फलीकरणानामाधाराभेदात् तन्त्रत्वम्। यज्ञपार्श्वे उक्तम्—'प्रतिप्रस्थाता न पत्नीः [2]संयाजयेदिति श्रुतिः' इति। तथाऽनुपदे–'अध्वर्योरेव गार्हपत्यान्वाहार्यपचन[3]संयुक्तानि' इति[4] ॥ ६७–६८ ॥

---

१. M °चार्योभ°. २. M Ad संयो°. ३. M Ad वच°. ४. M °युक्तानि.

संभरन्ति ॥ ६९ ॥ **तुषैश्च निष्कासेन चावभृथमवयन्ति** ॥ ७० ॥ **अत्र दशामेखले पर्यस्येते** ॥ ७१ ॥ 'उरुꣳ हि राजा' **इत्येतां त्रिरन्वाह** ॥ ४.२.३.७२ ॥ **[इति तृतीयः पटलः** (७)**]**

'उरुꣳ हि राजा' **इत्येतां त्रिरन्वाह** । '०वरुणश्चकार=विधश्चित्' **इति** ॥ १ ॥ 'शतं ते राजन् भिषजः' **इति यतोऽपः परापश्यति तद्वाचयति** । '०सहस्रमुर्वी गम्भीरा सुमतिष्टे अस्तु मुमुग्ध्य-स्मत्' **इति** ॥ २ ॥ 'अभिष्ठितो वरुणस्य पाशोऽग्नेरनीकमप आ विवेश' **इति बर्हिः प्रास्याभि-जुहोति** । '०अपान्नपात् प्रतिरक्षन्नसूर्यं दमेदमे समिधं यक्ष्यग्ने=न्तः स्वाहा' **इति** ॥ ३ ॥ **चतुर्गृहीतं गृह्णीते** ॥ ४ ॥ **अपबर्हिषश्चतुरः प्रयाजान् यजति** ॥ ५ ॥ **आज्यभागौ यजति** ॥ ६ ॥ **अप्सुमन्ता-वाज्यभागौ** ॥ ७ ॥ 'अग्नयेऽनुब्रूहि' **इत्याहाज्यस्य गृह्णानश्चतुः** ॥ ८ ॥ 'अप्स्वग्ने सधिष्टव' **इति यजति** ॥ ९ ॥ **वषट्कृते जुहोति** ॥ १० ॥ 'सोमायानुब्रूहि' **इत्याहाज्यस्य गृह्णानश्चतुः** ॥ ११ ॥

प्रणीतानिनयनादितन्त्रं परिसमाप्यावभृथस्य तन्त्रप्रक्रमः । अपूर्वोऽवभृथः । निर्गुणयोराज्यभागयोः पुनः श्रवणात् तत्र प्रयाजानूयाजा बर्हिर्वर्जा[१] विधीयन्ते नामधेयेन । तैरङ्गात्[२] पूर्वैः प्रयुक्ता धर्माः प्रवर्तन्ते ।

तत्र प्रयोगः । [३]आहवनीयकार्यापन्नास्वप्सु वेदोपवाजनं[३] कर्तव्यमिति वेदमुत्पादयन्ति केचित् । उपवाजनस्यावज्वलनार्थत्वादर्थलुप्तमित्यन्ये । स्फ्यमग्निहोत्रहवणीं स्रुवं जुहूमाज्यस्थालीमिति सादयित्वा पवित्रे आदाय 'यजमान वाचं यच्छे'त्युक्त्वा 'कर्मणे वामि'ति हस्तौ मार्जयित्वा प्रोक्षणीं[४] संस्कृत्य[४] पात्राणि प्रोक्ष्याज्यं निरुप्याधिश्रित्य पर्यग्निकृत्वा स्फ्येनावस्कभ्य संप्रेष्यति-'स्रुवं च स्रुचश्च संमृढ्याज्येनोदेही'ति । प्रैषार्थावाग्नीध्रः करोति । पत्नीमप्यवेक्षयति । ततोऽध्वर्युरुत्पवनान्तं कृत्वा पवित्रे[५] आहवनीयेऽनुप्रहरति । ततो दम्पती [६]ऊर्णासूत्रमये मेखले पर्यस्येते । वासो दशामये इत्यन्ये । ततस्तुषैश्च निष्कासेन चावभृथमवयन्ति । तुषा ऋजीषादीनां प्रत्याम्नायः । निष्कासः पुरोडाशस्य । तुषाणामत्र प्रतिपत्तिविधानात् प्राकृतं तुषोपवपनं न कुर्वन्ति केचित् । अपरे प्रकृतावपि[७] तुषाणामेकदेशस्यैवोपवपनं[७] कुर्वन्ति । तच्छेषैरवभृथावगमनमिति न निवर्तयन्ति[८] । एतत् सर्वमुपादाय यथोक्तमवभृथमव यन्ति[९] ॥ ४.२.३.७० ॥ **[इति तृतीयः पटलः** (७)**]**

'अग्नेरनीकमि'ति बर्हिःप्रासनमन्त्रः । 'अपान्नपादि'ति सकृद्गृहीतेन जुह्वा बर्हिरभिजुहोति । 'अग्नीदपस्त्रिः समृड्ढी'ति प्रेषितोऽग्नीदपस्त्रिः[१०] संमार्ष्टि । अथवाऽग्निसंमार्गस्यावज्वलनार्थत्वात् त्रिरुपवाजयतीति च ॥ ३ ॥

प्रयाजार्थं चतुर्गृहीतं जौहवैर्मन्त्रैर्गृहीत्वा प्रयाजान् यजति ॥ ४-५ ॥

[११]ध्रुवाकार्यस्याज्यस्थाल्या[१२] क्रियमाणत्वादाज्यभागयोरमन्त्रकं[१२] ग्रहणम् ॥ ६-८ ॥

---

१. M Ad बर्हिर्विधी°. **२.** M Ad °ङ्गापूर्वैः. **३-३.** M Ad °पन्ना ...वेदो°. **४-४.** M प्रो...स्कृत्य, Ad °क्षणी; thus T. **५.** T पवित्र आ°. **६.** M ऊ...येमे°. **७-७.** M प्रकृत ...णामेक°. **८.** M °र्तयन्त्ये, Ad °न्त्यन्ये. **९.** M T °थं यन्ति. **१०.** M °षितेस्त्रि°. **११.** M Ad स्रुवा°; thus T. **१२-१२.** M °स्थाल्या...त्वादाज्य°.

'अप्सु मे सोमो अब्रवीत्' **इत्यन्वाह**। '०अन्तर्विश्वानि=भेषजीः' **इति** ॥ १२ ॥ **जुषाणेनैव यजति** ॥ १३ ॥ **वषट्कृते जुहोति** ॥ १४ ॥ 'वरुणायानुब्रूहि' **इत्याहोपस्तृणानोऽवद्यन्** ॥ १५ ॥ **पश्चाच्च पुरस्ताच्च निष्कासानामवद्यति** ॥ १६ ॥ **अभिघारयति** ॥ १७ ॥ **प्रत्यनक्ति** ॥ १८ ॥ 'इमं मे वरुण' **इत्यन्वाह** ॥ १९ ॥ 'तत्त्वा यामि' **इति यजति** ॥ २० ॥ **वषट्कृते जुहोति** ॥ २१ ॥ 'अग्नीवरुणा-भ्यामनुब्रूहि' **इत्याहोपस्तीर्णाभिघारितान्निष्कासानादधानः** ॥ २२ ॥ 'त्वं नो अग्ने वरुणस्य विद्वान्' **इत्यन्वाह** ॥ २३ ॥ 'स त्वं नो अग्नेऽवमो भवोती' **इति यजति** ॥ २४ ॥ **वषट्कृते जुहोति** ॥ २५ ॥ **चतुर्गृहीतं गृह्णीते** ॥ २६ ॥ **अपबर्हिषो द्वावनूयाजौ यजति** ॥ २७ ॥ 'अवभृथ निचङ्कुण' **इति स्रुचमप्स्वस्यति**। '०निचेरु=कृतम्' **इति** ॥ २८ ॥ 'उरोरा नो देव रिषस्पाहि' **इति बिन्दून् प्रतिसूय** 'सुमित्रा न आप ओषधयः सन्तु' **इति प्राणेनापां भक्षयति**। '०दुर्मित्रा = द्विष्मः' **इति** ॥ २९ ॥ 'सं त्वा विशन्त्वोषधीरुतापः' **इत्यवभृथं संप्रकिरति**। 'यज्ञस्य त्वा=विधेम' **इति** ॥ ३० ॥ 'देवीराप एष वो गर्भः' **इति संप्रकीर्णमनुमन्त्रयते**। '०तं वः सुप्रतीतं=ब्रूताद्' **इति** ॥ ३१ ॥ 'प्रतियुतो वरुणस्य पाशः प्रत्यस्तो वरुणस्य पाशः' **इत्यप्सूत्तरसिचौ न्यस्यतः** ॥ ३२ ॥ 'इदमहं निर्वरुणस्य पाशान्मुच्ये' **इति वासोभ्यामभिनिर्वेष्टयेते** ॥ ३३ ॥ 'उदुत्तमं वरुण पाशमस्मद्' **इति दशामेखले विस्रंसयेते**। '०अवाधमं वि=तये स्याम' **इति** ॥ ३४ ॥ **अभ्यवेत्यान्योऽन्यस्य पृष्टीर्धावतः तौ** ॥ ३५ ॥ 'उद्वयं तमसस्परि' **इति प्रतिप्रस्थातोन्नयति**। '०पश्यन्तो= त्तमम्' **इति** ॥ ३६ ॥ 'एधोऽस्येधिषीमहि' **इत्यौदुम्बरीः समिधः कुर्वाते** ॥ ३७ ॥ **अप्रतीक्षमायन्ति** ॥ ३८ ॥ 'समिदसि तेजोऽसि तेजो मयि धेहि' **इत्याहवनीये यजमानोऽभ्यादधाति** ॥ ३९ ॥ **एवमेव गार्हपत्ये पत्नी** ॥ ४० ॥

उपस्तीर्य समस्तं निष्कासं सकृदेवावदाय द्विरभिघार्याग्नीवरुणौ[1] यजत्यर्धं स्रुवम्[1] ॥ १६-२५ ॥

अनूयाजार्थस्य चतुर्गृहीतस्य यजमानः 'सुवीर्याय' इत्यादिभिरनुमन्त्रयते ॥ २६ ॥

'देवौ यज यजे'ति प्रथमे, यजेत्युत्तरे ॥ २७ ॥

अवभृथं संप्रकिरति तुषान् ॥ ३० ॥

उत्तरसिचावुत्तरीये[2] वाससी वासोभ्यामभि निर्वेष्टयेते ॥ ३२-३३ ॥

निर्गच्छतो[3] दम्पती ॥ ३५ ॥

औदुम्बरीस्तिस्रः समिधः आधत्तो[4] दम्पती ॥ ३७ ॥

समित्सु[5] प्रत्येकं मन्त्र[5] आवर्तते। 'समिदसि' इत्यादयस्त्रयो मन्त्राः। तैः सस्वाहाकारैरादधाति ॥ ३९ ॥

तथा पत्नी तं तमग्निमुपस्थापयति ॥ ४० ॥

१-१. M ०र्याग्नौ वरुण य...स्रुव आनू० , Ad ०थार्याग्नौ वरुणौ यजत्यथ स्रुवं आनू० ; thus T. २. T उरसि०. ३. T ०गच्छन्तौ; thus M Ad. ४. M Ad T आदधाति. ५-५. M समित्सु...कर्मन्त्र; thus Ad T.

'अपोऽन्वचारिषम्' **इत्येनावुपस्थापयति।** '०रसेन=वर्चसा' **इति॥** ४१ ॥ **आगत्यापिसृजति पूर्वमग्निमपरस्मिन्नाहवनीये॥** ४२ ॥ **संस्थामनुहविषो निवर्तयते॥** ४३ ॥ **प्रसिद्धाः संभाराः॥** ४४ ॥ 'यो घर्मः पर्यवर्तयदन्तान्पृथिव्या अनु=अग्निस्तिग्मेन शोचिषा वैश्वानरस्य तेजसर्तेन त्वा निवर्तये सत्येन परिवर्तये शिवेन त्वोपवर्तये। तदृतं तत्सत्यं तद्व्रतं तच्छकेयं तेन शकेयं तेन राध्यासम्' **इति॥** ४५ ॥ **पुरस्तादग्रे वपतेऽथ दक्षिणतोऽथ पश्चादथोत्तरतोऽथ मध्ये॥** ४६ ॥ **सꣳस्थामनु हविषः प्रसिद्धम्॥** ४७ ॥ **पौर्णमासेन हविषा यजते॥** ४८ ॥ **देवव्रतानि चरति॥** ४.२.४.४९ ॥
[इति चतुर्थः पटलः (८)**]**

॥ इति चतुर्थप्रपाठके द्वितीयोऽनुवाकः ॥

अध्वर्युरागत्यापिसृजति पूर्वमग्निमपरस्मिन्नाहवनीये[१]। औत्तरवेदिकमुभौ [२]वा। अपिसर्गः[३] पशावाम्नातः। अवभृथगमनात्पूर्वम् 'आयुर्दा'[४] जुह्वति केचित्। 'आसां'[५] दशमी'मिति सोमसमिष्ट्यजुर्भिस्तुल्यवत् [६]प्रसंख्यानमविनाभावार्थम्। यत्र तानि गच्छन्ति तत्रैवेयमपीत्यन्ये न जुह्वति। नैष्ठ्ययनानि[७] सोमाभिषवनिमित्तानि अतोऽत्र तानि न प्रवर्तन्ते॥ ४२ ॥

संस्थामनुहविष इत्यादि व्याख्यातम्॥ ४.२.४.४७–४९ ॥ **[इति चतुर्थः पटलः** (८)**]**

॥ इति व्याख्यायां चतुर्थप्रपाठके द्वितीयोऽनुवाकः ॥

---

१. M Ad सृ=हवनीये; T सृ...हवनीये. **२.** M Ad औत्तरे वे°. **३.** M Ad T अविसर्गः°. **४.** M Ad आयुर्दा. **५.** M Ad आसन्दश°. **६.** M °वत्प्र...विना°. **७.** Ad नैष्ठ्यमना°.

॥ अथ चतुर्थप्रपाठके तृतीयोऽनुवाकः ॥

[साकमेधपर्व]

[अनीकवतीष्टिः]

श्वः कृत्तिकाभिः पौर्णमासीति यज्ञायुधानि संसाद्यापः प्रणीयाग्नयेऽनीकवते पुरोडाश–मष्टाकपालं निर्वपति साकं सूर्येणोद्यता ॥ १ ॥ **निरुप्ते प्राणग्रहांश्च पृश्नींश्च=दशहोतारं व्याचष्टे** ॥ २ ॥ **तस्यै वार्त्रघ्नावाज्यभागौ** ॥ ३ ॥ 'अग्नयेऽनीकवतेऽनुब्रूहि' **इत्याहोपस्तृणानो–ऽवद्यन्** ॥ ४ ॥ 'भद्रा नो अग्ने' **इत्यन्वाह** ॥ ५ ॥ 'भद्रं ते अग्ने सहसिन्ननीकम्' **इति यजति** ॥ ६ ॥ **वषट्कृते जुहोति** ॥ ७ ॥ **शर्धस्पत्यौ संयाज्ये** ॥ ८ ॥ 'जुष्टो दमूना अतिथिर्दुरोणः' **इत्यन्वाह**। '°इमं नो यज्ञ=भोजनानि' **इति** ॥ ९ ॥ 'अग्ने शर्ध महते सौभगाय' **इति यजति**। '°तव द्युम्नान्युत्तमानि सन्तु। सं जास्पत्यꣳ सुयममा कृणुष्व शत्रूयतामभि तिष्ठा महाꣳसि' **इति** ॥ १० ॥ **वषट्कृते जुहोति** ॥ ११ ॥ **सन्ततिमनु होतुराहुतिं जुहोति** ॥ १२ ॥ **प्रसिध्यति कर्म** ॥ १३ ॥ **सन्तिष्ठत एषेष्टिः** ॥ १४ ॥

[सान्तपनीयेष्टिः]

यज्ञायुधानि सꣳसाद्यापः प्रणीय मरुद्भ्यः सान्तपनेभ्यो मध्यन्दिने चरुं निर्वपति ॥ १५ ॥ **निरुप्ते प्राणग्रहांश्च पृश्नींश्च व्याचष्टे** ॥ १६ ॥ **समासन्नेऽपानग्रहांश्च पृश्नींश्च=**

श्वः[१] *कृत्तिकाभिः=सूर्येणोद्यता*। उद्यत्यादित्ये निर्वपति। द्रव्यदेवतासंबन्धविधिवाक्ये[२] श्रूय–माणो[२] गुणो भवत्यत एष कालो यागस्य। ननूक्तं कल्पवाक्यं न विधायकम्, ब्राह्मणवाक्येन विहित–स्यान्वाख्यानमिति। ब्राह्मणे हि 'यदग्नयेऽनीकवते पुरोडाशमष्टाकपालं निर्वपती'[३]त्यादिना वाक्येन यागं विधाय वाक्यान्तरेण 'साकं सूर्येणोद्यता निर्वपति'[४], साक्षादेवास्मा[४]अनीकानि जनयती'ति निर्वापसंस्कारो विहितः। अतो निर्वापस्य कालेन भवितव्यम्। ब्राह्मणेऽपि द्रव्यदेवतासंबन्धो वाक्य एव क्वचिद् 'अग्नयेऽनीक=णोद्यते'ति विहितम्। तत्र द्वयोर्वाक्ययोः किं बलवदिति विचार्या–ध्यवसायः कार्यः। तुल्यबलत्वे[५] विकल्पः। तुल्यबलत्वं[५] मन्यमानेनानुपदकारेणोक्तम्–[६]'इष्टिनाऽऽदित्यमाकाङ्क्षेत्साकं वा रश्मिभिः प्रचरेदि'ति। तथैव द्वेधा यज्ञपार्श्वे च। अतो विकल्पः[७] अग्निहोत्रं कालात्[८] प्रतिकर्षेद्वोत्कर्षेद्वा[८]। 'अनीकवतेऽग्निहोत्रं सवनकालात्प्रतिकर्षेदि'त्यनुपदम्। क्रैडिनेऽपि समानो[९] विचारः। [९]तत्र प्रतिकर्षं ब्रुवत आचार्यस्यापि प्रतिकर्ष[१०] एवाभिप्रेतः स्यात्। प्रहरणकाले परिधीन् विवर्त्य स्रुक्प्रसवादि[११] प्रतिपद्यते। शरमयं[१२] बर्हिर्यथास्तीर्णमेव शयितव्यम्[१३]। वेदतृणान्येवात्रानुप्रास्यति ॥ १ ॥

---

१. M Ad om; thus T. २–२. M °विधिवा...णो; thus Ad T. ३. T gives a reading from MS ख in the fn as निर्वपेदिती°. ४–४ M निर्व...देववस्मा. ५–५. M °बलत्वे... बलत्वं. ६. M Ad मुष्टिनानित्य°; thus T. ७. M Ad °पि कल्पो. ८–८. M Ad काले; thus T. ९–९. M समा...तत्र, Ad समानो विचार स तत्र. १०. M Ad प्रकर्ष; thus T. ११. M Ad स्रुक्प्रसावा°. १२. M Ad अयं; thus T. १३. M Ad शायि°; thus T.

दशहोतारं व्याचष्टे ॥ १७ ॥ **तस्यै वार्त्रघ्नावाज्यभागौ** ॥ १८ ॥ 'मरुद्भ्यः सान्तपनेभ्योऽनुब्रूहि' **इत्याहोपस्तृणानोऽवद्यन्** ॥ १९ ॥ 'सान्तपना इदꣳ हविः' **इत्यन्वाह** ॥ २० ॥ 'संवत्सरीणा मरुतः स्वर्काः' **इति यजति** ॥ २१ ॥ **वषट्कृते जुहोति** ॥ २२ ॥ **स्वस्तिमत्यौ संयाज्ये** ॥ २३ ॥ 'स्वस्ति नो दिवो अग्ने पृथिव्याः' **इत्यन्वाह** ॥ २४ ॥ 'यथा होतर्मनुषो देवताता' **इति यजति** ॥ २५ ॥ **वषट्कृते जुहोति** ॥ २६ ॥ **वर्तयति शंयुना बर्हिः** ॥ २७ ॥ **सन्ततिमनु होतुराहुतिं जुहोति** ॥ २८ ॥ **प्रसिध्यति कर्म** ॥ २९ ॥ **सन्तिष्ठत एषेष्टिः** ॥ ३० ॥

[गृहमेधीयेष्टिः]

निर्णिक्तया स्थाल्याऽवहतैस्तण्डुलैर्गा आयतीः प्रतीक्षते ॥ ३१ ॥ **सायꣳ सर्वासां दुग्धे गार्ह–**

निर्णिक्तया[१] =क्षते। गृहमेधीयस्यापूर्वत्वं केचिदिच्छन्ति। केचित्पूर्वत्वम्। कुत[२] एतत्। 'आज्य-भागौ[२] यजति। यज्ञस्यैव चक्षुषी नान्तरेती'ति चोदकप्राप्तस्याङ्गस्य पुनर्ग्रहणं परिसंख्यार्थम्। तत्र द्वयी गतिः। अङ्गमात्रं वा परिसञ्चष्टे, उत तुल्यजातीयान्यारादुपकाराण्यङ्गपूर्वाण्येव[३] वेति[३]। अङ्गमात्र–मिति वक्ष्यामः। कुतः। 'कस्मा इमं होष्याम' इति [४]श्रुतेर्देवताविचारश्रवणात्। कल्पे च 'गार्हपत्ये गृहमेधीयं चरुं श्रपयती'ति गार्हपत्यश्रवणात्। लोकाग्नावपि श्रपणमाशंकमानेनैव हि गार्हपत्यग्रहणं कृतम्। सिद्धं हि गार्हपत्ये हविषां श्रपणम्। निर्वापमनुक्त्वाऽवहतैस्तण्डुलैरिति प्रतिपन्नत्वात्। ननु 'न'[५] प्रयाजा इज्यन्ते नानूयाजा' इति प्रतिषेधात् प्रतिषिद्धवर्जानामङ्गानां प्राप्तिः। नैतदेवम्। आज्यभागयोः पुनः श्रवणान्निवृत्तानामर्थवादसंबन्धार्थं प्रतिषेधानुवादः। अवश्यमनूयाजप्रतिषेधानुवादत्वमभ्युप–गन्तव्यम्। इडान्तस्यैव विहितत्वात् तस्य। अन्ये वर्णयन्ति। अङ्गमात्रस्य परिसंख्याने सतीडान्तता न विधेया। अविधानादेव सिद्धत्वात्। अतस्तुल्यजातीयानां परिसंख्येति। धर्मकत्वेऽभ्याधानान्वाधान-परिस्तरणवेदकरणानि कृत्वा यथार्थं यज्ञायुधानि[६] संसाद्य पृष्ठ्यां स्तीर्त्वा पवित्रे आदाय 'यजमान वाचं यच्छे'त्युक्त्वा हस्तौ मार्जयित्वा बहून्व्रीहीन्निर्वपेत्[७]। अभ्यावापौ[८] वर्जयेत्[९]। त्रिष्फलीकरणान्तं कृत्वा गवामागमनमाकाङ्क्षमाण आस्ते॥ ३१ ॥

आगतासु महतीं स्थालीमधिश्रित्य सर्वा गा दोहयेत्। अग्निहोत्रीमपि दुह्यात्। द्रव्यान्तरेण सायंप्रातरग्निहोत्रं जुहुयात्। अस्मिन्काले पयः प्रणयन्ति केचित्। अपरे न प्रणयन्ति। काल एवान्यत् पय इत्यन्ये। स्थाल्यां तिरःपवित्रमप आनीय वेदं परिवासयेत्युक्त्वा तण्डुलान्निर्वपेत्। आज्यं निरुप्य प्रागवज्वलनात्कृत्वा लोम्नो व्यूह्य वा [१०]स्तम्बयजुर्हरेत्। करणच्छेदनयोयोपनवर्जं[११] प्राक् संप्रैषात्करोति[१२]। बर्हिष्येव योयोपनं केचिदिच्छन्ति। 'प्रोक्षणीरासादय स्रुवं च स्रुचौ च संमृड्ढि पत्नीं सन्नह्याज्येनोदेही'ति प्रैषः। पत्नीवर्जमित्येके। उक्तं च– 'नादिशन्ति तदाचार्याः पत्नीसन्नहनक्रियाम्' इति॥ ३२ ॥

---

१. M Ad ° क्ताया. २–२. M कु...आज्य°. ३–३. M Ad पूर्वाण्येवेति. ४. M Ad ° देव...चार°. ५. M Ad om. ६. T यज्ञसाधनानि. ७. M ° व्रीहीनि°. ८. M Ad ° वापेन; thus T. ९. M Ad वर्ध°. १०. T स्तम्बे य°. ११. M करणयोयोवन°, Ad ° छेदौयोयो°. १२. M Ad ° प्रेष्यत्.

पत्ये गृहमेधीयं चरुꣳ श्रपयति ॥ ३२ ॥ **तस्य शृतस्य त्रीनोदनानुपस्तीर्णाभिघारितानुद्धरति** ॥ ३३ ॥ **प्रथमोद्धृतं बहूपसिञ्चति** ॥ ३४ ॥ **अथेतरयोरुपसिञ्चति** ॥ ३५ ॥ **द्रुत्वाऽध्वर्युः परिधीन् संवर्तयति** ॥ ३६ ॥ **आहरन्त्योदनान्** ॥ ३७ ॥ **मध्यतः प्रथमोद्धृतमासादयति ध्रुवाभाजनम्** ॥ ३८ ॥ **तस्मा-दाज्यभागौ यजति** ॥ ३९ ॥ **तस्मादुपस्तरणाभिघारणं दक्षिणतश्चोत्तरतश्च** ॥ ४० ॥ **इतरावाज्य-भागौ यजति** ॥ ४१ ॥ **रयिमन्तावाज्यभागौ** ॥ ४२ ॥ 'रयिमतेऽग्नयेऽनुब्रूहि' **इत्याहाज्यस्य गृह्णान-श्चतुः** ॥ ४३ ॥ 'अग्निना रयिमश्नवत्' **इत्यन्वाह** ॥ ४४ ॥ **जुषाणेन यजति** ॥ ४५ ॥ **वषट्कृते जुहोति** ॥ ४६ ॥ 'सोमायानुब्रूहि' **इत्याहाज्यस्यैव गृह्णानश्चतुः** ॥ ४७ ॥ 'गयस्फानो अमीवहा' **इत्यन्वाह** ॥ ४८ ॥ **जुषाणेनैव यजति** ॥ ४९ ॥ **वषट्कृते जुहोति** ॥ ५० ॥ 'मरुद्भ्यो गृहमेधिभ्यो-ऽनुब्रूहि' **इत्याहोपस्तृणानोऽवद्यन्** ॥ ५१ ॥ **पश्चाच्च पुरस्ताच्च मध्यमस्यौदनस्यावद्यति** ॥ ५२ ॥ **एवं दक्षिणार्धस्यैवमुत्तरार्धस्य** ॥ ५३ ॥ **अभिघारयति** ॥ ५४ ॥ **प्रत्यनक्ति** ॥ ५५ ॥ 'गृहमेधास आगत' **इत्यन्वाह** ॥ ५६ ॥ 'प्र बुध्निया ईरते वो महाꣳसि' **इति यजति** ॥ ५७ ॥ **वषट्कृते जुहोति** ॥ ५८ ॥ 'अग्नये स्विष्टकृतेऽनुब्रूहि' **इत्याहोपस्तृणानोऽवद्यन्** ॥ ५९ ॥ **सकृदुत्तरार्धान्मध्यमस्यौदन-स्यावद्यति** ॥ ६० ॥ **एवं दक्षिणार्धस्यैवमुत्तरार्धस्य** ॥ ६१ ॥ **द्विरभिघारयति** ॥ ६२ ॥ **न प्रत्यनक्ति** ॥ ६३ ॥ **विराजौ संयाज्ये** ॥ ६४ ॥ 'प्रेद्धो अग्ने दीदिहि' **इत्यन्वाह** ॥ **६५** ॥ 'इमो अग्ने वीततमानि हव्या' **इति यजति** ॥ ६६ ॥ **वषट्कृते जुहोति** ॥ ६७ ॥ **संगृह्यैवैतान् परिधीननुप्रहरति** ॥ ६८ ॥ **तान् सꣳस्रावेणाभिजुहोति** ॥ ६९ ॥ **अत्याक्रम्य यथायतनꣳ स्रुचौ सादयित्वा मध्यम ओदन इतरयो-रिडाꣳ समवद्यति** ॥ ७० ॥ **उपहूतायामिडायामुत्तरमेवौदनमग्नीध उपोहति दक्षिणं ब्रह्मणे** ॥ ७१ ॥

प्रागाज्यग्रहणात्कृत्वा वेदिं प्रोक्ष्य निनीय प्रोक्षणीस्तूष्णीं स्रुचौ सादयित्वा[1] स्रुवमाज्य-स्थालीमादाय 'त्रीनोदनानि'त्यादि समभिघारणकाले ध्रौवैर्मन्त्रैर्मध्यमे गृहीत्वा चतुर्थो भूयोऽभ्यानयति। तस्मिन् संभविनो[2] ध्रुवाधर्माः सादनादयः क्रियन्ते। 'ध्रुवासदत् तां विष्णो पाही'ति मन्त्रसन्नामः[3]। प्रत्येकमोदनेषु 'यन्मे अग्ने' हविरुद्वासनानन्तरं [4]स्रुग्व्यूहनानन्तरं[4] वा परिधीन् संवर्त्याग्निं युनक्ति। इध्मकाष्ठाभावा[5]दाहवनीये बहूनि दारूण्यभ्यादधाति। आज्यभागप्रभृतीडान्तः[5] सन्तिष्ठते।

अधर्मकत्वे [6]अवहतास्तण्डुला गृह्यन्ते। निर्वापादयः[6] संस्कारा न सन्ति। उलूखलमूसलादीनि च[7] तन्त्रयुक्तानि[7] यज्ञायुधानि निवर्तन्ते। आगतासु च गोष्वन्वाधानादिहस्तसंमार्जनानन्तरं प्रोक्षणीः संस्कृत्य पात्राणि प्रोक्ष्य तच्छेषं[8] निधाय तदनन्तरं स्थालीमधिश्रित्य गा[9] दोहयित्वा तथैवानयति। समानमत ऊर्ध्वम्। 'देवस्त्वा सविते'ति वर्जयित्वोत्पन्नानां प्रतिपत्तिः कर्तव्या। युक्तानां विमोकश्च। होतुराहुतिर्हूयते[10]। इडान्तमातिथ्येनादृत्य[11] चतुर्होतुराहुतिं जुहोतीति। दृश्यते हि प्रागिडायाः परिधिप्रहरणं विदधत्। उत्पन्नप्रतिपत्तिमपि नेच्छन्तीति केचित्। ध्रौवस्याभावादाज्यस्थाल्याश्चतुर्होता

---

१. M Ad add च after °यित्वा. २. M Ad संभवनो; thus T. ३. T सन्नाम. ४-४. M Ad om, T स्रुगत्यूहना°. ५-५. M °भाव...आज्यभाग°. ६-६. M Ad अपहतास्तण्डुल...न्ते ...र्वा°. ७-७. M °खल...तत्रयु, Ad तत्रयु°; thus T. ८. M तच्छे...धाय. ९. M Ad गां; thus T. १०. T होत्याहूयत. ११. M Ad इडान्तेऽनादृत्य; thus T.

प्राश्नन्ति ॥ ७२ ॥ **मार्जयन्ते** ॥ ७३ ॥ **अग्निहोत्रमेवातो जुहोति** ॥ ४.३.१.७४ ॥ **[इति प्रथमः पटलः** (९)**]**

[अग्निहोत्रहोमः]

अग्निहोत्रमेवातो जुहोति ॥ १ ॥ **यत् स्थाल्यामतिशिष्यते तस्याध्वर्युश्च यजमानश्च प्राश्नीतः** ॥ २ ॥ **अन्य उपजनाः प्रतिवेशं पत्नियै पचन्ति** ॥ ३ ॥ **तस्य प्राश्नाति** ॥ ४ ॥ **अञ्जते** ॥ ५ ॥ **अभ्यञ्जते** ॥ ६ ॥ **अनुवत्सान् वासयन्ति** ॥ ७ ॥ **आज्येन स्थाल्या निष्कासमभ्यानीय गार्हपत्यस्यान्तिकं निदधाति** ॥ ८ ॥ **तं यजमान एव स्वयमनुतिष्ठेत्** ॥ ९ ॥ **तस्यौषसमध्वर्युरग्निहोत्रं हुत्वोपस्तीर्णाभिघारितं गार्हपत्ये पूर्णदर्वं जुहोत्यृषभस्य रवथमनु** ॥ १० ॥ 'पूर्णा दर्वि परा पत' **इत्यपरेणाग्निं तिष्ठन् पुरोनुवाक्यामन्वाह**। '°सुपूर्णा=शतक्रतो' **इति** ॥ ११ ॥ 'देहि मे' **इति यजति**। '°ददामि ते=मि ते स्वाहा' **इति** ॥ १२ ॥ **एतस्मिन् काले यजमान ऋषभ इव रूयात्** ॥ १३ ॥ **सवषट्कारमिव तदित्याहुर्यदृषभेणेति** ॥ १४ ॥ 'स्वाहा' **इति जुहोति** ॥ १५ ॥

[क्रीडीयेष्टिः]

यज्ञायुधानि सꣳसाद्याप: प्रणीय मरुद्भ्यः क्रीडिभ्यः पुरोडाशꣳ सप्तकपालं निर्वपति साकं सूर्येणोद्यता ॥ १६ ॥ **निरुप्ते प्राणग्रहाꣳश्च पृश्नीꣳश्च व्याचष्टे** ॥ १७ ॥ **समासन्नेऽपानग्रहाꣳश्च पृश्नीꣳश्च** *[1]**(व्याचष्टे** ॥ १८ ॥ 'ध्रुवा असदन्', 'यन्मे अग्ने' **इति समभिमृश्य)**

*[1]. Text abri. पृश्नीꣳश्च=दशहोतारं see above I.3.1.5-6.

हूयते। [1]अपरे चतुर्होतारं न व्याचक्षते[1], न च जुह्वति ॥ ४.३.१.३३-७३ ॥ **[इति प्रथमः पटलः** (९)**]**

अग्निहोत्रमेवातो जुहोति[2]। केचिदग्निहोत्रोत्तरकालं[3] गृहमेधीयस्य तन्त्रप्रक्रममामनन्ति। अस्माभिर्नेष्यते। कालातिपत्त्याशङ्क्या कर्ममध्ये [4]वेत्येवातः शब्दयोरुपयोगः ॥ १ ॥

अन्य उपजनाः[5] अन्येऽपि मनुष्याः पुत्रशिष्यबान्धवादयो हविःशेषप्राशनयोग्याः प्रतिवेशं समीपे ग्रामाग्नौ पत्न्यर्थं पचन्ति ॥ ३ ॥

'अञ्जत'[6] इत्यादि तृप्त्यर्थस्यान्नपानादेः प्रदर्शनम्। तथाहि वाक्यशेषः—'भ्रातृव्यायै=प्रहिणोती'ति ॥ ५-६ ॥

वत्सांश्च मातृभिः सह शाययन्ति ॥ ७ ॥

अनुतिष्ठेद् रक्षणं कुर्यात्। रक्षणार्थं जागरणमपीष्यते ॥ ९ ॥

[7]पूर्णदर्वमिति कर्मनाम। अतो होमपात्रं जुहूः। दर्व्यान्ये[8] जुह्वति। 'पूर्णा दर्वी'ति लिंगात् ॥ ४.३.२.१०-१२ ॥ **[इति द्वितीयः पटलः** (१०)**]**

१-१. M परे चतुर्होतार... व्या°, Ad तारो व्या°. **२.** T जुह्वति. **३.** M Ad °होत्रकालं; thus T. **४.** M °त्येवातच्छ°, Ad °त्येतावच्छ°. **५.** T उचज°. **६.** T आनुयाजत. **७.** M Ad पूर्णाद°; thus T. **८.** M Ad द्रव्या°.

दशहोतारं व्याचष्टे ॥ १९ ॥ **तस्यै वार्त्रघ्नावाज्यभागौ** ॥ २० ॥ 'मरुद्भ्यः क्रीडिभ्योऽनुब्रूहि' **इत्याहोपस्तृणानोऽवद्यन्** ॥ २१ ॥ 'क्रीडं वः शर्धो मारुतम्' **इत्यन्वाह** ॥ २२ ॥ 'अत्यासो न ये मरुतः स्वञ्चः' **इति यजति** ॥ २३ ॥ **वषट्कृते जुहोति** ॥ २४ ॥ **त्रिष्टुभौ संयाज्ये** ॥ २५ ॥ **सन्ततिमनु होतुराहुतिं जुहोति** ॥ २६ ॥ **प्रसिध्यति कर्म** ॥ २७ ॥ **सन्तिष्ठते एषेष्टिः** ॥ २८ ॥

[महाहविरिष्टिः]

महाहविरेवातः ॥ २९ ॥ **पूर्वेणाहवनीयं वेदिः क्लृप्ता भवति रथावकाशा** ॥ ३० ॥ **तस्यै स्तम्बयजुर्हरति** ॥ ३१ ॥ **वेदिं परिगृह्णाति** ॥ ३२ ॥ **करणं जपति** ॥ ३३ ॥ 'स्फ्यमुदपात्रम्' **इति संप्रेष्यति**। '०शम्यामाहरेहि यजमानाग्नीदुत्तरवेद्यामुपसीद' **इति** ॥ ३४॥ **उत्तरवेद्या आवृतोत्तरवेदिं निवपति** ॥ ३५ ॥ **इध्ममादीपयन्ति** ॥ ३६ ॥ **उपयमनीरुपकल्पयन्ति** ॥ ३७ ॥ **अग्नेरावृताग्निं प्रहरति** ॥ ३८ ॥ **प्रसिध्यति कर्माऽतिमुक्तिभ्यः** ॥ ३९ ॥ **अतिमुक्तीर्हुत्वा यज्ञायुधानि सꣳसाद्यापः प्रणीय महाहविर्निर्वपत्याग्नेयमष्टाकपालम्** ॥ ४.३.२.४० ॥ **[इति द्वितीयः पटलः** (१०)**]**

आग्नेयमष्टाकपालꣳ सौम्यं=कादशकपालमैन्द्रं चरुं वैश्वकर्मणमेककपालम् ॥ १ ॥ **निरुप्ते प्राणग्रहाꣳश्च पृश्नीꣳश्च व्याचष्टे** ॥ २ ॥ **तस्य हविष्कृता वाचं विसृज्य चतुर्गृहीतेन पञ्चहोतारमाहवनीये जुहोति** ॥ ३ ॥ **श्रप्यन्ते हवीꣳषि** ॥ ४ ॥ **शृतेषु हविःषु स्फ्यमादत्ते** ॥ ५ ॥ 'ब्रह्मन्नुत्तरं परिग्राहं परिग्रहीष्यामि' **इति प्रसूत उत्तरं परिग्राहं परिगृह्णाति** ॥ ६ ॥ **योयुपित्वाऽव-स्कम्भ संप्रेष्यति** 'प्रोक्षणीरासादयेध्मा=ह्याज्येनोदेहि पृषदाज्याय दध्याहरेहि यजमान' **इति** ॥ ७ ॥ **एतत् कुर्वन्ति** ॥ ८ ॥ **स्रुवं च स्रुचश्च संमार्ष्टि** ॥ ९ ॥ **आज्यानि गृह्णीते पृषदाज्यवन्ति** ॥ १० ॥ **इध्माबर्हिः प्रोक्षति** ॥ ११ ॥ **वेदिं प्रोक्षति** ॥ १२ ॥ **आसन्नं प्रोक्षति** ॥ १३ ॥ **अपो निनीय प्रस्तरं गृह्णाति** ॥ १४ ॥ **स्तृणाति बर्हिः** ॥ १५ ॥ **प्राङुत्सृप्य परिधीन् परिदधाति** ॥ १६ ॥ **समिधावाद-धाति** ॥ १७ ॥ **परिधिषु वाचयित्वाऽग्निं युनक्ति** ॥ १८ ॥ **आगत्य तिरश्ची सादयति** ॥ १९ ॥ **तिरश्च्योः प्रस्तरम्** ॥ २० ॥ **प्रस्तरे जुहूम्** ॥ २१ ॥ **बर्हिषीतरे** ॥ २२ ॥ **अलङ्कुर्वन्ति** ॥ २३ ॥ **उपस्तीर्णाभिघारितेषु हविःषूद्वासयति** ॥ २४ ॥ **समभिघार्य हवीꣳष्याहरन्ति** ॥ २५ ॥ **समासन्ने-ऽपानग्रहाꣳश्च पृश्नीꣳश्च व्याचष्टे** ॥ २६ ॥ **ध्रुवा असदन् यन्मे अग्ने इति समभिमृश्य पञ्च-होतारं व्याचष्टे** ॥ २७ ॥ **निर्मन्थ्येन चरति** ॥ २८ ॥ 'अग्नये समिध्यमानायानुवाच' **आह** ॥ २९ ॥ **सप्तदश सामिधेनीरन्वाह** ॥ ३० ॥ **अनूक्तासु सामिधेनीषु स्रुवेणाघारमाघार्याह** 'अग्नीदग्निं त्रिस्त्रिः संमृड्ढि' **इति** ॥ ३१ ॥ **स्रुग्भ्यामुत्तरम्** ॥ ३२ ॥ **असꣳस्पर्शयन्नत्याक्रम्य ध्रुवाꣳ समज्य सादयत्विा प्रवरं प्रवृणीते** ॥ ३३ ॥ **सीदति होता** ॥ ३४ ॥ **प्रसूतः स्रुचावादत्ते** ॥ ३५ ॥ **प्रयाजान् यजति** ॥ ३६ ॥ 'ओ श्रावय' **इत्याह** ॥ ३७ ॥ 'समिधो यज' **इति** ॥ ३८ ॥ 'यज यज' **इति** ॥ ३९ ॥ **चतुर्थेऽर्धꣳ समानीयाष्टमे सर्वꣳ समानयते** ॥ ४० ॥ **उपभृतोऽधि सर्वं प्रयजति** ॥ ४१ ॥ **प्रयाजानिष्ट्वाऽत्याक्रम्य ध्रुवामभिघारयत्यनुपूर्वꣳ हवीꣳषि** ॥ ४२ ॥ **पृषदाज्यमन्ततः** ॥ ४३ ॥ **नोपभृतꣳ रिक्ता हि सा भवति** ॥ ४४ ॥ **आज्यभागौ यजति** ॥ ४५ ॥ **वार्त्रघ्नावाज्यभागौ** ॥ ४६ ॥

'अग्नयेऽनुब्रूहि' **इत्याहोपस्तृणानोऽवद्यन्** ॥ ४.३.३.४७ ॥ **[इति *तृतीयः पटलः** (११)**]**

'अग्नयेऽनुब्रूहि' **इत्याहोपस्तृणानोऽवद्यन्** ॥ १ ॥ **प्रसिद्धाः षण्णाꣳ हविषां याज्यापुरोनु-वाक्याः** ॥ २ ॥ 'इन्द्रायानुब्रूहि' **इत्याहोपस्तृणानोऽवद्यन्** ॥ ३ ॥ 'इन्द्रसानसिꣳ रयिम्' **इत्यन्वाह** ॥ ४ ॥ 'प्र स साहिषे' **इति यजति** ॥ ५ ॥ **वषट्कृते जुहोति** ॥ ६ ॥ 'विश्वकर्मणेऽनुब्रूहि' **इत्याहोप-स्तीर्णाभिघारितमेककपालमादधानः** ॥ ७ ॥ 'विश्वकर्मन् हविषा वावृधानः' **इत्यन्वाह** ॥ ८ ॥ 'विश्वकर्मन् हविषा वर्धनेन' **इति यजति** ॥ ९ ॥ **वषट्कृते जुहोति** ॥ १० ॥ 'अग्नये स्विष्ट-कृतेऽनुब्रूहि' **इत्याहोपस्तृणानोऽवद्यन्** ॥ ११ ॥ **सकृदुत्तरार्धात्सर्वेषाꣳ हविषामवद्यति** ॥ १२ ॥ **एककपालस्यावदाय द्विरभिघारयति** ॥ १३ ॥ **न प्रत्यनक्ति** ॥ १४ ॥ **त्रिष्टुभौ संयाज्ये** ॥ १५ ॥ 'पिप्रीहि' **इत्यन्वाह** ॥ १६ ॥ 'अग्ने यदद्य विशो अध्वरस्य होतः' **इति यजति** ॥ १७ ॥ **वषट्कृते जुहोति** ॥ १८ ॥ **अत्याक्रम्य यथायतनꣳ स्रुचौ सादयित्वा प्राशित्रमवद्यति** ॥ १९ ॥ **अप उपस्पृ-श्येडामवद्यति** ॥ २० ॥ **उपहूतायामिडायामग्नीध आदधाति** ॥ २१ ॥ **प्राश्नन्ति** ॥ २२ ॥ **मार्जयन्ते** ॥ २३ ॥ **परिहरन्ति ब्रह्मणे** ॥ २४ ॥ **प्राशिते प्राशित्रे चरौ यजमानभागं प्रास्योद्वासयन्ति हवीꣳषि** ॥ २५ ॥ **अन्वाहार्ये वाचयति** ॥ २६ ॥ **सन्ततिमन्वष्टौ विष्टम्भान्वारोहाञ्जुहोति** 'सꣳसर्पाय स्वाहा', 'चक्षुषे स्वाहा', 'सूर्याय स्वाहा', ('ज्योतिषे स्वाहा') **इति विष्टम्भाः**, 'सहसे स्वाहा', 'सहस्याय स्वाहा', 'तपसे स्वाहा', 'तपस्याय स्वाहा' **इत्यन्वारोहाः** ॥ २७ ॥ 'एहि यजमान' **इत्युक्त्वाऽन्वा-रब्धे यजमाने होतुराहुतिं नवमीं जुहोति** ॥ २८ ॥ 'ब्रह्मन् प्रस्थास्यामः' **इति** ॥ २९ ॥ **पृषदाज्येन नवानूयाजान् यजति** ॥ ३० ॥ **आगत्य वाजवतीभ्याꣳ स्रुचौ व्यूहति** ॥ ३१ ॥ **शंयुना प्रस्तरपरिधि प्रकिरति** ॥ ३२ ॥ **परेत्य पत्नीः संयाजयन्ति** ॥ ३३ ॥ **फलीकरणहोमꣳ हुत्वा प्राडेत्य त्रीणि समिष्टयजूꣳषि जुहोति** ॥ ३४ ॥ 'यज्ञ यज्ञं=सुवीरः स्वाहा' **इति स्रुवेण हुत्वा ध्रुवामाप्याय्य** 'देवा गातुविद' **इति स्रुचा जुहोति**। '०गातुं वित्त्वा=वाते धाः' **इति** ॥ ३५ ॥ **प्रसिध्यति कर्म** ॥ ३६ ॥ **सन्तिष्ठते महाहविः** ॥ ४.३.४.३७ ॥ **[इति चतुर्थः पटलः** (१२)**]**

॥ इति चतुर्थप्रपाठके तृतीयोऽनुवाकः ॥

*. Commentory on the 3rd Paṭala (sūtra 1-47) is not given in the MSS.

महाहविषि समाप्त एतद् ब्राह्मण ऐन्द्राग्न इति वरुणप्रघासधर्मातिदेशादैन्द्राग्ननिष्कासेन तुषैश्चावभृथमवयन्ति। संस्थानानन्तरं पितृयज्ञ एवात इत्यतः परं पितृयज्ञ एवेत्यन्यन्नास्तीति ज्ञायत इति केचित् नावयन्ति। विद्यमानत्वस्यापि तदेव ज्ञापकमित्यपरे।[१] माहाहविष्कोऽवभृथोऽपि कार्यस्तु-षैरिति त्वेव वदन्ति केचिदित्युक्तम्। ऐन्द्राग्नतुषानप्सु प्रवेशयेदिति चामनन्ति केचित्॥ ४.३.४.३७ ॥ **[इति चतुर्थः पटलः** (१२)**]**

॥ इति व्याख्यायां चतुर्थप्रपाठके तृतीयोऽनुवाकः ॥

१. M Ad यज्ञपाक० ; thus T.

॥ अथ चतुर्थप्रपाठके चतुर्थोऽनुवाकः ॥

[पितृयज्ञः]

पितृयज्ञ एवातः ॥ १ ॥ तस्य संभाराः व्रीहियवाश्चाम्बरीषं चाभिवान्यायै च दुग्धमिक्षुशलाका च मूलच्छिद् वेदिस्तल्पावकाशाखाता यजमानसंमिता चतुःस्रक्तिः सर्वतः समेक्षणा च द्राघीयाꣳश्चेध्मः समूलं च बर्हिराञ्जनं च कशिपु दशोपबर्हणे च परिश्रयणं च ॥ २ ॥ दक्षिणेन गार्हपत्यं यज्ञायुधानि संसाद्यापः प्रणीय सोमाय पितृमते पुरोडाशꣳ षट्कपालं

पितृयज्ञ एवातः । 'अम्बरीषे धाना उपतपती'ति दर्शनात् तद्योग्यं पात्रमम्बरीषम्। अभिवान्या[१] मृतवत्सा याऽन्येन वत्सेन प्रत्ता दुह्यते। तस्याः पयः। इक्षुशलाका यथा मन्थनयोग्या तथा दण्डे प्रोता भवति मूलच्छिन्ना। वेदिस्तल्पावकाशा तत्प्रमाणा[२]। तल्पस्य च प्रमाणं पुरुषप्रमाणम्। पुरुषसंमितेत्यर्थः। अखातेत्युद्धननं प्रतिषिध्यते। चतुःस्रक्तिश्चतुष्कोणा। इमां दिशमिति सर्वनाम्ना विहिता। या 'उभये हि देवाश्च पितरश्चेज्यन्त' इति वाक्यशेषाद्दक्षिणा प्राचीति गम्यते। तथा चानुपदकारो विशिनष्टि– 'अग्रेणान्वाहार्यपचनं[३] यजमानमात्री वेदिर्भवति। दिक्षु स्रक्तिरित्येकेषा-मि'ति। सर्वतः समा पार्श्वतश्चोत्सेधतश्च। एकतो[४] निम्नतादिनिवृत्त्यर्थं च। प्राकृतादिध्माद्दीर्घतर इध्मो भवति। [५]स्तरणबर्हिः खात्वा गृहीतं भवति। कशिपुकुतपौ[६]। येन परिश्रयन्ति तत्परिश्रयणम्[७] ॥ १-२ ॥

यज्ञायुधानि संसाद्येति तन्त्रप्रक्रमप्रदर्शनम्। तद् 'दक्षिणेन गार्हपत्यमिति यज्ञायुधसंसादनस्य देशो विधीयते। अतो दक्षिणतो वा प्राचीनावीत्युत्तरत[८] उपवीती[८] निर्वपति। अन्य[९] आह—दक्षिणतो[९] निर्वापपक्ष एवेत्युच्यते। अत्र यज्ञायुधसंसादने इतरस्मिन्नुत्तर[१०] एवेति। तथावहननमपि दक्षिणार्धे। अधिश्रयणमप्युत्तरतो निर्वापपक्ष एवेत्युच्यते। पक्षाश्रितत्वमेषां ब्राह्मणे कल्पे वा नोपलभ्यते। अतो विशेषेण[११] विधिरानाय्यः[११]। कर्मणोऽपूर्वत्वं केचिदिच्छन्ति। कथम्। 'आघारावाघारयति यज्ञपुरुषो-रन्तरित्यै'। 'आज्यभागौ यजति[१२]' यज्ञस्यैव चक्षुषी नान्तरेती'त्याघाराज्यभागानां पुनः श्रवणादि-तरेषामङ्गानां निवृत्तिः। निवृत्तेषु च प्रयाजादयः सगुणा विधीयन्ते 'अपबर्हिष' इत्यादि नाम्ना विहिता-न्यङ्गपूर्वाण्यपि स्वान्[१३] धर्मानङ्गार्थानङ्गप्रधानार्थांश्च[१३] प्रयोजयन्ति। तथा प्राप्तयोरार्षेयहोतृवरणयोः प्रतिषेधः। आर्षेयवरणसंस्कृते ह्याहवनीये प्रयाजादयः प्रकृताविष्टाः। तथा प्राप्तानामेव[१४] वेद्यादीनां गुणा विहितास्तस्मादपूर्वमिति। कथं[१५] पुनः 'न पत्न्यन्वास्ते, न संयाजयन्ती'ति पत्नीसंयाजप्रतिषेधः। नित्यानुवादोऽयं भविष्यति। यथेडान्त आतिथ्यः[१६] सन्तिष्ठते। 'नानूयाजान् यजती'त्यस्य प्रतिषेधस्य

---

१. M Ad अभिमान्या; thus T. **२.** M Ad om; thus T. **३.** M Ad °वच°. **४.** M Ad °तोणिमन्नादि°. **५.** M स्तरणि....खात्वा, Ad °रणि° ; thus T. **६.** M Ad °तपे; thus T. **७.** M Ad °तत्परिश्रणं. **८-८.** M Ad °रतोपवीतीति. **९-९.** M अतः...दक्षिणतो, Ad अत दक्षिणतो; thus T. **१०.** M Ad उत्तरत एव° ; thus T. **११-११.** M विशेषेण...स्य, Ad विशेषेण विधानादस्य; thus T. **१२.** M Ad om; thus T. **१३-१३.** M Ad स्वन्ध° [Ad स्वंध°] र्मामङ्गप्रधा. **१४.** M Ad प्राप्त वेद्या° ; thus T. **१५.** M Ad om; thus T. **१६.** M Ad आदित्यः.

निर्वपति, पितृभ्यो बर्हिषद्भ्यो धानाः, पितृभ्योऽग्निष्वात्तेभ्योऽभिवान्यायै दुग्धे मन्थम्॥ ३॥

नित्यानुवादत्वं भवताभ्युपगम्यते।[१]तस्मादाघारादीनामेवानुवादत्वं नाभ्युपगम्यते। सर्वथा[२] नित्यानुवादत्वकल्पनायां वयं[३] न मुह्यामहे[४]। यश्चोभयोः पक्षयोर्दोषो न, तमेकश्चोद्यो भवति[५]। ततः प्राप्तानामेवाघारादीनामनुवादत्वं युज्यते, नाप्राप्तप्रतिषेधस्य। अतो धर्मवदेवेदं कर्म। तथा च प्रधानार्थं[६] प्रणीताप्रणयनं[६] धर्मवत्वं द्योतयति। तथा चानुपदकार आह—'पितृयज्ञे यावच्छ्रुतधर्माः प्रवर्तेरंस्तथैक आहुर्धर्मवदेव देवप्रवादेषु देवान् पितॄंर्नि'ति कुर्युरन्यत्र संस्कारेभ्यः इति।

ननु धर्मवत्वे प्राकृतानां धर्माणामुत्क्रमेण पाठो न युज्यते। उच्यते[७], नैतावता पूर्वत्वं कल्पयितुं शक्यते। अन्य[८] आह—धर्मवत्वेऽप्याचार्येणाम्नातं प्रमाणीकृत्य तेनैव क्रमेण कर्तव्यम्। आचार्य–प्रामाण्याच्छाखान्तरे तादृशः पाठोऽनुमीयत इति। ब्राह्मणे मन्थस्य गुणं विधाय वेद्यग्नीध्माबर्हिषां गुणा विहिताः। गुणविधिपाठश्च न क्रमकारणम्। यथा 'परिश्रयन्ति', 'समूलं बर्हिर्भवति' इत्युत्पत्तिविधि–पाठक्रमकारणब्राह्मणानुसारेणैवेहाप्याम्नातम्। अत एषां प्राकृत एव क्रम इति। तथा सत्यभ्याधान–मादितः कर्तव्यम्। तच्चाग्नावुत्पन्ने भवितुमर्हति। स चान्वाहार्यपचनात्प्रहृत्य वेदिमध्ये निधातव्यः। संस्कृता च वेदिर्भवति। तस्माद्वेदिकरणं[९] पूर्वं, ततोऽ[९]ग्निपरिहरणं, ततोऽन्वाधानादि। वेदिकरणे यदि[१०] दिक्षु[१०] स्त्रक्तयः स्युर्दक्षिणपूर्वा प्राची दिग्भवति। इतरस्मिन्पक्षे प्राच्येव। 'प्राची योयोपनान्तं वेदिं कृत्वाऽन्वाहार्यपचनादग्निं[११] प्रहृत्य मध्यतो वेद्यै सादयित्वोपसमाधायान्वादध्यात्[१२]। तस्मिन्नाहवनीयधर्माः[१३] प्रवर्तेरन्' इत्यनुपदम्। यद्येवं स्यात् ब्रह्मा मन्त्रेणैवोपविश्योत्तरं परिग्राहं प्रसुवति[१४]। प्रागुत्तरस्मात् परिग्राहाच्चेत् तूष्णीमेवोपविशति। अग्रेणाहवनीयं गत्वा पैतृयज्ञिक्या वेदेरपरेणाग्रेण[१५] वा ब्रह्मपथः[१६]। अपरेणैव[१६] यजमानस्य प्रागाज्यावेक्षणात् स्तम्बयजुरग्रेणाहवनीयं[१७] नित्यमुत्करं हरेत्। तस्या एवोत्तरत उत्करं कल्पयेद्वा। दक्षिणाग्निं गच्छतामपरेणाहवनीयमार्गः। अग्रेणेत्यन्ये। ततोऽग्निं प्रहृत्याभ्याधाय बर्हिः संभरेत्, तस्य समर्थत्वात्। असमर्थमसिदादि निवर्तते। खननयोग्यमुपादीयते। 'मूलं ते राध्यासमि'ति केचित्। अन्ये मूलेष्वपि सन्ति पर्वाणीति न[१८] विकुर्वते। 'आच्छेत्ते'ति मन्त्रो न विक्रियते। तत्रापि छेदनसंभवादाच्छेदनाभिमर्शनं नास्ति। तदुक्तं बोधायनेन—'समूलमेव बर्हिर्भवतीति बोधायनः'। तत्र नास्ति प्रत्यभिमर्श इति। आत्माभिमर्शनं न निवर्तते। परिस्तरणादीनां समूलता नास्ति। इध्मानां सामिधेनीविवृद्धौ[१९] वृद्धिः ह्रसे[२०] प्राकृतान्येवेति केचित्। अन्ये ह्रसेऽपि ह्रसमिच्छन्ति। तथा सति नवदारुरिध्मः। ततः परिस्तीर्य वेदं कृत्वा यदि वेदिं करणात्पूर्वं न कृतं दक्षिणेन

---

१. M Ad कस्मा°. **२.** M Ad सर्वदा. **३.** M Ad om; thus T. **४.** M Ad मुच्यामहे. **५.** Ad न. **६–६.** M Ad प्रधानताप्रणयनं; thus T. **७.** M Ad om; thus T. **८.** T takes it as additional hence puts this reading in fn. **९–९.** M Ad °करणतोऽग्नि°; thus T. **१०–१०.** M Ad यदिक्षु. **११.** M Ad °वचना°. **१२.** M Ad त्वोपसमादाया; thus T. **१३.** M Ad धर्मः. **१४.** M Ad °सुपति. **१५.** M Ad वेदे परेणा°. **१६–१६.** M Ad °पथो परे **१७.** M Ad °हवनीये. **१८.** M Ad om. **१९.** M Ad °वृद्धो. **२०.** M Ad प्रासे.

अवघ्नन्ति दक्षिणार्धे प्रतिपूरुषमेककपालाः स्त्रियम्बकान्, एकमतिरिक्तम् ॥ ४ ॥ **अम्बरीषेणान्वाहार्यपचने धाना उपतपति** ॥ ५ ॥ **ताः परिगण्य द्वेधा करोति** ॥ ६ ॥ **तासामर्धाः सक्तून् कुर्वन्ति** ॥ ७ ॥ **अन्वाहार्यपचनानि दक्षिणावृत्तस्तिष्ठन्नवहन्ति** ॥ ८ ॥ **अस्मा उपस्तीर्णा–**

गार्हपत्यमित्यादि। 'अपः प्रणेष्यामि'[१], 'वाचं यच्छे'ति प्रैषः। कुतः। 'अग्निं सकृत् सकृत्[२] समृद्धि, सीदे'त्येष एवात्र प्रवर इति दर्शनात्सर्वेषामृत्विग्यजमानवाचकानां शब्दानां निवृत्तिरिष्यत इति। तथा चानुपदे 'नर्त्विङ्नामधेयान्यभिपद्येत, न यजमानस्य। ऋत्विजामन्यत्र देवतानामधेयै रिमे वयं नरा मानुषाः स्मोऽस्मानि'त्येतानुत्सीदेयुरिति। 'अवन्त्वस्मानिमां वयं सुसंदृशं त्वा वयमि'ति दर्शनाद् वयमित्यादीनां निवृत्तिर्नेष्यत आचार्येण। पुरोडाशार्थं व्रीहीन्निरुप्य धानार्थमन्यान्[३] निर्वपति। 'उत्तरत आहवनीयस्य सादयति', 'आहवनीयं परेक्षत' [४]इत्यादिषु प्रणीत[४] एवाग्निराहवनीयकार्ये गृह्यते। न प्राकृतः। आहवनीयो वोत्तरवेदिकः। 'सुसन्दृशं त्वा वयम्' इत्याहवनीयमभिव्यनित्युपतिष्ठन्ते। आहवनीयस्यार्धमेतीति प्राकृतः। पुरोडाशीयानुत्तरेण गार्हपत्यं सादयति। प्रकृतिवत् दक्षिणतो वा। दक्षिणतोऽवहननदर्शनात्॥ ३ ॥

त्रयाणां निर्वापमुक्त्वा तान् दक्षिणेन[५] गार्हपत्यमित्यादिदर्शनाद् यवानुपनिधायोत्तरार्धे त्र्यम्बकार्थं प्रतिपूरुषमेककपालान्येकातिरिक्तान्युपदधाति। प्रतिपूरुषमिति व्याख्यातम्। करम्भपात्रेषु एककपाला–निति पुंल्लिंगश्रवणात्तेषु पुरोडाशा श्रप्यन्ते[६]। तत्र कर्तृनियमो नास्ति। धर्माश्रुतेः संस्कारनिवृत्तिः ॥ ४ ॥

[७]दर्वीहोमत्वात् षट् कपालोपधानान्ते तेनैवोपवेषेण 'अपाग्नेरग्निम्' इत्याद्युपक्रम्य प्रथमेन कपालमन्त्रेणाम्बरीषमधिश्रयति सामर्थ्यात् बह्वङ्गारेषु। सक्तुपेषणे कृष्णाजिनादीनां[८] तन्त्रत्वार्थं [९]पुरोडाशाधिश्रयमन्त्रेणाहितेन यवानम्बरीष औप्य तथैव प्रथममन्त्रेण [९]केनचिदालोडयन्ति[१०]। [११]ता यदा बहुरूपा भवन्ति [१२]तदावतार्य शूर्पे[१२] निवपति ॥ ५ ॥

[१३]अन्यस्मिन् वा निवपनसमर्थे[१३] ताः परिगण्य[१४] द्वेधा करोति। *परिगण्य परितो विकृष्य सक्तुयोग्याः[१५]। इतराश्च बहुरूपा विविच्य द्वेधा करोति*, विभागमन्त्रेण व्यादिशति च। 'पितृभ्यो बर्हिषद्भ्यो वः', पितृभ्योऽग्निष्वात्तेभ्यो वः' इति। पुरोडाशीयान् पिष्ट्वा सक्तून् प्रक्षिपेत्[१६] ॥ ६–८ ॥

तान् दुग्ध ओप्य[१७] सदुग्धानां सह पर्यग्निकरणमाप्येभ्यो निनीय [१८]स्फ्यमादत्ते। उत्तरं[१८]

---

१. M Ad प्रणयिष्या°. **२.** M Ad सकृत् once. **३.** M Ad रुप्याधानार्थान्यवान्निर्व°, T नार्थान्यपां (?). **४–४.** Ad om. **५.** M Ad दक्षिणे. **६.** M Ad श्रव्यन्ते. **७.** M Ad दर्वि°. **८.** M Ad °जिनादिनां. **९–९.** M °डाशा...हितेन°, Ad om text between मन्त्रेण and केन°. **१०.** M Ad °लोकयति; thus T. **११.** M Ad तदा; thus T. **१२–१२.** M तदावता... प्ये, Ad °वताप्य शूप्ये. **१३–१३.** M Ad अन्यस्मिन्वासमर्थे [Ad वा स], T अस्मिन्नपवपना स°. **१४.** M Ad °गण्य, T °खण्ड्य. ***–*.** T takes the text beginning with परिगण्य as additional, hence gives it in fn. **१५.** M Ad योऽन्या for योग्या. **१६.** M Ad पिंक्षेत्; thus T. **१७.** Ad औप्य. **१८–१८.** T °स्फ्यादानोत्तर°.

भिघारितं पुरोडाशमन्वाहार्यपचनान्यर्धम्, स तस्यालङ्कारः ॥ ९ ॥ आज्येन धानाः संयावयन्ति स तासामलङ्कारः ॥ १० ॥ अभिवान्यायै दुग्धेऽर्धपात्रमिक्षुशलाकया मन्थमुपमन्थति दक्षिणावृत्तोऽनारभ्य, स तस्यालङ्कारः ॥ ११ ॥ अन्वाहार्यपचनान्युप समादधाति ॥ १२ ॥ तस्यै मनसा स्तम्बयजुर्हरति ॥ १३ ॥ वेदिं परिगृह्णाति ॥ १४ ॥ करणं जपति ॥ १५ ॥ उदकुम्भमाहृत्य दक्षिणेऽꣳसे निदधाति ॥ १६ ॥ समूलं बर्हिराहृत्योत्तरत एवोपसादयति ॥ १७ ॥ द्राघीयाꣳसमिध्ममाहृत्योत्तरत एवोपसादयति ॥ १८ ॥ उदकुम्भमादाय परिषेक्ता त्रिरपसलैः परिषिञ्चन् पर्येति ॥ १९ ॥ निधायोदकुम्भं प्रतिपथं त्रिः पुनः पुनः परिद्रवति ॥ २० ॥ समूलं

परिग्राहमित्यादि योयोपनान्तायामग्निनिधाने[१] स्फ्यावस्कंभनादि पत्नीवर्जं संप्रेष्येत्[२]। अन्वाहार्यपचने स्रुक्संमार्गः वेद्यामेव। प्रकृतिवदाज्यग्रहणमन्वाहार्यसमीप एवान्ये गृह्णन्ति। प्रोक्षण्यासादनानन्तर-मु[३]दकुंभं दक्षिणार्धे संसादयति। यत्राज्यग्रहणं तत्र स्रुचासादनम्[३]। पत्नीसन्नहनाद्याहवनीयेऽधिश्रयती-त्यन्त[४] निवर्तते। आदानमन्त्रहरणमन्त्रवर्जमाज्यानि गृह्णीते। सर्वाणि षड् गृहीतानि समानयनस्य। बर्हिरर्थत[५] उपभृत्येकमेव षड्गृहीतमनूयाजहविरभिघारणार्थं चेज्जौहवेनैव क्रियते। इतरस्मिन् पक्षे द्वे षट् गृहीते उपभृति न संस्था। प्रयाजेषु तु जौहवस्य तस्मान्न। जुह्वां पितृशब्द उच्यः। स एवोपभृति स्रुवायां हवींषि गच्छति 'अभिघारणे तदि'ति ब्रुवत्याः सरस्वत्या न बर्हिरर्थमेव समानयनमित्यभि-प्रायः। अनुपदकारस्तु—'अवभृथपितृयज्ञयोर्न समानयनमि'त्याह। आज्यानि गृहीत्वोपस्तीर्णाभिघारितं पुरोडाशमुद्वासयति। धानाँश्च[६] कस्मिंश्चित्पात्र उपस्तीर्णाभिघारितान् संवपति ॥ ९-१० ॥

अभिवान्यायै दुग्धे। आधारभूतेन पात्रेणार्धपात्रे सक्तून् पूर्वमेव प्रक्षिप्तानिक्षुशलाकप्रोतया खेजकया [७]दक्षिणामुखोऽनारभ्य मन्थति। रज्ज्वा स्थूणादौ[८] बद्ध्वा हस्ताभ्यामेवेति केचित्। स्थाल्या उपरि पतितान् विन्दूनस्पृशन्नित्यन्ये। सक्तूनिवपनं[९] हविरधिश्रयणकाल एव। स्वक्रमे मन्थनमस्मिन् काले ॥ ११ ॥

तानस्मा अध्वर्यवेऽन्वाहार्यपचनसमीपमाहरति[१०]। तानसौ तत्र स्थापयति। ततो धरुण-प्रोक्षणादि ॥ १२ ॥

अत्यूह्य स्रुचमुदकुंभमादायेत्यादि ॥ १६-१८ ॥

परिषेको वेदिप्रोक्षणं न विकरोति प्रकृतिलिंगासंयोगात्। तत एव निनयनमपि न [११]विकरोति। प्रस्तरस्य पुरस्तात् ग्रहणं नास्ति। सन्नहनं निधाय मुष्टिमात्रेणाभिच्छाद्य 'उरु यज्ञाय' इत्यभ्यन्तरान्[१२] निःस्तृण्वन्[१३] पर्येति। उत्तराभ्यां लुप्तान्त्यपादाभ्यां द्विर्यथा स्तीर्णानां मूलान्यग्रैरभिच्छाद्यन्ते तथा स्तृणाति।

---

१. T °योपनतायाम° ; thus M Ad. **२.** M Ad °प्रेष्यद्. **३-३.** T takes the text from उदकुम्भं° = to °सादनम् as additional, hence gives it in fn. **४.** M Ad °त्यान्तं. **५.** M Ad °रर्थत्व; thus T. **६.** M Ad धानार्धश्च, T धानांश्च. **७.** T °क्षिणामुखेनाराभ्य; thus T. **८.** M °दाप, Ad °दाय. **९.** M Ad °पन; thus T. **१०.** M Ad °रन्ति. **११.** M Ad om वि. **१२.** M Ad °राणि. **१३.** M Ad om निः; thus T.

बर्हिरादाय त्रिरेवापसलैः परिस्तृणन् पर्येति॥ २१॥ निधाय प्रस्तरं प्रतिपथं त्रिः पुनः परिद्रवति॥ २२॥ प्रस्तरमादाय प्राङुत्सृप्य परिधीन् परिदधाति॥ २३॥ समिधावादधाति॥ २४॥ परिधिषु वाचयित्वाऽग्निं युनक्ति॥ २५॥ अपरेणाग्निं प्रस्तरं न्यस्यति॥ २६॥ समूलं तिरश्ची बर्हिराहरन्ति॥ २७॥ अस्मा एकꣳ स्रुवमेकां जुहूमेकामुपभृतमेकां ध्रुवामेकामाज्यस्थालीमेकं प्राशित्रहरणमेकं मेक्षणमेकं पुरोडाशमेकां धानाम् एकं मन्थमेकामिक्षुशलाकामेकमाञ्जन-मेकमभ्यञ्जनमेकं कशिपुमेकमुपबर्हणमेकं परिश्रयणम्॥ २८॥ एकैकमेवैनान्यनूचीनान्युदा-हरन्ति॥ २९॥ समासाद्य 'ध्रुवा असदन्', 'यन्मे अग्ने' **इति समभिमृश्य षड्ढोतारं व्याचष्टे॥ ३०॥** 'अग्नये देवेभ्यः पितृभ्यः समिध्यमानायानुब्रूहि' **इत्याहाज्यस्य गृह्णानश्चतुः॥ ३१॥** 'उशन्तस्त्वा हवामहे' **इत्येतां त्रिरन्वाह।** '०उशन्तः=अत्तवे' **इति॥ ३२॥ तानिध्मेन परीप्सति॥ ३३॥ अतिशिनष्टि समिधम्॥ ३४॥ अनूक्तासु सामिधेनीषु स्रुवेणाघारमाघार्याह** 'अग्नीदग्निꣳ सकृत् संमृड्ढि' **इति॥ ३५॥ उत्थाय प्रवरं प्रवृणीते॥ ३६॥** 'ओ श्रावय' **इत्याह॥ ३७॥** 'सीद होतर्' **इत्येष एवात्र प्रवरः॥ ३८॥ नार्षेयं वृणीते न**

'स्तृणीत बर्हिरिति' लुप्यते॥ १९-२१॥

तदेव त्रिवृत्पवित्रे अपिसृज्य प्रस्तरं निधाय प्रतिपथमित्याद्यपरेणाग्निं प्रस्तरं तूष्णीमेव न्य-स्यति॥ २२-२६॥

स्वयं तिरश्चीति तिरश्च्योर्निवृत्तिः॥ २७॥

ततः स्रुवादीन्येकैकमाहृतानि सादयति। मेक्षणं धानासंयवनार्थमर्थप्राप्तम्[1]। तदिक्षुशलाकया सहानुप्रहरति। कशिपूपबर्हणयोः प्रयोजनमाहरणमात्रमेव॥ २८॥

पुनरेकैकमेवैतानीति वचनमुक्तस्यैवोपोद्बलार्थम्[2]। यत् त्रीणि त्रीणीत्यभ्यासो हविःषु न संभवति सर्वाण्यभिप्रेत्य ब्राह्मणेऽभ्यास[3] इति। अनुपदयज्ञपार्श्वयोः[4] पितृयज्ञे व्रताभाव उक्तो यदि तदिष्यते। यजमानस्याध्वर्योश्च व्रतं नास्ति॥ २९॥

'अग्नये देवेभ्यः पितृभ्य' इत्यादि न प्राकृतस्य प्रैषस्योहः, प्रकृतस्य स्थाने विहितः॥ ३१॥

समिधस्त्रिषु प्रणवेषु विभज्याभ्याधानम्। अथवा द्वयोः प्रणवयोर्द्वे अन्त्येति[5] शिष्याः[5] सह सपक्ष[6] एकैकामेव॥ ३२॥

उत्थाय प्रवरं प्रवृणीते। उत्थायोत्तरमाघारमाघार्य प्रवरं प्रवृणीते। बर्हिर्मात्रमादाय प्रवराय आश्रावयति। होतृवरणाभावाच्छकलाभावः[7]॥ ३६॥

'सीद' इत्येष एवात्र प्रवर इति प्रवराभाव उच्यते॥ ३८॥

---

१. M Ad °नार्थं प्राप्तम्; thus T. २. M Ad द्बलनार्थं. ३. M Ad °ह्मणाभ्या. ४. M Ad °पदयज्ञायाः; thus T. ५-५. M अन्त्ये...स्सह, Ad अन्त्ये विशिष्याः, T अन्त्येति शिष्याः. ६. Ad सपक्षमे ए° ; thus T. ७. M °भावं

होतारम् ॥ ३९ ॥ **सीदति होता** ॥ ४० ॥ **प्रसूतः स्रुचावादत्ते** ॥ ४१ ॥ **अपबर्हिषश्चतुरः प्रयाजान् यजति** ॥ ४२ ॥ **आज्यभागौ यजति** ॥ ४३ ॥ **जीवमन्तावाज्यभागौ** ॥ ४४ ॥ 'अग्नयेऽनुब्रूहि' **इत्या-हाज्यस्य गृह्णानश्चतुः** ॥ ४५ ॥ 'आ नो अग्ने सुचेतुना' **इत्यन्वाह**। 'रयिं=जीवसे' **इति** ॥ ४६ ॥ **जुषाणेन यजति** ॥ ४७ ॥ **वषट्कृते जुहोति** ॥ ४८ ॥ 'सोमायानुब्रूहि' **इत्याहाज्यस्यैव गृह्णान-श्चतुः** ॥ ४९ ॥ 'त्वꣳ सोम महे भगम्' **इत्यन्वाह**। 'त्वं दूत=जीवसे' **इति** ॥ ५० ॥ **जुषाणेनैव यजति** ॥ ५१ ॥ **वषट्कृते जुहोति** ॥ ५२ ॥ **अत्याक्रम्य यथायतनꣳ स्रुचौ सादयित्वा प्राचीना-वीतानि कुर्वते** ॥ ४.४.१.५३ ॥ **[इति प्रथमः पटलः (१३)]**

प्राचीनावीतानि कुर्वते ॥ १ ॥ **आदत्ते दक्षिणार्ध्यं परिधिम्** ॥ २ ॥ **तं मध्यमं परिधिमनु निपातयति** ॥ ३ ॥ **परिश्रयन्ति** ॥ ४ ॥ **उत्तरां वेद्यै श्रोणिं प्रति परिश्रयणस्य सन्धिं कुर्वन्ति** ॥ ५ ॥ **विपर्यन्ति** ॥ ६ ॥ **उत्तरतो ब्रह्मा च यजमानश्चोपविशतो दक्षिणतो होता चाग्नीच्च** ॥ ७ ॥ **दक्षिणतोऽवदायोदङ्ङतिचङ्क्रम्यते** ॥ ८ ॥ 'आ स्वधा' **इत्याश्रावयति** ॥ ९ ॥ 'अस्तु स्वधा' **इति प्रत्याश्रावयति** ॥ १० ॥ 'स्वधा नमः' **इति वषट्करोति** ॥ ११ ॥ **वषट्कृते जुहोति** ॥ १२ ॥ 'सोमाय पितृमतेऽनु स्वधा कुरु' **इत्याहोपस्तृणानोऽवद्यन्** ॥ १३ ॥ **सकृत्पुरोडाशस्यावद्यति, सकृद्धानानाꣳ**

एतावतैव[१] सिद्धेः 'नार्षेयं वृणीते, न होतारमि'ति ब्राह्मणानुकरणम्। अन्य आह— आर्षेयहोतृवरणवर्जम् 'अग्निर्देव' इत्यादि वक्तव्यमिति पक्षान्तरमिति ॥ ४.४.१.३९ ॥ **[इति प्रथमः पटलः (१३)]**

प्राचीनावीतानि कुर्वत इति। प्रधानविषयमित्याचार्याभिप्रायः। 'प्राचीनावीती[२] सोमं यजतीति' प्रधानोपलक्षणत्वाद्[३] 'उत्तरत एवोपवीय[३] निर्वपेदि'त्युपक्रान्तत्वाच्च प्राचीनावीतत्वस्य[४] प्रधान-विषयत्वं युक्तम्। परिधित्रित्वादीनामपि तादृशं वचनमस्तीत्यवगन्तव्यम्' ॥ १ ॥

विपरीतगमने यथाप्रपन्नं गत्वा ब्रह्मयजमानावुपविशतः। अग्रेणैवाहवनीयमपरेण गार्हपत्यं दक्षिणेनैवान्वाहार्यपचनं[५] होताग्नीध्रौ[५]। स्थानान्तरत्वान्निरसनोवपेशने ब्रह्महोत्रोर्हविषामपि विपरिग्रहणमिष्यते ॥ ६-७ ॥

तत्र यथावस्थितानामेव जुहूं च षट्कपालं च तयोर्दक्षिणत उपभृद्धानाश्च ध्रुवां मन्थं च। स्वधादीनां तानि तान्यक्षराणि प्रकृतिवत् प्लवन्ते[६]। प्रतिदैवतं सर्वेभ्योऽवदाय यागः[७]। 'पञ्चकृत्वोऽवद्यति' 'सन्ततमवद्यती'त्यनयोरर्थ आचार्येण कल्पितः। स्वयंसम्पन्नं पञ्चावत्तिनां[८] पञ्चावत्तम्। अथवा इतरेषाम् अवदानादधिकं[९] प्रकृतिवदेकमवदेयम्। तथा हि सूत्रकार आमनति-

---

१. M एत...व. २. M Ad °वीतीति. ३-३. M °दुत्त...ापवीय. ४. T gives this reading from MS ख वीततस्य. ५-५. M पच ...ताग्नी°. ६. M Ad °वल्लभन्ते; thus T. ७. M Ad यागं. ८. M Ad पञ्चावर्तिनां; thus T. ९. M Ad °धिक.

सकृन्मन्थस्य ॥ १४ ॥ **अभिघारयति** ॥ १५ ॥ **प्रत्यनक्ति** ॥ १६ ॥ **द्वे द्वे पुरोनुवाक्ये अन्वाह** 'त्वꣳ सोम प्रचिकितो मनीषा=मघवा भवा नः' **इति** ॥ १७ ॥ 'आ स्वधा' **इत्याश्रावयति** ॥ १८ ॥ 'अस्तु स्वधा' **इति प्रत्याश्रावयति** ॥ १९ ॥ 'सोमं पितृमन्तꣳ स्वधा कुरु' **इत्याह** ॥ २० ॥ 'ये स्वधा' **इत्यागुरते** ॥ २१ ॥ 'त्वꣳ सोम पितृभिः संविदानः' **इति यजति**। '○अनुद्यावा=रयीणाम्' **इति** ॥ २२ ॥ 'स्वधा नमः' **इति वषट्करोति** ॥ २३ ॥ **वषट्कृते जुहोति** ॥ २४ ॥ 'पितृभ्यो बर्हिषद्भ्योऽनु स्वधा कुरु' **इत्याहोपस्तृणानोऽवद्यन्** ॥ २५ ॥ **सकृद्धानानामवद्यति सकृन्मन्थस्य, सकृत्पुरोडाशस्य** ॥ २६ ॥ **अभिघारयति** ॥ २७ ॥ **प्रत्यनक्ति** ॥ २८ ॥ 'बर्हिषदः पितर ऊत्यर्वाग्' **इत्यन्वाह**। '○इमा वो हव्या=गमिष्ठाः' **इति** ॥ २९ ॥ 'आ स्वधा' **इत्याश्रावयति** ॥ ३० ॥ 'अस्तु स्वधा' **इति प्रत्याश्रावयति** ॥ ३१ ॥ 'पितॄन्‌र्बर्हिषा स्वधा कुरु' **इत्याह** ॥ ३२ ॥ 'ये स्वधा' **इत्यागुरते** ॥ ३३ ॥ 'उपहूताः पितरः सोम्यासः' **इति यजति**। '○बर्हिष्येषु निधिषु=अवन्त्वस्मान्' **इति** ॥ ३४ ॥ 'स्वधा नमः' **इति वषट्करोति** ॥ ३५ ॥ **वषट्कृते जुहोति** ॥ ३६ ॥ 'पितृभ्योऽग्निष्वात्तेभ्योऽनु स्वधा कुरु' **इत्याहोपस्तृणानोऽवद्यन्** ॥ ३७ ॥ **सकृन्मन्थस्यावद्यति, सकृत्पुरोडाशस्य, सकृद्धानानाम्** ॥ ३८ ॥ **अभिघारयति** ॥ ३९ ॥ **प्रत्यनक्ति** ॥ ४० ॥ 'शृण्वन्तु नः पितरः सोम्यासः' **इत्यन्वाह**। '○अग्निष्वात्ता

'षडवत्तं पञ्चावत्तिनां, [1]पञ्चावत्तं च[1] चतुरवत्तिनां[2] द्विः प्रथमस्यावद्येत्[3] पञ्चावत्तिन[4]' इति ॥ ८-१४ ॥

पुरोनुवाक्ये द्वे अपि सप्रणवे[5] ॥ १७ ॥

प्राशित्रेडा षडवत्तवर्जं सर्वं हविःशेषकार्यं लुप्यते। शेषाणां पिण्डदानार्थमुपदिष्टत्वात् 'मार्जयस्वे'ति प्रैषवचनमञ्जलाववदानं चाध्वर्यम्। इतरत्सर्वं पिण्डदानं याजमानम्[6]। प्राग् [7]यज्ञोपवीतकरणात् ऋजुधा चरन्ति। आश्रावणादिषु विकारो नास्तीत्यर्थः। अस्य शंयुवाकान्तत्वं केचिद्वदन्ति। अन्ये प्रतिषिद्धवर्जं कुर्वन्ति। आश्वलायनेनोक्तम् —'सा[8] शंय्वन्ते'ति। आपस्तम्ब आह—'न पत्नीः संयाजयन्ति, न समिष्टयजुर्जुहोति। सर्वमन्यत् क्रियत' इति। शंय्वन्तत्वेऽप्युत्पन्नप्रतिपत्तिः कर्तव्या। युक्तविमोकश्चात्रैवेत्यादि। अस्मिन्नेवाग्नावित्यर्थः।

आहवनीयस्यार्धमेति यजमानः। ब्राह्मणे 'अग्नये देवेभ्यः पितृभ्य'[9] इति प्रैषं विधाय[10] 'उभये हि देवाश्च पितरश्चेज्यन्ते' इत्याह। तत्र देवाश्च पितरश्चेति व्यपदेशाद्देवेभ्योऽन्ये पितर इति गम्यते। तत्सर्वत्र देवप्रवादेषूभयं प्रयोक्तव्यम्। अतः[11] परं परिहाप्य यथा 'देवस्य त्वा सवितुः प्रसवे' इति, तथा। अनुपादकार आह- 'देवप्रवादेषु देवान् पितॄनिति कुर्युरन्यत्र सांस्कारिकेभ्यः' इति। बोधायनेनाप्युक्तम्—'देवानां पितॄणां परिषूतमसि। देवपितृबर्हिर्मा त्वान्वङ् मा तिर्यगि'ति। उदाहरणमात्रं दर्शयित्वैवमेवैतेष्वधिकरणेषु कुर्यात्, यत्र देवाश्च पितरश्च सन्निगच्छेयुरित्युक्तम्। एवं

१-१. M Ad om. २. M Ad °त्विदं; thus T. ३. M प्रथमस्य...त्. ४. M Ad °वर्तिन; thus T. ५. M Ad प्रणवे; thus T. ६. M Ad यज°. ७. M प्राग्य...तक°. ८. M Ad om. ९. M Ad om; thus T. १०. Ad विभाय. ११. M Ad तत्परं; thus T.

ऋतुभिः संविदाना भागं जुषाणा प्रथन्तां (...) भगमायजन्तु', 'वान्यायै दुग्धे जुषमाणाः करम्भमुदीराणा अवरे परे च। अग्निष्वात्ता ऋतुभिः संविदाना आसद्यास्मिन् बर्हिषि मादयन्ताम्' **इति** ॥ ४१ ॥ 'आ स्वधा' **इत्याश्रावयति** ॥ ४२ ॥ 'अस्तु स्वधा' **इति प्रत्याश्रावयति** ॥ ४३ ॥ 'पितर्निग्निष्वात्तान् स्वधा कुरु' **इत्याह** ॥ ४४ ॥ 'ये स्वधा' **इत्यागुरते** ॥ ४५ ॥ 'आगत्य पितरो मादयन्ताम्' **इति यजति**। '°अग्निष्वात्ता ऋतुभिः संविदानाः। भागं जुषाणा अवरे परे च। असुं य ईयुरवृका ऋतज्ञाः' **इति** ॥ ४६ ॥ 'स्वधा नमः' **इति वषट्करोति** ॥ ४७ ॥ **वषट्कृते जुहोति** ॥ ४८ ॥ 'अग्नये कव्यवाहनायानु स्वधा कुरु' **इत्याहोपस्तृणानोऽवद्यन्** ॥ ४९ ॥ **सकृत्पुरोडाशस्यावद्यति, सकृद्धानानाꣳ सकृदिक्षुशलाकया मन्थस्य** ॥ ५० ॥ **तामवदायाधोऽधः स्रुचावग्नीधे प्रयच्छति** ॥ ५१ ॥ **द्विरभिघारयति** ॥ ५२ ॥ **न प्रत्यनक्ति** ॥ ५३ ॥ 'यदग्ने कव्यवाहन' **इत्यन्वाह**। '°पितॄन् यक्ष्यतावृधः। प्र च=पितृभ्य आ, ये तातृषुर्देवत्रा जेहमाना होत्रावृधः स्तोमतष्टासो अर्कैः। आऽग्ने याहि सुविदत्रेभिरर्वाङ् सत्यैः कव्यैः पितृभिर्घर्मसद्भिः' **इति** ॥ ५४ ॥ 'आ स्वधा' **इत्या-श्रावयति** ॥ ५५ ॥ 'अस्तु स्वधा' **इति प्रत्याश्रावयति** ॥ ५६ ॥ 'अग्निं कव्यवाहनꣳ स्वधां कुरु' **इत्याह** ॥ ५७ ॥ 'ये स्वधा' **इत्यागुरते** ॥ ५८ ॥ 'हव्यवाहम्' **इति यजति**। '°अजरं पुरुप्रियमग्निं घृतेन हविषा सपर्यन्। उपासदं कव्यवाहं पितर्णिꣳ स नः प्रजां वीरवतीꣳ समृण्वतु' **इति** ॥ ५९ ॥ 'स्वधा नमः' **इति वषट्करोति** ॥ ६० ॥ **वषट्कृते जुहोति** ॥ ६१ ॥ **अनुप्रहरत्यग्नीदिक्षुशलाकाम्** ॥ ६२ ॥ **ताꣳ सꣳस्रावेणाभिजुहोति** ॥ ६३ ॥ **अत्याक्रम्य यथायतनꣳ स्रुचौ सादयित्वा प्राशित्रमवद्यति** ॥ ६४ ॥ **तदुत्तरतोऽत्यूह्य सादयति** ॥ ६५ ॥ **अप उपस्पृश्येडामवद्यति** ॥ ६६ ॥ **उपहूतायामिडाया-**

ब्रुवतामभिप्रायः प्रधानदेवताः पितरोऽङ्गदेवता देवा इति। एवं चेत्प्रधानार्थकरणेषु[1] देवशब्दमपनीय पितृशब्द एव प्रयोक्तव्यः। केवलाङ्गार्थेषु देवशब्द एव। उभयार्थेषूभयार्थमित्येवं ब्रुवते।

[2]'अग्नये देवेभ्यः पितृभ्य' इत्यादिना प्राकृतस्य प्रैषस्योहः प्रकृतस्य स्थाने विहितः।[2] 'अग्नये देवेभ्य = यानुब्रूही'त्याहेत्यस्य विध्युद्देशस्य स्तुत्यर्थम्। 'उभये हि देवाश्च पितरश्चेज्यन्ते' इत्युक्तम्। तथा च 'इमां दिशं वेदिमुद्धन्ती'त्यस्य च। तेन कथं सर्वत्र पितर्शिब्दान्वासङ्गो विधातुं शक्यते। अतो यथाप्रकृत्येव प्रयोग इति। ननु व्यपदेशात् ज्ञायते देवेभ्योऽन्ये पितर इति। अन्यत्वेऽपि व्यपदेशो भवति। यथा ऋषय आगता वसिष्ठोऽप्यागत इति। ननु लोकेतिहासपुराणेष्वन्ये देवा अन्ये पितर इति। सत्यमेवमेतत्। किन्तु पुराणादिप्रसिद्ध्या यज्ञकर्मणि कल्पयितुं न शक्यते। कल्प्यमाने हि द्रव्यगुणकालानां देवतात्वं व्याहन्येत। तथा सत्यव्यापित्वं स्यात्। के पुनरिह देवाः॥ ये च सूक्तं भजन्ते येभ्यश्च हविर्निरूप्यते ते देवाः[3] सूक्तभाजो हविर्भाजश्च। तस्मात्तेषामपि देवतात्वम्। देवदेवताशब्दौ[4] च समानार्थौ, स्वार्थे तद्धितस्मरणात्। स्मर्यन्ते[5] च कालानां देवतात्वं 'कालेभ्यो ह्यभवदि'ति[6]। अतो न पितृशब्दोऽनुषङ्ग[7] इति। तथा च सूत्रकारः—'पृथिवी देवपितृयजनी'-

---

१. M Ad °करेषु; thus T. २-२. M Ad om. ३. M Ad देवता; thus T. ४. M Ad देवदेवदेवता°. ५. M सूर्यन्ते, Ad सूर्यं ते. ६. M हपवदिति. ७. M Ad °शब्दानुषङ्ग.

मग्नीध आदधाति ॥ ६७ ॥ **अवजिघ्रत्यग्नीत्, न प्राश्नाति** ॥ ६८ ॥ **मार्जयते** ॥ ६९ ॥ **अवजिघ्रति होता, न प्राश्नाति** ॥ ७० ॥ **मार्जयते** ॥ ७१ ॥ **परिहरन्ति ब्रह्मणे** ॥ ७२ ॥ **अवजिघ्रति ब्रह्मा, न प्राश्नाति** ॥ ७३ ॥ **मार्जयते** ॥ ७४ ॥ **तान्यत्रैवेडापात्रे संप्रकिरन्ति** ॥ ७५ ॥ **अथ त्रीनुदपात्रान्नि-नयति** ॥ ४.४.२.७६ ॥ **[इति द्वितीयः पटलः** (१४)**]**

अथ त्रीनुदपात्रान्निनयति 'मार्जयन्तां पितरः' **इति दक्षिणायाः श्रोण्यां,** 'मार्जयन्तां पितामहाः' **इति दक्षिणेऽंसे,** 'मार्जयन्तां प्रपितामहाः' **इत्युत्तरेऽंसे** ॥ १ ॥ 'मार्जयस्व' **इत्याह यजमानम्** ॥ २ ॥ **तस्याञ्जलावुपस्तृणीते** ॥ ३ ॥ **सकृत् पुरोडाशस्यावद्यति, सकृद्धानानां सकृन्मन्थस्य** ॥ ४ ॥ **अभिघारयति** ॥ ५ ॥ 'एतत्ते तत' **इति दक्षिणायाः श्रोण्यां ददाति।** '॰याश्च त्वमन्वसि ये च त्वामनु ये च त्वामभितो ये च त्वया सह स्वधाक्षितिः' **इति** ॥ ६ ॥ 'इयमस्माकम्' **इत्यग्रेणाग्निमागत्योत्तरां वेद्यै श्रोणिमभिमृशति।** '॰इमां वयं जीवा जीवन्तोऽनुसञ्चरन्तो भूयास्म' **इति** ॥ ७ ॥ **उपस्तृणीत एवास्याञ्जलौ** ॥ ८ ॥ **सकृद्धानानामवद्यति, सकृन्मन्थस्य, सकृत्पुरोडाशस्य** ॥ ९ ॥ **अभिघारयति** ॥ १० ॥ 'एतत्ते पितामह' **इति दक्षिणेऽंसे ददाति।** '॰याश्च त्वमन्वसि ये च त्वामनु=क्षितिः' **इति** ॥ ११ ॥ 'इयमस्माकम्' **इत्येवाग्रेणाग्निमागत्योत्तरां वेद्यै श्रोणिमभिमृशति।** '॰इमां वयं=भूयास्म' **इति** ॥ १२ ॥ **उपस्तृणीत एवास्याञ्जलौ** ॥ १३ ॥ **सकृन्मन्थस्यावद्यति, सकृत् पुरोडाशस्य, सकृद्धानानाम्** ॥ १४ ॥ **अभिघारयति** ॥ १५ ॥ 'एतत्ते प्रपितामह' **इत्युत्तरेऽंसे ददाति।** '॰याश्च त्वमन्वसि ये च त्वामनु =क्षितिः' **इति** ॥ १६ ॥ 'इयमस्माकम्' **इत्येवाग्रेणाग्निमागत्योत्तरां वेद्यै श्रोणिमभिमृशति।** '॰इमां=भूयास्म' **इति** ॥ १७ ॥ **मार्जयते** ॥ १८ ॥ **यजमानः** 'अत्र पितरो यथाभागं मन्दध्वम्' **इत्युक्त्वोदञ्चो निष्क्रामति** ॥ १९ ॥ **आतमितोस्तिष्ठन्ति** ॥ २० ॥ 'सुसंदृशं त्वा वयम्' **इत्याहवनीयमभिव्यनिति।** '॰मघवन् मन्दिषीमहि। प्र नूनं पूर्णबन्धुरः स्तुतो = हरी' **इति** ॥ २१ ॥ 'अमीमदन्त पितरः सोम्याः' **इत्यभिपर्यावर्तते** ॥ २२ ॥ **यत् पात्रियामतिशिष्यते तत् त्रिरवजिघ्रति** 'ये सजाताः समनसो जी=शतं समाः' **इति** ॥ २३ ॥ 'नमो वः पित=वसिष्ठो भूयासम्' **इति** ॥ २४ ॥ **अथ त्रीनेवोदपात्रान्निनयति** 'मार्जयन्तां पितरः' **इति दक्षिणायाः श्रोण्यां,** 'मार्जयन्तां पितामहाः' **इति दक्षिणेऽंसे,** 'मार्जयन्तां प्रपितामहाः' **इत्युत्तरेऽंसे** ॥ २५ ॥ **ददाति कशिपूपबर्हणे आञ्जनाभ्यञ्जने** ॥ २६ ॥ 'आञ्जतां पितरः' **इति दक्षिणायाः श्रोण्यामानक्ति** ॥ २७ ॥ 'अभ्यञ्जतां पितरः आञ्जतां पितरः' **इति द्विरानक्ति सकृदभ्यनक्ति** ॥ २८ ॥ 'आञ्जतां पितामहाः' **इति दक्षिणेऽंसे आनक्ति** ॥ २९ ॥ 'अभ्यञ्जतां पितामहा आञ्जतां पितामहाः' **इति द्विरेवानक्ति**

त्यादीन्युदाहृत्य पुनराह—'अविकारो वा परवाक्यश्रवणादि'ति। भारद्वाजीयेऽपि तादृशं वचनमस्ति 'यथा प्रकृत्येव वर्तेरन्नि'ति। अन्वासङ्गपक्षे सर्वेषु देवशब्देषु तात्पर्यमतत्परत्वं च। प्रधानार्थत्वमुभयार्थत्वं च [1]सर्वमवेक्ष्यानुषक्तव्यम् ॥ ४.४.२.१८-७६ ॥ **[इति द्वितीयः पटलः** (१४)**]**

---

१. M Ad ससर्व॰.

सकृदभ्यनक्ति ॥ ३० ॥ 'आञ्जतां प्रपितामहाः' **इत्युत्तरेऽꣳसे आनक्ति** ॥ ३१ ॥ 'अभ्यञ्जतां प्रपितामहा आञ्जतां प्रपितामहाः' **इति द्विरेवानक्ति सकृदभ्यनक्ति** ॥ ३२ ॥ **दशां छिनत्ति** 'एतद्वः पितरो वासो=करोतु मामनेनसम्' **इति** ॥ ३३ ॥ **यज्ञोपवीतानि कुर्वते** ॥ ३४ ॥ **ऋजुधा चरन्ति** ॥ ३५ ॥ **सादयन्ति दक्षिणार्ध्यम्** ॥ ३६ ॥ **परिधिमवोद्धरन्ति** ॥ ३७ ॥ **परिश्रयणं विपर्यन्ति** ॥ ३८ ॥ **सन्ततिꣳ हुत्वा षड्ढोतुराहुतिं जुहोति** ॥ ३९ ॥ **संप्रेष्यति** 'ब्रह्मन् प्रस्थास्यामः समिधमाधायाग्नीदग्निꣳ सकृद् संमृड्ढि' **इति** ॥ ४० ॥ **अपबर्हिषौ द्वावनूयाजौ यजति** ॥ ४१ ॥ **आगत्य वाजवतीभ्याꣳ स्रुचौ व्यूहति** ॥ ४२ ॥ **शंयुना प्रस्तरपरिधि संप्रकिरति** ॥ ४३ ॥ **न पत्न्यन्वास्ते** ॥ ४४ ॥ **न संयाजयन्ति** ॥ ४५ ॥ **न समिष्टयजुर्जुहोति** ॥ ४६ ॥ **अत्रैव यत्पुरोडाशस्यातिशिष्यते यद्धानानां यन्मन्थस्य तत्सर्वꣳ संप्रकिरन्ति** ॥ ४७ ॥ **सन्तिष्ठते पितृयज्ञः** ॥ ४८ ॥ 'प्रजापते न त्वदेतान्यन्यः' **इत्याहवनीयस्यार्धमेति** । '°विश्वा=रयीणाम्' **इति** ॥ ४९ ॥ **कोशबिले त्र्यम्बकान् संप्रकिरन्ति** ॥ ५० ॥ **अन्तमं पलाशस्य पर्णमुपकल्पयते** ॥ ४.४.३.५१ ॥ **[इति *तृतीयः पटलः (१५)]**

अन्तमं पलाशस्य पर्णमुपकल्पयते ॥ १ ॥ **इमां दिशं प्राचीमुदीचीं चतुष्पथꣳ स्पाशयन्ते** ॥ २ ॥ **तमपरेणाखूत्करमन्यतममेकोल्मुकमादायोदपात्रं च कुमारीमामन्त्र्य त्र्यम्बकैरुत्परायन्ति** ॥ ३ ॥ 'यावन्तो गृह्याः स्मः' **इति गार्हपत्यमुपतिष्ठते** । '°तेभ्यः=शर्म मे यच्छ' **इति** ॥ ४ ॥ 'आखुस्ते रुद्र पशुः' **इत्याखूत्करे त्र्यम्बकमन्वस्यति** । '°तं जुषस्वैष ते रुद्र भागः=तं जुषस्व' **इति** ॥ ५ ॥ **चतुष्पथ एकोल्मुकꣳ सादयित्वोपसमादधाति** ॥ ६ ॥ **अन्तमे पलाशस्य पर्णे त्र्यम्बकाणाꣳ समवद्यति** ॥ ७ ॥ 'भेषजं गवे' **इत्यपरेणाग्निं पुरोनुवाक्यान्वाह** । '°अश्वाय पुरुषाय भेषज=मेष्यै कृधि' **इति** ॥ ८ ॥ 'अवाम्ब रुद्र मदिमहि' **इति यजति** । '°अव देवं त्र्यम्बकम्। यथा नः=व्यवसाययात्। यथा नः सर्वमिज्जगदयक्ष्मꣳ सुमना असत् स्वाहा' **इति** ॥ ९ ॥ **अनुप्रास्यति पर्णं कोशबिले** ॥ १० ॥ **त्र्यम्बकानुत्खिदति** ॥ ११ ॥ **तान् विमथ्नते** ॥ १२ ॥ **तान् समाहरन्ति** ॥ १३ ॥ **तान् यजमानस्याञ्जलावावपति** ॥ १४ ॥ 'त्र्यम्बकं यजामहे' **इति दक्षिणानूरूनाघ्नानाः प्रसलैः परियन्ति** । '°सुगन्धिं पुष्टिवर्धनमुर्वा=माऽमृतात्' **इति** ॥ १५ ॥ **तानेवोत्खिदति** ॥ १६ ॥ **तान्**

*. Commentory on the 3rd Paṭala (sūtra 1-51) is not given in the MSS.

कोशबिले। कोश इति प्रसिद्धः भस्त्रायामिति[१] । अन्ये त्र्यम्बकाणां सकृत्सकृदवदानमिच्छन्ति। अथैतेषां त्र्यम्बकाणां सकृदवदाय जुहोतीति केचित्पठन्ति ॥ १० ॥

उत्खिन्दति[२] ऊर्ध्वं क्षिपति[३] ॥ ११ ॥

यजमानस्तान् विमथ्नते ॥ १२ ॥

१. T भस्त्राया°. २. M Ad दन्ति; thus T. ३. M Ad °पन्ति; thus T.

विमथ्नते ॥ १७ ॥ **तान् समाहरन्ति** ॥ १८ ॥ **तान् यजमानस्यैवावपन्ति** ॥ १९ ॥ 'त्र्यम्बकं यजामहे' **इत्येव दक्षिणानूरुनाघ्नानाः प्रतिपथं परियन्ति** ॥ २० ॥ 'प्रेतो मुक्षीय माऽमुतः' **इति ह कुमारी वा पतिकामा ब्रूयात्** ॥ २१ ॥ **तस्या एनानञ्जलावावपन्ति** 'भगेन त्वा सꣳसृजामि मासरेण सुरामिव' **इति** ॥ २२ ॥ **तान्नु साऽन्ततो यजमानस्यैवाञ्जलावावपति** ॥ २३ ॥ **तान् मूतयोः कृत्वा विविधेनोदपात्रमादायाध्वर्युश्च यजमानश्च हस्ते शुष्के स्थाणावासजतः** 'एष ते रुद्र भागस्तं जुषस्व तेन=कृत्तिवासाः' **इति** ॥ २४ ॥ **अपः परिषिच्याप्रतीक्षमाव्रजते** ॥ २५ ॥ **आगत्य विसृजति पूर्वमग्निमपरस्मिन्नाहवनीये** ॥ २६ ॥ **पुनरेत्यापः प्रणीयादित्यं चरुं निर्वपति** ॥ २७ ॥ **निरुप्ते प्राणग्रहाꣳश्च पृश्नीꣳश्च व्याचष्टे** ॥ २८ ॥ **समासन्नेऽपानग्रहाꣳश्च पृश्नीꣳश्च व्याचष्टे** ॥ २९ ॥ 'ध्रुवा असदन्', 'यन्मे अग्ने' **इति समभिमृश्य दशहोतारं व्याचष्टे** ॥ ३० ॥ **तस्यै वार्त्रघ्नावाज्यभागौ** ॥ ३१ ॥ 'अदितिर्न उरुष्यतु' **इत्यन्वाह** ॥ ३२ ॥ 'महीमू षु मातरम्' **इति यजति** ॥ ३३ ॥ **वषट्कृते जुहोति** ॥ ३४ ॥ **त्रिष्टुभौ संयाज्ये** ॥ ३५ ॥ **सन्ततिमनु होतुराहुतिं जुहोति** ॥ ३६ ॥ **प्रसिध्यति कर्म** ॥ ३७ ॥ **सन्तिष्ठत एषेष्टिः** ॥ ३८ ॥ **सꣳस्थामनु हविषो निवर्तयते** ॥ ३९ ॥ **प्रसिद्धाः संभाराः** ॥ ४० ॥ 'य इमां महीं पृथिवीमृतुभिः पर्यवर्तयदन्तान् पृथिव्या अनु। अग्निस्तिग्मेन शोचिषा वैश्वानरस्य तेजसर्तेन त्वा निवर्तये सत्येन परिवर्तये शिवेन त्वोपवर्तये तदृतं तत्सत्यं तद्व्रतं तच्छकेयं तेन राध्यासम्' **इति पुरस्तादग्रे वपतेऽथ दक्षिणतोऽथ पश्चादथोत्तरतोऽथ मध्ये** ॥ ४१ ॥ **सꣳस्थामनु हविषः प्रसिद्धम्** ॥ ४२ ॥ **प्रसिद्धं पौर्णमासेन हविषा यजते** ॥ ४३ ॥ **देवव्रतानि चरति** ॥ ४.४.४.४४ ॥ **[इति चतुर्थः पटलः (१६)]**

॥ इति चतुर्थप्रपाठके चतुर्थोऽनुवाकः ॥

गृह्या यजमानस्य गार्हपत्योपस्थाने च तेषामेव 'माऽमुत' इत्यभिप्रेतस्य नाम्नः पञ्चम्यन्तस्य प्रयोगः। अथवा 'इतः' इत्यत्र कन्याभावादिति स्मरति। 'अमुत' इति वरेण योगादिति। यथाऽऽम्नातमेव प्रयोगः ॥ १८-२३ ॥

मूतयोः[1] कृत्वाऽपर्णसेवयोः[2] संभृत्योपनह्य विविधमध्य[3] आसज्य विविधप्रान्तयोरालभ्योभौ हरतः। पूर्वमग्निमौत्तरवेदिकं पाशुकेन विधानेन दक्षिणाग्नेः प्रणीतो लौकिको भवति[4] ॥ ४.४.४.२४ ॥ **[इति चतुर्थः पटलः (१६)]**

॥ इति व्याख्यायां चतुर्थप्रपाठके चतुर्थोऽनुवाकः ॥

---

१. M Ad T ऽमूत°. २. M पर्णदेसवयोः, T वर्णसेवयोः. ३. Ad T विविध°. ४. Ad wrongly gives at the end इति चतुर्थः प्रपाठकः समाप्तः instead of चतुर्थोऽनुवाकः.

॥ अथ चतुर्थप्रपाठके पञ्चमोऽनुवाकः ॥

[शुनासीरीयपर्व]

अद्य मृगशीर्षेण पौर्णमासीति यज्ञायुधानि संसाद्यापः प्रणीय शुनासीरीयं निर्वपत्याग्नेयमष्टाकपालꣳ सौम्यं चरुꣳ सावित्रं द्वादशकपालꣳ सारस्वतं चरुं वैष्णवं चरुमैन्द्राग्नं द्वादशकपालं वैश्वदेवं चरुमिन्द्राय शुनासीराय पुरोडाशं द्वादशकपालं वायव्यं पयः सौर्यमेककपालम् ॥ १ ॥ निरुप्ते प्राणग्रहाꣳश्च पृश्नीꣳश्च व्याचष्टे ॥ २ ॥ तस्य हविष्कृता वाचं विसृज्य चतुर्गृहीतेन पञ्चहोतारमाज्यस्याहवनीये जुहोति ॥ ३ ॥ श्रप्यन्ते हवीꣳषि ॥ ४ ॥ शृतेषु हविषुः स्तम्बयजुर्हरति ॥ ५ ॥ वेदिं परिगृह्णाति ॥ ६ ॥ करणं जपति ॥ ७ ॥ प्रसूत उत्तरं परिग्राहं परिगृह्णाति ॥ ८ ॥ योयुपित्वाऽवस्कभ्य संप्रेष्यति 'प्रोक्षणीरासादयेध्माबर्हिरुपसादय स्रुवं च स्रुचश्च समृड्ढि पत्नीꣳ संनह्याज्येनोदेहि पृषदाज्याय दध्याहरेहि यजमान' इति ॥ ९ ॥ एतत् कुर्वन्ति ॥ १० ॥ स्रुवं च स्रुचश्च संमृज्याज्यानि गृह्णीते पृषदाज्यवन्ति ॥ ११ ॥ इध्माबर्हिः प्रोक्षति ॥ १२ ॥ वेदिं प्रोक्षति ॥ १३ ॥ आसन्नं प्रोक्षति ॥ १४ ॥ अपो निनीय प्रस्तरं गृह्णाति ॥ १५ ॥ स्तृणाति बर्हिः ॥ १६ ॥ प्राङुत्सृप्य परिधीन् परिदधाति ॥ १७ ॥ समिधावादधाति ॥ १८ ॥ परिधिषु वाचयित्वाऽग्निं युनक्ति ॥ १९ ॥ आगत्य तिरश्ची सादयति ॥ २० ॥ तिरश्च्योः प्रस्तरम् ॥ २१ ॥ प्रस्तरे जुहूम् ॥ २२ ॥ बर्हिषीतरे ॥ २३ ॥ अलङ्कुर्वन्त्यनुपूर्वꣳ हवीꣳषि ॥ २४ ॥ उपस्तीर्णाभिघारितान्युद्वासयति ॥ २५ ॥ समभिघार्य हवीꣳष्याहरन्ति ॥ २६ ॥ समासन्नेऽपानग्रहाꣳश्च पृश्नीꣳश्च व्याचष्टे ॥ २७ ॥ 'ध्रुवा असदन्', 'यन्मे अग्ने' इति समभिमृश्य पञ्चहोतारं व्याचष्टे ॥ २८ ॥ निर्मन्थ्येन चरति ॥ २९ ॥ अग्नये समिध्यमानायानुवाच आह ॥ ३० ॥ सप्तदश सामिधेनीरन्वाह ॥ ३१ ॥ अनूक्तासु सामिधेनीषु स्रुवेणाघारमाघार्याह 'अग्नीदग्निं त्रिस्त्रिः संमृड्ढि' इति ॥ ३२ ॥ स्रुग्भ्यामुत्तरम् ॥ ३३ ॥ असꣳस्पर्शयन्नत्याक्रम्य ध्रुवाꣳ समज्य सादयित्वा प्रवरं प्रवृणीते ॥ ३४ ॥ सीदति होता ॥ ३५ ॥ प्रसूतः स्रुचावादत्ते ॥ ३६ ॥ नव प्रयाजान् यजति ॥ ३७ ॥ 'ओ श्रावय' इत्याह ॥ ३८ ॥ 'समिधो यज' इति ॥ ३९ ॥ 'यज यज' इति ॥ ४० ॥ चतुर्थेऽर्धꣳ समानीयाष्टमे सर्वꣳ समानयति ॥ ४१ ॥ उपभृतोऽधि सर्वं प्रयजति ॥ ४२ ॥

अद्य मृगशीर्षेणेत्यादि। व्याख्यातः कालविशेषः। वायव्यं पयः प्रातर्दोहं विकरोति। तत्र यद्यपि प्रकृतौ दर्भैः प्रातर्दोहाय वत्सा अपाकृताः, तथापीह [1]शाखामेवाहृत्य वत्सानपाकृत्य शाखापवित्रं कृत्वा दोहयति। अस्य पयसोऽधर्मकत्वं कात्यायनः किलाह—'अधर्मकं[2] वा प्रतिधुक् श्रुतेरि'ति ॥ ४.५.१.१ ॥ **[इति प्रथमः पटलः (१७)]**

---

१. T विशा° . २. M Ad धर्म° ; thus T.

प्रयाजानिष्ट्वाऽत्याक्रम्य ध्रुवामभिघारयत्यनुपूर्वꣳ हवींषि ॥ ४३ ॥ **पृषदाज्यमन्ततः** ॥ ४४ ॥ **नोपभृतः रिक्ता हि सा भवति** ॥ ४५ ॥ **आज्यभागौ यजति** ॥ ४६ ॥ **वार्त्रघ्नावाज्यभागौ** ॥ ४७ ॥ 'अग्नयेऽनुब्रूहि' **इत्याहोपस्तृणानोऽवद्यन्** ॥ ४.५.१.४८ ॥ **[इति प्रथमः पटलः** (१७)**]**

'अग्नयेऽनुब्रूहि' **इत्याहोपस्तृणानोऽवद्यन्** ॥ १ ॥ **प्रसिद्धाः सप्तानाꣳ हविषां याज्यापुरोनु-वाक्याः** ॥ २ ॥ 'इन्द्राय शुनासीरायानुब्रूहि' **इत्याहोपस्तृणानोऽवद्यन्** ॥ ३ ॥ 'इन्द्रं वयꣳ शुनासीरम्' **इत्यन्वाह** । '०अस्मिन् यज्ञे हवामहे आ वाजेरुप नो हवामहे' **इति** ॥ ४ ॥ 'प्र हव्यानि' **इति यजति** । '०घृतवन्त्यस्मै हर्यश्वाय भरता सजोषाः। इन्द्रर्तुभिर्ब्रह्मणा वावृधानः शुनासीरी हविरिदं जुषस्व' **इति** ॥ ५ ॥ **वषट्कृते जुहोति** ॥ ६ ॥ 'वायवेऽनुब्रूहि' **इत्याहोपस्तृणानोऽवद्यन्** ॥ ७ ॥ 'वायो शतꣳ हरीणाम्' **इत्यन्वाह** ॥ ८ ॥ 'प्र याभिर्यासि दाश्वाꣳसम्' **इति यजति** ॥ ९ ॥ **वषट्कृते जुहोति** ॥ १० ॥ 'सूर्यायानुब्रूहि' **इत्याहोपस्तीर्णाभिघारितमेककपालमादधानः** ॥ ११ ॥ 'उदु त्यं जातवेदसम्' **इत्यन्वाह** ॥ १२ ॥ 'चित्रं देवानामुदगादनीकम्' **इति यजति** ॥ १३ ॥ **वषट्कृते जुहोति** ॥ १४ ॥ 'अग्नये स्विष्टकृतेऽनुब्रूहि' **इत्याहोपस्तृणानोऽवद्यन्** ॥ १५ ॥ **सकृत्सकृदुत्तरार्धात् सर्वेषाꣳ हविषामवद्यति** ॥ १६ ॥ **आशयादेककपालस्यावदाय द्विः** ॥ १७ ॥ **अभिघारयति** ॥ १८ ॥ **न प्रत्यनक्ति** ॥ १९ ॥ 'अग्निꣳ स्तोमेन बोधय' **इत्यन्वाह** ॥ २० ॥ 'स हव्यवाड्' **इति यजति** ॥ २१ ॥ **वषट्कृते जुहोति** ॥ २२ ॥ **अत्याक्रम्य यथायतनꣳ स्रुचौ सादयित्वा प्राशित्रमवद्यति** ॥ २३ ॥ **अप उपस्पृश्येडामवद्यति** ॥ २४ ॥ **उपहूतायामिडायामग्नीध आदधाति** ॥ २५ ॥ **प्राश्नन्ति** ॥ २६ ॥ **मार्जयन्ते** ॥ २७ ॥ **परिहरन्ति ब्रह्मणे** ॥ २८ ॥ **प्राशिते प्राशित्रे चरौ यजमानभागं प्रास्योद्वासयन्ति हवीꣳषि** ॥ २९ ॥ **अन्वाहार्ये वाचयति** ॥ ३० ॥ **सन्ततिमनु द्वौ विष्टसम्भान्वारोहौ जुहोति** 'अभिषाहे स्वाहा' **इति विष्टम्भः**, 'सꣳसर्पोऽस्यꣳहस्पत्याय स्वाहा' **इत्यन्वारोहः** ॥ ३१ ॥ 'एहि यजमान' **इत्युक्त्वाऽन्वारब्धे यजमाने होतुराहुतिं तृतीयां जुहोति** ॥ ३२ ॥ 'ब्रह्मन् प्रस्थास्यामः' **इति** ॥ ३३ ॥ **पृषदाज्येन नवानूयाजान् यजति** ॥ ३४ ॥ **आगत्य वाजवतीभ्याꣳ स्रुचौ व्यूहति** ॥ ३५ ॥ **शंयुना प्रस्तरपरिधि संप्रकिरति** ॥ ३६ ॥ **परेत्य पत्नीः संयाजयन्ति** ॥ ३७ ॥ **फलीकरणहोमꣳ हुत्वा प्राडेत्य त्रीणि समिष्टयजूꣳषि जुहोति** ॥ ३८ ॥ 'यज्ञ यज्ञं गच्छ यज्ञ=सुवीरः' **स्वाहा इति स्रुवेण हुत्वा ध्रुवामाप्याय्य** 'देवा गातुविदः' **इति स्रुचा जुहोति** । '०गातुं वित्त्वा=स्वाहा वाते धाः' **इति** ॥ ३९ ॥ **सꣳस्थामनु हविषो निवर्तयते** ॥ ४० ॥ **प्रसिद्धाः संभाराः** ॥ ४१ ॥ 'एकं मासमुदसृजत= संवर्तयामि जीवसे। अग्निस्तिग्मेन शोचिषा वैश्वानरस्य तेजसर्तेन त्वा निवर्तये सत्येन परिवर्तये शिवेन त्वोपवर्तये। तदूतं=तेन राध्यासम्' **इति पुरस्ता**[*१] **(दग्रे वपतेऽथ दक्षिणतोऽथ पश्चादथोत्तरतोऽथ) मध्ये** ॥ ४२ ॥ **सꣳस्थामनु हविषः प्रसिद्धम्** ॥ ४३ ॥ **पौर्णमासेन हविषा**

[*१]. Text abri. पुरस्ता=मध्ये see IV.1.4.28.

यजते ॥ ४४ ॥ **देवव्रतानि चरति** ॥ ४.५.२.४५ ॥ **[इति द्वितीयः पटलः** (१८)**]**

॥ इति चतुर्थप्रपाठके पञ्चमोऽनुवाकः ॥

॥ इति चातुर्मास्याख्यः चतुर्थः प्रपाठकः ॥

□ □ □

इह 'देवव्रतानि' वचनम्[१] संवत्सरप्रयोगापेक्षम्। अनेकसंवत्सरप्रयोगे हि[२] 'इति चातुर्मास्ययाजिनः' इति वचनाद्यावत्प्रयोगं व्रतचर्याः[३]। अथवाऽन्यार्थवचने 'संवत्सरं हि व्रतं नातीयादि'ति हेतुनिर्देशात्संवत्सरपर्यन्तानि व्रतानि ॥ ४.५.२.४५ ॥ **[इति द्वितीयः पटलः** (१८)**]**

॥ इति व्याख्यायां चतुर्थप्रपाठके पञ्चमोऽनुवाकः ॥

॥ इति कल्पागमसंग्रहे चातुर्मास्याख्यः चतुर्थः प्रपाठकः ॥

□ □ □

---

१. M Ad देवव्रताव°. २. M Ad om; thus T. ३. M Ad व्रताचार्याः.

॥ अथ पञ्चमः प्रपाठकः ॥

[पशुबन्धः]

[संभारसंभरणम्]

पशुना यक्ष्यमाणः संभारान् संभरते ॥ १ ॥ द्वे रशने द्वे वपाश्रपण्यौ त्रयः कार्ष्मर्यमयाः

पशुना=भरते। पश्वाख्येन कर्मणा यष्टुकामस्तत्साधनानि उपकल्पयते। तत्र रशनादीनां द्रव्याणामनुक्रमणं[१] प्रदर्शनार्थम्। कुम्भीस्वधितीडसूनादीन्यप्यात्मसात्करणीयानि। पशुरपि [२]छागः। अध्रिगौ 'अन्वेनं[२] माता मन्यतामि'त्यादिदर्शनान्मातृमान् पितृमान् भ्रातृमान्[३] सगर्भिमान् सखिमानित्यादि गुणवत्त्वमिष्यते। अग्नीषोमीयविकारत्वे 'तस्मान्नु हैष आण्डीवलः[४] स्यादि'तीहापि च[५] तुल्यम्। सर्वाङ्ग इत्यच्छिन्नकरणत्वादि[६]। आत्मन्वी पीनः[७] बलवांश्च। अग्नीषोमीयविकारत्वेऽप्येते गुणा इष्यन्त एव। तथाहि विध्यवशेषेषु 'आप्लुतच्छागमकुण्यङ्गमि'त्याद्युक्तम्। [८]तथा च श्रुत्यन्तरेषु[८] 'अपशुर्वा एष योऽपन्नदत्, मलं वा एष पशूनां यो सिक्तरेता' इत्यादीनि निन्दावचनान्येतमेवार्थमुपोद्बलयन्ति। रशनादीनां दर्भाणां मुञ्जानां वेत्यादयो विशेषा विध्यवशेषेषु द्रष्टव्याः। कः पुनः पशुना यक्ष्यमाणः। आहिताग्निः। तस्य यथाऽग्निहोत्रं यथा दर्शपूर्णमासौ च तथेदमपि नित्यं कर्म। वक्ष्यति हि—'तमनीजानं संवत्सरो नाभ्यतीयादि'ति। अतीते प्रायश्चित्तीयतां मन्यमानेन ह्येवमभ्यधायि। अनुपदकारश्चाह—'तमनीजानं षण्मासः संवत्सरो वा [९]नाभ्यतीयात्, [१०]यद्यतीयान्मांसं नाश्नीयाद्'[११]। अथ कालातिनये अग्नये पथिकृते पुरोडाशमष्टाकपालं निर्वपेत्। वैश्वानरं द्वादशकपालम्, अग्नये व्रतपतये पुरोडाशमष्टाकपालं निर्वपेत्। सर्वेषां दर्शपूर्णमासप्रकृतीनां कालातिनय एतामेव निर्वपेत्। अथ सोमस्य कालातिनय एतां च सवनीयेष्टिञ्च निर्वपेत्। आग्नेयमष्टकपालमैन्द्रमेकादशकपालं वैश्वदेवं द्वादशकपालमि'ति। तस्य कालः 'पुरस्तात्प्रोष्ठपाद्यै पशुने'त्यविशेषेण पूर्वपक्षे प्राप्ते 'शातभिषज्यां पौर्णमास्यामि'ति वचनात् पौर्णमास्या उपवसथीयेऽहन्यालब्धव्यः। शातभिषजी प्रोष्ठपादीति च नार्थान्तरम्। ननु षट्सु षट्सु मासेषु पशुबन्ध इति। तदपि पक्षान्तरम्। तस्मिन् पक्षे माघस्य श्रावणस्य चामावास्ययोर्यजनीययोरह्नोरालम्भः। उभयोः पक्षयोरादिविकल्पत्वं केचिन्मन्यन्ते। अन्य आहुः—'यज्ञक्रतूनेतान् प्रोक्ष्यमाणो भवती'त्युपक्रम्य 'तस्यैवमेते यज्ञक्रतवः परिप्लवेरन्नि'त्यग्निहोत्रादीनां सोमान्तानां यावज्जीविकोऽभ्यासो विहितः। स च पाक्षिकः। तस्मिन्

---

१. T °मणप्रद°. २–२. T छागो वाध्रीगाव°, M Ad °ध्रिगाव°. ३. M Ad om; thus T. ४. M Ad आ = ण्डीवलः, T हैषकेवलः स्या°. ५. M Ad om; thus T. ६. M Ad °छिन्नकर्तृत्वादि, T °छिन्नकर्ण°. ७. M Ad पिनः. ८–८. M T takes it as additional hence gives in fn. ९. M Ad om; thus T. १०. M Ad om यद्यतीयात्; thus T. ११. M Ad नाग्नी°.

परिधय औदुम्बरो मैत्रावरुणदण्डो हृदयशूलो दधि पृषदाज्याय सक्तवः सक्तुहोमाय ॥ २ ॥ गार्हपत्य आज्यं विलाप्योत्पूय स्रुवं च स्रुचश्च संमृज्य प्राङेत्याहवनीयस्यार्धं चतुर्गृहीतं गृह्णीते ॥ ३ ॥ 'देवस्त्वा सविता मध्वानक्तु' **इत्येनः हिरण्यमन्तर्धायाज्येनानक्ति ॥ ४ ॥** 'ओषधे त्राय-

---

पक्षे षट्सु मासेषु चातुर्मास्यानां सोमस्य चाभ्यासः। संवत्सरे सकृत्। तत्र हि 'वरुणप्रघासेभ्योऽध्यर्धे मासि पशुबन्धेन यजेते'त्यारभ्य 'शुनासीर्यादर्धमासे पशुनेष्ट्वा तदहरेव दीक्षेते'ति[1] विहितमिति।

अत्र कश्चिदाह—'प्राक् सोमयागात् [2]सान्नाय्यविकाराणामप्रयोगः। पशुरपि[2] सान्नाय्यविकारः। अतः सोमेनेष्ट्वानधिक्रियते, नानिष्टसोम' इति। तथाऽयमप्याचार्यः 'ब्राह्मणमु वै[3] भवति नासोमयाजी =ततो दीक्षितमेवोपपरेयादि'ति प्रतिषेधोऽनर्थकः स्यात्। ज्योतिष्टोमप्रकृतयो हि सर्वे [4]सोमाः। अथा-तिरात्रस्यापि[4] प्रथमाहरत्वं[5] जैमिनीया आमनन्ति। तच्चाग्निष्टोमेनानिष्टवतो नोपपद्येत। चतुःसंस्थस्य ज्योतिष्टोमस्य समानविध्यादुपपद्यत इति चेत्, न। अग्निष्टोमस्यैव धर्मा इति वक्ष्यामः। इतरस्मिन्न-नतियागपक्षो नोपपद्यते। 'पञ्च वै ब्राह्मा' [6]इत्यस्मिन्ननुवाके[6] पक्षत्रयं विहितम्। पञ्चानामनुक्रमेण प्रयोगः[7]। दर्शपूर्णमासोत्तरकाले[8] सोमयागः। अग्निहोत्रमप्यनारभ्यैव सोमयागः। व्रतमेवाग्निहोत्रमि-त्यादि। तत्र कस्यचिदपि नापूर्वपक्षत्वमस्ति। ननु 'नासोमयाजी[9] सन्नयेदि'त्यादिना प्रथमः पक्ष उपोदितः[10]। एवं तर्हि[10] 'यथा ज्यायांसं[11] पर्यादधीते'त्यादि नान्ययोः पक्षयोरपवादः स्यात्। तथा सति न कस्यचित् प्रवृत्तिः स्यात्। वेदवाक्यानां शीलमेतद्वैकल्पिकानामेकस्य स्तुत्यर्थमितरस्य निन्दा। यथोदितानुदितहोमयोः प्रातः। 'प्रातरनृतं ते वदन्ति, पुरोदयाज्जुह्वति [12]येऽग्निहोत्रम्'। तस्मादुदिते होतव्यम्[13]। 'यदुदिते[13] सूर्ये प्रातर्जुहुयाद्, यथाऽतिथये प्रद्रुताय = तदेव संप्रतीति' च। तस्मात्सोम-यागात्प्रागपि पशुभिर्विहितः ॥ १-२ ॥

गार्हपत्य आज्यमित्यादि ॥ ३ ॥

उपांशुग्रहणं हिरण्यम् ॥ ४ ॥

यूपस्यार्धं यूपार्थस्य वृक्षस्य समीपमित्यर्थः। उपपरैतीति[14] यद्यप्येकवचनं तथाप्यध्वर्युयजमानावुत्थाय परा गच्छतः। 'यजमानेन यूपः संमितः' इति वचनाद् यजमानस्यारत्निभिर्विमितो हि यूपश्छिद्यते। तमुपतिष्ठते। जोषणवचनाद्विहितानां प्रशस्तानां च यूपगुणानां परिग्रहणार्थं यः प्रत्यङ्ङुपनतस्तं वृश्चेत्। 'यं कामयेत पशुमान् स्यात्' इति बहुपर्णं तस्मै बहुशाखं

---

१. T दीक्षितेति°. २-२. M Ad om; thus T. ३. Ad पै. ४-४. M सो...तिरात्र° ; thus Ad T. ५. M Ad °माहरत्वं. ६-६. M इत्य...क. ७. M Ad °योग. ८. M Ad काल, T कालं. ९. M Ad °याजि; thus T. १०-१०. M उपो...हि, Ad °दिक; thus T. ११. M Ad ज्यायां संपर्यादधीतेत्यादिति. १२. M Ad योऽग्नि. १३-१३. M °तव्यं...दिति; Ad यददिति. १४. M Ad °परेति°.

स्वैनम्' **इति बर्हिषा परिदधाति** ॥ ५ ॥ **यूपस्यार्धमुप परैति** ॥ ६ ॥ 'स्वधिते मैनꣳ हिꣳसीः' **इति स्वधितिना प्रहरति** ॥ ७ ॥ **यः प्रथमः शकलः परापतति तमुपनह्य निदधाति** ॥ ८ ॥ **अनक्षसङ्गं वृश्चति** ॥ ९ ॥ **प्राञ्चं वोदञ्चं वा प्रपातयति** ॥ १० ॥ 'दिवमग्रेण मा लेखीः' **इत्यनुमन्त्रयते**। '०अन्तरिक्षं मध्येन मा हिꣳसीः पृथिव्या सं भव' **इति** ॥ ११ ॥ 'वनस्पते शतवल्शो विरोह स्वाहा' **इति हिरण्यमुपास्य व्रश्चने जुहोति** ॥ १२ ॥ 'सहस्रवल्शा वि वयꣳ रुहेम' **इत्यात्मानं प्रत्यभिमृशते** ॥ १३ ॥ **अप उपस्पृश्य** 'यं त्वाऽयꣳ स्वधितिस्तेतिजानः प्रणिनाय महते सौभगाय' **इत्यन्वग्रꣳ शाखाः प्रहापयति** ॥ १४ ॥ 'अच्छिन्नो रायः सुवीरः' **इति परिवासयति** ॥ १५ ॥ **एवमेवोत्तरस्य स्कन्धस्य चषालं परिवासयति** ॥ १६ ॥ **चतुरङ्गुलश्रयमेतदाहरन्ति** ॥ १७ ॥ **यूप–**

वृश्चेदि'त्यादि निन्दाप्रतिषिद्धानां निराकरणार्थं च। 'यं कामयेतापशुः [1]स्यादित्यपर्णं तस्मै [1]शुष्काग्रं वृश्चेत्। न व्रततिं, न कुलायिनं, नोपदग्धं नासंस्थितं, न क्रिमिणम[2]नष्टसुषिरमिति।' 'यः पालाशं पशुबन्धयूपं कुरुत' (वाधू.अन्वा.३.२.३) इत्यादिनाऽन्वाख्याने पलाशस्य[3] नियमितत्वात्[3] पालाश एव भवति। तथा 'स प्राङ्ङनमत् तस्य[4] यः[5] पुरस्तादनमत् स[5] प्रत्यङ्ङनमद्' इति दर्शनादधस्तात् [6]प्रागानमनमुपरिष्टात् [7]प्रत्यङ्वनतमिच्छन्ति। तथा कौषीतकिनः समामनन्ति–'आहवनीयं पुनरभ्यावृत्त' इति ॥ ६ ॥

[8]स्वधितिर्वृक्षच्छेदनसमर्थः परश्वादिः[8] ॥ ७ ॥

अनक्षसङ्गं वृश्चति। स्थाणौ यथाऽक्षो न सज्यते तथा भूमिसमीपे वृश्चेदित्यर्थः ॥ ९ ॥

प्रपातयति[9] शाययति ॥ १० ॥

आव्रश्चनहोमं परिस्तीर्य जुहोति। [10]सर्वत्रानग्नावप्याहुत्यां हूयमानायां परिस्तरणमिच्छन्ति ॥ १२ ॥

'यं त्वाऽयमि'ति मन्त्रः प्रतिशाखं नावर्तते। पञ्चारत्निप्रभृतीनि पुरुषार्थानि यूपपरिमाणान्युक्तानि। तेषामेकं प्रथमं वा क्रत्वर्थं गृह्यते। [11]'त्र्यरत्निश्चतुररत्निर्वा पालाशः पशुबन्धयूप' इति श्रुत्यन्तरे वचनम्। सहोपरेण संख्या स्यात्। छेदने श्रवणात्। औदुम्बर्यास्तूपरादूर्ध्वं माने श्रवणात्॥ १४ ॥

एवमेवोत्तरस्य स्कन्धस्येति[12]। 'अच्छिन्नः' इत्यनेनैव मन्त्रेणेत्यर्थः ॥ १५–१६ ॥

यूपमष्टाश्रिं तक्ष्णुवन्ति। बहुवचननिर्देशाद् येनकेनचित् कुशलेन कर्तव्यम्। मध्यदेशादग्निष्ठायाः[13] स्वरुर्निस्तक्षणीयो[14] द्व्यङ्गुलं चतुरङ्गुलं वा। अष्टाश्रित्वं चषालस्यापि तुल्यम्। चषालादूर्ध्वमङ्गुलिपर्वमात्रं यूपस्यातिरिक्तं भवति। तेन[15] गृहेषु यजेतेत्याहुरिति[16]। अस्मिन् पक्षे

१–१. M Ad स्या=शुष्का°, T °त्।न शु°. **२.** T अनष्टसु°. **३–३.** M शन्य...मित°. **४.** M स प्र ङ न°. **५–५.** M Ad येपुरस्ताद = स. **६.** M Ad प्राङन; thus T. **७.** M Ad प्रत्यङ्ङुपनत° ; thus T. **८–८.** M Ad T give this text just after the comm. on *sūtra* 5.1.4. **९.** T प्र व्राययति. **१०.** T सर्वत्राग्ना°. **११.** M Ad °ऽत्यर; thus T. **१२.** M °न्धेऽस्येति, Ad स्कन्धेस्येति. **१३.** M Ad °देशामग्नि°. **१४.** M Ad स्वरूनिस्तक्षीण°. **१५.** M तेत्र, Ad तेऽत्र. **१६.** M Ad om इति.

मष्टाश्रिं तक्ष्णुवन्ति ॥ १८ ॥ **स यदि पुरस्तादिष्टिं कुर्वन्त्यन्वाहार्यपचने पितृभ्यो दत्त्वा यज्ञायुधानि सꣳसाद्याप प्रणीयाग्नयेऽष्टाकपालं निर्वपति** ॥ १९ ॥ **निरुप्ते प्राणग्रहाꣳश्च पृश्नीꣳश्च व्याचष्टे** ॥ २० ॥ **समासन्नेऽपानग्रहाꣳश्च पृश्नीꣳश्च व्याचष्टे** ॥ २१ ॥ **तस्यै वार्त्रघ्नावाज्यभागौ** ॥ २२ ॥ 'अग्निर्मूर्धा भुवः' **इति हविषः** ॥ २३ ॥ **त्रिष्टुभौ संयाज्ये** ॥ २४ ॥ **सन्ततिमनु होतुराहुतिं जुहोति** ॥ २५ ॥ **प्रसिध्यति कर्म** ॥ २६ ॥ **सन्तिष्ठत एषेष्टिः** ॥ २७ ॥ **यद्यु नेष्टिं कुर्वन्त्यन्वाहार्यपचने पितृभ्यो दत्त्वा पूर्वेणाहवनीयं वेदिं कल्पयन्ति रथावकाशाम्** ॥ २८ ॥ **संप्रति पुरस्ताद्वेद्यां तस्यै सन्धावुपरसंमितं यूपावटं खनति** ॥ २९ ॥ **तस्यै स्तम्बयजुर्हरति** ॥ ३० ॥ **वेदिं परिगृह्णाति** ॥ ३१ ॥ **करणं जपति** ॥ ३२ ॥ 'स्फ्यमुदपात्रम्' **इति संप्रेष्यति**। '°शम्यामाहरेहि यजमानोदपात्रेणावोक्ष' **इति** ॥ ३३ ॥ **चात्वालकालꣳ स्फ्येनोद्धृत्य** 'उन्नम्भय पृथिवीम्' **इत्युदपात्रे-**

समारोह्य सूयवसं गत्वा मथित्वा विहृत्य तथैव प्रतिपद्यते ॥ १८ ॥

इष्टौ विद्यमानायां पश्वर्थमुद्धृत एवाग्नाविष्टिः कर्तव्या ॥ १९ ॥

नेष्टिं संस्थाप्य पश्वर्थमुद्धरति। 'तस्मानु हैतावनुसंहितावेव स्याताम्' इतीष्टिपश्वोः सन्धानवचनमन्यथा नोपपद्येत। एतावदेव ह्यनुसंधानं न समानतन्त्रादि। तथा चानुपदकार 'इष्टिं विधाय धार्यत आहवनीय' इत्याह[१]। पितृदानं पिण्डपितृयज्ञः। पूर्वेणाहवनीयं वेदिं कल्पयति रथावकाशां, रथपरिमाणाम्[२]। कथं मीयते। रथेषया प्राची मातव्या। रथाक्षेण पश्चात्तिरश्ची रथयुगेन[३] पुरस्तात् तिरश्ची।

'अष्टाशीतिशतमीषा तिर्यगक्षश्चतुःशतम्।
षडशीतिर्युगं[४] चैव रथश्चारण उच्यते' ॥ इति ॥ २८ ॥

संप्रति मध्ये पुरस्तात्तिर्यङ् मान्या वेद्यन्तरस्य सन्धौ यथान्तर्वेद्यर्धं भवति बहिर्वेद्यर्धम्। अपरेण यूपावटं वितस्तिमात्रमवशिष्य शम्यामात्रपार्श्वमानीं समचतुरश्रामुत्तरवेदिं मिमीते। शम्या षट्त्रिंशदङ्गुलप्रमाणा, 'षट्त्रिंशच्छम्या बाहू' इति। वेदी[५] उत्तरवेदी अक्ष्णया मानेन प्रमाय कोणेषु शंकुं निहत्य समन्ततः स्पन्द्यया परितनोति ॥ २९ ॥

वेदिं कृत्वा तस्यै स्तम्बयजुर्हरतीत्यादि हस्तसंमार्जनान्तं करोति ॥ ३० ॥

ततः स्फ्यमुदपात्रमित्यादि ॥ ३३ ॥

चात्वालकालं स्फ्येनोद्धृत्य। कालशब्दः स्थानवाची[६]। कः पुनश्चात्वालस्य कालः[७]। महावेद्या उत्तरपूर्वार्धाच्छङ्कोः प्रत्यग्द्वादशभागे स्पन्द्यायां[८] चात्वालो दृष्टः। तथा षड्भागः उत्करोऽस्यामपि वेद्यां तथैव कर्तव्यः[९]। प्रक्रम उत्तरार्धाद्[१०] वेद्यै वा[१०]चात्वालस्योत्करस्येति प्रक्रमान्तरमिति विध्यवशेषेपूक्तम्।

---

१. M Ad वनीय इत्याह extra after इत्याह. २. M Ad माणं; thus T. ३. M °युगऽनु, Ad °युगेनु; thus T. ४. M Ad °शीतियुगं T °शीतिर्यु°. ५. M Ad वेद्युत्तरवेदि; thus T. ६. Ad चि]कः. ७. M Ad कालं. ८. M Ad स्फन्द्या°; thus T. ९. M Ad °र्तव्यं. १०-१०. M Ad वेद्यै चात्वा; thus T.

णावोक्षति। '०भिन्द्धीदं=वि सृजा दूतिम्' **इति** ॥ ३४॥ **शम्यया परिमिमीते** ॥ ३५ ॥ **दक्षिणतः प्राचीꣳ शम्यां निधाय** 'वित्तायनी मेऽसि' **इत्यन्तरतः स्फ्येनानुलिखति** ॥ ३६ ॥ 'तिक्तायनी मेऽसि' **इति पश्चादुदीचीम्** ॥ ३७ ॥ 'अवतान्मा नाथितम्' **इति पुरस्तादुदीचीम्** ॥ ३८ ॥ 'अवतान्मा व्यथितम्' **इत्युत्तरतः प्राचीम्** ॥ ३९ ॥ 'विदेरग्निर्नभो नामाग्ने अङ्गिरः' **इति मध्यतः स्फ्येन पुरीषस्योपहन्ति** ॥ ४० ॥ 'योऽस्यां पृथिव्यामसि' **इत्यादत्ते** ॥ ४१ ॥ 'आयुषा नाम्नेहि' **इति हरति** ॥ ४२ ॥ 'यत्तेऽनाधृष्टं नाम यज्ञियं तेन त्वाऽऽदधे' **इति पूर्वेणाग्नीधꣳ हत्वोत्तरवेद्याꣳ सादयति** ॥ ४३ ॥ 'अग्ने अङ्गिरः' **इति द्वितीयं प्रहरति** ॥ ४४ ॥ 'द्वितीयस्यां पृथिव्यामसि' **इत्यादत्ते** ॥ ४५ ॥ 'आयुषा नाम्नेहि' **इत्येव हरति** ॥ ४६ ॥ 'यत्तेऽनाधृष्टं नाम यज्ञियं तेन त्वाऽऽदधे' **इति पूर्वेणैवाग्नीधꣳ हत्वोत्तरवेद्याꣳ सादयति** ॥ ४७ ॥ 'अग्ने अङ्गिरः' **इति तृतीयं प्रहरति** ॥ ४८ ॥ 'यस्तृतीयस्यां पृथिव्यामसि' **इत्यादत्ते** ॥ ४९ ॥ 'आयुषा नाम्नेहि' **इत्येव हरति** ॥ ५० ॥ 'यत्तेऽनाधृष्टं नाम यज्ञियं तेन त्वाऽऽदधे' **इति पूर्वेणैवाग्नीधꣳ हत्वोत्तरवेद्याꣳ सादयति** ॥ ५१ ॥ **तूष्णीं चतुर्थꣳ हरति** ॥ ५२ ॥ **अद्भिः सन्तृप्य** 'सिꣳहीरसि महिषीरसि' **इति संयौति** ॥ ५३ ॥ 'उरु प्रथस्वोरु ते यज्ञपतिः प्रथताम्' **इति स्फ्येन प्रथयति** ॥ ५४ ॥ 'ध्रुवाऽसि' **इति त्रिः शम्यया सꣳहन्ति** ॥ ५५ ॥ **'सर्वतः प्रादेशमात्रीꣳ सुष्ठु चतुःस्रक्तिं कृत्वा** 'देवेभ्यः शुन्धस्व' **इत्यद्भिरवोक्षति,** 'देवेभ्य शुम्भस्व' **इति सिकताभिः** ॥ ५६ ॥ **अद्भिरेवोपरिष्टात्** ॥ ५७ ॥ **अनग्नामुत्तरनाभिं कृत्वा यन्ति** ॥

तथा सति स्फ्न्द्यायां[१] न भवतः। बहिर्वेदि भवतः। भागस्तु पूर्वोक्त एव ॥ ३४ ॥

'*शम्यया परिमिमीते*' इति वचनात् शम्याऽत्र समचतुरश्रा[२] ॥ ३५ ॥

'वित्तायनी मेऽसी'त्यादयः परिमाणमन्त्राः, नानुलेखनमन्त्राः। ब्राह्मणे तूत्तरवेदिपरिमाणे विहिताः, इह चात्वालपरिमाणे। तत्र [३]विकल्पो वा[३] स्यादभ्यासो वा। अनुपदकार उत्तरवेदिं प्रकृत्याह—'अत्र परिमाणमन्त्रानेके प्रयुञ्जते' इति ॥ ३६ ॥

[४]'विदेरग्निर्नभो नामे'त्युत्तरयो[४]रनुषजन्ति केचित् ॥ ४० ॥

'उत्तरवेद्यां सादयती'ति निमित्ते सप्तमी[५] उत्तरवेदिनिमित्त इत्यर्थः। [६]दृश्यते हि[६]—'उत्तरवेद्या आवृतोत्तरवेदान्निर्वपती'ति। तत एवैकदेशेनोत्तर[७]नाभिमपि तूष्णीम्। 'त्रिरागनीध्रश्चात्वालाद्धरेदुत्तर[८]नाभ्यर्थमि'त्यनुपदकार आह। अन्ये उत्तरनाभिमेव निवपन्ति। एवं कुर्वताम् 'उत्तरवेदिं निवपती'त्यादिषूत्तरवेदिग्रहणमुत्तरनाभ्युपलक्षणार्थं स्यात्। आहूतो हि[९] यजमानो ह्रियमाणान्यु[१०]प्यमानं चान्वारभते ॥ ४३ ॥

अद्भिरेवोपरिष्यत्तूष्णीम् ॥ ५.१.१.५७ ॥ **[इति प्रथमः पटलः]**

---

१. M Ad °स्फ्यन्द्या. **२.** M Ad °स्त्रः°. **३–३.** M वि...वा. **४–४.** M वदेर...त्यु°. **५.** T निमित्तिपञ्चमी; thus M Ad. **६–६.** M Ad om. **७.** M Ad °नोत्तरे ना°. **८.** M Ad °लाध्वरेदु°. **९.** T om; thus M Ad. **१०.** M Ad °माणन्यु° ; thus T.

५८ ॥ **शूर्पेण वा तृणैर्वा प्रच्छाद्येध्ममादीपयन्ति** ॥ ५९ ॥ **उपयमनीरुपकल्पयन्ति** ॥ ६० ॥ **उत्तरवेद्यै संभाराः** ॥ ५.१.१.६१ ॥ **[इति प्रथमः पटलः]**

[उत्तरवेद्यै संभारसंभरणम्]

उत्तरवेद्यै संभाराः—गुल्गुलुः सुगन्धितेजनं शुक्लोर्णास्तुकाः पौतुद्रवाः परिधय उपांशुग्रहणं प्रोक्षण्यः पञ्चगृहीतमाज्यम् ॥ १ ॥ **आदीप्त इध्मे चतुर्गृहीतं गृह्णीते** ॥ २ ॥ **तज्जुहोति** ॥ ३ ॥ **षड्ढोतारं मनसाऽनुद्रुत्यापरं चतुर्गृहीतं गृह्णीते** ॥ ४ ॥ **तज्जुहोति** ॥ ५ ॥ 'अन्वग्निरुषसामग्रमख्यद्' **इत्यनुख्यातिम्।** '०अन्वहानि=आ ततान स्वाहा' **इति** ॥ ६ ॥ **उद्यच्छन्त इध्मम्** ॥ ७ ॥ **उपयच्छन्त्युपयमनीः** ॥ ८ ॥ 'अग्नये प्रह्रियमाणायानुब्रूहि' **इत्याह।** '०एकस्फ्ययाऽनुद्रव' **इति** ॥ ९ ॥ **स्फ्येन लिखन्नेकस्फ्ययाऽनुद्रवत्योत्तरवेद्यै** ॥ १० ॥ 'कविर्यज्ञस्य वि तनोति पन्थाम्' **इत्यध्वर्युर्यजमानं वाचयति।** '०नाकस्य=सनीयान्' **इति** ॥ ११ ॥ **अनुद्रुत्य** 'इन्द्रघोषस्त्वा वसुभिः पुरस्तात् पातु' **इत्युत्तरनाभिं प्रोक्षति।** '०मनोजवास्त्वा पितृभिर्दक्षिणतः पातु', 'प्रचेतास्त्वा रुद्रैः पश्चात् पातु', 'विश्वकर्मा त्वाऽऽदित्यैरुत्तरतः पातु', 'बृहस्पतिस्त्वा विश्वैर्देवैरुपरिष्टात् पातु' **इति** ॥ १२ ॥ **यत्प्रोक्षणीनामुच्छिष्यते तद् दक्षिणत उत्तरवेद्यै स्फ्यस्य वर्त्मन्नुप निनयति** ॥ १३ ॥ **यं द्वेष्टि यजमानस्तं ध्यायति** ॥ १४ ॥ **अप उपस्पृश्य पञ्चगृहीतमादाय हिरण्यमुपास्याक्ष्णयोरुत्तरनाभिं व्याघारयति** ॥ १५ ॥ 'सिꣳहीरसि सपत्नसाही स्वाहा' **इति दक्षिणेꣳऽसे** ॥ १६ ॥ 'सिꣳहीरसि सुप्रजावनिः स्वाहा' **इत्युत्तरस्याꣳ श्रोण्याम्** ॥ १७ ॥ 'सिꣳहीरसि रायस्पोषवनिः स्वाहा' **इति दक्षिणायाꣳ श्रोण्याम्** ॥ १८ ॥ 'सिꣳहीरस्यादित्यवनिः स्वाहा' **इत्युत्तरेꣳऽसे** ॥ १९ ॥ 'सिꣳहीरस्या

उत्तरवेदिसंभाराः प्रसिद्धा एव। शुक्लोर्णास्तुकाः पेत्वस्य[1] शृङ्गमध्यादानेया[2] उत्तरनाभिपरिधानसमर्थाः परिधयः। प्रादेशमात्रा इत्यर्थः। [3]यथातथमितरेषां परिमाणम् ॥ १ ॥

पशुबन्धेन यक्ष्यमाणः षड्ढोतारमि'ति विहितस्यादावेव[4] प्राप्तस्यास्मिन्[4] काले विधानम्। 'स यत्राऽग्निं प्रहरति [5]तत् तस्य दीक्षे'ति वचनात्। एकां वाऽऽहुतिं पञ्च वा। पञ्चपक्ष एकैकस्मिन् वाक्ये ग्रहणमनुषज्य[6] जुहोति। अन्त्यवाक्यद्वयमेकीकृत्यानुषज्य पञ्चमीम्[7]। संग्रहस्य[8] समस्तस्यावृत्तिमेके मन्यते ॥ ४ ॥

एकस्फ्य[9] आग्नीध्र इध्ममुद्यम्य स्थित्वा होता यज्ञाय नीयत इत्युच्यमाने प्रहरति ॥ ९-१० ॥

प्रोक्षणे उत्तरनाभिग्रहणमुत्तरवेद्युपलक्षणार्थम्। ब्राह्मणे वा उत्तरवेदिग्रहणमुत्तरनाभ्युपलक्षणार्थम्। अथवोभयोर्विकल्पः। तथा व्याघारणे[10]। वाक्यबहुत्वात् प्रतिमन्त्रं यथालिङ्गं प्रोक्षति ॥ १२ ॥

अक्ष्णयोत्तरनाभिं व्याघारयति। मध्यत उपक्रम्याकोणादंसयोः। कोणत उपक्रम्य

---

१. M Ad वेत्वस्य; thus T. २. M म...दा...या, Ad ० दानेयोत्त० ; thus T. ३. M Ad यथातदर्थमि० ; thus T. ४-४. M Ad ० दावेवाप्रा० . ५. M Ad ० तत् = तस्य० . ६. M Ad ग्रहमनु० ; thus T. ७. M Ad पञ्चमी. ८. M Ad सग्र० . ९. M Ad एकस्याग्नी० . १०. M Ad प्पाघारेण० .

वह देवान् देवयते यजमानाय स्वाहा' **इति मध्ये** ॥ २० ॥ 'भूतेभ्यस्त्वा' **इति स्रुचमुद्गृह्णाति** ॥ २१ ॥

आमध्याच्छ्रोण्योः ॥ १५–२० ॥

स्रुचमुद्गृह्णाति ससंस्रावाम्[१]। यदा होता वदति प्रथमः 'सीद योनि'मित्यग्निं सादयेत्। पुरस्तात्प्रत्यगावृत्त इध्मम्। अतिमुक्त्यन्ते तन्त्रप्रक्रमोऽन्वाधानादि प्रतिपद्यते। पशोः सान्नाय्यविकारत्वादुत्पवनार्थं शाखापवित्रमपि केचिदिच्छन्ति। अपरे द्रवत्वादुत्पवनमर्थलुप्तमिति न गृह्णन्ति।

हविर्यज्ञविधे [२]व्रतमुपयन्ति न सवविधे[२]। अन्वाख्यानोक्तव्रतादीनां सप्तानामभावः सवविधः। तेषु विद्यमानेषु हविर्यज्ञविधः। बर्हिः संभृत्य परिस्तीर्याग्नीन् यज्ञायुधानि संसादयति औषधप्रयुक्तवर्जानि। सह स्रुवेण स्वधितिं सादयेत्। उभयतोऽश्रिं जुह्वा वसाहोमहवनीयमुपभृता पृषदाज्यग्रहणीम्। ध्रुवायां[३] ग्रहणपक्षे तामेव संयवनार्थाः। श्रद्धारम्भाद्यर्थाश्च यदि प्रणीताः स्युः। श्रद्धारम्भाद्यर्थानां सवविधे[४] प्रतिषेधो यदि केवलं संयवनार्था एव। 'आनर्थक्यात्तदङ्गेष्वि'ति पशुपुरोडाशे प्रतिषेधः। पूर्वस्मिन् पक्षे हविर्यज्ञविधे प्रणीतापात्रं साद्यते। श्रपणार्थत्वे[५] च तथा प्रतिभवि[६]। प्राशित्रमभिप्रेत्य प्राशित्रप्रतिषेधश्चेत् प्राशित्रग्रहणमपि। अथ न तस्यापि स एव न्यायः।

'आनर्थक्यात्तदङ्गेष्वि'ति पशुपुरोडाशे प्रतिषेधः। अन्वाहार्यस्थाली हविर्यज्ञविधे[७] साद्यते। कुम्भी[८]शूलवपाश्रपणीप्लक्षशाखेडसूनमपि साद्यते। पृष्ठ्याः स्तीर्त्वा पवित्रे आदाय हस्तौ मार्जयित्वाऽग्निहोत्रहवणीं तूष्णीमादाय प्रोक्षणीः संस्कृत्य पात्राणि प्रोक्ष्य 'वेदं परिवासये'त्युक्त्वा पवित्रे आज्यस्थालीं चादायाज्यं निरुप्याधिश्रित्य पर्यग्निकरोति। क्व पुनराज्याधिश्रयणं शालामुखीय आहोस्वित् पुराणगार्हपत्य इति। दूरमागत्य संदेहः क्रियते। अभ्याधानान्वाधानयोरेव सन्देहः कर्तव्यः। तत्र वैकल्पिकत्वशंकया[९] न चोदितम्। अनुपदकारस्तु दशपशोः प्रतिषेधति। 'उक्तानि सप्तान्वाधानं पृष्ठ्यास्तरणं याजमानमि'ति। आह हि—यत्र निःसन्दिग्धं तत्र चोदितं तदभिधीयते। अत्र विप्रतिपत्तिराचार्याणाम्। अग्नीषोमीयप्रकृतित्वमस्य[१०] केचिन्मन्यन्ते। तत्र हि [११]यूपाहुत्यादयो हृदयशूलपर्यन्ता[११] धर्मा विहिताः। सन्निधानतोऽन्येषां[१२] धर्मप्राप्तिरिति।

अन्ये वर्णयन्ति ऐन्द्राग्नमारभ्य होत्रस्य कृत्स्नाम्नानादस्यापि धर्मवत्वम्। तच्चोदकवाक्यवदेव श्रुत्यन्तरस्थमनुमीयते। श्रूयन्ते च—कापिष्ठलानां[१३] शाखिन ऐन्द्राग्नं निरूढपशुबन्धं प्रकृत्या साकल्येन पशुधर्मा नाम्नातवन्त इति। आचार्यप्रभृतिभिरप्युभयत्र[१४] धर्माणां कृत्स्नाम्नानमन्योऽन्याविकारत्वं ज्ञापयति। तस्मादयमप्यग्नीषोमीयवद् दर्शपूर्णमासविकार एवेति दैक्षस्य चेतरेष्वपि सौत्यादिविषय इति।

[१५]यद्यनग्नीषोमीयविकारः स्यात् पुराणगार्हपत्य एव हविरधिश्रयणम्। तथा च [१६]सौशारद

---

१. M Ad °स्रावम्. २–२. T takes this text as additional; thus in M and Ad. ३. M Ad स्रुवा°; thus T. ४. M Ad °विधेः; thus T. ५. M Ad श्रवणा°. ६. Ad प्रतिहावि. ७. M Ad om हविः. ८. M Ad °शूलपाश्र°. ९. M Ad परिकल्पयित्वाशं°. १०. M Ad °प्रकृतिम°; thus T. ११–११. M य...त्यादयो °न्तापि; Ad °न्ता अपि. १२. M Ad °धावतो°. १३. M Ad T कापिखलानां. १४. M Ad प्रवृत्तिरप्यु°. १५. M Ad यद्यप्यन°; thus T. १६. T चासौ शा°.

'विश्वायुरसि पृथिवीं दृꣳह' **इति मध्यमं परिधिं परिदधाति पौतुद्रवम्** ॥ २२ ॥ 'ध्रुवक्षिदस्यन्तरिक्षं दृꣳह' **इति दक्षिणार्ध्यम्** ॥ २३ ॥ 'अच्युतक्षिदसि दिवं दृꣳह' **इत्युत्तरार्ध्यम्** ॥ २४ ॥ 'अग्नेर्भस्मास्यग्नेः पुरीषमसि' **इति संभारान् निवपति** ॥ २५ ॥ 'तान् इडायै सृप्तं घृतवच्चराचरम्' **इति सꣳस्रावेणाभि जुहोति**। '०देवा अन्वविन्दन् गुहाहितम्। ये ग्राम्याः पशवो विश्वरूपा विरूपाः सन्तो बहुधैकरूपाः तेषाꣳ सृप्तानां मयि रन्तिरस्तु स्वाहा' **इति** ॥ २६ ॥ **उपनिवपत्युपयमनीः** ॥ २७ ॥ **सादयत्यग्निम्** ॥ २८ ॥ 'प्रजापतिरसि विश्कर्मा' **इति सन्नमुपतिष्ठते**। '०तदसौ सूर्यस्तदयमग्निः संप्रियः पशुभिर्भुवत्' **इति** ॥ २९ ॥ **आहुतिषाहेऽतिमुक्तीर्जुहोति** 'अग्निर्यज्ञं नयतु प्रजानन् मैनं यज्ञहनो विदन्। देवेभ्यः प्रब्रूताद्यज्ञं प्र प्र यज्ञपतिं तिर स्वाहा', 'वायुर्यज्ञं नयतु प्रजानन् मैनं यज्ञहनो विदन्। देवेभ्यः प्रब्रूताद्यज्ञं प्र प्र यज्ञपतिं तिर स्वाहा', 'सूर्यो यज्ञं नयतु प्रजानन् मैनं यज्ञहनो विदन्। देवेभ्यः प्रब्रूताद्यज्ञं प्र प्र यज्ञपतिं तिर स्वाहा', 'यज्ञो यज्ञं नयतु प्रजानन् मैनं यज्ञहनो विदन्। देवेभ्यः प्रब्रूताद्यज्ञं प्र प्र यज्ञपतिं तिर स्वाहा' **इति** ॥ ३० ॥ **स्फ्यमादायोत्तिष्ठन्नाह** 'ब्रह्मन्नुत्तरं परिग्राहं परिग्रहीष्यामि' **इति** ॥ ३१ ॥ **दक्षिणत उत्तरवेद्यै ब्रह्मोपविशति** ॥ ३२ ॥ **प्रसूत उत्तरं परिग्राहं परिगृह्णाति** ॥ ३३ ॥ **योयुपित्वाऽवस्कभ्य संप्रेष्यति** 'प्रोक्षणीरासादयेध्माबर्हिरुपसादय स्रुवं च स्रुचश्च संमृड्ढि पत्नीꣳ सन्नह्याज्येनोदेहि पृषदाज्याय दध्याहरेहि यजमान' **इति** ॥ ३४ ॥ **एतत् कुर्वन्ति** ॥ ३५ ॥ **स्रुवं च स्रुचश्च संमृज्याज्यानि गृह्णीते पृषदाज्यवन्ति प्रसिद्धम्** ॥ ३६ ॥ **जुहूपभृतोर्गृहीत्वा** 'महीनां पयोऽसि' **इति पृषदाज्यायोपस्तृणीते** ॥ ३७ ॥ 'विश्वेषां देवानां तनूः' **इति द्वितीयम्** ॥ ३८ ॥ 'ऋध्यासमद्य पृषतीनां ग्रहम्' **इति तिरःपवित्रꣳ स्रुचि दध्यानयति**। '०पृषतीनां ग्रहोऽसि' **इति** ॥ ३९ ॥ 'विष्णोर्हृदयमसि' **इति प्राप्य परिधिं परिदधाति** ॥ ४० ॥ 'विष्णुस्त्वाऽनु विचक्रमे' **इति द्वितीयम्** ॥ ४१ ॥ 'भूतिर्दध्ना घृतेन वर्धताम्' **इति वाचयति**। '०तस्य

उक्तम्— 'अग्नीषोमीयविकारेष्वविशेषं कुर्यात्, न चास्मिन्नर्थात् कुर्वीते'ति। अन्य आह—'यतः प्रणयति स गार्हपत्य इत्यनारभ्यवादः। अतोऽनग्नीषोमीयविकारत्वेऽपि शालामुखीय एवे'ति। तथाऽस्मिन्नेव पशावविशेषेणानुपदकारेणाम्नातम् 'उद्यत इध्मे शालामुखीये स्रुवाहुतिं जुहुयात्– 'यत्ते पावक चकृमा कच्चनागः पूर्वो यः सन्नपरो भवासि। घृतेन त्वं तनुवो वर्धयस्व मा मा हिंसीरधिगतं पुरस्तात् स्वाहे'ति। 'पूर्वो यः सन्नपरो भवासी'ति लिङ्गाच्छालामुखीयस्य गार्हपत्यत्वं ज्ञायते। अग्नीषोमीयविकारेष्वपि इहाम्नाता एव धर्मास्तत आगच्छन्ति 'नाग्नीदाज्यमधिश्रयेदि'त्यादयः। यदि तदनुवृत्तिरिष्येत[1], तदप्यामनेदग्निप्रणयनादिवत्॥ २१ ॥

स्फ्यमादायेत्यादि। ब्रह्मण इहोपवेशनवचनं [2]सवविधापेक्षम्। प्रणयनप्रतिषेधस्य पशुपुरोडाश-विषयत्वापेक्षं वा। अन्यथा प्रणयनकाल एवोपविष्टस्यापि इहोपवेशनवचनमनर्थकं स्यात्॥ ३१ ॥

स्रुवं संमृज्य संप्रैषानुपलक्षितमपि स्वधितिं स्वनामधेयोपलक्षितं संमृज्येत् स्रुवकार्यापत्त्येति ॥ ३६ ॥

---

१. M Ad ०रिष्यते; thus T. २. M Ad सेववि०.

मेष्टस्य=अस्तृतम्' **इति** ॥ ४२ ॥ **ध्रुवायै काल आज्यस्थालीमुपोद्यच्छति** ॥ ४३ ॥ **इध्माबर्हिः प्रोक्षति** ॥ ५.१.२.४४ ॥ **[इति द्वितीयः पटलः]**

[संभृतसंभाराणां प्रोक्षणादिकर्म]

इध्माबर्हिः प्रोक्षति ॥ १ ॥ **वेदिं प्रोक्षति** ॥ २ ॥ **आसन्नं प्रोक्षति** ॥ ३ ॥ **अपो निनीय प्रस्तरं गृह्णाति** ॥ ४ ॥ **स्तृणाति बर्हिः** ॥ ५ ॥ **परिगृह्य परिधीन् कार्ष्मर्यमयान् समिधावादधाति** ॥ ६ ॥ **परिधिषु वाचयित्वाऽग्निं युनक्ति** ॥ ७ ॥ **आगत्य तिरश्ची सादयति** ॥ ८ ॥ **तिरश्च्योः प्रस्तरम्** ॥ ९ ॥ **प्रस्तरे जूहूम्** ॥ १० ॥ **बर्हिषीतरे** ॥ ११ ॥ **समासाद्य** 'ध्रुवा असदन्', 'यन्मे अग्ने' **इति समुद्दिश्य**

ध्रुवायै काल आज्यस्थालीमुपोद्यच्छतीति । आज्यस्थाल्या ध्रुवाकार्येऽतिदेशाद्[१] ध्रुवायां [२]पृषदाज्यं गृह्यते, अन्यस्य पात्रस्याश्रवणात् । 'बर्हिषीतरे' इति दर्शनाच्चानूयाजद्रव्यधारणं प्रकृतावुपभृति कृतम् । तयैव होममपि वक्ष्यति 'एतां जुहूं यस्यां पृषदाज्यमि'ति । तच्च जुहू कार्यम् । अतस्तस्याः संमार्गमन्त्रः 'उपभृज्जुहूरसि प्रजां योनेश्चक्षुः श्रोत्रमि'त्युह्यः । तथा सादनमन्त्र इति केचित् । उपभृच्छब्दः क्रियायोगनिमित्तः । तच्चोपभरणमनया क्रियते । तथापि संमार्गोत्तरकालमाज्यस्थाल्या ध्रुवाकार्येऽतिदेशात् तस्यां ग्रहणमिति ज्ञातम् । तया होमोऽपि होमकाल इव विहितः । अतो ध्रुवाभूतायामेव गृह्यते । तथा हूयते चेत्यन्ये[३] । अन्य आह—'एकां[४] जुहूं यस्यां पृषदाज्यमि'ति सन्दिग्धवदतिदेशाद् ध्रुवायाम-न्यस्यां वा कस्यांश्चिदित्याचार्यस्याभिप्रायः । स्रुगन्तरोत्पादनपक्षे च धारणहोमयोर्होमस्य बलीयस्त्वात् [५]प्राधान्यादस्मिन् स्वव्यापारोत्तरकालं जुह्वा धारणस्य कृतत्वाद् यदुपभृत्याज्यं भवति तज्जुह्वमानीयेति जुहूजातीयया तत्संस्कारसंस्कृतया च भवितव्यम् । 'ध्रुवायै काल' इत्यपि [६]ध्रुवायामिति विपरिणम्य व्याख्येयम् । कालग्रहणमनूयाजद्रव्यग्रहणोत्तरकालमिति । आज्यानि गृह्णीत इति व्याख्यातम् । पदमव-विव्यर्थ[७] (?) एव । अन्यस्मिन्नपि पक्षे ध्रुवाया इति षष्ठ्या विपरिणामः कर्तव्य[८] एव । स्थाने योग्यया[९] कालसंबद्धया वा[१०] षष्ठ्या भवितव्यमिति प्रसिद्धम् । जुहूपभृतोर्गृहीत्वा न्यायं प्रज्ञातमित्यर्थः । किमुक्तं भवति । अनूयाजानां द्रव्यान्तरविधानादुपभृति प्रयाजार्थमेकमेव चतुर्गृहीतं गृह्णाति । द्वे हि प्रकृतौ चतुर्गृहीते प्रयाजार्थमनूयाजार्थं च । नैकम् । अष्टगृहीतं व्यासज्य वर्त्तीति[११] पृषदाज्यग्रहणेषु यजमानः 'सुवीर्याय त्वा' इत्यारभ्याभिमन्त्रयते ॥ ५.१.२.४३ ॥ **[इति द्वितीयः पटलः]**

पृषद्गुणविशिष्टं ह्याज्यमनूयाजद्रव्यमग्नीषोमीयविकारत्वे परिधानात्[१२] । अस्मिन् पक्षे 'प्रस्तरे जुहूम्'[१३] इति जात्यपेक्षमेकवचनम् । प्रस्तरे द्वयोः सादनम् । तथा 'धर्ता प्रयाजानामुतानूयाजानामि'ति लिङ्गम् ॥ १० ॥

तथा बर्हिषीतरे इति न विरोधः । अत्राध्वर्यू हविर्यज्ञविधे व्रतमुपेतः ॥ ११ ॥

---

१. M Ad कार्येति, देशा°, T gives a readding : कार्या° from ख–पाठः. **२.** M °वायां...दाज्यं. **३.** M Ad तेऽप इत्य° ; thus T. **४.** M Ad एताञ्जु° ; thus T. **५.** T प्रधा°. **६.** T विध्रुवा°. **७.** M Ad पदमवविव्यथ, T पदं विव्यर्थ. **८.** M Ad कर्तव्ये. **९.** M Ad योगया; thus T. **१०.** M Ad om; thus T. **११.** M Ad वत्ती इति, T वर्ती इति. **१२.** M Ad °धानम्; thus T. **१३.** M Ad जुहोमीति.

दशहोतारं व्याचष्टे ॥ १२ ॥ **अप उपस्पृश्य** 'देवस्य त्वा सवितुः प्रसवे' **इत्यभ्रिमादत्ते।** '०अश्विनो=नारिरसि' **इति** ॥ १३ ॥ 'परिलिखितꣳ रक्षः परिलिखिता अरातयः' **इति यूपावटं परिलिखति।** '०इदमहꣳ रक्षसो ग्रीवा=कृन्तामि' **इति** ॥ १४ ॥ 'प्रतिप्रस्थातः' **इत्याह।** '०एतं खनोपरसंमितम्' **इति** ॥ १५ ॥ **तष्टो यूपोऽष्टाश्रिः क्लृप्तचषालः** ॥ १६ ॥ **प्रक्षालितपूर्वेण यूपावट उपलिखितो भवति सह द्वाभ्याꣳ शकलाभ्याम्** ॥ १७ ॥ **तमुपरिक्रामन् संप्रेष्यति** 'यवमतीः प्रोक्षणीर्बर्हिराज्यमुपाꣳशुग्रहणमाहरेहि यजमान' **इति** ॥ १८ ॥ 'पृथिव्यै त्वा' 'अन्तरिक्षाय त्वा' 'दिवे त्वा' **इति यूपं प्रोक्षति** ॥ १९ ॥ 'शुन्धतां लोकः पितृषदनः' **इति यूपावटेऽपोऽवनयति** ॥ २० ॥ 'यवोऽसि यवयास्मद् द्वेषः' **इति यवान् प्रस्कन्दयति।** '०यवयारातीः' **इति** ॥ २१ ॥ 'पितृणाꣳ सदनमसि' **इति विषूचीनाग्रं बर्हिरवस्तृणाति** ॥ २२ ॥ 'पितृभ्यः स्वाहा' **इति हिरण्य-मन्तर्धायाज्येन जुहोति** ॥ २३ ॥ 'स्वावेशोऽस्यग्रेगाः' **इत्युक्त्वोत्तानं यूपशकलमवदधाति।** '०नेतर्णीं=तस्य वित्ताद्' **इति** ॥ २४ ॥ 'यूपायाज्यमानायानुब्रूहि' **इत्याह** ॥ २५ ॥ **अग्रमुदङ्मुख-स्तिष्ठन्** 'देवस्त्वा सविता मध्वाऽनक्तु' **इति प्रवृह्य चषालꣳ हिरण्यमन्तर्धायाग्रमनक्ति** ॥ २६ ॥ 'सुपिप्पलाभ्यस्त्वौषधीभ्यः' **इति प्रतिमुञ्चति** ॥ २७ ॥ **एवमेवाग्निष्ठामश्रिमनक्ति** ॥ २८ ॥ **नाभिदघ्ने त्रिः परिमृशति** ॥ २९ ॥ **आन्तमनक्ति** ॥ ३० ॥ 'उच्छ्रियमाणायानुब्रूहि' **इत्याह** ॥ ३१ ॥ 'उद्दिवꣳ स्तभान' **इत्युच्छ्रयति।** '०आऽन्तरिक्षं पृण पृथिवीमुपरेण दृꣳह' **इति** ॥ ३२ ॥ 'अभि तिष्ठ पृतन्यतः' **इत्यवदधाति।** '०अधरे सन्तु शत्रवः। इन्द्र इव वृत्रहा तिष्ठापः क्षेत्राणि सञ्जयन्' **इति** ॥ ३३ ॥ 'ते ते धामान्युश्मसि गमध्ये' **इति वैष्णवीभ्यां कल्पयति।** '०गावो यत्र भूरिशृङ्गा=युज्यः सखा' **इति** ॥ ३४ ॥ **यदाग्निष्ठामश्रिमाहवनीयेन संमिन्वन्त्यथ** 'तद्विष्णोः परमं पदम्' **इति चषालमुत्काशयति।** '०सदा पश्यन्ति=चक्षुराततम्' **इति** ॥ ३५ ॥ 'ब्रह्मवनिं त्वा क्षत्रवनिम्' **इति**

चतुर्होतृस्थाने दशहोतृपक्ष[1] उपस्पृश्येत्यादि। बर्हिःप्रोक्षणेन यूपप्रोक्षणमुक्तम्। यथालिङ्गं सकृदेवेति। मूलत आरभ्य पराञ्चं[2] प्रोक्षति ॥ १८-१९ ॥

आहूतो यजमानोऽध्वर्युणाऽवस्त्रावितेनाज्येनाग्निष्ठामश्रिं तीक्ष्णां पृथ्वीं वाऽञ्ज्यादान्तात् यूपमननुसृजन्। वक्ष्यति हि 'न पुरा परिव्ययितोर्यूपमनुसृजेदि'ति। तत्र न ज्ञायते कुत आरभ्येति। श्रुत्यन्तरे विशेषः 'अञ्जनादि यजमानो यूपं नानुसृजत्यापरिव्ययणादि'ति। एतज्ज्ञापयति इहानुक्तमपि शाखान्तरे पठितं ग्रहीतव्यमिति। तथा सति नोपरमनक्ति। पत्न्युपरमनक्तीति। एवमादीन्यपि[3] ग्रहीतव्यानीति[4] ॥ २८-३० ॥

याऽक्ता पृथ्वी तीक्ष्णा वा तामाहवनीयेन संमिनुयात्। चषालमुत्काशयति ईक्षयति शकलान्तं यूपमुत्सृजति स्वर्वपगूहनान्तमित्यर्थः ॥ ३५ ॥

---

१. M Ad दशहो = उप; thus T. २. M Ad परां च; thus T. ३. M Ad ०माद्यविग्रा; thus T. ४. M Ad ग्रहीतव्यमि०; thus T.

पुरीषेण पर्यूहति।'°सुप्रजावनिꣳ रायस्पोषवनिं पर्यूहामि' **इति** ॥ ३६ ॥ 'ब्रह्म दृꣳह क्षत्रं दृꣳह' **इति मैत्रावरुणदण्डेन दृꣳहति**। '°प्रजां दृꣳह रयिं दृꣳह रायस्पोषं दृꣳह सजातान् यजमानाय दृꣳह' **इति** ॥ ३७ ॥ 'उन्नम्भय पृथिवीम्' **इत्युदपात्रमुपनिनयति**। '°भिन्द्धीदं दिव्यं नभः उद्नो= दूतिम्' **इति** ॥ ३८ ॥ **न पुरा परिव्येतोर्यूपमनुसृजेत्** ॥ ३९ ॥ 'परिवीयमाणायानुब्रूहि' **इत्याह** ॥ ४० ॥ 'परिवीरसि' **इति नाभिदघ्ने परिव्ययति**।'°परि त्वा दैवीर्विशो व्ययन्तां=मनुष्याः' **इति** ॥ ४१ ॥ **त्रिः परिवीयाऽन्तं प्रवेष्टयति** ॥ ४२ ॥ **अणिमत् स्थविमत् प्रवयति** ॥ ४३ ॥ 'दिवः सानुरसि' **इति स्वरुमादत्ते** ॥ ४४ ॥ 'अन्तरिक्षस्य त्वा सानाववगूहामि' **इति मध्यमे परिव्ययेऽवगूहति** ॥ ४५ ॥ **शकलान्तं यूपमुत्सृजति** ॥ ५.१.३.४६ ॥ **[इति तृतीयः पटलः]**

॥ इति पञ्चमप्रपाठके प्रथमोऽनुवाकः ॥

'*न पुरा परिव्येतोरि*'त्युक्त्वा शकलान्तमित्यादि पदं ज्ञापयति बहूनां परिव्ययण एकैकस्या स्वर्वपगूहनान्तं[१] कर्तव्यमिति। शकलान्तं यूपमुत्सृजति। स्वर्ववगूहनान्तमित्यर्थः ॥ ५.१.३.३९–४६ ॥ **[इति तृतीयः पटलः]**

॥ इति व्याख्यायां पञ्चमप्रपाठके प्रथमोऽनुवाकः ॥

---

१. M Ad स्वर्ववगू°.

॥ अथ पञ्चमप्रपाठके द्वितीयोऽनुवाकः ॥

[उपाकरणीये होमादिकर्म]

'इषे त्वा' **इति बर्हिषी आदत्ते** ॥ १ ॥ 'प्रजापतेर्जायमाना' **इत्युपाकरणीये जुहोति।** '°प्रजा जाताश्च=मन्यताꣳ स्वाहा', 'इमं पशुं पशु=हव्यꣳ स्वाहा' **इति** ॥ २ ॥ 'उपवीरसि' **इति पुरस्तात् प्रत्यञ्चं पशुमुपाकरोति।** '°उपो देवा=रेवती रमध्वमिन्द्राग्निभ्यां त्वा जुष्टमुपाकरोमि' **इति** ॥ ३ ॥ **प्रजाते बर्हिषी निधाय** 'अग्नेर्जनित्रमसि' **इति शकलमादत्ते** ॥ ४ ॥ 'वृषणौ स्थ=जागतं छन्दोऽनु प्रजायस्व' **इति** ॥ ५ ॥ 'अग्नये मथ्यमानायानुब्रूहि' **इत्याह** ॥ ६ ॥ **मन्थन्त्यग्निम्** ॥ ७ ॥ 'जातायानुब्रूहि' **इत्याह** ॥ ८ ॥ 'प्रह्रियमाणायानुब्रूहि' **इत्याह** ॥ ९ ॥ 'भवतं नः समनसौ' **इति प्रहरति।** '°समोकसा=द्य नः' **इति** ॥ १० ॥ 'अग्नावग्निश्चरति प्रविष्टः' **इति प्रहृत्याभिजुहोति।**

'इषे त्वे'ति बर्हिषी आदत्ते। यथोक्तगुणं पशुं [१]पल्पूलयित्वाऽन्तरा चात्वालोत्करौ प्रपाद्य पुरस्तात् प्रत्यगावृत्तं स्थापयेत्। अयमेव पन्था ऋत्विक्स्वामिनाम्। आदौ विसंस्थिते [२]वाऽनुत्पन्नयोरुत्तरवेदिं चोत्करं च 'इषे त्वा' इत्येकवचनान्तत्वात्प्रत्येकमावर्तत इति केचित्। अन्ये 'इषे त्वे'ति बर्हिरादत्ते' इति। ब्राह्मणे एकवचनं जात्यपेक्षं, समुदायापेक्षं वा। तदिहापि तुल्यमिति। सहैवादत्ते। एतेनैवैकादशि-न्यादिषु व्याख्यातम्॥ १ ॥

'उपाकरणीये जुहोती'ति संज्ञया विधानं व्यवहारार्थम्। वक्ष्यति हि 'उत्सृजत्युपाकरणीययोः [३]पूर्वामि'त्यादि। उपाकरोति देवताभ्यां निर्दिशति। बर्हिरादानस्य दृष्टयर्थत्वादायतनाभ्यां संस्पर्शयति पशुम्॥ २-३ ॥

उक्तमग्निमन्थनमिह हौत्रवत्। एतावान् विशेषः। किन्तु 'आयुरसि' इत्यभिमन्त्रणमिह नोक्तम्। तस्य चास्मिन्नेव प्रकरणे मन्त्रब्राह्मणयोः[३] पठितस्य लोपो नोपपद्यते। तत्र द्वयी गतिः। अग्न्याधेयवदिहापि जातमेवाभिमन्त्रयते, तुल्यन्यायत्वात्[४]। अथ[५] 'उर्वश्यसी'त्यरणिमित्यादिग्रहणम्। द्वाभ्यां वाक्याभ्यामरण्यादानमेव च। 'आयुरसी'त्यग्न्यभिधानत्वान्नोपपद्यत इति चेत्। [६]कारणे कार्यवदुपचारोऽप्युपपद्यत एव। तथा च ब्राह्मणे—'उर्वश्यस्यस्यायुरसी'त्याह मिथुनत्वाये'त्यैक-मन्त्र्यमिव[७] लक्ष्यते। अन्येऽपि बौधायनादय एवमेवामनन्ति। 'शिशुं जातं न बिभ्रती'ति ॥ ४-८ ॥

श्रुत्वा परिह्रियमाणाय[८] चोदयति। '[९]आ स्वे [९]योनौ निषीदत्' इत्युच्यमानेऽनुप्रहरेत्। उत्तरं परिधिं परिहृत्य तच्छकलादानाद्यभिहोमान्तं निर्मन्थ्यं नाम। यत्र 'निर्मन्थ्येन चरती'ति कर्म चोद्यते [१०]तत्रैतावतो ग्रहणं प्रत्येतव्यम्। यत्र तु तदुद्धृत्यावोक्ष्य निर्मन्थ्यमग्निं मथित्वा निर्मन्थ्येनेष्टकाः पाचयेदिति द्रव्यप्रधानं तत्रासमारूढो निर्मन्थ्यः। तूर्णीं मथितो[११] निर्मन्थ्यः ॥ ९-१० ॥

---

१. M Ad पल्लूल°, Ad पल्ल°. **२.** M Ad °चानु°; T विसंस्मितेवानु°. **३-३.** M Ad om; thus T. **४.** M Ad न्याय्यत्वा; thus T. **५.** M Ad °वोर्वश्यसीत्यरणीमिः°; thus T. **६.** M Ad कारणकार्य°; thus T. **७.** T °त्येकमाभम°. **८.** M Ad प्रह्रिय°; thus T. **९-९.** M Ad आन्धे यो°; thus T. **१०.** M Ad अत्रै°; thus T. **११.** M Ad महितो°; thus T.

'°ऋषीणां पुत्रो अधिराज एष=भागधेयꣳ स्वाहा' **इति** ॥ ११ ॥ 'अप उपस्पृश्य देवस्य त्वा सवितुः प्रसवे' **इत्युत्तानेन हस्तेन रशनामादत्ते।** '°अश्विनोर्बाहुभ्यां पूष्णो हस्ताभ्याम् आददे' **इति** ॥ १२ ॥ 'ऋतस्य त्वा देव हविः पाशेनारभे' **इत्यक्ष्णया शृङ्गं पशोः परिहरति** ॥ १३ ॥ 'धर्षा मानुषान्' **इति नियुनक्ति** ॥ १४ ॥ **आहरन्त्यस्मै प्रोक्षणीः पात्रियाम्** ॥ १५ ॥ 'अद्भ्यस्त्वौषधीभ्यः प्रोक्षामि' **इति पशुं प्रोक्षति।** '°इन्द्राग्निभ्यां जुष्टम्' **इति** ॥ १६ ॥ 'अपां पेरुरसि' **इति पाययति।** '°स्वात्तं चित् सदेवꣳ हव्यमापो देवीः स्वदतैनम्' **इति** ॥ १७ ॥ **यदि न पिबेन्न वा उवेत्** 'न म्रियसे' **इत्यस्य दक्षिणं कर्णमाजपेत्।** '°न हन्यसे जीवन्निदेषि पथिभिः सुवर्ग्यैः। उज्जातेन भिनददुज्जनित्वैः स्वर्गे लोके यजमानꣳ हि धेहि मास्यै हास्या आहुत्यै यामुपेम' **इति** ॥ १८ ॥ 'शश्वद्धविः' **इत्येव वक्षः प्रोक्ष्य पृष्ठं प्रोक्षति** ॥ १९ ॥ **निपाय्योपोक्ष्य निधाय पात्रम् अग्नये समिध्यमानायानुवाच आह** ॥ २० ॥ **अनूक्तासु सामिधेनीषु स्रुवेणाघारमाघार्याह** 'अग्नीदग्निं त्रिः संमृड्ढि' **इति** ॥ २१ ॥ **स्रुग्भ्यामुत्तरम्** ॥ २२ ॥ **असꣳस्पर्शयन्नत्याक्रम्य** 'सं ते प्राणो वायुना गच्छताम्' **इति जुह्वा पशुꣳ**

उत्तानेन हस्तेन दक्षिणेन। 'एकाङ्गवचने दक्षिणं प्रतीयाद्। अनादेशे' इत्याश्वलायनः (आश्वश्रौ. १.१.१२-१३)। तथा स्मृतिरपि 'दक्षिणापचारेण कर्तव्यमि'ति ॥ १२ ॥

अक्ष्णया परिहरतीत्यस्य शेषः शृङ्गं पशोरिति। पशुः परिहरणीय[१] इति प्रकृतत्वात् प्राप्ते पशोः शृङ्गमिति परिहरणस्य विशेषमनुपदकार आह—'उदीचः प्राणानुत्सृजती'ति ॥ १३ ॥

'धर्षा मानुषानि'ति नियुनक्ति यूपरशनायाम्। नानैव नानादेवत्यान् रशनासु नियुनक्ति। 'समानस्यां प्राजापत्यान्' इति दर्शनादिति ॥ १४ ॥

पात्रीशब्दः स्रुचि वर्तते ॥ १५ ॥

वक्षः[२] प्रोक्ष्य पृष्ठं प्रोक्षति। पूर्वोक्तस्यैव प्रोक्षणस्य प्रकारो न प्रोक्षणान्तरं न च प्रोक्षणद्वयम्। वक्ष आरभ्य [३]आपृष्ठं प्रोक्षतीत्यर्थः ॥ १९ ॥

पायनमपि पूर्वोक्तम्। [४]एवमुपोक्ष्येत्यधस्तादुपोक्ष्येत्यर्थः। 'उपरिष्टात् प्रोक्षती'त्यादिना ब्राह्मणेन विहितस्य वक्षस आरभ्योपरिष्टात् प्रोक्षणं कर्तव्यमिति विशेषाभिधित्सया पुनर्वचनम् ॥ २० ॥

संयजत्रैरित्यत्रासामर्थ्यात् क्रियापदं नानुषज्यते। 'सं यज्ञपतिरि'त्यत्राप्यसामर्थ्य[५]व्यपेतत्वात्। आह-किं क्रियापदस्य लोपः कार्य एवम्, अथवा प्रकृतिरसामर्थ्याभावादनुषज्यते। सा च प्रकृतिः[६] प्रत्ययपरैव प्रयोक्तव्यैवेति[७] नियमात्समर्थप्रत्ययं लौकिकबहुवचनमुपादत्ते। तथा परस्तादप्येकवचनम्। यद्येवं सर्वत्रानुषङ्गः स्यात्किमनेन विचारेण। उच्यते[८]। अस्ति विशेषः[८]। प्रकृतिभ्रेषे श्रौतस्य भ्रेषो भवति। प्रत्ययभ्रेषे लौकिकस्य। तथा चानुपदे 'अत्रेडा[९]पशुं समञ्ज्यात्', 'सं ते प्राणो वायुना

---

१. M Ad °हरति य; thus T. २. M Ad वक्षं°; thus T. ३. M Ad om आ; thus T. ४. M Ad मुपाक्ष्ये°, T °मुपेक्ष्ये°. ५. T °प्यसमर्थव्य°. ६. M Ad twice. ७. M Ad °तव्यैवे°. ८-८. M त.....शेषः, Ad °तेतिशेषः. ९. M Ad त्रेधा; thus T.

समनक्ति। '०सं यजत्रैरङ्गानि सं यज्ञपतिराशिषा' **इति** ॥ २३ ॥ **ध्रुवाꣳ समज्य सादयित्वा प्रवरं प्रवृणीते** ॥ २४ ॥ **आश्रावयति** ॥ २५ ॥ 'ओ श्रावय' **इत्याह** ॥ २६ ॥ 'अग्निर्देवो होता देवाः प्रावितारः' **इति तद्धोतारं वृणीते** ॥ २७ ॥ 'को नामासि' **इत्येनमाह** ॥ २८ ॥ **नाम प्रबूते** 'असौ मानुषः' **इति** ॥ २९ ॥ **आहवनीये शकलं प्रास्यति यथा होतुर्नाम भवति** ॥ ३० ॥ **अत्याश्रावयत्येवातः** ॥ ३१ ॥ 'ओ श्रावय' **इत्याह** '०अग्निर्दैवीनां विशां पुरएताऽयं यजमानो मनुष्याणां तयोरस्थूरि गार्हपत्यं दीदयच्छतꣳ हिमाद्वायू राधाꣳसीत्संपृञ्चानावसंपृञ्चानौ तनुवः' **इति** ॥ ३२ ॥ **एतस्मिन् काले मैत्रावरुणाय दण्डं प्रयच्छति** ॥ ५.२.१.३३ ॥ **[इति प्रथमः पटलः (४)]**

[मैत्रावरुणाय दण्डप्रदानादिकर्म]

एतस्मिन् काले मैत्रावरुणाय दण्डं प्रयच्छति ॥ १ ॥ 'त्वां गावोऽवृणत राज्याय' **इति मैत्रावरुणदण्डेन ब्रह्मा यजमानं वाचयति।** '०त्वाꣳ हवन्त=वसूनि' **इति** ॥ २ ॥ **सीदति होता** ॥ ३ ॥ **प्रसूतः स्रुचावादत्ते** ॥ ४ ॥ **प्रयाजान् यजति** ॥ ५ ॥ 'ओ श्रावय' **इत्याह** ॥ ६ ॥ 'समिद्भ्यः प्रेष्य प्रेष्य' **इति** ॥ ७ ॥ **एकादश प्रयाजान् यजति** ॥ ८ ॥ **चतुर्थेऽर्धꣳ समानीयाष्टमे सर्वꣳ समानयते** ॥ ९ ॥ **उपभृतोऽधि स्रुच्येकादशं परिशिष्य दशेष्ट्वाऽत्याक्रामति** ॥ १० ॥ 'स्वरुः स्वधितिः' **इति** ॥ ११ ॥ **अक्ष्णया स्वरुं च स्वधितिं च संगृह्य** 'घृतेनाक्तौ' **इत्यन्तरतः स्रुचः स्वरुमनक्ति बहिष्टात् स्वधितिम्।** '०पशुं त्रायेथाम्' **इति** ॥ १२ ॥ **स्वधितिना प्रतिललाटं पशोरुन्मार्ष्टि** ॥ १३ ॥ 'एषा

गच्छतामि'ति ललाटे। 'सं ते यजत्रैरङ्गानि गच्छन्तामि'ति ककुदि, 'सं ते यज्ञपतिराशिषा गच्छतामि'ति श्रोण्याम्[1]। 'यदुपरिष्टात्पशुं समनक्ति [2]मेध्यमेवैनं करोति'[2] इत्येतावदेव ब्राह्मणे श्रूयते। वाक्यत्रित्वात् कर्मत्रित्वमपीष्यत एव। ललाटादिदेशविशेषो वाचनिकः ॥ २३ ॥

अत्याश्रावयत्येवातः। सोम एवैकेऽत्याश्रावणमामनन्ति। तदस्माभिर्नेष्यते। अतोऽत्याश्रावयत्येवेति ॥ ५.२.१.३१ ॥ **[इति प्रथमः पटलः (४)]**

अग्नीषोमीये पशावेतस्मिन् काल इति। 'क्रीते[3] सोमे मैत्रावरुणाय दण्डं प्रयच्छती'त्यनेन वैकल्पिकत्वप्रदर्शनार्थमाम्नातम्। इह पुनस्तदेवानूद्यते। सोमक्रयणाभावादयमेवात्र कालो मैत्रावरुण-दण्डेन दीयमान इति शेषः[4] ॥ १ ॥

'दुरः' प्रभृतयः षडागन्तवः प्रयाजाः। तेषां त्रयश्चतुर्थमन्त्राः त्रय उक्तविकाराः[5]। वर्मक्रियायां [6]तद्वदाहुतीनां स्थानम्। एकानीकपक्षे नास्ति विशेषः ॥ ८–९ ॥

'कः स्वधितिहस्तमि'ति शमितारमामन्त्रयत इत्यभिप्रायः। 'पशुं त्रायेथाम्' इति स्वरुणा [7]स्वधितिना च समनक्ति[7] ॥ ११–१२ ॥

स्वधितिना प्रतिललाटं पशोरुन्मार्ष्टीति विशेषः ॥ १३ ॥

---

१. M Ad श्रोत्रे...; thus T. २–२. M Ad om; thus T. ३. M Ad क्रियते; thus T. ४. M Ad शेषा. ५. M Ad उत्तमवि; thus T. ६. M Ad तद्वदेवाहुतीनां० T तद्वदाहु०. ७–७. M Ad twice.

तेऽश्रिः स्पष्टाऽस्तु' **इत्याह** ॥ १४ ॥ **शमित्रे स्वधितिं प्रयच्छति** ॥ १५ ॥ **अनया पशुꣳ स्पृशति** ॥ १६ ॥ **अवगूह्य स्वरुं यथायतनं स्रुचौ सादयित्वा** 'पर्यग्नयेऽनुब्रूही**'त्याह** ॥ १७ ॥ **आहवनीयाद-ग्नीदुल्मुकमादायान्तरा चात्वालोत्करौ निष्क्रम्य प्रसलैस्त्रिः पर्यग्निकरोति** ॥ १८ ॥ 'प्रजानन्तः प्रतिगृह्णन्तु पूर्वे' **इत्युल्मुकपाणिः परिद्रवति** ॥ १९ ॥ **पञ्चापाव्यानां यजूꣳषि जुहोति** 'प्राणम-ङ्गेभ्यः=शरीरैः स्वाहा', 'येषामीशे=नस्य सन्तु स्वाहा', 'ये बध्यमान=अग्निस्ताम्=विदानः स्वाहा', 'य आरण्याः पश=वायुस्ताँ=विदानः स्वाहा', 'प्र मुञ्चमाना=पाथः स्वाहा' **इति** ॥ २० ॥ 'एहि यजमान' **इत्युक्त्वाऽन्वारब्धे यजमाने होतुराहुतिꣳ षष्ठीं जुहोति** ॥ २१ ॥ **निधायोल्मुकमाग्नीध्रं प्रतिपथं त्रिः पुनः परिद्रवति** ॥ २२ ॥ **तदेवाग्नीदुल्मुकमादत्ते बर्हिषी अध्वर्युर्वपाश्रपण्यौ प्रतिप्रस्थाता** ॥ २३ ॥ **उल्मुकप्रथमा उदञ्चो यन्त्यन्तरा चात्वालं चोत्करं च** ॥ २४ ॥ **आश्राव्य** 'उप प्रेष्य होतर्हव्या देवेभ्यः' **इत्याह** ॥ २५ ॥ 'रेवतीर्यज्ञपतिं प्रियधाऽऽविशत' **इति वपाश्रपणी-भ्यां पशुमन्वारभन्ते**। '०उरो अन्तरिक्ष=यज्ञपतिं धा' **इति** ॥ २६ ॥ 'पृथिव्याः सम्पृचः पाहि' **इति बर्हिरुपास्य तस्मिन्नुपरि पशुं निक्षिणन्ति प्रतीचीनशिरसमुदीचीनपादम्** ॥ २७ ॥ 'अमायुं कृण्वन्तꣳ संज्ञपयत' **इत्याह** ॥ २८ ॥ 'संज्ञप्तं प्रब्रूताद्' **इति** ॥ २९ ॥ **तस्मात्** 'नानाप्राणो यजमानस्य पशुना' **इत्यध्वर्युश्च यजमानश्च व्यावर्तेते**। '०यज्ञो देवेभिः=कामाः' **इति** ॥ ३० ॥ **आगत्य**

---

[1]'एषा तेऽश्रिः [1]स्पष्टाऽस्त्वि'ति। एषा त्वया श्रीरपि स्मृता[2] भवतु। किं प्रयोजनम्। अस्य विशेषो विध्यवशेषेष्वाम्नातो विज्ञायते। यया पशुं समनक्ति न तया विशास्ति[3]। यया[4] विशास्ति[4] न तया श्रृतस्यावद्यति ॥ १४ ॥

पर्यग्नयेऽनुब्रूहीति[5]। *त्रिः पर्यग्निकरोति*। [6]'त्र्यावृद्धि यज्ञोऽथो रक्षसामपहत्यै'[6] इति विदधद् विस्रस्य पशुं तीर्थेन निष्क्रमय्य पर्यग्निकरोतीति ज्ञापयति। नैतदेवम्। पर्यग्निकृतान्पशून् यथापूर्वं स्थापयन्तीत्येकादशिन्यां दृश्यते। अतो यथावस्थितमेव निष्क्रम्य पर्यग्निकरोति। निष्क्रमणं वाच-निकम्। अन्य आह—'चात्वाले पशुपचनीं निधाय तया सह पर्यग्निकरणार्थमि'ति। अनुपदकार आह— 'पञ्चतयमिह पर्यग्निकुर्यात् पशुं यूपमाहवनीयं शामित्रदेशं[7] स्रुचश्च। चात्वाले पशुपचनीं निधाय तां पचनीम् पशुमेवेत्येक' इति ॥ १७-१८ ॥

[8]बर्हिषी अध्वर्युरुपाकरणार्थे ॥ २३ ॥

तस्मात्पशोः संज्ञप्यमानात्। अध्वर्युर्यजमानश्च मन्त्रेणावर्तेते[9]। प्रतिप्रस्थाताग्नीध्रश्च तूष्णीमेव ॥ ३० ॥

पृषदाज्यावेक्षणं सर्वेषाम् ॥ ५.२.२.३१ ॥ **[इति द्वितीयः पटलः** (५)**]**

१-१. M एष....स्पष्य; thus T. **२.** M Ad रविस्मृ° ; thus T. **३.** M Ad पिशा°. **४-४.** M Ad om; thus T. **५.** M Ad पर्यग्नयेऽनुब्रू=त्रि abri. text of *sūtras* 17-18. **६-६.** M Ad om; thus T. **७.** M Ad om; thus T. **८.** T बर्हिष्यध्व°. **९.** M Ad ° वर्तेत; thus T.

पृषदाज्यमवेक्षन्ते 'इह प्रजाः' **इति** ॥ ५.२.२.३१ ॥ **[इति द्वितीयः पटलः** (५)**]**

[वपाश्रपणपशुप्राणाप्यायनादिकर्म]

'इह प्रजा विश्वरूपा रमन्तामस्मिन् यज्ञे विश्वविदो घृताचीः। अग्निः कुलायमभि संवसाना अस्मानवन्तु पयसा घृतेन' **इति** ॥ १ ॥ **वाचंयमा अनवेक्षमाणा आसते** ॥ २ ॥ 'यत् पशुर्मायुमकृत' **इति संज्ञप्ते स्रुवाहुतिं जुहोति**। '॰उरो वा पद्भिराहते अग्निर्मा तस्मादेनसो विश्वान्मुञ्चत्वंऽहसः स्वाहा' **इति** ॥ ३ ॥ 'शमितार उपेतन' **इति वपाश्रपणीभ्यां पशुमुपायन्ति**। '॰यज्ञं देवेभि=परि' **इति** ॥ ४ ॥ **संवेष्ट्य रसनां ग्रीवासु पाशात्पशुं प्रमुञ्चति** 'अदितिः पाशं प्र मुमोक्त्वेतम्' **इति** ॥ ५ ॥ **विशालयोपसजति** 'नमः पशुभ्यः=पाशम्' **इति** ॥ ६ ॥ **ताः शुष्के स्थाणौ प्रतिमुञ्चति** ॥ ७ ॥ **यं द्वेष्टि यजमानस्तं ध्यायति** ॥ ८ ॥ **अपः परिषिच्याप्रतीक्षमाव्रजते** ॥ ९ ॥ **आनयति प्रतिप्रस्थाता पत्नीं सह पान्नेजनेन** ॥ १० ॥ **अन्तरा चात्वालं चोत्करं चोदङ्ङुप निष्क्रम्य** 'अनर्वा प्रेहि' **इत्युदीचीमानयति**। '॰घृतस्य कुल्या=रायस्पोषेण' **इति** ॥ ११ ॥ **आगत्य पशोः प्राणानाप्याय-यति** ॥ १२ ॥ 'वाक् त आप्यायताम्' **इति वाचम्** ॥ १३ ॥ 'प्राणस्त आप्यायताम्' **इति प्राणम्** ॥ १४ ॥ 'चक्षुस्त आप्यायताम्' **इति चक्षुः** ॥ १५ ॥ 'श्रोत्रं त आप्यायताम्' **इति श्रोत्रम्** ॥ १६ ॥ 'या ते प्राणाञ्छुग्जगाम' **इत्येतानेव पुनराप्याययति**। '॰या चक्षुर्या श्रोत्रं शुन्धताम्' **इति** ॥ १७ ॥ 'नाभिस्त आप्यायताम्' **इति नाभिम्** ॥ १८ ॥ 'पायुस्त आप्यायताम्' **इति**

अनवेक्षमाणः[1] संज्ञप्यमानं पशुं शमित्रा संज्ञप्त इत्युक्त आवृत्य संज्ञप्ताहुतिं जुहोति ॥ २-३ ॥

वपाश्रपण्योः सान्नाय्यस्थालीकार्यापन्नयोस्तद्धर्माः प्रवर्तन्ते। तयोर्यथार्थमूहः 'शमितार' इति मन्त्रमध्वर्युरेव वदति। नायमुपायनमन्त्रः ॥ ४ ॥

इतिकरणाभावेऽपि[2] 'अरातीयन्तम्' इत्यादि स्थाणौ जुहोति। 'मोचतः[3]। आव्रजत' इति दर्शनाद्यजमानोऽपि स्थाणुसमीपं गच्छति ॥ ७ ॥

'तमि'त्यत्र[4] यजमानस्य द्वेष्यं ध्यायति ॥ ८ ॥

सह पान्नेजनेन पादप्रक्षालनार्थेनोदकेन। पादप्रक्षालनेन पश्वाप्यायनं[5] लक्ष्यते। आदित्यमुत्काशयतीक्षमाणां[6] प्रणामयति ॥ १० ॥

आगत्य पशोः प्राणानाप्यायतोऽद्भिरभिषेकम्। अभिषिच्याभिषिच्य प्रत्येकं वक्ष्यमाणेषु प्राणस्थानेषु। आगत्येति क्त्वाप्रत्ययनिर्देशात् प्रतिप्रस्थाता च पत्नी चेति केचित्। अन्य आनयनमात्रं प्रतिप्रस्थातुराप्यायनेऽध्वर्युर्द्वितीयः। समानकर्तृकत्वावगमस्यापि पत्न्याः कृतार्थता। आगत्येति यत्नश्चानन्तर्यार्थः। 'आगतामध्वर्युरप्सु वाचयती'ति। तस्य पश्वाप्यायनं बौधायनीये विहितमिति। नात्र

---

१. M Ad ॰माणाः; thus T. **२.** M Ad ॰करणभावे॰. **३.** M Ad प्रतिमोचयतः, T मोचतः. **४.** M Ad T तस्मिन्नित्य॰. **५.** M Ad ॰प्ययनं; thus T. **६.** M Ad ॰यतिक्ष; thus T.

पायुम् ॥ १९ ॥ 'मेढ्रं त आप्यायताम्' **इति मेढ्रम्** ॥ २० ॥ 'शुद्धाश्चरित्राः' **इति पदः संनिधाय मार्जयति**। '°शमद्भ्यः शमोषधीभ्यः' **इति** ॥ २१ ॥ 'शं पृथिव्यै शमहोभ्याम्' **इत्यतिशिष्टा दक्षिणतोऽनुपृष्ठं वा निनयति** ॥ २२ ॥ 'आपो देवीः शुद्धायुवः' **इति निनीता अपोऽनुमन्त्रयते**। '°शुद्धा यूयं देवाँ ऊद्ध्वꣳ शुद्धा वयं परिविष्टाः परिवेष्टारो वो भूयास्म' **इति** ॥ २३ ॥ **प्रतिपरैति पत्नी** ॥ २४ ॥ 'कवोत्तानमिव पशुं कुरुत' **इत्याह** ॥ २५ ॥ 'तस्य ओषधे त्रायस्वैनम्' **इति दक्षिणेन नाभिं बर्हिषा त्वचमुप संगृह्णाति** ॥ २६ ॥ 'स्वधिते मैनꣳ हिꣳसीः' **इति स्वधितिना तिरश्चीनमाच्छ्यति** ॥ २७ ॥ **स्थविमतो बर्हिषश्छित्त्वोभयतः पशावनतिक्रम्य निरस्यति** 'रक्षसां भागोऽसीदमहꣳ रक्षोऽधमं तमो नयामि योऽस्मान् द्वेष्टि यं च वयं द्विष्म इदमेनमधमं तमो नयामि' **इति** ॥ २८ ॥ **अप उपस्पृश्य** 'इषे त्वा' **इति वपामुत्खिदति** ॥ २९ ॥ 'घृतेन द्यावापृथिवी' ॥ ५.२.३.३० ॥ **[इति तृतीयः पटलः (६)]**

[वपानिश्रपणादिकर्म]

'घृतेन द्यावापृथिवी प्रोर्ण्वाथाम्' **इति वपाश्रपणी प्रोर्णोति** ॥ १ ॥ **अविशालयोपतृणत्ति** ॥ २ ॥ 'अच्छिन्नो रायः सुवीरः' **इति परिवासयति** ॥ ३ ॥ 'देवेभ्यः शुन्धस्व', 'देवेभ्यः शुम्भस्व' **इति बर्हिषा परिवासनं प्रतियौति** ॥ ४ ॥ **उदपात्रेणाभिषिच्य** 'प्रत्युष्टꣳ रक्षः प्रत्युष्टा अरातयः' **इत्युल्मुकेन प्रतितपति शामित्रे** ॥५ ॥ **अङ्गारान् संप्रकृष्य** 'उर्वन्तरिक्षमन्विहि' **इत्युल्मुकप्रथमाः पुनरायन्त्यन्तरा चात्वालं चोत्करं च** ॥ ६ ॥ **वपाश्रपणी पुनरन्वारभन्ते** ॥ ७ ॥ 'उप त्वाऽग्ने दिवे-दिवे'

वाचयतीति दर्शनादन्येषु वाचनं गम्यते ॥ १२-२० ॥

कवोत्तानमिव ईषदुत्तानमिव। यथा दक्षिणे पार्श्वे आवर्ते विशसनं संभवति तथा स्थापयत हे शमितारः इति[१] ॥ २५ ॥

शिष्टेनोपाकरणबर्हिषा[२] त्वचमित्यादि। त्वचा सह बर्हिर्द्वेधा छिद्यते ॥ २६ ॥

तयोर्यत् स्थविमः तत्पुनर्द्वेधा कृत्वा द्वयोरपि स्थविमा[३] उभयतः पशौ लोहितमनक्ति ॥ ५.२.३.२८ ॥ **[इति तृतीयः पटलः (६)]**

बर्हिषा परिवासनं प्रतियौति। बर्हिषो मध्यमेन खण्डेन वपाया उपात्तावशिष्टं[४] प्रति निश्रयति छादयतीत्यर्थः[५] ॥ ४ ॥

उदपात्रेण वपामभिषिच्य शामित्रे पशुश्रपणप्रदेशे[६]। अथवा शामित्रोऽग्निस्तन्निमित्तमुल्मुकादङ्गारात्[७] संप्रकृष्य 'मातरिश्वनो घर्मोऽसी'ति तत्प्रथमाः पुनरायन्ति[८] ॥ ५-६ ॥

ये पशुं नीयमानमन्वारभन्ते ते[९] वपाश्रपणी पुनरन्वारभन्ते[९]। के पुनस्ते अध्वर्यू[१०]

---

१. M Ad om; thus T. **२.** M Ad नोपकरणबर्हिषि; thus T. **३.** M Ad °विमो; thus T. **४.** M Ad उपात्तातिशिष्टं; thus T. **५.** M छादयतीर्थः. **६.** M Ad श्रवण° ; thus T. **७.** M Ad °मुन्मुका° रान्. **८.** M Ad रादयन्ति. **९-९.** M Ad om; thus T. **१०.** T °ध्वर्युर्य°.

इति तिसृभिर्गायत्रीभिराहवनीयमुपायन्ति। '०दोषावस्त=स्वस्तये' **इति ॥ ८ ॥** 'प्रत्युष्टꣳ रक्षः प्रत्युष्टा अरातयः' **इत्याहवनीयस्यान्तमेऽङ्गारे प्रतितपति ॥ ९ ॥ तामेतेनान्तरा यूपं चाहवनीयं चातिहृत्य दक्षिणत उदगावृतः प्रतिप्रस्थाता वपाꣳ श्रपयति ॥ १० ॥ तस्यै** 'वायो वीहि स्तोकानाम्' **इत्यध्वर्युर्बर्हिरुपास्यति ॥ ११ ॥** 'त्वामु ते दधिरे हव्यवाहम्' **इति स्रुवाहुत्याऽभिजुहोति।** '०श्रृतं कतार=जुषस्व स्वाहा' **इति ॥ १२ ॥** 'स्तोकेभ्योऽनुब्रूहि' **इत्याह ॥ १३ ॥ यदैतं मैत्रावरुणः षड्चꣳ सूक्तमन्वाहाथ स्वाहाकृती: ॥ १४ ॥ प्रैषमादायाध्वर्युरत्याक्रामति ॥ १५ ॥** 'ओ श्रावय' **इत्याह ॥ १६ ॥** 'स्वाहाकृतीभ्यः प्रेष्य' **इति ॥ १७ ॥ वषट्कृते जुहोति ॥ १८ ॥ पृषदाज्यमभिघार्य वपामभिघारयति ॥ १९ ॥ आज्यं च हिरण्यशल्कं च ॥ २० ॥ वपाया उपस्तृणीत**

यजमानश्च ॥ ७ ॥

'उप त्वाऽग्न' इत्याग्नीध्रा सह सर्वेषां वपां सान्नाय्याधिश्रयणमन्त्रेणाधिश्रयति। तत्र यथार्थमूहः। अन्य आह—सान्नाय्ये स्थालीगतेनोष्मणा पाकः प्रार्थ्यते। संभवनधारणे अर्थकृते न च वपाश्रपणीगतेनोष्मणा[1] वपा पच्यते। अतः स्थालीधर्मा वपाश्रपण्यां न प्रवर्तन्त इति ॥ ८-१० ॥

बर्हिरुपास्यति। तस्या वपायाः श्रपणार्थं वपाविशसनछिन्नस्य बर्हिषो भागं समीपे क्षिपति ॥ ११ ॥

यद्यपि सूक्तानुवचनान्तरमित्युक्तं तथापि प्रतिष्ठाप्य समभिघार्याहृत्यासाद्य 'यन्मे अग्न' इत्यभिमृश्य ततः स्वाहाकृतीः ॥ १४ ॥

प्रैषमादायेत्यादि। स्वाहाकृतीः प्रैषो यत्र स्रुचावादायेत्यादि तत्र [2]स्रुगादापनस्यावृत्तावश्विनाध्वर्यू इत्यावृत्तिः ॥ १५-१७ ॥

पृषदाज्यमभिघार्य वपामभिघारयति। उपभृतमन्तत इत्यन्ते प्राप्तस्यानूयाजद्रव्याभिघारणस्य[3] वपायाः पूर्वत्वं विहितम्[4]। अतो [4]ध्रुवाभिघारणं न[5] निवर्तते। ततो ध्रुवामेव प्रथममभिघारयति। अन्य आह—'ध्रुवामेव प्रथममभिघारयत्यतो हि प्रथमावाज्यभागौ यक्ष्यन्भवती'ति श्रुतेः सवविधपक्षे प्राथम्यं नोपपद्यते। [6]सर्वार्थत्वाच्चानिवृत्तिरिति। ननु पशुपुरोडाशाभिघारणार्थं[6] किञ्चित् पात्रमुत्पाद्य तस्मिन्नानीय प्रयाजशेषः[7] स्थापयितव्यः। उच्यते। प्रयाजद्रव्यैकदेशेन कर्तव्यमभिघारणम्। जुह्वा रेच-नस्य दृष्ट्यर्थत्वात्। दृष्ट्यर्थस्य हविर्गतद्वितीयाश्रवणादपि[8] बलीयस्त्वादप्रयोजकं सत्[9] पात्रं नोत्पाद-यितुं शक्नोति। अतो विप्रकृष्टकालानां हविषामभिघारणं लुप्यते प्रयाजशेषेण। तदुक्तं[10] प्राजापत्या-धिकरणे— 'अभिघारणे विप्रकर्षादनूयाजवत्पात्रभेदः[11] स्यान्न वा पात्रत्वादपात्रैकदेशत्वात्'। हविर्यज्ञ-विधेऽत्राज्यभागौ यजति पुरस्तात्पुरोडाशस्य। सववविधे वपायां पञ्चावित्तनां महाहविर्यज्ञ[12] उक्तो

---

१. M Ad °श्रपणीतेनो° ; thus T. **२.** M Ad स्रुगादापास्या°. **३.** M Ad °द्रव्यस्याभि° ; thus T. **४-४.** M °हित....ध्रुवा° ; thus Ad T. **५.** M Ad om. **६-६.** M सर्वार्थत्वा ... शाभिधा°, Ad पशुपुरुषशपभिघा°. **७.** M Ad °शेषे; thus T. **८.** M Ad श्रपणा°. **९.** M सवत्रः, Ad सर्वत्र. **१०.** M Ad तद्युक्तं. **११.** M Ad °पात्राभेदः. **१२.** M Ad महापितृयज्ञ° ; thus T.

इन्द्राग्निभ्याम् ॥ २१ ॥ 'इन्द्राग्निभ्यां छागस्य वपाया मेदसोऽवदीयमानस्यानुब्रूहि' **इत्याह स्रुवेण वपाः संप्रलुम्पन्** ॥ २२ ॥ **हिरण्यशल्केन चैवाज्येन चोपरिष्टादभिघारयति** ॥ २३ ॥ **ते एतेनैव यथेतमाहृत्योत्तरतः प्रतिप्रस्थाता वपाश्रपण्यौ धारयंस्तिष्ठति** ॥ २४ ॥ 'ओ श्रावय' **इत्याह** ॥ २५ ॥ 'इन्द्राग्निभ्यां छागस्य वपां मेदः प्रस्थितं प्रेष्य' **इति** ॥ २६ ॥ 'स्वाहा देवेभ्यः' **इति पुरस्ताद् वपायै प्रतिप्रस्थाता स्रुवाहुतिं जुहोति** ॥ २७ ॥ 'जातवेदो वपया गच्छ देवान्' **इति वषट्कृते-ऽध्वर्युर्वपां जुहोति।** '०त्वः हि होता=दन्तु देवाः स्वाहा' **इति** ॥ २८ ॥ 'देवेभ्यः स्वाहा' **इत्यु-परिष्टात् स्रुवाहुत्याऽभिजुहोति** ॥ २९ ॥ 'स्वाहोर्ध्वनभसं मारुतं गच्छतम्' **इति विषूची वपा-श्रपणी प्रहरति, प्राचीं विशालां प्रतीचीमविशालान्ते** ॥ ३० ॥ **वपायै संस्त्रावेणाभि-जुहोति** ॥ ३१ ॥ **वपया प्रचर्य** 'आपो हि षष्ठा मयोभुवः' **इति तृचेन मार्जयन्ते चात्वाले** ॥ ५.२.४.३२ ॥ **[इति चतुर्थः पटलः** (७)**]**

॥ इति पञ्चमप्रपाठके द्वितीयोऽनुवाकः ॥

न्यायः ॥ १९ ॥

षडवत्तपक्षे वपां द्वेधा विच्छिद्य संप्रलुम्पति। अभितो वपां जुहोतीत्येकवचनोदितत्वात्[1] प्रतिप्रस्थातैवोपरिष्टादभि जुहोतीति केचित्। 'आरण्यानां पशूनां [2]निष्कृतीर्हुत्वा जुहोति 'हुताय स्वाहे'त्याद्युक्त्वा तासां चतसर्णामाहुतीनां पृथक् प्रयोजनं ब्रुवन्॥ २२ ॥

'देवेभ्यः स्वाहे'ति वपा एव तत्परिजुहोती'ति वचनादेकेनैव च तासां होत्रा भवितव्यत्वात् तत्र वचनमिति कल्पयितुमशक्यत्वादिहाध्वर्युणोपरिष्टाद्धोतव्यमित्यन्ये ॥ २९ ॥

वपाश्रपण्योः प्रहरणप्रसंगात्[3] प्रतिप्रस्थाता प्रहर्ता ॥ ३० ॥

चात्वाले मार्जनं[4] सर्वेषामृत्विक्स्वामिनाम्॥ ५.२.४.३२ ॥ **[इति चतुर्थः पटलः** (७)**]**

॥ इति व्याख्यायां पञ्चमप्रपाठके द्वितीयोऽनुवाकः ॥

अग्नीत्पशुपुरोडाश=एतत्कुर्वन्ति। प्रेषितास्त्रयोऽपि त्रीणि कर्माणि कुर्वन्ति। सामान्येनोक्त्वा पुनर्विशेषविवक्षयाऽधिकरोति ॥ १-२ ॥

---

१. M Ad वचनचोदि°. **२.** M Ad °कृति°, T निष्कृती°. **३.** M Ad °रणंप्रस°. **४.** M Ad मार्ज सर्वे°.

॥ अथ पञ्चमप्रपाठके तृतीयोऽनुवाकः ॥

[पशुपुरोडाशनिर्वपणादिकर्म]

'अग्नीत्पशुपुरोडाशं निर्वप' **इति संप्रेष्यति।** '°ब्रह्मन् पृषदाज्यं गोपाय', 'प्रतिप्रस्थातः पशुं विशाधि' **इति** ॥ १ ॥ **एतत् कुर्वन्ति** ॥ २ ॥ **अग्नीत्पशुपुरोडाशं निर्वपत्यैन्द्रमेकादशकपालम्** ॥ ३ ॥

अग्नीत्पशुपुरोडाशं निर्वपत्यैन्द्रमेकादशकपालमिति। अयं पशुपुरोडाशः पश्वङ्गत्वेन विहितः। स्वैः प्राकृतैरन्वाधानादिभिर्धर्मैर्धर्मवान् पश्वपूर्वायोपकर्तुं शक्नोति, न केवलः। अतोऽन्वाधानादयः सर्वे धर्माः प्राप्ताः। तत्राग्नीनां[1] यज्ञायुधानां च ये संस्काराः पश्वर्थानां पश्वङ्गार्थानां च कृतास्तेऽस्यापि प्रसज्यन्ते। आरादुपकारकाणि[2] चाङ्गपूर्वाणि च। तदुक्तं जैमिनिना–'तन्त्रमध्ये विधानाद्वा मुख्यतन्त्रेण सिद्धिः स्यात्, तन्त्रार्थस्यावशिष्टत्वा[3]दि'ति। बर्हिरादीन्यपि तद्वत् प्रधानाविरोधेनास्याप्युपकर्तुं शक्नु–वन्ति। अथ यानि पशुं[4] न प्रयोजयन्ति तानि संस्क्रियन्ते, यथा कपालादीनि। पशोः प्रतिषिद्धान्य–ङ्गपूर्वाणि चैतदर्थं क्रियन्ते, यथा सवविधे पशावाज्यभागौ यजन्ति। [5]प्रेषितोऽग्नीत् स्फ्यवर्जं[6] दश यज्ञायुधानि संसादयेत्। नन्वग्निहोत्रहवण्यपि संस्कृता। [7]सत्यं, संस्कृता[7], निवृत्तस्वव्यापारा[8]। क्व। अत्यूहनान्तें[8] स्वव्यापाराद् धरणाद्यपूर्व उपकारं निधाय संस्कारास्तिरोभवन्ति। उपकृतपरम्परया वा। अतोऽग्निहोत्रहवणी पुनः साद्यते। आप्रधानपरिसमाप्तेः[9] संस्कारा अवतिष्ठन्त इत्येके। एवं ब्रूवतामभिप्रायो युक्तविमोकादर्वाङ्न तिरोभवन्तीति। तेषां प्रतितन्त्रं[10] संस्कार इति सूत्रकारेणाप्युक्तम्। पिष्टसंयवनी पुरोडाशमेक्षणं [11]मदन्तीस्थालीं दारुपात्रीमुपवेषं च। प्रणीतापात्रप्राशित्रहरणयोः सादनं पुरस्तादेव विचारितम्[12]। [13]ते द्वे पश्वर्थे[14] प्रतिषिद्धे इह साद्येते। न चेदिहापि सवविधेन साद्यते[15]। पवित्रादानाद्याप्यनिनयनान्तमौषधप्रयुक्तं क्रियते। प्रणयनप्रतिषेधस्य पुरोडाशार्थत्वे सवविधे प्रैषः प्रणीतानयनं च लुप्यते। मदन्तीभ्यः स्रुवेणादायानयन्ति। 'प्रोक्षणीशेषेण संयुयादित्येके' इत्यनुपदम्। तथा च बोधायनेनोक्तम्—'प्रोक्षणीशेषेण पिष्टानि संयुयादेवं सवनीयानामि'ति। तथा सत्येतदन्ताः[16] प्रोक्षण्यः[17]। इतरस्मिन्पक्षे हविर्यज्ञविधे च पात्रप्रोक्षणान्ताः। ततः पवित्रे प्रस्तर एवापिसृजति ॥ ३ ॥

---

१. M Ad कर्त्राग्नी° ; thus T. २. M Ad °पकाराणि. ३. Ad °स्याविकृतत्वा° . ४. M Ad पशुर्न; thus T. ५. M Ad प्रैषि° ; thus T. ६. M Ad °वर्जा. ७–७. T takes the text as additional hence gives it in the fn. ८–८. M Ad °पारत्वादत्यूह° ; thus T. ९. M Ad आप्रदान° ; thus T. १०. M Ad प्रतियतन्तस्सं° ; thus T. ११. M Ad वामदन्तिस्था° . १२. M °रितः. १३. M Ad तेन; thus T. १४. M Ad पश्वर्थः; thus T. १५. M Ad साद्येत. १६. M Ad °दन्तां. १७. M °प्रोक्षण्यम्, Ad °क्षणम्.

ब्रह्मा पृषदाज्यं गोपायति ॥ ४ ॥ प्रतिप्रस्थाता पशुं विशास्ति ॥ ५ ॥ 'शमितर् हृदयं जिह्वां वक्षस्तानि त्रीणि, तनिम मतस्ने तानि त्रीणि, श्रोणिर्गुदो पर्याकृतस्तानि त्र्यङ्गाणि, सव्यं दोरेकचरं पार्श्वे प्रयवणीये दक्षिणाः श्रोणिमध्यूध्निं पिष्कलिं वनिष्ठुं यन्मेदस्तदवधत्तात्, त्रिः प्रच्युतस्य हृदयमुत्तमं कुरुतादि'**ति ॥ ६ ॥ अग्नीत् पशुपुरोडाशमुपस्तीर्णाभिघारितमासादयति ॥ ७ ॥ तयोर्द्वयोरुपस्तृणान आह—**

ब्रह्मा च पृषदाज्यमप्रमादेन रक्षति ॥ ४ ॥

प्रतिप्रस्थाता पशुं विशास्ति । पशुविशसनार्थं संशास्तीत्यर्थः । शमितृकर्म विशसनम् । दृश्यते हि अश्वमेधे 'स यत्राश्वं विशास्ति तत्संशास्ति 'शमितरित्याह माऽश्वस्य तिर्यग्लोम च्छेत्सी'रित्यादि ॥ ५ ॥

'तानि तानि त्रीणि' इति[१] वचनं सार्धक्रियार्थम् । 'तानि सार्धं कुरुतादि'ति बौधायनाः पठन्ति । किं प्रयोजनम् । हृदयस्याग्रेऽवद्यतीति । त्रयाणां क्रमेणावदानमिति व्याख्येयम् । 'अनुक्रम्य यथाकाममुत्तरेषामवद्यती'त्युक्तम् । तत्रैकं[२] त्रिकमन्येनाव्यवहितमवदेयमित्येवमर्थम्[३] । तथा सत्यत्रापि तानि त्रीणि सार्धं कुरुतादिति व्याख्येयम् । य एकचरमित्यादिषु कुरुतादित्येतदेव । विष्कलिं [४]वनिष्ठुमित्यत्रावधत्तादवधत्तादिति । अपर्याकृतो हस्ततले, अमण्डलीकृतः । लोकप्रसिद्धिमपेक्ष्य प्रतिषेधः । अथवा अपर्याकृत इति अविपर्यस्त उच्यते । पर्याकृतो विपर्यस्तः । उपलक्षितजघनार्धपूर्वार्ध इत्यर्थः । पार्श्वे प्रयवणीये प्रयवणार्हे । पार्श्वेन वसाहोमं प्रयौतीत्येकवचनश्रवणादेकस्यैव प्रयवणीयत्वं मा विज्ञायीत्युभयोः प्रयवणीयत्वम् । यत्र 'श्रीरसी'त्येकेन प्रयौति 'प्रयुतं द्वेष' इत्यनेन । अध्यूध्नीमूध्नोऽधिगताम्[५] अधोधिकां वा[५] । ऊधसा त्रिःप्रच्युतस्य त्रिर्विषण्णस्य हृदयमुपरिस्थिता [६]श्रपय हे शमितः । अध्रिगौ दृष्टमिहानुक्तमपि[७] कर्तव्यम् । एकधास्य त्वचमाच्छ्यतादूवध्यगोहं पार्थिवं खनतादि'ति । अथाध्वर्युः कुम्भीं स्थाल्यादानाधिश्रयणदृंहणमन्त्रैरादायाधिश्रित्य दृंहति । अन्ये स्थाल्यामानीतास्वप्सु स्थालीधर्मान् प्रयुञ्जते । तद्गतेनोष्मणावदानानि पच्यन्ते, न स्थालीगतेनेति । तथा सत्यप्छब्दस्य[८] बहुवचनान्तत्वादूहः । नैतदेवम् । कुतः । 'अर्णः'[९] (निघ. २.१२.१) इत्यादीन्युदकनामान्येकशतम् । तत्रैकवचनान्तान्यपि बहूनि सन्ति । कुत एतदप्छब्दस्य[१०] बहुवचनान्तत्वाद् ऊह इति । न चाप्छब्दस्य बहुवचनान्तत्वमर्थकृतम् । किं तर्हि, शब्दकृतं यथा 'दारा' इति । उदक्नामसु कस्यचिदपीह ग्रहणं नास्ति । तस्मात् तत्राप्यनूह[११] एव । तस्यां शमिताऽङ्गानि प्रक्षिप्य श्रपयित्वा यथोक्तं करोति ॥ ६ ॥

अग्नीत् पशुपुरोडाशमुपस्तीर्णाभिघारितमासादयति । आसादितं 'यन्म' इत्यभिमृशतः । अथ सवविध आज्यभागौ यजति । तस्य द्वयोरुपस्तृणान इत्यादि । हविर्यज्ञविधे प्राशित्रमवद्यति, प्राशित्रस्थाने सहैव पात्रिया पुरोडाशमिति ब्रुवन् । 'स यत्रास्मै पशुपुरोडाशं परिहरती'त्यादि प्राशित्रप्रतिषेधस्य पुरो-

---

१. M त्रीणि....ति. २. M Ad तत्रैकैकं. ३. M °दे...वमर्थं. ४. M Ad पनिष्ठुं. ५–५. M °गतां...वा. ६. M °स्थिता पय; thus T. ७. M °नूक्तम...कर्त°. ८. M Ad °सत्यच्छब्द°. ९. M Ad यार्णं; thus T. १०. M Ad एतच्छब्द. ११. M Ad तथाप्य°.

'प्रतिप्रस्थातरिन्द्राग्निभ्यां पशुपुरोडाशस्यावदीयमानस्यानुब्रूहि' **इति ॥ ८ ॥ पश्चाच्च पुरस्ताच्च जुह्वामवद्यति ॥** ९ **॥ अभिघारयति ॥** १० **॥ प्रत्यनक्ति ॥** ११ **॥ सकृदुत्तरादुपभृत्यवद्यति ॥** १२ **॥ द्विरभिघारयति ॥ १३ ॥ न प्रत्यनक्ति ॥** १४ **॥ सन्धायाध्वर्यव आदधाति ॥** १५ **॥ 'ओ श्रावय' इत्याह ॥** १६ **॥** 'इन्द्राग्निभ्यां पुरोडाशं प्रस्थितं प्रेष्य' **इति ॥** १७ **॥ वषट्कृते जुहोति ॥** १८ **॥** 'अग्नयेऽनुब्रूहि' **इत्याह पुरोडाशस्य स्विष्टकृतः समानयमानः ॥** १९ **॥**'ओ श्रावय' **इत्याह ॥** २० **॥** 'अग्नये प्रेष्य' **इति ॥** २१ **॥ वषट्कृते जुहोति ॥** २२ **॥ अत्याक्रम्य यथायतनं स्रुचौ सादयित्वाऽवदानानि संभिद्याभिघार्य होत्र इडामादधाति ॥** २३ **॥ उपहूतायामिडायामग्नीध आदधाति षडवत्तम् ॥** २४ **॥ प्राश्नन्ति ॥** २५ **॥ मार्जयन्ते ॥** २६ **॥ सहैव पात्रिया पुरोडाशं पूर्वेणाहवनीयं सहाद्भिर्ब्रह्मणे परिहरति ॥** २७ **॥ प्राश्नाति ब्रह्मा ॥** २८ **॥ मार्जयते ॥** २९ **॥** 'अग्नीदुत्तरबर्हिषा द्रव' **इति संप्रेष्यति।** '°प्रतिप्रस्थातः पशौ संवदस्व' **इति ॥** ३० **॥**

डाशविषयत्वं ज्ञापयति ॥ ७-८ ॥

इडामेके नावद्यन्ति। अत्राननुक्रान्तमिति। सहैव पात्र्या होत्र प्रयच्छतीति नोपपद्यते। इडायां विनियुक्तात् षडवत्तस्यैव[१] प्राशित्रत्वमिति बह्वसमञ्जसमश्रुतं कल्पितं भवति। अत[२] इडामवदाय तस्या अवान्तरेडामवद्येत्। यत्र होतृचमसमिडामादधाति पुरोडाशानामवान्तरेडामिति तत्रावदानं युज्यते। अथापि प्राप्तिमदप्रतिषिद्धं किमिति निवर्तेत। अनेनान्यैः प्राकृतपदार्थनिर्देशैरतुल्यो निर्देशः[३]। अवदानानि संभिद्याभिघार्येति। अन्यत्रापि उपस्पृश्येडामवद्यतीति। अतोऽभिहितमात्रेणैवात्र न भवितव्यम्। अथापि प्राजापत्ये पशौ 'प्राजापत्य इतरेषां हविषामिडामवद्यती'ति पशुपुरोडाशस्येडायां विनियोगे सामस्त्यमिव लक्ष्यते। अतः पात्रान्तरेऽवदानमाचार्येणानभिप्रेतमिति। यद्यप्याचार्यस्यैव-मेवाभिप्राय इति ज्ञातुं शक्यते, तथापीडार्थान्यवदानान्यनुपस्तीर्य पृथक् कृत्वाऽभिघार्येडां प्रयच्छेत्। शेषात् षडवत्तादि[४]। अन्यथोपयुक्तोपयोगोऽन्याय्यः[५] कर्तव्यः स्यात्।' यजमानभागः[६] चतुर्धाकरणे न स्तः। प्राशित्रावदानपक्षे पुरोडाशपरिहरणमपि नास्ति। अत्र दक्षिणां ददाति। तस्मात् 'पशुपुरोडाशे-डायामेवोपहूतायां दक्षिणां दद्यादि'ति [७]वचनादविशेषवचनात् गौः। संख्याश्रवणाच्चैका हविर्यज्ञविधे[८] अन्वाहार्यं च ददाति। उत्पन्नप्रतिपत्तिर्युक्तानां विमोकश्च कर्तव्यौ। फलीकरणान्याज्यव्यतिरिक्तान्येव हूयन्ते हविर्यज्ञविधे। सवविधेऽपि[९] केचित् जुह्वति। सवविधे विष्णुक्रमाः क्रम्यन्ते ॥ २३ -२४ ॥

अग्नीदुत्तरबर्हिषेत्याद्येतत्कुर्वन्तीति बहुवचनमविवक्षितम्। द्वयोरेव श्रवणात्। अथवा संवादे

---

१. M Ad षडवत्तं तस्यैव° . **२.** M Ad अथ; thus T. **३.** T ° पदार्थनिर्देशः, M Ad निर्देशः. **४.** M Ad ° वत्ताद्. **५.** M Ad ° योगो न्या° ; thus T. **६.** M य...दा न भाग; thus T. **७.** M Ad ° चना विशेष. **८.** M हविर्यज्ञ...अन्वा° , Ad ° विधेः अन्वा° , T ° विधेयान्वा° . **९.** M Ad om सवविधे; thus T.

एतत्कुर्वन्ति ॥ ३१ ॥ **अग्नीत् प्लक्षशाखामाहृत्य पर्णसून उपदधाति** 'देवानामवसे' **इति** ॥ ३२ ॥ **स्रुवेण प्रतिप्रस्थाता पृषदाज्यस्योपहन्ति** 'शुक्राणाꣳ शुक्रम्' **इति** ॥ ३३ ॥ **उत्क्रम्य स्रुचोपयम्य पृच्छति** 'शृतꣳ हवी३: शमित:' **इति** ॥ ३४ ॥ 'शृतम्' **इति स आह** ॥ ३५ ॥ 'तद्देवानां पूषा मा प्रपथात् पातु' **इति** ॥ ३६ ॥ **उत्क्रम्यैव पृच्छति** 'शृतꣳ हवी३: शमित:' **इति** ॥ ३७ ॥ 'शृतम्' **इति स आह** ॥ ३८ ॥ 'तद्देवानां पूषा मा पशुपा: पातु' **इति** ॥ ३९ ॥ **उत्क्रम्यैव पृच्छति** 'शृतꣳ हवी३: शमित:' **इति** ॥ ४० ॥ 'शृतम्' **इति स आह** ॥ ४१ ॥ 'तद्देवानां पूषा माऽधिपति: पातु' **इति** ॥ ४२ ॥ **पुराऽभिघारणाद्धृदयशूलेन हृदयꣳ सꣳस्पर्शयति** ॥ ४३ ॥ **तं प्रज्ञातं निदधाति** ॥ ४४ ॥ 'सं ते मनसा मन:' **इति पृषदाज्येन हृदयमुत्तमं कृत्वाऽभिघारयति।** '°सं प्राणेन प्राणो जुष्टं देवेभ्यो हव्यं घृतवत् स्वाहा' **इति** ॥ ४५ ॥ **तमन्तरा यूपं चाहवनीयं चातिहृत्य दक्षिणत उपसादयति** ॥ ४६ ॥ **तस्य चतसृषूपस्तृणान आह** 'प्रतिप्रस्थातर्मनोतायै हविषोऽवदीयमानस्यानुब्रूहि' **इति जुहूपभृतोर्वसाहोमीयां चेडापात्रे च** ॥ ४७ ॥ **द्विर्हृदयस्य जुह्वामवद्यति, द्विर्जिह्वायै, द्विर्वक्षस:, द्विस्तनिम्न:, द्विर्द्विर्मतस्नयोस्त्रियङ्गाणि** ॥ ४८ ॥ **विस्रस्य गुदं त्रेधा करोति** ॥ ४९ ॥ **तस्य मध्यमस्कन्धं द्वेधा विच्छिद्य जुह्वामवदधाति** ॥ ५० ॥ **स्थविमोपयड्भ्यो निदधात्यणिमत्**

सामर्थ्याक्षिप्तेन शमित्रा सह बहुत्वम् ॥ ३०-३१ ॥

देवानामव=पहन्ति[१] । आज्यग्रहणकाल एवान्यत् पृषदाज्यमुत्पाद्यमभिघारणार्थं वनस्पतियागार्थं [२]चानूयाजार्थत्वादि तस्याज्यं प्राकृतमेव कार्यस्य प्राकृतत्वात्। अन्य आह—'पृषदाज्यस्योपहत्याह 'वनस्पतयेऽनुब्रूही'ति। विद्यमानस्यावयव एव श्रूयते। न च पृषदाज्यान्तरस्योत्पत्तिरस्ति। अपि च स्विष्टकृद्विकारत्वाद्वनस्पते: [३]पारद्रव्यैकदेशवृत्तित्वम्। अत एवाप्रयोजकत्वम्। तस्मात् तत एव[३] कर्तव्यमिति। अनुपदकार आह—'पृषदाज्यं गृहीत्वा तूष्णीमन्यस्मिन् पात्रे तयैवा[४]वृता पृषदाज्य[४] गृह्णीयात् ततो वनस्पतिं यजेद् हृदयं चाभिघारयेदित्येक' इति। अभिघारणात्पूर्वं पर्यग्निकरणं प्रातर्दोहविकारत्वादभिद्योतनं नास्ति[५]। अन्य आह—'पर्यग्निकरणमपि पाशुकेनैव[५] पर्यग्निकरणेन निवर्तत' इति। सान्नाय्यप्रतिष्ठापनमन्त्रेण प्रतिष्ठापयति। तस्य यथार्थमूह:। पशुमासाद्य 'यन्मे अग्न' इत्यभिमृशत इत्येकादशस्वपि प्रत्यङ्गमावर्त्य। अङ्गेषु[६] गुद एवेति केचित् ॥ ३२-३३ ॥

स्विष्टकृतोऽप्रयोजकत्वादुपयागस्यापि[७] तत्र प्रयोजनवन्ति[७] साधनानि परिहृत्य तस्य[८] चतसृषूपस्तृणान इत्याद्यवदाय सर्वाणि पुन: प्रति परिहरति। उपस्तरणं जुहूपभृतोर्ध्रुवाया इडाचमस आज्यस्थाल्यां वसाहोमहवण्याम्। अपूर्वात् तथाभिघारणम् ॥ ४७ ॥

अथ त्र्यङ्गावर्जमुत्सादप्रदेशाद् द्विर्द्विरवद्यति। त्र्यङ्गेषु गुदस्य यथोक्तम्। त्र्यङ्गाणीति प्रथमा

---

१. T =पवहन्त्या°. **२.** M °ज्चा...र्थत्वादि. **३-३.** M परद्रव्यैकदे...त एवे; Ad °द्रव्यैकदेशवृत्तित्वमत एव कर्तव्य°; thus T. **४-४.** M तै...पृष°. **५-५.** M नास्ति...पाशु°. **६.** M Ad त्र्यङ्गेषु; thus T. **७-७.** M °यागस्या..वन्ति. **८.** M om; thus Ad T.

स्विष्टकृतम् ॥ ५१ ॥ **द्विः सव्यस्य दोष्णोऽवद्यति, द्विर्द्विः पार्श्वयोर्द्विर्दक्षिणायै श्रोण्या अध्युध्न्यै** ॥ ५२ ॥ **उत्तमाया अवद्यति** ॥ ५३ ॥ **यूष्णोपसिञ्चति** ॥ ५४ ॥ **यूषन्नवधाय मेदसा प्रोर्णोति** ॥ ५५ ॥ **अभिघारयति** ॥ ५६ ॥ **प्रत्यनक्ति पशुम्** ॥ ५७ ॥ **दक्षिणस्य दोष्णः स्थूलं पिशितमवद्यति** ॥ ५८ ॥ **तदुपभृत्यवदधाति** ॥ ५९ ॥ **अणिम्नो गुदस्योपभृत्येवावदधाति** ॥ ६० ॥ **सव्यायै श्रोण्यै स्थूलं पिशितमवद्यति** ॥ ६१ ॥ **तदुपभृत्येवावदधाति** ॥ ६२ ॥ **यूष्णोपसिञ्चति** ॥ ६३ ॥ **यूषन्नवधाय मेदसा प्रोर्णोति** ॥ ६४ ॥ **द्विरभिघारयति** ॥ ६५ ॥ **न प्रत्यनक्ति पशुम्** ॥ ६६ ॥ **वपाहोमं विश्राव्याभिघारयति** ॥ ६७ ॥ **अनस्थिकमिडापात्रे संप्रकिरति** ॥ ६८ ॥ **यूष्णोपसिञ्चति** ॥ ६९ ॥ 'ऐन्द्रः प्राणः' **इति पशुमवत्तं समभिमृशति।** '०अङ्गेअङ्गे नि देध्यदैन्द्रोऽपानो अङ्गे अङ्गे वि=मदन्तु' **इति** ॥ ७० ॥ 'श्रीरसि' **इति पार्श्वेन वसाहोमं प्रयौति।** '०अग्निस्त्वा=रोहिष्यै'
इ ि त ॥ ७ १ ॥
'प्रयुतं द्वेषः' **इति त्रिः प्रयौति** ॥ ७२ ॥ 'प्रयुतं द्वेषः' **इति यं द्वेष्टि यजमानस्तं ध्यायति** ॥ ७३ ॥ **ते प्रतिप्रस्थात्र आदधाति** ॥ ७४ ॥ **स्रुचोः पञ्चहोतारं व्याचष्टे** ॥ ५.३.१.७५ ॥ **[इति प्रथमः पटलः** (८)**]**

स्रुचोः पञ्चहोतारं व्याचष्टे ॥ १ ॥ **प्रतिपराहरन्ति विष्कलिं पत्नियै** ॥ २ ॥ **सन्धायाध्वर्यव आदधाति** ॥ ३ ॥ 'ओ श्रावय' **इत्याह** ॥ ४ ॥ 'इन्द्राग्निभ्यां छागस्य हविषोऽनुब्रूहि' **इत्याहो-**

निर्धारणषष्ठ्याः स्थाने सप्तम्या वा ॥ ४८-५२ ॥

उत्तमाया अवद्यतीति[1]। इह[1] पाठक्रमेणैव सिद्धे वचनं यथाकाममुत्तरेषाम्। अवद्यतीत्यस्मिन्नपि[2] पक्षेऽस्या एवोत्तमाया अवद्यतीत्येवमर्थम्[3]। गुदस्योक्तमवदानं[3] ब्राह्मणे विहितम्। तदनेन विकल्पते ॥ ५३ ॥

प्रत्यनक्ति पशुम्। अवत्तशेषस्य यागान्तरार्थस्य संस्कारः प्रत्यञ्जनम्। अतो गुदतृतीयस्य स्विष्टकृदर्थस्य प्रत्यञ्जनमुपयागार्थस्यापि केचिदिच्छन्ति, कारणस्याविशिष्टत्वात्[4]। 'त्र्यङ्गाणि [5]प्रत्यनक्ती'त्यनुपदम्[5] ॥ ५७ ॥

मतस्नूपरिगतेन मेदसा स्रुचौ प्रोर्णोत्यन्यन्मेदो वनिष्ठुं चेडायामवदधाति ॥ ६४ ॥

अनस्थिकेनावत्तशेषेण ॥ ६८ ॥

हृदयादिना सह पशुमवत्तं सहैवाभिमृशति चतुष्टयम् ॥ ७० ॥

'श्रीरसि' इत्येकेन प्रयुतमित्यन्येन ॥ ७१-७३ ॥

ते भक्षकाले प्रतिप्रस्थात्रे आदधाति प्रयच्छति ॥ ५.३.१.७४ ॥ **[इति प्रथमः पटलः** (८)**]**

१-१. M Ad ०द्यतीतिह, T द्यति इह. **२.** T ०स्मिन्नेव. **३-३.** M ०तीत्येवम...दावदानं, Ad ०स्योत्तमायावदानं. **४.** T ०स्यावशिष्ट० ; thus T. **५-५.** M प्रत्य...पदं.

त्तिष्ठन्नध्वर्युः ॥ ५ ॥ **वसाहोमं प्रतिप्रस्थाताऽऽदत्ते** ॥ ६ ॥ 'ओ श्रावय' **इत्याह** ॥ ७ ॥ 'इन्द्राग्निभ्यां छागस्य हविः प्रस्थितं प्रेष्य' **इति** ॥ ८ ॥ 'घृतं घृतपावानः पिबत' **इत्यर्धर्चे प्रतिप्रस्थाता वसाहोमं जुहोति।** '°वसां वपापावानः=स्वाहा' **इति** ॥ ९ ॥ **वषट्कृतेऽध्वर्युर्हविर्जुहोति** ॥ १० ॥ 'वनस्पतयेऽनुब्रूहि' **इत्याह स्रुवेण पृषदाज्यस्योपघ्नन् जुह्वामानीय** ॥ ११ ॥ 'ओ श्रावय' **इत्याह** ॥ १२ ॥ 'वनस्पतये प्रेष्य' **इति** ॥ १३ ॥ **वषट्कृते जुहोति** ॥ १४ ॥ 'अग्नये स्विष्टकृतेऽनु-ब्रूहि' **इत्याह हविषः स्विष्टकृते समानयमानः** ॥ १५ ॥ 'ओ श्रावय' **इत्याह** ॥ १६ ॥ 'अग्नये स्विष्टकृते प्रेष्य' **इति** ॥ १७ ॥ **वषट्कृते जुहोति** ॥ १८ ॥ **दिशो जुहोति** 'दिशे स्वाहा=उद्दिशे स्वाहा', 'आप्यायन्तां दिशो घृतेन स्वाहा', 'दिग्भ्यो नमो दिग्भ्यो स्वाहा' ॥ १९ ॥ **दिशोऽनु पञ्चहोतुराहुतिं जुहोति** ॥ २० ॥ **यं** *[1]**(द्वेष्टि यजमानस्तं ध्यायति** ॥ २१ ॥ **ते प्रतिप्रस्थात्र आदधाति** ॥ २२ ॥ **स्रुचो पञ्चहोतारं) व्याचष्टे** ॥ २३ ॥ **अत्याक्रम्य यथायतनꣳ स्रुचौ सादयित्वाऽभिघार्य प्रत्यङ्ङवृत्तहोत्र इडामादधाति मेदस्वतीम्** ॥ २४ ॥ **अवान्तरेडामादधाति** ॥ २५ ॥ **उपहूतायामिडायां वक्षो ब्रह्मण उपोहति** ॥ २६ ॥ **प्राश्नन्ति** ॥ २७ ॥ **मार्जयन्ते** ॥ २८ ॥ 'अग्नीदौपयजानङ्गारानाहर' **इति संप्रेष्यति।** 'उपयष्टरुप सीद ब्रह्मन् प्रस्थास्यामः समिधमा-धायाग्नीदग्निꣳ सकृत् संमृड्ढि' **इति** ॥ २९ ॥ **आहवनीयादग्नीदौपयजानङ्गारानाहृत्य पूर्वेण होतारं बर्हिषो व्यूह्य निवपति** ॥ ३० ॥ **गुदेनोपयष्टोपसीदति** ॥ ३१ ॥ **पृषदाज्यस्यानूयाजान् यजति** ॥ ३२ ॥ **उपभृतमेवोपभृतं कुरुत एतां जुहूं यस्यां पृषदाज्यम्** ॥ ३३ ॥ 'ओ श्रावय' **इत्याह** ॥ ३४ ॥ 'देवेभ्य प्रेष्य' **इति** ॥ ३५ ॥ 'प्रेष्य प्रेष्य' **इति** ॥ ३६ ॥ **एकादशानूयाजान् यजति** ॥ ३७ ॥

***१.** Text abri. यं=स्रुचोः=व्याचष्टे see V.3.1.73-75.

याज्याया[1] अर्धर्च उक्ते प्रतिप्रस्थाता वसाहोमं जुहोति ॥ ९ ॥

वषट्कृते हविर्हुत्वा प्रदक्षिणमावृत्य 'वनस्पतयेऽनुब्रूही'त्यादि स्विष्टकृतम्। अन्विति यत्न आनन्तर्यार्थः। अन्तःपरिधिबहिःपरिधिहोमयोरपि पूर्वे यथा स्यादिति ॥ १०-११ ॥

दिशोऽन्विति। समानकर्तृकत्वार्थम्। तथा च व्याख्यातैव। हूयते अप्राकृतत्वाच्चापूर्वेणैव ॥ २०-२३ ॥

सन्ततिं हुत्वाऽग्नीदौपयजानित्येतां [2]जुहुमित्याद्युक्तम्। अनूयाजेषु द्वितीयादयः षडागन्तवः। नवमदशमौ च। तेषां तृतीयादयः[3] प्रथमविकाराः, पञ्चमादयो मध्यमविकाराः। नवमदशमयोरुत्तमविकारत्वे प्राप्ते लिङ्गाद् दशमः प्रथमविकारः। षष्ठे विवदन्ते। लिङ्गादुत्तमविकार इति केचिद्। [4]होतृशब्दद्वित्वाद्धोताराविति ॥ २९-३० ॥

---

१. T याज्यया. **२.** M Ad °त्येताञ्जु [Ad °न् जु] होमि°. **३.** T द्वितीया°. **४.** M Ad चिद्धातृशब्दवत्वा°. **५.** M मैत्रावरुणे...होऽध्वं°. **६.** T यजेदिति. **७.** M Ad द्वियजित्वमत्वा.

यदाऽऽह मैत्रावरुणो 'यज' **इत्यथोपयष्टोपयजति** 'समुद्रं गच्छ स्वाहा' **इति गुदस्य प्रच्छेदम-संभिन्दन्नपर्यावर्तयन्** ॥ ३८ ॥ 'अग्निं वैश्वानरं गच्छ स्वाहा' **इति सर्वमन्ततो गुदं जुहोति** ॥ ३९ ॥ 'अद्भ्यस्त्वौषधीभ्यः' **इति बर्हिषि हस्तौ निमृष्टे** ॥ ४० ॥ 'प्राणान् मनो मे हार्दि यच्छ' **इत्युपयष्टा यजमानं वाचयति।** '°तनूं त्वचं पुत्रं नप्तारमशीय' **इति** ॥ ४१ ॥ **अनूयाजानिष्ट्वोपपरिक्रम्य स्वरुमनक्ति** 'यन्ता रन्ता रायः' **इति** ॥ ४२ ॥ 'इह धृतिः' **इत्येनꣳ स्रुच्युद्दधाति।** '°इह विधृतिरिह स्वधृतिः' **इति** ॥ ४३ ॥ 'दिवं ते धूमो गच्छतु' **इत्येनं जुहोति।** '°अन्तरिक्षमर्चिः पृथिवीं भस्मना पृण स्वाहा' **इति** ॥ ४४ ॥ **अत्र यूपमनुप्रहरति** ॥ ४५ ॥ **यद्यनुप्रहृष्यन्तो भवन्त्यागत्य वाजवतीभ्याꣳ स्रुचौ व्यूहति** ॥ ४६ ॥ **शंयुना प्रस्तरपरिधि संप्रकिरति** ॥ ४७ ॥ **परेत्य विष्कल्या पत्नीः संयाज-यन्ति** ॥ ४८ ॥ **आज्यस्य सोमं यजति** ॥ ४९ ॥ **आज्यस्य त्वष्टारम्** ॥ ५० ॥ **आज्यस्य राकाम्** ॥ ५१ ॥ 'देवानां पत्नीभ्योऽनुब्रूहि' **इत्याहोपस्तृणानोऽवद्यन्** ॥ ५२ ॥ **पश्चाच्च पुरस्ताच्चोत्तानायै विष्कल्या अवद्यति** ॥ ५३ ॥ **अभिघारयति** ॥ ५४ ॥ **प्रत्यनक्ति** ॥ ५५ ॥ 'ओ श्रावय' **इत्याह** ॥ ५६ ॥ 'देवानां पत्नीर्यज' **इति** ॥ ५७ ॥ **वषट्कृते जुहोति** ॥ ५८ ॥ 'अग्नये गृहपतयेऽनुब्रूहि' **इत्याहो-पस्तृणानोऽवद्यन्** ॥ ५९ ॥ **नीच्यै विष्कल्या उत्तरार्धाच्छूलं पिशितमवद्यति** ॥ ६० ॥ **द्विरभिघार-यति** ॥ ६१ ॥ **न प्रत्यनक्ति** ॥ ६२ ॥ 'ओ श्रावय' **इत्याह** ॥ ६३ ॥ 'अग्निं गृहपतिं यज' **इति** ॥ ६४ ॥ **वषट्कृते उत्तरार्धेऽतिहाय पूर्वा आहुतीर्जुहोति** ॥ ६५ ॥ **उत्तानाया इडामादधाति** ॥ ६६ ॥ **नीच्या अग्नीधे शंयुवन्तम्** ॥ ६७ ॥ **एतत्कृत्वाऽऽज्यस्यैव फलीकरणहोमꣳ हुत्वा प्राडेत्य त्रीणि समिष्टयजूꣳषि जुहोति** 'यज्ञ यज्ञं गच्छ=वाते धाः' **इति** ॥ ६८ ॥ 'अयं ते योनिर्ऋत्वियः' **इत्यरण्योरग्निꣳ समारोहयते** ॥ ५.३.२.६९ ॥ **[इति द्वितीयः**

मध्यमोत्तमविकारेषु मैत्रावरुणेन[1] सहाध्वर्युरपि 'यज' इति[1] ब्रूयात्।[2]द्वियजिमत्वात्। तेषामुपयष्टा प्रतिप्रस्थाता। गुदस्य जघनार्धादारभ्य तस्यास्तस्या आहुतेर्भागं प्रच्छिद्याहुत्यर्थं गृहीतं शिष्टेन सन्दधदपर्यावर्तयन् यथावस्थितस्यैवादायोपयजति ॥ ३८ ॥

'प्राणान्' इत्यादिवाचनमन्त्रः[1] ॥ ४१ ॥

स्वरुं[1] प्रागग्रम्। पुरस्तात्प्रत्यङ्तिष्ठन् जुहोति ॥ ४२ ॥

यूपः प्रत्यगग्रः ॥ ४५ ॥

यद्यनुपहृष्यन्तो भवन्ति। [3]गृहेष्टिक्रियमाणेऽनुप्रहरणम्। उदवसाय चेत् तिष्ठेदेव। स्रुग्व्यूहनेऽनूयाजहोममात्रमपि जुह्वा सह व्यूहन्ति केचित्, [3]निवृत्तसंस्कारत्वात्। यद्ययमभिप्रायः[4] स्यात् स्रुचो[4] व्यूहतीत्यवक्ष्यदित्यन्ये[5] न कुर्वन्ति ॥ ४६ ॥

विष्कली[6] जाघनी ॥ ४८ ॥

आज्यस्यैव फलीकरणहोमं हुत्वेति हविर्यज्ञविधापेक्षम्। समिष्टयजूंषि हुत्वा तत्प्राकृतं[7] करोति। 'हृदयशूलान्ते पत्नीं[8] विसर्जयती'त्यनुपदम् ॥ ५.३.२.६८ ॥ **[इति द्वितीयः पटलः** (९)**]**

१–१. M Ad °मन्त्र...रुपं, Ad स्वरूपं. २. M Ad °ष्टिः. ३. T °निवृतसं. ४–४. M °मभिप्रो...स्रु°. ५. M Ad °त्यनेन; thus T. ६. M वल्कली, Ad विकली, T पिष्कली. ७. M Ad तत्कृतं; thus T. ८. M Ad om.

पटलः (९)]

'अयं ते योनिर्ऋत्विय' इत्यरण्योरग्निꣳ समारोहयते। '०यतो=रयिम्' इति यद्युदवस्यति॥ १॥ यद्यु न शकल एव पूर्वमग्निꣳ समारोह्य 'अहं त्वदस्मि' इत्यपरस्मिन्नाहवनीये विसृजति। '०मदसि=जातवेदः' इति॥ २॥ 'यत्कुसीदमप्रतीत्तं मयि' इत्युत्तरां वेद्यै श्रोणिमुपोषति। '०येन यमस्य बलिना चरा=भवामि' इति॥ ३॥ 'विश्वलोप विश्दावस्य त्वाऽऽसञ्जुहोमि स्वाहा' इत्यञ्जलिना सक्तून् प्रदाव्ये जुहुतो यजमानश्च पत्नी च॥ ४॥ 'अग्धादेकः' इति हस्तान् संप्रघ्नाते। '०अहुतादेकः स=रेण्यम्' इति॥ ५॥ 'अयं नो नभसा पुरः' इत्याहवनीयमुपतिष्ठते। '०सꣳस्फानो=सन्' इति॥ ६॥ 'स त्वं नो नभसस्पते' इति वायुम्। '०ऊर्जं नो=कृधि' इति॥ ७॥ 'देव सꣳस्फान' इत्यादित्यम्। '०सहस्रपोषस्ये=स्वस्तिम्' इति॥ ८॥ 'आशासानः सुवीर्यम्' इति यूपम्। '०राय=मानाय तिष्ठ' इति यदि तिष्ठति॥ ९॥ 'इमं विष्यामि वरुणस्य पाशम्' इति यद्यनुप्रहृतः॥ १०॥ स्फ्यमादायोदपात्रं च हृदयशूलेनोत्परायन्ति॥ ११॥ अन्तरा चात्वालं चोत्करं च गत्वा पूर्वेण यूपं बहिर्वेदि स्फ्येनोद्धत्य 'उन्नम्भय पृथिवीम्' इत्युदपात्रेऽवोक्षति। '०भिन्द्धीदं=दृतिम्' इति॥ १२॥ 'शुगसि' इति शुष्कस्य चार्द्रस्य च सन्धौ पराञ्चꣳ हृदयशूल-मुद्वासयति। '०तमभि शोच योऽस्मान् द्वेष्टि यं च वयं द्विष्मः' इति॥ १३॥ 'धाम्नो धाम्नो राजन्' इत्युपतिष्ठते। '०इतो वरुण=मुञ्च', 'अप्सु राज्ञो वरुणस्य गृहो हिरण्ययः कृतस्ततो धृतव्रतो राजा विश्वा धर्माणि पश्यति' इति॥ १४॥ 'सुमित्रा न आप ओषधयः सन्तु' इत्यपः परिषेच्याप्रतीक्षमायन्ति। '०दुर्मित्रा=द्विष्मः' इति॥ १५॥ उदवसायैता आहुतीर्जुहोति यद्युदव-स्यति॥ १६॥ यद्यु नात्रैव चतुर्गृहीतेन दशहोतारं गार्हपत्ये जुहोति, षड्ढोतारमन्वाहार्यपचने, पञ्चहोतारममात्ये, चतुर्होतारꣳ सभायाम्॥ १७॥ आगत्य द्विराज्यस्योपस्तृणीते॥ १८॥ दध्या-नयति॥ १९॥ द्विरेवाभिघारयति॥ २०॥ तज्जुहोति 'इडायै सृप्तं घृतवच्चराचरम्' इत्याहवनीये।

उदवसानपक्षे वास्तोष्पतीयं[१] हुत्वा समारोप्य[१] प्रयाति॥ १॥

इतरस्मिन् शकल एव पूर्वमग्निमित्यादि वेद्युपोषणमप्युदवसानपक्ष एवेति केचित्॥ २॥

अनुपोष्य प्रयायादिति[२] प्रयाणसंबन्धादित्यविशेषेणैव अन्ये कुर्वन्ति॥ ३॥

प्रदाव्यो[३] वनाग्निः। एतस्यैव वेद्युपोषणार्थस्य प्रदाव्यशब्देनोपचार[४] इत्यन्ये[४]। हृदयशूलचर्या सर्वेषाम्। तत्रैकवचनमतन्त्रम्। उद्धननावोक्षणोद्वासनान्यध्वर्युरेव करोति। उपस्थानादि सर्वे॥ ४॥

'तमभि शोचे'त्यादौ यजमानस्य द्वेष्यं ध्यायति॥ १३॥

१-१. M ०तीय...मारोप्य. २. M Ad प्रायादिति; thus T. ३. M Ad प्रभाव्यो; thus T. ४-४. M ०चार...न्य; thus Ad T.

'०देवा=रन्तिरस्तु स्वाहा' **इति** ॥ २१ ॥ 'पुनरूर्जा निवर्तस्व' **इति दध्ना गार्हपत्ये जुहोति।** '०पुनः=विश्वतः स्वाहा' **इति** ॥ २२ ॥ 'सह रय्या निवर्तस्व' **इत्यन्वाहार्यपचने जुहोति।** '०अग्ने पिन्वस्व=स्परि स्वाहा' **इति** ॥ २३ ॥ **पूर्णाहुतिमेवातो जुहोति** ॥ २४ ॥ **परिश्रित्याहवनीयं चतु–र्गृहीतं गृह्णीते** ॥ २५ ॥ **अभिपूर्य सप्तहोतारं व्याचष्टे** ॥ २६ ॥ 'सप्त ते' **इत्येतामृचं मध्यतो दधाति** ॥ २७ ॥ **समिधमाधाय होतुराहुत्या जुहोति** ॥ २८ ॥ **वरमस्मै ददाति** ॥ २९ ॥ **सन्तिष्ठते पशुबन्धः सन्तिष्ठते पशुबन्धः** ॥ ५.३.३.३० ॥ **[इति तृतीयः पटलः** (१०)**]**

॥ इति पञ्चमप्रपाठके तृतीयोऽनुवाकः ॥

॥ इति पशुबन्धाख्यः पञ्चमः प्रपाठकः ॥

□ □ □

दध्ना गार्हपत्ये पयसाऽन्वाहार्यपचन[1] इति केवलाभ्यामेव ॥ २३ ॥

पूर्णाहूतिमेवातो[2] जुहोति। परिश्रित्याहवनीयमत[3] उत्तरं पूर्णाहुतिमेव जुहोति। नेष्टिरस्माभिरिष्यत इति। पर्युपयुक्तावेवातः शब्दौ। कुत एतत्। पठन्ति हि केचित्। 'पशाविष्टिरुभयतोऽन्यतरो वाऽऽग्नेयी वाऽग्नावैष्णवी वा उभे वा इति ॥ २४–२५ ॥

सन्तिष्ठते पशुबन्धः। सर्वप्रकरणेऽभ्यासो मङ्गलार्थः ॥ ५.३.३.३० ॥ **[इति तृतीयः पटलः** (१०)**]**

॥ इति व्याख्यायां पञ्चमप्रपाठके तृतीयोऽनुवाकः ॥

॥ इति कल्पागमसंग्रहे पशुबन्धाख्यः पञ्चमः प्रपाठकः ॥

□ □ □

---

१. M Ad °वचन. **२.** M °मेव...होति. **३.** M Ad परि=नी°.